Acknowledgments

Without the help of my wife Galina in tasting, testing, and criticizing so many recipes and so much good and bad food, this book would not have been conceived in the first place.

Without the encouragement and enthusiasm of my editor, Elisabeth Scharlatt, this book would not have been written.

Without the efforts of my agent, Diane Cleaver, this book would not have been published.

Without the impeccable attention to detail by my copyeditor, Amy Mantell, and her staff, this book would have more errors and less polish.

Without the resources of the New York Public Library and the efficiency of its staff, this book would have less credibility than it does.

And without the information provided by the following people, this book would have been a lot less enjoyable to write. Thanks to Patricia Brown, Elaine Chaika, A. Craig Copetas, Stephanie Curtis, Lessie Davison, Rick Easton, Barbara Ensrud, Michel Fitoussi, Eunice Fried, Lila Gault, Marion Gorman, John Gottfried, Emanuel Greenberg, Burks Hamner, Kevin and Denise Harrigan, Claus Hattasch, Nika Hazelton, Paul Kovi, Leon Lianides, Sirio Maccioni, Tom Margittai, Peter Meltzer, Charles Mueller, Fenella Pearson Kirwin, Lisa Roberts, Nikki Singer, Marie-Claude Stockl, Richard Story, Patrice Tanaka, Gisela Vaughan, and Terri Woods.

Last, I owe a great debt to my mother and father, Renee and Eligio Mariani, who truly believed that setting a good table was an expression of love and one of the highest traditions of a culture.

For Galina

High praise for a new American classic

"John Mariani has given us our own *Larousse Gastronomique*, written with care, intelligence, and passion. A must for every kitchen library. This is a delightful book, full of all sorts of facts and anecdotes."
— Anthony Dias Blue

"America's answer to the *Larousse Gastronomique*; a valuable work."
— Laurie Burrows Grad

"One of the most entrancing books I've come across in a long time. The author of this American equivalent of the French *Larousse Gastronomique* — joy of joys — a man who can write with wit, eloquence, and elegance. Here, for the first time, we have a true chronicle and explanation of American foods."
— Nika Hazelton

"Required reading. Some food authorities have compared *The Dictionary of American Food & Drink* with *Larousse Gastronomique*. We beg to disagree: Mariani's delightful romp through this country's culinary heritage is *far* more entertaining than its Gallic counterpart."
— *Dallas Morning News*

"A lexicographical bouillabaisse of information for the chef, historian, linguist, sociologist, as well as the average American cook. From Mickey Finn to the Volstead cocktail, a tasty dish for every reader."
— *Los Angeles Herald Examiner*

"Filled with information to intrigue and inform the scholar, the trivia buff, and the cook."
— *New York Times*

"Informative, entertaining, and full of surprises."
— *Christian Science Monitor*

"An invaluable reference compendium for everyone, amateur or professional. In addition, it's a book written in an engaging style that makes for engaging reading from cover to cover. You'll have a hard time putting it down."
— *White Plains Reporter Dispatch*

"If you have a kitchen reference library, this book should be in it."
— *Saturday Review*

"A valuable companion for adventurous eaters and armchair connoisseurs of American food. We won't leave home without it."
— Jane and Michael Stern

THE DICTIONARY OF
AMERICAN
FOOD
AND
DRINK

John F. Mariani

12/7/84

NEW YORK

TICKNOR & FIELDS

Library of Congress Cataloging in Publication Data

Mariani, John.
The dictionary of American food and drink.

Bibliography: p.
Includes index.
1. Cookery, American—Dictionaries. 2. Food—
Dictionaries. 3. Beverages—Dictionaries. I. Title.
TX349.M26   1983   641.5973′03′21   83–4977
ISBN 0–89919–199–1
ISBN 0–89919–359–5 (pbk.)

Printed in the United States of America

V 10 9 8 7 6 5 4 3 2

Contents

Preface

In 1977 my wife and I drove crosscountry for eleven weeks, with no firmer commitment than to see what we had not seen, learn what we did not know, and savor what we had not tasted. We began in New York, went south, then west across Texas and over the mountains to California. Our return took us through the Grand Canyon, the flatlands of Kansas, and the snowy hills of the Midwest before ending on the edges of New England.

At that time I had no intention of compiling a gastronomic dictionary nor even of writing a book of any kind about American food. In fact, most of our meals on the road were disappointing, consumed in restaurants recommended by friends, editors, and guide books, the most thorough of which was the multivolumed *Mobil Travel Guide,* an oil company's Baedeker with the uncanny ability to choose the most restaurants specializing in steaks, chops, and prime ribs. Depending on such a guide would lead a traveler to believe that Americans live on nothing but steak and potatoes—a prevailing view in most people's minds anyhow, and one the compilers of the *Mobil Travel Guide* took to heart.

One can hardly blame them, since even in the large cities and small towns of the South and West our request for a good meal was usually answered with directions to the nearest steak house. The "best" restaurant in town was invariably the kind of place peripatetic author Calvin Trillin spoke of when he described "some purple palace that serves 'Continental cuisine' and has as its chief creative employee a menu-writer rather than a chef." My wife was almost brought to tears at a penthouse restaurant atop a hotel in Birmingham, Alabama, when a waiter tried to make up for some stale shrimp cocktail with a sweet lime sherbet intended to "clear the palate" before moving on to a tough, burned steak.

What we found difficult to believe was that restaurants serving traditional, fine American cuisine are exceedingly difficult to find. The boardmembers of local chambers of commerce, the businesspeople, and the tourist-information agents may eat in a wonderful little barbecue place on the outskirts of town, but without fail they will send the traveler to one of those hotel dining rooms where decor and situation mean far more than quality or integrity of food. So we'd ply our way through a wretchedly made béarnaise, wilted stringbeans *amandine,* filet mignon topped with canned liver pâté, and *mousse au chocolat* with all the taste and texture of shaving cream.

Only with the greatest and most insistent effort did we ferret out a good American restaurant serving old-fashioned fare or just plain, well-made contemporary cookery. We found that most of the cooking of this sort, as the Time-Life *American Cooking* series indicated, was being done in the homes of Americans who were upholding a long and honorable heritage of baking, roasting, grilling, barbecuing, and mixing—from frosted silver mugs of mint julep to tortillas with a salsa cruda more complex than any Gallic *rouille.*

We sampled excellent cornbread, made without sugar in the South, and crabmeat dishes in Charleston that were creamy and full of the flavor of the Caribbean, and in the Southwest a bowl of fresh, fragrant guacamole.

But it was not only in the homes that we began to find American food: there were cafeterias serving well-made stews and perfect pies; diners where the German chocolate cake was hot out of the oven; a barbecue pit set up in what was once an Army barracks; and pastry shops that served up the best muffins I've ever had.

In New Orleans we had red beans and rice and sampled beignets and chicory coffee in the French Market there. There were walnut waffles in Greensboro, and deep-fried, cornmeal-dusted catfish at a Vicksburg restaurant where we were entertained by an organ player wearing a VFW cap. We couldn't get enough of those succulent Gulf shrimp or pecan pie with peach ice cream, and in Texas a meal of chili and ice-cold beer seemed one of the best things in the world as we listened to a juke box full of Hank Williams classics. We were introduced to chimichangos in Arizona, enjoyed fresh game in Nevada, burgers of real substance in Los Angeles, and exquisite wines in the Napa and Sonoma valleys. Traveling back across the western plains we had fine roast beefs and sturdy pot roasts, breakfasts with hefty side orders of bacon, ham, grits, hashed browns, and the inevitable orange slice. In a ski town in Pennsylvania we warmed up with a white bean soup, and in New England a pot of chowder made with quahog clams and topped with common crackers. Back in New York we threw ourselves into every imaginable ethnic cuisine— from Czech to Greek, from Sichuan to Hunan, from Moroccan to Korean. And there were plenty of prime steaks, black on the outside, pink within, sidled with crisp, golden onion rings and cottage fries. We were soon trying to make up our minds whether to buy a Jewish cheesecake on the Lower East Side or an Italian cheesecake in Little Italy.

In the years since then Americans have become more interested in more kinds of food than anyone might have imagined a decade before. Much of the writing on food and wine continued to praise the products and preparations of chefs in Lyons, Munich, Florence, and Hong Kong, but along with the growth of the delicacy or "gourmet" shops in American cities came a reevaluation of the conclaves of ethnic cooking in our immigrant cities, which in turn led to a reappreciation of regional American dishes. And although the new boom towns like Houston and Atlanta made fast progress in installing deluxe French restaurants in their new hotels, there arose an attendant interest in American cookery. Trendy city magazines might review the new *nouvelle cuisine* dining room downtown, but they would also scour the countryside to find the best pizza, the best cheesecake, the best ice cream, the best chili, or the best hamburger in the state. Even Julia Child began demonstrating how to prepare American dishes on her TV show.

Ironically, the very critics who had argued that complexity meant excellence now began to see the virtues of simplicity in a well-grilled piece of fish or a beautifully roasted loin of pork with fresh applesauce. The idea of a clambake on a beach was taking on fashionable social overtones, and no one would argue that a Maine lobster, just boiled and then served with butter, accompanied by a baked Idaho potato and a glass of California Chardonnay could ever be improved upon by any chef in the world.

I thought about all this after that trip in 1977, and I was encouraged to write this book when I could find no gastronomic dictionary or encyclopedia that traced the origins, terminology, slang, and methods of American cookery, except as part of a larger international cuisine. I decided I needed such a book, and so I wrote it.

Introduction

TOWARD A MISUNDERSTANDING
OF AMERICAN FOOD

In 1947 expatriate American author Henry Miller wrote, "Americans can eat garbage, provided you sprinkle it liberally with ketchup, mustard, chili sauce, cayenne pepper, or any other condiment which destroys the original flavor of the dish."

Miller might have gone on with such hyperbolic scorn by noting that the French will eat anything with a cream sauce, Italians anything with tomato and garlic, Indians anything with curry powder, and Chinese anything with soy sauce—all to cover up the original flavor of the dish.

None of these assertions holds true, but such facile and offhanded criticism of American food, wine, and drink has become almost a tradition; by now it is a gastronomic cliché to identify American food as hamburgers, hot dogs, Coca-Cola, and ice cream—a list that would not even adequately describe the offerings at a summer's baseball game. More than once the response of friends to the news that I was preparing this book has been, "But what *is* American food? Fried chicken and pizza?", as if to suggest that all American food is prepared at fast-food outlets and dispensed by young people wearing silly hats.

Others would argue that there *is* no such thing as American food (except, perhaps, whatever it was the Indians ate before the coming of the white man) because everything was brought over by Europeans, Africans, and Asians or that, even if "created" here, an American dish is merely an adaption of or variation on a foreign dish—as evidenced by America's distressing fondness for chop suey, spaghetti and meatballs, and "Chablis" made in the hills of California. Jambalaya, these critics will assert, is little more than a Louisiana version of Spain's *paella;* New England clam chowder derives from French seafood soups cooked in a copper pot called a *chaudière;* even a quintessentially American cocktail like the Harvey Wallbanger depends for its effectiveness on Galliano, an Italian liqueur.

Such allegations completely and conveniently ignore how every culture in the world has borrowed, absorbed, and been changed by the food and drink of other cultures, either through conquest, assimilation, or mere emulation. It has long been debated whether Marco Polo brought noodles back from the Orient, but we do know he returned with recipes for frozen milk desserts that may have been the first European sherbets. Had India not been dominated by the Persian Moghuls, the cuisine of Punjab, Kashmir, and Uttar Pradesh would be utterly different from what it is, and Japan would not have its *tempura* dishes had Portuguese traders not introduced the idea there three hundred years ago. Italians will always be delighted to remind their French neighbors that Gallic cookery was forever transformed after Caterina de' Medici (who became Catherine de Médicis) brought her Italian chefs with her in 1547 when she set up her French court.

So, too, the influence of the American cornucopia on the rest of the world has been enormous, from the time the tomato was first introduced to Italy in the sixteenth century, through the era of triangular trade between England, Africa, and New England, based on American cod and West Indies sugar, and up to the modern age, when American food-processing technology and agricultural surpluses have not only saved nations from starvation but altered the diets of their people. Even the American-inspired "Japanese steak house" has become popular in Tokyo, while the McDonald's hamburger stand on the Champs-Elysées is flocked with young Parisians who undoubtedly douse their burgers with ketchup, mustard, and the rest of the condiments Henry Miller deplored. Nor shall the *vignerons* of Bordeaux and Burgundy ever forget that it was grafts from American vines that salvaged the French wine industry after the phylloxera blight of the nineteenth century.

The simple truth is that there is no national cuisine that has ever sprung entirely and ingenuously from its own kitchens. Thus, the United States—a stewpot of cultures—has developed a gastronomy more varied, more distinctive, and more colloquially fascinating than that of any other in the world, all based on an astounding bounty of meat, fruit, vegetables, grains, dairy products, and fish, as well as an incomparable system of transportation that makes finding Pacific salmon on a New York dinner plate an unremarkable occurrence. In any major American city one will find restaurants representing a dozen national cuisines, including northern Italian trattorias, bourgeois French bistros, Portuguese seafood houses, Vietnamese and Thai eateries, Chinese dim sum parlors, Japanese sushi bars, and German rathskellers. Add to these an endless array of regional delicacies—Creole gumbo, Philadelphia scrapple, Texas chili, Maryland she-crab soup, Detroit bullshots, Florida Key lime pie, Napa Valley zinfandels, North Carolina pork barbecue, Arizona chimichangos, Rhode Island johnnycakes, Long Island ducks, Boston scrod, New Orleans Sazeracs, Kentucky bourbon, Minnesota blue cheese, and thousands of others—and one must marvel at the diversity and breadth of American food and drink.

"In nothing is there more evolution than the American mind," wrote Walt Whitman, and this is as true of an American's food as it is of his politics, his art, or his treasured mobility, which allowed him to maintain his immigrant heritage while assimilating a new one. The apple may have been brought to

America by the Pilgrims, but it was a gentle Swedenborgian named John Chapman, better known as Johnny Appleseed, who extended the fruit into the western territories and helped turn the United States into the world's largest grower of apples. An ex-slave named George Washington Carver revived the depleted economy of the South through his experiments in and promotion of peanut farming. A movement of men and beasts from Texas to Kansas after the Civil War resulted in a cattle industry that determined the social, political, and even literary character of the Midwest. In 1840 a German-American Philadelphian named John Wagner produced a light lager that immediately became the dominant style of beer in America and led to the establishment of the great brewery families that shaped the destinies of cities like Milwaukee and Portland, Oregon.

For all this, however, American gastronomy has been chronically under-rated, constantly satirized, and continuously characterized as unimaginative, unsophisticated, and unredeemedly bland, depending more on portion size than preparation time for its effect. Such bias began early in our history, coming from both European and native gastronomes who found the American way of eating all at odds with civilized behavior. It became fashionable for French travelers to shudder at the barbaric table manners and eating habits of Americans. Constantin François de Chassebœuf, Count Volney, showed his disdain for American palates in a report published in 1804 in London:

> In the morning at breakfast they deluge their stomach with a quart of hot water, impregnated with tea, or so slightly with coffee that it is more colored water; and they swallow, almost without chewing, hot bread, half baked, toast soaked in butter, cheese of the fattest kind, slices of salt or hung beef, ham, etc., all of which is nearly insoluble. At dinner they have boiled pastes under the name of puddings, and their sauces, even for roast beef, are melted butter; their turnips and potatoes swim in hog's lard, butter, or fat; under the name of pie or pumpkin, their pastry is nothing but a greasy paste, never sufficiently baked. To digest these viscous substances they take tea almost instantly after dinner, making it so strong that it is absolutely bitter to the taste, in which state it affects the nerves so powerfully that even the English find it brings on more obstinate restlessness than coffee.

Europeans gasped at the amount of salt pork, lard, oysters, and pastries Americans consumed, and in much of the criticism there is a strong hint of envy, for Americans, on the whole, ate far better than any other people on the face of the earth. After the initial years of starvation faced by the earliest settlers, the American land gave up its bounty, as the forests and lakes and seas had done immediately. There seems no exaggeration in the reports of the first Europeans on these shores about hundred-pound cod, forty-pound wild turkeys, six-foot lobsters, and game birds so numerous as to blacken the sky when they flew. In his first dispatch to England in 1606 Captain John Smith asked with a proud immigrant's exuberance, was it not wonderful to be in a land "where man, woman and childe, with a small hooke and line, by angling, may take divers sorts of excellent fish, at their pleasures? And is it not a pretty sport, to pull up two pence, six pence, and twelve pence, as fast as you can haule and veare a line?" This was written at a time when the great majority of Europeans lived on nothing but bread or porridge, when they could get it at all.

Certainly deprivations persisted, but not for lack of abundance. The diets of African slaves on southern plantations were severely restricted by their owners, usually insufficient for good nutrition and rarely augmented by foraging in the fields and forests. The diet of the indentured servant was little, if at all, better. But for others the American larder was full and fully utilized. Hogs, brought to the West Indies by Columbus and introduced to Jamestown by the English, proliferated so well that by the end of the seventeenth century Virginia and Maryland were exporting pork back to Europe. Corn, a native grain, became the most important crop in the States; molasses fueled the economies of several nations; and oysters were so plentiful that by the late eighteenth century they had become the staple of the urban poor's diet.

With the establishment of strong, well-governed colonies came wealth, and with wealth came refinement both in the arts and at the dinner table. For the most part food remained plain—fried or roasted meats and game, boiled fish, cider to drink, and hot breads. Involved sauces were frowned upon as Gallic kickshaws and the food of fops. Yet there were large numbers of "cookery books" (most of them British until the publication in 1796 of *American Cookery,* a forty-seven-page volume by "An American Orphan" named Amelia Simmons), which gave involved, though less than detailed, recipes for stewed carp in a sauce of claret, anchovies, and shallots thickened with butter and egg yolks; ice creams and purées of fruits; and all manner of pastries. Few Americans of the eighteenth century ever made or even came across such dishes, but, it must be stated forcefully, neither did most Europeans. The fallacy of the myth of European taste and elegance lies in its microcosmic scope; it involved no more than a small percentage of the population and focused on only two classes of people—the gentry and the *nouveau riche.* Nevertheless, tables set by Americans like Thomas Jefferson easily rivaled in gastronomic interest those presented at the finest dining salons of France or England.

Jefferson's passion for good food was merely an extension of his voracious appetite for knowledge in every form. His experiments in farming and gardening were directly involved with his experiments in cooking, and he was forever fascinated by foreign foods, methods of preparation, and botanical distinctions that affected the flavors of things. He even installed a French chef in the White House, then brought in two black women to apprentice with the master and learn his techniques. Jefferson brought back a waffle iron from Holland, a pasta machine from Italy, and imported all sorts of plants, fruits, and even olives from Europe. Though criticized by Patrick Henry for renouncing American victuals, Jefferson was not at all interested in turning Monticello into a Virginian Petit Trianon nor in turning his back on American food: indeed, he was, in Evan Jones's words, "determined to surround the best of Virginia food with the best from European cuisine." As Jefferson told his friend Lafayette, if a man wishes to learn about French food he must "ferret people out of their hovels, as I have done, look into their kettles, eat their bread."

By the nineteenth century American cooking had developed quite naturally along regional lines and European traditions, always modified by the exigencies of the land. Foods that were major items in one region's diet may have been marginal in another's, but Americans did share a certain manner of cooking and eating by the middle of the nineteenth century. The cuisine of New Orleans was easily the most distinctive of all the gathered strains of American cookery, but there were dishes to be found in New England—Joe Froggers, Deacon Porter's hat, rum tum tiddy, Harvard beets, and Parker House tripe, to name a few—unlikely to be encountered in the South, while a South Carolinian spending a week in Vermont would be hard put to find a kitchen serving cooter stew, Lady Baltimore cake, mint juleps, hopping john, or benne brittle.

The farther west settlers trekked, the more culinary cohesion Americans took on, for although the Midwest was settled largely by people of German extraction who continued making many dishes from the Old Country, the new territories and broad farms provided such a wealth of grain, fruits, vegetables, and livestock that the whole country began eating much the same diet, still buoyed by copious portions of meat. Barbecue grew out of the South and Southwest, and there was considerable Mexican influence along the Rio Grande. The food of the pioneers was often horrifying, meant only to keep body and soul, though not appetite, together during the push across the wilderness. The stories of these settlers are harsh, full of tales of starvation and revulsion for a diet that never varied from St. Louis to Oregon. Mostly they ate preserved foods, salt pork, jerky, dried corn, and dried-apple pies. Trappers might make a "butter" from buffalo marrow, blood, and boiling water, while others survived on insects, vultures, and reptiles.

After the Civil War beef asserted itself as a most desirable alternative to pork, and by the twentieth century "steak and potatoes" had become synonymous with the American diet; at the same time the American "sweet tooth" developed with the drop in sugar prices. There were by the end of the nineteenth century lavish restaurants serving the most extravagant meals, bars serving all manner of beers and cocktails to a public that never lacked for ice, and everyone ate at chowder houses, delicatessens, coffeehouses, and tamale stands. Even as far west as Denver, in 1892 a hotel like the Brown Palace could put up a spread that included littleneck clams, consommé renaissance, trout ravigote, Maryland terrapin, German wines, and French champagne. This was as nothing compared to the meals created in New York's Delmonico's, Boston's Parker House, or Chicago's Sherman House, where ten-course meals were everyday suppers.

In fact, it was the virtue of such restaurants to bring America into gastronomic repute. They impressed even European visitors who previously had expected the kind of disastrous dining experiences noted by Charles Dickens, who described dinner, supper, and breakfast aboard a Pennsylvania canal boat as identical to one another—tea, coffee, bread, butter, salmon, shad, liver, steak, potatoes, pickles, ham, chops, black puddings, and sausages, all consumed by gentlemen who "thrust the broad-bladed knives and the two-pronged forks farther down their throats than I ever saw the same weapons go before except in the hands of a skillful juggler."

By the same token the opulent restaurants and grand hotels of the Gilded Age focused attention on the gluttonous nature of dining among the newly rich, which led quite naturally to a general criticism of all Americans' eating habits. And the menus of such establishments—fussed up with French dishes and French terminology for American dishes—scorned the food of the common man in an attempt to elevate the status and palate of the American trying desperately to appear civilized.

As a result, regional American cuisine became a subject of homely virtues, expressive of the gracious and genteel traditions of Victorian womanhood. Old recipes for local delicacies were not so much forgotten as ignored, so that the first edition in 1896 of Fannie Merritt Farmer's extraordinarily successful *Boston Cooking-School Cook Book* contained sensible, well-tested recipes for *potage à la reine, maître d'hôtel* butter, charlotte russe, and cutlets *à la Maintenon* (along with hints on how to clean mirrors, remove wine stains, and sweep carpets) and had a three-page glossary composed almost entirely of French terms.

Nothing so relegates a culture to mediocrity as to be thought quaint, and by the beginning of the twentieth century American cookery had entered just such a phase, largely as a reaction to the ways in which the populace had come to enjoy its meals—at beer halls, at ball parks, at county fairs, on boardwalks, at roadside stands, at soda fountains, at lunch counters, at pizzerias, at hash houses, at saloons, at spaghetti joints, at barbecue pits. Food was taken on the run, eaten on park benches, wolfed down at taverns, consumed at beach parties, and all of it was ingested too quickly. Concerns about the health of the population not only led to a reassessment of the nutritive values of foods, but also resulted in federal regulations to combat corrupt and sickening practices in the meat and agriculture industries. These concerns ultimately led, with a strident moralism, to Prohibition, which radically altered the manner in which people cooked, ate, and dined out for more than a decade.

The so-called ladies' books had long imitated Victorian hesitancy when describing food in print—rice would be called "farinaceous dishes" and a meal was "a simple repast"—and this tradition continued well into the present century. There was an attempt to ban the use of the term *hot dog* from all vendors' signs in Coney Island, lest people think their frankfurters really contained dog meat. And the vitality of lunch-counter speech—*cat's eyes* for tapioca, *baby* for glass of milk, *jerk* for ice cream soda, and *Adam and Eve on a raft* for fried eggs on toast—had a raciness about it that many people sought to put an end to in the 1930s.

More profound than any other factor affecting the image of American cookery in this century was the pervasive influence of immigrants on the culture. The waves of new settlers driven to the American shore were inspired not by a belief that the streets were paved with gold but by sheer, basic hunger. What the Poles, Jews, Italians, Irish, Germans, Armenians, and others found in America was far more valuable than gold: it was a constantly available source of fruits, fresh water, good grains, green vegetables, annual harvests of plenty, and safe, healthful milk.

The immigrants immediately set about adapting their native cookery to what was available in the American marketplace. Certain vegetables were not readily found here, and the water was different, as were the flour, the butter, the meat, and the wonderful cookstoves (by the 1930s gas and electric stoves, too). These differences altered traditional cooking methods and changed the tastes and textures of their foods.

Lox, so closely associated with Jewish-Americans, was unknown to European Jews; the Italian pizza, once a staple of the Neapolitan poor, became an American snack food; *gulyás,* in Hungary a dried meat carried by shepherds, became in America goulash, a kind of peppery stew; chop suey and chow mein came out of the makeshift kitchens of Oriental workers on the western railroads; and wines from native American grapes were labelled "Green Hungarian," "Chianti," and "Sauterne."

The culture was immeasurably enriched by the influx of the immigrants, as was the language of our gastronomy: Americans spoke with evident familiarity about beerfests, wieners, bagels, tutti-frutti, hamburgers, Swedish meatballs, ravioli, smorgasbords, Danish pastries, liverwurst, vichyssoise, chow-chow, lager, curry, matzo ball soup, halvah, tortillas, paprika, baklava, moussaka, and sukiyaki, and they visited bodegas, delicatessens, trattorias, sushi bars, taco stands, Greek coffee shops, dim sum parlors, pizzerias, rathskellers, and bistros. All these foods and all these places were transformed into American institutions, for better or for worse. Add to these the extraordinary growth of the processed-food and confections industries, with items like Coca-Cola, Crisco, Sugar Daddy, Eskimo Pies, Cheerios, Grape Nuts, Pork n' Beans, Niblets, and thousands of others, and one begins to sense the dimensions of American gastronomy.

It is, of course, legitimate to suggest that many of these items fall far short of the culinary sublime or that much of the "ethnic" food on this side of the Atlantic bears scant resemblance to that in the Old Countries. But such a criticism assumes three claims:

First, that people in France, Germany, Italy, or China at the turn of the century were eating splendid meals on a daily basis—that a citizen of Bordeaux sat down each evening to a fine *coq au vin* made with a bottle of excellent claret; that a peasant of Sicily each afternoon enjoyed a steaming plate of macaroni with a rich tomato-and-garlic sauce, followed by fresh mussels and a glass of Marsala with dessert; or that a worker in Canton province regaled his neighbors with a meal of lobster steamed with ground pork or chicken with wild mushrooms.

Second, that the transformation of a dish, especially by Americanized immigrants, is always inferior to the original. Yet, except for certain classic and mannered dishes in French and other gastronomies, there are really very few dishes in the world that have not been modified or radically altered by inventive cooks. In northern Italy the cooks look down with dyspepsia on the olive-oil-and-garlic-rich cuisine of the south, while the people from one province to another regard the butter and wines of their direct neighbors with disdain. A French *cassoulet* will have as many variants as there are households in Toulouse, and every Moroccan will argue vociferously that her *cous-cous* is the only "authentic" one in her village. (This same form of debate rages among American cooks who consider the alteration of a single ingredient in a southern fried chicken recipe or the use of the wrong kind of cornmeal in a jonnycake as tantamount to bona fide heresy and sacrilege.)

Third, that American cuisine is nothing more than the cookery of peasants, dispossessed people, and uneducated amateurs whose foods may taste wholesome, even delicious, but rarely sublime. Such a position is not only snobbish but misses the whole thrust of American cookery—or any nation's cookery, for that matter. The cuisine of the royal courts, the gentry's manors, and the entrepreneur's townhouses is never the cuisine of a country. Fabled dishes—from excesses like *tournedos rossini* to glories like *poularde à la Perigourdine*—are not to be found simmering in the kettles of French kitchens, but hearty *choucroute,* aromatic *bouillabaisse,* and oxtail stew are. For every Carême or Escoffier in France there are a million unheralded home cooks whose cuisine truly carries on the reputation of France over the centuries.

Yet French deluxe cuisine—meaning that prepared only in the greatest, most expensive, and most socially exclusive restaurants—continues as the measure of a country's culinary culture and sophistication, a criterion rigidly promoted by those who own, cook, and dine in such places. The notable restaurants of the nineteenth and early twentieth centuries in America were designed not for an appreciative mass of middle-class eaters—and certainly not for the new immigrant class—but for the wealthy, who did not expect to find on the menu homely dishes like peanut soup, barbecued spareribs, spoon bread, ham with redeye gravy, and fudge cake, much less Polish sausage, manicotti, and Irish soda bread. (To be fair, restaurants like Delmonico's, Rector's, and others offered a wide variety of American game, pies, and desserts, though usually described on the bill of fare as *à la* this or *au* that.) By the turn of the century hotel restaurants like the Waldorf's Palm Garden had hired tyrannical maître d'hôtels like Oscar Tschirky, an ex-busboy who rose to near royalty in New York society by decreeing who was and was not fashionable in his dining room, which served a menu rife with Gallicisms. A menu of 1904 served to William Howard Taft, then Secretary of War, read as follows:

Cocktail *aux Huitres, Consommé de Volaille, Printanière, Tortue Verte Claire, Radis Olives Celeri Amandes Salées, Coquilles de Bass à la Virchow, Concombres Marines,*

Couronne de Ris de Veau avec Champignons Frais, Mignons de Filet de Boeuf à la Cardinalice, Pommes de Terre Sautées en Quartiers, Petits Pois à la Française, Fond d'Artichauts Frais à la Dubarry, Sorbet de Fantasie, Pluviers d'Herbes Rôtis, Gelée de Groseilles Salade Chiffonade, Glaces à la Grenadine, Petits Fours, Fruits, Cigars, Café. [The wines were all French.]

Ironically, the Waldorf could turn out some very "American" meals—dishes like Colombine of Chicken California Style, Ruddy Duck, and the famous Waldorf Salad. Even in the French dishes the chefs used excellent-quality American ingredients, a fact that should not be lost on those current-day practitioners of what is called "The New American Cuisine," which uses American ingredients and French techniques.

But reputations were not built on serving the kind of food that might just as easily be turned out by immigrant housewives or black cooks. Interestingly enough, it was the black cooks who maintained, even in restaurants, the great traditions of southern cuisine in cities like New Orleans, Charleston, Richmond, and Savannah and who kept up the strain of northern cookery in Boston, Philadelphia, and Chicago. None of these cooks, however, was known to anyone except steady customers, who might have called them by their first names. Professional American cooks were known only as "Jimmy" or "Thomas" or "Henry" to their public, and the fame of ethnic cooks in the northern cities was enshrined in the names of the restaurants themselves—Tony's, Haussner's, or O'Brien's, for example. Memoirs of the first half of this century speak of ethnic restaurants with believable affection, but rarely with high regard for the food, except to say that it was cheap, belly-filling, and honestly prepared.

It is significant that of the more than fifty volumes in the American Guide Series published under the Federal Writers Program during the Depression, only a handful mention the food of a region, and fewer still mention restaurants at all. American cooking was simply not considered worthy of critical scrutiny, even though a work like Irma S. Rombauer's *Joy of Cooking,* which first appeared in 1931 and has gone through several revisions, remains a thorough and authoritative collection of American recipes and kitchen techniques.

American food was looked upon as rib-sticking, plain, sometimes wholesome, sometimes not, fun to eat, fast to eat, and never anything to be fussed with or over. Writers took true delight in exalting the lowliest of sandwiches, the greasiest of meats, the hottest of preparations, and the gloppiest of desserts with a kind of deliberate thumb-to-the-nose attitude that only hardened the opinions of gastronomic critics who believed all along that Americans reveled in bad taste. Or, as Henry Miller wrote, Americans would eat garbage if you put ketchup on it. We Americans prided ourselves on the number of hot dogs we could eat, the amount of candy we could consume, the intensity of hot peppers we could abide, and the time in which we could devour all of it. None of these achievements was likely to build a national reputation for gastronomic excellence.

At the same time Americans were being taunted by one of the most unreasonable and baffling forms of temperance, which sprang not from a nutritional argument but, for the most part, from a religious one. We are the only people in the world who, possibly because of our abundance, have been made to feel guilty about our good fortune. In a mild form this self-recrimination is evident in the pangs of conscience a person feels when he goes off his diet and in the ridiculous way chocolate is described as "devil's food," especially considering that other cultures call chocolate the "food of the gods" (*Theobroma* in the Linnaean system), and rich desserts as "sinfully delicious." Clearly it was the duty of American religious crusaders to point out the sins of dissolution that result from too much wine, spirits, and extravagant food, but this was far more a position of the established English and German religions than of the new immigrant faiths.

Nevertheless, the passage of the Volstead Act in 1919 only ostensibly cut off most Americans from the enjoyment of wine and spirits (and actually led to more crime, corruption, and "sin") while severely crippling an already struggling wine industry in California, New York, and other states. To survive such a blow, vineyard owners turned to raisin production and selling grape juice for jams and jellies.

Prohibition also destroyed any possibility that American restaurants would develop a reputation for fine dining, much less a distinctive cuisine based on American fare. Even the first-class speakeasies of the era were not places one went to for great food. As Michael and Ariane Batterberry note in their book, *On the Town in New York* (1973), "The depressing truth was that New Yorkers could not be enticed into a dry restaurant, no matter how superior the food; on the other hand, they seemed perfectly content to eat sawdust as long as it came with a drink."

The era of the grand banquets and twelve-course meals had vanished too, as did Delmonico's and Louis Sherry, two of the outstanding restaurants of pre–World War I days. Ethnic restaurants—tellingly referred to as "joints"—provided the cities with considerable liveliness, and the speakeasies provided gossipmongers with a new "Café Society" to write about.

After Prohibition ended in 1933, there was no scramble to restore the opulent dining of the past, though the enjoyment of good food was considerably more enjoyable now that wine and spirits were again available. Major cities began to nurture truly fine restaurants, like New York's Le Pavillon, which opened in 1941, but again, most of these were French or described by a new word—*Continental*. Continental restaurants aimed to please everyone's palate, serving up a melange of dishes that ranged from filet mignon and clams casino to striped bass *à la meunière*, beef Wellington, and baked Alaska, usually with an emphasis on French and Italian items. This approach to menu-planning was precisely what gourmets might have expected from inferior kitchens, and, too often, the results were as expected.

If a restaurant was not dishing out such international approximations of authentic "classics," it was busy gearing everything, including the food and service, to a "theme," created so that people who felt uneasy about ordering a meal at a fancy, formal restaurant, where one had to dress and act in a certain way, could casually enter dining rooms that were decorated like pirates' coves, Wild West saloons, colonial taverns, or Roman temples, where all the waiters were dressed appropriate to the idea and where the food was described in the most expressive prose since *Euphues*. The most extravagant of such eateries were run by New York's Restaurant Associates, which could certainly turn out good meals on occasion but did so according to a "concept." Thus, at the Forum of the Twelve Caesars the menu was in Latin (with English subtitles), dishes were named after Cleopatra and Nero, and there were even barbaric puns on notable American dishes, like caesar salad ("The Noblest Caesar of Them All").

The theme concept was quickly adapted throughout the country, and one never quite knew what to expect when one walked through the swinging doors of a restaurant called the Auto Pub or Long John Silver's; certainly one's gustatory expectations were not very high.

Restaurants with a superb view of the city became faddish by the 1970s; some dining rooms even revolved atop bank buildings as customers wolfed down plates of "Mile-High Pie." Waiters themselves were encouraged to become so friendly as to announce their first name to customers, whether or not the customer wanted to know it. This practice expressed a democratic spirit of such insecurity that implicit in the act was the common understanding that having a swell time was more important than having a great meal. What did it matter if the fish had been frozen and cooked by microwave or that the entire entree had been packaged in a New Jersey food-processing plant and merely needed to be heated up in order to serve a customer a perfectly proportioned meal, complete with bright green beans and bright orange carrots and a rim of powdered mashed potatoes caressing the veal parmesan?

The advent of frozen foods in the 1940s and 1950s made life easier and, to be sure, offered a new diversity of food items to a large number of people. The labor involved in cooking was reduced, and the guesswork and worry over a poorly wrought meal was removed. Another advance was "instant" foods— powdered puddings, potatoes, and cereals, prepackaged pancake batter, vegetables sealed in plastic pouches, and other less than delectable but wholly efficient preparations that seized the American imagination and made convenience a virtue far outweighing matters of taste and flavor.

Yet for all the criticism of such foods (and of an agricultural industry that propagated fewer varieties but hardier breeds of fruits and vegetables), the next phase of frozen, instant, and packaged foods was even worse—"gourmet dishes," such as fettuccine Alfredo, asparagus with hollandaise sauce, and "Oriental" vegetables, a seemingly complete contradiction in terms. The final blow to American taste came with the plethora of "diet foods," which were either traditional processed foods made with less sugar, oil, or syrups or smaller portions of the same old stuff. In recent years diet beer and diet wine have enjoyed tremendous popularity, even though almost no one vouches for their having much flavor at all.

It is no wonder, then, that American food deserved the hard knocks it has taken in the last twenty years. Indeed, Americans seemed proud of their so-called junk food, which at first meant snacks, candies, and other less than nutritious items but came to encompass "fast foods" sold at roadside stands usually run by nationwide chains. Several such operations have specialized in some of the more obvious items in the American kitchen—hamburgers, hot dogs, fried chicken, french-fried potatoes, apple pie, and ice cream—serving them lickety-split from assembly lines of griddles and deep-fryers at the hands of patently chummy young people in standardized uniforms. Cheap, casual, and geared for ingestion of product rather than the pleasure of dining, these places reduced the flavor of such foods to the point where Henry Miller's comment about drowning the original taste with sweet-and-sour condiments began to make sense.

More disturbing was the fact that small, family-owned restaurants, where such food was traditionally made according to old recipes, were being nudged aside in favor of the fast-food eateries, so that even American institutions like the diner and the cafeteria, where excellent American fare could be had, found it difficult if not impossible to compete with the fast-food places' prices and "fun atmosphere."

The reaction to all this was the development of a culinary elitism that once again pronounced the excellence of French, Italian, and Oriental cuisines and the horrid state of American gastronomy. Even a charming Boston woman named Julia Child enjoyed a long run on Public Television showing Americans how to cook not turkey with stuffing, clam chowders, or scrod, but *rôti de porc poele, canard à l'orange,* and *choux de Bruxelles.* Credit must be given to such a television program and to Mrs. Child for relieving the inferiority complex American cooks had about French food and complex cooking processes in general. Her tone was typically Yankee and refreshingly reassuring, and she taught a generation how to care about excellent ingredients and attention to detail.

There also appeared in the 1970s a number of works by authors who began seriously to restore traditional American fare to its proper perspective. James Beard, Craig Claiborne, James Villas, and Waverly Root spoke with authority and great affection of their childhood memories of catfish, Dungeness crab, pork barbecue, grits, blueberry bread, hot chilies, New England boiled dinner, Pacific oysters, potato salad, and scores of other delectables that many people had forgotten could be so very good until prepared with care and love and served with those same homely virtues.

At the same times, food magazines like *Gourmet, Cuisine, Food & Wine,* and others began devoting more space to American cookery, and even the Culinary Institute of America, a cooking school in Hyde Park, New York, long devoted to continental cuisine, opened a separate course of study on American food.

A crucial event in the renaissance of American cuisine came with the publication in 1970 of a beautifully produced seven volumes entitled *American*

Cooking in Time-Life's Foods of the World series. Well-written, gorgeously illustrated, and full of well-tested, explicit recipes, these volumes on New England, Creole and Acadian, Northwest, Eastern Heartland, Southern Style, Great West, and Melting Pot regional cooking showed just how diverse this nation's cookery is. They reveal the wealth of tradition and history behind each dish and a people's pride in every preparation.

Other regional cook books have appeared since 1970 ranging from specific books on a single item like chili or cheesecake to thick volumes of recipes compiled by women's organizations throughout the United States. Several excellent histories of American food and drink have appeared within the last decade, along with delightful compendiums of lore and anecdotes on everything from candy bars and ice cream to North American fish. American wines, which in the 1970s became internationally respected, have been boosted by wine writers and recorded in narratives and encyclopedias with care and devotion to accuracy. Things seem to be on the right track again.

American food is diversified, modified, substantial, complex, heterogeneous, subtle, humdrum, exciting, excessive, embracing, soul-warming and stomach-filling, hot, cold, prepared with honesty, concocted with audacity, promoted with passion, consumed with courage, debated with conviction, tossed in a pot, simmered in a kettle, fried in a skillet, chilled in a bowl, shaken in a cannister, brewed in an urn, topped off, tossed out, shoved down, pushed aside, got through, held up, wriggled on the end of a pole, brought down with an arrow, skinned with a knife, tested with a finger, squeezed with a hand, sniffed at, cursed at, argued over, and beloved by a people who will try anything once.

What *is* American food?

It is this—

A Guide to the Dictionary

No one ever starts writing a dictionary of anything believing it will be a complete record of its subject. Even a compiler of known facts on Etruscan art hopes that tomorrow a new shard of pottery will be unearthed that will add to or alter his work in small but important ways. The subject of a country's food, more than most others, is as inexhaustible as language itself, for each generation renames, reworks, and reevaluates the culture that produced it, discarding some prejudices and reenforcing others. Two of the most American of American animals—the buffalo and the turkey—were misnamed from the start (the American buffalo is really a bison, and the turkey was confused with a guinea fowl brought from Turkey), yet we retain their appellations proudly. Other foods go through so many mutations that they bear scant resemblance to the original. The Sazerac cocktail, originally made with absinthe and named after Sazerac brandy, is no longer made with either ingredient, yet it still is a quintessential drink of New Orleans.

No county worth its salt has less than six different names for the same kind of regional fish, all of which differ from the next locality's names for the same creature. And what Yankees refer to as a "partridge" is really a ruffed grouse, while a southerner who points out a "partridge" is really indicating a quail. The American who calls a sweet potato a "yam" has never seen a true yam.

Language is consistent only in its mutability, as is the food and drink we eat, celebrate, and argue over. A Texan would never dream of letting a kidney bean near his chili, but a midwesterner couldn't imagine chili without a whole mess of beans. (A *mess*, incidentally, may mean a lot of food sloppily thrown together, but an older usage connotes nothing more than an assemblage of people eating together or a portion of food.)

Etymologists will argue forever as to the true origins of the martini cocktail (indeed, the word *cocktail* itself is still under linguistic scrutiny), the exact derivation of Harvard beets, the root for the deep-fried rice cakes of New Orleans called "calas," and the way doughboys got their nickname. Who can say just when the old usage of *truck farm,* meaning a fresh-produce market, took on the contemporary usage of the farm on which the produce sold at market is grown? Why and when did Americans show a preference for *hot dogs* over *weenies* or *bar* over *saloon?*

My aim in this dictionary is to demonstrate both the array of American food, wine, and drink and the way Americans speak of it, consume it, and have changed it over the centuries. In each case I have tried to answer the questions I myself would ask were I looking for information on an apple or a tamale, a brief history of Prohibition, or a slang term for a bartender. I have endeavored to include as much as possible about American gastronomy, but no book of this sort could include everything, just as the standard dictionaries on the English language differ on what they list.

More important than all-inclusiveness is accuracy, and I hope that my research has been fruitful enough to turn up the best information and the most reliable anecdote on a particular subject, although I have been quick to point out when this or that story is mere legend. Sometimes a story is so enjoyable it begs inclusion, if even with my strong objection to its veracity.

While I regret any errors or omissions, I welcome corrections and addenda from the reader, and I fully expect to hear what I hope will be sympathetic words from people all over the country who can enlighten me as to the precise origin of a dish or the only correct way to mix a drink.

This volume is not a history of gastronomy or the American language, nor is it a cookbook. It assuredly is not a book to tell the reader the best way to skin a rabbit or skim a broth. There are several books available on each of these subjects. This book contains elements of all of them, gathered into a survey, from A to Z, of the origins, changes, and current status of food and drink items, terms of culinary interest, and slang.

Although my own background is academic and journalistic, my approach has been to inform the general reader in as readable and entertaining a way as possible. I have, therefore, kept abbreviations to a minimum and discarded footnotes in favor of giving full credit in the body of the text or in the bibliography and acknowledgments. While I hope every sentence makes a good point, I sometimes cannot resist an anecdote that I believe the reader will enjoy.

My dependence on the work of others who have labored for a lifetime in the fields of etymology and linguistics has been enormous, and I take scant credit for illuminating dark corners where others' lights have failed to find a convincing explanation. I merely suggest what seems to me plausible, and then throw it open for discussion with the reader. I stand humbly in the shadow of H. L. Mencken, who wrote in the preface to his second supplement to *The American Language* (1948), "I am not trained in linguistic science, and can thus claim no profundity for my book. It represents gatherings, not of an expert in linguistics, but simply of a journalist interested in language, and if there appears in it any virtue at all it is with the homely virtue of diligence. Someone had to bring together the widely scattered field material and try to get some order and coherence into it, and I fell into the job."

MAIN ENTRIES

Main entries are listed alphabetically, sometimes as a general heading for a specific food or drink. Under the more general topics, for example, APPLE, BEER, PANCAKE, there may very well be dozens of more specific terms, types, species, regional variants, slang, or ancillary items within the body of the entry. The reader is urged to check the index for those items not found as a main entry. Within the main entries these subitems may be printed in small capital letters, indicating that there is further information on that particular subject as a main entry.

RECIPES

The recipes that follow a main entry's description of an item are chosen in most cases to be *representative* of a dish or item; the directions have been kept deliberately simple and brief. In some cases a recipe is taken from a quoted source, especially if it is of historical importance or if it is the original source of the dish or drink. Recipes from an original source are always thus credited, as, for example, Parker House roll or Trader Vic's Mai Tai. I have also included recipes from historical sources, either to give a sense of a food's original form or because such dishes are rarely, if ever, made anymore. Hartshorn jelly, for instance, was a well-known eighteenth-century confection, but as it is unlikely to be found today, I have provided an eighteenth-century recipe and noted the origin.

By a representative recipe I mean one that seems close to the way in which such a dish is usually made. I am well aware that there may be hundreds of variations on a "classic" recipe, but I have tried to choose the one that represents the principal ingredients and method of preparation that would be used by a wide range of cooks. I have not tried to choose the *best* recipe I've ever found for a specific dish for the reason that it may very well *not* be representative of the way Americans cook. (Recipes for some of the finest desserts, pastries, and cookies I know come from several cook books written by Maida Heatter, but they often do not represent the way most American cooks would prepare an item; they represent the unique and imaginative talents of this singularly remarkable woman.)

Many readers may find the recipes stingy with details and not specific enough in comparison with many cook books that lead the reader by the apron strings, explaining everything from how to peel a carrot to how to beat an egg. I have assumed that the user of this book possesses a certain culinary acumen —as did his or her ancestors, who cooked by very simple directions—and I simply did not have the space to include instructions on how to whip an egg white to "soft, glistening peaks" every time such a preparation was called for. So, too, if a cooked-sugar recipe calls for bringing the caramel to a "hard-ball" or "soft-ball" stage, the reader is assumed to be familiar with such terms but is nevertheless provided with a temperature to test for on a candy thermometer. The details of making a dough and letting it rise in bulk are kept to a minimum, and often I will instruct the reader only to "make a pastry crust," rather than tell again how to make one.

This is not a book on nutrition, and I have tried to keep clear of arguments for or against the "healthfulness" of this or that dish or spirit. Nor is this an industry manual meant to contain hints on how to best cut, package, and store meat, fish, or fowl.

One rule I do advise the reader to follow with these recipes is to pay attention to the order in which ingredients are listed, for the order indicates at what point they should be added to a preparation. Although in many cases the addition of several spices or seasonings at once is justified, I have attempted to indicate the moment at which the next ingredient should be added, and it is best to blend thoroughly each new addition before putting in the next one. Cooks more or less familiar with the routine of such matters will know when this is important or not.

As for the terminology of cooking, I have conservatively adhered to level teaspoons and standard measurements in ounces and pounds and avoided old-fashioned instructions like "add a wine glass of" such and such. On the other hand, I see no reason to be stringently specific about what constitutes a *dash* or a *pinch,* long-honored terms that make sense to anyone who cooks regularly. (There is an apocryphal story about Fannie Merritt Farmer giving instructions on making a martini that go, "to one cup gin, add. . . .")

The recipes themselves come from a wide variety of sources from three centuries of American cookery, but the bulk come from cookbooks of the last thirty years for the reason that it is impossible to gauge the success factor of a recipe from an era when flour, yeast, molasses, baking powder (which only came along in the 1850s), wine, spirits, and even ovens were very different from what they have become in the past quarter century. Despite the prejudice of those who believe that cookbooks of the eighteenth and nineteenth centuries represented American culinary arts at their highest, there is really no way to reproduce recipes that call for ingredients like isinglass, pearl ash, and sack. Others would shudder at the thought of my including recipes from "ladies' magazines," because such journals often try to oversimplify or change recipes to suit some imaginary housewife who has access only to processed and packaged foods. The point is well taken, especially since many of these magazines depend on the advertising of the very products they recommend in a recipe. But if one is to compile a dictionary of gastronomy that tells the reader how Americans actually do cook and eat, such recipes play an important part. I have, for the record, never recommended margarine where butter is preferred, but it may be argued that Americans cook with far more margarine and shortening than butter. So, too, I have avoided brand names of products, except where they seem an intrinsic part of a recipe—Tabasco sauce, for example.

I claim no originality for any of these recipes—that would defeat the whole point of the book—and I have tried to cull workable recipes from reliable sources and to stay clear of arguments as to the "correct" method of preparing a dish. "Correct methods" are usually those that an individual believes to be the *best* method or those derived from a recipe of antique interest. American cookery has very few "classic" recipes; even those that originated at a specific place and time have been changed, sometimes for the worse, often for the better. That is the role of a good cook, for absolute imitation is the drudgery of the slave or the pedant.

WHAT IS AND IS NOT INCLUDED

As I have indicated, there is no workable definition of what constitutes American cuisine. Most American dishes are essentially variations or derivatives, which is true of almost every dish in the world. "The discovery of a new dish is more beneficial to humanity than the discovery of a new star," wrote Brillat-Savarin (who rather liked American food when he visited here in 1794), but every new dish is really a variation on an old one. Anyone who has ever paged through Escoffier's *Le Guide Culinaire* will immediately be struck by the minor modifications of one dish that allow it to be called something entirely different; the same is true of *Larousse Gastronomique,* in which one finds that the addition of one standard sauce or another to poached chicken deserves a new appellation and brief cooking instructions.

Certain dishes or drinks indisputably originated in America: Key lime pie, cornbread, bourbon, fudge, and hundreds of others. Other dishes, like jambalaya, gumbo, beignets, and much of the cuisine of the Creoles and Cajuns, were derived from European, Caribbean, Indian, and African sources, but were then turned into distinctive American foods. Beverages like shrubs, flips, grogs, and punches became popular in Great Britain and America at the same time, while turkey, buffalo, and numerous species of fish were exported to Europe, where they became delicacies.

I have been liberal in my choice of what to include, but I believe I have good reasons to keep many items out. While it may be true that the Bloody Mary cocktail was "created" in Paris in the 1920s (when it was called the "Bucket of Blood"), the drink caught on here, not there, and has remained a standard American bar item ever since the 1930s. On the other hand, even though Americans drink more Scotch than any other people outside England, the fact is that by law Scotch is produced only in Scotland and has no business being in a dictionary of American gastronomy.

The real problem develops when one deals with the foods brought over by the immigrants of the late nineteenth and early twentieth centuries. (Fifty years from now it will be interesting to see how many Korean, Vietnamese, and Thai dishes have become standard menu items here.) What is the rationale for including dishes like veal parmigiana or chili con carne or vichyssoise? These three are easily defensible: There *is* no such dish in Italy by the name "veal parmigiana" (much less "veal parmesan"); chili con carne is a Texas dish, frowned upon by most Mexicans; and vichyssoise was created at New

York's Ritz-Carlton Hotel dining room by chef Louis Diat, who named it after a French spa. Such dishes are simply *inspired* by Italian, Mexican or French notions.

Other ethnic foods have been so transformed over the years that they bear scant resemblance to their ancestral origins. Read, for example, the bewildering difference between the recipe given for *filets de sole Marguery* in *Larousse Gastronomique,* supposedly provided by the original chef, and that attributed to George Rector, Jr., who brought the recipe back from France for the delectation of Diamond Jim Brady and, afterwards, for the approval of generations of American cooks (see SOLE MARGUERY). The original recipe for fettuccine Alfredo—ubiquitous here, rarely found in Italy by this name—contains no cream at all, which in America is the main ingredient. English muffins are never called by that name in England. And *french fries* refers not to potatoes as invented by some Frenchman, but to the way in which they are sliced, or "frenched."

My rule of thumb, then, with regard to such transformed dishes has been to include them if they have really been changed over the years by American cooks or if they have become so popular here as to be immediately identifiable by the majority of Americans. Certain items, like Cornish pasties, are so associated with the miners of Michigan that to exclude them would be to omit one of the dishes that helps define the region's gastronomic character. The same would be true of many Pennsylvania Dutch or Moravian items, delicacies of New Orleans, or the dishes of New York's Jews.

By the same token I cannot in good conscience include foreign dishes that may still be prepared in the traditional way for special feasts among a certain group of people. My wife, for instance, prepares traditional Russian foods at Easter, but none of them—such as the tall cake called *"kulich"* or the pot cheese dessert called *"paskha"*—has been Americanized, nor are they known outside of the Russian families that still make them in this country. So, too, Czech families in this country may still make *brněnský řízek,* Greeks their *entrada,* Austrians their *haussulz,* and Japanese their *kyogashi,* but these foods are still uncommon, especially among second- or third-generation ethnic Americans.

As for drinks and cocktails, I have tried to list those that are well known today or that have some historic interest. These would include everything from Coca-Cola and Tab to the numerous slang terms for coffee and the various kinds of beer and alcoholic beverages enjoyed both regionally and nationally, such as mint juleps, screwdrivers, and Manhattans. I have avoided listing alcoholic concoctions that seem to have been invented and forgotten almost in the same night. As far as I have been able, I have traced the origins of these drinks and provided recipes according to current tastes, with notes on how such beverages may have changed through the decades.

Last, I have no intention of declaring my own fondness or antipathy for certain dishes or terms, nor do I ever want to get in between two southerners debating the right way to make hush puppies. Even though I will never understand all the fuss about chicken-fried steak or grits, I happily include them here. As someone who grew up on Bronx egg creams, I can understand others' astonishment that such a confection could have inspired so many New Yorkers to praise it.

If it's true—and it is—that we are what we eat, then what is included here is all about what we are.

THE DICTIONARY OF
AMERICAN FOOD
AND DRINK

abalone (Genus *Haliotis*). Any of a variety of univalve gastropods having an ear-shaped shell. The name is from the Spanish, *abulón,* was introduced into English in 1850 and in 1883 appeared in George Brown Goode's *Fisheries and Fishery Industries of the United States.* There are about a hundred species of abalone in the world, eight of which inhabit the waters of the Pacific coast and are commercially harvested, by prying them from rocks they attach themselves to, in California and, to a lesser extent, in Washington. All species are edible, but the flesh is rubbery and must be pounded. Abalone is usually dredged with flour and sautéed in butter. The main American species are black abalone *(Haliotis cracherodii),* green abalone *(H. fulgens),* pink abalone *(H. corrugata),* red abalone *(H. rufescens),* white abalone *(H. sorenseni),* flat abalone *(H. walallensis),* threaded abalone *(H. assimilis),* and pinto abalone *(H. kamt-schatkana).*

Aberdeen angus. Also "Angus" or "Black Angus." A breed of black, horn-less steer originally bred in Scotland, this variety was brought to the United States in 1873 and quickly replaced the **longhorn** as a beef steer. The name comes from two counties in northeastern Scotland, Aberdeen and Angus.

absinthe. A green cordial derived from wormwood *(Artemisia absinthium).* Absinthe is anise-flavored and rather bitter, has a proof of 136, and was first used as a stomach tonic concocted by French doctor Pierre Ordinaire in Switzerland. In 1797 the recipe was sold by the physician's heirs to the firm of Henri-Louis Pernod, which sold it commercially. The drink was reputed to have aphrodisiacal qualities and became extremely popular in New Orleans, which came to be known as the absinthe capital of the world and where the liqueur found its way into cocktails, such as the **Sazerac.** One of the city's most famous restaurants, Brennan's, was called the Old Absinthe House in the 1860s. (The recipe for absinthe frappé below is from this establishment.)

Absinthe was usually diluted by dripping it through a perforated spoon containing a sugar cube and then dripping water through the absinthe, which turned the liqueur cloudy.

Wormwood was discovered to have harmful effects on people's health and to be habit-forming. It was banned in Switzerland in 1908, then in America in 1912, and replaced in cocktails by anise-flavored liqueurs like Ojen, from Spain, or Herbsaint, made by a New Orleans pharmacist named J. Marion Legendre in 1934.

ABSINTHE FRAPPÉ:
(From *The Picayune's Creole Cook Book* [1901]) Mix 1 tbs. absinthe (now Herbsaint or Pernod) with a dash of anisette and pour into small, thin glasses filled with crushed ice and water; let the mixture get very cold and serve. (The absinthe frappé may be served without the anisette. Some add the white of an egg.)

ABSINTHE SUISSESSE:
Combine 1 1/2 oz. Herbsaint or Pernod with 2 tbs. cream, 1 tbs. orgeat syrup, 1 egg white, and crushed ice and shake (or mix in an electric blender) till completely blended. Pour the unstrained liquid into a chilled glass.

acorn. A hard-shelled nut, the fruit of an oak tree, that in some varieties can be poisonous. The word is from Old English, *æcern.*

Acorns are rarely eaten by Americans, but they were once an important food of the Indian. Of the sixty species of oak in America, twenty-seven yielded acorns that were eaten by about half the Indians in North America and that provided for California Indians a staple of their diet. Because of their bitter, sometimes poisonous character, the acorns were cracked with a hammer, ground up with a mortar and pestle, and then leached in a stream by rinsing with several changes of water. They were then often boiled or roasted.

Some of the more important species for the Indians were *Quercus emoryii, Q. reticulata, Q. grisea,* and *Q. arizonica.*

acorn squash. An acorn-shaped **squash** weighing between one and two pounds, measuring four to seven inches in length, with a dark-green-and-orange-streaked fluted rind. Sometimes called a "Des Moines squash," this American winter fruit has long been favored by the Indians. The name first appears in American print in 1937.

Adam's ale. Slang for water. A colloquialism based on the assumption that the only drink Adam had in the Bible was water; this term is often heard in soda fountains and at LUNCH COUNTERS.

additive. Any substance added either directly or indirectly to a food product. About twenty-eight hundred substances, ranging from vitamins to preservatives, are added directly, while more than ten thousand—including pesticides used on growing plants, drugs added to animals' diets, and chemicals from wrapping materials—enter indirectly.

Most of the time, the term refers to those substances added directly and intentionally for a wide variety of reasons that include:

1. Maintaining freshness by adding nitrites and sodium nitrates to protect

cured foods from bacterial toxins such as botulin. Antioxidants such as butylated hydroxyanisole (BHA) help prevent discoloration; vitamin C keeps peaches from turning brown.

2. Maintaining or improving nutritional value by adding vitamins, iodine to SALT, and other minerals. Often this is done after processing has already removed many of the same nutrients from a food item like bread.

3. Making food more appealing to the eye by adding coloring agents.

4. Making food tastier by adding natural or synthetic flavors, enhancers such as MONOSODIUM GLUTAMATE (MSG), various sweetening agents such as SUGAR, corn syrup, and SACCHARIN, or just plain salt and pepper.

5. Aiding processing and preparation by adding emulsifiers to give consistent texture, thickeners to prevent the formation of ice crystals, and humectants to retain moisture. Yeasts and BAKING POWDER are leavening additives essential in baked goods.

In recent years there has been a great deal of concern, and not a little paranoia, over food additives, and health food zealots damn them all without considering the virtues of or necessity for some. Many harmless additives add immeasurably to the appearance, freshness, and edibility of food items, and the availability of certain foods year-round is due to the preserving additives that have revolutionized the marketplace throughout the world and made scarcity far less severe than it might be.

The first governmental attempts to oversee food additives came with the 1906 Food and Drugs Act, followed by the Food, Drug and Cosmetic Act of 1938, which helped remove some dangerous and poisonous elements from processed food. In 1958 the Food Additives Amendment established specific laws, bolstered two years later by the color additive amendments, authorizing the Food and Drug Administration (FDA) to monitor and regulate additives for safety, although no power was given the FDA to limit the number of additives in a food or the reasons for their being added. Approval of a new additive comes after a long, thorough process of experimentation, and there is a "100-fold margin of safety" rule that dictates that only one one-hundredth of the maximum amount of an additive that has been found *not* to produce any harmful effects in test animals may be used by a manufacturer of a food item. Under the Delaney Clause, no substance that has been shown to cause cancer in man or animal may be added to food in any amount.

Exempt from such tests are what are known as "generally recognized as safe" substances (GRAS) in use before the passage of the amendments, and "prior sanctioned substances" that had already been approved before 1958, although substances in both of these categories are under constant review. Currently thirty-one color additives are fully approved.

Listed below are the most commonly used additives. The reader is encouraged to look under main entries for many of the following.

1. Substances to maintain or improve nutritional quality: ASCORBIC ACID, beta carotene, iodine, iron, niacinamide, potassium iodide, riboflavin, thiamine, tocopherols (vitamin E), vitamin A, and vitamin D (D$_2$, D$_3$).

2. Substances to maintain product quality: ascorbic acid, butylated hydroxyanisole (BHA), butylated hydroxytoluene (BHT), butylparaben, calcium lactate, calcium propionate, calcium sorbate, citric acid, ethylenediaminetetraacetic acid (EDTA), heptylparaben, lactic acid, methylparaben, potassium propionate, potassium sorbate, propionic acid, propyl gallate, propylparaben, sodium benzoate, sodium diacetate, sodium erythorbate, sodium nitrate, sodium nitrite, sodium propionate, sodium sorbate, tertiary butyl hydroquinone (TBHQ), and tocopherols (vitamin E).

3. Substances to aid in processing and preparation: acetic acid, acetone peroxide, adipic acid, ammonium alginate, arabinogalactan, azodicarbonamide, benzoyl peroxide, calcium alginate, calcium bromate, calcium phosphate, CALCIUM PROPIONATE, calcium phosphate, calcium silicate, carobbean gum, CARRAGEENAN, cellulose, citric acid, diglycerides, dioctyl sodium sulfosuccinate, gelatin, glycerine, glycerol monostearate, guar gum, gum arabic, gum ghatti, hydrogen peroxide, iron-ammonium citrate, karaya gum, lactic acid, larch gum, lecithin, locust-bean gum, mannitol, modified food starch, monoglycerides, pectin, phosphates, phosphoric acid, polysorbates, potassium alginate, potassium bromate, popylene glycol, sodium acetate, silicon dioxide, sodium aluminum sulfate, sodium bicarbonate, sodium calcium alginate, sodium citrate, sodium stearyl fumarate, sorbitan monostearate, sorbitol, tartaric acid, tragacanth gum, and yellow prussiate of soda.

4. Substances that affect appeal characteristics: annatto extract, beta carotene, canthaxanthin, caramel, citrus Red No. 2, cochineal extract, corn endosperm, corn syrup, dehydrated beets, dextrose, disodium guanylate, disodium inosinate, dried algae meal, Blue No. 1, Red No. 3, Red No. 40, Yellow No. 5, fructose, glucose, grape-skin extract, hydrolyzed vegetable protein, invert sugar, iron oxide, mannitol, monosodium glutamate (MSG), paprika, riboflavin, saccharin, saffron, sorbitol, spices, sucrose, tagetes (Aztec Marigold), titanium dioxide, toasted partially defatted cooked cottonseed flour, turmeric, ultramarine blue, vanilla, vanillin, yeast-malt sprout extract.

5. Outlawed substances: dulcin, safrole, Green No. 1, cobalt sulfate, cyclamate, Violet No. 1, Red No. 2.

agave *(Agave palmerii* and *Agave parryi).* Also called "mescal" and "century plant," so named because it may live thirty or forty years. *Agave,* in New Latin, means "noble," for the plant's height. Edible species of this fast-growing, golden-flowered plant thrive in Arizona, New Mexico, southeastern California, southern Utah, and northern Mexico. The plant was extremely important to the Indians of the Southwest, especially the Mescalero Apaches, who held to a lengthy ritual in cooking the agave. The crowns of the plant were carefully placed in a pit three- to four-feet deep, covered with bear grass and a thick layer of earth, then roasted for about two days, during which the tribe refrained from both drinking and sexual activity (an incomplete baking was blamed on the incontinence of some of the women). When fully cooked, the centers of the crowns could be eaten immediately or dried in the sun. The leaves were consumed like artichokes or boiled into a syrup. Ground agave would be mixed into a drink.

The Chiricahua Apaches referred to blooming agaves as "woman" plants and nonblooming ones as "man" plants.

The agave also makes an alcoholic drink known to both the Indians and the Mexicans, who call the drink *"mescal";* the fermented pulp of the agave is called *"pulque."* This drink is similar to, but not the same as, TEQUILA and sotol.

In her book *American Indian Food and Lore* (1974), Carolyn Niethammer says the plant has a "pleasant, sweet flavor" but that eating it raw is poisonous. It is best baked or made into a nutbutter or syrup.

akule *(Selar crumenophthalmus).* A food fish of Hawaii, known on the mainland as "bigeye scad." Hawaiians usually salt and dry the fish.

Albany beef. A nineteenth-century slang term for **sturgeon,** so called because the specimens taken from the Hudson River near Albany, New York, could weigh up to two hundred pounds. The term was used at least as early as 1791.

albóndiga. A meatball flavored with vegetables and served with a sauce. Albóndiga (the name is the same in Spanish) is a popular dish in the Southwest and comes from Mexico.

> Combine 1/2 lb. each of ground pork, beef, and veal, add 1/2 cup bread crumbs, 1 chopped onion, 1/2 tsp. cumin, salt and pepper, and 1 beaten egg. Form into 1 1/2-in. balls, roll in flour, and sauté in a skillet till browned. Remove from skillet. Purée 3 chili peppers with 1/2 cup warm water. In skillet sauté 1 clove minced garlic, 1 chopped onion, and then the chili purée. Add 2 cups peeled, seeded, chopped tomatoes and sauté for 5 min. Add 1 cup beef stock, season with salt and pepper and 1/4 tsp. sugar, simmer, add the meatballs, cook for about 20 min. Serve with rice. Serves 6.

algin. A thickening agent derived from seaweed and used in processed foods to maintain desired texture. Propylene glycol alginate thickens soda pop, ice cream, candy, yogurt, and stabilizes the foam in beer.

alligator *(Alligator mississippiensis).* A large, lizardlike reptile that may grow up to nineteen feet in length. It is a dangerous denizen of the Louisiana and Gulf States swamplands, having been introduced into the Rio Grande in Texas. The name is from the Spanish, *el lagarto,* and ultimately from the Latin, *lacertus,* "lizard." As *lagarto* the name appears in English print first in 1568.

The alligator in American waters is, with the crocodile (from the Greek, *krokodilus,* "worm of the pebbles," for its habit of lying on pebbles to absorb the sun's heat) of the Florida Keys, occasionally caught and consumed by local inhabitants, particularly the Cajuns of Louisiana. The meat of the tail is particularly relished and usually cooked in a form of stew.

almond *(Prunus amygdalus).* A tree native to the Mediterranean and a member of the rose family whose nut is widely used in desserts, candy, and garnishes and as a SNACK. The name is from Greek, *amugdale,* and is first found in English print about 1300.

Almonds were introduced to California in the mid-1800s, and that state now produces half the world's crop.

American almonds are often roasted and ground as a topping for ice cream or cakes, made into a marzipan paste, or coated with candy or chocolate.

amaretto. A cordial with the flavor of almonds, though it may contain no almonds at all and is often made from apricot pits. The original formula, called "Amaretto di Saronno," comes from the Italian town of Saronno. (*Amaretto* in Italian means "a little bitter.") A wholly unsubstantiated legend, promoted by the producers' American distributor, Glenmore Distilleries of Lexington, Kentucky, tells of how Renaissance artist Bernardino Luini came to the town of Saronno in 1525 to paint a fresco in the sanctuary of Santa Maria delle Grazie. One of his models was a widow who gave him the liqueur that came to be called *"amaretto."*

The drink was imported into the United States in the 1960s, and by 1980 it had become the second-best-selling cordial here (after Kahlúa), causing several American producers to make their own amarettos in American distilleries.

Amaretto is sometimes used as a topping for ice cream desserts, and used as a flavoring for cakes and pies or coffee.

ambrosia. A cocktail reputedly first concocted at Arnaud's restaurant in New Orleans immediately following the end of Prohibition. The name, from the Greek *ambrotos,* "immortal," refers to the food of the Roman and Greek gods, thought to bestow immortality.

> Shake together the juice of 1 lemon, 1 oz. applejack, 1 oz. brandy, 1/2 oz. Cointreau, and top with champagne.

ambrosia. A nineteenth-century dessert made from fruits and grated coconut, most popular in the South.

> Peel and slice 3 oranges into 1/4-in. wedges and place a layer in a bowl. Sprinkle with confectioners' sugar and about 1 tbs. grated coconut. Make another layer the same way, and another, until the oranges are used up. Chill before serving. Serves 4.

Anadama bread. A bread made from cornmeal and molasses.

If it were not for the frequency of their citation, it would be difficult to believe the stories of how this New England bread got its name. The story most often cited is of a Gloucester, Massachusetts, fisherman's wife named Anna, who gave her husband nothing but cornmeal and molasses to eat every day. One night the fisherman got so angry he tossed the ingredients in with some yeast and flour and made a bread in the oven while muttering to himself, "Anna, damn her!"

A more affectionate story has a New England sea captain referring to his wife with the same expletive as a phrase of endearment. This Anna was apparently adept at bread baking, and she became well known for her corn-meal-and-molasses loaf among the fishing crews who appreciated this long-lasting, hearty bread. There was, supposedly, a gravestone to this legendary woman that read, "Anna was a lovely bride, but Anna, damn 'er, up and died."

One source contends that a commercial bakery called its product "Annadammer" or "Annadama" bread.

> Combine 3 cups all-purpose flour, 1 cup cornmeal, 2 pkgs. dry yeast, 1 tbs. salt together in a bowl. In another bowl mix 2 cups hot water, 4 tbs. butter, and 1/2 cup molasses, then add to flour mixture. Beat and knead to form a stiff dough. Place in greased bowl and let rise till doubled. Punch down, shape into two balls and place in greased 8-in. cake tins. Let rise till doubled. Bake at 375° for about 1 hr., till deep brown in color.

anchovy (Family Engraulidae). A small herringlike fish that travels in large schools. Anchovies are generally packed in oil and canned for the American market, even though there are sixteen species in United States waters and they are abundant on both coasts. The word is from the Spanish *anchova,* and was first printed in English in Shakespeare's *Henry IV, Part One* (1596). Anchovies are often used as an ingredient on pizza or as a part of several salad preparations.

andouille. A smoked pork sausage made from neck and stomach meat. This specialty of CAJUN cookery takes its name from a French word meaning "sausage."

angel food cake. Also called "angel cake." A very light, puffy cake, perhaps of Pennsylvania Dutch heritage, made without yeast and with several beaten egg whites. The egg whites give it a texture so airy that the confection supposedly has the sublimity of angels. Angel food cake was known by the 1870s in America and served as a sensible usage of leftover egg whites.

> Sift three times 1 1/2 cups sugar with 1 cup flour. Beat till stiff 13 egg whites with 1 tsp. cream of tartar and 1/8 tsp. salt. Fold in the flour, add 1 tsp. vanilla and 1 tsp. almond extract. Do not overmix. Pour into a greased tubular mold and bake at 325° for about 45 min.

apee. A cookie made from butter, sugar, and sour cream. The word derives from the name of the cookie's creator, Ann Page, a Philadelphia cook who carved her initials into the tops of the confection. This was first noted in print in J. F. Watson's *Annals of Philadelphia* (1830) to the effect that Ann Page, then still alive, "first made [the cookies] many years ago, under the common name of cakes."

Cream 1 cup butter with 1 tsp. vanilla and 1 1/3 cups sugar till very smooth. Add 2 eggs. Sift 2 1/3 cups flour, 1/4 tsp. cream of tartar, and 1/4 tsp. salt, then stir into mixture with 2/3 cup sour cream. Drop by spoonfuls onto buttered cookie sheet, bake for 10 min. at 375°. Cool on rack. Makes about 70 cookies.

apple (*Malus,* of the family Rosaceae). A sweet fruit with a firm flesh and thin skin found in temperate regions. The apple is native to Europe and Asia, though the United States now produces about one-quarter of the world's crop. There are probably tens of thousands of apple varieties, and more than seven thousand are classified in the United States alone, but most apples sold at market come from no more than fifty varieties and the consumer is unlikely to encounter more than a half-dozen of the most successfully propagated varieties. The annual crop in America, grown in thirty-five states, is approximately 145 million bushels.

The apple (the word is from the Old English *æppel*) has been a favorite fruit for millennia; it was known to the people of the Iron Age and cultivated four thousand years ago in Egypt. The Roman Pliny the Elder listed thirty-six varieties in the first century A.D., and the fruit has mythological associations in many different civilizations.

There were no native American apples when the first settlers arrived on these shores. (The custard apple [*Annona reticulata*] of the American tropics and the May apple or mandrake [*Podophyllum peltatum*] of eastern North America are not true apples.) The first apple seeds were brought by the Pilgrims in 1620, and there were plantings in New Jersey as of 1632. Governor John Endecott of the Plymouth Colony traded five-hundred three-year-old apple trees for two hundred acres of land in 1649, and Governor Peter Stuyvesant brought to New Amsterdam in 1647 a Dutch apple tree that flourished until it was accidentally knocked down in 1866.

The French brought the apple to Canada, and the fruit was grown up and down the thirteen colonies. In 1730 the first commercial apple nursery was opened on New York's Long Island, and by 1741 apples were being shipped to the West Indies. The proliferation of the fruit into the western territories came by the hand of an eccentric but gentle man named John Chapman, affectionately known as Johnny Appleseed. Born in Leominster, Massachusetts, in 1774, Chapman left his father's carpentry shop to explore the new territories and to preach a Swedenborgian philosophy of life. Beginning in Pennsylvania in 1800—barefoot, wearing a saucepan for a hat, and subsisting on a vegetarian diet of buttermilk and "beebread" (pollen)—Chapman planted apple trees and started nurseries over ten thousand square miles of American frontier. (He did not, as folklore would have it, merely toss apple seeds to the ground in the faith that they would grow true.) He got as far as Fort Wayne, Indiana, where he died at the age of seventy-one in 1845.

Apples were introduced in the Northwest by Captain Aemilius Simmons, who planted seeds at Fort Vancouver in Washington in 1824. His first tree grew but one apple, but the seeds of that single fruit bore future generations of hardier stock. Commercial growing of apples in the Northwest began with two Idahoans, Henderson Luelling and William Meek, who became the fathers of Washington's major crop and made the state the top producer of apples in the United States.

Apples were among the most versatile and long-lasting of fruits for the early settlers, and they have long been stored for the winter in "dry houses" or made into cider. By the year 1800 there were a hundred American-bred varieties, and Downing's *Fruits and Fruit Trees in America* (1872) listed more than a thousand varieties of apples bred in America. Most of these have been forgotten or are grown only in "collectors' orchards," where varieties such as the Roxbury Russet, Golden Russet, Black Gillflower, Chenango, Black Esopus Spitzenburg, Sweet Bough, and Winter Banana are still sustained. But the majority of the most important varieties still marketed date from before 1850, and only one, the Cortland, is the result of experiments by a scientific plant breeder; the rest come from seedlings.

The early apple storage cellars, called "common storages," lasted well into the nineteenth century. One of the first commercial cold storage plants for apples was established in 1870 in Niagara County, New York, but not until 1915 was a refrigerated storage facility possible. A method of slowing apple maturation by what is called "controlled atmosphere storage" (pioneered by Frenchman Jacques Bérard in the early 1800s) extended the life of apples so that they have become available yearround. This method increasingly is being used throughout the United States to preserve apples.

Almost half of the American apple crop is turned into products such as CIDER or juice, applesauce, canned slices, apple butter, and other packaged items.

Apple-harvest time is a festive and social occasion in America, and "apple bees" used to be held to core apples to be dried for the winter. At Halloween children "bob for apples," that is, they attempt to pick up apples floating in a large tub of water with their teeth, a pastime that may derive from Druidic or Roman harvest rites.

The following list of American apple varieties includes the most popular and most important ones sold and cultivated. In addition to these common varieties, some newer apples that show promise for the future include Kendall (a cross between McIntosh and Zusoff); Spartan (McIntosh and Yellow Newtown); Idared (Jonathan and Wagener); and Jondel (Jonathan and Delicious).

Baldwin. Red-skinned; harvested in autumn. An all-purpose apple not easily found anymore except in New England and New York retail outlets in the autumn months. The Baldwin appeared around 1740 as a seedling on the farm of John Ball in Wilmington, Massachusetts. For a long while the apple was called "Butters' apple," after the name of the next farmer who owned the land. Butters himself called it "Woodpecker." The variety was publicized by Colonel Baldwin of Woburn, Massachusetts, who gave his name to the apple, and after 1850 it was introduced into New York, where it was the major variety for years. Since 1945 the Baldwin has declined in popularity, though it is still used by commercial processors.

Cortland. Red-skinned; September–April. An all-purpose apple that stores well. The only major variety that is the result of scientific breeding, the Cortland was first propagated at the New York State Agricultural Experiment Station at Geneva, New York, and introduced in 1915 as a cross between the McIntosh and the Ben Davis.

crab. Red-skinned. Used primarily in cooking, the crab apple is small and deep-hued. It is a wild species and goes by the names "American sweet" or "garland" *(Malus coronaria)* and "prairie crab apple" *(Malus ioensis).*

Delicious. Red-skinned; mid-September–August. A heart-shaped eating apple also called the "Red Delicious." This variety is the largest apple crop in the United States, with several sports, strains, and tree types. It was discovered by a farmer named Hesse Hiatt at Peru, Iowa, in 1872 near an old Yellow Bellflower apple tree. Hiatt cut it down twice because of its irregular growing pattern, but it grew back, and, finally, Hiatt named it the "Hawkeye." In 1895 rights to the variety were bought by a commercial nursery, Stark Brothers, that renamed it the "Delicious." Today the eastern variety of Red Delicious is often possessed of better flavor than the western variety of the same name.

Golden Delicious. Gold-skinned; late September–August. An eating apple with a long peak season, the Golden Delicious bruises less readily than other varieties and is preferred for eating rather than cooking. It was discovered in 1914 on the Anderson Mullens farm in West Virginia, possibly from a Grimes Golden variety pollinated by the Golden Reinette. First called "Mullens' Yellow Seedling," the variety was purchased by the Stark Brothers nursery as a companion to their Red Delicious and is now the second largest apple crop in the United States.

Gravenstein. Yellow-skinned; early fall. An all-purpose apple of uncertain origins. Some authorities hold that the variety came from the eighteenth-century garden of the Duke of Augustinberg, in Gravenstein, Germany, but others cite the Grafenstein garden in Sleswick, Germany. Still others trace the variety to Italy. No one knows who first introduced the breed to the United States, but it was apparently grown in New York prior to 1826, and Russians planted the variety in Bodega, north of San Francisco, by 1820. Today the Gravenstein is still better known as a California breed, where it is a major variety for applesauce. A Nova Scotia variety of Gravenstein, the Banks, discovered by C. E. Banks in 1880, is still widely propagated there.

Jonathan. Red-skinned; mid-September–March. A highly aromatic, spicy apple good for eating, pies, and applesauce. Discovered in 1800 in Woodstock, New York, where it was originally called the "Rick," after farmer Philip Rick, who found it among his trees, the variety was popularized by Jonathan Hasbrouk and Judge J. Buel of Albany, New York, and took the former's first name. The Jonathan may be a seedling of the Esopus Spitzenburg variety. The Jonathan grew better in Michigan and the Ohio Valley than in the East and became a major variety in the Midwest and as far as Idaho and Colorado.

McIntosh. Red-skinned; mid-September–July. A round, all-purpose apple, the McIntosh is excellent for crossbreeding and has given us varieties such as the Cortland, Spartan, Melba, Macoun, Niagara, Puritan, and others.

A plaque in Dundas County, Ontario, across the Lawrence River from Massena, reads, "The original McIntosh red apple tree stood 20 rods North of this spot. It was one of a number of seedlings taken from the border of the clearings and transplanted by John McIntosh in the Year 1796." John McIntosh took seedlings from the brush near his home near Dundela, Ontario, and planted them in his garden. By 1830 only one tree had survived, and this was the original tree that, with some grafting assistance given by an itinerant peddler five years later, resulted in a nursery of identical trees that gave excellent, sweet fruit. McIntosh's wife Hannah took care of the nursery, and neighbors took to calling the apple "granny's apple" after her, though a son, Allan, gave the family name to the variety, and other relatives began propagating it in New York and Vermont. It became the predominant variety of the Northeast (the original Ontario tree was burned in a fire and died in 1910), especially in New York State, where it is grown in the Hudson Valley, the Champlain Valley, and near Lake Ontario. The largest orchard, Chazy Orchards Inc., located in Chazy, New York, has nine hundred acres devoted to McIntosh.

Newtown Pippin. Greenish-yellow-skinned; mid-September–April. An all-purpose apple of uncertain origins, also called the "Albemarle." The original seedling may have come from Gersham Moore's estate in Newtown, Long Island, though it is not certain whether the fruit of the original tree, which died in 1805, was yellow or green. Both varieties go by the name "Newtown Pippin," with the yellow primarily grown in the West and in Virginia (where Albemarle County lent its name to the variety, brought from Philadelphia in 1755 by Dr. Thomas Walker). Today the variety is a major export apple, and Oregon is the major grower.

Northern Spy. Red-skinned, with some blush; mid-October–February. A robust eating and cooking variety produced mainly in New York, Michigan, and Ontario, the Northern Spy is not widely available. It originated as a seedling in an orchard planted in 1800 by Herman Chapin in East Bloomfield, New York, from Salisbury, Connecticut, seeds. The origin of the name, however, is obscure. Some say it may derive from the fact that Bloomfield was a site of activity for the Underground Railroad, a secret system by which slaves were brought North to freedom.

The original seedling died but the first apple from the seedling's transplanted suckers came from the farm of Roswell Humphrey, and it became an important apple throughout the northern states. Owing to its tendency to appear only in alternate years, the variety has declined in popularity, but many people consider Northern Spy apples among the very best in America.

Rhode Island Greening. Yellow-green-skinned. A baking or cooking apple considered best for apple pie, the Rhode Island Greening is produced mainly in New York and is commercially processed for applesauce and frozen pies, and, therefore, rarely seen in the market. The variety began in Green's End, Rhode Island, about 1748 through the efforts of a tavern keeper named Green. It was carried from Newport to Plymouth, Massachusetts, then to Ohio by 1796 and established in a nursery at Marietta.

Rome Beauty. Red-skinned; late September–July. An excellent baking apple, originally propagated by Alanson Gillett from a discarded tree given him by his brother Joel, of Proctorville, Ohio. The variety was named by George Walton about 1832 for the township of Rome, where the Gillett farm was located. The Rome Beauty has given us hybrids like the Gallia Beauty, Monroe, and Ruby. The Rome Beauty is produced in all the apple-growing regions of the United States.

Stayman. Red-skinned; early October–May. An eating apple grown throughout Appalachia with some uses for cooking. The variety came from a Winesap seedling, discovered in Leavenworth, Kansas, in 1866 by Dr. J. Stayman. It is sometimes called "Stayman's Winesap" or "Stayman Winesap." After 1900 extensive plantings took place in the East and Midwest.

Winesap. Red-skinned; late October–June. A tart, crisp apple for eating. The Winesap is of obscure origins, possibly of New Jersey stock before 1800. Its long keeping time made it popular until controlled atmosphere storage made other varieties even more so. It is now produced mainly in Washington, Virginia, and West Virginia.

York Imperial. Red-skinned; mid-September–May. A good baking apple, first discovered near York, Pennsylvania, about 1830 by a man named Johnson. Johnson took it to nursery owner Jonathan Jessup, who in turn produced the variety and called it "Johnson's Fine Winter Apple," but had little success with it. Other farmers planted the discarded variety, and it took on its noble name from horticulturist Charles Downing, who promoted its long keeping qualities in the mid-1800s. It is now a processing apple.

apple butter. A Pennsylvania Dutch dish, dating at least to the 1770s, made by puréeing apples with cider.

Cook 3 qt. cider over high heat until reduced by half. Quarter 8 lb. unpeeled, cored apples, add to cider and cook till tender. Work through a sieve or purée the mixture, then add 2 1/2 cups brown sugar, 1/2 tsp. ground cloves, 1 1/2 tsp. cinnamon, 1 tsp. allspice, and 1/2 tsp. salt. Cook till the mixture thickens, then pour into jars for keeping. Makes about 4 jars.

apple cake. Sift together 2 cups flour, 3 tbs. sugar, 1 tsp. salt, and 2 tsp. baking powder. Whip a cup of heavy cream, mix in the dry ingredients, then spread in a greased pan. Pare and core 4 apples, slice them thin and arrange on the dough. Over the top sprinkle a mixture of 1/4 cup sugar and 1/2 tsp. cinnamon, then pour 2 tbs. melted butter over the top. Bake for about 30 min. at 400°.

apple dumpling. A baked dessert made of apples wrapped in pastry dough.

Peel and core an apple and fill center with a mixture of brown sugar, a touch of cinnamon, nutmeg, and 1 tsp. butter. Wrap a pastry crust around apple, forming it to shape the fruit. Moisten edges of pastry and close at top, then prick in several spots with a fork. Let chill in refrigerator for 1 hr., then bake in 450° oven for 10 min. Lower heat to 350° and bake for another 30–35 min. Serve with maple syrup.

apple fritter. An apple slice that has been covered with a batter and fried in hot oil. Apple fritters have been popular since the middle of the eighteenth century.

Peel and core 4 apples and cut into 1/4-in.-thick slices. Mix together 2 cups flour, 2 beaten eggs, 1 tbs. dark rum, 1/4 tsp. salt, and 1 cup milk. Dip apple slices in batter, then deep-fry. Serve with powdered sugar and/or sour cream and maple syrup.

apple snow. A dessert popular in the early part of this century.

Beat 3 egg whites, add 1/4 cup sugar and 1 cup applesauce, and serve with whipped cream or custard sauce.

baked apple. Apples that are baked in the oven may be unspiced or seasoned with cinnamon, cloves, or nutmeg, stuffed with MINCEMEAT, nuts, or other fruits, and slathered with maple syrup, corn syrup, wine, or fruit syrups. To bake an apple, merely core it, flavor it with any of the above, and bake at 400° until tender.

fried apples. A popular country dish of sliced apples fried in hot fat and sprinkled with sugar.

Apple Annie. A term for any vendor who sold apples on city street corners during the Great Depression of the 1930s. Most were very poor people with no other trade and no other wares to sell at regular markets.

apple brown Betty. A layered dessert of apples and buttered crumbs. The origin of the name is unknown, but the dish was first mentioned in print in 1864.

Mix together 1 1/2 cups dry bread crumbs with 1/4 cup melted butter and place one-third of the mixture in a buttered baking pan. Slice 4 pared and cored apples into 1/4-in.-thick slices and place a layer on top of the crumbs. Cover with part of a mixture of 1 tsp. cinnamon, 1/4 tsp. ground cloves, 1/4 tsp. nutmeg, and 1 tsp. grated lemon rind. Repeat layers of bread crumbs, apples, and spice mixture, then sprinkle the top with a mixture of the juice of 1 lemon and 1/4 cup water. Bake at 400° for 10–15 min. Serve with whipped cream or ice cream.

apple charlotte. A dessert of French origins made of cooked apples and bread slices. Apple charlotte is distinguished from charlotte russe, a creamy pudding placed in a deep mold lined with lady fingers, a dessert generally credited to Frenchman Antonin Carême, who first called it *"Charlotte parisienne."* But apple charlotte predated charlotte russe. In France it was called a *"Fruit Charlotte"* and, according to André Simon's *A Concise Encyclopedia of Gastronomy* (1952), was named after Charlotte Buff, on whom the heroine of Johann Wolfgang von Goethe's *Die Leiden des Jungen Werthers* (1774), a tremendously popular epistolary novel of the time, was based. Apple charlotte became a fashionable dessert in America soon afterwards, as a rather fancy version of APPLE BROWN BETTY.

> Line the bottom and sides of a charlotte mold with thin bread slices (which may be cut into the shape of hearts) that have been soaked in melted butter. Slice up a dozen apples that have been peeled and cored, and place in a saucepan with 3 tbs. butter. Add 2 tbs. powdered sugar, 1/4 tsp. cinnamon, 1/2 tsp. grated lemon rind, and 1/4 tsp. vanilla extract. Cook till apples have broken down, then add 4 tbs. apricot jam. Stir and blend. Fill the mold, place buttered bread slices on top, trim, then cook in a 350° oven for 40 min. Let rest for a few minutes, then turn out on a plate. Serve with apricot sauce, if desired.

applejack. Apple cider or a brandy made from apple cider. Apple brandy was particularly favored in early New England, where any household might have the means to make the spirit, and the United States continues to be a major producer. (France is another principal source for apple brandy, their best being Calvados, from around Normandy.)

In the United States applejack must spend at least two years in wood casks, though most are aged much longer, and the proof is 100, or, if blended with neutral spirits, 80.

As a term for cider, *apple jack* dates back at least to 1816. Later in the century it was also referred to as *apple john,* which in England is a term for a specific type of apple. For more information on apple cider, see CIDER.

apple-knocker. A club used to loosen fruit from trees, or a person who picks apples very fast.

apple pandowdy. A dish of sliced apples covered with a crust, sometimes referred to as "apple Jonathan" in the Northeast. First mentioned in print in 1805, apple pandowdy seems to be specifically American by name, and Nathaniel Hawthorne mentions the dish in his *Blithedale Romance* (1852). The name's origins are obscure, but perhaps its homely simplicity connotes a "dowdy," that is, unstylish, appearance.

> Core, peel, and slice 4 apples and place in a buttered dish. Pour 1/2 cup cider over them, sprinkle with 1/2 tsp. cinnamon, 1/8 tsp. ground cloves, 1/8 tsp. nutmeg, 3/4 cup light brown sugar, 1/4 cup maple syrup, and dot with butter. Cover with a

biscuit dough about 1/4-in. thick, then slit the top to allow for the escape of steam. Bake in 350° oven till apples are tender. Serve with cream.

apple pie. If something is said to be as "American as apple pie," it is credited with being as American as the *Star Spangled Banner*. In fact, apple pies were very popular in Europe, especially in England, before they came to epitomize American food. But Americans popularized the apple pie because we became the world's most important apple-producing nation.

There are hundreds of apple pie recipes from every region of the country, some with a top crust, some without, some with bottom crust, some without, some with raisins or dates or nuts or cranberries, some with buttery crumbs on top. The most popular kind is referred to as "deep dish apple pie," meaning it is baked in a pie pan of at least 1 1/2 inches in depth.

Cut up 2 1/2 lb. of apples that have been peeled and cored. Blend with 1/4 cup sugar, 1 tbs. rum, 1/8 tsp. ground cloves, and 1/4 tsp. cinnamon. Let stand till apples have exuded juice. In a pie pan spread a 9-in. crust and trim edges. Place the apple mixture in the crust, then cover with another crust. Primp the sides at the rim, decorate if desired with dough designs, and brush with a wash of egg whites and water to glaze the surface. Bake at 375° for about 45 min. to 1 hr.

applesauce. A purée of apples, sugar, and, sometimes, spices. In New England it is often called "apple sass."

Quarter 3 lb. unpeeled, cored apples and place in a saucepan with 1/3 cup water. Cook till they fall apart, then strain through a food mill. Add sugar to taste.

apricot *(Prunus armeniaca).* A tree native to western Asia and Africa that gives a yellow-orange fruit. The word is from the Latin, *praecoquere,* "to ripen early," and first appears in English print in 1551.

The apricot reached North America sometime in the eighteenth century when Spanish monks brought it to California, which now produces 90 percent of the American crop (with the rest from Washington and Utah). About 65 percent of the crop is canned, 20 percent dried, 5 percent frozen, and only 10 percent sold fresh. The major cultivated varieties are Royal, Blenheim, Tilton, Chinese, and Riland.

Arbuckle's. A brand name for coffee in the Old West. Arbuckle's coffee was so ubiquitous that recipes for coffee would read, "Take a pound of Arbuckle's. . . ."

armadillo. Any of a variety of New World mammals of the family Dasypodidae having bony plates resembling armor, especially the nine-banded armadillo *(Dasypus novemcinctus).* The name comes from the Spanish, *armado,* "armored," ultimately from the Latin, *arma,* "arms," and first appears in English print in 1577.

The armadillo is rarely eaten in the United States today, but by some westerners it was considered an unusual delicacy, usually to be stewed.

arroz con pollo. A Hispanic dish of rice with chicken. The dish, whose name is from the Spanish, is part of Hispanic-American culture. The term was first mentioned in print in 1938.

> Brown cut up pieces of 1 chicken in 4 tbs. olive oil till browned, add 6 chorizo sausages cut into chunks, and brown with the chicken. Add 2 cups cooked rice to the skillet. In another pan sauté 2 chopped cloves of garlic, 1 chopped onion, 1 chopped green bell pepper, and add to the chicken and rice. Mix 1/4 tsp. crumbled saffron in 6 cups chicken stock and add to rice. Add 4 peeled and chopped tomatoes and 1 cup peas. Cover and bake at 350° for 1 1/2 hr. Garnish with pimiento strips. Serves 8.

artichoke *(Cynara scolymus).* A tall plant native to the Mediterranean bearing a large, globular flower head with scaly, thistlelike bracts. The artichoke is eaten as a vegetable, usually boiled and served with butter or stuffed with bread crumbs and other seasonings and baked.

The word is from the Italian dialect word *articiocco,* ultimately from the Arabic *al-kharshūf,* first mentioned in English print in 1530.

The Spanish introduced the artichoke to California, but it was almost unknown to most Americans until well into the twentieth century, when its cultivation in the South and, principally, in California gave the vegetable a popularity that today is equalled only in France and Italy. The only commercial kind grown in the United States is the common or globe artichoke.

ascorbic acid. Vitamin C. Ascorbic acid can be used as an antioxidant or a nutrient and color stabilizer; it also prevents the formation of nitrosamines (cancer-causing chemicals).

Ashley bread. A southern batter bread, similar to SPOON BREAD, made from rice flour. The name may commemorate Anthony Ashley Cooper, first Earl of Shaftesbury (1621–1683), who was one of the first proprietors of the royal colony of Carolina, for which he had John Locke draw up the first constitution. The following recipe is from Panchita Heyward Grimball, of the Wappaoolah Plantation, Cooper River, South Carolina, as printed in *200 Years of Charleston Cooking* (1930).

> Mix and sift 1 cup rice flour, 1/2 tsp. salt, 1 1/2 tsp. baking powder; beat 1 egg with 1 cup milk and add to the dry ingredients. Stir in 1 1/2 tbs. melted butter and turn batter into well-greased shallow pan. Bake at 350° for about 45 min. Makes 8 large pieces.

asparagus (Genus *Asparagus*). Any of 150 species of a Eurasian plant with long branchlets that is a very popular vegetable and is usually boiled or steamed. The name is from the Greek, *asparagos,* and first appeared in English print around the year 1000 A.D. Though mentioned in America in cookery books of the latter eighteenth century, it is not known when the vegetable arrived in North America, where it has flourished, especially the common asparagus *(A. plumosus)*. A particularly hardy variety, the Mary Washington, was developed by the United States Department of Agriculture.

Most American asparagus is sold fresh.

aspartame. An artificial sweetener of aspartic acid and phenylalanine developed in 1965 by chemist James M. Schlatter, it is two hundred times sweeter than sugar. Currently manufactured by G. D. Searle & Company, aspartame is used in processed foods and as a substitute for sugar. The company markets a form of aspartame for table use called "Equal," which appeared in 1982.

atol. A cornmeal or porridge used in the Old West. The name is from the Spanish.

Automat. An inexpensive and informal restaurant where food is displayed in small compartments whose windows open when the required number of coins is deposited. The term comes from the Greek, *automatos,* "self-acting." The first such establishment was Joseph V. Horn and F. Hardart's Automat, opened in 1902 in Philadelphia and using German equipment, but it was in New York ten years later that the concept became an important part of city life. So linked to the idea of the automat were its originators' names that Americans more often than not referred to such places as "Horn and Hardarts." These often grand eateries became representative of Americans' love of economy coupled with a mock grandiosity that resulted in a period of lavish automats full of white tile and Carrara marble. They were kept spotlessly clean, and it was quite normal to find everyone from unemployed drifters lingering over a cup of five-cent coffee to the brightest of Broadway's celebrities there. Silver-ornamented spigots dispensed coffee, tea, and hot chocolate. Stews, desserts, rolls, and sandwiches were offered in profusion. By the 1930s New York had more than forty such restaurants, but after World War II FAST-FOOD restaurants and hamburger stands ascended in popularity while the automats declined, so that today there are very few left in the country. Robert F. Byrnes wrote of the Horn & Hardart Company in its heyday: "If you were the young man who had escaped from Easton, and you went to Horn & Hardart for Thanksgiving and for company, after you ate your fill you could walk back to your furnished room and write to your sister about the great meal. You could say you went in with a dollar in your pocket, and came out with 50 cents."

avocado *(Persea gratissima* or *P. americana).* Also, "alligator pear." A tropical tree that bears a globular green fruit with a large seed and tough skin. The name is from the Nahuatl, *ahuacatl,* "testicle" (because of its shape), and entered English via the Spanish, first appearing in print in the seventeenth century and in America in 1751.

The Aztecs ate avocados, as was noted by the early Spanish explorers, but it was long considered a rather tasteless food, enjoyed only in Central and South America and in the Caribbean, where it acquired its alternative name "alligator pear," possibly because it grew where there were alligators, as in Florida. Horticulturist Henry Perrine planted the first avocados in Florida in 1833, but it was not until the turn of the century that the plant took on commercial importance. Even then avocados were not particularly relished by most Americans, and only in California, Florida, and Hawaii, the major producing states, was it much appreciated until it became popular as a salad item in the 1950s.

The three major varieties grown are the Mexican, the Guatemalan, and the West Indian.

The avocado is the major ingredient of GUACAMOLE.

Awenda bread. A Carolinas bread made from hominy grits, perhaps of Indian derivation.

Push 1/2 cup cooked hominy grits through a sieve, beat in 1 egg, 1/2 cup cornmeal, 1 tsp. sugar, 1 tsp. salt, 1 tsp. baking powder, and 3/4 cup milk to make a thin batter. Grease a 1-qt. baking pan, pour in batter, and cook 40–50 min. at 350°. Serve with butter.

baby beef. Western term since the 1890s for young cattle killed for market. Today the term refers to a calf several months old and weaned from its mother. This is often sold as VEAL, though it is not considered of the highest quality because of its age.

Bacardi cocktail. A cocktail made with lime juice, sugar, grenadine, and Bacardi light rum. The name is directly associated with the firm Bacardi Imports, Inc., of Miami, Florida, and in 1936 a New York State Supreme Court ruled that to be authentic a "Bacardi cocktail" had to be made with Bacardi rum, since the name "Bacardi" was a registered trademark.

> Shake together with ice 2 tsp. lime juice, 1/2 tsp. sugar, 1 tsp. grenadine, and 1 1/2 oz. Bacardi light rum. Strain into chilled cocktail glasses.

bachelor's button. A cookie with a cherry set on top and made to resemble a button. The cookie has nothing to do with the flower called by the same name, except for its similar shape.

> Cream 1 3/4 cups sugar with 2/3 cup butter. Add 2 beaten eggs, 1/2 tsp. salt, 3 cups flour, 2 tsp. baking powder, and 1 tsp. vanilla. Cut with cookie cutter, place on buttered cookie sheet, top with cherries, and bake at 450° for 8–10 min.

backdaag. "Baking Day," which was Friday, on Pennsylvania Dutch farms. One day was set aside for baking because occasional baking of one or two items could not satisfy the needs of the hard-working farmers.

bacon. Salted and/or smoked meat taken from the sides and back of a pig. Bacon is cut in slices and fried, usually as a breakfast item, or used as larding in certain dishes. It is customarily served with broiled or fried calf's liver.

The word derives from Frankish, *bako,* "ham," and Common Germanic, *bakkon,* and in Middle English was spelled either "bacon" or "bakoun," which was also a more general term for pork well into the sixteenth century. In America bacon has long been a staple of most households, largely because of a long history of PORK consumption and hog butchering on farms. "Bacon pigs" are animals especially grown for their bacon, often from breeds like the Yorkshire and Tamworth.

Bacon may be cured at home with salt and some sugar, but factory bacon is dry-salted then cured with brine (often pumped into the arteries and muscles). Most bacon is sold already sliced and packaged, though slab bacon may be bought at groceries and butchers for slicing to suit one's preferences. Country-style bacon is usually a generously sliced, well-cured bacon, while thick-sliced (or thick-cut) bacon is cut about twice as thick as regular bacon. Canned bacon is usually precooked and used where there is little access to kitchen stoves and equipment. Bacon bits are preserved and dried (though there are also artificial "bacon-flavored" bits sold in jars), usually for tossing with a salad dressing.

Canadian bacon (called "back bacon" in Canada) is cut from the loin or eye muscle along the pig's back. It is a leaner, drier, fully-cooked meat usually sold in a packaged hunk. The reason for the name is not clear.

Salt pork is a very fatty cured pork (also called "white bacon") generally used as a cooking fat or flavoring for other dishes.

bagel. A round yeast bun with a hole in the middle. The bagel is a staple of Jewish immigrants' Sunday breakfasts that has become a reasonable substitute for sandwich bread in many American cities where DELICATESSANS exist. Traditionally the bagel is eaten with such delicacies as LOX, Nova Scotia salmon, and slices of white onions; the most classic match is cream cheese (an American creation) and lox or cream cheese and jelly. Bagels are sometimes toasted, and one will find them studded with onion flakes, sesame seeds, poppy seeds, or raisins or made from dark flours. The bagel was first mentioned in American print only in 1932.

The origins of the bagel are lost somewhere in the history of the Ashkenazi Jews, who brought Yiddish culture to America. The word *bagel* derives from a Yiddish word, *beygel,* from the German *Beugel,* for a round loaf of bread. There is a story that the word may also derive from the German word *buegel,* meaning "stirrup," according to a legend that the bakers of Vienna commemorated John III's victory over the Turks in their city in 1683 by molding their bread into the shape of stirrups because the liberated Austrians had clung to the king's stirrups as he rode by. But Leo Rosten in *The Joys of Yiddish* (1968) notes that the first printed mention of the word *bagel* is in the Community Regulations of Cracow for 1610, which stated that the item was given as a gift to women in childbirth.

Mix together 1 1/2 cups flour, 3 tbs. sugar, 1 tbs. salt, and 1 pkg. yeast. Add 1 egg yolk and 1 1/2 cups water and beat with electric mixer for 2 min. Add 1/2 cup more flour and beat for 2 more min. at high speed. The dough should be soft. Knead for 8–10 min. Let rise for 20 min. in an ungreased, covered bowl. Punch down, place on floured board, cut into 10 equal pieces, and roll each piece to make a rope. Form into circles and pinch ends to close. Place on ungreased cookie sheet, cover, and let rise for 20 min. In a large shallow pan boil 2 cups water. Stir in 1 tbs. honey. Lower heat, add bagels, a few at a time, and simmer for about 7 min. Allow to cool on clean towel for 5 min., then place on ungreased cookie sheet. Bake at 375° for 10 min. Remove from oven, brush with a mixture of egg white and water, return to oven for 20 min. more. Cool on wire rack.

bait. Food or a meal to westerners. A "bait can" was a lunch pail used by loggers.

Baked Alaska. A dessert made of sponge cake covered with ice cream and a meringue that is browned in the oven.

The idea of baking ice cream in some kind of crust so as to create a hot-cold blend of textures occurred to Thomas Jefferson, who in 1802 served minister Manasseh Cutler a puddinglike dish that included "ice cream very good, crust wholly dried, crumbled into thin flakes." And a report in the French journal *Liberté* for June, 1866, indicates that the master cook of the Chinese mission in Paris imparted a technique for baking pastry over ice cream to the French chef Balzac of the Grand Hotel. But Baked Alaska as we know it today may be traced to the experiments in heating and cooking conducted by Benjamin Thompson (1753–1814), born in Woburn, Massachusetts, who became a celebrated scientist both at home and in England, where he was awarded the title of Count Rumford for his work (the name Rumford came from the town of Rumford [now Concord], New Hampshire, where his wife was born). His studies of the resistance of egg whites to heat resulted in the browned topping that eventually became the crown for a dish called "Alaska-Florida" that was popularized at Delmonico's restaurant in New York City in the nineteenth century. In Europe the dessert was called *"Omelette à la norvégienne"* and was popularized by chef Jean Giroix of the Hôtel de Paris in Monaco in 1895. The term *Baked Alaska* came somewhat later and was used by Fannie Merritt Farmer in the 1909 edition of her cookbook.

> To make Baked Alaska, trim a sponge cake to a 1-in. thickness and cover with about 3 in. of ice cream. Freeze until very firm. Beat 5 egg whites till stiff with 1 tsp. vanilla, 1/2 tsp. cream of tartar, and 2/3 cup sugar. Remove the ice cream cake from freezer and spread the egg whites in swirls around the ice cream into the shape of a dome. Bake in a 500° oven till the top is golden brown, about 3 min. Serve immediately.

baking powder. A combination of sodium bicarbonate and acid salt that became popular in the 1850s as a leavening agent in baking what came to be called "quick bread," "lightnin' bread," or "aerated bread." By 1854 Americans had self-rising flour, which was baking powder mixed with flour. By the 1870s *baking soda* was the new term for the less desirable potassium or sodium bicarbonate, also called "saleratus."

bald face. Nineteenth-century slang term for inferior whiskey.

baldface dishes. Cowboy slang since 1840 to describe real china plates and dishes, in contrast to the tin or granite dishes usually used on the trail.

bamboo cocktail. A drink made with a dash of orange bitters, 1 oz. sherry, and 1 oz. dry vermouth, stirred with ice, strained, and served in a wine glass with a lemon peel. The drink is said to have been invented about 1910 by bartender Charlie Mahoney of the Hoffman House in New York.

banana. Any of a variety of tropical or subtropical trees of the genus *Musa* bearing clusters of long, yellow or reddish fruits. The name is from Portuguese and Spanish, via a West African name, and was first printed in English in the seventeenth century.

The banana, which has been traced to southern Asia and India, may have been cultivated as long ago as 1000 B.C. in Assyria. The Arabs brought the fruit to Egypt in the seventh century, and Portuguese navigators found them in 1482 on Africa's west coast and thereafter transplanted them to the Canary Islands. The early Spanish explorers of the New World remarked on the "bananas" in the West Indies, but actually had seen plantains *(Musa paradisiaca)*. In 1516, on the island of Hispaniola, Friar Tomás de Berlanga planted the first banana trees in the West Indies, but propagation of the fruit was limited to the islands until well into the nineteenth century. The first bananas entered the United States only in 1804, when they were brought from Cuba to New York City by Captain John Chester on the schooner *Reynard*. But no further shipments arrived in the city, or anywhere else in North America, until 1830, when Captain John Pearsall brought in fifteen hundred stems on the schooner *Harriet Smith*. By the 1840s New York markets were receiving frequent shipments of bananas, and in 1870 Captain Lorenzo D. Baker of the *Telegraph* brought a cargo of the fruit to Boston from Jamaica, leading to a partnership with a fruit broker named Andrew Pearson. Together they founded the Boston Fruit Company and introduced the banana as an exotic fruit wrapped in foil and sold for a dime at the Philadelphia Centennial Exposition of 1876. The Boston Fruit Company was merged by Samuel Zemurray and Minor Keith into the United Fruit Company (later United Brands) in 1899, which, with the introduction of refrigerated cargo holds, began shipping bananas to new ports and markets in the United States. The success of the banana after the turn of the century led to widespread involvement of American companies and the federal government in the affairs and politics of the Caribbean and Central and South America. Plantations were established in what came to be called "banana republics" run for the benefit and interests of the fruit companies in the United States, often to the detriment of the inhabitants in those countries.

Although Hawaii had long grown bananas (discovered there by Captain James Cook in 1799), the state has never had a significant commercial banana industry. Most bananas eaten in the United States—between 70 million and 80 million bunches a year, making it Americans' most popular fruit—are shipped in from Costa Rica, Guatemala, and other countries, with the majority being the common banana *(M. sapientum),* of which the Gros Michel variety is most frequently found in American markets. The red banana and the plantain are rarely seen in most American markets outside Florida and the Gulf States.

Americans eat bananas raw, in salads, in various desserts, and as a flavoring for breads and other confections.

BANANA CREAM PIE
(popular at least since the 1920s): In a double boiler blend 1 1/3 cups milk with 3 1/2 tbs. flour. Blend 2 beaten egg yolks with milk mixture and add gradually to 2/3 cup sugar, stirring to dissolve. Add 2 tbs. butter, cook about 20 min., till thickened, add 1 tsp. vanilla, and cool. Pour into baked pie crust, alternating with layers of sliced bananas. Cover with meringue and brown in oven.

banana bread. Also, "banana cake." A loaf with a cakelike consistency made from flour and mashed bananas. Fannie Merritt Farmer's cookbook makes reference in 1896 to a "banana cake," which was really a cake with sliced bananas on top. But in the 1960s and 1970s, during a period of delight in hearty, fresh-made breads, banana bread took on a certain faddishness.

Cream together 1/4 cup shortening with 1 cup sugar. Add 2 beaten eggs, 3 tbs. buttermilk, 1 tsp. baking soda, and fold in 3 mashed bananas. Bake for 1 hr. in a greased pan at 350°.

bananas Foster. A dessert made from sliced bananas cooked with butter, brown sugar, rum, and banana cordial and served with vanilla ice cream. The dish was created in the early 1950s at Brennan's Restaurant in New Orleans as part of a Breakfast at Brennan's promotion that has since become a city tradition (the restaurant was opened in 1946). It was named after a regular customer, Richard Foster, owner of the Foster Awning Company in New Orleans. The chef responsible was named Paul Blange. The recipe below is from Brennan's.

Melt 4 tbs. butter over an alcohol burner or flambé pan. Add 1 cup brown sugar, 1/2 tsp. cinnamon, 4 tbs. banana cordial, and mix well. Heat for a few minutes, then place 4 bananas that have been cut in half lengthwise and then halved widthwise in pan and sauté until soft. Add 1/4 cup rum and allow to heat well, then tip pan so that flame from burner ignites alcohol. Allow to burn until flame dies out. Serve over vanilla ice cream by placing 4 pieces of banana on each portion, then spooning hot sauce from the pan onto the bananas and ice cream.

bannock. A nineteenth-century New England cornmeal cake derived from a Scottish barley or wheat pancake of the same name. Sometimes this was called "White Indian bannock," because of the use of white "Indian" cornmeal.

Scald 1 qt. milk and pour over 1 cup cornmeal. Cook in a double boiler over low heat till thick and lukewarm. Add 5 beaten eggs, 2 tbs. sugar, 1/2 tsp. salt. Pour into greased pan and bake for 30 min. at 350°.

Baptist cake. A New England deep-fried doughnutlike confection. Baptist cakes are risen dough balls that have been "immersed," like Baptists who are immersed in water at their baptism, in hot oil. In Connecticut they are called "holy pokes," in Maine "huff juffs," and in other parts "hustlers."

bar. Also, "bar room" or "barroom." A tavern or room where alcoholic beverages are served, or the long counter at which one stands or sits to have such beverages. The word derives from the more general meaning of a long slab or block of wood or other material used to separate or support, and in this sense derives from Vulgar Latin, *barra.* In its usage for a tavern, the word dates from the sixteenth century, when bars would be pulled across the counter at closing time. *Bar room* came into the language in the late eighteenth century, and in America *bartender* (one who tends the bar) was known by 1836; ten years later *bar keep* was also used. *Bar-counter* was used by Dickens in his *American Notes* (1842), and by 1857 there were female hostesses called, with some condescension, "bar-girls."

By the 1830s *saloon* (from the French word for "room," *salon*) was an alternative word for *bar,* and there were many other less savory terms, like *gin mill, rum hole, whiskey joint,* and, later, *juke joint,* to join the more refined, post-Prohibition *cocktail lounge. Dram-shop* first saw print in 1839.

Today the word *bar* suggests an establishment where the principal business is the dispensing of alcoholic drinks, while *tavern* is somewhat quaint and *saloon* a bit dated, except when it is used as a deliberately nostalgic reference. *Bar and grill* conveys some culinary interest at such a place, while *lounge* refers more to a bar's booths-and-tables section than to its counter, which is usually flanked by "bar stools" (first noted in Arthur Koestler's novel *Twilight Bar* in 1945) and a "bar rail," on which to rest one's foot.

barbecue. Also "Bar-B-Q" and other variations. A method of cooking meat, poultry, or fish over an open pit fire, often with the whole animal skewered on a spit and almost always done out of doors. Barbecues are as much a social ritual in America as they are a means of cooking, for they are held as often for large parties, celebrations, and political rallies as for cooking a family's meal. Barbecuing methods go back to the earliest days, when man first used fire to cook his food, but the term barbecue comes from the Spanish and Haitian word *barbacoa* ("framework of sticks"), which referred first to a kind of latticework bench but soon after was adapted to mean the grill on which meat was roasted. The *Dictionary of American English* shows that the word was in use in America at least by 1709, and by 1733 it had taken on the implications of a social gathering. By 1836 barbecues were popular in Texas, and in 1850 a barbecue was held in Kansas whose menu included six cattle, twenty hogs, fifty sheep, pigs, and lambs, a hundred hams, and hundreds of baked goods.

Because of the outdoor nature of the barbecue (although indoor pit barbecues are found in restaurants throughout America), the use of charcoal, fruit woods, and mesquite (especially in the West) is easily managed, and even backyard barbecues, which are usually large metal saucers supported on legs and outfitted with metal grills, utilize store-bought, packaged briquets of compressed charcoal. A favorite backyard barbecue would include American staples like steak, hot dogs, hamburgers, and baked potatoes cooked in aluminum foil, but the two most traditional regional barbeques are made with pork or beef, the former in the South, the latter in the West.

BEEF SPARERIB BARBECUE:
Sauté 3 cups coarsely chopped onions and 1 1/2 tbs. minced garlic in 4 tbs. oil till soft but not brown. Add one 1-lb. can drained, chopped tomatoes with liquid, 2 tbs. dry mustard, 2 tbs. sugar, 1 1/2 tbs. vinegar, 3/4 cup tomato paste, salt, pepper, and about 6 seeded chilies (or add chilies to taste). Bring to a boil and reduce till thickened. Correct seasoning and remove from heat. Skewer spareribs, baste lavishly with sauce, and grill over hot coals, basting often, for about 30 min. Serve with heated sauce on side. (This same sauce may be used for chicken barbecue.)

PORK BARBECUE:
In a large kettle brown 3 lb. pork shoulder in 3 tbs. fat. Mix together 1/2 cup ketchup, 1 tsp. chili powder or cayenne, 1/2 tsp. nutmeg. 1/4 tsp. cinnamon, 1 tsp. celery seed, 1 tsp. sugar, 1/2 tsp. nutmeg, salt and pepper, 1/3 cup vinegar, and 1 cup water. Bring to a boil and cook for 10 min. Pour over pork, cover, and bake at 325°, basting often, for about 1 1/2 hr. or more, till pork is very tender and comes away easily with knife and fork. Remove all meat from bone and chop into fine pieces or shreds, then add salt, pepper, and hot sauce to taste. Serve with cole slaw and corn bread.

bar dog. A cowboy term for a bartender.

barfly. A term dating from 1910 for someone who stays too long at a saloon. Harry MacElhone, owner of Harry's New York Bar in Paris, founded a less-than-serious organization called "International Bar Fly" or "IBF" in 1924, which now supposedly has more than eighty thousand members.

bar glasses. Any of the various types of glassware used at a bar. There are dozens of such glasses (*Grossman's Guide to Wines, Beers, and Spirits,* by Harold J. Grossman, revised by Harriet Lembeck [1977], shows thirty-seven different glasses), but few bars or restaurants stock more than a few useful kinds such as those listed below:

cocktail glass. A 2 1/2-ounce stemmed glass with a tapered bowl used to serve COCKTAILS. A larger 4 1/2-ounce cocktail glass with a wider rim is preferred, especially for MARTINIS, and this glass is usually called a "martini glass."

collins glass. A cylindrical 12-ounce glass for long drinks like the TOM COLLINS.

highball glass. A cylindrical 8-ounce glass for mixed drinks on the rocks.

jigger. A short, squat, thick glass used to hold 1 1/2 ounces of spirits, it is often used as a measuring glass or shot glass.

old-fashioned glass. A short, cylindrical 6-ounce glass with a thick bottom, used for serving short drinks on the rocks, like the OLD-FASHIONED. This glass is sometimes stemmed.

pilsener glass. A long, conical glass of at least 10 ounces used to hold BEER. Its design helps to maintain a foamy head on the beer.

pony or liqueur glass. A 1-ounce glass that is stemmed and tubular in shape, used for CORDIALS.

saucer glass or champagne glass. Traditionally (though not recommended by connoisseurs) used for serving CHAMPAGNE and sparkling drinks, this stemmed 5-ounce glass has a flat, saucerlike bowl.

sherry glass. A slightly fluted 2-ounce glass used for sherry and cordials.

shot glass. A short, squat, thick-bottomed glass used to serve a "shot" of whiskey or other spirits. It is often called a "cheater" because the customer often does not receive a full ounce.

sour glass. A stemmed 6-ounce glass for serving SOURS.

wineglasses. According to the WINE served, these glasses may be of various heights, shapes, and stems. The all-purpose wineglass holds between 6 1/2 and 8 1/2 ounces of liquid. White wines are customarily served in long-stemmed glasses with a medium-size bowl; Bordeaux and other red wines are served in glasses with a slightly larger bowl; Burgundy and other red wines are considered best served in a balloon glass with a large bowl; German wines customarily are served in a small-bowled, long, green-stemmed glass; BRANDIES are served in snifters, glasses with short stems and large-bottomed bowls.

barley (Genus *Hordeum*). A grain of the grass family that was brought to the United States by early settlers, who ground the seed for use as a cereal, in breads and cakes, and as "barley sugar." The word is from Old English, *bærlic*.

Today the United States is the second largest producer of barley, after the Soviet Union. Most barley is used for livestock feed or for making beer, but it is still also used in cakes, breads, and mixed CEREALS.

barracuda (Genus *Sphyraena*). Any of various long, silvery tropical fishes with a row of sharp, long teeth. Barracudas are often poisonous to eat, though the Pacific barracuda has long been a California delicacy, where it is sold fresh. The fish, which is voracious and feared, may be broiled, grilled, or smoked.

The word is from the Spanish, and its first reference in English was in 1678.

Basque barbecue. A barbecue made from lamb, so called by cowboys because many nineteenth century sheepmen were of Basque ancestry.

bass. Any of a variety of salt- or freshwater fish, whose general name derives from Old English *bærs* and has German roots that mean "bristle," which describes the spiny appearance of any number of fish of the perch and other families. *The American Heritage Dictionary of the English Language* defines bass, first, as "Any of several North American freshwater fishes of the family Centrarchidae," and, second, as "Any of various marine fishes of the family Serranidae."

Some sea PERCHES, groupers, jewfishes, and others go by the name "bass," but the only fish in Europe by this specific name is what the French call *"loup."*

The reader should look under main entries for the following: BLACK BASS, BLACK SEA BASS, GROUPER, JEWFISH, and STRIPED BASS.

bath towel. Meatpacker's term for beef tripe.

batter bread. An old cornmeal bread often associated with Virginia and first mentioned in print in 1897. The following recipe by Houston Eldredge appeared in *Famous Old Receipts,* published in Philadelphia in 1908.

> Scald 1/2 pt. cornmeal, cool, then beat in 1/2 pt. clabber with 1 tsp. melted butter, 1 tbs. flour, 1 tsp. salt, and another 1/2 pt. clabber. Dissolve 1/2 tsp. baking soda in 1/2 cup clabber, beat into mixture, place in buttered pudding dish, and bake at 425° for about 30 min.

bean. Any of variety of pods from plants in the genus *Phaseolus,* and, for culinary purposes, especially *Phaseolus vulgaris,* of which there are more than a thousand varieties. The word is from the Old English, *bēan.*

Beans have been enjoyed for thousands of years throughout the world, and the oldest domesticated beans in the Americas were found in the Ocampo Caves of Mexico, dating back to 4000 B.C. Beans were often planted in the same fields with corn and were carried to North America from Mexico.

The two main types of beans grown and eaten in the United States are field beans, including the pea or NAVY BEAN, the BLACK BEAN, the KIDNEY BEAN, and others raised in Michigan, California, Idaho, New York, Colorado, New Mexico, and elsewhere; and garden beans, including the STRING BEAN, the butter or LIMA BEAN, and the wax bean. Soybean *(Glycine max),* whose seeds are called "soya" or "soyabean," are generally used for fodder, though some oil, soy sauce, and bean curd is made from them too.

bean eater. Cowboy slang for a Mexican, because beans were a predominant ingredient in Mexican cooking. Also, since 1881, a slang term for a Bostonian, because of the association with BOSTON BAKED BEANS.

bean-hole cookery. A method of baking, used by the Indians of the Northwest, by which a hole in the ground is filled with very hot stones on which is placed an earthenware pot filled with beans. This is then covered further with hot stones, then earth, and left to bake for hours.

bear. Any of a variety of large, shaggy-furred mammals in the family Ursidae, especially in North America the black bear *(Ursus americanus),* also called the "brown bear" and "cinnamon bear," the grizzly bear *(U. horribilis),* also called the "silver tip," and the polar bear *(U. maritimus).*

Omnivorous and ferocious, bears have been among the most sought after game, for their fur, their fat, and their meat, all of which the Indian used long before the arrival of the European trappers, who hunted the animal mainly for its coat and nearly drove the beast to extinction in the East. Because of bear's gaminess, young bear was the most desirable, and bear meat, needing to be marinated or covered with a strongly seasoned sauce to make it palatable to most tastes, was available in city markets of the nineteenth century.

Today bear occasionally shows up in some specialty restaurants, usually as a stew.

bear sign. Cowboy's term for a doughnut.

beef. The meat of a full-grown steer, ox, cow, or bull. Beef, in preparations ranging from steak and stews to HAMBURGERS and BARBECUES, is one of the most important meats in the American diet.

The word is from the Latin, *bōs,* "ox," which in Middle English became *boef* or *beef.*

Cattle for beef have been domesticated for millennia, all descended from the wild bulls of Europe called "aurochs" *(Bos primigenius).* By 3500 B.C. cattle were being raised in Egypt, and the ox is constantly used as a symbolic animal of the Old and New Testaments. By 500 A.D. the aurochs had been brought to England to be bred with the native "shorthorn," and most American breeds are descendants of English cattle, though the Spanish were the first to bring cows to Florida in 1550. Jamestown had cattle by 1611, but there was no commercial meat-packing in the colonies until William Pynchon set up a slaughterhouse in Boston in 1662. PORK was much preferred for meat in those days because pigs were easier to care for and feed, whereas cattle often ran off to the woods, where they became wild. Still, although beef was not so common as pork, the early settlers had sufficient land on which to raise enough beef for their needs, and the word *beef-steak* was in use since the late seventeenth century. In 1711 a "Beef-Stake Club" was thriving in London and later was imitated in Philadelphia, where a similar organization under the same name met at Tunn Tavern as of 1749. In those days a beef-steak was a flattened piece of beef that was usually fried and served with gravy. The English liked it served very rare, and so the American colonists followed suit. By the 1760s some cities had "beef steak houses." Nineteenth-century American cookbook authors insisted that beef should be cooked till very well done.

Most of the beef consumed, however, was salted or corned, and little meat was shipped over long distances. By 1767 the Franciscan friars of California had enlisted Mexicans and Indians to herd cattle, and Americans were involved in similar activities in Texas by the 1820s, where the LONGHORN steer, which was actually herded as far as New York in 1854, became an important breed in the decades to follow. By the 1850s Chicago had already established itself as a meat-packing center, but again, the industry produced mainly salted or corned meat products. After the Civil War the demand for beef increased with the rise in population and the decrease in forage land east of the Mississippi River, and on September 5, 1867, the first cattle were shipped by railroad car out of Abilene, Kansas, a town that livestock trader Joe McCoy bought for $4,250 as a central depot for cattle movements out of Texas. This began the era of the great cattle drives and the expansion of the West's mythos into romance and literature, with the cowboy as the central figure of America's seemingly unending destiny. According to Edwin C. McReynolds in *Oklahoma: A History of the Sooner State* (1954), the total number of cattle driven from Texas to Kansas City between 1866 and 1885 was six million head, with a peak of six hundred thousand in 1871. But the cattle drives were short-lived for several reasons. The introduction of barbed wire in 1875 and the intrusion of more farm families into the western territories meant an end to free access to land. Then, over the winter of 1886–1887, a bitter cold spell wiped out 90 percent of the herds, and the end came quickly.

Americans had developed a great appetite for beef by the turn of the century, and, after Detroit meat-packer G. H. Hammond brought out the refrigerated railway car in 1871, chilled carcasses became readily available in the East, though fresh beef was still not common in the outer reaches of the western frontier. Still, by the 1880s beef was being shipped even to England, and "steakhouses" were among the most popular restaurants in large American cities.

A hardy American breed of cattle called the "Santa Gertrudis," developed from shorthorns and Brahmans at the King Ranch in Texas, became an extremely adaptive steer for the beef market, though ABERDEEN ANGUS, Herefords, and Galloways were also important in the late nineteenth century. Slaughterhouses of this era were primitive and generally unhygienic, leading to frequent campaigns to correct their abuses and to the passage in 1906 of the Pure Food and Drug Law, to a large extent the result of the impression made on the public by Upton Sinclair's accusatory novel about the meat-packing industry, *The Jungle* (1906).

By the 1920s beef had become a competitor with pork in terms of consumption, and Europeans began characterizing Americans as a "nation of beefeaters." To be sure, a meal of a two-inch-thick steak and a baked potato or FRENCH FRIES became an icon of American gastronomy and remains so to this day, despite the fact that beef consumption has begun to decrease in recent years. In 1952 the average American ate 62 pounds of beef per year; by 1960, 99 pounds; by 1970, 114 pounds. But in 1983 the figure stood at only 78.2 pounds. The decrease is due both to Americans' desire to cut out excessive fat and cholesterol from their diet and to the current high price of beef. There have in recent years been attempts by meat producers to change the federal regulations on meat quality (based on marbling, color, and texture), but for the moment the standards are as follows: prime, choice, good, standard, commercial, utility, cutter, and canner. These standards are enforced by the Department of Agriculture and stamped on the outside of each carcass. The lowest five grades are generally available only in processed or canned meats, while the top grade, prime, is most often encountered at the better steakhouses or butchers.

The terminology of American butchering is often confusing, and many terms are used as synonyms for poorly defined standard cuts. The most commonly used terms are explained below.

primal brisket. The breast section of the animal, just under the first five ribs of the chuck. The brisket, which is usually braised or pot-roasted, is cut into two pieces, the flat half and the point half.

primal chuck. The shoulder and part of the neck. Chuck is usually ground for hamburger or other meat dishes. The cross-rib roast (also called "English" or "Boston" cut) is usually pot-roasted, as is the next cut, the arm pot roast (also called "shoulder roast"). The blade cut, which may be made into a roast or steak, is next. This may be further divided into the chuck eye (also called "market" or "Spencer" roasts), the chuck steak (or "flat iron" steak), and the mock tenderloin (or "Scotch tender," "Jewish fillet," and "chuck eye").

primal flank. Meat from the belly section below the loin. It is usually braised or, if marinated, grilled for LONDON BROIL.

primal plate. From the chest in front of the flank steak. It is cut into short ribs or braised without the bone. PASTRAMI is often made from this cut, as is the skirt steak, a diaphragm muscle that is braised or ground.

primal rib. The meat between the primal chuck and short loin containing seven ribs. Prime rib, often encountered on menus and considered the most desirable part of the animal, is from this section. A boned rib roast is often called a "Delmonico steak" (after Delmonico's restaurant in New York, where it was a popular cut of the nineteenth century). A standing rib roast includes the seven ribs of this section.

primal round. Meat from the hind leg of the animal, from the end of the primal loin to the hock or ankle. This is divided into several other cuts: the top round (often sold as LONDON BROIL), the bottom round, the eye of the round, the sirloin tip, the heel of the round, and the shin.

primal shank. Meat taken from the shin section of the front leg of the animal. Primal shank requires braising or grinding.

primal short loin. Meat from the hindquarter between the pinbone of the primal sirloin and the small end of the rib. It is considered the best cut for steaks, which include the PORTERHOUSE (containing the top loin, the tenderloin, and the tail and retaining the T-bone); the T-bone steak (which first appeared as a term in 1928), comprised of meat that is often the same as the porterhouse; the club steak, sometimes called a "Delmonico steak," having no tenderloin or flank attached; the TENDERLOIN, also called "filet mignon," "tournedos," and "chateaubriand" (though this last is also the name of a recipe for a porterhouse steak); and the strip steak or strip roast, which contains the top loin muscle and bones and is called in some parts of the country "New York strip," in others "Kansas City strip," and "shell" in others.

primal sirloin. The meat on the animal's hip, which may be cut into pinhouse sirloin, flat-bone sirloin, round-bone sirloin, wedge-bone sirloin, cut-with-the-grain tenderloin, cut-with-the-grain bottom sirloin, and whole sirloin roast.

The varieties of ground beef recognized by the United States Department of Agriculture include the following:

ground beef. Meat from any part of the animal, except "undesirable" parts, such as ears, snout, and innards.

ground sirloin. Meat specifically from the primal sirloin section.

ground round. Meat exclusively from the primal round section.

ground chuck. Meat exclusively from the primal chuck.

hamburger meat. Meat that is intended for use in meat patties; however, this is a confusing and ambiguous term.

beef head. Slang for a Texan, used by cowboys and other westerners because of Texans' association with the beef industry and because of the popularity of that meat with Texans.

beef herd. A herd made up of STEERS, as opposed to a cow herd, made up of steers and cows.

beef-on-weck. A Buffalo, New York, specialty, made of thin slices of roast beef topped with its own juices and served on a hard, caraway-seeded roll called a *kummelweck,* from German, *Kümmel,* "caraway," and *Weck,* "roll." Usually eaten with horseradish.

beer. A low-alcohol beverage made from fermented barley and other grains and flavored with hops. Beer is easily the most popular of all alcoholic drinks enjoyed by Americans, with a per capita consumption in 1982 of 24.4 gallons and a market expenditure of $34 billion—more than half the total expenditures for all alcoholic beverages in the United States.

The word *beer* comes from the Middle English, *ber(e),* and, ultimately, from Latin, *bibere,* "to drink." The beverage in various forms has been made for at least eight thousand years, evidence having been found in Babylonian records of beer being used in sacrificial rituals. Egypt, China, and India all made beer, as did the Incas in Peru. Beer was well known throughout Europe even before viticulture had developed to any significant degree, and the addition of hops (the dried flowers of vines of the genus *Humulus*) to give a characteristic bitterness has been traced at least as early as 768 A.D. By 1376 there were more than a thousand brewmasters in Hamburg alone, and the popularity of the drink became good reason to tax it.

The first brewery in America was set up by the Dutch in New Amsterdam in 1612, and Governor Peter Minuit (1580–1638) established the first public brewery in 1632. The Pilgrims, who had intended to settle in Virginia in 1620, instead landed at Plymouth Rock, Massachusetts, because, according to a chronicler, "we could not now take time for further search or consideration, our victuals being spent, especially our beer."

Early settlers in America made beer from all sorts of substances, including corn, pumpkins, and persimmons, sometimes flavored with sassafras or pine. Early colonial breweries generally reflected the preference for English-style beers, strong, lusty, and dark, over the lighter German styles. By 1629 there were breweries in Virginia, and eight years later the first licensed brewhouse was opened in Massachusetts. (*Brewery* entered the language a century later.) During the seventeenth century beer was considered a light, everyday "small drink," consumed by men, women, and children throughout the day. Before that time ale (from Old English, *ealu*) was distinguished from beer because it contained no barley or hops. When brewers added both to ale in the seventeenth century, the two terms became synonymous, with Englishmen preferring to keep the name *ale* and Americans *beer*. Both were "top fermented," meaning the spent yeasts rose to the top of the barrel.

Beer was a perfectly respectable beverage among the founding fathers of the country. William Penn (1644–1718) set up Philadelphia's first brewhouse in 1685, and Jefferson, Madison, and Adams all had interests in such establishments, while George Washington maintained his own brewhouse at his Mount Vernon home.

Several kinds of beer were available to the Americans of those days. Stout, a strong English beer or ale, was dark in color and bitter in taste; porter, which originated in England about 1722, was a blend of ale and beer. Its name derived from its popularity among the eighteenth-century porters who carried produce to London's Covent Garden. Porter was heavily malted and had a slightly sweet taste. In America it was purveyed at porterhouses, and the proprietor of one such place, Martin Harrison, became known for his cut of beef, which was called after 1814 a "porterhouse steak." And then there was spruce beer, made with the tops of spruce trees, which became so popular during the Revolutionary War that the Continental Congress in 1775 decreed that the American troops should receive a choice of one quart of either cider or spruce beer daily.

After the turn of the century the arrival of German immigrants in Philadelphia made that city a major brewing center, and German-style beers became increasingly available. Then, about 1840, John Wagner of Philadelphia began making a lager (from the German, *lager bier,* "storehouse beer") that was "bottom fermented," that is, the yeast sank to the bottom, making the beer lighter and somewhat weaker than top-fermented beers. Wagner's German contemporaries followed suit, building special facilities to keep the beer cool during fermentation and to age the product for two to three months. Although some immediately dismissed these light lagers (also called "Pilsner" or "pilsener," from the Pilsner Urquell beer of Pilsen, Czechoslovakia, where quality beer had been made since 1292) as a "woman's drink," they caught on rapidly, at first in German communities, where beerhalls and beergardens flourished in midcentury, and afterwards in every major city in America.

Beerhalls—some of which could hold up to twelve hundred people—became social centers for the lower and middle classes, and one moralist of the day wrote of their lavish and bawdy atmosphere: "The quantity [of lager] sold in a day is enormous. A four-horse team from the brewery . . . finds it difficult to keep up the supply."

Soon *lager* and *beer* were interchangeable terms, and the golden, effervescent beverage (sometimes called "a bucket of suds") surpassed cider and all others in popularity. The cities of the Midwest—Cincinnati, St. Louis, Chicago, and, particularly, Milwaukee—grew powerful as brewing centers, all following the lead of John Wagner's Philadelphia. One of the first in the new market, however, was a New York family, Frederick and Maximilian Schaefer, who purchased the Sebastian Sommers Brewery in New York City in 1842 and began making lager there under their own name. Two years later Jacob Best, Sr., and his four sons opened a brewery on Chestnut Street Hill in Milwaukee that later came under the control of Frederick Pabst, who increased output to half a million barrels in 1889 and by 1902 had built the first plant in America equipped to carry the fresh beer from brewery to bottler. (Bottled beer was first produced in 1875 by the Joseph Schlitz Brewing Company, which advertised its product as "The Beer That Made Milwaukee Famous." Before then all beer was drawn from a spigot and referred to as "draft beer," also then called "shenkbeer" [from the German, *Schenkbier*].)

By 1900 the brewery facilities of Anheuser-Busch covered sixty acres of St. Louis. The firm had forty-two branches in other cities and even operated its own railroad. Jacob Schmidt built another great brewery in Minneapolis-St. Paul, while Henry Weinhard and Arnold Blitz merged resources to make Portland, Oregon, a major beer producer. In San Francisco, where the shortage of ice in midcentury was a factor in making decent lager, there developed STEAM BEER, so called because of the high amount of pressure built up in the barrel through a special process of fermentation (see main entry for more information on this beer). By 1870, however, American refrigeration techniques made it possible to make beer year-round without regard to temperature. By 1876 there were more than 4,000 breweries in the United States.

PROHIBITION in America (1920–1933, with some states banning alcoholic beverages, that is, "going dry," as early as 1916) was a disaster for the beer industry, which survived by producing malt and yeast and by providing ice. The Volstead Act defined a forbidden beverage as one containing 0.5 percent alcohol (regular beer varies from 3.2 to 4 percent by weight), so a market developed for "near beer," which had been made since 1909 as a substitute for the real thing and contained 0.4 percent alcohol. If illegal spirits were added to near beer, it was called "needle beer" or "needled beer." On April 7, 1933, President Franklin D. Roosevelt signed the Cullen-Harrison Act, which raised the definition of nonintoxication to 3.2 percent, and people started referring to such brews as "3.2 beer." Of course, illegal beer was made throughout

Prohibition, often at home, where it was called "home brew." When Prohibition finally ended in 1933, only 750 breweries reopened, and though new ones opened and demand for beer grew rapidly through the 1930s and 1940s, competition drove many breweries into consolidation or out of business. One of the greatest boons for the industry was the introduction in 1935 by the Adolph Coors Company of beer in cans, which led to increased home consumption. The nonreturnable bottle became the norm in the early 1950s, further increasing the ease of the consumer to enjoy his beer at home. With this expansion of the market came increased competitiveness. Price cutting among the largest breweries drove the small, local breweries out of the market, so that today there are only about seventy breweries left in the United States, even though we are the largest beer-producing country. (Germans, however, are the largest beer drinkers, per capita, in the world; Americans rank twelfth worldwide.)

Making beer in America is a complex process, beginning with the malting of barley, which is combined with a cereal like corn that has been cooked. The two are mixed and mashed to convert starch to maltose and dextrin. This is called "wort" and is filtered through a "lauter tun," which separates wort from grain (the latter is used for cattle feed). Hops are added to the wort for flavor, and high heat is added until the wort is completely soluble (called the "hot break"), before being run through a "hop strainer" or "hop jack," which removes the hops and leaves "hot wort." This is cooled, yeast is added, and fermentation begins. Beer is usually fermented between thirty-seven and forty-nine degrees Fahrenheit, whereas ale, which uses a different type of yeast, ferments at temperatures between fifty and seventy degrees. Brewer's yeast is used in beer, and, in lagers, it settles to the bottom. Ale's yeasts settle at the top. The beer ferments for eight to eleven days, ale five to six. The beer is then stored and kept close to the freezing temperature to precipitate out the yeast and solids. As the beer mellows over the next month or two, it takes on its final character before having carbon dioxide (CO_2) added to give it effervescence. This carbon dioxide comes from that thrown off during fermentation or from a process called "*kräusening,*" by which a small amount of still fermenting young beer is added to produce a short second fermentation. The beer is then refrigerated, filtered, and, if intended for bottling or canning, usually pasteurized. (Beers put in strong aluminum or stainless-steel kegs are usually not pasteurized, because they are likely to be consumed faster and therefore would not undergo any further fermentation, which could cause additional carbon dioxide to burst cans or bottles.) Peak drinking time for canned beer is considered to be about four months; for bottles, six. Some bottled or canned beer that has not been pasteurized goes under the name *draft beer,* but *draft brewed* and *draft beer flavor* are phrases used on bottles and cans that may contain pasteurized beer, as long as the pasteurization is noted on the label.

Other beer terms include:

ale. Once a term for a brew of malt and cereal without hops or barley. In the seventeenth century hops and barley were added and the distinction between ale and beer disappeared for a hundred years, until the lagers of the 1840s became synonymous with beer while ale continued to be made in an older, more flavorful style. Ales average 4.5 percent alcohol by weight, slightly higher than beer.

bock beer. Also, "bockbier." In Germany bock beer was usually brewed in the spring and was a heavier, darker beer than most lagers. In America its style and taste is a matter of individual companies' definition and marketing.

malt liquor. A malt beverage that is higher in alcohol than beer, up to 8 percent by weight in some states.

The taste of beers in the United States has been mellow and, to some, lacking in distinction from one major brand to another. There has been a great increase in the importation of stronger beers from other countries (currently about 3 percent of the American market). Nevertheless, the same brand of beer may taste different from state to state because the alcoholic content is regulated by each individual state's legislation. Federal law requires a minimum alcohol level for beer of 0.5 percent, but sets no maximum.

beer bash. Campus or young people's term for a party at which the primary beverage is beer, often served from a keg.

beet *(Beta vulgaris).* A dark, reddish purple fruit of a plant with leafy greens sometimes eaten as a vegetable on their own.

The name is from the Latin, *bēta,* which in Middle English became *bete.* The vegetable is a native of the Mediterranean, but it was not of much gastronomic interest until the nineteenth century in France, and, afterwards, in America, where most of the beet crop is canned, or sometimes pickled. The most popular varieties are the Detroit Dark Red, Egyptian, and Eclipse. Swiss chard is also known as the "spinach beet."

beignet. A puffy yeast pastry deep-fried and served with sugar. The beignet (whose name is French, for "fritter") is a traditional food item of New Orleans.

In the French Market in New Orleans's Vieux Carré, beignets are served with CHICORY coffee for breakfast and as an afternoon snack.

Sprinkle 1 pkg. yeast over 1/4 cup lukewarm water, let stand 3 min., then stir. Let stand for 10 min. till proofed. Combine 1/4 cup sugar, 2 tbs. shortening, and 1/2 tsp. salt, then pour in 1/2 cup boiling water and blend well. Stir in 1/2 cup cream, yeast, and 1 beaten egg. Add 2 cups flour, followed by another 2 cups to make a smooth dough. Gather dough into ball, roll out into rectangle about 1/4-in. thick, then cut into 5-in. squares and drop one by one into hot oil, turning to coat with oil and cooking till browned. Drain, sprinkle with confectioners' sugar.

belly-wash. Cowboy slang for weak coffee. Also, logger slang for a soft drink.

bend an elbow. To drink whiskey. The term dates at least to the 1830s.

bender. Slang term for a drunken spree. The term goes back at least to the 1820s.

best ever. A phrase used by cooks to describe with considerable hyperbole a prized recipe, as in "best ever cake," "best ever cookies," or "best ever frosting." It is a twentieth-century term, probably from the 1940s.

beta carotene. A coloring agent added to butter, margarine, and nondairy products used as shortening. The body converts beta carotene to vitamin A.

bialy. A Jewish-American baked roll sprinkled with onion flakes. The name, first mentioned in print in 1965, comes from the Polish city of Bialystok.

bière douce. A Louisiana Creole beer made from the skin of the pineapple, sugar, rice, and water. The term is from the French for "sweet beer."

big antelope. A cowboy term for an animal belonging to someone else and killed for food. Ramon F. Adams, in his *Western Words* (1968), notes, "It was the custom in the old days for a ranchman never to kill his own cattle for food, and many an old-timer was accused of never knowing how his own beef tasted."

billi-bi. A soup made from mussels, cream, and seasonings. Under the name *mouclade* it is a well-known soup of Normandy, where the mussels are left in the final preparation; in a true billi-bi they are removed before straining the soup.

Billi-bi (sometimes spelled "Billy By") is a popular soup in American restaurants, but its origins are in France. Some have claimed that the soup was named after William Bateman Leeds, Sr. (1861–1908), president of the American Tin Plate Company, at Maxim's restaurant in Paris. But Jean Mauduit in his book, *Maxim's, soixante ans de plaisir et d'histoire* (1958), wrote "The recipe was created by chef [Louis] Barthe to please an old regular customer who nourished an exclusive passion for mussels; the success of the dish was so great that they named it, as an honor, with the diminutive and the initial of the customer's name, even though he was not really the creator [my translation]." Mauduit gives the man's name as William Brand. The current management of Maxim's, however, says that Barthe created the dish for Brand ("an American client of Maxim's") in 1925, but not at Maxim's; instead Barthe created the dish at Ciro's restaurant in Deauville.

> Clean 2 lb. mussels, place in kettle with 2 chopped shallots, 2 chopped onions, 2 sprigs parsley, salt and pepper, 1/8 tsp. cayenne pepper, 1 cup white wine, 2 tbs. butter, 1 bay leaf, and 1/2 tsp. dry thyme. Cover, bring to a boil, lower to simmer and cook for 10 min., till mussels have opened (discard those that do not). Strain soup through cheesecloth, reserve mussels for other use. Return soup to kettle, bring to boil, add 2 cups heavy cream, remove from heat, add 1 beaten egg yolk, and return to heat to thicken. Sprinkle with Parmesan cheese. Serves 6.

binder. Also called an "extender." A food additive that binds meat and poultry products together and helps retain moisture. Binders are sometimes used as a supplement for nutrients in the meat or merely to add bulk. A nonmeat binder would be SOY PROTEIN.

bird's nest pudding. Also, "crow's nest pudding." A very old New England apple pudding.

> Pare and core 4 apples, place them in a buttered dish, and fill the centers with seedless raisins. Mix 4 beaten eggs, 1 cup sugar, 1/8 tsp. nutmeg, salt, and 3 cups milk, and pour over apples. Bake at 325° till custard curdles, about 45 min.

biscuit. A small leavened and shortened bread served with meals. The word derives from the Latin words *bis,* "twice," plus *coctus,* past participle of *coquere,* "to cook." In England, a "biscuit" is what Americans usually call a CRACKER. The American meaning for *biscuit* was first noted by John Palmer in his *Journal of Travels in the United States of North America, and in lower Canada* (1818), and by 1828 Webster defined the confection as "a composition of flour and butter, made and baked in private families." In general usage such puffy leavened little breads were called "soda biscuits" or "baking-soda biscuits," in contrast to the unleavened cracker type.

Recipes for soda biscuits are found in every nineteenth-century cookbook, especially with reference to the cookery of the South, where biscuits with ham was a specialty. The South is also home of the "beaten biscuit," which was first mentioned in the 1870s. This curious confection, known in Maryland as a "Maryland biscuit," is rarely made today, but was once common in the South, where the sound of a mallet beating the biscuit dough was a nostalgic sound of morning. This process made for a very hard, crisp biscuit that is the antithesis of the soft, puffy biscuits usually encountered.

Biscuits are sometimes made with buttermilk. Usually they are broken open and buttered or served with slices of ham and gravy.

> Sift together 2 cups flour, 1 1/2 tsp. salt, and 4 tsp. baking powder. Cut in 2 tbs. butter or lard with a fork till it has the texture of coarse meal. Add 3/4 cup milk and blend quickly. Knead for about 30 sec., then roll out to 1/2-in. thickness on floured board. Cut out in 2-in. circles, let stand, bake for 20 min. at 425°.
>
> BEATEN BISCUITS:
> Combine 1/2 cup lard with 4 cups flour and 1 tsp. salt till the texture is like that of coarse meal. Add 1/2 cup milk and ice water mixed together, then add 1 beaten egg white. Beat with a mallet for 30 min. or more, till dough is blistered and smooth. Roll out on floured board to 1/2-in. thickness, cut in 2-in. circles, prick with fork, and bake for 25 min. at 350°.

biscuit roller. Cowboy slang for the cook on a ranch, used since the 1870s. Also called a "biscuit shooter," which was sometimes applied to a restaurant waitress as well.

bishop. A drink of mulled wine, sugar, spices, and citrus fruit. The name possibly derives from its red color, as in a bishop's robes. Jonathan Swift was the first to mention the drink in print as of 1738, and James Boswell in his *Life of Johnson* (1790) says that it was a favorite drink of his subject, as it was in America throughout the eighteenth and nineteenth centuries. Often, as in the recipe below, the citrus fruit is first roasted.

> Insert about 1 doz. cloves into the rind of an orange and roast it for about 15 min. Cut into quarters, place in a saucepan with 1 qt. port or wine and 1 tbs. sugar, and simmer on a very low flame for about 30 min.

bishop's bread. A sweet bread made with dried fruit. According to the *Better Homes and Gardens Heritage Cook Book* (1975), it is a bread of the American nineteenth-century frontier, when settlements would be visited by traveling clergymen. Legend has it that "one early Sunday morning a circuit-riding bishop in Kentucky dropped in on one family unexpectedly for breakfast. The resourceful hostess invented a quick fruit bread for the occasion [and] named it Bishop's Bread in honor of her guest."

There is, however, a similar bread traditionally made in Germany by this same name, *bischofbrot*.

> Combine 2 1/2 cups flour, 1 3/4 cups packed brown sugar, 1 tsp. ground cinnamon, and 1/2 tsp. salt. Cut in 1/2 cup butter till the mixture resembles coarse meal. Stir in 1/2 cup chopped nuts. Remove 1/2 cup of the mixture and set aside. Mix 1 tsp. baking soda into rest of mixture. Mix 1 cup buttermilk and 2 beaten eggs, then add 1/2 cup raisins or currants and stir into flour mixture just to moisten. Turn batter into 2 greased and floured pans, sprinkle reserved flour mixture over tops, and bake for 35 min. at 350°.

bite and stir box. A box used by the New York Dutch with two compartments—one containing sugar lumps that one may bite and chew, and one holding granulated sugar to use in one's tea or coffee.

bitters. Aromatic, bitter blends of various spices, herbs, and alcohol. Bitters are usually sold as a digestive or medicinal aid, but several bottlings of bitters are used specifically as seasonings in foods and alcoholic beverages. Peychaud's bitters was an essential ingredient in many Louisiana cocktails, and many recipe books call for angostura bitters as a matter of course.

The herbs most often used would include gentian, orange, quinine, and ginger. Bitters have been spoken of in England since the early eighteenth century.

black and white. A term used to describe several soda fountain confections mixing chocolate and vanilla flavors, although it may also refer to black coffee with a container of cream on the side. In the East, *black and white* usually refers to a chocolate soda made with vanilla ice cream. Elsewhere it may be a chocolate MILK SHAKE with vanilla ice cream blended in (a black and white float would have the vanilla ice cream floating on top of the milk shake) or even a sundae made with vanilla ice cream and chocolate sauce.

black bass (Genus *Micropterus*). A member of the SUNFISH family, Centrarchidae, these freshwater fish of North America have been widely introduced throughout the United States. Because of the difficulty in catching black bass, they became popular for consumption only during the nineteenth century, when they were shipped from eastern to western waters for sport fishermen. Black bass are now found in forty-nine states of the union. The best black bass are those under three pounds; they are prepared in all manner of ways, grilled, poached, fried, or broiled. The following list includes the principal kinds of black bass for eating:

> **largemouth bass** *(Micropterus salmoides).* Found throughout the United States, the largemouth bass thrives in lakes and ponds and may weigh up to twenty pounds. It has a black band underneath a green back.

> **redeye bass** *(M. coosae).* A river bass of the South, the redeye bass is small, rarely weighing more than a pound. It is sometimes called the "mountain trout."

> **smallmouth bass** *(M. dolomieui).* In wide distribution, the smallmouth bass may run up to twelve pounds, though it is usually much smaller. It inhabits clear rocky lakes and rivers.

> **spotted bass** *(M. punctulatus).* With its yellow back and black blotches, this southern United States fish lives in streams and deep pools. It weighs about three pounds.

black bean *(Phaseolus vulgaris).* A bean usually cooked in a soup called "black bean soup." The bean, which is known to have been eaten in Mexico as much as seven thousand years ago, is used throughout the Caribbean. Venezuelans refer to the bean as *caviar criolo,* "creole caviar," and Brazilians make it part of their national dish, *feijoada.* In America the black bean has long been part of southern diets, and in Florida it is a favorite dish of the Cuban-American communities.

The following recipe is from The Coach House restaurant in New York City.

BLACK BEAN SOUP:
Brown 3 lb. beef bones, 1 lb. beef shin, and 3 lb. ham shank with rind in a 400° oven for about 20 min. Cut off meat and place in a kettle with 15 cups water, 3 cloves, 1 tsp. black peppercorns, and 3/4 tsp. celery seed. Bring to a boil, simmer with lid ajar for 8–10 hr. Strain, remove meat for other purposes, and refrigerate stock. Soak 2 1/2 cups black beans overnight in the refrigerator. Remove congealed fat from stock, reserving 2 tbs. Melt fat in skillet and sauté 1 cup chopped onion and 1/2 cup chopped celery till soft. Drain beans and add to skillet. In a kettle add beans and vegetables, 2 cups water, and 7 cups stock. Add 2 tsp. chopped garlic, simmer for

2 1/2 hr., stirring occasionally. Coarsely purée the bean mixture through strainer or in blender. Reheat, add salt and pepper. Before serving add a dash of dry sherry. Top with lemon slice and garnish, if desired, with chopped boiled egg.

blackberry. Any of a variety of plants in the genus *Rubus* that bear black, sweet berries. The berry is often called a "bramble" because it grows on prickly shrubs.

Blackberries have long flourished in North America, where the majority of the crop is produced in Texas, Oklahoma, and Arkansas, with a great amount of wild blackberries growing throughout the Southwest. Americans have always cherished the blackberry, and Walt Whitman wrote in *Song of Myself* (1855) that "the running blackberry would adorn the parlors of heaven."

Two important hybrids of the blackberry were discovered by Americans: the loganberry (possibly a cross between the blackberry and RASPBERRY), found by Judge J. H. Logan of California, in 1881; and the boysenberry (a cross of the loganberry and blackberry), developed by horticulturist Rudolph Boysen in 1923. The DEWBERRY is another form of blackberry particularly beloved in the South.

The most important cultivated varieties include the Himalaya, the Lucretia, the Black Diamond, the Agawam, the Lawton, and the Snyder.

"Blackberry winter" is the period of cool weather in May when the blackberries are in bloom. The term dates back at least to the turn of the present century.

black bottom. A term describing either of two confections: a sundae made with chocolate ice cream and chocolate syrup; or a pie made with a chocolate custard topped with rum custard and whipped cream.

The term derives from what the *Oxford English Dictionary* describes as "a low-lying area inhabited by a coloured population," first mentioned in print as of 1915 but probably older. The black bottom pie probably derives its name directly from this usage, and, notes James Beard in his *American Cookery* (1972), this recipe "began appearing in cookbooks around the turn of the century."

The black bottom sundae, on the other hand, probably gets its name from a popular dance of and following 1926 called the "black bottom," which itself may have come out of black culture.

BLACK BOTTOM PIE:
Dissolve 1 tbs. unflavored gelatin in 1/4 cup cold water. Scald 2 cups milk over low heat. Mix together 1/2 cup sugar, 1/4 tsp. salt, 2 tbs. flour, and 4 beaten egg yolks. Pour in some of the hot milk till blended, then pour this mixture into the rest of the hot milk. Stir over low heat to thicken (about 15 min.), remove from heat, and remove 1 cup of custard. Add 2 oz. unsweetened chocolate and 1/2 tsp. vanilla, blend well, then cool. Add gelatin to remaining custard and blend well. Add 2 tbs. dark rum. Chill. Spread chocolate mixture into chilled baked graham cracker crust and

refrigerate. Beat 3 egg whites with 1/4 tsp. cream of tartar and, gradually, 1/3 cup sugar. Fold into gelatinized custard and spread over chocolate layer. Top with whipped cream and garnish with shaved chocolate.

black cake. An old Virginia/Maryland cake made from molasses, spices, and fruit.

Combine 5 beaten eggs, 1 cup flour, 1/2 lb. butter, 1/2 lb. sugar, 1/2 pt. molasses, and 1 tsp. baking soda dissolved in 1/2 pt. sour cream. Add 4 tsp. ginger, 1 tsp. cinnamon, 1/4 tsp. ground cloves, 1/4 tsp. allspice, and 3/4 cup raisins or currants. Bake at 375° till an inserted knife comes out clean.

black cow. Any of a variety of ice cream sodas made with a scoop of vanilla ice cream. Usually the soda itself is either chocolate, sarsaparilla, or root beer, and the name refers to the mixture of dark soda with the white dairy item floating in it. If made with chocolate soda (that is, seltzer, milk, and chocolate syrup), it might be called a BLACK AND WHITE, especially in the East. In the 1930s plain root beer sometimes went by this term, as did chocolate milk in the 1940s, especially at lunch counters.

black drink. A drink of the boiled leaves of *Ilex cassine* in water, used by the Gulf State Indians as a purification medicine. The drink sometimes induced a nervous state of mind and was drunk as part of a ritual. The Catawba Indians called it "*yaupon,*" the Creeks "*ássi-lupútski*" ("small leaves"), and the English traders named it the "black drink" or "Carolina tea."

blackjack steer. Cowboy term for a scrawny steer from the timber country, where there would not be good grazing pasture.

black Mike. Logger's term for stew made from meat and vegetables.

black sea bass *(Centropristis striata).* Also, "blackfish," but different from the true blackfish or TAUTOG. A carnivorous fish that ranges from Maine to Florida, though most come from the coast between North Carolina and New York. The black sea bass has always been a highly valued eating and sport fish, and, as A. J. McClane notes in *The Encyclopedia of Fish Cookery* (1977), "Party boats already in vogue [in the early nineteenth century] (the first record is of George Washington chartering a boat to fish the banks off Sandy Hook) became so popular that woodcut posters were distributed around New York depicting men carrying great strings of sea bass."

Sea bass usually run between one-and-a-half and five pounds at market, and they are a major fish in Chinese-American recipes.

blackstrap. Also, "blackstrap molasses." A very dark molasses often used to make cattle feed or industrial alcohol. The term also refers to a mixture of rum and molasses in New England.

blended whiskey. A whiskey blended from at least 20 percent straight whiskey together with varying amounts of grain spirits, light whiskeys, or neutral spirits. About half the American whiskey consumed in the United States is blended. It is sometimes erroneously called "rye," but a true rye must contain at least 51 percent of that grain. The word was first printed in 1940.

blind tiger. A term used to describe an illegal establishment serving alcoholic beverages. It may also mean a cheap or inferior whiskey, though the phrase is no longer used in either sense.

The *Dictionary of Americanisms* cites an 1857 account in a sportsmen's gazette called *Spirit of the Times* as the term's first appearance in print: "I sees a kinder pidgeon-hole cut in the side of the house, and over the hole [a sign,] '*Blind Tiger,* ten cents a sight.' Says I to the feller inside, 'here's your ten cents, Walk out your wild-cat.' . . . I'll be dod-busted if he didn't shove out a glass of whiskey. You see that 'blind tiger' was an arrangement to evade the law, which won't let 'em sell licker there, except by the gallon."

An alternate term, *blind pig,* appeared in print in 1872.

blintz. A form of pancake with any of several fillings, such as cheese, jam, fish, fruits, or potatoes. The word is from the Yiddish, *blintseh,* via the Russian, *blinyets,* and first appears in English print in 1903.

American Jews usually eat blintzes with sour cream. Although they are traditionally served at the Jewish feast of Shevuoth, they have become a year-round snack, sometimes sold from pushcarts in large cities.

> Make a batter from 3 beaten eggs, 3/4 cup matzo meal, 1/2 tsp. salt, and 1 1/2 cups water. Pour a very thin layer of batter into a frying pan brushed with fat and brown on one side. Continue to make pancakes till all batter is used. Mix 1 lb. cottage cheese with 2–3 tbs. sugar and 2 tbs. sour cream. Fill pancakes with mixture, fold over three sides, and roll into envelope shape, tucking in the flap to seal. These may be fried or baked. Serve with sour cream. Serves 6.

Bloody Mary. A cocktail made of tomato juice, vodka, and seasonings, by far the most popular alcoholic drink with Americans, especially as part of weekend BRUNCHES.

Ernest Hemingway wrote in 1947 that he had introduced the Bloody Mary to Hong Kong in 1941, an act he said "did more than any other single factor except the Japanese Army to precipitate the Fall of that Crown Colony." But the drink seems to have originated in Paris, under another name, at Harry's New York Bar. Bartender Ferdinand "Pete" Petiot was experimenting with vodka, to which he'd been introduced in 1920, and a year later came up with the blend of tomato juice, vodka, and seasonings that American entertainer Roy Barton christened the "Bucket of Blood," after a nightclub in Chicago. The drink did not then become popular in Paris, but in 1933 Petiot was brought to New York by Vincent Astor to man the King Cole Bar at the St. Regis

Hotel, where the drink caught on—particularly as a supposed cure for hangovers—under the less sanguine name *Red Snapper*. Just when other bars around town began calling it the Bloody Mary (after Mary Tudor, Mary I of England and Ireland, known for her bloody reign against Protestants) is vague, but entertainer George Jessel has been credited with calling the drink a Bloody Mary (after friend Mary Geraghty) about 1929.

> Shake with ice cubes 1 1/2 oz. vodka, 2 oz. thick tomato juice, 1 dash lemon juice, 2 dashes salt, 1 dash black pepper, 2 dashes cayenne pepper, and 3 dashes Worcestershire sauce. The Bloody Mary is often served with a celery stick or a slice of lemon or lime.

Bloody Marys have been made with gin or rum, and replacing vodka with tequila and the lemon juice with lime gives one a Bloody Maria. By using Japanese *saké*, the drink becomes a Bloody Mary Quite Contrary, and not using any alcohol at all makes the drink a Virgin Mary, which some imbibers have called a "Bloody Shame."

blueberry. Any of a variety of native North American shrubs of the genus *Vaccinium* bearing deep-blue berries, which give the fruit and shrub its name. Blueberries, first noted by Captain James Cook in the late eighteenth century, are often confused with HUCKLEBERRIES, for both grow wild.

Blueberries are cultivated in Michigan, Maine, New Jersey, North Carolina, Washington, and elsewhere; commercially grown varieties account for more of the crop than do the wild ones. The most important variety is the highbush blueberry *(V. corymbosum)*, while the wild lowbush berry *(V. angustifolium* or *V. pennsylvanicum)* is important as a crop in Maine. Other varieties include the dryland blueberry *(V. ashei)* of the South and the evergreen blueberry *(V. ovatum)* of the Northwest.

Blueberries are eaten raw, with cream, and baked in muffins or pies.

> BLUEBERRY PIE:
> Wash and drain 1 qt. blueberries, pour into pie crust, sprinkle with a pinch of nutmeg, 3/4 cup sugar, and dot with 3 tbs. butter. Cover with top crust or pastry strips, allowing vents for steam to escape, and bake at 450° for 10 min., then reduce to 350° for about 30 min. till crust is golden brown.

blue blazer. A cocktail made from Scotch sweetened with honey and dramatically ignited to form a blue flame that is passed back and forth from one mug to another. The drink was the creation of Professor Jerry Thomas, bartender at San Francisco's El Dorado Bar in the 1860s and author of *How to Mix Drinks* (1862) and other recipe books. The story goes that Thomas made the drink for a weary miner whose time away from civilization made him long for something out of the ordinary. Thomas came up with the blue blazer, cautioning the amateur mixer "to practise for some time with cold water."

The name *blue blazer* refers to the blazing blue flame passed between mugs, but it has also come to share its meaning with the men's jacket with brass buttons named after the colorful jackets worn by the crew of the Lady Margaret Boat Club of St. John's College, Cambridge.

The drink's pyrotechnical display is no longer ordinary in the bars of this century.

> In a silver mug dissolve 1 tbs. honey in 4 oz. boiling water. Put 4 oz. Scotch in another mug and ignite, passing the liquid back and forth between the mugs till the flame dies out. Pour into a glass and garnish with lemon peel and grated nutmeg.

bluefish *(Pomatomus saltatrix).* Also, "snapper" (though no relation to the true SNAPPER), "tailor," and other names. A warm-water fish found from Maine to the Gulf of Mexico, the bluefish is ferocious and a great sport fish, nicknamed "bulldog of the ocean" for its tenacity. Early English settlers on Nantucket caught bluefish in abundance as of 1659, but a hundred years later the schools had vanished and did not reappear until 1800. They became abundant again about 1825, when bluefish sailing parties were organized for both men and women of Connecticut and New York.

Bluefish may have a strong flavor and must be dressed quickly.

blue lagoon. A cocktail made first at Harry's New York Bar in Paris about 1960 by Andrew MacElhone, son of the original owner, Harry MacElhone.

> Shake together one part blue curaçao, one part vodka, and one part lemon juice, strain, and pour over an island of crushed ice in an oval, clear glass bowl. Serve with straws piercing a slice of lemon and orange, and add a few cherries.

blue meat. Rancher's term for the meat of an unweaned calf.

boardinghouse man. Logger's slang for the cook at a camp.

bobotee. A puddinglike dish of milk, bread crumbs, almonds, onions, and Tabasco. The word, first printed in 1870, is from the Afrikaans, possibly derived from Malay or Javanese, and was well known to seamen of the nineteenth century. The dish is mentioned in Sarah Tyson Rorer's *McIlhenny's Tabasco Sauce Recipes* (1913), from which the following recipe is taken:

> Sauté 1 chopped onion in 2 tbs. butter till browned. Add 1 cup soft white bread crumbs, 1 cup milk, 1/2 tsp. salt. Stir and cook 1 min. Add 12 almonds, 5 drops Tabasco, 3 beaten eggs, and blend well. Squeeze the juice of half a lemon into a buttered baking dish, pour in the batter, and cook at 325° for about 20 min. till the pudding sets. Serve with boiled rice.

boiler. A logger's slang term for a cook.

boilermaker. A shot of straight whiskey followed immediately with a beer, called a "chaser" or "helper." Sometimes the whiskey is poured right into a glass of beer. The term has been used at least since the 1920s and is often associated with the Southwest and with stevedores. A "boilermaker's delight" is MOONSHINE or inferior whiskey.

In the Montana mining camps of the early part of this century a similar drink, called a "Shawn O'Farrell" or "Shawn O'," probably a catch-all reference to the number of Irish in the mines, was served as the workers came off their day's shift.

bologna. Also, "baloney" and "boloney." A smoked, seasoned sausage made from a variety of meats and popular as a SANDWICH meat or COLD CUT. The word derives from the Italian city of Bologna, where it was supposedly first produced, an observation first made in print in 1596. In the United States bologna (pronounced more like *baloney*) is usually made of pork and beef and is sold in groceries where it is sliced from a whole sausage.

The first mention of the word in American print was in 1850.

bolted meal. Corn that has not been home-ground.

bombo. A North Carolina term for a badger since the mid-nineteenth century. It is also an eighteenth-century term from the same region for equal parts of rum, water, and New England molasses, possibly named after British Admiral John Benbow (1653–1702).

bongo bongo soup. An oyster-and-spinach soup created by Vic "Trader Vic" Bergeron, owner of Trader Vic restaurants in San Francisco and elsewhere. Bergeron contends he tasted the soup during World War II in New Zealand, made with *toheroa* clams. On his return Bergeron substituted oysters for the unavailable *toheroas.*

> In a saucepan heat 2 1/2 cups half-and-half to simmer. Poach and purée 10 oz. oysters and add 1/4 cup spinach purée, 2 tbs. butter, 1 1/2 tsp. monosodium glutamate, 1 tsp. A.1 sauce, salt, pepper, a dash of garlic salt, and a dash of cayenne. Simmer, add 2 tsp. cornstarch dissolved in 2 tbs. water. Simmer and thicken, top with whipped cream, and slip under broiler till browned. Serves 8.

boova shenkel. A Pennsylvania Dutch stew-and-dumpling dish. The term means "boys' legs," but the origins of the meaning are obscure.

> Simmer 1 1/2 lb. beef, 1 tsp. salt, and 1/8 tsp. pepper, in a kettle of water to cover. Cook about 2 1/2 hr. Drain 6 cooked riced potatoes, and 1 tbs. butter, 1 tbs. minced onion, 1 beaten egg, and let stand. Sift 1 1/4 cup flour, 1 tsp. baking powder, 1/2 tsp. salt, and cut in 2 tbs. butter till of a crumbled texture. Add 3 tbs. water to make a dough. Roll into 10-in. circles and spread potato mixture on top. Fold in half-circles, press together, and place on top of hot meat and broth. Cover and boil for 25 min. Brown 1/2 cup bread cubes in 2 tbs. butter, stir in 1/4 cup milk, and arrange with meat and pastry. Serve with sauce from kettle. Serves 4.

bop. An old North Carolina confection made by mixing 2 cups milk, 3 beaten eggs, 1 tbs. butter, and 4 tbs. flour, and baking the batter in a pan at 450° until brown. The name seems to describe the puffy nature of the item.

borracho. A southwestern border term since 1836 for a drunkard, from the Spanish.

borscht. Also "borsch." A traditional beet-and-cabbage soup of Russian and Polish origins, borscht was particularly popular with American Jews who emigrated from those countries, so much so that in the 1930s people began referring to Catskill resorts featuring Jewish entertainers and, often, KOSHER food for their largely Jewish clientele as the "Borscht Belt." The word itself refers to a Russian word for cow parsnips, which originally went into the soup.

The soup may be served hot or cold, often with a dollop of sour cream floated on top. The word was first printed in 1884.

> Sauté till soft 1 cup finely chopped onions and 2 cloves minced garlic in butter. Add 1 lb. trimmed, coarsely grated beets, 1 cup celery root, 1 cup parsley root, 2 skinned, seeded chopped tomatoes, 1 cup parsnip coarsely grated, 1/2 tsp. sugar, 1/4 cup wine vinegar, 1 tbs. salt, and 1 1/2 cups beef stock. Bring to a boil, partially cover pot, lower heat, and simmer for 40 min. Pour 2 1/2 cups beef stock into large casserole, add 1 lb. potatoes in chunks, 1 lb. coarsely shredded cabbage, bring to a boil, then simmer partially covered for 20 min., till potatoes are tender. Add the first mixture of vegetables to this casserole along with 2 skinned, seeded, coarsely chopped tomatoes and 1 lb. boiled brisket cut into 1-in. chunks. Simmer for 15 min.

bosk. Also, *"boos-ke-tan."* The so-called green corn dance, an eight-day ritual of the Gulf State Indians, during which they drank the BLACK DRINK that had the effect of altering their state of mind in ways they believed increased the spirituality of the feast.

Boston baked beans. A dish of navy beans made with molasses and salt pork or bacon. Some authorities contend that baked beans were introduced to the American colonists by the Indians, but novelist Kenneth Roberts, in an essay on "The Forgotten Marrowbones," printed in Marjorie Mosser's *Foods of Old New England* (1957), argues that baked beans had long been a traditional Sabbath dish among the North African and Spanish Jews, who called it *"skanah."* Roberts also cites *Riley's Narrative* (1816), by James Riley, as a source and supposes that New England sea captains brought the idea home with them from Africa.

Nevertheless, the dish became closely associated with the city of Boston and with the Puritan women who baked beans on Saturday, served them that night for dinner, for Sunday breakfast with codfish cakes and Boston brown bread, and again for Sunday's lunch. No other cooking was allowed during the Sabbath, which ended Sunday evening. Sometimes the housewives would hand over their pots of uncooked beans to a community oven, often located in a tavern cellar, to be baked.

Because of the association between Bostonians and beans, the city came to be called "Bean Town." *Boston baked beans* was a term known by the 1850s, and *Boston strawberries* was a restaurant slang term for the same beans in the late nineteenth century.

Rinse 32 oz. of pea (navy) beans in cold water. Heat beans over high heat in large pot, add 4 tsp. salt, 8 cups boiling water, and boil for 2 min. Cover and let stand for 1 hr. Reboil beans, then turn heat to low and simmer for 1 hr. Mix together 1/4 cup dark molasses, 1/4 cup dark brown sugar, 1 tsp. pepper, 1 tsp. dry mustard, and stir into beans. Alternate layers of beans with slices of browned salt pork and molasses mixture, adding onion to the middle if desired. On top lay strips of salt pork or bacon, and bake in a covered pot at 250° for about 7 hr., adding more water if necessary to keep the beans moist. Serves 12.

Boston brown bread. A rye-flour bread made with molasses. Boston brown bread was well known among the Puritans, who served it on the Sabbath with BOSTON BAKED BEANS. It is often made with graham flour. The name has been in use since the middle of the nineteenth century.

Sift together 1/2 cup rye flour, 1/2 cup whole wheat or graham flour, 1/2 tsp. baking soda, 1/2 tsp. baking powder, 1/2 cup cornmeal, and 1/2 tsp. salt. Mix in 1 1/2 cups buttermilk and 1/2 cup dark molasses, then pour into 1-qt. buttered baking pan or tall pudding mold, and cover tightly. Place in kettle of boiling water until mold is immersed halfway. Cover and steam in 300° oven for about 3 hr., then place bread, uncovered, in oven to dry for a few minutes. Serves 6.

BAKED BOSTON BROWN BREAD:
Sift 4 1/2 cups graham flour with 3/4 cup sugar, 1/2 tsp. salt, and add 1 cup dark molasses, 2 beaten eggs, and 2 cups buttermilk in which 2 tsp. baking soda have been dissolved. Add 2 cups raisins if desired. Pour into greased pans and let rise for 1 hr. Bake at 300° for 1 hr.

Boston butt. Also, "Boston shoulder." A late-nineteenth-century term for meat cut from the top of the shoulder of a California ham and consisting of about two-thirds lean and one-third fat. The term was first used in print in 1903.

Boston cracker. A large, thin semisweet biscuit, similar to a COMMON CRACKER and eaten with cheese or other savories. Boston crackers were first mentioned in 1818.

Boston cream pie. A pie made of white cake and custard filling or topping. If chocolate icing is added, it is called "Parker House chocolate pie," after the Parker House hotel in Boston, Massachusetts, where the embellishment was first contrived.

The pie goes back to early American history, when it was sometimes called "pudding-cake pie," or, when made with a raspberry jelly filling, "Mrs. Washington's pie." The first mention of the dessert as "Boston cream pie" was in the *New York Herald* in 1855.

Mix together 1 cup cake flour, 3/4 cup sugar, 6 tbs. softened butter, 1/3 cup milk, 1 1/2 tsp. baking powder, 1 1/2 tsp. vanilla, 1/4 tsp. baking soda, a dash of salt, and 2 beaten eggs. Pour into greased pan and bake at 375° for 25 min., or until inserted knife comes out clean. Cool on cake rack. In a saucepan stir 2 cups milk, 1/4 cup sugar, 3 tbs. cornstarch, 1/4 tsp. salt, and 2 beaten egg yolks. Cook till thickened, boil for 1 min., stir in 1 tsp. vanilla, and remove from heat to cool. Spread thickly onto cake and cool in refrigerator for 30 min.

PARKER HOUSE CHOCOLATE PIE:
In a saucepan melt 2 squares semisweet chocolate, 1 tbs. butter, and remove from heat. Beat in 1/2 cup confectioner's sugar and 3 tbs. milk till smooth. Spread over two-layer cake made with custard, as directed above. Chill.

bottled water. Any water sealed in bottles and intended for drinking. This designation would include mineral water, which usually comes from a source of water containing various minerals rather than water to which have been added such minerals.

Bottled waters took on a certain fashionability, both as an alternative to alcoholic or carbonated drinks and as a weight-reducing aid, after an intensive advertising campaign by Perrier, a French water bottling company, in 1977.

boudin. A Louisiana sausage of two varieties: boudin rouge (French for "red pudding"), which is a blood sausage, and boudin blanc (French for "white pudding"), which is made with pork shoulder. Boudin is customarily made and served at hog-butchering parties called "boucheries," still held occasionally in the Cajun country during autumn or winter.

BOUDIN ROUGE:
Finely mince 2 onions and sauté in 2 tbs. pork fat. Add 1 clove minced garlic. Grind 1/2 lb. pork fat and mix with 1 lb. pork blood. Add the onion and garlic and season to taste with allspice, salt, pepper, cayenne pepper, mace, nutmeg, clove, and *fines herbes*. Fill sausage casings, wash the sausage, and make strings about 2-ft. long and tie casings in 3-in. lengths. Cook in tepid water until no blood emerges when sausages are pricked. Remove, dry, and cool. Sausages are then fried in boiling lard or broiled.

BOUDIN BLANC:
Grind 1 lb. white chicken meat, 1 lb. pork shoulder, and 1 lb. pork fat. Season with salt, pepper, cayenne pepper to taste, 1 minced onion, and 1 minced garlic clove. Soak 1/2 cup bread in milk, squeeze out excess liquid, and blend into meat mixture. Cook for 15 min. in 1 pt. cream. Add 2 beaten egg yolks, then cool. Fill sausage skins and boil in a mixture of half milk and half water for 20 min. Prick gently and broil. May be served as an appetizer.

boula. A green-pea-and-green-turtle soup, flavored with sherry and topped with whipped cream and cheese. The dish is described in *The White House Cookbook* (1964) as "an old favorite which was served in President Martin van Buren's day. President and Mrs. John F. Kennedy served it at the White House and, as sports enthusiasts, renamed it for the old college song, 'Boula-Boula!' "

Theodora FitzGibbon in *The Food of the Western World* (1976) notes that the soup "came originally from the Seychelles."

Combine 1 can pea soup with 1 can green turtle soup, boil, season with 3/4 cup sherry and a dash of ground pepper. Fill bowls and top with whipped cream and a sprinkle of Parmesan cheese. Place under broiler till lightly browned. Serves 4–6.

bounce. A fermented beverage popular in colonial days, made by pouring spirits such as rum or brandy over fruit, adding sugar, citrus fruit, spices, and water. Bounce is similar to, and perhaps interchangeable with, shrub, which is strained and sweetened with brown sugar. The former's name probably derived from its ability to give the imbiber a bounce, the latter's possibly from the Arabic, *shurb,* "drink."

Pour 1 qt. rum or brandy over 5 pt. pitted cherries or other fruit, and let stand to ferment for a week. (For a shrub, strain the liquid and add brown sugar to taste.) Bottle and let stand another week.

Benjamin Franklin gave the following recipe for making orange shrub:

"To a Gallon of Rum two Quarts of Orange Juice and two pounds of Sugar— dissolve the Sugar in the Juice before you mix it with the Rum—put all together in a Cask & shake it well—let stand 3- or 4-weeks & it will be very fine & fit for Bottling—when you have Bottled off the fine pass the thick thro' a Philtring paper pout into a Funnell—that not a drop may be lost.

"To obtain the flavour of the Orange Peel paire a few Oranges & put it in Rum for twelve hours—& put that Rum into the Cask with the other—

"For Punch thought better without the Peel."

bourbon. A spirit distilled from a fermented mash of grain, at least 51 percent of which must be corn. Bourbon is bottled between 80 and 125 proof and must be aged at least two years in new, charred, white-oak barrels. Only limestone-filtered spring water may be used to lower alcoholic proof.

Bourbon is a distinctly American spirit, and in the South it was traditionally synonymous with WHISKEY. It is the essential ingredient of a Kentucky MINT JULEP and finds its way into many sweet confections such as bourbon balls and cakes.

The name comes from Bourbon County, originally in Virginia but now part of Kentucky. (The Bourbons were a line of European monarchs whose subjects settled colonies in the Americas.) Corn spirits had been made as early as 1746 in America, but legend has it that a Baptist minister, Reverend Elijah Craig, gave corn whiskey its distinctive flavor in 1789. At first this was called merely "corn whiskey" or "corn," but by the middle of the nineteenth century the spirit was so associated with Bourbon County, Kentucky, that it was called, simply, "bourbon," and often "Kentucky bourbon," although bourbon is made elsewhere in the United States.

Most bourbon uses sour mash—that is, a part of the spent beer, or distiller's beer (a residue from a previous mash run), allowed to sour overnight and then added to a new batch of mash.

The law requires the use of new, charred, white-oak barrels to give the bourbon its character, part of a tradition whose origins are obscure. In *American Cooking: Southern Style* (1971), Eugene Walter gives three stories of how the distilling method came about:

> One story tells of a careless cooper who drowsed while some dampened staves were steaming by the fire. The staves burned but he made the barrels with them anyway, and a new flavor was imparted to the contents. Another tarrydiddle would have it that a thrifty cooper, intending to resell some barrels in which salted fish had been shipped, carefully burned out the interiors to get rid of every trace of fishiness. My own favorite explanation holds that a Kentucky farmer buried several barrels of whiskey under his barn to age. Lightning struck the barn, it burned down and a few years later, digging there, the farmer rediscovered the barrels, charred black but with the honey-red liquid unharmed, and noticeably better than any other whiskey he had made.

Bourbon is drunk STRAIGHT, ON THE ROCKS, ideally with so-called BRANCH WATER, or in SOURS and other mixed drinks. Bourbon makes up about 15 percent of the United States spirits market, with some 66 million gallons sold annually.

James Villas, in *American Taste* (1982), notes that "Dixie Nectar," "Liquor Joy," "Milk of Old Age," "Old Friend," "Good Company," and "Constant Companion" are all well-known synonyms for bourbon.

KENTUCKY COLONEL:
Shake with ice 2 1/2 oz. bourbon and 1/2 oz. Benedictine. Strain into an old-fashioned glass.

BOURBON BALLS:
Mix 1 cup confectioner's sugar with 2 1/2 cups finely crushed vanilla wafers, 1 cup finely chopped walnuts, 1/4 cup bourbon, 2 tbs. cocoa, and 3 tbs. corn syrup. On waxed paper sprinkle some confectioner's sugar and shape mixture into small, 1-in.-diameter balls, rolling them in confectioner's sugar. Makes about 3 1/2 dozen.

bramble jelly. An eighteenth-century jelly made from crab apples and blackberries. It originated in England.

branch water. Supposedly the clearest, purest water from a small stream called a branch. "BOURBON and branch water" is a nostalgic request in the South, but one that can hardly be fulfilled unless the bartender has access to such a stream's water supply. The term was first printed in 1850.

Brandon puff. A South Carolina muffin of flour and cornmeal. The origin of the name may in some way refer to Charles Brandon, first Duke of Suffolk (died 1545).

> Combine 1 qt. flour, 3/4 cup melted cooled butter, 4 beaten eggs, 1 yeast cake, and enough milk to make a muffin batter. Let rise overnight. Add 1 tsp. cornmeal, pour into muffin tins, bake till brown at 425°, about 10–15 min.

brandy. A spirit obtained from distilled wine or the fermented mash of fruit. The word comes from *brandewijn,* a Dutch word meaning to "burn" or "distill." In America most brandy is made in California (about 72 percent) from grapes such as the THOMPSON SEEDLESS and the Flame Tokay, although some is made from fruits such as apples (APPLEJACK), peaches, and others. About 20 percent of the distilleries use a "pot still" (or "alembic") by which the wine is heated in a pot, becomes vaporized, and condenses into a receptacle. The rest of the brandy is produced in a "continuous still," which allows brandy to be produced without pausing between batches and gives off a very clean product.

Brandies are aged in fifty-gallon white-oak barrels that add flavor and slight color.

A "brandy smash" is a cocktail of the mid-nineteenth century made from brandy, crushed ice, and mint.

brandy Alexander. A cocktail made from brandy, cream, and a chocolate cordial. The origin of the name is unknown, as is its date of concoction, but it probably came out of the Prohibition era. For a long time it was considered a "ladies' cocktail"—an alcoholic beverage for those who were not used to drinking.

If made with gin instead of brandy, the drink is called a "Panama," after the country in Central America.

> Shake with ice cubes 1 1/2 oz. brandy, 1 oz. chocolate cordial, and 1 oz. light or heavy cream. Strain into cocktail glass.

brasserie. In France, a small, inexpensive restaurant serving various types of beer, or a brewery itself, although the term has also come to mean a restaurant serving simple, neighborhood fare. In America, *brasserie* more often approximates this second meaning, usually connoting a place serving inexpensive French food in informal surroundings.

bread. One of the world's basic foods, made from flour and water, often with the addition of yeast, salt, and other ingredients. Shaped into loaves, rolls, flat cakes, or rings, bread is one of man's earliest foods, dating back more than ten thousand years, soon after man cultivated cereal grains and pounded them to make porridge (which may have been baked as the first breads). The word itself is from the Old English, *brēad.*

The bread of the American Indians was based on cornmeal and included a wide variety of preparations. Piki bread was very thin, often made from blue cornmeal batter on a hot stone. This was the bread of the Hopi; the Zunis call it *"hewe,"* the Tewa call it *"mowa,"* and the Indians of San Ildefonso call it *"bowahejahui"* ("put it on, take it off"). As Carolyn Niethammer notes in her *American Indian Food and Lore* (1974), "Piki making is an art and a ritual. . . . Years ago a young woman was required to demonstrate that she had mastered the art of piki-baking before she was considered a suitable bride, . . . but today the number of those who excel in this art is dwindling." The TORTILLA, common still in Mexican-American restaurants, was originally an Indian cornmeal bread. Later, after Columbus brought wheat to the New World in 1493, tortillas were also made with wheat flour. Other breads were baked in adobe ovens or in a hole in the earth. Niethammer describes *kinaalda,* a bread measuring eight inches deep and five feet across, as "the traditional food for the Navajo girl's puberty ceremony."

The Indians of the East Coast also used corn exclusively for their bread, and as of the 1650s the European settlers called this "Indian bread," as an alternative to the earlier *pone* (from an Algonquian word, *apan,* "baked"). The colonists immediately adapted cornmeal as a flour and made their own "cornbread" (first mentioned in 1750) or combined rye, molasses, cornmeal, and yeast to make RYE 'N' INJUN BREAD. Yeast was easily obtainable from beer brewers, and there was also a whole range of steamed breads like BOSTON BROWN BREAD. BISCUITS were found throughout the United States, especially after the new leavenings like pearl ash, saleratus, BAKING POWDER, and baking soda came into use during the mid-nineteenth century, thereby creating a new variety of "quick" or "lightnin' breads." Home baking was further helped along with a novelty of the 1850s, self-rising flour, and an increase in store-bought and bakery bread was spurred by the invention in 1834 of the Swiss steel roller that processed flour finely and uniformly.

During the Gold Rush in California in 1849 an old-fashioned form of bread was revived—SOURDOUGH—that has since been associated with San Francisco's history. During a period of deprivation in the Civil War, a wing of the United States Senate in Washington was turned into an enormous oven to bake sixteen thousand loaves of bread a day for the Union troops.

After the Civil War bakeries grew in number, especially in large cities with new immigrant populations, and there was a trend toward purer, whiter bread. Before this time bakers were accused of adulterating their bread with lime. Ready-made, packaged yeast was available for the homemaker by 1868, and for the rest of the century most bread was still made at home. By 1900, 95 percent of the flour produced was sold to home bakers. But in 1911 the National Association of Master Bakers quoted a study showing the percentage had changed radically: 60–65 percent of the city families did not make their own bread any longer. Today only 15 percent of the flour bought is used by home bakers.

The twentieth century also brought innovations in technology that produced a loaf whiter but less nutritious than those previously baked. The whiteness represented purity to those brought up on dark, coarse breads (however full of nutrients they were), but the new loaves were made by extracting 28–30 percent of the wheat kernel's bulk, thereby eliminating the bran and wheat germ. This resulted in 1941 in a federal law requiring that such breads be "enriched" with thiamine, niacin, riboflavin, and iron, an action that seemed to placate nutritionists for two decades until the "HEALTH FOOD movement" pointed out the contradictory idea of removing nutrients only to replace them in another form. Today some commercial breads are in fact jammed with vitamins and minerals ordinary breads do not have; but, then, bleached-flour breads lack the other nutrients derived from the bran and wheat germ.

Sliced bread, also called a "sandwich loaf," was introduced during the 1920s, and most American bread is bought in this form. There has, however, been a trend in the last fifteen years to produce commercial breads of coarser textures and varied grains, ironically often sweetened with sugar, molasses, or honey. At the same time the growth in packaged mixes for breads, rolls, muffins, and biscuits has grown tremendously, as have frozen breads and pastries or "heat-and-serve" (also, "brown-and-serve") varieties that need no true baking, only warming.

Peak consumption of white bread in the United States was 9 billion pounds in 1963. Since then consumption has declined steadily to 6.2 billion pounds in 1982, with per capita consumption about twenty-seven pounds a year. Total consumption of bread products, however, has increased, including buns for hot dogs and hamburgers, whole-grain breads, and other forms.

Italian bread is a long, cylindrical bread with blunt, pointed tips. It is slightly fatter or wider than French bread as sold in American groceries. Pita bread is a flat Middle Eastern–style bread that is often called "pocket bread." Raisin bread is a popular sweet variety, while rye and PUMPERNICKEL are used for sandwiches. See also CORNELL BREAD, SOURDOUGH, BOSTON BROWN BREAD, MONKEY BREAD, and ANADAMA BREAD.

WHITE BREAD:
To 1 cup scalded milk, add 1 cup hot water, 1 1/2 tbs. shortening, 1 1/2 tbs. butter, 2 1/2 tsp. salt, and 2 tbs. sugar. Soak 1 cake or 2 pkgs. of yeast in 1/4 cup tepid water. When milk has cooled to lukewarm, add to yeast. Sift 6 1/2 cups flour, add milk-and-yeast mixture, and knead well until elastic. Place in greased bowl, cover with cloth, and let rise till doubled. Punch down, knead briefly, and let rise again. Cut dough into desired number of loaves, let rest for 5 min., then place in bread pans that have been greased and dusted with cornmeal. Let rise again, covered with damp cloth. Preheat oven well to 450°. Bake bread for 10 min., then reduce heat to 350° and bake for another 30 min. Remove from pans and cool on rack.

WHOLE WHEAT BREAD:
Dissolve 2 pkgs. yeast in 3/4 cup warm milk and 1 tsp. sugar. Place 2 cups rolled oats in bowl with 2 1/2 cups boiling water. Let stand to soften, stir, and let cool. Heat 3/4 cup dark molasses, 1 1/2 tbs. butter, and 1 tbs. salt, stir in oats, then yeast. Blend well, add 3 1/2 cups flour and 3 1/2 cups whole wheat, and mix well with

hands. Cover and let rise till doubled. Knead again, let rise again. Cut and shape into loaves, let stand for 5 min., and place in buttered bread pans dusted with cornmeal. Let rise again. Bake at 350° for 1 hr. Remove from pans, let cool on rack.

bread line. A term first used in 1900 to describe the lines of poor, hungry people who received loaves of bread and other food from charitable institutions. Bread lines became a common sight in American cities during the Great Depression of the 1930s.

breakfast. The first meal of the day. The word means "to break one's fast" and dates back at least to the middle of the fifteenth century.

The Indian breakfast consisted of cornmeal mush and perhaps corn bread, both items the first European settlers adapted for their own breakfasts. The settlers also breakfasted on a quickly prepared porridge called "hasty pudding," made with cornmeal and molasses. Later bread or toast and coffee or tea were the usual breakfasts, while in the nineteenth century affluence brought more variety to the diet and larger portions of meats, fish, cheese, bread, jams, and, often, a tot of rum or cider. Scotsman John Melish visited America in 1811 and reported in his *Travels in the United States of America* on "A Backwoods Breakfast," at which his humble hostess sought to wring the necks of two chickens.

> I told her to stop, and she gave me a look of astonishment. "Have you any eggs?" said I. "Yes, plenty," replied she, still keeping in a stooping posture, with the chicken in her hand. "Well," said I, "just boil an egg, and let me have it, with a little bread and tea, and that will save you and I a great deal of trouble." She seemed quite embarrassed, and said she never could set down a breakfast to me like that. ... She detained me about half an hour, and at last placed upon the table a profusion of ham, eggs, fritters, bread, butter and some excellent tea. . . . I mention the circumstance to show the kind of hospitality of the landlady, and the good living enjoyed by the backwoods people.

Also popular were PANCAKES, especially buckwheat pancakes, which were consumed in stacks with butter and molasses or maple syrup. Of these the English author of *Mrs. Beeton's Every-Day Cookery* (1909 edition) wrote, "Hot cakes at breakfast are quite a national institution [in America]. These are made with soda and baking-powder, and must be regarded as somewhat beyond the capacities of average digestive organs."

In different parts of the United States different food items are served for breakfast, although a meal of eggs, bacon, toast, and coffee seems ubiquitous, with the addition in the South of GRITS, ham, or BISCUITS, in the West with CHILI peppers, in the Northeast with sausages and hash-brown potatoes, and in urban restaurants with preparations of EGGS BENEDICT, finnan haddie, melon, FRENCH TOAST, CAVIAR, WAFFLES, DANISH PASTRY, fruit, ENGLISH MUFFINS, and many other items. In Jewish communities breakfast may consist of BAGELS and cream cheese.

The popularity of breakfast CEREALS began in the middle of the nineteenth century and has continued since then, especially as a children's breakfast item. Americans have to some extent curbed their hearty breakfasts in recent years because of dietary concerns (although the midmorning "coffee break" often serves to bolster an early light breakfast with a roll or muffin), saving the tradition of a big breakfast for weekends or Sunday BRUNCH. Business breakfasts held at hotel dining rooms are also popular, for, as James Villas contends in *American Taste* (1982), "Show me the fool who finds something sensible and dignified about offering plastic cups of instant coffee and a puny piece of bread as an excuse for a business breakfast, and I can only hope that he collapses from lack of adrenaline before the meeting is finished."

The American food industry has marketed scores of breakfast foods designed to save time in the kitchen, including frozen waffles, packaged pancake batter, heat-and-serve eggs, powdered eggs, imitation CREAM, already cooked sausage, fake bacon, canned fruit, and tarts shaped to fit conveniently into the toaster. FAST-FOOD restaurants also offer standard fare, such as scrambled eggs, sausage, pancakes, and coffee, and many restaurants, diners, and luncheonettes advertise the fact that "breakfast is served 24 hours a day."

breakfast cream. A New Orleans term for light cream.

brick cheese. A smooth, cow's-milk cheese created in 1877 by John Jossi of Wisconsin. It is formed into bricks about five pounds in weight, has small holes, and is aged about three months.

broccoli *(Brassica oleracea botrytis).* A plant in the mustard family having a flowery green head and related to CABBAGE and CAULIFLOWER. The word is from the Italian, *broccolo,* "cabbage sprout," and was first recorded in English in 1699 as a plant from Naples. The plant arrived in England about 1720, and John Randolph of Williamsburg wrote of it in *A Treatise on Gardening by a Citizen of Virginia* (1775) that "the stems will eat like Asparagus and the heads like Cauliflower." Nevertheless, broccoli virtually disappeared from American soil until its reintroduction in the twentieth century, and its popularity in this country dates only from the 1920s. In the United States the green sprouting varieties are most often grown. Broccoli is usually boiled or steamed and served with butter sauce. Americans ate 1.9 pounds per person in 1982.

Bronx cocktail. A cocktail made of gin, sweet and dry vermouths, and orange juice.

According to Michael and Ariane Batterberry in *On the Town in New York* (1973), the drink was created by bartender Johnnie Solon at the Waldorf-Astoria hotel in New York City. The first appearance of the cocktail in American print was in 1906. "Until this historic moment," wrote the Batterberrys, "no more than a dozen oranges had been used daily by the bar. With the advent of the Bronx cocktail [supposedly named after the Bronx Zoo], a case had to be delivered every morning."

The additicn of an egg yolk to the following recipe makes the drink a "silver Bronx," while the juice of a blood orange makes it a "bloody Bronx."

> Shake over ice cubes 1 1/2 oz. gin, 1/2 oz. dry vermouth, 1/2 oz. sweet vermouth, and 1/2 oz. orange juice. Strain into cocktail glass and serve over ice cubes.

Brooklyn cake. A nineteenth-century light cake whose name probably has nothing to do with the borough of New York City, but rather with Brooklyn, Connecticut, or, perhaps, a misreading of Brookline, Massachusetts. The recipe given in *The Pentucket Housewife* (1882) calls for a batter of 1 1/2 cups sugar, 6 egg whites beaten with 1 tsp. cream of tartar folded into 1/2 cup creamed butter, 1/2 tsp. baking soda, 1/2 cup cornstarch, 1 1/2 cups flour, and lemon juice.

Brother Jonathan's hat. A suet pudding of nineteenth-century New England. The name derives from a derisive term used by the British and the Loyalists during the Revolutionary War for American rebels. Later the name was applied to any American citizen, and the *Dictionary of Americanisms* disputes the claim that it originally referred to Governor Jonathan Trumbull (1710–1785) of Connecticut. As a dish it seems to be synonymous with DEACON PORTER'S HAT (see main entry for recipe), but may predate the latter.

brown bag. A term used to describe a meal packed in a brown paper bag, usually for lunch consumed at work. Brown paper bags were first made in Pennsylvania in 1852, and by 1870 there was a machine that fabricated the paper into a flat-bottomed, easily folded bag that became the standard of the food-service industry.

Today there are about 60 million Americans who eat lunch out of a brown bag, and the phrase *to brown bag it,* meaning to eat one's lunch in this manner, goes back at least to the 1950s, according to David Lyon, head of the Brown Bag Institute in Connecticut.

brownie. A rich chocolate cake cut into squares and eaten as a dessert or snack. The name comes from the deep-brown color of the confection, and it has been an American favorite since the nineteenth century, first appearing in print in the 1897 *Sears, Roebuck and Co. Catalog.* Some brownies are quite moist at the center, while others are more cookielike. The following recipe is for the former type.

> Combine 2 cups sugar, 1/2 cup flour, and 1/2 cup cocoa. Add 4 beaten eggs, 1/2 lb. melted cooled butter, 2 tsp. vanilla, and 1 cup chopped pecans or walnuts. Pour into buttered pan and place in a larger pan half-full of hot water. Bake for 45 min. at 300°.

bruiss. A dish of boiled bread and milk. The origin of the name is unknown, but the dish is mentioned in *The Pentucket Housewife* (1882) with the instructions to add milk to crusts of bread, boil slowly, and add salt and butter.

brunch. A portmanteau word combining *breakfast* with *lunch* for a meal taken late in the morning or just around noon. According to the English magazine *Punch* for August 1, 1896, brunch was "introduced . . . last year by Mr. Guy Beringer, in the now defunct *Hunter's Weekly,* and indicating a combined breakfast and lunch," probably one taken just after arriving home from hunting.

The practice of having brunch did not really take hold in the United States till the 1930s, but today it is part of many hotel and restaurant menus on weekends, as well as a popular form of social entertaining for weekend hosts. "There may be some perfectly nice people who use the word 'brunch,'" commented humorist Heywood Broun, "but I prefer not to know about them."

The foods served at a brunch might include any or all of the following: pancakes, omelettes, sausage, smoked salmon, fruits, salads, quiche, coffee, tea, orange juice, and Bloody Mary cocktails.

Brunswick stew. A stew made originally with squirrel, now made with chicken or other meats. There have been many claims as to the dish's origins, especially from the citizens of Brunswick County, North Carolina, but the most creditable claim comes from Brunswick County, Virginia, where in 1828 Dr. Creed Haskins of the Virginia state legislature requested a special squirrel stew from "Uncle Jimmy" Matthews to feed those attending a political rally. This original Brunswick stew was said to have contained no vegetables but onions, but it soon went through several transformations before the squirrel itself dropped from most recipes after the turn of the century.

brush roast. A North Carolina term for a dish of oysters cooked on a wire netting over a wood fire and served with butter, chow-chow, and corn bread.

Brussels sprout (*Brassica oleracea gemmifera*). A small cabbage of the mustard family originally developed from primitive cabbage in fourteenth-century Brussels, Belgium. It is first mentioned in English print in 1796, but did not enter England until the mid-nineteenth century. In the United States Brussels sprouts are grown predominantly in California and New York, with the most popular variety being the Improved Long Island.

buck. Originally a Prohibition-era drink made with gin (and called a "gin buck"), ginger ale, and the juice of a lemon whose shell was then added to the drink. It contains no sugar. Later bucks were made with other carbonated drinks and spirits.

> Over ice cubes pour 1 1/2 oz. gin, squeeze the juice of half a lemon into the glass, add the lemon shell, and top with ginger ale.

buck and breck. A cold pickle condiment like CHOW-CHOW, it is an Old Virginia dish. The origin of the name is unknown.

To 1 gallon of vinegar add 1 lb. brown sugar, 1 cup salt, 2 oz. black pepper, 2 oz. ginger, 2 oz. white mustard seed, 2 oz. dry mustard, 2 oz. cloves, 2 oz. celery seed, 1 oz. turmeric, 1 cup grated horseradish, 2 oz. cloves, 2 chopped onions, 1 head of chopped cabbage, 2 lb. chopped, peeled tomatoes, 2 each of red and green peppers, mix, pour into bottles, seal, and, according to old advice, "let stand until Thanksgiving."

bucket of blood. A westerner's term for a very tough saloon or bar. Originally the term referred to the Bucket of Blood saloon owned by Shorty Young in Havre, Montana, the fame of which became the basis for describing any similar establishment by the same name by about 1880. One may also find such places referred to as "bucket shops." See also BLOODY MARY.

buckwheat. Any plant of the genus *Fagopyrum,* whose seeds are coarsely ground to make flour. The name is from the Middle Dutch, *boecweite,* "beech wheat," so called because the seeds resemble the nuts of the beech tree. The word was first recorded in English in 1548. The plant is a native of Central Asia, but it was propagated in the New World for fodder and cereal, as is known through a reference by Adam Smith in 1776. Buckwheat cakes, PANCAKES made with buckwheat flour, were popular everywhere in the country in the nineteenth century. "It is hard for the American to rise from his winter breakfast without his *buckwheat cakes,*" wrote English traveler George Makepeace Towle in *American Society* (1870). It was American painter James Abbott McNeill Whistler (1834–1903) who introduced buckwheat cakes to London society.

Slip go down is a slang term for buckwheat PUDDING.

buffalo. An erroneous name for the American bison *(Bison bison),* a shaggy-maned, short-horned, hoofed mammal of the cattle family with a large, low-slung head and massive hump, reaching a height of five feet, a length of nine feet, and a weight of twenty-five hundred pounds. The word *buffalo* correctly applies to various species of Asian or African oxen, but Americans have called their native bison by this name ever since explorer Hernando de Soto spotted the animal in the New World in 1544 and called it by the Spanish, *bufalo.*

Once the buffalo population in this country spread on both sides of the Mississippi River in thick waves, numbering more than 60 million at the beginning of the nineteenth century. The Indians' respect for the buffalo was borne out of their total dependence on its meat and hide for sustenance, clothing, tepee coverings, and rope, while other parts of the beast went into making utensils, medicines, even children's toys. The buffalo was deified by the Great Plains Indians for good reason.

By slicing the meat from the carcass and drying it in the sun or smoking it in their tepees, the Indians produced a jerky they called "pemmican," which they pounded and preserved in buffalo-skin pouches and often enriched with fat and wild berries.

Despite their respect for the buffalo, the Indians engaged in wanton killing of the herds, sometimes driving them off a cliff into a ravine. But this was as nothing compared with the deliberate and wholesale slaughter of the herds brought on by the easterners who killed the buffalo for its hide, for sport, and for its importance to the Indian tribes. Buffalo hunters sent back tens of thousands of pelts to be made into coats. The Kansas Pacific Railroad, desiring an efficient way to remove the herds from their westward path, arranged special hunting tours on which well-dressed easterners with long rifles shot from the moving train windows and cut down the animals, only to have them rot where they fell. But the main reason for the deliberate destruction of the herds was to eliminate the life-sustaining animal as a resource for the Indians, who were the real object of the slaughter.

By the mid-nineteenth century the buffalo was extinct east of the Mississippi, and by the end of the century less than a thousand remained on the whole continent. Only the interdiction of President Theodore Roosevelt, who in 1905 established in Kansas and Montana two protected reservations for the beast, saved the buffalo. Today they number nearly twenty thousand. The state of Kansas named the buffalo its state animal, and for a time this most American of cattle appeared on the nickel coin.

The buffalo has never been of much gastronomic interest to Americans, although today there is a certain exotic curiosity about the meat, which is occasionally found on menus. The early pioneers were forced to eat buffalo meat and Indian pemmican on the long trek westward, but later on the cattle breeders preferred the more passive longhorn steer to the ornery bison. A few attempts have been made to breed the buffalo with other cattle. One such crossbreed, by Charles Goodnight, between a bison and a Polled Angus steer produced the "cattalo," and since 1973 there has been some interest in a hybrid called the "beefalo," a cross between the buffalo and a Hereford or Charolais. There is even an American Beefalo Association, with 950 members worldwide.

The beefalo was said to be easier and faster to bring to full weight, and its meat was leaner. Still, the beefalo has never fulfilled its early promise as the "meat of the future."

Buffalo meat itself tastes a good deal like beef and has no pronounced gamey flavor. Young bulls make for the best meat, especially if marinated.

Buffalo cider is a euphemism for the liquid in a buffalo's stomach that a Great Plains hunter would drink if he were far from water. A "buffalo pound" is a place where buffaloes congregate during the winter. "Buffalo chips" are dried buffalo manure used as fuel in the Old West. "Buffalo grass" is a low-lying prairie grass.

Marinate a 5-lb. haunch of buffalo in 1 cup red wine, 2 bay leaves, 1/2 cup chopped onion, 1/2 cup chopped celery, 1/4 cup parsley, salt, and pepper. Dredge the meat in 1/4 cup flour, season with salt and pepper, and brown in a large kettle. Add the marinade and 8 oz. canned tomatoes. Cover and bake for 3 hr. at 325°. Serves 8.

Buffalo chicken wings. Deep-fried CHICKEN wings served with a HOT SAUCE and a blue cheese dressing.

The dish originated at the Anchor Bar in Buffalo, New York, in 1964, when owner Teressa Bellissimo received a large order of chicken wings from her supplier and served them with a hot pepper sauce. They became an immediate sensation at the restaurant, and soon Buffalo chicken wings (sometimes called "Western New York chicken wings") were being served all over the city. Today they can be found in other cities and states, particularly Florida. In 1977 the city of Buffalo declared July 29 "Chicken Wing Day."

> Separate the wing bone at the joints of 20 chicken wings, then cut off the tip of each wing. Deep-fry in peanut oil for about 10 min., till golden brown and cooked through.
>
> Melt 4 tbs. butter in a saucepan and add 4 tbs. bottled red hot pepper sauce. Add salt and pepper to taste, and a dash of cayenne pepper. For the dressing, blend 1 cup mayonnaise with 2 tbs. chopped onion, 1 tsp. minced garlic, 1/2 cup sour cream, 1 tbs. white vinegar, and 1/4 cup blue cheese. Serve chicken wings with the sauce and the dressing. Serves 4.

bug juice. Schoolboy slang term for a sweet, usually noncarbonated soft drink, so called for its ability to draw bugs to its sugar. Also a cowboy term for whiskey, at least since 1869, or a trucker's term for gasoline.

bull and bear. A sandwich created at the Caucus Club restaurant in Detroit, Michigan, made with corned beef, chopped liver, lettuce, tomato, cole slaw, and Russian or Thousand Island dressing. The name has nothing to do with the ingredients, but instead with the traditional symbols of buyer and seller on the stock exchange, which provides much of the Caucus Club's clientele.

A bull and bear cocktail, also created at the Caucus Club, is made with 1 1/2 oz. vodka, 1/2 oz. clam juice, 1/2 oz. beef bouillon, a slice of lemon, and a dash each of celery salt, A.1 sauce, and Tabasco sauce.

bull cheese. A Western term of the nineteenth century for dried strips of buffalo meat. The Spanish words *carne secco* were also used for the same item.

bullshot. An alcoholic drink made with vodka, beef bouillon, and seasonings. The drink originated at the Caucus Club restaurant in Detroit, Michigan, in the early 1960s when then-owner Lester Gruber and a representative of a national soup company created the cocktail together. The name, a play on the expletive *bullshit,* derives from the blend of beef bouillon and shot of vodka.

> Mix 1 1/2 oz. vodka with 3 oz. beef bouillon. Add dashes of Worcestershire sauce, A.1 sauce, Tabasco, and angostura bitters. Stir, pour over ice, and garnish with slice of lemon and a sprinkling of celery salt.

A Danish bowl cocktail, also invented at the Caucus Club, substitutes aquavit for vodka in the recipe.

buñuelo. A round pastry deep-fried and sprinkled with sugar, very popular in the Southwest. Buñuelos were brought from Mexico, where hot chocolate and buñuelos are part of the Christmas Eve meal.

Beat 4 eggs and add 1/2 cup milk, 1/4 cup melted butter, 3 cups sifted flour, 1 tbs. sugar, and 1 tsp. salt. This should form a nonsticky dough. Roll in the palms of one's hands to make balls the size of walnuts, then with a rolling pin make these into pancakes about 6–8 in. in diameter. Fry in hot fat till golden, drain, and sprinkle with cinnamon and sugar.

Buñuelos are often served with a syrup of 2 cups brown sugar, 2 cups water, 1 stick of cinnamon, and 1 clove boiled together.

burbot *(Lota lota).* A freshwater cod found on both coasts and throughout the Great Lakes. The burbot has a slightly oilier flesh than the saltwater varieties. The name is from Middle English, *borbot,* and Old French, *bourbeter,* "to burrow in mud."

burgoo. A southern stew of various meats and vegetables. Burgoo is often associated with Kentucky and is frequently seen at political rallies in the South. One authority believes the word may derive from a mispronunciation of *barbecue,* but the word was known to British sailors at least as early as 1740 as a kind of oatmeal porridge, making some etymologists suspect that it may derive from the Turkish wheat pilaf called *burghul* (or *bulgur*), meaning "bruised grain." No one knows how this might have become an American stew by the time the word appeared in print in 1750. There is another, highly suspect story about a Civil War soldier with a speech impediment who cooked up some blackbirds in a five-hundred-gallon copper kettle used for making gunpowder. When he called his fellow soldiers to dinner, the word came out, not *bird stew,* but *burgoo.*

Whatever its origins, it was a very popular stew. In 1895 Gus Jaubert cooked up a batch for the Grand Army of the Republic that came to six thousand gallons, and the so-called Kentucky burgoo king, James T. Looney, was used to serving crowds of people numbering up to ten thousand. A recipe for a mere five thousand people was printed in the *Louisville Courier-Journal* not long ago that called for 800 lb. of beef, 200 lb. fowl, 168 gal. tomatoes, 350 lb. cabbage, 6 bu. onions, 85 gal. tomato purée, 24 gal. carrots, 36 gal. corn, 1,800 lb. potatoes, 2 lb. red pepper, 1/2 lb. black pepper, 20 lb. salt, 8 oz. angostura bitters, 1 pint worcestershire sauce, 1/2 lb. curry powder, 3 qt. tomato ketchup, and 2 qt. sherry.

A somewhat less gargantuan portion printed in the same journal goes as follows:

Place in a large kettle 2 lb. pork shank, 2 lb. veal shank, 2 lb. beef shank, 2 lb. breast of lamb, one 4-lb. hen, and 8 qt. water. Bring slowly to a boil and then simmer till meat falls from bones. Pare and dice 1 1/2 lb. Irish potatoes and 1 1/2 lb. onions. Remove and chop up the meat, discard the bones. Return to stock with potatoes and onions, together with 1 bunch scraped, chopped carrots; 2 seeded, chopped green peppers; 2 cups chopped cabbage; 1 qt. tomato purée; 1 cup whole corn; 1 pod red pepper; 2 cups diced okra; 2 cups lima beans; 1 cup diced celery. Add salt, cayenne pepper, Tabasco, A.1 sauce, Worcestershire sauce to taste. Cook about 10 hr. or until thick but still soupy. Stir frequently. Add chopped parsley.

burrito. A wheat-flour tortilla rolled with various fillings and usually fried. The filling may be meat, poultry, vegetables, beans, or cheese. Burritos are a Mexican-American staple. The word, from Spanish for "little donkey," first saw print in America in 1957.

busboy. A restaurant worker who clears ("buses") and sets a table. The term derives from the Latin *omnibus* ("for all"), and was first in print in 1913.

butter. An emulsion of fat made from churned milk, usually whitish yellow to yellow in color and used as a cooking fat or as a spread on bread and other preparations. The word is from the Greek, *bouturon,* "cow cheese," becoming in Middle English, *buter.*

Butter has been widely used for centuries as a cooking fat, at first by herdsmen, and it is mentioned several times in the Bible. It was not until the Middle Ages, however, that Europeans began to use butter extensively, but because of its tendency to turn rancid quickly, it was not a preferred food till well into the eighteenth century. Even today other oils are preferred for cooking in warm Mediterranean countries.

There is no evidence that the American Indians made butter, but the early European settlers made their own with whirling wooden blades inside a butter churn. The surplus was sold to neighbors and local stores, for there was no commercial creamery in the United States until the mid-nineteenth century; possibly the first was opened in 1856 in Orange County, New York, by R. S. Woodhull. Today very little butter is made at home, and, in fact, Americans now buy more butter substitutes, such as MARGARINE, than the real thing, with volume sales of butter equaling only 18 percent of the total market in spreads, of which margarine accounts for the other 82 percent.

All American butter is made from cow's milk and is pasteurized, that is, heated to 163° for thirty minutes or to 182° for ten minutes (called "high temperature short-time pasteurization"). It is then cooked and churned. F.D.A. gradings of AA, A, B, and C are then assigned.

Only after 1900 was creamery butter widely available, and new processes in the 1930s that allowed continuous production boosted sales. Today the United States and the Soviet Union are the world's leading producers. The leading butter states are Minnesota, Wisconsin, and Iowa, with the butter industry as a whole using up 20 percent of all milk produced.

Sweet butter, or unsalted butter, contains no SALT. Sweet cream butter has some salt added. Whipped butter is combined with air to give a more spreadable texture when cold. Clarified butter is made in the kitchen by melting butter and letting the casein and other nonfat ingredients drop out, thereby creating a clear liquid with a higher burning point but less flavor. Buttermilk is the liquid left after butter granules have reached the "breaking point" on the milk's surface during the production process (see also MILK).

Let stand 1/2 pt. cream having 30 percent butterfat for 10 min. at room temperature. Beat 20–30 min. with a hand beater, or 3–5 min. with an electric one. Pour off the buttermilk, work well with a spoon, wash butter with cold water, and add 1/4 tsp. salt. Blend well.

butterfish *(Peprilus triacanthus).* A fatty fish ranging from Nova Scotia to Cape Hatteras that grows up to twelve inches and one-and-a-half pounds. Butterfish are usually found fresh in summer in New York and Boston markets. Its name goes back at least to the 1880s.

buttermilk cow. A cowboy term for a bull steer.

butterscotch. A confection made from butter, brown sugar, and lemon juice, so called probably because it originated in Scotland. Butterscotch sauce, or butterscotch topping, is an American dessert sauce with the flavor of butterscotch candy and is served over ice cream (for a butterscotch sundae), on pound cake, and on other sweets. The word was first printed in 1855.

BUTTERSCOTCH:
Combine 1/2 cup butter with 1 lb. brown sugar, heat to 290° (use a candy thermometer), and flavor with 1 tbs. lemon juice. Beat to make creamy in texture, then pour out on a marble slab and let cool.

BUTTERSCOTCH SAUCE:
In a double boiler combine 2 cups brown sugar, 1/2 cup butter, 1/4 pt. heavy cream, and 1 tbs. lemon juice. Cook for about 1 hr., stirring to thicken.

cabbage *(Brassica oleracea capitata).* A plant whose large head of tightly wrapped leaves is eaten in a variety of ways—boiled, stuffed, or raw, as in COLE SLAW. The word is from Vulgar Latin, *bottia,* "bump," which in Middle English became *caboche.*

The term *cabbage* includes BROCCOLI, BRUSSELS SPROUTS, CAULIFLOWER, KALE, and collard greens, but it usually refers more specifically to the white and red cabbages, as well as the purple and green varieties, with their characteristic large heads and firmly packed leaves. The savoy cabbage, mostly grown in Europe, is considered among the finest, while Chinese cabbage *(B. pekinensis),* also called "petsai," is an Oriental cabbage of a different species.

Cabbages were brought to the New World by the European settlers, and the plant grew well in temperate climates, particularly in the Middle Atlantic colonies. German immigrants especially valued the cabbage, which was a major vegetable in their diet, and the Dutch made cole slaw from it. After the Civil War, with the proliferation of railroads, cabbage became widely available to all Americans, and it remains a very popular garden plant.

Cabernet Sauvignon. A variety of Vinifera grape that makes a rich, tannic red wine with a distinctive varietal character. This is the predominant grape in the wines of Bordeaux and has in recent years become one of the premium grapes of California and the Northwest, where the best examples may contain 100 percent Cabernet Sauvignon (often called "cab" for short). In 1981 there appeared a booklet entitled *California Wine List: Cabernets,* edited by David Holzgang, which rated 144 California Cabernet Sauvignons under 120 labels, and that was not a complete list. Cabernet Sauvignon is also grown in other parts of the United States. The word was first printed in 1941.

According to "Peter Quimme" (a pseudonym for Elin McCoy Walker and John Frederick Walker) in *The Signet Book of American Wine* (1980), "California Cabernet Sauvignons range from light red to ruby to purple red, the deepest colors usually indicating a 'bigger' style of winemaking. The lightest specimens are sometimes so stripped of their character by overfiltering that they are thin and sharp after a half-dozen years; excellent specimens come into their own only after ten to twenty years of bottle age."

cabinet. A Rhode Island name for a soda fountain confection of milk, syrup, and ice cream blended in a mixer. The name probably derives from the container in which it was made, for mixers were often encased in square wooden cabinets. Elsewhere this drink is called a MILK SHAKE.

cackleberry. A logger's term for an egg. The cackle refers to the sound made by chickens, and in prison lingo eggs are referred to as "cacklers" (or "shells").

caesar salad. A salad of romaine lettuce, garlic, olive oil, croutons, Parmesan cheese, Worcestershire sauce, and, often, anchovies. It was created by Caesar Cardini, an Italian immigrant who opened a series of restaurants in Tijuana, Mexico, just across the border from San Diego. On Fourth of July weekend in 1924 at Caesar's Place, Cardini concocted the salad as a main course, arranging the lettuce leaves on a plate with the intention that they would be eaten with the fingers. Later Cardini shredded the leaves into bite-sized pieces. The salad became particularly popular with Hollywood movie people who visited Tijuana, and it became a featured dish at Chasen's and Romanoff's in Los Angeles. Cardini was adamant in insisting that the salad be subtly flavored and argued against the inclusion of anchovies, whose faint flavor in his creation he believed may have come from the Worcestershire sauce. He also decreed that only Italian olive oil and imported Parmesan cheese be used. In 1948 he established a patent on the dressing, which is still packaged and sold as "Cardini's Original Caesar dressing mix," distributed by Caesar Cardini Foods, Culver City, California. Cardini himself died in 1956, and the business is now carried on by his daughter, Rosa Cardini. The caesar salad was once voted by the International Society of Epicures in Paris as the "greatest recipe to originate from the Americas in fifty years."

The following recipe is the original and does not include anchovies.

Cut up white bread into 1/2-in. pieces to make about 2 cups. Mash 2 cloves garlic in some olive oil. Dry out the croutons in the oven, basting them with the garlic and oil. Strip the leaves from 2 medium heads of romaine lettuce to provide 6 to 8 leaves per person. Wash gently, shake dry, and refrigerate in a plastic bag until ready to serve. Purée 2 cloves mashed garlic with 1/4 tsp. salt and 3 tbs. olive oil, strain, and place in frying pan. Add croutons, heat briefly, and toss, then turn into serving bowl. Boil 2 eggs exactly 1 min. Grate 1/4 cup Parmesan cheese. In a very large bowl pour 4 tbs. olive oil over the lettuce leaves and scoop in large motions to coat. Sprinkle lettuce with 1/4 tsp. salt, 8 grinds of fresh black pepper, and 2 more tsp. oil, toss again, add juice of 1 lemon, 6 drops Worcestershire sauce, and break in eggs. Toss and add cheese. Toss and top with croutons. Serve on a chilled plate.

café brûlot. A dark coffee mixed with the flavors of citrus rind and brandy. The name of this traditional New Orleans coffee is a compound of the French *café*, "coffee," and *brûlot*, "burnt brandy." Although it is not mentioned in

The Picayune's Creole Cook Book (1901), it is apparently an old recipe, since flame-proof brûlot bowls made especially for the coffee were known before 1900.

> In a fireproof brûlot bowl or saucepan place 2 sticks of cinnamon, 6 cloves, 1 1/2 tbs. sugar, the rind of 1 lemon, and 3 oz. brandy. Heat to below boiling point, ignite with a match, and mix. Pour strong, hot coffee into bowl, then pour into small coffee cups.

cafeteria. A restaurant at which people move along a line and select the food and drinks they want, then carry them on trays to a table to eat their meals. The word is an American rendering of a Spanish word for coffee shop, a meaning it had back in the 1830s. The modern cafeteria began in 1885 in New York City, although women were not allowed in. At Chicago's 1893 World's Columbian Exposition, self-service restaurants (called "conscience joints" because customers tallied up their own bill) catered to the tourist trade there, and within two years the city had at least four cafeterias operating around town.

Later the word *cafeteria* also came to mean a student's dining hall, where in many public schools such meals were not paid for by the children.

Cafeterias are still very popular throughout the South and Southwest, usually run by franchised chains. To a large extent regional cookery is preserved in such places, along with the usual FAST-FOOD items.

The suffix *-eria* has led to all manner of words meaning a kind of shop—*pizzeria, chocolateria, fruiteria, meateria,* and so on.

caffeine. An alkaloid found in coffee, tea, kola nuts, and other plants. It can also be synthetically produced from uric acid. Caffeine has a stimulating effect on the heart rate and rhythm, which is one reason for its desirability in coffee, tea, soft drinks, and cocoa, but some authorities warn of its adverse effects on ulcers, the heart, and the circulatory system and of its contribution to insomnia and restlessness.

Cajun. A descendant of the French Acadians who settled in Lousiana after the British deported them from Acadia in Nova Scotia and the Maritime Provinces of Canada in 1755 for refusing to pledge allegiance to England. In Louisiana these people were soon called " 'Cadians," and, by 1868, "Cagians."

Cajun cuisine, with its French, Spanish, Negro, and Indian influences, is distinctive, but Louisiana authorities and gastronomes have argued for decades about just what is and is not Cajun cookery. Few would refuse to list the following dishes in the Cajun canon: JAMBALAYA, étoufée, coush-coush, PIG'S EARS, BOUDIN, ANDOUILLES, grattons, CHAUDIN, LA CUITE, GUMBO, and all manner of crab dishes and dishes requiring heavy doses of TABASCO sauce.

Each year a good number of Cajun festivals revolve around food, including the Breaux Bridge Crawfish Festival, a yam festival, *boucheries* (large-scale butchering parties), and *fais dodos* (all-night parties; the phrase means "go to sleep"), where Cajuns consume prodigious amounts of food and drink and everyone works hard to live by the Cajun motto, *Laissez le bon temps rouler* — "Let the good times roll."

In *American Cooking: Creole and Acadian* (1971), Peter S. Feibleman wrestled with the problem of defining Cajun cookery and finally realized there was no final word on the matter:

> What, then, is the difference between the terms *Creole* and *Acadian* as applied to food? Most authorities will start with a simple answer: they will tell you that it is the difference between city French cooking and country French cooking. But then the reservations and qualifications begin. Both Creole and Acadian cooking are *Louisiana* French in style, of course—which (authorities will add) isn't French at all. Is that clear? No? Well, Acadian cooking is a little spicier than Creole— sometimes, not always. Acadians like a lot of rice—well, of course, the Creoles like a lot of rice, too. Acadian cooks are likely to put all the ingredients for a course into one big pot, while Creoles like these ingredients separate. Yes, that's true—at least, *most* Creoles like them separate. "Look [the authorities will finally say], maybe you'd better just taste it. . . ."

cake. A baked confection usually containing flour, butter, eggs, and sweetener, although some cakes do not contain flour. The word derives from Old Norse, *kaka*, which in Middle English became *cake*.

Until the last quarter of the nineteenth century cakes were usually baked in pans shaped to resemble bread loaves and were often studded with fruit. With the availability of the more modern bake ovens after 1870, it became possible to make much lighter cakes with the new baking sodas and powders.

In the twentieth century packaged cake mixes became very popular. Cake flour is regular white soft-wheat flour often containing a proportion of baking powder and salt.

calabash. Also, "calipash," "capapash," and other forms. This word refers to two plants, one an Old World vine *(Lagenaria siceraria)*, the other a tropical American tree *(Crescentia cujete)*, also called the "bottle gourd" for its large, round shape. The word is from the Spanish, *calabaza*, "gourd."

In South Carolina *calabash* was also the name for a dish of turtle cooked in its shell, now served rarely. In North Carolina "calabash style" refers to batter-fried fish; the term is from the town of Calabash, where many restaurants specialize in this style.

calas. A New Orleans Sunday-morning breakfast confection made of rice that is mixed with flour, spices, and sugar and then deep-fried. Calas were sold by black street vendors in the city's French Quarter, and one would hear the cry, *"Belles calas tout chauds!"* The word's origins are obscure. (*Calas* is also a term for a shoulder cut of ham, usually referred to as "shoulder bacon," "picnic ham," or "California ham.")

> Mix 3 cups cooked rice, 3 beaten eggs, 1/4 tsp. vanilla, 1/4 tsp. nutmeg, 1/4 tsp. cinnamon, and 1/4 tsp. lemon rind. Sift 1/2 cup flour with 1/2 cup sugar, 3 1/2 tsp.

baking powder, and 1/2 tsp. salt. Stir into rice. Drop by spoon into deep, hot fat and fry for about 2 min. Sprinkle with confectioners' sugar. Makes about 2 dozen.

calcium (or sodium) propionate. A preservative used to prevent the growth of mold in bread products.

calcium (or sodium) stearoyl lactylate. An additive mixed with dough to strengthen its texture. It is also used in artificial whipped cream, cake fillings, and processed egg whites.

cale-cannon. A dish of cabbage and potatoes. The name comes from an Irish dish, traditionally served at Halloween and known at least since the eighteenth century, called "colcannon," in which *cole* refers to cabbage and *cannon* is of obscure origins (though the *Oxford English Dictionary* notes, "it is said that vegetables such as spinach were formerly pounded with a cannon-ball"). Colcannon is also a Scottish Highland dish of cabbage, potatoes, turnips, and carrots mashed and cooked with butter.

In her *Directions for Cookery* (1837) Eliza Leslie says to boil potatoes and cabbage together in a ratio of two parts to one, add butter and salt, and serve with corned beef.

calf fry. The testicle of a bull calf, usually fried—a Western delicacy.

calibougas. A beverage of rum, spruce beer, and molasses known since the middle of the eighteenth century, but a word of unknown origins.

cambric tea. Also called "hot water tea," cambric tea is merely hot water, milk, sugar, and perhaps a dash of tea, given to children to make them feel part of a social gathering. The term comes from cambric fabric, which is white and thin, as is cambric tea; it is American slang, used at least since 1888.

canaigre *(Rumex hymenosepalus)*. Also called "wild rhubarb" and "tanner's dock." Canaigre is a species of buckwheat found from Wyoming to Utah, Western Texas, New Mexico, Arizona, and California. It has long green leaves and a reddish stem. The Indians of the Southwest, including the Maricopa, Pima, Navajo, and Hopi, prepared it in various ways, and the plant was used for soothing sore throats and for tanning leather. The Maricopas used the seeds in a flat bread; the Navajos blended them into a mush.

In her book *Pima Cookery* (1968), Elizabeth Hart gives the following recipe for what is called "Sivitcult Pie":

Collect the stems of 4 cups of canaigre and cut into 1-in. lengths. Put in a saucepan with enough water to cover, and steam till tender with the lid on the pan. Add 1/4 cup flour, 1 1/2–2 cups sugar, 1 tbs. butter, and cook till sugar is melted and juice thickened. Pour into pie shell and cover with top crust. Slit top of crust to allow steam to escape, and then bake at 450° for 10 min. Reduce heat to 350° and bake for 40–45 min.

canapé. A slice of thin toast or cracker spread with any of a variety of meats, vegetables, cheeses, or fish, which is usually served on trays before the first course. *Canapé* is often synonymous in America with *hors d'oeuvre.* The word is from the French, for "couch," and Medieval Latin, *canapeum.* According to the *World Famous Chefs' Cook Book* (1941), compiled by Ford Naylor, "It is correct to offer [canapés] to guests in the living room, just before dinner; or as a first course at luncheon or dinner; or at receptions and teas. When canapés or tidbits are served with relishes, the combination is known as an hors d'oeuvre."

Canapé first appears in English print in 1890 as a reference to a tidbit served with anchovies, still a popular canapé. Other canapés might include hard-boiled, minced eggs, sliced olives with pimiento, cheese puffs, ham, liver or fish pâté, smoked salmon, pickles, small frankfurters wrapped in pastry (called "pigs-in-a-blanket"), and oysters wrapped in bacon (an English canapé known as "angels on horseback").

candy. Any of a wide variety of sweet morsels, bars, lozenges, figures, or other confections eaten on their own, as a snack or treat beyond the usual mealtime foods. Candy may take the form of fluffy marshmallow, chocolate-covered nuts, citrus rinds, spun sugar, bars with cream centers, tiny hard drops, gums, and many other shapes and types. Many are based on crystallized sugar, whose once high price made such sweet confections a delicacy indulged only by the wealthy. The ancient Egyptians preserved nuts and fruits with honey, and by the Middle Ages physicians had learned how to mask the bad taste of their medicines with sweetness, a practice still widespread. Boiled "sugar plums" were known in seventeenth-century England and soon were to appear in the American colonies, where maple-syrup candy was popular in the North and benne-seed confections were just as tempting in the South. In New Amsterdam one could enjoy *marchpane,* or marzipan, which is a very old decorative candy made from almonds ground into a sweet paste.

While the British called such confections "sweetmeats," Americans came to call them "candy," from the Arabic, *gandī,* "made of sugar," although one finds *candy* in English as early as the fifteenth century. Originally Americans used the word to mean a "toffee" (a hard candy made from sugar and butter), but by the nineteenth century *candy* was a general term for all kinds of sweet confections.

CARAMELS were known in the early eighteenth century, and LOLLIPOPS by the 1780s, as were PRALINES—named after French diplomat César du Plessis-Praslin, later Duc de Choiseul—a candy that became particularly well known in Louisiana.

Hard candies made from lemon or peppermint flavors were popular in the early nineteenth century, and Eliza Leslie, in her *Directions for Cookery* (1837), speaks of chocolate-covered nuts and bonbons (from the French, for "good-good") wrapped in papers on which were printed lines of verse. Peppermint sticks were enjoyed by midcentury, as was HOARHOUND CANDY and other lozenges used as sore-throat remedies. Soft, chewy TAFFY was made at taffy pulls during this period, and people also delighted in peanut brittle and a candy so hard it was called a "jawbreaker." Vinegar candy was boosted by being continuously mentioned throughout the popular series of *Dotty Dimple Stories* of 1867–1869 by Rebecca Sophia Clarke, whose pen name was Sophie May. By the 1860s there were gum drops.

A significant moment in candy history occurred at the 1851 Great Exhibition in London, where "French-style" candies with rich, cream centers were first displayed. These caught on immediately in America, and within a few years there were more than 380 candy factories in the United States, many turning out candy that cost one cent (called "penny candy"), a price that extended well into the twentieth century. Most of these candies were sold in batches or by the pound and displayed behind glass cases. Hard, clear candies, traditional at Christmas, were made at home in patterned molds, most of which were made by Thomas Mills and Brothers, a Philadelphia company established in 1864.

Flavored gums from tree resins had been known throughout the nineteenth century, but chewing gum did not come along until the 1870s. Bubble gum appeared by the end of the century.

FUDGE originated at women's colleges in the late nineteenth century, sourballs appeared by the turn of the last decade, and Cracker Jacks were the hit of Chicago's Columbian Exposition of 1893. Jelly beans came along in 1905.

But it was the discovery of milk chocolate in Switzerland in 1875 that made the American CANDY BAR such a phenomenon of the late nineteenth century. The first such chocolate bar was produced by Milton Snavely Hershey, and there soon followed an endless array of candy products containing peanuts, cream centers, fruit fillings, nougat, coconut, and many other sweet fillers with names like "Milky Way," "Snickers," "3 Musketeers," "Mary Jane," "Goo Goo Cluster," and hundreds of others. (For a fuller discussion, see CANDY BAR.)

In 1912 Americans began buying Life Savers, made by Clarence A. Crane of Cleveland, Ohio. These were round, white peppermints with distinctive holes in the middle (thus, their resemblance to a life preserver on a boat); later five more flavors were added. According to Ray Broekel in *The Great American Candy Bar Book* (1982), about 30 billion rolls of Life Savers have been made since their appearance.

Nineteen twelve was also the year NECCO Wafers (an acronym for the New England Confectionary Company) appeared. These were previously called "Peerless wafers" and had been carried to the Arctic and South Pole by Donald MacMillan and Richard Byrd (Byrd allegedly brought two-and-a-half tons of them with him). In 1920 the newest candy on the market was JUJUBES, tiny morsels of hard colored candy, and Juicyfruits, shaped into fruit forms.

Americans went to the "candy shop" specifically to buy various kinds of candies, usually sold by the pound or produced in bars by the shop itself.

"Candy stores" were small shops selling mostly commercially produced, packaged candies, as well as everything from newspapers and magazines to ice cream sodas and cigars, and, in fact, were more or less synonymous with "soda fountains" and "cigar stores" by the twentieth century. At such stores a child could purchase penny candy, which sometimes was merely icing in a little tin plate, or malted-milk balls, or strings of licorice, or sweet liquids inside small wax bottles. One favorite was hard pellets of candy stuck to long strips of paper.

Cotton candy, made by spinning colored sugar in a centrifuge, causing it to puff into cottonlike strands, came along in the 1920s and was usually sold at carnivals, circuses, and state fairs, rarely at candy stores.

Today Americans consume about 16.2 pounds of candy per person each year (including "healthful" candy bars like Nature Valley Granola Bars, created in 1975 by General Mills, Inc.), but not including chewing gum. The American candy industry turns out more than two thousand different items.

candy apple. Also, "candied apple." A confection made by immersing an apple in a red syrup that forms a hard, candylike crust on the fruit. Candy apples are usually eaten on a stick and are a specialty of carnivals and county fairs.

> Combine 4 cups sugar, 1/2 cup light corn syrup, and 1 1/2 cups water in a saucepan and bring to a boil till sugar dissolves to a temperature of 285°. Stir in 1/4 tsp. red food coloring. Dip apples, fixed on the end of a stick, into mixture and let them cool on waxed paper. They will have a hard, crisp shell.

candy bar. A bar of candy, usually coated with or containing chocolate, that may include nuts, jellies, peanut butter, fruit, nougat, caramel, coconut, cookie wafers, and other fillings.

The first candy bars may have been made in Victorian England, and by 1842 Birmingham's Cadbury Limited offered eating chocolate for sale through its catalog. But the candy bar as we know it was the idea of Milton Snavely Hershey, who manufactured the first American chocolate bars, the Hershey Almond Bar and the Hershey Mild Chocolate Bar, in 1894 after seeing some German chocolate-making machines at the 1893 World's Columbian Exposition in Chicago. Hershey had before then made caramels at his Lancaster (Pennsylvania) Caramel Plant, which he sold in 1900. After a trip to Europe Hershey built a plant in Derry Church, Pennsylvania, and opened the Hershey Company in 1904.

Before long the Bunte Brothers were making chocolate-coated bars, and by 1912 the Standard Candy Company of Nashville, Tennessee, produced the first combination bar, called the "Goo Goo Cluster," which contained caramel, marshmallow, peanuts, and milk chocolate. Peanut-butter bars had been around since 1905. After World War I the candy-bar craze swept the country, giving impetus to dozens of candy manufacturers, including the Curtiss Candy Company, the Fox-Cross Candy Company, Peter Paul Candies, the Clark

Company, Mars Candies, the Charles N. Miller Company, and many others. During the war candy bars were given to servicemen for nourishment, to provide quick energy, and to build morale.

The first candy bars sold for ten cents, which at the time was too much for a public not hooked on such confections, especially when a pound of loose candy cost the same price. After World War I a drop in the prices of sugar and chocolate helped lower the price of candy bars to five cents, and a nickel was the prevailing price of most candy bars until the 1960s. By 1968 the average candy bar cost ten cents again, and by 1980 thirty-five cents was the usual tab for a bar that changed shape, size, and weight through competition and as the result of falling or rising sugar prices.

Today candy bars represent endless variations on the basic ingredients of the first such confections sold after World War I. Although there have been a few attempts to make "health bars," containing honey instead of sugar, carob instead of chocolate, and vitamins instead of caramel, the American candy bar remains a persistent reminder of the American sweet tooth.

Some of the most famous and popular candy bars over the years include:

Baby Ruth (1920). A chocolate-covered bar with caramel-and-peanut center produced by the Curtiss Candy Company of Chicago. The item was apparently not named after New York Yankee baseball player George Herman "Babe" Ruth (1895–1948), but instead honored the daughter of former President Grover Cleveland, whose name was Ruth and who as a child had won the hearts of the nation.

Bit-o-Honey (1924). A bar made of almond bits and honey-flavored taffy, produced by the Schutter-Johnson Company of Chicago, now produced by the Chunky Corporation of New York City.

Charleston Chew (1922). A chocolate-covered bar with a vanilla nougat center, manufactured by the Fox-Cross Candy Company of Emeryville, California. The current producer is Nabisco Confections, Inc.

Chuckles (1921). A jellied candy coated with sugar crystals, created by Fred W. Amend of Chicago and now produced by Nabisco Confections, Inc.

Chunky (Mid-1930s). A square chunk of chocolate containing Brazil nuts, cashews, and raisins, created by New York confectioner Philip Silverstein, who named the candy after his "chunky" little daughter. It is now manufactured by the Ward-Johnston Division of the Terson Company.

Clark (1917). Usually referred to as the "Clark bar," it was made by the D. L. Clark Company and contained roasted peanuts and a milk-chocolate covering. The company is now merged with the M. J. Holloway Company, a division of the Beatrice Foods Company.

5th Avenue (1936). A peanut-butter-and-almond bar covered with milk chocolate, first produced by William H. Luden of Reading, Pennsylvania.

Goo Goo Cluster (1912). The first combination bar of milk chocolate, caramel, marshmallow, and peanuts. The Goo Goo Cluster was made by the Standard Candy Company of Nashville, Tennessee, and is a great favorite in the South.

Heath Bar (1932). Introduced as "Heath's English Toffee" in 1928 by L. S. Heath, this chocolate-covered toffee bar was considered a premium item because it was smaller than most other candy bars. People often referred to it as the "H and H Bar," because the two *H*'s in the word *Heath* were capitalized between lower-case letters *eat.*

Junior Mints (1949). These small morsels with a creamy mint center covered with chocolate were produced by the James O. Welch Company (now part of Nabisco Confections, Inc.). Welch himself named the candy after seeing a performance of a Broadway play entitled *Junior Miss,* based on the *New Yorker* short stories by Sally Benson.

Hershey's Kisses (1907). Small chocolate droplets wrapped in foil and with identifying paper plumes. Kisses were made by the Hershey Company, although the Wilbur Chocolate Company of Lititz, Pennsylvania, had been making similar candies called "Wilbur Buds" since 1894.

M & M's Plain Chocolate Candies (1941). Usually called "M & M's," these chocolate morsels coated with colored sugar shells were produced by M&M Limited of Newark, New Jersey. In 1954 M & M's Peanut Chocolate Candies appeared, and both are known by the slogan, "The Milk Chocolate Melts in Your Mouth—Not in Your Hand."

Mary Jane (1914). A molasses-and-peanut-butter candy bar made by the Charles M. Miller Company.

Milk Duds (1926). Caramel-and-chocolate morsels, first made by the Holloway Company of Chicago, now by Beatrice Food Company.

Milky Way (1923). Introduced by Frank C. Mars, this bar of chocolate nougat, caramel, and chocolate covering has been one of the most popular of all candy bars.

Mr. Goodbar (1925). A chocolate-and-peanut bar produced by the Hershey Company.

Mounds (1922). A double bar of dark chocolate covering and coconut center, manufactured by Peter Paul Halajia of Naugatuck, Connecticut. In 1948 a similar bar using milk chocolate and almonds became another success for the company, who called the new candy "Almond Joy."

Oh Henry! (1921). Made by the Williamson Candy Company of Chicago, this milk-chocolate-and-peanut bar was not named after short-story writer William Sydney Porter, whose pen name was O. Henry. According to Ray Broekel in *The Great American Candy Bar Book* (1982),

Mr. Williamson was operating a combination retail and wholesale candy store, and every day about the same time, a young fellow named Henry would come into the store and kid around with the girls who were making candy. Before long, the girls got into the habit of asking Henry to do little odd jobs and favors for them . . . [and] you'd hear, "Oh, Henry, will you get me this?" Or, "Oh, Henry, will you get me that?"

Later in the year, when it came time to find a name for the nut roll that was being manufactured, Mr. Williamson's salesmen said, "All we hear around here is 'Oh, Henry,' so why not call the candy bar Oh Henry!"

Reese's Peanut Butter Cups (1923). Produced by H. B. Reese in Hershey, Pennsylvania, these chocolate-and-peanut-butter candies came in waxed paper containers. The candy is now made by the Hershey Company.

Sky Bar (1937). A combination bar of chocolate segments containing centers of caramel, vanilla, peanut, or fudge, made by the Necco Company of Cambridge, Massachusetts.

Snickers (1930). A bar of peanut-butter nougat, peanuts in caramel, and a milk-chocolate coating. Snickers was produced by Frank C. Mars of Chicago and is the largest-selling candy bar in the United States.

3 Musketeers (1932). Originally three bars of chocolate coating on fluffy chocolate nougat, these were named after the 1844 novel by Alexandre Dumas, *The Three Musketeers*, and were created by the Mars Company. Today the item is one long bar.

Tootsie Roll (1896). Leo Hirschfield of New York City named these chocolate, chewy morsels after his daughter, Clara, whose nickname was Tootsie. In the 1930s he came up with Tootsie Roll Pops, which were lollipops filled with the original product's chocolate.

canoe race. A campus phrase for drinking beer in relay teams, not an official college sport by any means.

cantaloupe *(Cucumis melo reticulatus).* A musk melon, elsewhere called the "netted" or "nutmeg" melon, that is round or oval, weighs about two to four pounds, has orange flesh, and is known for is sweetness. The word is from the name of a papal villa near Rome, Cantalupo, where the fruit was supposedly first grown, but in Europe the cantaloupe is specifically *C. melo cantalupensis.* The melon is first mentioned in American print in 1839. It may have been first brought here by Columbus before March 29, 1494, when the first European melons were planted.

Americans often eat cantaloupe for breakfast, sometimes with cottage cheese.

cantina. A saloon in the Southwest; also, "canteen," which has the additional meaning of a metal flask used to carry water. The word *cantina* is from the Italian (for "wine cellar") and the Spanish (for "wine cellar" or "storage room"); by extension it came to mean a place where one could buy a drink of wine or spirits. The word was first printed in 1844.

canvasback duck *(Aythya valisineria).* A wild North American duck found throughout the United States whose name derives from the light color of its neck and back. Thomas Jefferson first mentioned the bird by this name in 1782, and it has long been considered one of the tastiest of all American fowl, its flavor the result of its wild celery diet. The most preferred canvasbacks came from the Chesapeake Bay, Long Island Sound, and along the Delaware and Susquehanna rivers; for these gastronomes paid a high price and Europeans had the ducks imported. In the Chesapeake Bay region the canvasback almost became extinct after Army Ordnance appropriated some of the fowl's feeding grounds in 1917.

Cape Cod turkey. A euphemism for baked codfish at least since 1865. The term may have derived from the gratefulness of Cape Codders for nature's bounty of cod, their major industry in the eighteenth and nineteenth centuries. So, perhaps in the spirit of the Thanksgiving turkey, the people called the fish by this name. Others believe it may derive from Boston Catholics' attempt to make more palatable the thought of eating fish every Friday, when no meat was allowed for religious reasons.

> Season a 3-lb. cod with salt and pepper, then fill its cavity with 3 cups bread crumbs, 1 chopped onion, 2 tbs. parsley, 1/3 cup dill pickle, salt, pepper, 3 beaten eggs, and 4 tbs. melted butter. Close cavity and bake for 45 min. at 350°. Serves 6.

caper *(Capparis spinosa).* Any of 150 species of shrub bearing a flowered bud pickled for use as a condiment. Capers may have originated in Asia Minor; the word is from the Greek, *kapparis,* which became in Middle English *caperis.*

Capers are grown in the United States in Florida and California.

cappuccino. A dark coffee served with a foamy head of milk or cream. A traditional beverage of Italy, cappuccino is made by forcing steam through milk or cream to form a creamy topping for the coffee, though in America it may be served simply with whipped cream on top. The drink is supposedly named after a Capuchin monk in whose garden coffee was grown in Brazil in 1774. The word is first found in American print in 1948.

caramel. A confection made from sugar, cream, butter, and flavorings, or merely melted sugar used as a flavoring, topping, or coloring in soups, desserts, and spirits.

The term came into English from the French, via Old Spanish, and, ultimately, the Greek, *kalamos.* It first appears in English print in 1725, referring to the melted-sugar variety. The candy caramel was first mentioned in 1884 by the *Philadelphia Times.* To caramelize sugar is to heat it to the melting stage, just before it begins to burn. Some recommend the addition of a small bit of water during the cooking of caramel.

CARAMEL CANDY:
In a saucepan place 2 1/2 cups sugar, 3 cups heavy cream, 5 tbs. dark corn syrup, and 1 vanilla bean and bring to boil, carefully scraping down the crystallized sugar on the pan's sides with a moistened utensil. When the caramel begins to form a thread, add 7 tbs. butter cut into pieces and cook until caramel enters the soft-ball stage. Remove vanilla bean. Remove from heat, pour onto greased marble slab to

form a thickness of about 1/4 in., and cool. Cut into squares. Caramels may also be flavored with coffee, chocolate, or nuts.

CARAMEL SAUCE:
Mix together 1 cup light brown sugar, 1/4 cup granulated sugar, 1/2 cup corn syrup, and 1 cup heavy cream. Cook till temperature reaches 238° on candy thermometer.

caribou *(Rangifer tarandus).* Also, "cariboo," "carraboo," and other spellings. A large wild deer of the arctic and subarctic regions of North America, taxonomically the same as the reindeer but never domesticated. The domesticated reindeer, on the other hand, was introduced into Alaska from Siberia only in the 1890s and became an essential part of the Alaskan Eskimo's way of life.

The caribou has shaggy hair, grows to about eight feet in length and four feet in height at the shoulder, migrates in herds, and is highly prized by hunters. The name comes from French Canadian, in turn from Micmac *khalibu* or other Indian words meaning "pawing the snow," and has been traced to 1610. By 1972 it had other Indian names, such as "maccarib" and "Pohano."

Usually caribou meat would be marinated and stewed. *Nipku* is a Canadian Eskimo trail food made by partially thawing chunks of the meat, slicing them very thin, and drying the slices on bushes.

carp *(Cyprinus carpio).* A warm-water fish native to Asia and introduced to the United States from Germany in 1876 by the United States Fish Commission. The fish proliferated so fast that 260,000 carp were distributed throughout 298 congressional districts in an effort to make fishermen out of the constituencies. It propagated so successfully that it invaded the habitats of trout and other fish, and efforts were made to eradicate the oversupply of carp. Despite its widespread distribution in muddy waters throughout the United States, the carp has never been favored by Americans as an eating fish, although it has been a principal ingredient used by Jewish-Americans to make GEFILTE FISH.

The name of the fish is of unknown origins and is first mentioned in English in 1440.

carpetbag steak. A grilled steak of beef into which is cut a pocket enclosing a stuffing of oysters. The name derives from a handbag for travelers that was popular from about 1840 to 1870. The dish resembles the sacklike bag with its top closure. There does not seem to be any specific association with an American slang term, *carpetbagger,* for a hated post–Civil War opportunist who took advantage of both white and black southerners politically and economically. In fact the carpetbag steak is much more popular in Australia and is only mentioned in American print for the first time in 1958.

The following recipe is from New York City's Fraunces Tavern restaurant, where the dish is referred to as a "carpetbagger steak."

Cut a pocket in the edge of a trimmed 8-oz. shell steak and season with salt and pepper. In 2 tbs. butter sauté 2 oz. finely chopped shallots, then remove from heat. Add 6 oysters and bind with 4 oz. bread crumbs and 1 tbs. chopped parsley. Stuff steak pocket, secure with skewers, and grill on both sides to desired doneness.

carrageenan. A thickening and stabilizing agent obtained from Irish moss seaweed, often added to ice cream, chocolate milk, and infants' formula.

carrot *(Daucus carota)*. A long, orange root vegetable having fine leaves called "carrot tops." The carrot originated in the Middle East but is now propagated worldwide. The word is from the Greek, *karōton,* and first appears in English print in 1538.

The carrot was not much appreciated in Europe until the sixteenth century, but the roots were brought to America by the early English settlers, and, with improved types developed in France around 1830, the vegetable took on commercial interest. Today carrots are grown in half the states in the Union, especially in Texas, California, Michigan, and Wisconsin.

Americans nibble on carrots raw, often cut into "carrot sticks" served as appetizers at parties. They are also boiled and buttered, sometimes made into puddings, and often baked into a cake, especially popular since the 1960s, topped with a cream cheese frosting.

CARROT CAKE:
Mix 1 cup sugar with 1/2 cup butter, 1 1/2 cups flour, 2 tsp. baking powder, 1/2 tsp. salt, 1/4 tsp. nutmeg, 1/2 tsp. baking soda, 1 tsp. cinnamon, and 1/8 tsp. allspice. Add 1 cup grated, raw carrots. Add 2 eggs and beat well, then add 1 cup chopped walnuts or pecans. Place in buttered pan and bake for 60 min. at 350°. Spread with frosting made by beating 1/4 cup cream cheese with 1 1/4 cups confectioners' sugar, 1/2 tsp. vanilla, and 1 slightly beaten egg white.

casaba. A variety of winter melon *(Cucumis melo)* with a yellow skin and sweet, white flesh. The name comes from the Turkish town of Kasaba (now Turgutlu). The melon may have been brought to California by Turkish or Armenian immigrants, although, notes Waverly Root in *Food* (1980), "The first officially recorded import . . . seems to have been the Netted Gem variety, imported from France in 1881. This started commercial melon cultivation in the United States, though not until 1895 did they develop reliable quality in this country, starting in Colorado."

casserole. A dish or pot made from a material such as glass, cast iron, aluminum, or earthenware in which food is baked and, often, served. The word may also refer to the food itself, as, for example, a *tuna casserole.* It is from the French and was first printed in English in 1706.

Cooking in such dishes has always been part of most nations' gastronomy, but the idea of casserole cooking as a "one-dish meal" became popular in America in the twentieth century, especially in the 1950s when new forms of lightweight metal and glassware appeared on the market. The virtues of easy-to-prepare meals were increasingly promoted in the women's magazines of the era, thereby supposedly freeing the housewife from the lengthy drudgery of the kitchen. Casserole cooking also coincided with the popularity during this same era of buffets, brunches, patio parties, and other casual social meals at which guests could help themselves from a common dish. By the 1970s "casserole cookery" took on a less-than-sophisticated image, even though many such dishes were still served at formal dinners and casual meals without characterizing them by the name.

TUNA-NOODLE CASSEROLE:
Combine 2 1/2 cups canned tomatoes, 1 chopped onion, 1 minced clove garlic, salt and pepper, and 1/4 chopped parsley. In a buttered baking dish place 2 oz. cooked noodles, half of the tomato mixture, 1/2 cup chunk-style tuna, and 1/4 lb. Cheddar cheese slices. Add another 2 oz. cooked noodles, the rest of the tomato mixture, 1/2 cup tuna, and 1/4 lb. Cheddar cheese slices. Bake, uncovered, for 40 min. at 350°.

Catawba. An American Labrusca grape originally found growing along the banks of the Catawba River in North Carolina in 1823 and popularized by John Adlum of Washington, D.C. It became a popular wine grape of Ohio in 1842, when Nicholas Longworth made the first American CHAMPAGNE from it. Catawba is still widely used in the East to make sweet red, white, and rosé wines, often blended with the DELAWARE grape.

catfish (Family *Ictaluridae*). Any of a wide range of spiny, scaleless fish with eight barbels (or "whiskers") on the snout, jaw, and chin. Catfish have bristle-like teeth and some species contain a poison gland at the base of the pectoral spines. There are two thousand species of catfish, whose name, derived from its whiskered appearance, was first mentioned in print in 1612.

North America has twenty-eight species of catfish, about a dozen of which are eaten and three of which make up the most important edible species: the channel catfish *(Ictalurus punctatus),* the white catfish *(I. catus),* and the blue catfish *(I. furcatus),* also called the "Mississippi catfish." Smaller catfish, called "mad toms" (genus *Noturus*), are used mainly for bait.

Catfish are greatly enjoyed in the South, where they are usually dredged in cornmeal and fried. These are usually served with hushpuppies and cole slaw on the side. In the southern states catfish are produced on fish farms (90 percent in Mississippi) and sold fresh or frozen.

Cut catfish fillets in half crosswise. Combine 1/2 cup cornmeal, salt, and pepper, dredge the catfish fillets in the mixture, and cook in deep, hot oil for 5–10 min. till browned and crisp. Serve with lemon wedges.

cauliflower *(Brassica oleracea botrytis).* A plant with a large head of crowded white flowers, related to the cabbage and broccoli. The word is probably from the Italian, *caoli-fiori,* "flowered cabbage," and is first recorded in English in 1597. Cauliflower originated in Asia Minor and did not reach America until the seventeenth century, when it was first grown on Long Island, New York, where it has been cultivated ever since. The most popular United States variety is the snowball. Cauliflower is usually boiled and served as a vegetable with meats.

caviar. Specifically, the eggs or roe of the STURGEON, but generally referring to the eggs of other fish as well, such as TUNA, lumpfish, and SALMON. The word *caviar* originates in the Turkish, *havyār,* and for most of man's history the eggs of the sturgeon were consumed as a matter of course throughout the Middle East and eastern Europe. It was hardly considered a delicacy in nineteenth-century America, when caviar was given away in saloons as part of the FREE LUNCH designed to build a thirst for beer. At the end of the nineteenth century America was the largest supplier of caviar in the world. American caviar was obtained from Atlantic sturgeon (or "sea sturgeon"), which Henry Hudson had noted in abundance in 1609 but which were not much prized as a food fish among the white settlers, though a mainstay of the Indians' diet.

In 1873 German immigrant Henry Schacht set up a caviar business near Chester, Pennsylvania, catching his sturgeon in the Delaware River and shipping his product to European markets for a dollar per pound. Seven years later another plant opened in Bay Side, New Jersey, and business boomed for the next quarter century. So successful was the sturgeon industry in those years that it soon depleted its own product, so that by 1900 such fisheries found themselves without a source of supply. Sturgeon fisheries were also established along the Columbia River in the Northwest in 1888, and by 1892 six million pounds of the fish were caught. By 1900 these, too, were depleted almost to the point of extinction.

During those boom years America shipped much of its caviar supply to Europe and then imported it back again under the label "Russian caviar," for ever since the word *caviar* was first printed in English in 1591, the best examples were thought to come from Russian rivers. With the end of the American sturgeon industry, caviar prices jumped wildly and true Russian and Iranian caviar needed to be imported.

Americans not willing to pay such prices were forced to switch to domestic fish roe. In the 1960s the Romanoff Caviar Company (which began when German immigrant Ferdinand Hansen came to Pennsgrove, New Jersey, in 1859 to supervise caviar production and which is now owned by Iroquois Foods) began marketing more affordable varieties made from the roe of salmon (called "red salmon caviar"), lumpfish, and, in 1982, whitefish (called "golden whitefish caviar").

F.D.A. regulations forbid the use of the word *caviar* alone on a label unless it is truly from sturgeon roe; if other fish roe is used, the name of the fish must precede *caviar.* During the 1970s there was increased interest in the production of domestic sturgeon caviar because of an encouraging rise in the number of the fish in Arkansas, Oklahoma, and Oregon rivers. (California also has sturgeon, but it is illegal to catch them for commercial purposes.) Domestic production is now in excess of thirty metric tons.

Caviar is traditionally made by pushing the roe through a sieve in order to remove fatty tissue and membranes. It is then salted and packed in tins or jars.

cayenne pepper. Also, "cayenne." A seasoning of pulverized chili peppers and salt. The word comes from the seasoning's association with the peppers of Cayenne Island, French Guiana, but the powdered peppers were made elsewhere. Eliza Leslie, in her *Directions for Cookery* (1837), gives the following instructions, advising one to "wear glasses to save your eyes from being incommoded by [the peppers]."

> "Dry ripe chilis before a fire the day before. Trim the stalks, pound the pods in a mortar until powdered, add one-sixth their weight in salt."

celery *(Apium graveolens dulce).* A plant of the CARROT family, related to the PARSNIP and PARSLEY, used as a flavoring or vegetable in soup, salads, and sauces or eaten raw as an appetizer. The word derives from the Greek, *selinon,* and first appears in English print in 1664, thirty-two years after its first cultivation in France as a soup ingredient. Celery grows wild in Europe and Asia, and some wild varieties, which are believed to have escaped from cultivated varieties, are found in California. Florida and California grow most of the United States celery crop, and most of that is of the Pascal variety.

Celery salt was first advertised in 1897 in the *Sears, Roebuck and Co. Catalog* and is still used as a milder flavoring.

cereal. Generally, any edible grain, such as wheat, oats, barley, or corn. In America, however, the word (from the Latin, *cereālis,* "of grain") has since the end of the nineteenth century meant a breakfast food prepared from such grains. Such dishes are often called "breakfast cereals," such as oatmeal, corn flakes, and Cream of Wheat, which first appeared on the market in 1894.

The first examples of American cooked cereals were the corn mush porridges adapted from Indian cookery. But the interest in nutrition in the midnineteenth century as promoted by Reverend Sylvester Graham (1794–1851), creator of graham flour, led to pronouncements on the value of grain in the diet. One of Graham's followers, Dr. James Caleb Jackson of New York, created the first packaged breakfast cereal, which was called "Granula."

In the 1890s another nutritionist, Dr. John Harvey Kellogg (1852–1943), head of the Battle Creek Sanatorium in Battle Creek, Michigan, doled out portions of "Battle Creek health foods" to his patients, who consumed great quantities of bran and zwieback. Kellogg developed packaged cereals at this time—the first named "Granola," quickly changed to "Granose" to avoid conflict with Jackson's Granula. Later Kellogg created one of the most popular and enduring of all American breakfast cereals, Kellogg's Toasted Corn Flakes, introduced in 1907.

One of Kellogg's patients, Charles William Post (1854–1914), founded the

Postum Cereal Company in 1896, marketing a coffee substitute made from cereal and called "Postum Cereal Food Coffee," and, in 1898, a wheat-and-malted barley cereal called "Grape-Nuts" (which contained neither grapes nor nuts; Post claimed grape sugar was formed in the baking process). Post's other contribution of that era was a corn-flake cereal he originally called "Elijah's Mann" in 1906, but, owing to criticism of his use of a biblical name, changed it to "Post Toasties" two years later. In 1892 a Denver lawyer named Henry Perky traveled to Watertown, New York, to work with William Ford on a corn cereal, but discovered instead a process for pressing wheat into shreds that could be formed into biscuits. These he called "Shredded Wheat" and returned to Denver to open a bakery and restaurant and sell the item door to door by wagon. He set up the Shredded Wheat Company, which was bought in 1928 by the National Biscuit Company (today called Nabisco Brands, Inc.).

Maltex, a toasted-wheat-and-barley cereal, made by the Standard Milling Company of Kansas City, Missouri, appeared in 1899. Wheaties, a wheat-flake cereal, was accidentally created when a Minneapolis health theorist named Mennenberg (or perhaps Minniberg) spilled some gruel on a hot stove, making a crisp wheat flake. The Washburn Crosby Company (changed in 1928 to General Mills, Inc., of Minneapolis, Minnesota) bought the rights to this cereal and introduced it in 1924. The same company's corn-puff cereal, Kix, was marketed in 1937, and their ring-shaped oat cereal, Cheerioats, appeared in 1941. Three years later the name was changed to "Cheerios." In 1935 the Ralston Purina Company of St. Louis, Missouri, came out with Shredded Ralston, a cereal of small wheat squares in a waffle pattern. Later the name was changed to "Wheat Chex," and "Rice Chex" and "Corn Chex" followed.

Because of criticism of breakfast cereals in the 1960s as being of little nutritional value on their own, many cereal manufacturers have since added vitamins and minerals to their products and cut down on the sugar content, which had become very high in cereals aimed at the children's market. Many of these were named after cartoon or movie characters like Dracula ("Count Chocula," chocolate-flavored), Frankenstein ("Frankenberry," fruit-flavored), and others.

Also in the 1960s there was a surge of interest in "natural grain" cereals that were supposedly unadulterated by sugar and additives, although many of these contained high amounts of honey, brown sugar, or raisins, as well as dried fruits. The most successful was Granola, a mixture of various cereal grains. Wheat germ was also promoted as an additive giving a nutritional boost to packaged cereals.

Hot cereals made from grains include cream of wheat, farina, and oatmeal, which are all variations of basic porridge.

challa. Also, "challeh" or "challah." A shaped loaf of white, slightly sweetened bread coated with an egg-white glaze. Challa is a traditional Jewish bread served on the Sabbath and assumes different shapes at different holiday feasts: for Shabbat it is braided; for Rosh Hashanah and Yom Kippur it is rounded and might be topped with a dove-wing or ladder pattern made from the dough. By tradition, when the bread is baked a small morsel is thrown into the oven as a sacrifice to commemorate the Hebrew term *challa*, "the priest's share," mentioned in the Bible, Num. 15:20 and Ezek. 44:30.

> Dissolve 2 pkgs. yeast in 1/2 cup warm water. Add a pinch of saffron that has steeped in some hot water to 2 cups boiling water, 3 tbs. vegetable oil, 1 tbs. salt, and 1 tbs. sugar. Cool to lukewarm and add yeast. Add 2 beaten eggs and mix with 3 cups flour. Set aside for 10 min., add enough flour to make a dough, and knead. Shape into a ball, grease the surface and cover to let rise till doubled. Knead again, then cut dough into two loaves. Cut each half into three long pieces, fasten the ends together, and braid. Place on greased sheet, let rise till doubled, brush with egg white in 1 tbs. water, bake at 400° for 15 min., reduce to 350°, and bake for 45 min.

chalupa. A tortilla formed in the shape of a little boat (from the Mexican) and filled with various ingredients, such as shredded pork, beef, poultry, tomatoes, onion, or cheese. Chalupas are often served as an appetizer and are a staple of Mexican-American menus.

Champagne. A sparkling wine. True champagne comes from the Champagne region of France, northeast of Paris, which is centered around the cities of Reims and Epernay.

Sparkling wines (as opposed to the still wines produced in the same region) were produced in the seventeenth century in the Champagne area, but much credit has been given to a Benedictine monk named Dom Pérignon, cellarmaster at the Abbey of Hautvillers until his death in 1715, for his work in stopping the bottles from exploding because of the excessive effervescence by using better corks and thicker bottles. Dom Pérignon is also credited for important work in the blending of champagnes.

Champagne became extremely popular at the French court, and soon afterwards it came to be considered a wine for special occasions and lavish dinners; to this day it is still so used to celebrate weddings, anniversaries, births, holidays, and other feasts in America and the rest of the world.

Champagne is made by any of three methods: the first, called the "Champagne process" (*méthode champenoise* in French), involves pressing the grapes and fermenting them for about three weeks. The wine is then chilled either by fresh winter air or refrigerated tanks, and a small amount of sugar dissolved in old wine is added to initiate a second fermentation in the bottle. The yeasts and sugar create additional carbon dioxide and alcohol. Sediment in the bottle is positioned in the neck by a process called "riddling," or turning the bottles periodically to force the sediment down the neck. This process, traditionally done by hand, is now occasionally done by machine. The sediment is then disgorged from the bottle by freezing the neck and removing the cork with the sediment behind it. The wine lost in disgorging is replaced with more wine and with a concentration of sugar dissolved in mature wine. This last addition gives the wine its final degree of sweetness, which ranges from "*brut*" (very dry), to "extra dry" or "extra *sec*" (dry), to "dry" or "*sec*" (somewhat sweeter), to "*demi sec*" (quite sweet), to "*doux*" (very sweet). The bottle is then recorked.

The second method is called the "Charmat" or "bulk process," invented by French enologist Eugene Charmat in 1907. Fermentation takes place in large tanks and bottling is done under pressure all in a continuous process.

The third method is a transfer process, developed in Germany, in which a second fermentation does take place in the bottle but in which the bottles are not riddled. Instead the cork is removed after being chilled, the sediment is twice filtered out under pressure, and the wine is put into clean bottles.

Although all three processes are used in American sparkling wines, the transfer and bulk methods are by far the most frequent.

The first American champagnes were made in 1842 by Nicholas Longworth from Catawba grapes grown on twelve hundred acres of vineyards near Cincinnati, Ohio, and these wines enjoyed great success and acclaim even in England, where a writer for the *Illustrated London News* reported that Longworth's sparkling wine "transcends the Champagne of France." There were other attempts after Longworth's, including those of Arpad Haraszthy in California's Sonoma Valley in the 1860s, based on methods learned at France's Moët et Chandon cellars, but his efforts failed. In 1884 French-born Paul Masson brought champagne-making equipment to his employer Charles Lefranc in Santa Clara, California, and began making sparkling wine there after the phylloxera blight destroyed the French vineyards. In 1892 Masson founded his own Paul Masson Champagne Company, and his wines won awards both in America and abroad, including honorable mention at the Paris Exposition of 1900. Masson prospered and became known for his lavish parties, at one of which singer Anna Held took a notorious bath in Masson champagne in 1917. During Prohibition Masson continued to make some champagne for "medicinal purposes," but federal agents raided his winery in 1929 and severely crippled the operations there.

Another name in California champagne making of that era is that of the Korbel brothers, whose winery dates to 1886 but whose first sparkling wines were not made until 1896 by winemaker Franz Hazek from Prague. Both the Paul Masson Vineyards and Korbel Champagne Cellars thrive today.

New York State also produced champagne in the nineteenth century. In 1860 Charles Davenport Champlin opened the Pleasant Valley Winery in Hammondsport in the Finger Lakes district. By 1865 Champlin had made the first New York champagne from Catawba grapes, and he won an honorable mention at the 1867 Paris Exposition. In 1870 the winery blended Catawba with Delaware grapes; on tasting it, horticulturist Colonel Marshall Wilder said, "Truly, this will be the great champagne of the West!" (meaning west of Europe), and soon afterwards the wine was called Great Western, which took a gold medal at the 1873 Vienna Exposition. Great Western was an enormous success, and the company even built a railroad in 1872 to haul their product. It was called the Bath & Hammondsport Railroad, but was nicknamed "The Champagne Trail."

Today sparkling wine accounts for a large proportion of the wines made in New York.

Although the French rage at the practice of American wines being labelled "champagne," there is nothing in United States law to prevent it. (It is interesting to note that when the French champagne producers Moët-Hennessey built a winery in California's Napa Valley in 1973, they labelled their product "sparkling wine," refusing to call it "champagne.") Americans have also referred to their sparkling wines as "the bubbly" since the 1890s, and, more colloquially, "gigglewater" by the 1920s. There are also other American wines labelled "Sparkling Burgundy" or "Sparkling Moscato" that may or may not possess any of the characteristics associated with the true wines of Burgundy or Italy.

American champagnes have traditionally been fermented somewhat sweeter than their European counterparts, although this has changed in the last decade, as drier wines have become more popular. The grapes used in the production of California champagne include the traditional PINOT NOIR and CHARDONNAY used in France, along with French Colombard, CHENIN BLANC, Sémillon, Folle Blanche, and others. New York State champagnes are principally made from Catawba and Delaware varieties.

In 1981, 34 million gallons of American sparkling wine were shipped.

Chardonnay. A white Vinifera grape that produces a well-balanced, fruity wine. It is the grape used in the finest whites of Burgundy and within the last twenty years has become the premium white grape of California and the Northwest. Some plantings are also found in the East. The label on American Chardonnays may read "Pinot Chardonnay," but the grape is not now believed to be related to the Pinot family. The word was first printed circa 1941.

Charlie Taylor. A mixture of sorghum or syrup and bacon grease, used by westerners as a substitute for butter.

chaser. A drink imbibed immediately after swallowing a first, different drink; for instance, a *beer chaser* would be a glass of beer drunk after one has had a jigger of spirits. The term has been in use since the 1890s.

chaudin. A stuffed pig's stomach that is browned and then cooked in a kettle. It is a traditional Cajun dish, and the word is derived from the French, *chaud,* "hot." The pig's stomach itself is called a "ponce" (French, *panse,* "belly"). The recipe below is adapted from Peter S. Feibleman's *American Cooking: Creole and Acadian* (1971):

Soak 1 1-lb. pig's stomach in cold water for 2 hr. Rinse and dry. Combine 3 slices white bread with crusts removed and 1/2 cup milk, let stand until all liquid is absorbed, and press out excess milk through a sieve. Sauté in 2 tbs. butter 1/4 cup finely chopped onions, 1/4 cup finely chopped green peppers, 1/4 cup finely chopped scallions, and 1 1/2 tsp. finely chopped garlic for about 5 min. Remove and let cool.

Mix together cooked vegetables and bread, add 1 1/2 lb. ground pork, 2 diced yams, 1 beaten egg, 1/2 tsp. cayenne pepper, 2 tsp. salt, and a dash of pepper. Knead till light and fluffy. Sew up one end of the stomach and stuff the other end with mixture. Sew up this end, then sauté stomach in 2 tbs. oil in a large casserole till browned. Pour in 1 cup water, bring to boil, cover tightly, reduce and cook for 3 hr., keeping water to depth of 1/2 inch. Transfer the stomach to platter, let stand for 10 min. before serving. Boil down remaining liquid till it forms a thin gravy. Carve the meat into crosswise slices.

chayote *(Sechium edule).* Also, "vegetable pear" and, in Louisiana, "mirliton." A squashlike fruit often served as a vegetable. The name derives from the Spanish, via Nahuatl, *chayotli.* Chayote is pale green in color and shaped like a pear. It is raised throughout the Caribbean and Latin America, as well as in small gardens of Louisiana, where stuffed mirlitons are served as a main dish. The word was first mentioned in 1887.

STUFFED MIRLITONS:
Cook mirlitons in boiling salted water for about 20 min., remove, drain, and cool. Scoop out the pulp, chop, and set aside. Sauté 5 strips of bacon till almost crisp, add 1 chopped onion, 1/2 cup chopped green pepper, 3 tbs. chopped celery, 1 clove chopped garlic, 1 chopped tomato, 1/2 cup chopped shallots, 1 1/2 tsp. salt, 1/2 tsp. black pepper, 1/2 tsp. thyme, 2 bay leaves, 3 tbs. minced parsley, and 1/8 tsp. cayenne. When onions and tomatoes begin to soften, add 1 lb. peeled shrimp, then 1/2 cup dampened, crumbled bread. Cook till shrimp turn pink, stuff mixture into mirlitons, then place in 350° oven for 30 min. Serves 4.

Cheddar. A cow's-milk CHEESE produced in many states, ranging from mild to quite sharp in taste and from white to pumpkin-orange in color (the deeper hues come from the American annato-bean vegetable dye).

The name and the cheese derive from the village of Cheddar, a district of Somerset, England, where it has been made at least since the sixteenth century.

American Cheddars are usually made in blocks, with a firm, not crumbly, texture, or they may be dipped in paraffin. The main varieties are:

coon. Very sharp, aged for more than a year and cured at high temperatures. Coon has a more crumbly texture than other Cheddars.

Goat's Milk Cheddar. Made in Iowa, this variety is not commonly found in the rest of the states. It is rich and has a slightly sweet flavor.

New York Cheddar. Some varieties are white and sharp, like Herkimer Cheddar; mild and yellow, like Cooper Cheddar; or smoked.

pineapple Cheddar. Made in Litchfield County, Connecticut, pineapple Cheddar is now uncommon. Its name derives from its hanging shape in the netting during the curing process.

Tillamook. A highly esteemed, yellow Oregon Cheddar that may be well aged, but may also range from mild to sharp.

Vermont Cheddar. A sharp cheese, light yellow in color, and distinctive in taste—especially the Crowley variety, which may have a tangy taste after aging. Vermont sage Cheddar is flavored with sage.

Wisconsin Cheddar. Wisconsin produces the most Cheddar cheeses in the country, ranging from Colby (after the town in Wisconsin where it was created), to Longhorn, which is somewhat mild. In the 1964 World's Fair in New York a six-ton Cheddar, made from Wisconsin and Canadian cheese, was exhibited; it was later served in a London restaurant.

Cheddar cheese is often served in New England with a slice of apple pie and coffee. It also makes a fine soup in winter.

CHEDDAR CHEESE SOUP:
Melt 2 oz. butter in a double boiler. Add 2 tbs. chopped leeks, 1/4 cup chopped carrots, 1/4 cup chopped celery, 1 grated lemon rind, 1 1/4-in. piece of bay leaf, 1/4 tsp. white pepper, and 1/2 tsp. dry mustard. Pour in 1 qt. chicken stock, simmer for 20 min., then whip in 6 oz. sharp Cheddar. Combine 2 tbs. butter, 2 tbs. flour, and 1 pt. hot milk, and whip into mixture. Let stand 10 min., then strain. Add 1 1/2 tsp. Worcestershire sauce. Add salt and Tabasco to taste.

cheese. A food made from the pressed curd of milk. The word is from the Latin, *cāseus,* and became *cese* in English about the year 1000. Medieval monks raised cheesemaking to a sophisticated and diverse craft, and the French developed so many varieties in so many regions that Charles de Gaulle was quoted in 1962 as saying, "How can you be expected to govern a country that has two hundred and forty-six kinds of cheese?" (De Gaulle was giving a conservative figure.)

Americans developed their own cheesemaking talents mainly from English traditions, although German methods had a distinct effect on the production of nineteenth-century cheeses and Scandinavians who settled in the Midwest brought their own talents to bear. American colonists in the North loved cheese and enjoyed it frequently; the Dutch of the Middle Atlantic colonies ate it twice a day, and it was certainly a staple of the Germans' diet in New Jersey and Pennsylvania. Most of the cheese eaten by English colonists was imported from the mother country, and after the Revolution high duties were placed on imported Cheshires and CHEDDARS. In the South, where fresh milk quickly soured in the heat, cheese was brought in from the North. As in other countries, cheese was a delectable way to preserve milk all over the United States. The basic technique for cheesemaking begins with mixing milk with rennet, the stomach lining of a slaughtered calf. The rennet curdles the milk, leaving the whey on top to be drawn off. The curds are then pressed into a mold and eaten fresh or aged for flavor and texture. Cheese was used with other foods of the colonial period as barter for goods.

Good cheeses were considered something of a luxury, however, and served as part of celebrations. On New Year's Day, 1802, President Thomas Jefferson was presented at the White House with a 1,235-pound Cheshire cheese from Cheshire, Massachusetts. A 1,400-pound cheese was delivered to President Andrew Jackson's last reception in 1837—the ten thousand citizens who attended left the cheese and the White House in shambles. It is said the smell of the cheese lingered in the carpets and furniture for a month afterwards.

The most popular cheese of the nineteenth century was Cheddar. American varieties of this English cheese were sold in every New England grocery as "store cheese," largely as a result of improved techniques developed by Englishman Joseph Harding. Vermont and New York became famous for their Cheddars. In the years following the California Gold Rush of 1849 in Monterey farmer David Jacks created a cheese called "Monterey Jack" that was similar to cheeses made by the Spanish friars. A Wisconsin farmer named Adam Blumer, recently arrived in the United States from Switzerland, began making imitation Swiss cheese, complete with the identifying holes, about 1850. Brick cheese was made first in Wisconsin, about 1877; Liederkranz was the creation of Swiss-born Emil Frey of Monroe, New York, in 1892. Creditable Limburgers, first made in Belgium, were produced by the German immigrants in upstate New York and became a standard item at beerhalls, where the drinks were accompanied by large slabs of cheese and pumpernickel bread.

The best-known United States cheese is termed, simply, "American cheese" or "American Cheddar," so called after the Revolutionary War when proud dairy workers scorned English items. This factory-made cheese was popularized further when a Chicago grocery clerk named J. H. Kraft had the idea of wrapping individual portions of cheese for his customers to buy and, as of 1903, of selling his cheese door to door by horse and wagon.

Today the United States is the largest producer of cheese in the world, even though the yearly American per capita consumption of about ten pounds of cheese is far below that of many other countries. New York State alone produces about twenty-six pounds of cheese for every American. The total United States cheese production for 1981 was 5.2 billion pounds, much of which was bought by the federal government as part of a dairy support price system. Cheese is made in thirty-seven states. Wisconsin, Minnesota, and New York are the country's largest cheese producers, making all sorts of traditional cheeses, as well as process cheese spread, pasteurized process cheese food, and other dairy products.

Several small commercial cheese producers have experimented with French-style cheeses, goat cheese, and other varieties heretofore not available. Also in recent years there has been a growth in the amount of mozzarella cheese (primarily used on pizza), low-fat cottage cheese (used on diets), and cream cheese, while imported cheeses sold at "cheese stores" have become readily available year-round.

The following list of American-made cheeses includes the main varieties, which may have separate main entries in this book, and lesser varieties of regional interest:

American. A form of Cheddar; see description above.

Amish Baby Swiss. Produced by Ohio Amish farmers; sometimes smoked.

baker's. Made from skim milk for commercial use.

Bandon. An Oregon-produced Cheddar.

Bel Paese. An Italian cheese (the name means "beautiful country," the title of a children's book by Father Antonio Stoppani) also produced in America.

bierkäse. In Germany this cheese is called *Weisslacker,* but it is made in Wisconsin. *Bierkäse* means "beer cheese" and is associated with the strong-tasting cheeses, like Limburger, usually consumed with beer.

blue. A blue-veined cheese under various names. Originally made from goat's milk by the United States Department of Agriculture and California Experiment Station in 1918 by using *Penicillium roqueforti,* American blue cheeses were later made with cow's milk after further successful experiments in universities in Washington and the Midwest.

brick. A semisoft cheese with holes developed in Wisconsin. (See BRICK CHEESE.)

Brie. A French cheese now made in small amounts by small dairies in the United States. Brie is creamy inside and has a white rind.

Camembert. A soft-centered cheese originally made in France's Normandy, but for some years made in the United States. The best known is Borden Camembert, made by the Borden Company in Van Wert, Ohio.

Cheddar. Originally made in Cheddar, England, now available in many American versions. Cheddar is the most popular cheese in the United States. (See CHEDDAR.)

cheese food. Cheese that has been processed with cream, milk, skim milk, cheese whey, or whey albumin. Under F.D.A. regulations, at least 51 percent of the product must be pure cheese.

Colby. A granular cheese first made at the end of the nineteenth century by the Steinwand family in Colby, Wisconsin. Colby is now made outside the United States as well. F.D.A. standards require that it contain not less than 50 percent milk fat.

coon. A sharp American Cheddar, usually aged a year or more.

Cornhusker. Developed by the Agricultural Experiment Station at the University of Nebraska about 1940, this cheese is similar to Colby.

cottage. An unripened, fresh cheese made with or without rennet. (See COTTAGE CHEESE.)

Cougar Gold. A form of Cheddar first made at the State University of Washington at Pullman.

cream. A very smooth, creamy cheese often made with gum arabic to give it a firm texture. (See CREAM CHEESE.)

Creole. A very rich and moist New Orleans cheese made from clabber and heavy cream.

Cup. A cheese made in Pennsylvania Dutch country whose the name derives from the white china cups in which it was carried to market. According to Evan Jones in *The World of Cheese* (1979), "Berks Cup Cheese is the result of baking curds in the oven, with new curds added each day for a week. The baked curds are poured into a heated pan and simmered slowly to a boil, without stirring; salt, cream, butter, and baking soda are added, and the mixture is boiled 15 minutes, during which time eggs are mixed into the curds. The cheese is cooled in cups."

coldpack. A cheese made from one or more varieties of Cheddar. Flavorings, such as wine, are sometimes added to this unheated, tangy cheese, which may also be called "club cheese."

Edam. Originally a cheese of Holland, Edam is formed into a ball and usually coated with a red covering of paraffin or other substances. It must contain not less than 40 percent milk fat.

farmer. A general term applied to fresh cottage cheese, although there are regional farmer cheeses of firmer textures.

goat. Called *chevre* in France, this is a fresh, sourish cheese made from goat milk by a few small producers around the United States, including California, Iowa, New Jersey, and Pennsylvania.

Gold'N'Rich. A semisoft loaf developed from Port Salut cheese at Elgin, Illinois.

Gorgonzola. A crumbly, blue-veined cheese of Italian origin (named after a town in Piedmont), Gorgonzola is injected with *Penicillium glaucum*. The American version must contain at least 50 percent milk fat.

Gouda. Named after a Dutch town, this is a firm cheese formed into a compressed sphere. It is similar to Edam and must contain not less than 46 percent fat solids.

Herkimer. An American Cheddar made in New York's Herkimer County.

Liederkranz. A strong, soft cheese developed by Emil Frey in 1892. (See LIEDERKRANZ.)

Limburger. A strong cheese of Belgian origins, it was made popular by German cheesemakers of the nineteenth century and served at beerhalls with pumpernickel bread, onions, and draughts of beer.

Longhorn. An American Cheddar.

Minnesota Slim. An orange, loose-textured cheese good for melting developed by the University of Minnesota. It was named at Minneapolis's Lund Market.

mozzarella. Of Italian origins, this fresh white cheese comes in two forms in America: a mild unsalted cheese made in Italian-American groceries and kept fresh in water, and a firmer, salted cheese made in factories and used primarily for putting on top of pizza. Both must have at least 45 percent milk fat.

Monterey Jack. A mild cheese that originated in Monterey, California, and resembles the cheeses made by the early Spanish friars in that territory. It is named after David Jacks, who first made the cheese right after the Gold Rush years. Today it is an essential ingredient in much Mexican-American food.

Muenster. Of Alsatian origins, this is a cheese developed by the monks of medieval monasteries (the name is related to the Latin, *monasterium*).

In America the name is spelled "Muenster" or "Munster," and must contain not less than 50 percent milk fat.

New York. A well-aged Cheddar produced in New York.

Nuworld. A white-mold cheese developed by the universities of Wisconsin and Minnesota after the Second World War. It must contain at least 50 percent milk fat.

Parmesan. This cheese, which in Italy is called *"parmigiano,"* takes its name from the city of Parma. It is both an eating and a grating cheese, although in America it is primarily a grating cheese and can contain no less than 32 percent milk fat. It is sometimes called "reggiano," after the Italian town of Reggio.

pecorino. Although in Italy this is made from sheep's milk (the name derives from the Italian, *pecora,* "sheep"), in America it is a cow's-milk grating cheese, quite firm and sharp.

pineapple. A pineapple-shaped cheese said to have been developed in 1845 by Lewis M. Norton of Litchfield, Connecticut, who by hanging his Cheddars in a net gave them the characteristic shape. A variety of "pine apple" cheese was mentioned in print in 1830.

process. A product made from melting various kinds of cheeses with emulsifiers, acids, flavorings, and colorings to produce a smooth consistency. A process cheese food contains less real cheese than process cheese spread, whereas process cheese spread has more moisture and less butterfat than cheese.

ricotta. A fresh, moist white cheese originating in Italy, where its name means "recooked." Ricotta is similar to cottage cheese in the United States and most often used in making lasagna.

romano. A hard grating cheese whose name derives from the Italian city of Rome. American versions are salty and used to grate on spaghetti and other Italian pasta dishes.

Swiss. This is a generic term for all imitations of the original Swiss Emmenthaler, and the words *Imported Swiss* on a label mean only that the cheese is of this type and not necessarily that it is from Switzerland. Swiss cheese made in America is aged about four months, has holes, and originated in the work of Wisconsin's Adam Blumer about 1850.

Teleme Jack. A good melting cheese not associated with the brine-cured cheeses of Rumania of the same name. According to Evan Jones's *World of Cheese* (1979), "this California product is labeled variously as 'Teleme,' 'Cream Jack,' or 'High Moisture Jack,' and is said to have been originated about 1922 by makers of Monterey Jack who had immigrated from Greece and applied the Middle Eastern word to their new cheese." It may have somewhat more moisture content than regular Monterey Jack.

Tillamook. An American Cheddar made in Oregon's Tillamook County.

Trappist. A generic term for cheese made by monks of the Trappist order. A form of this cheese is made by Trappists near Gethsemane, Kentucky.

cheesecake. A dessert cake or pie made with cream, cottage, or ricotta cheese. Various forms of cheesecake have been popular for centuries; the first mention of such a dessert was in 1440, and recipes for the dish can be found in cookbooks throughout the eighteenth and nineteenth century.

American cheesecakes in the present century are primarily of two ethnic kinds—Jewish cheesecake, with a smooth, cream cheese filling; and Italian cheesecake, with a ricotta cheese filling. Both may have a pastry or graham cracker crust, originated in the immigrant neighborhoods of New York at the turn of the century, and have since become standard items in steak houses across the country, with the preferred nod given to the Jewish variety, which is often called (outside New York) "New York cheesecake." Occasionally a French pastry maker in the United States will advertise French cheesecake, but this usually refers to the Jewish variety.

The following recipe for Jewish cheesecake is the one made famous at Lindy's restaurant in New York City.

LINDY'S CHEESECAKE:
Combine 1 cup flour, 1/4 cup sugar, 1 tsp. grated lemon rind, and a dash of vanilla. Make a well in the center, add 1 egg yolk and 1/4 lb. softened butter, adding water if necessary to make a pliable dough. Wrap in waxed paper and chill 1 hr. Meanwhile, combine in an electric mixer 2 1/2 lb. cream cheese, 1 3/4 cups sugar, 3 tbs. flour, and 1 1/2 tsp. each of grated orange and lemon rind. Add 5 whole eggs and 2 egg yolks, 1/4 tsp. vanilla, beat well, add 1/4 cup heavy cream, and blend thoroughly. Butter the sides and bottom of a 9-in. springform pan. Roll out one-third of the dough to a 1/8-in. thickness and mold to pan's bottom. Bake at 400° for 15 min., till lightly browned, then cool. Place the top of the pan over the base, roll remaining dough to 1/8-in. thickness, cut into strips and press into pan to line the sides completely. Pour in cheese mixture, bake for 10 min. at 550°, reduce heat to 200°, and continue to bake for 1 hr.

ITALIAN CHEESECAKE:
Combine 2 cups flour sifted with 1/2 tsp. salt, cut in 1 cup butter or lard till coarse and crumbly. Make a well and add 2 beaten egg yolks and 1–2 tbs. cold water. Make a pliable pastry dough and roll into a thickness of about 1/8 in. Place in buttered pan, trim edges, set aside. Beat till light in color 4 eggs, gradually adding 1 cup sugar. Combine 3 cups ricotta cheese, 1/4 cup flour, 2 tsp. candied fruit (if desired), 2 tbs. each of grated orange and lemon rind, 1 tbs. vanilla extract, and 1/8 tsp. salt. Beat in egg mixture till smooth, pour into pastry, bake for about 1 hr. at 350°. Cool before serving. If desired, dust with 2 tbs. confectioners' sugar.

Chenin blanc. A white Vinifera grape that makes a spicy wine that is sometimes slightly sweet. It is an important grape of France's Loire Valley and has been used by high-volume California wineries. According to Leon D. Adams in his *Wines of America* (second edition, revised, 1978):

Before Prohibition, California vineyardists grew a luscious white grape they called "White Zinfandel." After Repeal, when varietal labels were first becoming popular, they learned that one of the names of the grape in France is Pineau Blanc de la Loire, so they began selling its dry wine as "White Pinot." In 1955, the Mondavi brothers of the Charles Krug winery [in the Napa Valley] made a semi-dry version of the wine and introduced it under the grape's French name, Chenin Blanc.

Most Chenin blanc is grown in California's Central Valley.

cherry. Any of a variety of trees of the genus *Prunus* (especially *P. avium,* the sweet cherry) bearing small, red berries that are eaten raw, baked in pies, made into relishes, ice creams, cordials, and brandies, and used as flavorings. The word is from the Greek, *kerasos,* and in Middle English became *chery.*

The cherry originated in Asia but was widely dispersed in Europe and North America in prehistoric times. European colonists found wild cherries in America and cultivated them, also crossbreeding them with European varieties.

One of the enduring, though wholly apocryphal, stories of American folklore involves a cherry tree and the "Father of Our Country," George Washington, as a young boy. As told by Parson Mason Weems in the 1806 edition of his *Life of George Washington* (1800), the boy chopped down the tree with his hatchet but, because of his ingrained honesty, admitted the fact to his father, saying, "I cannot tell a lie."

The United States is today the leading producer of cherries, with 85 percent of the country's crop grown in Michigan, California, Oregon, and Washington. The total crop breaks down as follows: 44 percent is canned, 35 percent is sold fresh, 20 percent is dried, and 1 percent is frozen. The leading variety is the Bing cherry, developed in 1875 by S. Lewelling of Milwaukie, Oregon, but called "Bing" only as of 1925. Other leading varieties are the Lambert and the Napoleon (or the Royal Ann).

chervil *(Anthriscus cerefolium).* An aromatic plant used in soups and salads. It originated in Russia, and the name is from the Greek, *khairephullon,* becoming in Middle English *cherville.* The herb is raised to some extent in the northeastern United States.

chestnut. Any of a variety of trees in the genus *Castanea* that bear a sweet nut that is eaten roasted, boiled, in stuffing, or as a flavoring. The name is from the Greek, *kastenea,* which in Middle English became *chesten.*

The first colonists in North America found the land covered with sturdy, tall American chestnut trees *(C. dentata)* whose nuts were eaten by the Indians, but the Europeans also brought their own varieties with them. In 1904 Far East varieties were planted on Long Island, New York, carrying a chestnut blight *(Endothia parasitica)* that virtually wiped out the native chestnut trees over the next three decades.

Most chestnuts are still imported from Europe, especially the Spanish chestnut or European chestnut *(C. sativa)* and the Chinese chestnut *(C. mollissima),* this last now grown in the United States.

The horse chestnut *(Aesculus hippocastenum)* is almost never eaten because of the work required to make it edible; the water chestnut *(Trapa natans)* is not related to the true chestnut.

chewing gum. A sweet, flavored chewable substance made from chicle, enjoyed as an idle snack. The word *gum* is from Middle English, *gumme.*

Americans had long chewed gum resins from trees, as they had seen the Indians do. Spruce gum was particularly popular in the early eighteenth century. In the 1870s a chewing gum was created from chicle (from the Nahautl, *chictli*), a gummy juice of the tropical evergreen, by a Staten Island, New York, inventor named Thomas Adams, who had observed the exiled Mexican General Santa Ana chewing the substance. As Stuart Berg Flexner tells it in *Listening to America* (1982):

> [Adams] mixed [the chicle] with hot water, rolled it into balls and persuaded a Hoboken, New Jersey, druggist to sell his chewable chicle balls at one cent each, and had another son, Thomas Adams, Jr., a traveling salesman, sell it all the way to the Mississippi. Later Adams, Sr., packaged his gum as "Adams' New York Gum —Snapping and Stretching." Since chicle will also carry a flavor, Adams next introduced the first flavored gum, flavored with sassafras; when that failed he introduced the very successful licorice-flavored *Black Jack.*

Peppermint gum came along in the 1880s. It was introduced by William White, whose Yucatan brand was the first chewing gum to contain corn syrup, and by the turn of the century New Yorkers were buying their chewing gum from vending machines, or gumball machines, located at train platforms.

Flexner goes on to note the contribution of soap salesman William Wrigley, Jr., who became the largest chewing-gum producer in the world with brands such as Spearmint, Juicy Fruit, and Doublemint. Bubble gum, which was more elastic and easy to blow into large bubbles, was the creation of Frank Fleer, whose Double Bubble was a great success in the 1930s. Fleer's brother, Henry, invented Chiclets, which were candy-coated gum pieces, at the turn of the century.

In 1969 the first sugarless gum was marketed for those watching their calories, and today there are a wide variety of flavored gums, including some with liquid centers. One of the great pastimes of American children is the trading of bubble gum cards, photos of baseball, football, and movie or television heroes printed on thin cardboard and packed with a sheet of bubble gum. This marketing ploy, which began with cigarette packs in the 1880s, had the effect of selling enormous amounts of gum that was never eaten; Topp's chewing gum cards totalled a quarter of a billion by the end of the 1970s.

Chicago. A slang term for a pineapple, or, as in "Chicago sundae," a sundae made with pineapple. The term refers to the city of Chicago, Illinois, and dates from the 1920s, when the gangsters of that city used hand grenades called "pineapples" as weapons in their intraregional disputes.

chicken *(Gallus domesticus)*. A common name for the domestic fowl that is raised throughout the world as a food and cooked in every conceivable way, except as a dessert. The word is from the Old English, *cīcen*.

The domesticated chicken first appeared about 2000 B.C. in India, bred from the wild red jungle fowl *(G. gallus)*. Although this variety began appearing on European tables about five hundred years later, chickens were not a common dish, and the heartfelt wish of France's Henry IV (1553–1610) on his coronation in 1589 was that "there would not be a peasant so poor in all my realm who would not have a chicken in his pot every Sunday." The tradition of eating chicken on Sunday continued well into the twentieth century, for the fowl was not as cheap a food as it now is, though the colonists brought these easily transportable birds to America very early (the first were brought by Columbus in 1493) and no part of the bird was wasted in the kitchen. In the South chickens were often fried in lard and this dish has become known as SOUTHERN FRIED CHICKEN; in New England chicken POTPIES were popular in the nineteenth century, as was chicken salad by the 1850s.

In Hawaii European travelers found a domesticated fowl called the *"moa,"* a descendant of a wild jungle fowl probably brought from Malaysia. In 1826, however, the ship *Wellington* docked in Hawaii, taking on fresh water and dumping its old water (remaining from its voyage from Mexico), which contained mosquito larvae carrying a bird pox or "bumblefoot" that immediately infected the Hawaiian chickens and devastated the birds of the island.

In the nineteenth century poultry breeding in America resulted in some excellent stocks that have continued to be commercially important. The Plymouth Rock was noted in 1849 to have been "recently formed"; the Wyandotte received its name from a Mr. Houdette of Worcester, Massachusetts, in 1883. The state bird of Rhode Island, the Rhode Island Red, was developed in 1902 by William Tripp of Little Compton, Rhode Island, by crossing a Brown Leghorn with a Malay hen. The Rhode Island White was developed in 1926.

In the United States federal law sets the following standards for chickens: a broiler, almost always raised from crossbreeds like the White Plymouth Rock, may weigh up to two-and-a-half pounds and be between four to six weeks old; a fryer (also sometimes called a "spring chicken") may weigh up to three-and-a-half pounds; a roaster may be up to five pounds but less than eight months old; a capon ranges up to ten pounds. Above this weight or an age of a year-and-a-half, the bird is called a "hen," "boiling fowl," or "stewing chicken."

The Cornish game hen, developed from a Plymouth Rock and a Cornish game cock, weighs between one and two pounds. A squab chicken is not related to a true squab, but instead is a very small chicken weighing between three-quarters and one-and-a-half pounds.

The Department of Agriculture grades for chickens include grades A, B, and C, though grade A is the most readily found in groceries.

Chickens are sold "fresh-killed," which may mean they have been shipped at about the standard 35° refrigeration or that they have been shipped in shaved ice (called an "ice pack") or at 30° ("deep-chilled"), which is about two degrees above the point at which chickens will freeze. Birds are also shipped frozen, canned, or freeze-dried.

Americans eat about thirty-three pounds of chicken a year (and about 270 eggs), preparing the fowl in many ways, including such standard dishes as CHICKEN À LA KING, CHICKEN TETRAZZINI, CHICKEN CACCIATORE, COUNTRY CAPTAIN, BARBECUE chicken, and many others.

chicken à la king. A dish of chicken with a cream sauce garnished with pimientos. There are several stories as to its origins, all dating from the last quarter of the nineteenth century. One credits its creation to New York's Brighton Beach Hotel, where chef George Greenwald supposedly made it for the proprietors, Mr. and Mrs. E. Clark King III. Another claim, by chef Charles Ranhofer of the original Delmonico's restaurant in New York City, suggests that Foxhall P. Keene, son of Wall Street broker and sportsman James R. Keene, was the originator of the dish at Delmonico's in the 1880s. A third story credits James R. Keene himself as the namesake and the time and place of origin as Claridge's restaurant in London after Keene's horse won the 1881 Grand Prix. However the dish got its name, first mentioned in print in 1912, it became a standard luncheon item in the decades that followed, often served from a chafing dish or with rice or on a pastry shell. The recipe below is from Nika Hazelton's *American Home Cooking* (1980):

> In a saucepan stir 4 tbs. flour in 4 tbs. butter and cook for about 2 min. Add 2 cups chicken broth and 2 cups light cream, thicken, and remove from heat. In a skillet sauté 1 tbs. minced onion, 1/4 lb. sliced mushrooms, and 1 sweet green pepper cut in strips. Add 1/2 cup chopped pimiento and 3 cups diced cooked chicken. Season with salt and pepper. Spoon a little sauce into 2 beaten egg yolks, then stir eggs and all the sauce into chicken mixture, and cook over low heat for 1 min. Remove from heat and stir in 1/2 cup sherry and 1/2 cup blanched toasted almonds. Serve on toast, rice, or pastry shells. Serves 6.

chicken bog. North Carolina slang for a chicken PILAU. A bog is a section of wet, soggy ground, and the chicken in this dish would be mixed with wet, soggy rice.

chickenburger. A patty of ground chicken broiled, grilled, or fried to resemble a BEEF hamburger. The chickenburger followed the latter sometime in the first quarter of this century.

> Grind 1 lb. chicken meat, mix with 2 tbs. chopped parsley, 1/2 cup bread crumbs, salt and pepper to taste. Form a patty about 1/2" thick, brush with butter, broil, grill or fry and serve with a mustard sauce or on a hamburger roll.

chicken cacciatore. A dish of chicken cooked with mushrooms and, often, tomato sauce. It is an Italian-American specialty whose name means chicken "hunter's style," in the assumption that it is a hearty dish made with forest mushrooms. There is, however, no traditional dish by this name in Italy, and it only became a standard Italian-American restaurant item after World War II.

> Cut a chicken in several pieces, dredge in flour, and sauté in 3 tbs. olive oil. Add 1 lb. sliced mushrooms and cook together. Add 1 sliced onion, then 1 1/2 cups seasoned tomato sauce, and salt and pepper. Cook, covered, till chicken is tender.

chicken-fried steak. A beefsteak that has been tenderized by pounding, coated with flour or batter, and fried crisp. It is a specialty of the South, Southwest, and Midwest. Usually a lesser cut of beef is used. The name seems to refer to the style of cooking, which is much the same as for SOUTHERN FRIED CHICKEN. Chicken-fried steak is of rather recent origins, probably the 1950s, for it is rarely mentioned in any American cookbooks before the 1970s.

> Pound till thin and tender 4 slices of beefsteak. Dip in a mixture of 1 beaten egg and 1 cup milk, dredge in flour seasoned with salt and pepper, and fry in shortening or other oil till crisp and well done. Pour off the oil. Sprinkle 1 tbs. flour into skillet and cook with pan drippings till browned. Add 1 cup milk and bring to boil, then lower to simmer and cook till thickened. Pour gravy over steaks.

chicken-in-the-shell. A dish of chicken in a creamed mushroom sauce served in a cockleshell; well known in San Francisco at the turn of the present century, it was first served at the Iron House on Montgomery Street.

> In a pot cover with water 1 chicken, 1 onion, 1 bay leaf, 2 cloves, a blade of mace, and 6 peppercorns. Bring to boil, then simmer for 1 hr. Cool, remove from kettle, and dice the chicken. Mix 1 tbs. butter, 1 tsp. flour, and 1/2 pt. cream in a skillet. Add salt and white pepper, stir till sauce comes to a boil, then add sliced truffle, 2 doz. chopped mushrooms, and then the chicken meat. Let the mixture heat through, add the yolks of 2 eggs, cook for 2 min., stir in 1/2 cup sherry, and serve in cockleshells.

chicken tetrazzini. A dish of chicken (though turkey is often substituted) in a cream sauce, served over spaghetti and browned in the oven with bread crumbs and Parmesan cheese. It is named after the Italian coloratura soprano opera singer Luisa Tetrazzini (1871–1940), who was extremely popular in the United States after 1908. It is not known when or where the dish was created (some say it was in San Francisco), and Tetrazzini herself does not mention the dish in her autobiography, *My Life of Song* (1921). The rather stout singer did write of her eating habits, however: "I eat the plainest food always, and naturally, being Italian, I prefer the foods of my native land. . . . I allow the tempting pastry, the rich and over-spiced patty, to pass by untouched, consoling myself with fruit and fresh vegetables." The dish was first mentioned in print in 1951.

> In a saucepan make a roux of 4 tbs. flour and 4 tbs. butter, add 2 cups heavy cream and 1 cup chicken broth, stir, and cook till thickened. Remove from heat, blend in

3 cups cooked chicken meat cut into small pieces. In a buttered dish place 3/4 lb. cooked buttered spaghetti, pour chicken mixture on top, spread with bread crumbs and Parmesan cheese, and brown in oven or under broiler. Serves 6.

chick-pea *(Cicer arietinum).* A hard seed of a plant indigenous to the Mediterranean and central Asia. The chick-pea is not actually a pea, though both are of the same subfamily, *Papilionoideae.* The name for the seed comes from the Latin, *cicer,* but in the United States, where it was introduced by Hispanics, it is called a "garbanzo" (a word that worked its way from Latin, *ervum,* "bitter vetch," through Old Spanish, *arvanço,* to Spanish, *garbanzo*). The word was first printed in 1548. Chick-peas are usually soaked for several hours, roasted, and eaten as a snack or put into stews and salads.

chicory. American nomenclature is very confusing for this salad green called *Cichorium intybus,* with its curly leaves and bright blue flowers (it is sometimes called "blue sailors"). Chicory is quite bitter and is often mixed with other salad greens.

The same plant's roots are dried and ground into a granular powder, often referred to as "succory," that resembles coffee and is used as an additive to or substitute for real coffee in Creole and Cajun cooking, a legacy of the French influence on these cuisines.

The confusion begins with what Americans call "endive," which is a form of *Cichorium intybus* cultivated to produce silky white leaves for salad and which is often referred to as "Belgian endive" or "witloof." The Belgians, however, call that *"chicon."*

True endive is another variety, called *Cichorium endivia,* with curly, succulent leaves, more commonly known in America as "escarole."

chicory coffee. Adding chicory to coffee began in New Orleans during the food-scarce Civil War. Chicory adds a bitterness to coffee, which may be moderated with milk to make café au lait, although morning coffee tends to be black, café noir. In New Orleans the coffee and chicory can be bought already blended into light or dark mixtures, and it is meant to be made by a drip method. Most of this chicory is imported from Spain. There is an old saying among Catholic Creoles in New Orleans to the effect that "Good coffee and the Protestant religion can seldom if ever be found together." And the same people are fond of the description of chicory coffee as being "Black as the devil, / Strong as death, / Sweet as love, / Hot as Hell!"

chiffon. A very light, sweet, fluffy filling for a pie, cake, or pudding. The word is from the French, meaning "rag," and ultimately the Middle English word *chip,* as *chiffon* also refers to pieces of sheer, delicate ribbon or fabric for women's clothing.

Chiffon pie is first mentioned in American print in 1929 as a "chiffon pumpkin pie" in the Beverly Hills Women's Club's *Fashions in Foods.* The 1931 edition of Irma S. Rombauer's *Joy of Cooking* gives a recipe for lemon chiffon, and the *Better Homes and Gardens Heritage Cook Book* (1975) says that "chiffon cake was invented by a professional baker and introduced in May, 1948. Made with cooking oil instead of solid shortening and beaten—not creamed—this light cake was the first new cake to have been developed in one hundred years of baking."

PUMPKIN CHIFFON PIE:
Soften 1 tbs. gelatin in 1/4 cup cold water. Combine 1 1/2 cups cooked pumpkin, 1/2 cup sugar, 1 tsp. salt, 1 tsp. cinnamon, 1/2 tsp. ginger, 2 beaten egg yolks, and 1 cup milk. Cook in double boiler 5 min., stirring constantly, then add gelatin and stir till dissolved. Chill till slightly thickened. Beat 1/4 cup sugar into 2 stiffly beaten egg whites, fold into pumpkin mixture, pour into baked pie crust. Chill till firm.

PINEAPPLE CHIFFON CAKE:
Sift together 2 1/4 cups cake flour, 1 1/4 cups sugar, 1 tbs. baking powder, and 1 tsp. salt. Blend in separately 1/2 cup vegetable oil, 5 egg yolks, and 3/4 cup unsweetened pineapple juice. Beat 8 egg whites till stiff, then fold into mixture. Bake in ungreased tube pan at 350° for 1 hr. Invert, cool, split into 2 layers, ice with topping of 2 cups whipped cream blended with 20 oz. crushed pineapple.

child care food program. A federally sponsored program to provide cash and commodities for meals served at day-care centers, nursery schools, and homes for orphans.

chiles rellenos. A Mexican dish of fried stuffed chili peppers (the term means "stuffed chilies"), served throughout the Southwest and in Mexican-American restaurants.

Peel 12 charred chilies, leaving on the stems, and slit them open to remove seeds. Stuff the pockets with 8 oz. of Monterey Jack cheese cut in thin strips. Sift together 1 cup flour, 1 tsp. baking powder, 1/2 tsp. salt, 3/4 cup cornmeal, and add 1 cup milk blended with 2 beaten eggs. Dip the chilies in the batter and cook in hot oil till golden. Drain and serve with guacamole, onions, and other Mexican condiments. Serves 4.

chili *(Capsicum frutescens).* Also, "chilli," "chile," and "chili pepper." A very hot red, green, or yellow fruit of a New World plant, or the powder made from this fruit. The word is from the Nahuatl, *chilli,* and came into English in the mid-seventeenth century via the Spanish. Christopher Columbus found that the Indians of the New World had cultivated the plant and used the fruit as a principal seasoning for their food. In fact, the Indians of Central and South America had done so for several thousand years before Christ. The chili was brought back to Spain as early as 1514, where it was called *"ají,"* but a German botanist named Leonhard Fuchs, believing Columbus had landed in India, called the chilis "Calcutta peppers" despite the fact that chilis were not true peppers (nor did they reach India until 1611). Nevertheless the English and Americans have continued to refer to the plant as the "chili pepper."

The chili was also pounded into condiments and powders that took names like CAYENNE, TABASCO, and, in Hungary, paprika, and throughout the Caribbean and Gulf states such seasonings are used to give regional cookery its distinctive tastes. In Texas it forms the basis of CHILI CON CARNE, and it is a prime ingredient in TEX-MEX and Mexican-American cuisine, including stuffed chilis called CHILES RELLENOS.

The main varieties of chili used in the United States include the ancho (dark red, mild, sold dried), the jalapeño (green, about two inches long, hot), the serrano (green, small, hot), the Anaheim or Californian (green, long, fairly mild), the Fresno (small, cone-shaped, fairly hot), and others.

There are about two hundred varieties of chili in the world, and the major United States growing regions are New Mexico, California, Texas, and Arizona, where several hybrids have been created.

chili con carne. Also, "chile con carne," or, simply, "chili." A dish of well-seasoned and well-cooked beef with chili peppers. Chili con carne is one of the most famous dishes of Texas, although wide variations are known throughout the United States.

The term is Spanish-American for "chili pepper with meat" (see CHILI) and first appeared in a book by S. Compton Smith entitled *Chile Con Carne, or The Camp and the Field* (1857). It came into more common usage only at the end of the century. As Waverly Root and Richard de Rochemont point out in *Eating in America* (1976), "One Mexican dictionary even goes so far as to define chili con carne as 'a detestable food with a false Mexican title which is sold in the United States from Texas to New York,' " and until recently many San Antonians regarded the dish with disdain. In 1902 a German immigrant in New Braunfels, Texas, created a chili powder that helped popularize the dish across the country.

Although it originated in Texas and has become a staple of TEX-MEX cooking, chili con carne is found throughout the United States in diverse forms. Some recipes call for chopped chili peppers, others for chili powder. In New Mexico one may find LAMB or MUTTON used instead of beef, while Cincinnati chili and many other northern versions contain red kidney beans, a variant that Texas purists would consider tantamount to a criminal act. In chili's native state there are several quasi-organizations devoted to the glories of the dish, and every year there are several chili contests held. The most famous is the Annual World Championship Chili Cookoff in Terlingua, Texas, sponsored by the Chili Appreciation Society International and begun in 1967 as a promotional aid for restaurateur Frank X. Tolbert's book, *A Bowl of Red: The Natural History of Chili with Recipes.* (*Bowl of red* is a common term for chili con carne in Texas.) The championship is held on the first Saturday of November, with participants from all over the world. Although the hotness of the chili is a virtue, it is the blend of flavors that ultimately decides a champion recipe.

Chili con carne has even become a partisan issue in the United States Senate. In 1974 Arizona Senator Barry Goldwater challenged Texas Senator John

Tower on the floor of the Senate to a cooking contest with the words, "A Texan does not know chili from the leavings in a corral." The following spring a panel of five "experts" judged chilis made by the two legislators and Goldwater's came out the best of the lot.

Today chili con carne is sold in restaurants called "chili parlors." It is also available in cans. The Department of Agriculture stipulates that products labelled "chili con carne" must contain at least 40 percent meat; "chili con carne with beans" at least 25 percent meat; "chili hot dog with meat" 40 percent meat; "chili mac" (with macaroni and beans) at least 16 percent; and "chili sauce with meat" at least 6 percent. In the Old West cowboys would often throw bull's eyes into their chili. There is one company that markets its chili in degrees of hotness: "One-," "Two-," and "Three-Alarm" chili.

CHILI CON CARNE:
Cut up 4 lb. beef chuck into cubes and brown in hot oil, then remove and drain off excess grease. Brown in oil 1 1/2 cups chopped onions with 6 green or red chili peppers, then add to meat and mix well. Add 3 tbs. cumin, 2 tbs. oregano, 1–2 bay leaves, 3/4 cup hot paprika, 1 1/2 tbs. chili powder, 3 tbs. chopped coriander (cilantro), 5 cloves chopped garlic, 1/4 tsp. ground pepper, 1 tsp. salt, and 1 cup water. Simmer till meat is tender, add a little water if necessary, adjust salt, pepper, and hot seasonings to taste. Serves 10.

BARRY GOLDWATER'S CHILI WITH BEANS:
Brown 1 lb. coarsely ground beef and drain off excess grease. Add 1 lb. pinto beans (if dried, soak overnight in water), one 6-oz. can tomato puree, and 2 cups chopped onion. Into 1/2 cup water stir 3 tbs. chili powder, 1 tbs. cumin, and 1/2 tsp. salt. Bring to a boil, add meat, reduce heat, and simmer till meat is tender.

Chili con carne is traditionally served with rice and beer.

chili con queso. An appetizer dip made of chili peppers and cheese (the Spanish term means "chili pepper with cheese"), it is a staple of Tex-Mex and Mexican-American menus.

Melt 1 cup Monterey Jack cheese with 3/4 cup sharp Cheddar in a double boiler. Add 1/4 cup heavy cream and blend with 1 chopped tomato, 1 chopped onion, 1 chopped charred chili pepper, and 1 clove minced garlic. Serve with corn chips.

chili queen. A Texas slang term for a Mexican in the downtown section of San Antonio who sold tamales from quickly set up stands. These stands were prohibited for sanitary reasons by Mayor Charles Kennon Quin in 1937. According to Green Peyton in his book, *San Antonio: City in the Sun* (1946), "The singers still gather around your car and serenade you. But without the chili queens to exchange the anatomical insults with them in sonorous Spanish, they seem a bit lackadaisical and depressed."

chimichanga. A deep-fried wheat tortilla stuffed with minced beef, potatoes, and seasonings. The term may be a nonsense word—a Mexican version of *whatchamacallit* or *thingamajig*. It is reputed to have been first coined in the

1950s in Tucson, Arizona. Diana Kennedy, in her *Cuisines of Mexico* (1972), notes, however, that fried burritos in Mexico are called by the similar name *chivichangas.*

> Coarsely chop 2 lb. chuck steak, add 2 diced potatoes, 6 green or red chilis that have been charred, peeled, and deseeded, 1 onion, 3 cloves garlic, 1 tsp. oregano, salt, pepper, and enough water to cover. Boil, then lower heat and simmer for 1 hr., till meat is tender and texture is stew-like. Place the mixture in 12 wheat tortillas and fold into a packet, then fry in hot oil till golden brown. Drain, serve with shredded lettuce, sour cream, guacamole, and chili sauce. Serves 6.

chipped beef. Dried beef. The term derives from early English usage of the word *chip,* "to strip or pare away a crust." The dish has been known at least since 1819.

Dried beef was a staple of the early American diet, and even much later, when more desirable forms of beef were readily available, chipped beef in a flour-based gravy continued to be a popular luncheon or buffet item.

> CREAMED CHIPPED BEEF:
> Shred 1/2 lb. dried beef into strips. Melt 1/2 cup butter in pan and brown meat. Add salt and pepper and sprinkle with 6 tbs. flour. Add 2 pt. milk gradually, stirring constantly till blended, and cook till it boils. Lower heat and simmer till thickened. Serves 12.

chitterlings. Also, "chitlins." A hog's innards, which are either fried or boiled, most popular in the South and as soul food in the Northern cities. Because of their association with lower-class cooking, chitterlings were rarely found in American cookbooks until recently. Most black Americans pronounce the word "chitlins," but the origins of the word are in Middle English (*chiterling,* "body organs"), German (*kutteln,* same meaning), and Danish (*kuit,* "fish roe").

> Chitterlings should be well washed so as to remove any residue. For 5 lb. of chitterlings, add 1 large chopped onion, 1 tsp. salt, 1/4 cup vinegar, and about 1/2 cup water, simmer for 2 hours, stirring occasionally, then cut into smaller pieces and continue cooking for two more hours. Correct seasoning and add water as necessary.
> To fry chitterlings repeat steps above, but do not cut up into small pieces. Make a batter from 2/3 cup milk, 1 beaten egg, 2/3 cup flour, 1/2 tsp. baking powder, 1/4 tsp. salt, and stir until smooth. Dip chitterlings in batter and fry in hot fat.

choc. An inferior beer originally made by the Choctaw Indians. The term came to mean any such low-grade beer.

chocolate. Both chocolate and cocoa come from the tropical bean known as *Theobroma cacao.* The use of chocolate in everything from hot and cold drinks to candy making to pastries and other confections makes it one of the world's most versatile flavorings. The word *chocolate* comes via the Spanish from the Aztec Indian word *xocolatl,* meaning "bitter water." The Aztecs drank the pounded beans with spices but no sugar and believed that the bean was brought from the heavens by the gods (indeed, *Theobroma* means "food of the gods"). So valuable were these beans that a hundred of them were worth the price of a slave in Mexico, where they were used as currency.

Some authorities say Columbus brought cocoa beans to Spain, but they were of little interest until Hernando Cortés returned with the beans and some Aztec hints on how to process them. Cortés first tasted chocolate at a ceremony with the Aztec king Montezuma, who reputedly believed in the drink's aphrodisiac powers and consumed up to fifty large cups a day. The Aztecs also enjoyed chocolate with red peppers and chilled with snow. The Spanish found their bitterness off-putting, but, with the addition of sugar, a chocolate drink was prepared that became immediately popular throughout Europe. The term *chocolate* appears in print in England as of 1604, and by 1657 a Frenchman had opened a "cocoa house" in London that sold prepared chocolate at the very high price of ten to fifteen shillings per pound.

Chocolate became the fashionable drink in Europe in the eighteenth century, and was first manufactured in America in 1765 at Milton Lower Mills, near Dorchester, Massachusetts, with beans from the West Indies. By 1780 John Hanan had opened the first chocolate factory under the financing of Dr. James Baker (there is still a product called "Baker's Chocolate" made by General Foods, Inc.). Cocoa powder was first produced in 1828.

But hard chocolate, of the consistency of candy, was still unknown at the beginning of the nineteenth century, while the liquid form was promoted mainly as a restorative. (Thomas Jefferson believed chocolate superior to tea or coffee in this regard).

On the basis of a Mexican Indian's process of using sifted wood ashes to refine the raw cocoa into a more digestible form, Holland's C. J. Van Houten found a way to alkalize chocolate and make it darker through a process, which also released cocoa butter, that came to be called "dutching." When combined with sugar and chocolate, the butter enabled processors to make a hardened candy bar, and by 1842 the Cadbury Company of England was selling such confections and Americans were eating "chocolate creams" (candies with sugar-cream centers) by the 1860s.

In 1875 a Swiss chocolate manufacturer named Daniel Peter combined his product with sweetened condensed milk, recently discovered by Henri Nestlé, a Swiss chemist, thereby creating the first milk chocolate, which became extremely popular in Europe and the United States. The Nestlé Food Company opened facilities in New York in 1905 to act as a sales agency for its products. But America's first mass-produced milk-chocolate candy was the Hershey Bar, manufactured in 1894 by Milton Snavely Hershey of Lancaster, Pennsylvania.

In the present century chocolate took powerful hold of the candy and confections market, and cocoa—a mixture of cocoa powder, sugar, and milk or water—became a popular wintertime beverage, especially with children.

After World War II powdered and sugared chocolate were processed so that they would dissolve in cold milk, and chocolate milk became a household word. Chocolate is also made into syrups, sodas, milk shakes, fudge, cookies, cakes, and every imaginable kind of dessert. Its association with Valentine's Day (February 14)—represented by giving chocolate hearts or boxes of gift-wrapped chocolate candies filled with sweet sugar creams, fruits, liqueurs, or nuts—was well promoted by the 1890s. Chocolate Easter bunnies and Easter eggs have made that feast a rather sweet one, and one may as well throw in chocolate Santas for Christmas. Commercial chocolate kisses (a large droplet of milk or other chocolate shaped something like an acorn cap), now made by the Hershey Company, were called "Wilbur Buds" when they were first introduced in 1893 by a manufacturer of that name (although there are recipes for kisses before then). Chocolate babies (once called NIGGER BABIES, in less enlightened times), tiny figures of babies molded in chocolate, have been known since the 1890s.

Within the last decade the world consumption of cacao beans has averaged 600,000 tons annually, most of it coming from Africa. The "chocolate belt" of countries producing the bean extends around the middle of the tropical regions of the earth, from places like Guatemala, Nicaragua, Panama, Costa Rica, Nigeria, Trinidad, and the Ivory Coast. The largest producer is Ghana, where the Forastero type of bean constitutes the staple of the world's consumption. The Maracaibo bean, from Venezuela, and the Puerto Cabello, also South American, are highly prized and are blended in the more expensive chocolates.

The production of chocolate begins with the picking of the pods with a "cacao hook." Each pod on the tree contains between twenty and forty beans, which are removed from the pods by hand and then left in the open air before fermenting in "sweating boxes," boxes with perforated slats that allow the beans to drip their juices. The beans are then dried, washed, and put in sacks for shipping. At the chocolate plants the beans are roasted in various ways to produce several different flavors that will be blended. The shells are removed by a machine, called a "cracker and fanner," that separates the nibs and shells and blows away the debris.

The beans are approximately 50 percent fat, called "cocoa butter," and 50 percent liquid, called "chocolate liquor." The former is expressed as a gold liquid, while the latter becomes a thick paste that, unsweetened, is turned into baking or cooking chocolate. Cocoa powder is made by melting the chocolate liquor and pressing out more of the cocoa butter. The remaining hard mass is then ground into a fine powder and sold, either as a flavoring or for making cocoa and hot chocolate.

To make sweet chocolate for candy and other confections, sugar and a little vanilla are mixed with the chocolate liquor. It is then processed to a smooth texture in the form of a paste, to which is added cocoa butter before being hardened by cooling. Milk chocolate is mixed from this sweetened chocolate and more cocoa butter, sugar, and milk and then processed to remove moisture and to give smoothness. Semisweet chocolate has a lower quantity of sugar than sweet chocolate.

In 1981, Americans consumed 9.3 pounds of chocolate per person per year, 96.7 percent of which was made in the United States. Most American chocolate is made with large amounts of cocoa powder and some lecithin emulsifier to reduce the required amount of cocoa butter.

chocolate velvet cake. A very rich, densely textured chocolate cake that originated at the Four Seasons restaurant in New York. It was the creation of the first pastry chef, Albert Kumin, in 1959. Since then chocolate velvet cake has become synonymous with very rich, thick cake with a fudgelike consistency. The recipe below is from the Four Seasons:

> Completely line a 1-qt. baking mold with a thin layer of sponge cake. Mix 3 egg yolks, 1 tbs. instant coffee, 1/4 cup Kirsch, 1/4 cup rum, 1/4 cup creme de cacao, and 1/3 cup firmly packed praline paste. Beat till smooth and add 6 tbs. cooled melted butter. In a double boiler melt 1 1/2 lb. semisweet chocolate and add to mixture. Beat 3 egg whites till soft peaks are formed, adding 1/4 cup confectioners' sugar. Continue beating till egg whites are very stiff. Fold egg whites and 2 cups unsweetened whipped cream into mixture, pour into mold, chill in refrigerator till firm, about 2 hr. Cover top with thin slice of sponge cake, loosen from mold, turn upside down, and ice with semisweet chocolate glaze made by melting 5 squares semisweet chocolate in double boiler, adding 1 cup boiling water, and blending till smooth.

chop suey. A Chinese-American dish of widely varying ingredients, but usually containing bamboo shoots, water chestnuts, bean sprouts, celery, soy sauce, and either pork or chicken. *Chop suey* first appeared in print in 1888, but must be older.

Chop suey was a mixture of vegetables and meat concocted by the Chinese cooks who fed the workers on the Pacific railroad lines in the middle of the last century. Although there is no such dish in China, the Mandarin words for chopped up odds and ends, *tsa sui,* would approximate the sound of "chop suey" as spoken by Western Americans.

Americanized Chinese dishes such as this and chow mein were served in Chinese restaurants to American customers, but rarely would a Chinese indulge in such a food. In his book *Bohemian San Francisco* (1914), Clarence E. Edwards noted that after the earthquake of 1906 "a number of places [in Chinatown] have been opened to cater to Americans, and on every hand one sees 'chop suey' signs and 'Chinese noodles.' It goes without saying that one seldom sees a Chinaman eating in the restaurants that are most attractive to Americans." "American chop suey" is a New England dish of ground beef, noodles, and tomato sauce.

> Slice 2 chicken breasts into thin strips, then sauté in 2 tbs. oil till lightly cooked. Add 1 cup sliced button mushrooms, 1 chopped green pepper, 1/2 cup sliced water chestnuts, 1 can Chinese vegetables, 1 chopped stalk of celery, 3 tbs. soy sauce, and 1/2 cup chicken broth. Bring to a boil, then simmer for 3 min. Blend 1 tbs. cornstarch

into 4 tbs. cold water, mix, then add to simmering chicken. When thickened remove from heat and serve over hot white rice.

chorizo. A spicy sausage found in Hispanic cooking from Spain to California. Called "chaurice" in Louisiana, chorizo is used in egg dishes and tortillas, as appetizers, or as part of a main dish. The word was first printed in 1846.

chow. A slang term, especially popular with American servicemen, for food served to them by the cook. It also referred to mealtime, although "chow time" was also heard. A "chowhound" was someone who was first in line for food. These were well-known terms by World War I, but the word *chow* goes back to the era when Chinese laborers worked on the Pacific railroads during the 1850s. The word may have been picked up by sailors from Pidgin English, which in turn got it from the Mandarin Chinese *ch'ao,* "to fry or cook."

chow-chow. A relish of pickles or other vegetables. The word may be from the Mandarin Chinese *cha,* "mixed," and dates from the 1840s, when Chinese laborers worked on the railroads of the American West.

> Mix together 1 qt. small cucumbers, 1 qt. large cucumbers, 1 qt. sliced green tomatoes, 1 qt. sliced onions, 1 qt. small onions, 1 qt. chopped cauliflower, and 4 chopped peppers. Cover with 1 cup salt in 4 qt. water. Let stand for 24 hr., then heat until scalded. Drain. Mix 1 cup flour, 1 1/2 cups sugar, 6 tbs. mustard, and 1 tsp. turmeric with 1 pint vinegar. Pour into 2 pt. vinegar and heat in double boiler till thickened. Add to vegetables and pack into clean jars and seal.

chowder. A seafood soup associated with New England, the most popular of which is clam chowder. The term may also describe a buttery, hearty soup made with corn, chicken, or other chunks or bits of food still evident in the blend.

The origins of the word *chowder* are somewhat obscure, but most authorities believe it derives from the French word for a large cauldron, *chaudière,* in which Breton sailors threw their catch to make a communal stew. This custom was carried to Newfoundland, Nova Scotia, and down to New England in the seventeenth and eighteenth centuries. In his booklet *Down East Chowder* (1982), John Thorne contends that evidence for such a derivation is very tenuous, noting that "the phrase *'faire la chaudière'* seems no longer to exist in Brittany, while *chaudrée,* another touted source of origin, resembles chowder no more and no less than any fish soup resembles another. (The French word for cauldron, by the way, is *'chaudron,'* not *'chaudière'*—that latter word has more the meaning of a steam boiler.)"

Although the *Oxford English Dictionary* suggests *chaudière* as the etymological link, it also lists *chowder* as a dialectical variation of an old Cornwall or Devonshire word, *jowter,* for a fish peddlar. Certainly fish stews existed in almost every sea-bound country in the world, and the distinction between these and the earliest chowders of New England are a matter of interpretation.

The first New England "chowders" have been known at least since the 1730s, and were first mentioned in print by a New England diarist in 1732, by which time salt pork seemed to have already attained the status of a prerequisite ingredient. By 1751 the *Boston Evening Post* had published a recipe containing onions, salt pork, sweet marjoram, savory, thyme, biscuit, and fish, to which was added a bottle of red wine. This and other early chowders were undoubtedly more like a pudding or thick stew than a soup, a perfect consistency for onboard consumption, especially since, as Thorne notes, "it uses a minimum of one of the most precious of shipboard supplies: water."

The first American cookbook to give a chowder recipe is Amelia Simmons's *American Cookery* (1800). It called for bass, salt pork, crackers, and a side dish of potatoes. Ketchup and flour were suggested to thicken the dish in early-nineteenth-century recipes, by which time New England chowders had become more like a soup. Although by 1836 clam chowder was known in Boston, where its associations are still strong, throughout the century chowder was less commonly a dish of clams than of fish, usually cod or haddock, and by the 1840s potatoes had become a traditional ingredient.

Chowder was a staple dish of New Englanders, and for sailors merely another way to make a constant diet of fish palatable. In *Moby-Dick* (1851) Herman Melville wrote of the Try Pots, a chowder house in Nantucket, where one might have a choice of either cod or clam chowder. Melville ordered the latter: "Oh! sweet friends, hearken to me. It was made of small juicy clams, scarcely bigger than hazel nuts, mixed with pounded ship biscuits, and salted pork cut up into little flakes! the whole enriched with butter, and plentifully seasoned with pepper and salt." Melville went on to describe the menu at the Try Pots—"Chowder for breakfast, and chowder for dinner, and chowder for supper, till you began to look for fish-bones coming through your clothes."

By the end of the century certain New England regions became known for their various interpretations of chowder—one might find cream in one spot, lobsters in others, no potatoes elsewhere—but most were by then a creamy white soup brimming with chopped fish or clams, crackers, and butter. In Rhode Island, however, cooks often added tomatoes to their chowder, a practice that brought down unremitting scorn from chowder fanciers in Massachusetts and Maine, who associated such a concoction with New York because the dish came to be called, for no discernible reason, "Manhattan clam chowder" sometime in the 1930s. By 1940 Eleanor Early in her *New England Sampler* decried this "terrible pink mixture (with tomatoes in it, and herbs) called Manhattan Clam Chowder, that is only a vegetable soup, and not to be confused with New England Clam Chowder, nor spoken of in the same breath. Tomatoes and clams have no more affinity than ice cream and horseradish." In her 1954 *New England Cookbook* she goes on to note that Rhode Islanders and Connecticut cooks believe Cape Cod milk chowder is fit "only for babies and sick people," to which Early replies, "Nonsense! Cape Cod is full of happy octogenarians." She nevertheless includes a recipe for tomato-laden Rhode Island clam chowder.

The issue of whether one should add tomato to chowder is merely a regional preference, for tomatoes fill the fish stews of many countries' kitchens, and neither Manhattanites nor Rhode Islanders are original or adamant on the matter.

Today chowders made with clams predominate, but fish chowders are also popular. Noting that in Oregon a "first-rate chowder is made with corn and fresh salmon," John Thorne recommends cod, haddock, whiting, flounder, cusk, hake, and halibut. The best clams for a chowder are traditionally the large quahogs.

CLAM CHOWDER:
Shell 3 doz. clams, remove tips and chop up coarsely. Peel and dice 5 potatoes. Fry 1/4 lb. salt pork with 2 diced onions till soft. Add potatoes to 1 qt. boiling water, then add pork and onions. Cook till tender. Scald and strain 1 1/2 cups clam liquid, then add to kettle. Add clams, bring to a boil, add 1 qt. milk, pepper to taste, and several common crackers. Serve when warm.

FISH CHOWDER:
Cook 3 diced onions in 2 tbs. salt pork till soft. In 2 cups water boil 4 diced potatoes till tender, add onions, 2 lb. cut-up fish, 1/2 lb. butter, salt, pepper, 1/4 tsp. savory, 1 can evaporated milk, and 3 cups milk. Heat but do not boil. Serves 6.

MANHATTAN CLAM CHOWDER:
Brown 2 oz. salt pork in a skillet, then remove and drain. In a large kettle place the salt pork, 1 pt. opened clams chopped fine, 1 1/2 cups clam liquid, 2 peeled and diced potatoes, 1/2 cup water, 1 chopped onion, 1 stalk celery, 1 chopped carrot, 6 peeled, seeded, chopped tomatoes, 1 chopped green pepper, 1/3 cup tomato paste, 1 bay leaf, 1/2 tsp. thyme, salt, and pepper. Bring to a boil, reduce heat, and simmer for 2 hr.

chow mein. A Chinese-American dish made of stewed vegetables and meat with fried noodles. The term comes from Mandarin Chinese, *ch'ao mien,* "fried noodles," and probably was brought to the United States by Chinese cooks serving the workers on the western railroads in the 1850s. The word first appears in print in 1903. Although most chow mein bears scant resemblance to true Mandarin cooking, it has become a staple in Chinese-American restaurants. H. L. Mencken notes that at least one Chinese authority vouched for the Chinese origins of the dish, though in America it is " 'a bit flavored up for Western palates.' " Owing to its inexpensive ingredients, chow mein has long been a lunch dish in American school cafeterias.

A wide variety of ingredients may go into a chow mein, which is often the same as CHOP SUEY in some kitchens.

Heat 3 tbs. oil in a saucepan over high heat, and sauté 1 cup sliced beef or chicken till brown. Add 1 cup sliced celery, 1 cup diced onion, and 1 cup water. Stir and cook till tender, covered. Add 1 can of Chinese vegetables, 3 tbs. flour mixed with 1/2 cup water, 2 tbs. soy sauce, 1 tsp. salt, 1/2 tsp. paprika, and 1/4 tsp. celery salt. Serve on rice and top with 1 can Chinese fried noodles.

Christy Girl. A cocktail that originated at the Howard Chandler Christy Room of New York's Sherry-Netherland Hotel. Christy (1873–1952) was a prominent illustrator of the early part of this century and later a sought-after portrait painter. His illustrations of the American girl as a perky outdoors-woman of considerable daring for the era inspired the cocktail, though it is rarely ordered today.

> Shake together 1/2 jigger peach brandy, 1/2 jigger dry gin, a dash of grenadine, and the white of 1 egg with ice cubes. Strain into a cocktail glass and decorate with a maraschino cherry.

chuck. A western term for food of any kind, dating back to the late nineteenth century; also used as a verb, "to eat." A "chuck habit" is a fear of or obsession for a certain kind of food.

Chuck is also a butcher's term for a cut of beef extending from the neck to the ribs, including the shoulder blade. This cut is often used to make hamburgers and a rib roast (or "blade roast"). One oval-shaped part of the chuck may be sliced into slabs to make "chicken steaks," which are quickly grilled or pan-fried.

chuck wagon. A converted farm wagon that served as a mobile kitchen and center of social activity in the West. The chuck wagon was manned by a cook who had to store utensils and food enough to feed the range cowboys three hot meals a day. Early Texans called it the "commissary," and other terms were *mess wagon* and *growler.* A "chuck box" of shelves and storage space, attached to the rear of the wagon, swung down on hinges as a work table. Underneath was a dishpan called a "wreck pan," and under that a "cooney," a piece of dried cowhide slung to carry firewood and buffalo or cow chips. A good chuck wagon was one that could carry at least a month's provisions. The word was first printed in 1890; by the 1940s *chuck wagon* was also used for a roadside or neighborhood lunch counter.

chuck-wagon chicken. A cowboy term for fried bacon.

chug-a-lug. A campus term, dating from the 1950s, that describes the sound of someone drinking a long draught of beer or spirits. Usually to chug-a-lug a drink means to swallow it down without pausing between gulps.

cíbola. A southwestern cowboy term, from the Spanish, for buffalo. A "cibolero" is a buffalo hunter.

cider. Pressed apple juice that is used to make both vinegar and an unfermented drink called "sweet cider" or a slightly fermented drink called "hard cider." The word derives from the Hebrew, *shēkār,* which in Middle English became *cidre.*

Cider was by far the most popular drink of colonial America. Everyone, including children, drank it, and it was bought very cheaply by the barrel, if not made at home. Ciderkin was a diluted form of cider made from a second pressing of the apple pulp residue and more water. Cider royal was a more pungent form that might be mixed with brandy or boiled down for strength. If mixed with rum it became a drink called "stonewall."

There was not only variety but a great range of quality in ciders, and the French gastronome Jean Anthelme Brillat-Savarin (1755–1826), who spent three years in America, pronounced the native product "so excellent that I could have gone on drinking it forever." President John Adams (1735–1826), who lived to be ninety-one, prided himself on drinking a pitcher of cider every morning.

The popularity of cider waned in the nineteenth century as beer predominated with the adult population, but cider is still extremely popular with Americans, especially in autumn when the pressings take place. Hard ciders range from 3–7 percent alcohol, while sweet cider's alcohol content must fall below 3 percent. Above 7 percent alcohol the drink becomes wine or APPLEJACK.

In the eighteenth century the word *cider* was occasionally applied to drinks made from the pressings of other fruits, like peaches and pears.

cinderella. A muffin flavored with wine or sherry and nutmeg. The name comes from the heroine of the old fairy tale and may have something to do with the muffin's fancy appearance, just as Cinderella emerged as a grand, fancily dressed girl for the prince's ball. The recipe is from *Directions for Cookery* (1837) by Eliza Leslie, who notes that these muffins are also sometimes called "German puffs."

> Beat 8 eggs till light in color, mix in 8 tbs. flour, 1 qt. milk, 1/2 lb. cooled melted butter, 1/4 tsp. powdered nutmeg, and 1 tsp. cinnamon. Make a smooth batter. Fill in buttered muffin tins, bake for 15 min. at 375°. Turn muffins out on rack and sprinkle sugar over them. Serve hot with whipped cream flavored with sherry and nutmeg.

cioppino. A fish stew associated with San Francisco at least since the 1930s and still served in that city as a specialty in many restaurants. The word is Italian, from a Genoese dialect, *cioppin,* for a fish stew, and the dish seems to have originated with the Italian immigrants of San Francisco, who often used the crabmeat available in the city's markets.

> In a large kettle with 4 tbs. olive oil sauté 4 chopped onions, 8 chopped garlic cloves, 1 diced carrot, 1 diced leek, 1 diced celery stalk, till limp. Add 1 cup tomato purée and 1/3 tsp. crumbled saffron. Add the meat from 2 or more crabs, 10 shrimp that have been peeled and deveined, 2 doz. clams, 2 doz. mussels, 1/2 lb. bay scallops, 8 oz. each of two or more fish (such as snapper or sea bass), and stir to coat with

oil and other ingredients. Add 2 cups white wine, 3 cups fish stock, 2 bay leaves, 1/2 tsp. oregano, 1/2 tsp. thyme, salt, pepper, and 4 peeled and seeded chopped tomatoes. Cover, bring to a boil, then simmer for 15 min. Remove fish and reduce stock for 15 min. Return fish to stock, bring to a boil, then serve. Serves 8.

citric acid. Abundant in citrus fruits, this is used as an additive (as an antioxidant and flavoring agent), imparting a tart flavor to processed food.

clabber. Sour, curdled milk, rarely seen now in the United States because most milk is pasteurized and will not naturally turn to curd before it goes bad. In the South clabber was often eaten with sugar, or even with black pepper and cream. *New York Times* food writer Craig Claiborne recalled that "it was a common dish of my Southern childhood. My father raised and milked cows. The milk was allowed to stand in churns and more often than not became clabber, a semifirm, very white liquid on the bottom and a semifirm layer of yellow cream on top. The clabber was a pure product, the result of a natural bacterial action. Clabber tends to 'break apart' when dipped into. It is quite sour but of a different texture and flavor than yogurt. When you 'churned' the clabber, you wound up with butter (from the top cream layer) and buttermilk." The word comes from the Irish *bainne clabair* (literally, "thick milk"), in English, "bonny clabber."

clam (Class Pelecypoda). Any of a variety of bivalve mollusks that burrow in sand in both salt and fresh water. The word derives from Old English, *clamm*, "bond" or "fetter," for its clamped shell. The mollusk has had this name in English at least since the end of the fourteenth century, although a Scot may mean a scallop when he says "clam."

Clams, of which there are more than two thousand species, exist in most regions of the world and have been consumed since prehistoric times. The earliest white settlers of North America found clams to their liking, and the Indians used the clam shell as money, or *wampum*. The Indians also showed the New England colonists how to hold "clambakes"—social gatherings, often held at the beach after a fresh catch, which have endured to this day in that region.

The two main varieties of clams eaten on the East Coast are the soft-shell *(Mya arenaria)* and the hard-shell *(Mercenaria mercenaria)*, better known as the "quahog" (from the Narraganset word, *poquaûhock*), and as the "round clam." *Quahog* in English dates at least to 1753.

The soft-shell clam, found from the Arctic Ocean to Cape Hatteras and introduced to Pacific waters north of San Francisco, is generally used for making clam CHOWDER and frying, though it is most commonly steamed. Soft-shell clams are often called "steamers."

The hard-shell clam is preferred raw and in chowders, its size sometimes determining its use. The smallest quahogs are called "littlenecks" (after Littleneck Bay on Long Island, New York; but William and Mary Morris in their

Morris Dictionary of Word and Phrase Origins [1971] give "Little Neck" as a clamming region of Ipswich, Massachusetts); the next size is "cherrystone" (after Cherrystone Creek, Virginia); still larger quahogs are called "chowder clams" and used for that purpose.

The razor clam of the East *(Ensis directus)*, so called because of its sharp shell, is not as popular because it is difficult to catch. The bar clam *(Spisula solidissima)*, also called the "Atlantic surf clam" and "skimmer clam," is used for chowders or deep-fried.

There are several clams of culinary interest on the West Coast: the razor clam *(Siliqua patula* and other species) is not related to the eastern variety named above; the Pacific littleneck *(Protothaca staminea* and others) is not related to the eastern variety either, nor is the Philippine littleneck *(Tapes philippinarum);* the California bean clam *(Donax californicus)* is eaten in soups; the geoduck *(Panope generosa),* pronounced "gooey-duck," is very large, up to eight inches in length and five pounds in weight, and has a tough texture. Its name, first appearing in English in 1883, is most probably from the Nisqualli Indian for "digging deep."

This last species is dug out of beds twenty to seventy feet deep, and most of the supply is shipped to Japan, where it is considered a great delicacy. Americans may find the clam on Pacific beaches during very low tides. The process of catching one is described by Lila Gault in *The Northwest Cookbook* (1978):

The digger must first find the neck of the geoduck, which is directly below the "mark," and then center a stovepipe over it. The stovepipe is then driven into the sand as deeply as possible and the fun truly begins. The neck is held with one hand and the other scoops sand away from it, making a large hole in the process. Unlike razor clams, geoduck do not move their bodies when disturbed. Once the neck is grabbed, if the diggers are persistent, they will always get their clam! When the body of the clam is reached, often two and sometimes as much as four feet below the surface, the geoduck can be lifted out of the hold. This chase and capture actually works better with two or three people at work—a single digger must be extremely agile and tenacious to get even one of these clams.

STEAMED CLAMS:
Clean soft-shell clams thoroughly and place them in a deep kettle or clam steamer with a tight lid. Pour in about 1 1/2 in. clam broth or seasoned water and cook just until clams have opened.

GEODUCK STEAK:
(From Lila Gault's *Northwest Cookbook* [1978]) Cut a live geoduck into 4-in. steaks. Combine 2 beaten eggs with 1 cup cracker crumbs, salt, and pepper. Dredge the clam steaks in the mixture and fry 4–5 min. in oil at least 400°.

CLAMBAKE:
Build a fire in a deep pit, place a layer of large, flat rocks on top of the burning wood, and repeat procedure with more wood and rocks twice more. Let burn until very hot. Rake the fire, retaining embers, and lay on top wet seaweed to a depth of about

6 in. Then place clams, mussels, lobsters, potatoes, corn, and onions on top. Cover
with layers of wet canvas, cook about 1 1/2 hr. Serve with butter.

clam fritter. A deep-fried clam in batter, supposedly first made at Woodman's
Restaurant in Essex, Massachusetts, on July 3, 1916. Clam fritters are also called
"fannie daddies" on Cape Cod or "boat steerers" in other parts of New England.

> Beat 2 egg yolks, add 1/2 cup milk, 1 tbs. butter, 1 cup flour, salt, pepper, and 1 tbs.
> lemon juice. Beat in 2 stiffly beaten egg whites, mix in 1 pt. clams, and chill for
> several hours. Fry small amounts in hot oil till golden brown.

clams posillipo. An Italian-American dish of clams cooked with garlic, red
peppers, tomatoes, and seasonings. The dish is named after the cape of Posillipo near Naples, Italy, but there is no specific, traditional dish by this name
in Italy. It is a creation of Italian immigrants based on home-style recipes of
Naples and the surrounding area.

> Wash and drain 4 doz. clams (littlenecks or cherrystones). In 1/2 cup olive oil sauté
> 1 1/2 tbs. minced garlic and 2 seeded dried red peppers for about 1 min. Add 1/2
> cup dry white wine, reduce by half, add 3 cups canned tomatoes and 1 tbs. tomato
> paste. Add salt and pepper, 1 tbs. oregano, and 1/4 cup chopped parsley. Cover,
> bring to a boil, then simmer for 15 min. Add clams, cover, and cook till clams open,
> about 8–10 min. Serves 4–5.

club. A term for a bill or check for one's meal. It was first mentioned in print
in 1793 but is now obsolete.

club sandwich. A sandwich usually made with three slices of toast enclosing
fillings of lettuce, mayonnaise, cooked chicken breast, tomato slices, cooked
bacon strips, and a garnish. James Beard, in *American Cookery* (1972), however, insists that the original club sandwiches were made with only two slices
of toast (and calls the three-slice rendition "a horror"). He also gives the
alternate name of "clubhouse sandwich," which suggests its origins were in the
kitchens that prepared food for men's private social clubs. The first appearance
of the club sandwich in print was in Ray L. McCardell's *Conversations of a
Chorus Girl* in 1903, indicating that the item was known specifically by that
name as of the turn of the century.

Food writer James Villas in a letter to the *New York Times* (March 9, 1983)
contends the sandwich originated on the two-decker "club cars" (a term first
recorded in 1895) of the "streamliner trains" (although *streamlining* dates a bit
later, to 1909). In the same number of the *Times* another letter-writer cites an
explanation of the sandwich's origins in a book entitled *New York, a Guide to
the Empire State* (1962): "In 1894 Richard Canfield (1865–1914), the debonair
patron of art, purchased the Saratoga Club [in Saratoga, New York] to make
it a casino. Canfield Solitaire was originated in the casino's gambling rooms
and the club sandwich in its kitchens."

cobbler. A cold drink made from wine, sherry, liquor, or other alcohol with citrus juice and sugar. The word's origins are obscure; one conjecture has it associated with a shortened form of *cobbler's punch,* meaning that it had the effect of "patching up" the imbiber. Washington Irving's reference to a "sherry-cobbler" in his *Knickerbocker's History of New York* (1809) is the first appearance of the word, used to describe a drink, in print.

Another kind of cobbler is a western deep-dish pie with a thick crust and a fruit filling. This dish is called BIRD'S NEST PUDDING or "crow's nest pudding" in New England; it is served with a custard but no topping in Connecticut, with maple sugar in Massachusetts, and with a sour sauce in Vermont.

cocktail. A beverage combining liquors with juices, sodas, or other ingredients. Examples would include MARTINIS, MANHATTANS, SAZERACS, and SCREWDRIVERS. The term does not usually refer to punches or any hot drinks and is usually associated with apéritifs served at the "cocktail hour," that is, the period before dinner when such libations would be enjoyed.

The word *cocktail* has been a subject of some controversy among etymologists and historians. H. L. Mencken, in his first supplement to *The American Language* (1945), notes seven sources of origin for the term, including references to the British "cock ale," a seventeenth-century concoction of chicken broth and ale. The *Dictionary of American English* traces *cocktail* to 1806 in print, but it appears to be somewhat older than that. Stuart Berg Flexner, in *Listening to America* (1982), strongly supports the contention that the word derives from the French, *coquetier,* for "egg cup," the container in which French apothecary Antoine Peychaud served his concoction of bitters and Sazerac-du-Forge brandy after his arrival in New Orleans about 1795. Other authorities have problems with this assertion, including Professor Arthur Schlesinger, who wonders how the word could have so quickly found its way into a Hudson, New York, newspaper (the *Balance*) by 1806 if it had only recently been coined from the French word for egg cup. Finally, in a column in the *New York Times,* William Safire considers the options and comes down on Flexner's side, but adds the remark, "If you think this controversy is a waste of time, and believe that great minds should stick to elevated notions, consider the significance of the coinage: Were it not for this word, nobody could put on a cocktail dress, go to a cocktail party, put feet up on a cocktail table, listen to a cocktail pianist or order a nonalcoholic bitters-less shrimp cocktail. The word goes to the heart of our way of life and deserves sober second thought."

A "cocktail dress" would be a fancy dress worn by a woman to a "cocktail party," a social gathering that became popular in the 1920s, during Prohibition when alcoholic drinks were hard to find outside the home, except illegally. A "cocktail table" is a low table, usually set between sofa and chairs, around which guests sit and enjoy cocktails. A "cocktail pianist" is an entertainer who plays while people sip cocktails. A "shrimp cocktail" was a variation on the "oyster cocktail," created about 1860 by a San Francisco miner who dipped his oysters in ketchup. "Cocktail lounges," where one would go to enjoy cocktails, have been so called since the 1930s.

By the nineteenth century any mixture of various whiskeys was called a "cocktail." Since the 1870s a mixture using champagne or a sparkling wine was called a "champagne cocktail." A "cocktail shaker," in which to mix cocktails with ice, was created as of the 1860s.

coconut. Also, "cocoanut." The large pod fruit of the coconut palm (*Cocos nucifera*). The interior white meat of the fruit and its milky liquid are eaten fresh or dried as desserts, as a garnish, or as an oil for cooking. The word is a combination of a Portuguese children's term, *coco,* for the "goblin" shell of the fruit, and the English word *nut.* The fruit was first mentioned in English print in 1555, and the first American reference was in 1834.

The origins of the coconut have never been fully understood, but some believe it is native to tropical America and was dispersed to Pacific islands by the drift of the pods through the ocean. Coconuts were known in Egypt by the sixth century A.D., and Marco Polo noted it in India and elsewhere in the Far East. Certainly coconuts were encountered on the Pacific shores of South America and Hawaii, but coconut is not a major crop of the latter. Most of the coconut enjoyed by Americans is imported from Indonesia, the Philippines, and other Pacific countries. Half the coconuts used in the food industry actually come from noncultivated trees.

The dried meat of coconut, called "copra" (probably from the Hindi, *khoprā,* for "coconut") is shredded or flaked, often sweetened, or processed to make coconut oil. Americans eat coconut fresh, but most often use it in its dried form in desserts such as coconut cake, known at least since 1830. By 1909 coconut ices were enjoyed. Coconut cream, a viscous, sweet liquid made with coconut and various thickeners, was first marketed in the early 1950s and is principally used to make cocktails like the PIÑA COLADA.

COCONUT FROSTING:
Boil 1 cup sugar with 1/2 cup water till syrup spins a thread. Pour slowly into 2 stiffly beaten egg whites, beat till smooth, add 1 cup shredded or flaked coconut, and blend well. Use to ice cakes.

cod (Family Gadidae). Also, "codfish." Any of a variety of marine fishes in this family. Cod is one of the most important food fishes in the world, both fresh and, especially, salted and dried. The word is possibly related to the Middle English word *cod,* meaning a "bag," the shape of which resembles the hefty codfish. The first printed mention of the word as a fish was in 1460.

Cod is a fish inextricably linked to the history and fortunes of America; the fish's abundance in eastern waters was excitedly noted by Venetian navigator Giovanni Caboto (who sailed for England as "John Cabot") on his exploration of Newfoundland in 1497. An English adventurer, Bartholomew Gosnold, found so many of the fish when he sailed south of Nova Scotia in 1602 that he named the arm of land in those waters "Cape Cod," later a center of the

New England fishing industry. In 1630 Francis Higginson wrote, "The abundance of Sea-Fish are almost beyond beleeving, and sure I whould scarce have baleeved it except I had seene it with mine owne eyes." Ten years later Massachusetts, whose fishing industry had begun in Gloucester in 1623, sent 300,000 dried codfish to market.

The cod trade developed rapidly. American shipbuilders in 1713 created the New England schooner for fishing in the worst of weather, and the newly rich fishing families of the region were slightingly referred to as the "codfish aristocracy." So important was the cod to the livelihood of Massachusetts that the state's House of Representatives voted in 1784 to hang a white-pine carving of the "Sacred Cod" in their meeting room, where it is still displayed today.

Cod also had a role in maintaining the lucrative triangular trade between England, the North American and West Indian colonies, and Africa. Dried cod would be shipped to Europe, the boats would then pick up slaves in Africa, stop in the Caribbean to load on molasses and sugar, and sell the latter goods to New England rum distilleries, a continual journey of economic barbarism that lasted for more than eighty years.

The American Revolution's peace treaty included provisions for American boats to fish in English waters, thanks to Massachusetts's John Adams.

Young cod is called SCROD, which is also the name of a dish of young cod baked with white wine and milk.

The principal types of cod found in American waters include:

Atlantic cod (*Gadus morhua*). This enormous cod dominates the industry, with nearly 7 billion pounds caught annually around the world. It ranges the North Atlantic, rarely going as far south as Virginia. It is sometimes called "rock cod."

haddock (*Melanogrammus aeglefinus*). Ranging throughout the North Atlantic as far south as New Jersey, the haddock usually weighs between two and five pounds and is preferred fresh rather than salted. "Finnan haddie" (from a Scottish port, Findhorn, and the Scottish word for haddock) is a smoked haddock popularized by John Ross, Jr., in the nineteenth century.

COD CAKES:
Clean and soak in salted water 1/2 lb. cod. Dice well and boil with 2 1/2 cups potatoes for 15 min. Mash together till smooth, add 1 beaten egg, 2 tbs. butter, and a dash of pepper. Shape into cakes about 3 in. wide, coat with cracker crumbs, and deep-fry on both sides till golden. Makes 12 cakes.

coddes. Breaded and deep-fried cod cakes, a specialty of Maryland and pronounced "coddees."

coddle. To cook in a liquid just below the boiling point, as with eggs. Coddled apples are made by cooking apple slices in a syrup of water and sugar in the ratio of two to one. The term goes back at least to the sixteenth century.

coffee. Roasted, ground beans from the coffee plant (genus *Coffea*), or a beverage made from these beans. The main species, *Coffea arabica,* indigenous to Ethiopia, is now grown throughout the so-called coffee belt, with temperatures of 70° and good rainfall throughout the year, that rings the world between latitudes of twenty-five degrees North and thirty degrees South.

Coffee plants originated in Ethiopia, and the word's etymology derives either from its shipping point, Kaffa, in that country, or from the Arabic, *quhiya,* or Turkish, *kahveh,* which referred to a wine tonic that restored the appetite.

There are several legends as to who first brewed coffee: one story involves a goatherd of Kaffa named Kaldi whose goats were particularly sprightly after consuming the caffeine-rich coffee beans. This activity was noticed by a local monk named Mullah, who brewed a beverage from the beans and spread word of its restorative virtues throughout the region. An Arab legend of the fifteenth century contends that the ninth-century mufti of Aden was the first to make the drink, after which it became a favorite of the Middle Eastern courts.

The first mention of coffee in English is in 1598, but the word itself did not appear in print until 1659. Coffee had been brought to Italy by 1615, to France in 1644. It became a most fashionable drink at the court of France's Louis XIV in 1669, thanks to the efforts of Suleiman Aga, the Turkish ambassador there. Louis introduced a single coffee seedling to the Caribbean island of Martinique and began a spread of the plant throughout Central and South America that eventually made Brazil the world's largest coffee producer. (The Dutch introduced the plant to Indonesia and Java, and *java* became an American slang term for all coffee as of the mid-nineteenth century.)

The first coffee house in London was opened in 1688 by Edward Lloyd (who later built the insurance company Lloyd's of London), and more sprouted quickly, as they did in America, where the Dutch had introduced coffee by 1670. The Merchants Coffee House in New York had by the middle of the eighteenth century become known for entertaining several of the leading revolutionary dissenters of the day. In protest against the high taxes imposed by the British on tea, Americans turned to coffee; according to Flexner in *Listening to America* (1982), Revolutionary War coffee sales had increased 600 percent. But coffee's own high price prevented it from becoming a truly popular drink for decades afterwards, and mock coffee made from rye (called "Boston coffee"), peas ("Canadian coffee"), and burnt bread ("crumb coffee") was often substituted.

In the 1860s tea importers George Huntington Hartford and George Gilman organized the American Coffee Corporation to buy beans directly from Brazil and Colombia, thereby making coffee less expensive for the American consumer—twenty-five cents per pound, as compared with the two dollars per pound Americans had paid before—and helping it to become America's favorite beverage.

Americans got the coffee percolator from the English, but *drip pot* was an American term by the end of the century. In 1878 James Sanborn and Caleb

Chase produced the first ground coffee sealed in tin cans. The American taste in coffee was largely due to a blend developed by Joel Cheek of Nashville, Tennessee, and served in the 1880s at the Maxwell House hotel in that city. It became extremely popular, especially after President Theodore Roosevelt (1858–1919; President, 1901–1909) pronounced the coffee "good to the last drop," which is the motto of the brand, Maxwell House, to this day.

In New Orleans, the people were drinking chicory coffee, a more bitter brew than most American blends. In 1903 a caffeine-free coffee called "Sanka" (from French, *sans caffeine,* "without caffeine") was developed but was not successful until it was promoted in the 1930s by the General Foods company.

Powdered coffees had been known as of the eighteenth century, but it was not until G. Washington, an Englishman living in Guatemala, discovered in 1906 a practical process of condensing coffee so that it could be reconstituted merely by adding boiling water in a cup that real "instant coffee" became available.

Coffee is almost always a blend of beans from various sources. Brazil provides the beans for one-third of the world's consumption, Colombia is the second largest producer, and there are large plantations in Costa Rica, Mexico, Cuba, India, Java, and various African countries. Some of the best beans come from Jamaica, and Hawaii produces a coffee, known as "Kona," that is highly esteemed. Ninety million Americans drink coffee daily.

Americans have generally preferred a lighter, less robust coffee than the rest of the world, and instant coffee makes up a great share of the domestic market. The term *American coffee* has become useful to restaurants within the last decade to describe a blend that is percolated, as opposed to ESPRESSO, *café filtre,* or Hispanic coffees, which are very hearty and rich and brewed by a drip method. An "American roast," also called a "regular roast," is somewhat heavier than a "light roast." A "heavy roast" (sometimes called "Dark French") is extremely dark, while "Italian roast" (preferred for espresso) is glossy and dark brown. "Viennese roast" is a blend of one-third heavy and two-thirds regular, while "European roast" transposes the ratio. "Mocha" is either a coffee from Ethiopia (whose name is derived from the city of Mocha there) or a Yemeni coffee having a taste of chocolate. *Mocha* may also refer to a beverage made with coffee and cocoa mixed together with water or milk or to any flavor derived from these two beans. *Jamoke* (also, *jamoca*) is an early-twentieth-century term for coffee in general, a combination of *java* and *mocha.*

Americans drink coffee with breakfast, in the middle of the morning at a "coffee break" (so called since the mid-1940s), at lunch, with snacks (especially DOUGHNUTS), and with or after dinner. In many restaurants the coffee cup and saucer will be placed on the table at the start of the meal. Coffee mugs are popular at inexpensive restaurants, diners, and lunch counters, and take-out eateries offer plastic or cardboard coffee cups. Americans take their coffee either "black" (with no sugar, milk, or cream), "light" (with a lot of milk or cream), or "regular" (which usually refers to coffee with some sugar and milk or cream, although regional differences may eliminate one or the other in usage).

coffee klatch. An informal get-together over coffee. The term, which comes from a similar German term, *kaffee-klatsch* ("coffee gossip"), first in English print in 1895, was especially popular during the 1950s and 1960s.

coffee milk. A blend of a little coffee in a glass of sweetened milk. In Rhode Island this drink is very popular and may be purchased in containers. The citizens of that state are also very fond of flavoring milk with sweet coffee syrup.

cold cut. Usually meant to refer to a thin slice of meat served cold for lunch, either on a SANDWICH or with various salads, mayonnaise, vegetables, mustard, and snacks. The most common meats are bologna, liverwurst, beef, turkey breast, chicken, tongue, pastrami, and various salamis.

The first printed reference to the term appeared in 1945.

Cold Duck. A mixture of American sparkling red and white wines, it is a semisweet, low-alcohol beverage that achieved widespread popularity in the 1970s and then faded by the beginning of the 1980s.

There are several versions of how Cold Duck got its name, though most authorities agree that it is a mistaken transformation of the German words *Kalte Ende*, "cold ending." Some assert the drink originated in Bavaria, where hunters would begin the day with a glass of sparkling wine. The unused wine was then mixed together with other leftover wines and drunk cold at the end of the day. Another story credits the court of Wilhelm I (1797–1888), emperor of Germany (1871–1888) and king of Prussia (1861–1888), with the drink's origins. General Von Pape, attending a dinner at the emperor's, remarked that he preferred a "cold ending" rather than coffee at the end of a meal and proceeded to mix *Sekt* and a Moselle wine with lemon juice. *Kalte Ende* became popular after that. Somehow *Kalte Ende* was erroneously transformed, perhaps in dialect, into *Kalte Ente,* meaning "cold duck."

The drink came to America by way of a German immigrant named Harold Borgman, original owner of the Pontchartrain Wine Cellar in Detroit, Michigan, where, he contended, he first made the drink with champagne and still Burgundy wine in 1935. It remained a local favorite until, in 1963, the general manager of an importing firm sampled the drink and talked one of his suppliers into bottling the concoction. A year later the first commercially sold Cold Duck was produced, followed by examples from California and Michigan. American Sparkling Burgundy replaced the still Burgundy used originally, and American CHAMPAGNE was used instead of *Sekt* or true champagne. (Germany has bottled a lemon-flavored version of *Kalte Ente* since 1948 and a red variation called *Turkenblut.*) After 1971 Cold Duck was a semisweet apéritif with enormous sales in America, but the American palate soon grew tired of the soda-poplike quality of the beverage, and sales had dropped precipitously by the end of the decade.

Cold Water Regime. A humorous description of President Rutherford B. Hayes's administration (1877–1881), owing to the fact that he served no spirits during his tenure in the White House. The phrase was first seen in print in 1884.

cole slaw. Shredded cabbage, mayonnaise, and seasonings, usually served cold as a side dish. The words are from Dutch, *koolsla,* a combination of *kool,* "cabbage," and *sla,* "salad," a dish that was known in America by 1792. Because it is usually served cold, some have called the dish "cold slaw," in contrast to "hot slaw," but there is no relation to the temperature in the etymology.

> In a large bowl stir together 1 cup mayonnaise, 1 tbs. lemon juice, 4 cups shredded cabbage, and 1 1/2 cups shredded carrots. Add 1/2 cup raisins if desired. Makes about 5 cups.

common cracker. Very crisp, hard, thick wheat-flour cracker that may be split and grilled with butter or Cheddar cheese, ground into breadcrumbs, or eaten in chowders; similar to BOSTON CRACKER. One manufacturer claims common crackers were first baked by Charles Cross about 1830 in his Montpelier, Vermont, bakery, and were called "Cross crackers" or "Montpelier crackers."

But in Eleanor Early's *New England Cookbook* (1954), the crackers' invention was credited to Artemus Kennedy of Menotomy, Massachusetts, almost two hundred years ago. Early writes that "Artemus had a large family and it was said that the children learned to retrieve the crackers [that Artemus tossed on the floor of a big Dutch oven] . . . before they could walk. Baking was done three times a week, and Artemus rode about the countryside on his horse, selling them from his saddlebags."

Whatever their origins, common crackers are no longer easily found, and the news that a Rockingham, Vermont, citizen named Vrest Orton had bought the original Charles Cross machinery and begun to sell common crackers again in 1981 was greeted with considerable interest by those who remember the taste of dry, crisp morsels split opened and eaten with good Vermont Cheddar. See also TRENTON CRACKER.

A recipe from Louise Andrews Kent's *Mrs. Appleyard's Kitchen* (1942), reprinted in the *New York Times* in 1981, gives the following directions for making "Puffed Montpelier Crackers."

> "1. Allow at least two whole crackers per person. Split each cracker in half.
> "2. Put ice cubes into a large bowl of cold water. When the water is very cold, put in the split cracker halves. . . . At the end of three minutes—or sooner, if they seem to be getting too soft—remove the crackers from the ice water.
> "3. When they have drained about five minutes, put them into iron dripping pans and dot them thickly with soft butter. Dust them with paprika, if you wish. Heat

the oven to 450 to 500 degrees and bake them until they are puffed, crisp, and golden brown. They should be done in 25 to 35 minutes."

common doings. A frontier term since the 1830s for any plain food.

commons. A college or university dining hall, where the students are served a "common" meal. It may also refer to the food itself, a meaning dating to the sixteenth century in England.

conch (Genus *Strombus*). A brightly colored gastropod mollusk eaten in the Caribbean and Florida. The word (which is pronounced "conk") is from the Latin, *concha,* and as slang has been applied at least since 1852 to the inhabitants of Key West, Florida, especially to those with a Bahamian ancestry of mixed Cockney and Negro blood, probably because of their fondness for the marine food. (North Carolinians have also been called "conchs," for reasons that have nothing to do with the mollusk or Bahamians.)

Conch is tough and must be pounded or finely chopped. It is often served in salads, as fritters, or in a chowder.

CONCH CHOWDER:
Fry 1/4 lb. diced salt pork till crisp, add 2 chopped onions, and sauté until limp. Add 1 chopped green pepper. Place in a large pot with 1 can of tomatoes, 4 conchs ground well, 3 diced potatoes, and 2 qt. water. Bring to boil, then simmer till potatoes disintegrate and begin to thicken the soup. Allow to cool, then reheat and serve.

Concord. A Labrusca hybrid grape used to make wine and jelly, jam, and preserves. Introduced in 1849, this dark red grape was propagated from a seedling grown in Concord, Massachusetts, by Ephraim Wales Bull, whose discovery enriched others but not himself: his gravestone reads, "He sowed, but others reaped."

Concord was especially successful in New York State, both as a wine grape and as an eating grape. Oversupply in the 1890s led to a bust, which in turn prompted two dentists named Welch to set up the world's first large grape-juice plant at Westfield, New York. The Welch Grape Juice Company prospered under Prohibition by selling "unfermented wine" and the juice to make jellies, jams, and preserves. Jacob Merrill ("Jack") Kaplan bought the company in 1945 and began making a very sweet kosher wine from Concord grapes. He neglected to put the word *kosher* on the label, however, and thereby lost out to other kosher-wine producers like Manischewitz and Mogen David.

Today more than 80 percent of New York's vineyards are planted with Concord grapes, the majority going to make jams, jellies, and preserves as well as grape juice and concentrates.

coney. A pork frankfurter or hot dog. A coney is whitish in color, like a German Weisswurst, and is a specialty of Syracuse, New York. The name derives from Coney Island, an amusement park in Brooklyn, New York, where hot dogs first became popular.

cookbook. A term for a book of recipes. Before 1809 such volumes were referred to as "cookerie books," "recipe books," "receipt books," or "culinary reviews." The first American cookbooks were family collections of favorite recipes handed down from one generation to the next, and many were only American editions of English volumes. But in 1796 Amelia Simmons, who called herself "An American Orphan," published the forty-seven-page *American Cookery, or the art of dressing viands, fish, poultry and vegetables, and the best modes of making pastes, puffs, pies, tarts, puddings, custards and preserves, and all kinds of cakes, from the imperial plumb to plain cake. Adapted to this country, and all grades of life.* It was the first published volume to include recipes for specifically American dishes such as cranberry sauce and pumpkin pie.

Cookbooks began appearing rapidly after Simmons's successful venture. Lydia Child's *The American Frugal Housewife* (1832), Mary Randolph's *Virginia Housewife* (1824), Eliza Leslie's *Directions for Cookery* (1837), Sallie Rutledge's *Carolina Housewife* (1847), Elizabeth H. Putnam's *Mrs. Putnam's Receipt Book* (1850), and others were very popular. Catharine Esther Beecher's *Treatise on Domestic Economy for the Use of Young Ladies at Home and at School* (1841) and *Miss Beecher's Domestic Receipt Book* (1846) were significant for their tips on food storage and the use of ovens and kitchen utensils.

In 1896 Fannie Merritt Farmer published *The Boston Cooking-School Cook Book,* which for the first time applied scientific terms and precise measurements to recipes. In it appeared the first American instructions to use a "level teaspoon," rather than the usual "dash" or "pinch" other writers decreed. Farmer's cookbook, originally published in a three-thousand-copy edition at her own expense, was an immediate and tremendous best-seller, and she was to become one of the most important women in America for changing the way women of the period cooked and managed their households.

In the twentieth century cookbooks were often issued by food companies to promote their product, cooking institutes to promote their schools, and newspapers to promote their sales. The *Boston Post Cook Book,* for instance, sprung from "The Great Breakfast Table Paper of New England," listed favorite dishes of famous American women, including Mrs. Calvin Coolidge, and pages of "household hints" ranging from the use of a corn popper to methods for removing tea stains. Various food-industry organizations—for apple growers or meatpackers, for example—offered cookbooks to the public, and there is a long tradition of church groups, Junior Leagues, and women's clubs that publish their own, usually based on members' own recipes. Some of these grew into best-selling books, such as *The Joy of Cooking,* by Irma S. Rombauer and Marion Rombauer Becker, published in numerous editions since 1931. Other popular cookbooks issued forth from the editorial departments of the "ladies' magazines," such as *Better Homes and Gardens,* *McCall's,* and *Good Housekeeping.*

Ethnic foods formed but a small section of most of these books, and only after World War II did ethnic cookbooks begin to interest the American public, although the authors almost always "adapted" foreign recipes to an American palate that supposedly did not care for highly seasoned or spicy foods or for dishes that took much time to prepare and cook. Such modifications led to a mistaken notion among many Americans about the true nature of ethnic foods, and foreign restaurateurs followed by catering to the same conventions about adaptions or transformations of dishes on their menus.

In the 1950s and 1960s there appeared a number of very popular cookbooks that were sold on gimmickry, from an attempt to sympathize with the housewife who really did not much enjoy cooking (with titles such as the *I Hate to Cook Book*) to small volumes, often enhanced by strong graphic design, that catered to a specific approach to cookery, such as "patio," "fondue," "backyard," or "hibachi" cookbooks in which every recipe was adapted to the book's idea.

Also in the 1960s, however, came the first series of serious, specialized, and challenging cookbooks that demonstrated some of the more sophisticated and authentic techniques of preparing French, Italian, Chinese, and other ethnic cuisines, beginning with Julia Child's *Mastering the Art of French Cooking,* first published in 1961 and keyed to a very well received public television show. Mrs. Child abated the fears of some American cooks who regarded French classic cuisine as intimidating, and there quickly followed volumes by other authors on regional Italian cookery, authentic Cantonese and Sichuan cookery, and true Mexican cookery. Later came Vietnamese, Indian, and Thai cookbooks of great authority, as well as translations of the cookbooks of the French practitioners of *la nouvelle cuisine.*

In the late 1960s and 1970s there appeared a series of beautifully designed and thoroughly researched volumes by Time-Life Books, under the general editorship of Richard L. Williams, entitled *Foods of the World.* These books surveyed the cuisines of Japan, Russia, Italy, and other countries along with several volumes on American cooking, from the South to the Northwest, including a volume gathering up the various ethnic influences in American food entitled *The Melting Pot.*

Today there are hundreds of cookbooks published each year, though only a handful reach a large public.

cookhouse. A ranch building where food is prepared and served. Cookhouses were also called "feed bags" or "feed troughs" (referring to the bags and troughs from which horses fed on grain).

cookie. A small, flat, sweet cake eaten as a snack or with other desserts. The word is from the Dutch, *koekje,* "little cake," and first appears in print in 1703. In England the term is little used, and in Scotland it refers to a small bun. In

America the cookie has long been a favorite snack food since the Dutch made them popular in their early settlements.

One finds dozens of cookie recipes in eighteenth- and nineteenth-century cookbooks, but the most popular cookie in America today—the chocolate chip or TOLL HOUSE cookie, created by Mrs. Ruth Wakefield, who owned the Toll House Inn in Whitman, Massachusetts—did not appear until after 1930.

In 1982 Americans bought $2.5 billion worth of cookies.

OATMEAL COOKIES:
Sift 1 1/2 cups flour, 1 tsp. baking soda, and 1 tsp. salt. Cream 1/2 lb. butter, 1 cup brown sugar, and 3/4 cup sugar. Beat in 2 eggs and 1 tsp. vanilla extract. Add flour mixture, blend well, stir in 3 cups uncooked oats, and drop onto buttered cookie sheet. Bake at 350° for 12–15 min.

BUTTER COOKIES:
Blend 1/2 cup butter and 1/2 cup brown sugar till creamy. Add 2 egg yolks, 1/2 tsp. vanilla, 1 cup flour, and a dash of salt to form a dough. Chill for several hours, roll out to 1/8-in. thickness, cut out with cookie cutter, and bake on buttered pan at 375° for 10–12 min. Dust with sugar or cinnamon if desired.

cookie. A nineteenth-century term used by ranchers or cowboys for a cook or by sailors for a cook's helper.

The ranch cook was responsible for three hot meals a day, and he had to possess a good deal of imagination to please his men with dishes that often had to be prepared from meager sources on the open range.

A "cook's louse" was a cook's helper, and a cowboy's cook might also be called a "coosie" (from the Spanish, *cocinero*), as well as a "bean master," a "belly cheater," a "belly robber," a "biscuit roller," a "boardinghouse man," a "boiler," a "dinero," a "dough-belly," a "dough-boxer," a "dough-puncher," a "dough roller," a "dough wrangler," a "flunky," a "grease ball," a "grease burner," a "grease belly," a "GRUB spoiler," a "grub worm," a "gut burglar," a "gut robber," a "HASH burner," a "hash slinger," a "kitchen mechanic," a "lizard," a "scorcher," a "mess moll," a "MULLIGAN mixer," an "old woman," a "pothook," a "pot rustler," a "Sallie," a "sheffi," a "sizzler," a "sop and 'taters," a "SOURDOUGH," a "star chief," a "stew builder," a "stomach robber," a "swamper," and, doubtless, scores of other appellations.

cookie pusher. A cowboy term for a restaurant waitress.

cooking wine. Any wine primarily intended to be added to cooked foods for flavor. The alcohol in cooking wine is burned off, leaving a faint taste of the wine. Although gourmets recommend using a good wine for cooking, most wines used for this purpose are inexpensive and lack distinction. During Prohibition many of these wines were salted so as to make them undrinkable.

cooter. A southern dialect word for a box TURTLE. From either a West African word, *kuta*, or a Kongo word, *nkuda*, it was first printed in English in 1832, though probably used for a long while before that on southern plantations. Cooter stew is still part of southern cookery.

coquina soup. A Florida soup of periwinkle clams. *Coquina* is an Americanism that usually refers to a build-up of marine shells bound by calcareous cement and used as a building material, but this soup seems to derive from the original Spanish word meaning "shellfish."

> Rinse clams in water several times, cover with water, bring to boil, and simmer 10 min. Pour through sieve and serve.

cordial. A sweet, syrupy spirit, synonymous with *liqueur,* which is the preferred term in England and France, though it is often heard in America. *Cordial* derives from the Medieval Latin, *cordiālis,* from the Latin, *cor,* "heart."

Cordials once had medicinal uses, and the oldest known cordial dates back to Hippocrates, who concocted one of cinnamon and wine-sweetened honey about 420 B.C. The tradition was carried on by European monks, and many cordials now made commercially were first created by such men of the cloth.

Cordials are made by three processes: infusion (or maceration), in which the flavorings steep in alcohol; percolation, in which the alcohol percolates above the flavorings; and distillation, in which ingredients are distilled directly from their extracted flavors in copper stills, a method that results in clear, colorless liquids of varying proofs. A fruit-flavored brandy is a cordial made with a brandy base, but other spirits are used for other kinds of cordials.

Most American cordials are quite sweet, with up to 35 percent sugar, and are made from various fruits, beans, and herbs, ranging from cherry to chocolate to mint. Some are milk-based, with low alcohol. A "dry" cordial must have less than 10 percent sugar, but no cordial may have less than 2 1/2 percent sugar by weight.

In 1981 cordials accounted for 9.9 percent of the spirits market in America.

corn. Any of a variety of a cultivated cereal plant, *Zea mays,* yielding a sweet kernel that is made into oil, eaten fresh, or cooked in a wide variety of dishes. The word in Britain refers generally to any major cereal crop and was applied to this new cereal they found in North America in 1608. But the word *maize* (from the West Taino Indian, *mahiz*) was more common in the New World. Because the cereal was so associated with the Indians, it was soon being called "Indian corn" by the white settlers, to distinguish it from their own cereals such as barley and wheat.

Corn was not only a staple crop of the New World Indians, it was the staff of life for many tribes ranging from Canada to South America long before Columbus arrived in the West Indies. It was grown in Mexico in prehistoric times and reached the territory that is now the United States more than two millennia ago, where it became part of Indian rituals and religion. Many legends and deities were devoted to the cycle of raising corn. The Indians called the cereal "Sacred Mother" and "Giver of Life," and the Zunis dusted their doorways with cornmeal in the belief its miraculous powers would prevent the marauding conquistadores from entering. According to Alfred Whiting in *Ethnobotany of the Hopi* (1966), the Hopi of the Southwest had at least twenty different varieties of cultivated corn in a rainbow of colors, each of which was symbolic in some way.

The Indians roasted their corn and ground it into meal to make cakes, breads, and porridges. Tortillas were made with cornmeal before the Spanish introduced wheat, and succotash was an Indian vegetable stew that provided a great range of nutrients. When the Spanish landed on Cuba on November 5, 1492, they were treated to *mahiz* in at least two forms, baked and in flour.

When Captain John Smith explored the Virginia territory in 1607 he commented on "great heapes of corn" stored away by the Indians, and the colonists from the ship *Susan Constant* were met at Chesapeake Bay in April 1607 by friendly Indians led by Powhatan, who gave them a feast of cornbread, venison, and berries. When Miles Standish alighted from the *Mayflower* at Plymouth in 1620 he immediately came upon an Indian cache of corn and collected it for the winter ahead. By the following spring the Pilgrims were planting corn in the Indian method, by poking a hole in the ground and putting in the corn kernels with a dead fish that served to fertilize them. By the fall twenty acres of corn were harvested—the European grains of barley and wheat having failed —and served at the first THANKSGIVING. The Indians even brought a remarkable delicacy to the feast—POPCORN.

The new cereal was precious and helped the early settlers to survive those first harsh years. There is a record of a public whipping in the Plymouth Colony in 1622 of settlers who dared eat the new corn before it was fully ripe. Before long uniquely American dishes were being developed on the basis of this new grain, including an Indian bread called "pone" or "corn pone" (from the Algonquian word, *apan*, "baked") made of cornmeal, salt, and water. This was later called "corn bread" and has been a staple of American cooking to this day. HOMINY was, as of 1629, a term for a cornmeal porridge, though it referred specifically to dried, hulled corn kernels. Once the crops took hold throughout the colonies, cornmeal foods were everyday fare, and slaves on the southern plantations lived on a diet of corn bread and water, as did the poorest white settlers. "Dodger" was a corn cake first mentioned in 1831.

Sweet corn fit to be boiled and buttered was first found along the banks of the Susquehanna River in an Indian village in 1779, but it was not until the 1820s that it garnered much attention among farmers and not until the 1840s that it became a ubiquitous item on American dinner tables. In fact, the term *corn on the cob* only entered the language as of 1876.

Throughout the nineteenth century the corn crop increased as the settlers moved into the western territories. It was utilized both for food and fodder, and by 1882 people were referring to the great corn-producing states of the Midwest as the "corn belt." Corncrackers, mills for grinding corn, were known by 1844, and corn poppers were marketed in the 1870s. A breakfast cereal called "corn flakes," developed by Dr. John Harvey Kellogg of Battle Creek, Michigan, made its appearance in the market in 1907. Corn roasts were popular social events by 1899, and corn syrup was known by 1903.

From 1877 through 1920 American horticulturists developed many new hybrids that became standard on the country's farms, including Golden Chaff, shoepeg, Country Gentleman, and Bantam.

The major varieties of corn include dent (so called because the kernel becomes dented in shrinking), flint (very hardy), flour (preferred by the Indians), waxy (introduced from China as a tapioca substitute in 1907), and popcorn, also called rice or pearl corn.

Today the United States corn crop is equal to the combined crop of wheat, oats, barley, rice, rye, and sorghum, although most is used for feed. The principal corn-producing states are Ohio, Indiana, Illinois, Nebraska, South Dakota, and, the largest, Iowa.

Depending on the region of the country they live in, Americans often stand firmly on the merits of either white or yellow cornmeal in their recipes, white generally being preferred in the South and Midwest.

Americans enjoy their corn in a wide variety of ways, especially in late summer when the fresh corn on the cob is boiled and buttered. Corn on the cob is also available frozen, and shucked corn kernels are widely bought in cans. Creamed corn, sold canned, consists of whole or partially whole cut kernels packed in a creamy liquid from the kernels or other ingredients (including monosodium glutamate, starch, butter or margarine, and often pieces of green or red peppers).

Aside from those recipes given below, many corn items and dishes will be found under main entries, including HUSH PUPPIES, crackling bread, SPOON BREAD, INDIAN PUDDING, SUCCOTASH, TORTILLAS, and others.

CORN BREAD:
Pour 2 tbs. butter or bacon fat into a skillet and place in 450° oven to heat up. Combine 2 cups cornmeal, 4 tsp. baking powder, and 1 1/2 tsp. salt. Beat 1 egg in 1 1/2 cups milk, combine with dry ingredients, pour into skillet, and bake for 20–25 min.

CORN MUFFINS:
Follow recipe above and pour into buttered, heated muffin tins.

CORN STICKS:
(Recipe from The Coach House restaurant in New York City) Combine 3 cups yellow cornmeal, 3 cups flour, 2 tbs. baking powder, 3 tbs. sugar, and 1 1/4 tsp. salt. Add 4 eggs, one at a time, mixing well after each addition. Blend in 4 cups milk, add 1/2 cup melted butter and 1 cup heated but not thoroughly melted vegetable shortening, mix well, cover, and refrigerate 1 hr. Grease corn stick molds and set in 500° oven till very hot. Using pastry bag, lay batter into molds about three-quarters full. Bake at 400° for 15–20 min. till golden brown. Serve with butter or honey.

CORN CHOWDER:
Brown 1/4 lb. salt pork and add 1 chopped onion. Put in 4 cups peeled potatoes, 2
cups water, salt, and pepper, and simmer till potatoes are tender. Stir in 4 cups
scalded milk and 2 cups kernel corn. Correct seasonings, serve with pat of butter.
Serves 6.

corn. Logger's slang term for a poor grade of whiskey.

corn dog. Sausage in cornbread on a stick, created in 1942 by Texan Neil
Fletcher and called Fletcher's Original State Fair Corny Dog.

Fry 1/2 lb. mashed spicy sausage with 1 chopped onion, 1 tsp. cayenne, and 2 tbs.
beef stock. Grease corn stick pans and heat in 375° oven. Mix together 1 cup
cornmeal, 1 cup flour, 2 tbs. melted butter, 3 tsp. baking powder, 1/4 tsp. salt, 2
beaten eggs, and 3/4 cup milk. Fill corn stick pans, cover each stick with some of
the sausage mixture, cover with more corn mixture, and bake at 375° for 25 min.

corned beef. Beef that has been cured in salt. Corned beef is served either
as a main dish or as a sandwich in America. The term has nothing to do with
American corn, but rather with an English term, *corn,* for any small particle,
such as a grain of salt. Beef brisket is the usual cut, although rump, eye round,
bottom round, and tongue may also be used.
Saltpeter (sodium nitrate or potassium nitrate) is added to most of the
corned beef sold in the United States. Little curing is done in America.

To make corned beef, prepare a corning solution having a ratio of 10 parts water
to 1 part salt. For each 2 1/2 qt. water, add 1 cup salt and 3 tbs. pickling spice. Bring
to a boil in a large kettle. Cool to room temperature, then pour over the meat in
a nonmetal bowl to cover completely. Store, covered, in a cool place (below 60°) for
1 to 2 weeks, depending on the thickness of the meat. Rinse off any mold before
cooking.

Cornell bread. A bread made with soya flour, wheat germ, and nonfat dry
milk. It was developed as a high-protein bread in the 1930s by Clive M. McKay,
professor of animal nutrition at Cornell University in Ithaca, New York.
Originally created with the help of the Dry Milk Institute as a way of improving the diet of patients in mental hospitals, Cornell bread became popular
during World War II at a time when meat was rationed or increasingly
expensive and a high-protein alternative was needed.
The formula called for adding to the bottom of each cup of white flour in
a bread recipe one tablespoon soya flour, one tablespoon dry milk solids, and
one teaspoon wheat germ. The rest of the cup would then be filled with sifted
unbleached white flour.

corn syrup. A sweet, thick liquid derived from cornstarch treated with acids
or enzymes and used to sweeten and thicken candy, syrups, and snack foods.

cottage cheese. A moist, soft white cheese made from skimmed milk. Cottage cheese may be eaten on its own, in a salad, or with melon and is sometimes used as a substitute for ricotta in American lasagnas. It is consumed fresh, not aged.

After milk has soured it solidifies into a wet mass called "clabbered milk," which leaves behind the curds as the liquid ("whey") drops away. Sometimes this process is hastened by the addition of rennet. Cottage cheese is the product of one of the first stages of the process.

In the early part of the nineteenth century the name for such cheese was *pot cheese,* which today is almost synonymous with *cottage cheese,* though sometimes the term suggested a cheese that has drained for a longer period and acquired a slightly sour taste. By the 1820s *smear case* (from German, *Schmier-käse,* a spreading cheese) was also heard, particularly in Pennsylvania Dutch communities, and by midcentury the name *cottage cheese* entered the language.

Today cottage cheese may be bought in various forms. Sweet-curd cottage cheese is mild because it has been washed to remove acid; creamed cottage cheese contains 4–8 percent cream; and California-style or small-curd cottage cheese has smaller curds than regular cottage cheese. Medium-curd and large-curd cottage cheese, also sometimes called "popcorn cheese," is also available.

cottage pudding. A plain cake that is smeared with a sweet sauce. It was mentioned by O. Henry in 1909, and was listed in the *Fannie Farmer Cookbook* by 1943.

> Sift 1 3/4 cups flour, 1 1/4 cups sugar, 1 tsp. salt, and 2 1/2 tsp. baking powder and blend with 1/3 cup butter and 2/3 cup milk. Beat, then add 1 egg, 1/3 cup milk, and 1 tsp. vanilla. Butter an 8-sq.-in. cake pan, smear the bottom liberally with heated marmalade, pour in the batter, and bake at 400° for 25 min. Serves 6.

country captain. A curried chicken dish often attributed to Georgian origins. Eliza Leslie, in her mid-nineteenth-century cookbooks, contended that the dish got its name from a British army officer who brought the recipe back from his station in India. Others believe the dish originated in Savannah, Georgia, a major shipping port for the spice trade.

> Fry 4 bacon strips till crisp. Remove from pan, then sauté in 2 tbs. bacon fat 1 chopped green pepper, 1 chopped onion, 2 minced garlic cloves, and 1/2 cup celery for about 5 min. Add 6 chopped tomatoes and 1 cup orange juice, sprinkle in 2 tbs. curry powder and 1/2 tsp. thyme. Bring to a boil, then simmer for 5 min. Add 8 slices chicken breast and cook 30 min. Garnish with chutney or sprinkle with dried currants, roasted almonds, and minced parsley.

cowboy cocktail. Straight whiskey.

cowboy coffee. Black coffee without sugar, a term dating back to the 1940s. Cowboys themselves called their coffee "Arbuckle's," "belly-wash," "blackjack," "black water," "brown coffee," "jamoka" (from the words *java* and *mocha*), "six-shooter coffee" (strong enough to float a six-shooter pistol), and "Indian coffee" (which was a weakened, reboiled coffee made from used grounds that was considered not fit for cowboys but good enough for Indian visitors).

cowcumbers. Cowboy slang term for pickles.

cow grease. Cowboy slang for butter. Also called "cow salve."

cowpea. *(Vigna sinensis).* Also, "black-eyed pea," so called because of a black rim on the inner curve of the coat seam. Cowpea is a native Asian vine bearing pods, also used in Africa as food and fodder and probably brought to the West Indies in 1674 during the slave trade. It is said that James Oglethorpe brought the cowpea to Georgia in 1734, after which it became an important crop in the South and one of the staples of the Negro diet. Today it is still a cherished ingredient of black SOUL FOOD. The cowpea has been known by that name at least since 1776.

Many local names for the cowpea have been recorded—"Jerusalem pea," "field pea," "whippoorwill," "marble pea," "Tonkin pea,"—and George Washington Carver listed varieties called the "Extra Early Black-Eye," "New Era Lady Cuban Blackeye," "Iron," "Speckled," "Groot," "Clay," "Red Ripper," "Brabham," and "White Crowder." The most popular name, "black-eyed pea," was first mentioned back in 1738. Thomas Jefferson instructed his Monticello overseer to plant a plot of them.

Cowpeas are the legumes used in a dish of beans and rice called HOPPING JOHN, and, with green peppers, green onions, vinegar, and red peppers, "Texas caviar."

crab (Order Decapoda). Any of a large variety of crustaceans, mostly inhabiting salt water, with a hard shell and five pairs of legs, the front ones having pincers. There are more than forty-four hundred species, all edible, ranging from tiny pea crabs to giant, thirty-pound Tasmanians. After shrimp, crab is the most popular crustacean on American dining tables. Scores of preparations have been created region by region for the shellfish, and there are more varieties in North America than anywhere in the world. Crabs from Maryland's Chesapeake Bay are particularly savored in the East, while the Pacific's Dungeness and king crabs are highly popular in the West. Southerners pride themselves on their many different crab recipes, from crab cakes to gumbos.

The word is Middle English in origin.

The most important crabs in American cookery are:

   blue crab *(Callinectes sapidus).* With its blue-green shell and romantic Latin name, which means "beautiful swimmer," the blue crab is the most important species on the East Coast. The female carrying eggs is called by various names—"sponge," "ballie," "punk," and others. The shedding crab, called a "buster," is particularly valued for its culinary interest.

Dungeness crab. See main entry.

king crab *(Paralithodes camtschaticus).* A large Pacific crab, also called "Alaska crab," "Japanese crab," and "Russian crab," which derives its name from its regal size. However, only about 25 percent of the crustacean is actually edible, and most Americans buy its claws frozen.

land crab *(Cardisoma guanhumi).* Also, "mulatto" or "white crab." Land crabs are found throughout the Gulf of Mexico and the Caribbean. A. J. McClane, in his *Encyclopedia of Fish Cookery* (1977), notes that "this species was so abundant in south Florida until the 1950s that our streets were often overrun at night with migrating crabs. Evidently their place has been usurped in a changing ecology."

rock crab *(Cancer irroratus).* An East Coast crab that lives among rocks and in deep water, similar to the Jonah crab *(Cancer borealis).*

spider crab *(Libinia emarginata).* With its spindly legs that make it resemble a spider, this crab is given market names that would make a consumer less squeamish, such as "snow," "tanner," and "queen crab."

stone crab. See main entry.

Much American crab is marketed as "crabmeat," either frozen or vacuum-packed, which constitutes the overwhelming majority of crab used in restaurants. Crabmeat may be labelled "lump" meat, "flake" (small pieces), or "flake and lump," mostly from blue crabs.

See recipe at SHE-CRAB SOUP.

crab butter. The white-yellow fat inside the back shell of a large crab. Crab butter is much prized as a delicacy and is often added to a dressing or sauce.

LEMON CRAB BUTTER:
Mash crab butter from 2 crabs (about 1/2 cup) and beat in 4–5 tbs. olive oil, 3 tbs. lemon juice, pepper, salt, and a dash of hot pepper seasoning or cayenne. Serves 2.

crabmeat Louis. A dish made from crabmeat and a dressing of mayonnaise, chili sauce, grated onion, and various other seasonings. The origins of the dish are somewhat obscure, except that it is believed to have been created on the West Coast, probably in San Francisco, around the turn of the century. Helen Brown in her *West Coast Cookbook* (1956) contended that the dish was first made at San Francisco's Solari restaurant, while others credit the St. Francis Hotel in that city. The dressing may also be used for lobster or shrimp.

Combine 1 cup mayonnaise, 1/2 cup cream, 1/4 cup chili sauce, 1/4 cup chopped scallion, 1/4 cup chopped green pepper, 2 tbs. chopped green olives, salt, and the juice of 1/2 lemon. Combine with crabmeat, set on a bed of lettuce, and garnish, if desired, with sliced olives and sliced hard-boiled eggs.

crabmeat Remick. A dish made from crabmeat, chili sauce, mayonnaise, and other seasonings. It was created in 1920 at the Plaza Hotel in New York City by chef Albert Leopold Lattard in honor of William H. Remick (1866–1922), president of the New York Stock Exchange from 1919 to 1921.

Combine 1 cup chili sauce, 1 cup mayonnaise, 1/2 oz. dry mustard, 1 tsp. paprika, 1 tsp. celery salt, 1/2 tsp. Tabasco sauce, and 1/2 tsp. Worcestershire sauce. Blend half of this mixture with 1 lb. crabmeat. Spoon the crabmeat mixture into 2 doz. empty clam shells, pour the rest of the sauce mixture on tops of shells, sprinkle with Parmesan cheese, and set in 350° oven till sauce bubbles.

crab Norfolk. A dish of crabmeat baked and seasoned with vinegar, Tabasco, and Worcestershire sauce. The name supposedly derives from the city of Norfolk, Virginia, where the dish was made in what was called a "Norfolk aluminum pan," a small, oval cooking pan in which the crabmeat was placed. According to Craig Claiborne of the *New York Times*, the dish was created by W. O. Snowden at the Snowden and Mason Restaurant in Norfolk, which opened in 1924.

Combine 1 lb. crabmeat with 2 tbs. vinegar, 1/2 tsp. Tabasco sauce, 1/2 tsp. Worcestershire sauce, salt, and pepper. Place portions in small pans each containing 1 tbs. melted butter. Bake in 350° oven till well heated.

cracker. A thin, unsweetened wheatflour wafer made from unleavened dough and usually eaten as a snack, as a canapé, with soups, and with dips. The word comes from the "cracking" sound it makes when broken. Since the eighteenth century Americans have spoken of these wafers by this term, first appearing in print in 1739, and it is still a word rarely used in England, where *biscuit* is preferred. (To Americans, a biscuit is a small, yeast-dough form of bread.) In the 1830s Americans called the wafers "soda crackers," and COMMON CRACK-ERS or oyster crackers were placed in New England chowders or split and buttered. Graham crackers are sweet and made with GRAHAM FLOUR, while Saltines is a trademark of the National Biscuit Company ("Nabisco") for a very popular cracker made with salt on top. See also TRENTON CRACKER.

In the nineteenth century crackers were sold at grocery stores from cracker barrels or packaged in cracker boxes or Boston tins.

cracker barrel. A large barrel, found in turn-of-the-century groceries and general stores, for holding crackers that were to be sold in quantity. The term first appeared in print in 1905.

crackling. A crispy morsel left over after most of the fat has been rendered by cooking pork, a meaning the word has had since the beginning of the eighteenth century. Cracklings may be added to a variety of dishes—beans and other vegetables, for instance—and a particular favorite in the South is "crackling [or cracklin'] bread."

In Cajun Louisiana cracklings are called "grattons," from the French, *gratter,* "to scrape."

CRACKLING BREAD:
To 1 qt. cornmeal, add enough boiling water to make a stiff dough. Add 1 cup cracklings, mix and form into oblong cakes. Bake at 400° till inserted knife comes

out clean and top is golden-brown. (Modern-day recipes usually include eggs and butter.)

crackseed. A snack in Hawaii available in scores of varieties and eaten like candy. Crackseeds are made by smashing the seed of a fruit and preserving the pulp with salt; they have a salty-sweet pungency with a faint taste of licorice. Some of the varieties sold in small packages include sweet *li hing mui* (plum), rock salt plum, salted mango, wet lemon peel, and wet *li hing mui.*

cranberry *(Vaccinium macrocarpon).* A very tart red berry grown in bogs from low, trailing vines. Cranberries are used in sauces, jellies, and beverages and as a traditional accompaniment at Thanksgiving dinners. There are several species of wild cranberry in the world, but the American or large cranberry is the only one in wide cultivation. This variety makes up a major crop of Massachusetts, New Jersey, Wisconsin, and Oregon. Cranberry bogs are sandy and often flooded, and some continue to be productive after a century. In New England the bogs are picked between Labor Day (when the Early Blacks ripen) and the end of October (when the Late Howes are brought in).

The Indians of New England, who called them *"sassamanesh,"* long enjoyed cranberries, both raw or sweetened with maple sugar, and they often added them to their PEMMICAN. The first European settlers found the fruit similar to their lingonberry but somewhat too tart unless sweetened or made into a condiment.

There is no hard evidence that the Pilgrims had cranberries at the First Thanksgiving, held in October of 1621, but it is a fair assumption that the Indians might have brought them to the feast at a time when the cranberries were at their ripest in that region. The name *cranberry* was not English, however; the settlers probably called the berries "fenberries," after a fruit they knew at home. Years later the Dutch introduced the word *kranbeere* (from the Low German, *kraanbere*, "crane berry," because its stamen resembled a beak). Others referred to them as "bounce berries," because of their bouncey quality. There is a story that a New Jersey grower named John I. Webb ("Peg-Leg John") initiated the development of the first cranberry separator after he transferred the berries from his loft to the ground by allowing them to tumble down the stairs—the ripest, firmest berries bounced to the ground, the bruised fruit remained on the steps. Commercial cranberry cultivation began after another accidental discovery, this time on Cape Cod about 1816. Henry Hall noticed that bogs that had had sand blown over them produced a sturdy crop of cranberries, so he spread some sand on his own property and duplicated the results. There is a cherished legend on Cape Cod about how the cranberry bogs began there. It seems that an Indian medicine man cast a spell over the Reverend Richard Bourne and then mired him in quicksand. For the next fifteen days the two men waged a battle of wits, during which the motionless Reverend Bourne was sustained only by a white dove who fed him cranberries. The Indian fell exhausted from the strain, and the spell was lifted from the minister. The story goes on to tell how one of the berries fell to the ground and became rooted forever in the Cape Cod soil, which is acknowledged to produce some of America's best cranberries.

Today the cranberry is most often used as a sweet relish served with poultry and fowl, and contains either the whole berry or is made as a jelly. It has long been a beverage berry in New England, but only since 1967 has it been promoted as a "cranberry cocktail" in the rest of the United States by the largest producer, Ocean Spray, Inc., which runs the Cranberry World Visitors Center in Plymouth, Massachusetts.

CRANBERRY SAUCE:
A very simple old recipe calls for washing and stewing cranberries in water, then adding their weight in sugar just before removing them from the fire.

CRANBERRY RELISH:
Wash 2 lb. fresh cranberries and coarsely grind them in a blender or food processor. Place them in a large kettle with the grated rinds of 3 oranges, 3/4 cup raisins, and 4 cups sugar. Heat to simmer, stirring frequently, for about 1 1/2–2 hr. Cool.

CANDIED CRANBERRIES:
Spread 1 lb. fresh washed cranberries on a greased baking pan, then sprinkle with 2 1/2 cups sugar. Let stand for about 1 hr., then cover with foil and bake in 350° oven for about 45 min., stirring occasionally. Chill and serve with whipped cream.

CRANBERRY-NUT PUDDING:
Sprinkle 1/4 cup brown or maple sugar over 1 1/4 cups cranberries in a bowl. Add 1/4 cup chopped walnuts. Beat 1 egg and add 1/2 cup sugar, then 1/2 cup flour and 1/3 cup melted butter. Pour this over cranberries and bake in a pie plate for 45 min. at 325°. Serve with whipped cream or ice cream.

CRANLILLI:
Grind coarsely 1 cup fresh washed cranberries, 1 chopped onion, and 1 green pepper. In a covered saucepan simmer the cranberry mixture with 1/2 cup sugar, 1/2 cup vinegar, and 1/2 tsp. salt for about 10 min. Uncover and simmer 10 min. more. Served chilled with meat or poultry.

crayfish. Also, "crawfish" and "crawdaddy." Any of various freshwater crustaceans of the genera *Cambarus* and *Astacus*. Although considerably smaller, the crayfish resembles the LOBSTER, and there are 250 species and subspecies found in North America alone. The name is from Middle English, *crevise*, and, ultimately, from the Frankish, *krabītja*.

Crayfish was a significant part of the diet of the American Indians of the South, and crayfish still achieve their highest status among the Cajuns of Louisiana, which harvests about 18 million pounds of the crustacean annually. Louisianans are crazy about crayfish (which they pronounce "crawfish," but also call "mudbugs," "creekcrabs," "freshwater lobsters," "yabbies," and other names) and hold "crawfish boils" as often as possible. Breaux Bridge, Louisiana, calls itself the "Crawfish Capital of the World" and holds a yearly festival of eating and drinking to prove it, cooking up crayfish in pies, gumbos, stews, and every other way imaginable. Louisiana produces 90 percent of the crayfish crop.

Crayfish are commercially harvested in waters of the Mississippi basin, most of them of the Red Swamp and White River varieties. These are eaten with the fingers, picking or sucking the white meat out of the body, claws, and head.

CRAWFISH ÉTOUFFÉE:
(A Louisiana specialty; *étouffée* is a French term that means "smothered.") Sauté 1 chopped onion, 1/2 cup chopped green pepper, 2 chopped shallots or scallions, and 2 chopped cloves of garlic in 6 tbs. butter for about 15 min. Add 3 lb. crayfish and continue cooking for another 15 min. Add salt and pepper to taste, 1/4 tsp. cayenne, and enough water to moisten bottom of pan. Bring to boil, simmer for 5 min., basting crayfish. Serve over boiled rice.

cream. The fat-rich, unhomogenized part of the milk that rises to the surface. F.D.A. Standards of Identity mandate that a product cannot be called "cream" unless it contains at least 18 percent butterfat.

half-and-half. A mixture of half cream and half whole milk.

heavy cream. Must contain not less than 36 percent butterfat; may contain emulsifiers, stabilizers, nutritive sweeteners, and flavoring ingredients.

light cream. Also called "coffee cream." Light cream must contain less than 30 percent, but not less than 18 percent, butterfat and may contain emulsifiers, stabilizers, nutritive sweeteners, and flavoring agents.

light whipping cream. Must contain not less than 30 percent but less than 36 percent butterfat and may contain emulsifiers, stabilizers, nutritive sweeteners, and flavoring ingredients.

sour cream. Cream that has been treated with lactic acid producing bacteria and containing not less than 18 percent butterfat. Sour cream may contain optional ingredients such as rennet, salt, sodium citrate, and flavoring ingredients.

cream cheese. A cow's-milk cheese with a very smooth consistency and a mild, slightly tangy flavor. Under F.D.A. regulations cream cheese must contain not less than 33 percent milkfat and not more than 55 percent moisture. The cheese is not aged, but gum arabic may be added to increase firmness and shelf life. Diluted cream cheese may be called "imitation cream cheese" (although this may also refer to a nondairy product).

Cream cheese became available to everyone after the Breakstone Company produced Breakstone's Downsville Cream Cheese (named after the New York community where it was made) in 1920. It became immediately popular among Jewish communities in New York City as a spread for BAGELS.

Creole mustard. A hot, spicy mustard made from seeds marinated in vinegar. It is a specialty of Louisiana's German Creoles, who brought the mustard seeds from Austria and Holland.

crib. A miner's term for lunch, derived from the crib-shaped boxes in which lumber was sorted.

Crisco. The trademark of a shortening made from vegetable oils, principally soybean. By a process called "hydrogenation" the oils are suspended in fat solids so as to form a white, soft mass that is packed in air-tight tin cans.

The product is manufactured by the Procter & Gamble Company, which began marketing the new shortening in 1911. Its virtues over lard, butter, and other vegetable oils at that time were that it did not pick up odors or flavors from foods fried in it, did not smoke when heated, and could be kept for long periods without going rancid. (In the early 1960s the product was altered to double the amount of polyunsaturates, considered by some scientists to be important to health.)

The name *Crisco* was the result of a contest held among Procter & Gamble employees. The two leading choices were *Krispo* and *Cryst,* meant to suggest the hissing sound of the shortening in the pan, and these were combined into *Crisco.* From the beginning the product was marketed with recipes attached, and the name became fairly synonymous with *shortening,* especially *white shortening,* and was used as an alternative to heavier fats such as lard. It has been particularly favored in the South, where, according to James Villas in *American Taste* (1982), it is the essential ingredient in making good **southern fried chicken.**

crust coffee. A coffee substitute known in nineteenth-century New England. It was made by toasting bread till almost burned, pouring boiling water on it, straining the liquid, and drinking with sugar and cream.

Cuba libre. A cocktail made from rum, cola, and lime juice. The name in Spanish means "free Cuba," but its origins are obscure, possibly dating from the Spanish-American War (1898) when Cuba was "liberated" from Spanish rule.

According to a deposition by Fausto Rodriguez on October 24, 1965, this blend of ingredients was made in August of 1900 by a "Mr. X," who worked in the office of the United States Signal Corps in Cuba. (Mr. Rodriguez was a messenger for the Corps.) The drink became immediately popular among the American soldiers.

Combine 1 oz. light rum, 1/2 oz. 151-proof rum, 1/2 oz. Coca-Cola, 1/2 oz. lime juice, and 1/2 tsp. sugar. Serve over ice cubes and garnish with a lime peel.

cucumber *(Cucumis sativus).* A long, green vegetable in the gourd family that is generally eaten raw, as in a salad.

The word is from the Latin, *cucumis,* which in Middle English became *cucumer.*

Though long believed to have originated in India, there is now evidence that the cucumber came from Thailand and was cultivated there ten thousand years before Christ. By the fourteenth century A.D. it was being cultivated in England. Spaniards brought the cucumber to America, and it was then readily cultivated by the Pueblo Indians. Today it is a very important crop in the United States. Americans ate 4.1 pounds per person in 1982.

curaçao. A cordial based on the flavor of green oranges from the island of Curaçao in the Caribbean. It is an ingredient in scores of cocktails and was first mentioned in print in 1813. Curaçao recipes were, however, listed in cookbooks in the middle of the nineteenth century, as the one below, called "curacoa," from Sarah J. Hale's *Mrs. Hale's New Cook Book* (1857) shows:

> Wash 1 lb. of the dried peel of Seville oranges in lukewarm water. Put peel in jars and add a mixture of 8 pt. brandy and 2 pt. water. Let stand for 2 weeks, shaking often. Strain. Melt 5 lb. sugar in 3 pt. water, mix with liquor, strain.

currant. Any of a variety of prickly shrubs of the genus *Ribes* that bear small, dark berries that are often dried and used as a flavoring. The word is from Old French, *Corinthe,* referring to Corinth, because the berries were called in Middle English "raysons of coraunte"—that is, "raisins of Corinth."

Currants first began to appear in England in the seventeenth century and were brought to America soon afterwards, even though there were already native varieties in the New World, specifically the American black currant *(R. americanum).* Until the present century currants were cultivated in the United States, but their growth has now been discouraged because currants carry the parasite *Cronartium ribicola,* which does not harm the plant itself but attacks precious white pines in its vicinity. Most currants on the American market are therefore dried and imported.

cush. A cornmeal pancake made in the South. The name (first recorded in 1770) arrived in America with the African slaves brought to the Caribbean and the South; it derives from the Arab, *kuskus,* "to grind small," and the grain dish of Morocco called "couscous." In Louisiana "coush-coush caille" is a dish of cornbread and clabber.

COUSH-COUSH:
Combine 2 cups yellow cornmeal, 1/2 cup flour, 1 tbs. baking powder, 2 tsp. salt, and 2 tsp. sugar, then add 1 1/2 cups water to make a paste. Melt 1/4 lb. lard in a skillet, add the cornmeal paste, and fry for about 10 min. Stir to incorporate brown bits of crust, then lower heat and cook for another 15 min. Serve as a cereal with cream, sugar, or cane syrup.

cushaw *(Cucurbita moschata).* An American crook-necked SQUASH popular among the Cajun people of Louisiana. The name comes from the Indian, probably the Algonquian of North Carolina and Virginia, *coscushaw,* and first appears in English in 1588.

> Wash 1 cushaw, cut into small pieces, boil till tender, drain, and scoop out the pulp. Mash the pulp together with 1/2 lb. butter, 2 cups sugar, 1 1/2 cups milk, 4 beaten eggs, 1/2 tsp. nutmeg, 1/2 tsp. allspice, and 1/4 tsp. salt. Bake at 300° for about 30 min. Serves 6–8.

cyclone candy. A sweet confection mentioned by Marjorie Mosser in her *Foods of Old New England* (1957). The reasons for its name are unknown.

> Cook 1 cup sugar with 1 cup molasses, 3 tbs. vinegar, and 2 tbs. butter to the hard-ball stage. Add 1 tsp. vanilla, 1/4 tsp. baking soda, stir, and pour into buttered pan. Cool and cut into candy-size pieces.

Dagwood sandwich. A sandwich made with many slices of bread enclosing various kinds of meats, lettuce, vegetables, and other condiments. The name derives from the comic-strip character Dagwood Bumstead, created and drawn by Murat Bernard. ("Chic") Young (1901–1973) for *Blondie,* which began on September 8, 1930, as part of the King Features Syndicate.

The sandwich first appeared in the comic strip on April 16, 1936, and, according to Dean Young, son of Chic Young and now co-author of the strip with Bill Yates, "it was not at first as colossal a sandwich as it eventually became through the years." The character and the sandwich became immediately linked, and Americans began referring to such overstuffed items as "Dagwoods." The sandwich was also a regular feature in the series of twenty-eight *Blondie* motion pictures made from 1938 to 1951 and in two television series, in 1954 and 1968, of the same name.

daiquiri. Sometimes "Daiquiri." A cocktail made from rum, lime juice, and sugar. It is named after the town of Daiquirí, near Santiago, in Cuba, where, after the Spanish-American War (1898), Americans came to work the mines, retiring on weekends to the Venus Hotel to drink such a cocktail. Chief engineer Jennings S. Cox has been credited with naming the drink in 1900 after the mines. Some say he himself invented the cocktail. The *Oxford English Dictionary,* however, finds the first printed reference in F. Scott Fitzgerald's novel, *This Side of Paradise,* in 1920.

The frozen daiquiri, for which crushed ice is added before blending, was supposedly created at the La Florida Bar (known to customers in Ernest Hemingway's day as the "Floridita") in Havana, Cuba.

> Combine 2 tsp. lime juice, 1/2 tsp. superfine sugar, and 2 oz. light rum over ice, shake and strain into a chilled cocktail glass. Sometimes the rim of the glass is sugared. A "frozen daiquiri" is made by adding about 4 ice cubes to the mixture and pulverizing it in an electric blender; a "pink daiquiri" by adding 1 tsp. each of maraschino and grenadine. See also BACARDI COCKTAIL.

daisy. A cocktail made from citrus fruit juice, a cordial or fruit syrup, and liquor. Daisies are generally synonymous with "fixes," which were originally based on pineapple syrup while daisies were based on raspberry or grenadine, but these distinctions have blurred since the mid-nineteenth century, when both drinks were especially popular. The name probably derives from a slang term meaning "something excellent," rather than directly from the flower.

dandelion *(Taraxacum officinale).* A native Eurasian plant that has become naturalized as a weed in North America. Its leaves are sometimes added to salads, and is flowers are used to produce a HONEY, especially in Colorado.

The word is from the Medieval Latin, *dens leōnis,* "lion's tooth," via Old French.

Danish pastry. Also, "Danish." A term encompassing a variety of yeast-dough pastries rolled and filled with cheese, prune, almond paste, fruit preserves, nuts, or other condiments. These pastries are a staple breakfast item, especially on the East Coast, where one orders a "Danish" prefixed by the filling desired. Although the pastries may have Danish origins, these flaky buns and rolls are more often associated with New York Jewish delicatessans and bakeries.

With this meaning the word first appeared in print, according to *Webster's Ninth,* in 1928.

> Dissolve 1 pkg. yeast in 1/4 cup warm water. Mix 1/3 cup sugar with 1 tsp. salt, 1/4 cup butter, 1 cup scalded milk, and cool. Beat in 2 eggs, add yeast, 1/4 tsp. vanilla, 1/4 tsp. lemon extract, 1/4 tsp. mace, and 3 cups flour, and make an elastic dough. Cover, let rise till doubled. Roll out to 1/3-in. thickness, dot with 1/2 cup soft butter, fold and seal. Roll dough, place in greased bowl, let stand for 20 min., then roll out to a thickness of 1/3 in., place on buttered baking sheet, and let rise till doubled. Sprinkle with ground nuts and bake at 475° for 10 min. Glaze top with sugar. If a filling is desired, it should be rolled into the dough before the second rising.

date. The fruit of the date palm *(Phoenix dactylifera),* a tropical tree. The sweet fruit is especially popular in Asia and the Middle East. The name is from the Greek, *daktulos,* "finger," after the shape of the fruit. The date began to be cultivated in California about 1902, principally from the variety deglet noor. More than 99 percent of the dates marketed in the United States are grown in California.

Deacon Porter's hat. A suet pudding steamed in a long, cylindrical mold. It is possibly the same pudding as BROTHER JONATHAN'S HAT. According to Eleanor Early in her *New England Cookbook* (1954), "When this pudding ... made its first appearance at dinner one noon in 1837, a student [at] Mount Holyoke Female Seminary, cried, 'Oh, see the Deacon's hat!'," referring to Deacon Andrew W. Porter, a member of the school's first board of trustees, who wore a stovepipe hat every day. Early also notes that "there is said to have been a light-colored pudding, made in a similar mold, called the Deacon's Summer Hat, but that is only a legend."

> Mix 3 cups flour, 1 tsp. baking soda, 1 tsp. cinnamon, 1/2 tsp. nutmeg, 1/2 tsp. ground cloves, 1/2 tsp. ginger, and sift thoroughly. Chop finely 1 cup suet and add to 1 cup molasses and 1 cup milk. Combine with flour mixture, pour into greased 2-qt. mold, and steam for 3 hr. Serve warm with hard sauce.

dead soldier. Also, "dead marine." An empty beer bottle. The term began sometime during World War I.

Delaware. An American red Labrusca grape that makes wines that rarely need the sugaring that other eastern varieties require. It was introduced in the 1840s and is today used as a table grape as well as a champagne grape.

delicatessen. A grocery store that usually sells cooked meats, prepared foods, and delicacies. The word is from the German, *Delikatesse,* "delicacy," and, ultimately, from Latin, *dēlicātus,* "delicate." In the 1880s it referred to preserved foods, and a "delicatessen shop" or "delicatessen store" was a place that sold such items. By the turn of the century the store's name was shortened to *delicatessen,* and, somewhat later, as slang, *deli* or *delly,* which now may also refer to the food itself.

These stores were usually owned by Jews in New York (who sometimes preferred the non-German word *appetizing* for their establishment), and to call a store a "Jewish delicatessen" is something of a tautology. Today there are delicatessens in most large eastern cities, though New York is still the hub for such places, which may or may not be kosher.

Delicatessens specialize in serving pastrami, potato salad, pickles, rye bread, liverwurst, and many other items enjoyed by the Jews of the eastern cities.

Delmonico potatoes. Potato balls boiled and buttered and sprinkled with lemon juice, parsley, pepper, and salt. The dish was featured at New York's Delmonico's restaurant in the nineteenth century.

Democrat. A sweet, baked buttermilk confection of the nineteenth century. The nature of the connection is obscure, but the dish somehow refers to the Democratic Party.

> Combine 1 pt. buttermilk with 1 cup confectioners' sugar, 3 beaten egg yolks, 1/2 cup butter, 3 tsp. baking powder, and 1 qt. flour. Fold in 3 stiffly beaten egg whites. Bake in muffin tins, 1 tbs. of batter to a tin, for about 20 min. at 375°.

deviled. Also, "devilled." Any of a variety of dishes prepared with hot seasonings, such as cayenne or mustard. The word derives from its association with the Satanic demon that dwells in hell, from the Greek, *diabolos,* "slanderer." In a culinary context the word first appears in print in 1786; by 1820 Washington Irving had used the word in his *Sketchbook* to describe a highly seasoned dish similar to a curry.

Deviled dishes were very popular throughout the nineteenth and into the twentieth centuries, especially for seafood preparations and some appetizers.

DEVILED CRAB:
Simmer 1/2 lb. crabmeat with 2 chopped shallots in 4 tbs. butter. Add 1 cup cream sauce, salt and pepper, 1 tsp. hot mustard, 1/2 tsp. Worcestershire sauce, and 1 dash cayenne pepper, and remove from heat. Bind with 2 beaten egg yolks. Fill crab shells with mixture, sprinkle with bread crumbs, dot with butter, and bake in 400° oven until crusted and browned. Serves 4.

DEVILED EGGS:
Remove the shells from hard-boiled eggs, cut into halves, and remove yolks. Crush the yolks and combine with various seasonings that might include vinegar, mayonnaise, lemon juice, dry mustard, ketchup, Worcestershire sauce, cayenne, cheese, chives, or parsley. Stuff egg-white halves with mixture and chill.

devil's food. A cake, muffin, or cookie made with dark chocolate, so called because it is supposedly so rich and delicious that it must, to a moralist, be somewhat sinful, although the association is clearly made with humor. Its dark color contrasted with the snowy white of ANGEL FOOD CAKE, an earlier confection. The first devil's food recipe appeared in 1905.

Cream 1/4 lb. butter with 1 1/4 cups sugar. Add 2 eggs, one at a time, then 1 3/4 cups flour, 1 cup milk, 1 tsp. baking powder, 2 squares baking chocolate, melted, 1 tsp. vanilla, and a pinch of salt. Pour into 2 buttered cake pans, bake for 25 min. at 350°, cool on rack, then spread both layers with vanilla or chocolate frosting. Stack layers and spread completely with frosting.

dewberry (Genus *Rubus*). Any of a variety of trailing forms of the BLACK-BERRY. In his *Soul Food Cookbook* (1969), Bob Jeffries refers to dewberries baked in pastry as "dubies." The word first appeared in print in 1578.

dextrose. A sugar (also called "glucose" or "grape sugar") derived from the sap and juice of grapes and other plants. Dextrose provides the major source of energy in animals and is used to thicken and sweeten caramel, soda pop, baked goods, and candy.

dill (*Anethum graveolens*). An herb, native to the Old World, used as a seasoning in sauces, soups, and salads. Its name derives from the West Germanic, *dilja*. Pickles are often flavored with dill, which in the United States is grown primarily in Ohio and the Midwest. In *Food* (1980), Waverly Root notes that "the Romans mixed aneth oil in their gladiators' food in the belief that it was a tonic, and it may have been for the same reason that dill seeds were given to American children a century or two back to chew in church, perhaps to keep them awake during long sermons, for which reason they were called 'meetin' seeds.' "

dinner. The main meal of the day. Until the 1820s this was commonly the midday meal, supper being a lighter meal at the end of the workday. Today, dinner is usually the evening meal.

The word *dinner,* dating to the thirteenth century in England, derives from the French, *diner,* ultimately from the Latin, *dis-,* "away," plus *jejunus,* "fast." *Supper* is also found in English as of the thirteenth century, from the French, *so(u)per,* itself possibly related to *soup,* which was often the simple repast of the evening meal.

In America the tradition of eating the heaviest meal at midday was superseded in the 1820s by the demands of workers whose mealtime was often not paid for by their employers, thereby necessitating a quick, light meal before getting back to work. This became known as LUNCH, and the main meal of the day, dinner, was consumed after work ended. The tradition of eating the main meal in the afternoon was carried on as the "Sunday dinner," since Sunday was for most people the only day of the week off from work. Even after the five-day work week became the norm, the Sunday dinner, held anywhere from noon onwards, continued to be an American family gathering.

Today southerners still speak of "supper" as the evening meal, though it may be eaten somewhat earlier than in the rest of the country. Most Americans refer to the evening meal as "dinner," although there is occasional reference made to "pre-theater suppers" or "after-theater suppers" in New York City restaurants that cater to theater-goers who must make an eight-o'clock curtain or wish to eat lightly after the show.

dip. A condiment, often made with mayonnaise or sour cream, into which one dips any of a variety of vegetables or snacks. Dips are usually served with party food. In the mid-nineteenth century *dip* referred to a sauce of pork fat served on fish, and the first references in print to items like clam dip, cheese dip, and mushroom dip were only as recent as 1960, although the term in this context must be somewhat older.

CREAM CHEESE DIP:
Mix 1 3-oz. pkg. cream cheese with 1 1/2 tbs. light cream. Add 1/2 tbs. mayonnaise, 1/4 tsp. paprika, salt and pepper, 2 finely chopped garlic cloves, 1/2 tsp. Worcestershire sauce, 1 tsp. lemon juice, and 1/2 tsp. mustard.

ONION DIP:
Mix 1 pkg. onion soup mix with 2 cups sour cream.

CHILI SAUCE DIP:
Combine 1/2 cup chili sauce, 1/4 cup horseradish, 1 tsp. Worcestershire sauce, 1 tsp. minced onion, 1/4 tsp. minced garlic, 1/2 tsp. salt, 1/8 tsp. pepper, 1 tbs. veinegar, 1/4 tsp. bottled meat sauce, 1 tsp. celery salt, and 2 tbs. sugar and chill.

dirty rice. A Louisiana Cajun dish of rice cooked with chicken gizzards and livers, so called because the meat gives the rice a "dirty" appearance.

Boil 10 each of chicken gizzards, necks, livers, and hearts in 2 qt. water till tender. Remove and retain liquid. Fry 4 lb. hot sausage and retain fat. Sauté 2 minced onions, 1 minced bell pepper, and 4 stalks minced celery in 3 tbs. of the retained fat, then add 5 chopped scallions and cook for about 10 min. Add 1 cup chopped ham and chicken mixture, 8 tbs. melted butter, and 2 tbs. chopped parsley. Add water from kettle, salt, and pepper, and let simmer for 15 min. Blend in 3 lb. cooked rice.

Dr. Brown's Cel-Ray Tonic. A celery-flavored carbonated beverage first bottled in 1868 and now bottled by the American Beverage Company in Brooklyn, New York. Its unique flavor, from celery seeds, has long been popular with New York City's Jewish community, and its label proudly proclaims that it "contains vitamins G B D." "Dr. Brown" is a trademark, but there was never such a person connected with the drink.

dog *(Canis familiaris).* A domesticated carnivorous mammal of many breeds. In America the dog has never been a food animal except among Indians and Hawaiians. In fact most Americans and Europeans, who have traditionally used dogs as pets and domesticated them for hunting and herding, find the idea of eating the animal abhorrent, although the first settlers from England who landed in Virginia in 1607 staved off starvation by boiling and eating their mastiffs.

In precolonial Hawaii dogs, which were brought from Polynesia, were called *"ilio"* and raised in large herds for food; they were actually preferred to pig in those days, and in 1830 the Reverend William Ellis reported that dogs were "mostly fed on vegetables; and we have sometimes seen them kept in yards, with small houses to sleep in. A part of the rent of every tenant who occupies land, is paid in dogs for his landlord's table." Ellis claimed to have seen two hundred dogs baked at one time for a feast and to have heard that when King Taumuarii of Tauai visited the governor of Hawaii, Kuakini, four hundred dogs were baked for the dinner.

doggie bag. A bag in which a customer may carry home the edible remains of a restaurant meal to be eaten the next day, though its name suggests—in a rather too-cute manner—that the contents will be fed to one's pet. The term dates in print to 1963 and became so popular by the 1970s that some restaurants even had special bags imprinted with the words *doggie bag* on them.

Dolly Varden *(Salvelinus malma).* This char or TROUT, which grows up to three feet in length, is a multicolored, spotted fish found from Alaska to Northern California in both salt and fresh water. Its beautiful markings have caused some Alaskans to call the fish "golden trout" or "golden-finned trout," but the more common name, "Dolly Varden," comes from a character in Charles Dickens's novel *Barnaby Rudge* (1841) who wore a tight-fitting dress with a flowered skirt over a brightly colored petticoat.

The *Yreka Union* (California) of June 3, 1876, insisted the fish were "first caught in McCloud River by white men—Messrs. Josiah Edson of Shasta Valley and Geo. Campbell of Soda Springs, and were given the name of Dolly Varden by Elda McCloud, a niece of Mr. Campbell." But Goode's *Fisheries* (1884) contends that "in the Sacramento the name 'Dolly Varden' was given to [the fish] by the landlady at the hotel, and this name it still retains in that region."

"Dolly Varden" is also the name of a New England cake, mentioned in *The Pentucket Housewife* (1882).

DOLLY VARDEN CAKE:
Beat 4 egg yolks separately from 4 egg whites. Fold the two together, add 1 cup creamed butter, 2 1/2 cups sugar, 1 cup milk, 4 cups flour, 1/2 tsp. baking soda, and 1 tsp. cream of tartar. Divide the mixture in two. To each half of the mixture add 1 tbs. molasses, 1 tsp. spices, and some raisins and currants. Pour each mixture into separate loaf pans and bake in medium-hot oven.

dolphin. Either of two varieties of marine fish, *Coryphaena hippurus* or *C. equisetis,* ranging in size from two pounds to fifty pounds or more and inhabiting both oceans of North America. These food-fish dolphins are not in any way related to the mammals of the same name. The word comes from Greek, *delphis.*

These varieties are better known in Hawaii as *"mahimahi,"* and there are considered a delicacy. They are also sought in Florida, where the roe is eaten.

dope. Slang term in the South for cola drinks, probably an allusion to the illusion that the caffeine in some soda pop acts as a slight stimulant. Originally it applied to true narcotics, especially heated opium, which became a gloppy substance like the Dutch sauce called *"doop,"* from which the word derives.

doughnut. A deep-fried yeast pastry that has a hole in the middle. Doughnuts are a favorite snack and confection throughout the United States and are known in other forms throughout Europe.

The first American doughnuts did not have holes at all; they were quite literally little "nuts" of dough. The Pilgrims, who had spent the years 1607–1620 in Holland, learned to make doughnuts there and brought them to New England; the most direct antecedent of the pastry seems to be of German origin, and these doughnuts came in all shapes and sizes. The first mention of the term in print was in Washington Irving's *Knickerbocker's History of New York* (1809), in which he describes the Dutch settlers of New Amsterdam in the seventeenth century: "[The table] was always sure to boast an enormous dish of balls of sweetened dough, fried in hog's fat, and called doughnuts or olykoeks [oil cakes]—a delicious kind of cake, at present scarce known in the city, excepting in genuine Dutch families."

Eliza Leslie's *New Cookery Book* (1857) refers to the German origins of the doughnut, which by then had become quite popular. The Pennsylvania Dutch traditionally served doughnuts called *"fossnocks"* or *"fastnachts"* on Shrove Tuesday (Fastnacht) as the last sweet before Lent; at other times of the year they were called *"Fett Kucke"* or "fat cake." On Fastnacht Day these doughnuts are served at breakfast (the last person to arrive at the table is labelled a lazy *fastnacht* and served the last of the dough).

The Pennsylvania Dutch were probably the first to make doughnuts with holes in their centers, a perfect shape for "dunking" (Pennsylvania Dutch, *tunke;* German, *dunke*) in coffee, which has become a standard method of eating doughnuts for Americans. There seems little real evidence to support the story of a Rockport, Maine, sea captain named Hanson Crockett Gregory, who claimed to have poked out the soggy centers of his wife's doughnuts in 1847 so that he might slip them over the spokes of his ship's wheel, thereby being able to nibble while keeping an even keel. Nevertheless, in 1947 a centenary plaque commemorating Gregory's alleged culinary creation was placed on the house where he had lived.

By the middle of the nineteenth century the hole must have been widely accepted, because a housewares catalog of 1870 shows a doughnut cutter including a corer, as does the 1897 *Sears, Roebuck & Co. Catalog,* which priced the gadget at four cents.

"Crullers" (Dutch, *krullen*) were an early egg-dough pastry shaped by the New Amsterdam Dutch into "love knots" or "matrimony knots" or the elongated shape that became familiar throughout the country. Sometimes crullers were called "wonders," and, among the Creoles, *"croque-cignole."*

By the twentieth century doughnuts, dusted with powdered sugar or cinnamon, iced, or stuffed with jelly, had become a great American favorite.

It is improbable that American soldiers in France during World War I were called "doughboys" because of their affection for the confection, or, as Evan Jones asserts in *American Food* (1981), that the name "doughboy" appeared after a Salvation Army worker in France made a batch for the soldiers away from home. The term *doughboy* goes back at least to the Civil War, for Elizabeth Custer (widow of General George Custer) referred to the name as having been derived from the similarity of doughnuts' shape to the infantry's globular brass buttons. There are other associations: a pipe clay, called "dough," with which the infantry cleaned their white belts, and a slang term of southwestern Hispanics for American soldiers quartered in adobe structures. The term is found even in a British soldier's reference in 1809 to Lord Wellington's retreat after the battle of Talavera in Spain. Wellington's soldiers made bread by grinding wheat flour with their hands and stones—"from which wretched practice we christened the place Dough Boy Hill."

Doughboy is also a Rhode Island term for deep-fried and sugared dough. *Doughgod* is a variant term, used in the Northeast and West, for the same confection.

Doughnuts, often spelled "donuts," are as popular as ever, and shops specializing in selling them have been around for decades, sometimes called "doughnuteries." Although the majority of home-made doughnuts are still deep-fried in oil, there are on the market electric appliances for making dough-nuts without having to deep-fry the dough.

Sinker, once a term applied to a pancake or roll, became by the 1920s a term for a very heavy doughnut.

REGULAR DOUGHNUTS:
Sift 2 cups flour, 1/2 cup sugar, 1 tsp. salt, and 3 tsp. baking powder. Beat 1 egg with 1/2 cup milk and 2 tbs. cooled melted butter. Mix with flour and knead the dough lightly. Roll on a board to 1/4-in. thickness and cut with doughnut cutter. Deep fry in a light oil heated to 360°–375° and of a depth that allows doughnuts to float to surface. Brown on one side, turn over, and brown other side. Drain on brown paper or crisp in warm oven.

CINNAMON DOUGHNUTS:
Add 1/4 tsp. cinnamon to dry ingredients listed above. Dust with cinnamon and sugar.

RAISED DOUGHNUTS:
Cream 1 cup butter with 1/2 cup sugar, then add 3 eggs, 1 tsp. salt, 1 cake yeast dissolved in lukewarm milk, and the grated rind of one lemon. Blend in 3 cups flour and knead into an elastic dough. Cover and let rise overnight in a warm place till doubled. Roll into 1/4-in. sheet, cut into rings, let stand again till doubled, then fry in deep oil. Drain and roll in powdered sugar.

FASTNACHTS:
Cook 1 potato till very tender and drain, reserving 1 1/2 cups of potato water. Mash the potato to a smooth paste till you have about 1/2 cup. Beat in 4 tbs. butter and keep warm. When lukewarm, pour 1/4 of the potato paste into a bowl and add 1 package dry yeast and 1 tsp. sugar. Let stand for a few minutes, then set in warm place for 5 min. till yeast bubbles and mixture doubles. Put the paste into a well of 6 cups flour sifted with 1/2 cup sugar. Pour in the yeast mixture, 2 eggs, and 1 1/4 cups potato water. Knead to make a firm, elastic dough. Set the dough in a greased bowl and turn to coat the dough. Cover and let rest till doubled in bulk, about 1 1/2 1 hr. Place the dough on a floured board and roll to 1/2-in. thickness. Cut into 2-in. squares and cut a 1-in. slash in the center of each, then arrange them about 1 inch apart on baking sheets lined with waxed paper. Let them double again. Heat a light oil to 375° and fry the dough squares, turning them till golden on all sides. Drain, then shake in a bag of sugar.

Dresden dressing. A cold sauce, made with hard-boiled eggs, onion, mustard, and other seasonings, to accompany meats. The name derives from the German city of Dresden, and the sauce itself may be of German origins, though it first appears under the name "Dresden dressing" in American cookery of the nineteenth century.

Separate yolks and whites of 3 hard-boiled eggs. Rub yolks through a fine sieve and combine with 1/3 cup minced onion, 1 tsp. sugar, 1 tsp. salt, and 1 pinch of dry mustard. Slowly beat in 1/4 cup corn oil. When mixture thickens slowly add 1/4 cup vinegar. Chill and serve with meats. Makes about 1 cup.

dried apple. A staple of early American tables and traveler's provisions. Apples left to dry over the winter were often made into pies on the trail westward, causing one passenger on the overland stagecoaches to remark that it was "apple pie from Genesis to Revelation along the Platte." A bit of doggerel from the same period goes:

> Spit in my ears
> And tell me lies,
> but give me no
> dried apple pies.

See also MCGINTY.

drum (Family Sciaenidae). Any of a variety of fish that inhabit temperate and tropical marine waters, with species ranging from those weighing less than eight ounces to giant "totuava" that may reach 225 pounds or more. The name comes from a "drumming muscle" that makes a drumlike sound when expanded against the gas bladder. The fish was so called at least as early as 1676. Many species are called "croakers," because the sound resembles croaking. Some of the more important drums for culinary purposes include the Atlantic croaker *(Micropogon undulatus);* banded croaker *(Larimus fasciatus);* black drum *(Pogonias cromis);* freshwater drum *(Aplodinotus grunniens),* also called "sheepshead," "crocus," "gaspergu," "jewelhead," and other names; red drum *(Sciaenops ocellata),* also called "channel bass" and redfish; spot drum *(Leiostomus xanthurus),* also called "Lafayette," after a visit to New York City by General Lafayette at a time when the fish was particularly numerous in the harbor; white sea bass *(Cynoscion nobilis);* and yellowfin croaker *(Umbrina roncador).*

drunk. Intoxicated with liquor. This word is only the most easily identifiable among hundred of others to indicate intoxication. As Stuart Berg Flexner writes in his appendix to the *Dictionary of American Slang* (second supplemented edition, compiled with Harold Wentworth, 1975):

> The concept having the most slang synonyms is *drunk.* This vast number of drunk words does not necessarily mean that Americans are obsessed with drinking, though we seem obsessed with talking about it. Many of these words are quite old. . . . Later immigrant groups brought their own words for drink and drunkenness, and it seems that some, during their first period of adjustment had a fair number of members who turned to whiskey as a compensation for the rejection they suffered as newcomers to a strange land. Most of the words for drunk, however, originated or became popular during Prohibition.

Flexner's list included 353 terms ("and I didn't exhaust the subject," he wrote later).

The American penchant for *drunk* slang was first noted by Benjamin Franklin in the *Pennsylvania Gazette* in 1737, when *have a glass eye, loose in the hilt, nimtopsical, moon-eyed, top heavy,* and *been to Barbados* were all used to describe drunkenness. Franklin listed 228 terms, ninety of which (as pointed out by Edward D. Seeber in *American Speech* [February 1940]) were not listed in either the *Oxford English Dictionary* or the *English Dialect Dictionary.*

The following list gives only a small sampling of the more familiar terms for drunk, with the dates of their first appearance in print in parentheses: *soused* (sixteenth century), *blind* (seventeenth century), *oiled* (1737), *stewed* (1737), *bent* (1833), *stinking* (1837), *lushed* (1840), *tight* (1843), *pixillated* (1850s), *swizzled* (1850s), *D and D*—that is, an abbreviation for the legal phrase *drunk and disorderly* (1870), *paralyzed* (1888), *looped* (1890), *pickled* (1890s), *woozy* (1897), *tanked* (1905), *plastered* (1912), *hooted* (1915), *potted* (1922), *dead to the world* (1926), *bombed* (1940s), *shit-faced* (1940s), *feeling no pain* (1940s), *sloshed* (1950s), and *zonked* (1950s).

duck. Any of a variety of webbed-footed birds of the family Anatidae that may be either wild or domesticated and that inhabit open water, marshes, ponds, lakes, and rivers. The word is from Old English, *dūce.*

Ducks have been esteemed for their culinary value by most cultures of the world, and it is possible that the Indians in Central America domesticated the bird even before the Chinese did. The first European explorers were amazed at the numbers of ducks in American skies and soon commented on the delicious and distinctive flavor of the native CANVASBACK, whose name figures in every cookbook of the nineteenth century, to the extent that no banquet would be considered successful without the serving of the fowl.

On March 13, 1873, however, the arrival in New York of a Yankee clipper ship with a tiny flock of white Peking ducks—one drake and three females—signaled the beginning of a domestic industry of immense proportions. The birds were introduced to Connecticut and then to eastern Long Island, where they propagated at an encouraging rate. Domestic ducks were bought mostly by newly arrived immigrants, who bought them plucked, cooled, and packed in a barrel (called "New York Dressed"). Only in this century did the fowl, by now called the "Long Island duckling," attain gastronomic respect; Long Island now produces half the ducks sold in America and exports some as well.

In the nineteenth century wild ducks were usually eaten rare, but today domestic ducks are generally preferred cooked with a very crisp skin and served either roasted with applesauce or in the classic French manner, with orange sauce. *Peking duck* now refers to a Chinese dish of specially prepared duck skin and meat detached and served in thin pancakes or buns with scallions and a sweet sauce.

The wild ducks of culinary importance to Americans include the canvasback *(Aythya valsineria),* the redhead *(Aythya americana),* the mallard *(Anas platyrhynchos),* the black duck *(Anas rubripes),* the ring-necked duck *(Aythya collaris),* and the scoters *(Melanitta fusca, M. perspicillata,* and *M. nigra),* also called "coots." The mergansers (any of a variety in the genus *Mergus,* which derives its name from the Latin, *mergus,* "diver," and *anser,* "goose") are not preferred and are often referred to by hunters as "trash ducks."

The Muscovy duck *(Cairina moschata)* was originally called the "musk duck" for its distinct, musky smell. Its first printed mention, in 1774, notes that the name "Muscovy duck" had already been erroneously applied to the bird, which was native to South and Central America. Because of the bird's strong flavor it has been domesticated and crossed with other breeds. It is sometimes called the "Barbary duck," because it was assumed to be an African bird.

The Muscovy duck is available at American markets in the fall and winter. It is usually roasted.

The United States Department of Agriculture grades ducks as it does chickens, grade A being the highest, grade B next, and grade C the lowest.

duff. A steamed pudding containing fruit, as an apple duff or plum duff. The word is a nineteenth-century English rendering of "dough," pronounced like "rough."

du jour. A French term meaning "of the day" that in America is usually attached to *soup, fish, dish,* or even *quiche.* It refers to a special item on the menu for that particular day.

Dungeness crab. *(Cancer magister).* A Pacific crab that is found from Alaska to Baja. It is one of the rock crabs, colored pinkish green and yellow and weighing between one-and-three-quarters and four pounds. It is named for a small town on the Olympic Peninsula in Washington, where it was first commercially harvested. Only males at least six and a quarter inches long may be harvested, mainly during the winter months. Today the Dungeness is a major industry of the Northwest, and each season in San Francisco Bay a Roman Catholic priest blesses the fishing fleet that will bring in the crabs. It is a very popular seaside delicacy sold by vendors who get "cracked crabs" fresh from the boat, scoop out the yellow-white fat called CRAB BUTTER, and serve them with mayonnaise. The term was first printed in 1925.

dusty miller. A sundae made with powdered malted-milk topping. The term derives from a noctuid moth of the same name whose speckled wings resemble the dusty topping on the sundae. The moth's name is first mentioned in print in 1909; the sundae probably dates from the 1920s.

Dutch courage. A slang term (dating back at least to 1812) for false courage induced by alcohol. Also, an English term for gin imported from Holland.

Dutch grocery. A slang term for a dirty grocery store. It was in use in the last quarter of the nineteenth century.

Dutch oven. Also, "Dutch bake oven." Usually a large, covered cast-iron kettle used for slow cooking. It may indeed have been of Pennsylvania Dutch heritage, though the word itself first appears in print in 1769. In colonial America such kettles were often hung from a hook in the open fireplace, while at other times set on legs over the fire. In the West the term referred to a thick, three-footed skillet used as an all-purpose cooking utensil that was placed over hot coals, with more coals placed on the lid in order to brown baked items like biscuits. In this century a wall oven may also be called a "Dutch oven."

eatin' iron. Cowboy slang term for a knife, fork, or spoon.

eau sucrée. This French-Creole term, which means "sugar water," refers to a glass of water in which has been dissolved one tablespoon sugar. Eau sucrée is drunk after a heavy meal, supposedly to ease digestion, and, notes *The Picayune's Creole Cook Book* (1901), it "is used by all Creole mothers as a sedative for their little ones. Just before kissing her babes 'Good-night,' the Creole mother will give them a small glass of 'Eau Sucrée.' It is claimed that it insures easy digestion and perfect sleep."

Eau sucrée parties were frequent in old New Orleans, often held as a substitute for the more lavish parties of wealthier Creoles but no less enjoyed for their simple pleasures.

EDTA. (Ethylenediaminetetraacetate). An additive, used in mayonnaise and other processed foods, for preventing trace metals from mechanical rollers, blenders, and containers from causing rancidity.

eel *(Anguilla rostrata).* A long, snakelike fish of the order Anguilliformes, found in eastern waters. The word is from Old English, *ǣl.*

Eels, long considered a delicacy by Europeans and Asians, have not been of much gastronomic interest to most Americans, but in colonial New England "eel time" in autumn was anticipated with the same enthusiasm as attended the run of the shad or the apple harvest. Later, Mediterranean immigrants—the Italians, Greeks, Portuguese, and others—kept their traditions of eating eel on certain holidays, especially Christmas, and the eel industry in America is still seasonal. Eels are prepared in diverse ways, boiled, steamed, stewed, grilled, or fried.

egg. A shelled ovum of a bird, especially from domesticated fowl. The word is from Old Norse.

Eggs are a staple food of the world's people, and although the eggs of wild fowl, turkeys, geese, doves, and other birds are eaten, it is the egg of the chicken that is most widely cultivated. Americans consume about 270 eggs per capita each year.

The Indians did not have chickens until the Europeans brought them to America, but wild fowls' eggs—quail, geese, turkey, and pigeon—were part of the Indian diet, as were turtle and crocodile eggs in the territories near the Gulf of Mexico. Columbus brought chickens to the West Indies in 1493, and the Puritans and English settlers of Jamestown brought them to North America. Since chickens—and, therefore, eggs—were common but not abundant enough to provide everyday meals in the colonial era, they remained expensive items well into the nineteenth century, especially in the West, where domesticated fowl were rare. In fact, the dish called the HANGTOWN FRY was made in the California Gold rush days from the two most expensive ingredients of the kitchen—eggs and oysters.

Today egg production is a finely mechanized science, overseen by both federal and state inspectors. Eggs are sized by weight, averaged by the dozen. Jumbo eggs must weigh 30 ounces or more, extra large between 27 and 30, large between 24 and 27, medium between 21 and 24, small between 18 and 21, and peewee between 15 and 18. Eggs are also graded on the basis of physical condition, with the more viscous yolks scoring highest, from grade AA (Fancy Fresh) to A, B, and C. About 10 percent of the country's eggs goes into egg products, such as frozen and dried eggs.

Americans eat their eggs poached (in New England called "dropped eggs"), boiled (or hard-boiled), as an omelette, or, since 1864, scrambled, that is, sautéed in butter by mixing the eggs around in a skillet. Americans also created the term *shirred eggs* as of 1883, for eggs cooked unshelled in molds. A well-known egg sandwich or omelette is the WESTERN, made with green pepper, chopped ham, and eggs on toast. A Spanish omelette is made with onions, peppers, tomatoes, and other seasonings. See also main entries for EGGS BENEDICT, EGGS SARDOU, and EGG NOG.

SCRAMBLED EGGS:
Beat 2 eggs lightly with 1 tbs. milk, salt, and pepper. Pour into heated skillet with 1 tbs. butter and work with fork to give a fluffy, moist texture. Serve with toast.

SHIRRED EGGS:
Into each of several buttered ramekins, break 1 egg, add salt to taste, sprinkle with 1 tsp. cream, and bake for 8–10 min. at 350°.

SPANISH OMELETTE:
Sauté 3 tbs. chopped green pepper and 4 tbs. chopped onion in 2 tbs. butter. Add 1 cup sliced mushrooms, 1 1/2 cups cooked tomatoes, 1 clove chopped garlic, salt and pepper, and 1/4 tsp. Tabasco sauce and simmer till thickened. Make an egg omelette, fill with mixture, and roll carefully. If chopped green chilies are added to mixture, this dish becomes a Mexican omelette.

egg bread. A cornbread without leavening, known since the middle of the nineteenth century. It was first mentioned as an American bread in 1854.

egg butter. A sweet spreading butter made with molasses. *The Buckeye Cookbook* (1883) gives the following recipe:

Boil 1 pt. molasses slowly for 15–20 min., stirring frequently. Add 3 beaten eggs, stirred in quickly so as not to curdle. Boil a few minutes longer, partially cool, and add lemon juice to taste.

egg cream. A New York City soda fountain confection made from chocolate syrup, milk, and seltzer. The simplicity of the egg cream is deceptive, for its flavor and texture depend entirely on the correct preparation. There is no egg in an egg cream, but if the ingredients are mixed properly a foamy, egg-white-like head tops off the drink. Egg creams became popular in New York City soda fountains and candy stores from the 1930s onward, and they are difficult to make correctly at home because fountain seltzer, not bottled club soda, is of prime importance. The term was first printed in 1954.

In a paper cone cup, squirt 1 1/2 oz. chocolate syrup, add 1 1/2 oz. ice-cold milk (ideally, the milk should have small ice crystals floating in it), stir, then fill to the top with a fast jet of seltzer deflected off a spoon, which should create a foamy, white head.

egg foo yung. A dish of scrambled eggs and Chinese vegetables. Egg foo yung is a Chinese-American menu item not found in authentic Chinese cooking. The name has no specific meaning.

The following recipe is from Trader Vic's restaurants in San Francisco, New York, and other locations.

Beat 4 eggs lightly and combine with 1 cup bean sprouts, 1 tbs. chopped scallions, 1 tbs. bamboo shoots, 1 tbs. water chestnuts, 1 tsp. monosodium glutamate, and salt to taste. Add 3/4 cup chopped seafood or cooked meat. Mix well. In a skillet or wok with 3 tbs. oil, drop 1/3 cup egg and vegetable mixture in small cakes and cook till browned. Pile cakes together and pour over them sauce made from 1 cup chicken broth, 1/4 tsp. sugar, salt, 2 tbs. soy sauce, 2 tsp. monosodium glutamate, and 1 tbs. cold water in which 1 tsp. cornstarch has been dissolved.

egg nog. Also, "eggnog." A rich beverage made with eggs and spirits traditionally served in America at Christmastime. The word *nog* is an old English term for ale, a meaning known since the late seventeenth century. In England the drink was often made with red Spanish wine, but in America, where the first printing of the word was in 1775, rum and later other spirits were substituted.

According to F.D.A. standards, commercially produced egg nog must contain at least 1 percent by weight egg-yolk solids and must be pasteurized; it may also be homogenized.

Separate 6 eggs and beat the yolks with 1/2 cup sugar till light yellow. Add 1/2 cup bourbon or blended whiskey and 1/2 cup brandy and blend well. Chill in refrigerator for several hours. Beat egg whites till soft peaks are formed. Whip 1 1/2 pt. heavy cream till slightly thickened, then fold into yolk mixture. Fold in egg whites, chill again. Serve with a sprinkling of grated nutmeg.

eggplant *(Solanum melongena)*. The plump, deep-purple fruit of a plant in the potato family native to India. The name, derived simply from the egglike shape of the fruit, was first mentioned in English print in 1767.

Thomas Jefferson has been credited with introducing the eggplant to America, though it has never achieved great popularity with most of the population. It is usually sautéed or baked, often as eggplant parmigiana, an Italian-American dish of breaded, sautéed eggplant baked with tomato sauce.

eggs Benedict. English muffins topped with a slice of ham or Canadian bacon, poached eggs, and a hollandaise sauce. It is a very popular BRUNCH and breakfast item. The word first appeared in print in 1928.

The *Dictionary of Americanisms* and the *Morris Dictionary of Word and Phrase Origins* agree on the story of how the dish got its name, with Morris reporting: "The legendary Delmonico's Restaurant in New York City has been the birthplace of eggs Benedict. According to a well-founded report, two of the regular customers were Mr. and Mrs. LeGrand Benedict. One Saturday at lunch Mrs. Benedict complained that there was nothing new on the menu, so the maître d'hôtel asked what she might suggest. Out of their colloquy came the now internationally famous recipe." Another story attributes the dish's inspiration to Wall Street broker Lemuel Benedict, and food writer George Lang contends that the famous maître d'hôtel of the Waldorf-Astoria restaurant and hotel in New York City, Oscar Tschirky, changed the recipe by adding truffles and a *glace de viande*, but *The Waldorf Astoria Cookbook* (1981) follows the traditional form of earlier years.

Still others will always associate eggs Benedict with breakfast at Brennan's restaurant in New Orleans, though no claim for its creation has been established there.

> Split two English muffins and toast lightly. Spread with butter. Sauté in butter 4 slices baked ham or Canadian bacon and place one slice on each muffin half. Keep warm in slow oven. Boil water and add 1 tbs. vinegar and 1 tsp. salt. Lower heat to a simmer and poach 4 eggs for about 5 mins. Remove and drain, then place over muffins. Pour over them a freshly made hollandaise sauce.

eggs Sardou. A dish of poached eggs with artichoke hearts, anchovies, chopped ham, truffle, and hollandaise sauce. Eggs Sardou is a specialty of New Orleans, and, specifically, of Antoine's restaurant, where it was created by owner Antoine Alciatore (1824–1877) on the occasion of a dinner he hosted for French playwright Victorien Sardou (1831–1908), author of a satire on America entitled *L'Oncle Sam* (1873).

> Place 2 cooked artichoke hearts on a serving dish, set 4 anchovy fillets and 2 poached eggs on top, and pour 1/3 cup hollandaise sauce over them. Sprinkle with 1 tbs.

chopped ham and garnish with a slice of truffle. Serves 1. (Some recipes call for creamed spinach to be set under the artichoke hearts.)

election cake. A raised fruitcake of New England, first mentioned by Amelia Simmons in her *American Cookery* as early as 1800. The name comes from the tradition of serving this cake on election days to those who voted with the host party. Although this practice spread throughout the Midwest and West in the nineteenth century, the cake is usually associated with Hartford, Connecticut, and, by the 1830s, was often called "Hartford election cake." There were also "election buns," which were doled out along similar party lines.

Heat 1/2 cup dry sherry in a saucepan, add 1 1/2 cups raisins, and remove from heat. Let stand several hours till raisins soften and absorb sherry. Heat 1 1/2 cups milk to lukewarm and remove from heat. Combine 1 1/2 cups flour, 1/3 cup sugar, 1 pkg. yeast, and 1/2 tsp. salt. Add milk, blend, cover, and let rise till doubled. Punch dough down. Mix together 3/4 cup butter, 1/2 cup brown sugar, 2 beaten eggs, and 3 1/2 cups flour. Add 1 tsp. ground cinnamon, 1/2 tsp. ground nutmeg, 1/4 tsp. ground cloves, 1 cup chopped pecans or walnuts, and 1/2 cup candied citron. Drain the raisins, but reserve the sherry. Add sherry to yeast flour, then into egg flour, blend well together, add raisins, and place batter in greased and floured 10-in. tube pan. Let rise again, bake at 350° for 1 hr., covered with aluminum foil for the last 15 min. Invert on rack and cool. Combine 2 cups confectioners' sugar, 1 tsp. vanilla, and 2 tbs. sweet sherry to make an icing. Frost cake, garnish with nuts and flower shapes of citron.

el presidente. A cocktail whose name is Spanish for "the president." The drink supposedly was named after (perhaps concocted by) General Marco García Menocal y Deop (1866–1941), who was called "Menocal," President of Cuba from 1913 to 1921.

Shake with ice 1 1/2 oz. gold rum, 1/2 oz. dry vermouth, 1 tsp. dark rum, 1 tsp. curaçao, 1/4 tsp. grenadine, 2 tsp. lime juice. Serve in a chilled cocktail glass.

Emmaline sauce. A nineteenth-century flavoring sauce included by Sarah Tyson Rorer in *McIlhenny's Tabasco Sauce Recipes* (1913). The origin of the name is not known.

Pare and grate raw pumpkin, squash, pawpaw ("custard apple") to make 1 pt. Add 1 chopped Spanish onion, 4 mashed garlic cloves, 1 tsp. celery seed, 2 red peppers, 2 green peppers, 1 tsp. turmeric, and 1 bottle Tabasco. Add 1 pt. vinegar, stir, then bring to boil and simmer for several minutes. Bottle and seal. Use as a flavoring for soups or stews.

empanada. A fried turnover pastry of Mexican origins and now a staple of Mexican-American restaurants. The word was first printed in 1922. *Empanar* in Spanish means "to bake in pastry."

Dissolve 1 pkg. yeast in 1/2 cup lukewarm water. Cut 4 tbs. lard or butter into 4 cups flour, add 1 tsp. salt and 1 tbs. sugar. Pour in yeast and make a dough. Roll into thin sheet and cut into rounds. Fill with mincemeat or fruit preserves, moisten edges of dough and seal one round to another. Deep-fry in hot oil to a golden-brown, drain, and dust with powdered sugar or cinnamon.

enchilada. A TORTILLA stuffed with various fillings of meat, cheese, chili pepper sauce, chorizo sausage, and other ingredients. *Enchilada* is an American-Spanish term meaning "filled with chili" and was first printed in America in 1887. The dish has now become a staple of Mexican-American restaurants.

> In a blender purée one 16-oz. can tomatoes, 2 red chili peppers, 1/2 tsp. salt, and 1/4 tsp. pepper. Add 1 cup sour cream. Mix 2 cups chopped cooked chicken with 1/2 cup shredded Monterey Jack or Cheddar cheese. Sauté briefly a dozen tortillas in 1 tbs. oil till golden on both sides. Drain and spread chicken on each tortilla, roll up, and place in greased baking dish. Pour tomato and chili mixture over them, cover with aluminum foil and bake at 350° for 30 min. Remove foil, sprinkle with more cheese, place under broiler till top melts and browns. Serves 6.

English muffin. A round, flat muffin made from white flour, yeast, malted barley, vinegar, and farina. English muffins are usually split and toasted, buttered and spread with jam or preserves. Although tea muffins that were once popular in England resembled the American "English muffin," there is no single muffin in Britain by this specific name. Nor do Americans often make English muffins at home, preferring to buy those sold at a grocery. Most of these store-bought varieties derive from those made by the S. B. Thomas Company of New York, whose founder, Samuel Bath Thomas, emigrated from England with his mother's recipe and began making muffins at his New York bakery in 1880. The name was first printed in 1926.

John Thorne, in his booklet *The English Muffin* (1980), gives a lengthy recipe for the item, but it does not contain several ingredients used in Thomas's English muffins.

Recipes for English muffins generally do not contain many of the ingredients in the Thomas's formula. For muffin rings, *The Joy of Cooking* (1964) by Irma S. Rombauer and Marion Rombauer Becker recommends using "small unlacquered fish cans and deviled meat cans [with the] tops and bottoms removed and the rims . . . thoroughly scrubbed."

> Combine 2 tsp. sugar, 1 tsp. salt, 1/2 cup scalded milk, and 1 cup hot water. In 2 tbs. warm water dissolve 1 cake yeast and let stand about 10 min. Combine yeast with water-and-milk mixture, beat in 2 cups flour, cover with damp cloth, and let rise for 1 1/2 hr. Beat in 3 tbs. butter and 2 cups flour, let rise again till doubled in greased muffin rings half filled with dough. Bake on a hot, well-buttered griddle, turning once, till golden brown on both sides. Cool on rack. Makes 20 muffins.

entrée. The main course of a meal, or, occasionally, a dish served between two chief courses. The word is French for "entry," and in France the word formally has the second meaning, as it does in England, where it might also be called a "made dish." In America menus usually list the entrée as the main course, although this has been its principal usage only over the last forty years. Noted Ford Naylor in 1941 in his *World Famous Chefs' Cook Book,* "It is only in the less expensive restaurants and lunchrooms, where the word 'entrée' has come to describe any main dish, including roasts." Often in America the word is spelled without the accent mark, and first appeared in 1759.

espresso. A very dark, bitter Italian coffee, often incorrectly spelled "expresso." The name has nothing to do with the idea of "a quick cup" of coffee, but everything to do with the Italian meaning "pressed out," for in the preparation of this coffee the essence of freshly ground beans is pushed out of a special espresso machine by steam and water, creating a very concentrated half-cup of brew. In America, espresso often comes out as a full cup of less-strong Italian coffee. Espresso may also be prepared in a drip pot, but this is wholly an Italian-American substitution. Often in America espresso will be garnished with a sliver of lemon peel, and a generous restaurateur may offer a complimentary shot of Sambucca or anisette liqueur to be added to the cup, but this too is almost never seen in Italy.

The only way to make true espresso is to buy the beans fresh from an Italian grocer, grind them just before you make the coffee, and use an espresso machine, which is a very expensive investment; for this reason Italians almost always drink their espresso at a café.

The word *espresso* first appears in English print in 1945.

estomacs mulâtres. Louisiana gingerbread made with flour and cane syrup. The name is from the French, "mulatto stomachs," and refers to the puffy, light brown color of the little confections.

fast food. A term referring to food dispensed quickly at inexpensive RESTAU-RANTS where only a few items are sold, often precooked or prepackaged. These items include hamburgers, hot dogs, french fries, pizza, milk shakes, soda, and ice cream. As an adjective, the term was traced to 1969, although as a noun it must precede that date by a few years.

Most of the fast-food restaurants are drive-ins, places where one drives to, parks, and buys one's meal either in the restaurant or from one's car. Fast-food restaurants proliferated in the 1960s when a variety of chain restaurants (usually franchised) expanded, including McDonald's, Burger King, Pizza Hut, Wendy's, Kentucky Fried Chicken, Arby's, Roy Rogers, and many others.

Today the term *fast food* is often synonymous with *junk food,* which also appeared in the 1960s or 1970s but which includes store-bought items such as potato chips, candy, brownies, cakes, and cookies, considered to have little nutritional value or to contain "empty calories."

F.D.A. See Food and Drug Administration.

fettuccine Alfredo. A dish of fettuccine noodles mixed with butter, Parmesan cheese, and cream. The dish has been a staple of Italian-American restaurants since the mid-1960s. It was created in Rome in 1920 by Alfredo di Lellio, owner of a restaurant on the Via della Scrofa, supposedly to restore the appetite of his wife after she gave birth to their son. The original dish was made with a very rich triple butter di Lellio made himself, three kinds of flour, and only the heart of the best *parmigiano.* The dish became well known when Hollywood movie actors Douglas Fairbanks and Mary Pickford came to Rome on their honeymoon in 1920 and dined at Alfredo's daily. At the end of their stay they presented the owner with a gold-plated spoon and fork with which to mix the pasta. The *Rector Cook Book* gave a recipe for the dish in 1928.

Di Lellio moved after World War II to the Piazza Augusto Imperatore, and in the 1950s his restaurant became a mecca for visiting Americans, most of whom came to sample fettuccine Alfredo. (The grandson of the original Alfredo now runs three restaurants called "Alfredo's—the Original of Rome" in the United States.)

Because most American cooks could not reproduce the richness of the original butter, today the dish almost always contains heavy cream. (In Italy this would be called *"fettuccine alla panna"* or *"alla crema."*)

Boil in salted water 1 lb. fresh fettuccine *al dente.* In a saucepan melt 7 tbs. butter with 7 tbs. Parmesan cheese and 1 cup heavy cream. Drain fettuccine, add to sauce and toss. Serve with more grated Parmesan. Serves 4–6.

fiddlehead fern *(Matteucia struthiopteris, Amsinckia intermedia,* and *Phacelia tanacetifolia).* Also, "fiddleneck." Several ferns having tips shaped like a violin's scroll fall under this name, though the cinnamon, brake, and, especially, the ostrich fern are the varieties most commonly referred to. Ostrich ferns from Maine are highly valued and are sometimes found canned or frozen. Because of their delicacy, fiddleheads should be eaten immediately after picking, boiled in salt water, and served with butter or in a salad. The earliest citation of a fern by this name, in reference to the cinnamon variety, was in 1902.

fig *(Ficus carica).* A sweet multiseeded fruit of the fig tree or shrub, usually eaten dried. It originated in northern Asia Minor. The word is from the Latin, *ficus.*

Figs were introduced into America in the sixteenth century by the Spaniards, and the Mission fig owes its name to the Spanish missions set up in California, where most of the crop is cultivated. Figs had not been a very important crop until 1900. Today the most important varieties of figs cultivated are the Calimyrna, the San Pedro, the Mission, the Kadota, the Adriatic, and the Brown Turkey.

Most of the fig crop goes into making a sweet filling for Fig Newtons, cookies baked by Nabisco Brands, Inc., of East Hanover, New Jersey. The cookie was first produced after James Mitchell developed a machine in 1892 to combine a hollow cookie crust with a jam filling. This machine he brought to the New York Biscuit Company, which tried it out in Cambridgeport, Massachusetts, and the resulting cookie was christened "Newton's cakes," after the nearby Boston suburb of Newton. In 1898 the company combined with others to form the National Biscuit Company (now Nabisco Brands). The most frequently used jam in the cookie was fig, and soon the name became "Fig Newton."

filet mignon. A very tender cut of beef. The term, first used in O. Henry's *The Four Million* (1906), is from the French words *filet,* "thick slice," and *mignon,* "dainty."

Fish House punch. A PUNCH made of lemon juice, brandy, and peach brandy. It was first created about 1732 at Philadelphia's Colony of the State in Schuylkill (reorganized in the Revolutionary War as the State in Schuylkill) Fishing

Club, which was limited to thirty members, all of whom were expected to be good cooks. Each meeting is opened with a toast and a glass of Fish House punch and closed with a glass of Madeira and a toast to the memory of George Washington, who, legend has it, once dined at the club and for days afterwards left blank pages in his diary. There are many variations of Fish House punch, some made with brandy, some made with rum or other whiskeys.

> Dissolve 3/4 lb. sugar in a little cold water, add 1 qt. lemon juice, 1 qt. brandy or rum, 2 qt. water, 1 cup peach brandy, and a large lump of ice. Let stand for 2 hr. Makes 1 1/2 gal.

fish muddle. A North Carolina term for a fish stew. *Muddle* refers to a jumble or something mixed up together.

fish stick. A fillet of fish that has been sliced into sticks about one-inch wide, battered or rolled in bread crumbs, and fried or baked. *Time* magazine reported in 1953 the sale of frozen fish sticks made by the Birds Eye Company (now owned by General Foods of White Plains, New York).

flat car. A Negro slang term for pork chops. Now rare, it was heard earlier in this century in the South.

flauta. A tortilla that is rolled with various fillings and then fried. Flautas, whose resemblance to a flute gives them their Mexican name, are made by heating in an oven a cornmeal tortilla, rolling a filling of meat or poultry in the center, and frying the roll in hot oil. They are then drained and garnished with shredded lettuce and a chili sauce.

fletcherism. A fad of the early twentieth century based on *The ABC of Nutrition* (1903), by Horace Fletcher (1849–1919), in which the author mandated that each mouthful of food be chewed exactly thirty-two times—once for each tooth in the mouth. *To fletcherize* meant to chew one's food thoroughly. The theory had the support of many prominent Americans, including John D. Rockefeller, William James, and Thomas Edison. After Fletcher's death in 1919 his theories quickly lost their bite.

flip. A drink made with beer, sugar, molasses, dried pumpkin, and rum, all heated with a hot iron. A fireplace poker was called an "iron flip dog," hence the drink's name. A "yard of flannel" was flip with a beaten egg added, which gave it a flannellike appearance on top. Flip is first mentioned in 1695 in England, and Herman Melville's hero Ishmael in *Moby-Dick* (1851) expounds on the drink:

> Flip? Did I say we had flip? Yes, and we flipped it at the rate of ten gallons the hour; and when the squall came (for its squally off there by Patagonia), and all hands— visitors and all—were called to reef topsails, we were so top heavy that we had to swing each other aloft in bowlines; and we ignorantly furled the skirts of our jackets

into the sails, so that we hung there, reefed fast in the howling gale, a warning example to all drunken tars. However, the masts did not go overboard; and by and by we scrambled down, so sober, that we had to pass the flip again, though the savage salt spray bursting down the forecastle scuttle, rather too much diluted and pickled it for my taste.

floating island. A dessert made with fluffs of meringue set in a custard sauce. The dish originated in France but became known in America by the late eighteenth century. The term is a translation of the French *île flotante*, and *Larousse Gastronomique* describes another version of the dessert made with sponge cake spread with jam, whipped cream, and nuts and set in a bowl of custard. Benjamin Franklin mentions eating a "custard with floating masses of whipped cream or white of eggs" in his *Letters* (1771), and Thomas Jefferson called the dessert "snow eggs," a translation of the French, *oeufs à la neige*. By the nineteenth century the dish was well known and served at lavish dinners. Today floating island is still occasionally seen, though it is not as popular as it once was.

> Combine 6 egg yolks, 1/2 cup sugar, and a pinch of salt in a double boiler. Heat 3 cups light cream and slowly add to egg mixture. Stir in 2 tsp. vanilla and cook till thickened, being careful not to curdle the eggs, then cool the custard. Beat 4 egg whites with a pinch of salt, a pinch of cream of tartar, and 1/2 cup sugar till soft peaks are formed. Poach tablespoons of the egg whites in hot, not boiling, water, for about 2 min. Drain meringues and set in bowl of custard, then chill before serving. Serves 4.

flounder. Any of a variety of flatfishes in the families Bothidae and Pleuronectidae, sometimes erroneously sold as SOLE. The name comes from Norman French, *floundre*. The main American species of fish that fall under the name include: American plaice *(Hippoglossoides platessoides)*, also called the "dab" or "sanddab" (*plaice* is from the Latin, *platessa*, "flatfish"); Atlantic halibut *(H. hippoglossus)*; California halibut *(Paralichthys californicus)*; Pacific halibut *(H. stenolepsis)*; Pacific sanddab *(Citharichthys sordidus)*; Southern flounder *(P. lethostigma)*; starry flounder *(P. stellatus)*; fluke *(P. dentatus)*, also called "summer flounder"; winter flounder *(Pseudopleuronectes americanus)*, also called "blueback flounder," "blackback flounder," and "lemon sole."

flour. A powdery substance made by grinding and sifting grains such as wheat, corn, rye, and others. The word is from the Middle English.

American Indians used corn flour almost exclusively for their breads, porridges, and other staple foods, and corn was the flour most readily available to the first settlers who came from Europe, their own grains, like wheat and barley, having failed in several instances. Cornmeal and flour continued to be the most important variety until well into the nineteenth century, when wheat became a major crop in America. The production of wheat flour picked up after the invention in 1834 of the Swiss steel roller that ground the meal very finely. After 1900 American wheat flour was processed to appear white by bleaching and removal of the wheat germ and other flecks of grain, thereby lessening its nutritive value. Today there has been a trend favoring unbleached and whole wheat flours.

The main types of flour available in the American market include:

hard wheat flour. Milled from winter or spring wheat grown mainly in North and South Dakota, Montana, and Kansas. Hard wheat flour has a higher gluten level than other flours and is excellent for bread making.

soft wheat flour. Milled from winter wheat and grown mostly in Illinois and Indiana. Soft wheat flour is used for biscuits and pastries.

all-purpose flour. A blend of hard and soft wheat flours suitable for general use in all baked goods. Now enriched with thiamine, niacin, iron, and riboflavin and available bleached or unbleached, this is the flour usually meant when no other is specified.

whole wheat flour. Also called GRAHAM FLOUR. Whole wheat flour is made from the entire wheat kernel, and for baking is usually combined with a white all-purpose flour.

cornstarch. Also called "corn flour." A flour made from corn, although cornmeal is not quite as fine but used more frequently for cornbread, muffins, and other confections, as well as in baked puddings and porridges. Cornstarch is used as a thickener in gravies and sauces.

barley meal. A coarse whole-kernel flour made from barley.

rye flour. A coarse whole-kernel flour milled from rye.

stone-ground flour. A coarse flour milled with stone rather than steel rollers.

cake flour. A flour made from soft wheats, although the term may also refer to a self-rising flour that contains baking powder and salt.

pastry flour. A finely milled, soft, low-gluten flour found in the South, where it is used to make pastries.

semolina. A granular durum-wheat flour used to make macaroni, spaghetti, and other pastas. It is high in gluten.

farina. A flour made from hard, but not durum, wheat.

gluten flour. A starch-free flour made by washing the starch from a high-protein wheat flour.

rice flour. A flour made from milled rice, often combined with all-purpose flour in recipes.

potato flour. A flour made from potatoes, used primarily as a thickener in gravies and sauces or in sponge cakes.

tapioca flour. A flour made from the cassava root, used primarily as a thickener in sauces and gravies.

arrowroot flour. A flour made from the arrowroot plant, used mainly as a starch for thickening sauces and gravies.

oat flour. A flour milled from oats, rarely used. But oatmeal, with a much coarser texture, is used for a porridge and in breads and cookies. Flakey rolled oats are used the same way.

fonda. A hotel or restaurant in the West. The term dates back at least to 1844 and derives from the Spanish.

fondant. A sugar paste eaten as candy or as icing. The word is from the French, from the past participle of *fondre,* "to melt." The word first appeared in English in the 1877 edition of the *Encyclopaedia Britannica* and has become a general cooking term in England and America.

> Mix 4 cups sugar with 1 cup hot water, add a pinch of salt, and 1/8 tsp. cream of tartar. Heat to boil till mixture spins a thread (238° on a candy thermometer). Remove from heat, add 1 tsp. vanilla extract, and beat until creamy. To use as candy, press into balls the size of a nut.

fondue. A method of fast cooking by which bite-size pieces of meat, fruit, or bread are impaled on skewers and dipped into a bubbling liquid either to be quickly cooked or coated. Individual eaters insert their own skewers into the pot, and, because of the communal nature of the activity, fondue cooking has been very much part of social gatherings and parties.

Fondue originated in Switzerland, where it was part of peasant families' one-pot cooking methods and a means of using hardened cheese. The word comes from the French verb *fondre,* "to melt." The classic fondue, called *fondue neuchâteloise,* is made with Emmenthaler or Gruyère cheeses and a Swiss white wine intended to provide acidity. This mixture is placed in a flame-heated earthenware pot called a *caquelon* and melted; a cherry brandy such as Kirsch is added, and skewered crusts of bread are dipped into the blend. *La fondue bourguignonne* is made by dipping cubes of meat into hot oil and is accompanied by various condiments and sauces such as béarnaise or hollandaise. This dish was popularized in Switzerland during the 1950s.

Although the French gastronome Brillat-Savarin referred to fondue in the nineteenth century, the dish actually remained a peasant meal of little interest until it was introduced in the United States in the 1950s. In 1956 chef-owner Konrad Egli of New York's Chalet Swiss restaurant made a *fondue bourguignonne* that became an overnight sensation that spread rapidly to other restaurants. In the early 1960s Egli, who noticed that many of his diet-conscious customers avoided his rich chocolate desserts, consulted with his public-relations agent, Beverly Allen, and came up with a chocolate fondue into which one dipped pieces of cake, fruit, or cream-puff pastry—a variation completely unknown in Switzerland but one that became popular even there within the last few years.

These various fondues were enormously popular as party food with Americans, particularly during winter and especially on skiing holidays. Fondue pots and skewers were a standard entertaining item in American homes throughout the 1960s, but the popularity of the dish has faded considerably since then.

BASIC CHEESE FONDUE:
Rub a fondue pot with a clove of garlic and set over heat. Add 1 tbs. lemon juice and gradually add 1 lb. shredded or diced Swiss cheese. Add 3 tbs. Kirsch or other

brandy and white pepper to taste, and bring to a bubbly consistency. Each person skewers cubes of French or Italian bread for dipping into bubbling cheese mixture.

FONDUE BOURGUIGNONNE:
Fill the fondue pot halfway with cooking oil or clarified butter. Skewer cubes of tenderloin or filet mignon, dip into boiling oil, cook to desired degree, and serve with accompaniments of béarnaise, hollandaise, chutney, horseradish, mustard, ketchup, and other condiments.

CHOCOLATE FONDUE:
Break 8–9 oz. of good Swiss chocolate (preferably Toblerone brand with honey and crushed almonds) into fondue pot, add 1/2 cup heavy cream and 2 tbs. Kirsch or other brandy. Skewer morsels of any or all of the following—cake, fruit, cream-puff pastry—and dip in bubbling chocolate.

Food and Drug Administration (F.D.A.). An agency of the Public Health Service division of the United States Department of Health, Education and Welfare whose purpose is to protect public health by monitoring standards of the food and drug industries.

The Food and Drug Act of 1906 was the first instance of such monitoring, and in 1931 the F.D.A. was formed. The Food, Drug and Cosmetic Act of 1938 (amended in 1958 and 1962) increased the powers of the agency.

The F.D.A. controls bureaus of Food, Product Safety, Drugs, and Veterinary Medicine, and its role in drawing up "standards of identity" has helped enormously in defining what American food products may or may not be or contain by law. For example, a product labeled "fruit jam" must contain forty-five parts fruit and fifty-five parts sugar or other sweetener, while "raisin bread" must have raisins equalling 50 percent of the weight of the flour. Skim milk is required to have two thousand International Units of Vitamin A in each quart. "Standards of quality" set minimum specifications for such factors as tenderness, color, and freedom from defects in canned fruits and vegetables, limiting, for example, excessive peel in tomatoes, hardness in peas, or pits in pitted canned cherries. These standards are not to be confused with the Department of Agriculture's U.S.D.A. voluntary grades of meat.

The F.D.A. also monitors "fill-of-container standards," setting requirements as to the volume of food product that must be packaged in a container, sometimes specifying minimum weights of solid food that must remain after the drainable liquid has been poured off (referred to as "minimum drained weight"). Other items must have a minimum fill in terms of the total food as a percentage of the container.

The F.D.A. may take the following actions against those who violate these standards: seizure of the product itself; prosecution of the packer or distributor with possible fines or jail sentence; and court injunction to prohibit shipment of illegal goods.

food stamps. A federally funded program designed to provide nutritional assistance to the poor in America by giving them coupons that may be exchanged at grocery stores for food products. About 22 million people, or one of every eleven Americans, had received food stamps as of 1983, at a cost of $11.3 billion.

During the Depression the federal government alleviated both hunger and surplus farm products by allowing families to exchange money for stamps of equal value and additional stamps with which to buy food. Reduced surpluses during World War II cancelled such federal programs, but in 1961 President John F. Kennedy directed the Agriculture Department to establish an experimental program, which in 1964 became a full-fledged program under the Food Stamp Act. By 1971 Congress had established uniform standards of eligibility. Since then various changes in the regulations and funds available for food stamps have occurred under different administrations.

forbidden fruit. A logger's term for pork.

Franconia potatoes. Boiled potatoes baked with butter. The name refers to the Franconia range of the White Mountains in New Hampshire. The recipe below is from a 1944 cookbook.

> Boil potatoes in salted water, place on a buttered pan, pour melted butter over them, season with salt and pepper, and bake till browned at 400°.

free lunch. A midday meal offered free of charge to saloon customers in order to entice them to drink more beer or spirits. The *Dictionary of Americanisms* traces the first appearance of the word in print to 1854, although the term is somewhat older. In her book, *The New Orleans Restaurant Cookbook* (1967), Deirdre Stanforth contends that the practice began in the New Orleans French Quarter at the St. Louis Hotel and was created for the business clientele who could not get home for lunch. So successful was the free lunch that the management sought to stop it, but by then it had become firmly entrenched and before long was practiced in other restaurants across the country, and especially in beerhalls. In those days the free lunch might consist of large platters of beef, ham, soup, potatoes, caviar, and oysters, all set on the bar, but as time went on sliced meats, cheese, and bread became more the norm. By the middle of the twentieth century the free lunch had deteriorated into a complimentary snack of pretzels, potato chips, or other cocktail nibbles, though one occasionally will still find a crock of Cheddar cheese and crackers set out on a bar.

French Colombard. A white Vinifera grape used both in blending wines and as a varietal. In France the grape is known as the "Colombard" and by other names, but in California, it has been called "West's White Pacific" in the nineteenth century (when West & Sons of Stockton, California, brought it back from France) and "Winkler" (after viticulturist Dr. Albert J. Winkler) after the repeal of Prohibition. Later it was identified by enologist Harold P. Olmo of the University of California as French Colombard. The first varietal from this grape appeared in 1964 under the Parducci Wine Cellars label. It is second only to Zinfandel in total acreage planted in California and makes up nearly half of the state's white-wine crush.

French dressing. A salad dressing made by mixing three parts oil to one part vinegar, though some other seasonings may be added. The term was first recorded in 1884, and a recipe was given by the *Ladies' Home Journal* in 1900.

french fry. A method of cooking potatoes or other vegetables cut into narrow strips or rounds. French fries are easily the most popular form of potato preparation in America and are a staple of FAST-FOOD restaurants. In France they are called *"pommes frites"* and in England "chips." The term *french fry* has nothing to do with the country of origin, but instead refers to a method, called "frenching," of cutting the potatoes into narrow strips. The *Oxford English Dictionary,* which traces *french-fried potatoes* back to 1894, suggests the terms are American in origin. *French frieds* dates to the 1920s; *french fries* to the 1930s. *French-fried onions* appears in print in 1945.

Most of the commercial french-fried potatoes are precut, partially cooked, and frozen for delivery to groceries and restaurants. In fact, it is now infrequent to find freshly made french fries outside the home. An American will order the item by asking for a "side of fries," adding salt, pepper, and perhaps ketchup to the finished product. At home the potatoes may be fried in pure lard, but vegetable oil is the preferred medium today. "Steak fries" are usually cut thicker than regular french-fried potatoes. "Onion rings" are usually battered in flour, milk, and cornmeal before frying.

> Slice a baking potato (preferably from Idaho) into strips about 1/3-in. thick. Soak in ice water for 15 min., drain, pat dry, and fry in hot oil till pale gold. Remove, drain, set aside for a few minutes, return to hot oil, and cook till golden brown. Drain and salt.

French 75. A cocktail made from gin, Cointreau, lemon juice, and champagne, though ingredients vary with different recipes. Count Leon Bertrand Arnaud Casenove, owner of Arnaud's restaurant in New Orleans, which opened in 1917, claimed to have created the drink, but *Harry's ABC of Mixing Cocktails* (1919, revised 1939) refers to a " '75 Cocktail" made from 1 tsp. absinthe plus two parts Calvados and one part gin as "the original 1915 recipe of the French '75 Cocktail," and gives another recipe for a French '75 calling for 2 ounces gin, the juice of a lemon, sugar, ice, and champagne as having originated at Harry's New York Bar in Paris in 1925. David A. Embury, in his *Fine Art of Mixing Drinks* (1958), notes unpersuasively that "gin is sometimes used in place of cognac in [a French 75], but then, of course, it no longer should be called French." Embury's version calls for the juice of 1 lime or half a lemon, 2 teaspoons sugar syrup, and 2 ounces cognac. The drink is named after a French 75-millimeter Howitzer cannon.

Arnaud's recipe for a French 75, given in Deirdre Stanforth's *New Orleans Restaurant Cookbook* (1967), is as follows:

Shake with ice the juice of 1 lemon with 1 oz. gin and 1/2 oz. Cointreau, strain into a champagne glass, and top with champagne and a lemon twist.

French toast. A breakfast dish made from white bread dipped in an egg-and-milk mixture, then fried in butter and served with either syrup or powdered sugar. It is a very popular item both at home and in restaurants, and it is often accompanied by bacon, ham, or sausage.

The dish does have its origins in France, where it is known as *"ameritte"* or *"pain perdu";* in Spain it is called *"torriga"* and in England "Poor Knights of Windsor," which is the same name for the dish in Denmark *(arme riddere)* and Germany *(arme Ritter).* At one time or another in America it has been referred to as "Spanish," "German" or "Nun's toast," and its first appearance in print as "French toast" was in 1870. In her 1893 cookbook Mary Lincoln calls it "egg toast," but the dish gets no mention in Fannie Merritt Farmer's 1896 cookbook.

The term *pain perdu* ("lost bread") has persisted, however, in Creole and Cajun cookery (although *The Picayune's Creole Cook Book* of 1901 gives an alternative name of "egg toast"), and it is one of the most treasured dishes in that part of the country. The bread used is a stale, day-old French loaf.

FRENCH TOAST:
Dip a slice of white bread into a batter made from 1 beaten egg and 1/4 cup milk or cream. Sauté in butter till brown on both sides. Serve immediately with maple syrup, cinnamon, powdered sugar, or honey.

PAIN PERDU:
Beat 1 egg in a bowl with 1 tsp. brandy, 1 tsp. orange flower water, and 1 tsp. sugar. Add 1/2 tsp. lemon zest. Remove the crust from a loaf of French bread and cut into slices (many recipes call for bread with the crust intact). Let 2 slices sit in egg mixture for a half hour. Sauté in 2 tbs. sweet butter, drain, sprinkle with powdered sugar and nutmeg, if desired, and serve hot.

fried chicken. A cowboy term for bacon that is rolled in flour and then fried.

frogs' legs. Any of various preparations using the legs of three United States species of frog, the green frog *(Rana clamitans),* the American bullfrog *(R. catesbeiana),* or the northern leopard frog *(R. pipiens).* The majority of these are caught in Florida and Louisiana, where they are a delicacy, either deep-fried or made with a spicy sauce.

DEEP-FRIED FROGS' LEGS:
In a bowl with 1 cup vinegar, 1 sliced onion, and 3 chopped cloves of garlic marinate 2 doz. frogs' legs for about 3 hr. Make a batter of 1 beaten egg, 1 cup flour, 1/2 cup milk, 1/4 tsp. cayenne pepper, and 1 tsp. salt. Drain frogs' legs, dip in batter, fry in deep fat at 375° till golden brown.

frosted. A half-frozen citrus juice drink, made by freezing a fruit juice till almost firm, then whirling it through a blender. Frosteds may also be made by putting ice cubes made from one fruit juice, such as grapefruit, into a glass containing another fruit juice, like lemonade. An infrequently heard usage of *frosted* is to describe a MILK SHAKE. Both usages date from the first quarter of the twentieth century.

fruit cocktail. A cup of various fruits served as an appetizer, usually containing pineapple slices, grapefruit slices, and, if canned, a sweetened liquid. For the origins of the name, see COCKTAIL, for the term *fruit cocktail* seems an extension of the use of the word *cocktail.* In the 1850s recipe books called the item a "fruit salad." The term *fruit cocktail* is first used in print in the *New York Hotel Review* for 1922; *fruit cup* follows in print in 1931.

fry bread. A bread of the Southwest Indians, particularly the Navajos and Hopis, deep-fried and sometimes served with honey and powdered sugar. Wheat flour was brought to the Americas by the Spanish, and this is one of the few Indian breads not based on corn flour.

Fry breads are often featured at county fairs and Indian festivals throughout the Southwest, and a fry-bread contest, overseen by a Navajo woman named Hazel Yazza since 1946, is held annually at the Navajo Nation Fair and Rodeo in September.

> Mix 2 cups flour with 2 tbs. baking powder and 1 tsp. salt. Add 1/2 cup warm water, or more, to achieve an elastic dough. Divide into 2-in. balls, roll out to a 1/4-in. thickness, and fry in hot oil. Drain and serve with honey, cinnamon, or confectioners' sugar. (If Navajo bread is desired, punch a hole in the center of each flattened piece before frying, since Navajos lowered their bread into the oil with a stick, leaving hole in the bread.)

frying-pan bread. Cowboy's bread made in a skillet from flour, water, and baking powder made into a thin batter that was spread on a skillet placed over hot coals.

fudge. A semisoft candy made from butter, sugar, and various flavorings, the most usual being chocolate, vanilla, and maple. The candy was first made in New England women's colleges. The origins of the term are obscure. The *Oxford English Dictionary* suggests it may be a variant of an older word, *fadge,* meaning "to fit pieces together." The term *fudge* had been used to mean a hoax or cheat since about 1833, and by midcentury "Oh, fudge!" was a fairly innocuous expletive. It has also been speculated that the college women, using candy making as an excuse to stay up late at night, applied the then-current meaning to the new candy. *Fudge* as candy first showed up in print in 1896, though it was quite commonly associated with college women by that time and was responsible for helping many students gain their "Freshman Fifteen," that is, fifteen pounds gained during the first year at college. Recipes of the period and later more often than not refer specifically to "Wellesley fudge," "Vassar fudge," and other schools' recipes, while "divinity fudge" (known by this name at least since 1913), made with egg whites and candied cherries, came along about 1910 and was especially popular during the holidays.

The majority of all fudge is made from chocolate, though vanilla and maple are very popular, as is fudge riddled with walnuts or pecans. Fudge brownies are more cakelike than fudge, but have a similar semisoft, moist texture.

CHOCOLATE FUDGE:
Combine 2 cups sugar, 2 tbs. corn syrup, 2/3 cup evaporated milk, 2 oz. unsweet-ened chocolate, and 3 tbs. butter in saucepan, bring to boil, and cook to 236° on a candy thermometer. Pour mixture onto marble slab and turn edges in with spatula until glossy sheen is gone. Add 1 tsp. vanilla and, if desired, chopped nuts.

DIVINITY FUDGE:
Boil 2 cups sugar, 1/2 cup corn syrup, and 1/2 cup water to 245° on a candy thermometer. Slowly pour into 2 stiffly beaten egg whites, stirring constantly. Beat with whisk till cool, add 1 cup walnuts, 1 tsp. vanilla, and 3/4 cup candied cherries. Turn out onto greased pan, let cool, and cut into pieces.

fumaric acid. An additive used to give a tartness to the flavor of processed foods like pie fillings, gelatin, and powdered drinks.

funeral pie. A Pennsylvania Dutch pie traditionally baked before the imminent death of a family member for the purpose of easing the grief of the mourners at the funeral. The pie is also sometimes called a "rosina" or "rosine" pie, because *Rosine* in German means "raisin."

Soak 1 cup raisins in 2 cups warm water for 2 hr. In a double boiler combine 1 1/2 cups sugar, 4 tbs. flour, 1 beaten egg, the juice of 1 lemon and the lemon rind, 1/4 tsp. salt, then raisins and water. Cook for 15 min., pour into unbaked pie shell, top with a lattice of dough, and bake at 375° for 45 min.

funnel cake. A deep-fried pastry made from batter dripped through a funnel. This Pennsylvania Dutch breakfast dish is swirled in a spiral in hot fat and then served with sugar or maple syrup.

Combine 1 cup flour, 3/4 cup milk, 1 tsp. baking powder, 1/8 tsp. salt, and 1 egg to make a batter. Let stand for 10 min. Drip the batter through a funnel, swirling to form a spiral design, in very hot fat or oil. Turn when browned and brown the other side. Drain and serve with powdered sugar or maple syrup.

gap 'n swallow. Described by Josephine H. Pierce in *Coast to Coast Cookery* (1951) as "an emergency pudding made of cornmeal, much like Hasty Pudding. Also a plum pudding served with maple syrup." It is an old New England dish, whose name is a fanciful description of opening one's mouth and swallowing the dish either with relish or mere endurance.

Garbo. Also, "garbo." An uncommon term for a toasted English muffin, perhaps named after movie actress Greta Garbo (1905–).

garden vegetables. The American gardening tradition is basically derived from English roots. But the availability of fruits and vegetables at American markets has made a food-producing garden on one's own property more of a hobby than a necessity. On southern plantations before the Civil War, slaves were often encouraged to keep their own gardens to add to their own diet; if there was a surplus, the food would be sold.

During World War I Americans were urged to plant "liberty gardens" in vacant lots or their own backyards in order to release other foodstuffs for shipment overseas to troops. This same practice came about again in 1942, when such plantings were called "victory gardens."

During the 1960s gardening took on a revival owing to studies that showed many commercially grown fruits and vegetables were treated with pesticides and chemicals that rendered some items dangerous to consume. Many books appeared that encouraged Americans to raise some of their own food on their own land, while at the same time food raised without any chemical additives were pronounced natural or "organically grown."

Today more than half of all American households grow some or all of their own food—in 1982, 44 million Americans did so, 38 million working their own backyard or community gardens and 6 million gardening in pots on rooftops and patios. The Midwest has the most home gardeners, the South the least, and the average yield is $470 in food value. The tomato, grown by 94 percent of home gardeners, is easily the most popular vegetable among such planters.

garlic *(Allium sativum).* An onionlike plant having a bulb that is highly aromatic and distinctly flavored. The word is from Old English, *garlēac,* "spear leek." The plant is native to Central Asia and has long been enjoyed as a seasoning in Asia, Africa, and Europe, especially around the Mediterranean.

In America there grew a wild garlic *(A. canadense)* eaten by pre-Columbian Indians, but the familiar market varieties (American, Creole, Mexican, Italian, and Tahitian) came via Europe and were only appreciated as a seasoning in those regions bordering the Gulf of Mexico, where the French, Spanish, African, and Caribbean influences were the strongest. In the rest of the country garlic's usage was confined to ethnic neighborhoods in large cities until the middle of the present century. "Garlic has been the vehicle in the United States of a self-reversing snobbery," wrote Waverly Root in *Food* (1980). "Before I left America to live in Europe in 1927, you were looked down upon if you ate garlic, a food fit only for ditchdiggers; when I returned in 1940, you were looked down upon if you *didn't* eat it. It had become the hallmark of gastronomic sophistication, and I was overwhelmed by the meals offered by thoughtful friends, who catered to my supposedly acquired dashing Gallic tastes by including garlic in every dish except ice cream."

Garlic salt, a milder-flavored seasoning from processed garlic, appeared in the 1930s; in the late 1940s garlic bread was being served in Italian-American restaurants as a standard item.

Lunch-counter slang terms from the 1920s and 1930s for garlic include *Bronx vanilla, halitosis,* and *Italian perfume.*

GARLIC BREAD:
Spread a sliced loaf of Italian bread with a mixture of butter in which minced garlic or garlic salt has been added. Toast under broiler or in oven till crisp and browned.

gazpacho. Also, "gaspacho." A cold tomato-and-vegetable soup popular as summer fare and a staple of American restaurant menus, especially in the West. Another rendering of the dish is "gazpacho salad," a layering of greens, sliced tomatoes, cucumbers, onions, bread crumbs, and French dressing. As such it was characterized by Mrs. Mary Randolph in *Virginia Housewife* (1796). As a soup, *gazpacho* has been in print since 1845.

Although antecedents of the soup are mentioned in the Bible and Greek and Roman literature (the word comes from the Arabic for "soaked bread"), gazpacho is more specifically an Andalusian dish, itself open to numerous interpretations—some thick, some hot, some cold—and often served with several garnishes, such as chopped eggs, bread cubes, peppers, onions, and scallions. In fact, *Cassell's Spanish Dictionary* defines *gazpacho* as an "Andalusian dish made of bread, oil, vinegar, onions and garlic; crumbs of bread in a pan" and makes no mention of the strained tomatoes that most identify gazpacho for Americans.

Although long known in this country, its popularity was for a great while confined to the South. Later, in the West, it took on a vogue that has made it one of the most often found contemporary soups on a menu.

> Peel and seed 2 tomatoes and chop together with 1 seeded sweet red pepper, 2 cloves garlic, and 2 tbs. seasonings, such as basil, tarragon, parsley, scallion, onions, and chives. Add 1/2 cup olive oil, 3 tbs. lime juice, and about 3 cups chicken broth. Purée in a food blender or food mill, add salt, pepper, and chopped cucumber, and chill for several hours. Serve with bread crumbs or bread cubes and white onions.
>
> GAZPACHO SALAD:
> Blend 1/2 cup chili sauce, 2 tbs. vinegar, and 2 tbs. peanut oil. Shred 1 head of iceberg lettuce and line a plate with the shreds. Top with slices of peeled cucumber, 1 sliced green pepper, 1 cup pitted black olives, and 1 diced, seeded tomato. Pour on dressing and sprinkle with chopped scallions.

gefilte fish. Also, "gefulte fish." A fish loaf or cake seasoned with chopped eggs, onion, and pepper, which according to tradition should be made from several varieties of freshwater fish. The dish is frequently served at Jewish-American homes on Friday night. The term is from the German for "stuffed fish." The term is first mentioned in English print in 1892.

> Fillet 3 lb. whole fish of two or three varieties, such as whitefish, carp, or pickerel. Lightly salt the fillets and chill for several hours, then grind finely, adding 2 eggs, 1/2 cup water, 3 tbs. matzo meal, 2 tsp. salt, and 1/8 tsp. pepper. Chill for 10 min., shape into loaves.
>
> Salt and chill the bones, skin and head of the fish, rinse, and place in large pot with 2 chopped onions and 3 chopped carrots in a layer. Season with salt and pepper, cover with water, and bring to boil. Cook for 5 min., then add fish mixture to broth and place sliced carrots on top. Cover, bring to boil, simmer gently for 1 hr. Cool slightly before serving, garnished with carrots, broth, horseradish, and dill pickles. Serves 6.

gelatin. A thickening agent used in powdered desserts, yogurt, puddings, ice cream, cheese spreads, and other foods. Gelatin is a protein derived from animal bones, hoofs, and other parts.

Gibson. A MARTINI cocktail garnished with a small white onion. The drink was apparently named after the American illustrator Charles Dana Gibson (1867–1944), famous for his drawings of the turn-of-the-century "Gibson Girl." The story goes that Gibson ordered a martini—usually served with an olive —from bartender Charley Connolly of The Players in New York City. Connolly found himself out of olives and instead served the drink with two tiny white onions. The drink caught on, took the name of the more famous of the two men, and ever since has caused confirmed martini drinkers to shudder at the thought of drinking their favorite cocktail with such a garnish. The recipe, however, differs not at all from that of a dry martini. The cocktail is first mentioned in print in 1930.

gimlet. A drink of gin and lime juice. The word derives from a term for a boring tool (from Middle English and, ultimately, Middle Dutch, *wimmelkijn*), which supposedly was used to puncture the kegs of lime juice shipped after 1795 to the British colonies as a preventative for scurvy. As a cocktail, the word first appears in print in 1928.

Bartenders disagree as to the proportions for a gimlet, some adding carbonated water as with a gin RICKEY, others not. In America carbonated water is not usual. In his novel, *The Long Goodbye* (1953), Raymond Chandler insists "a real gimlet is half gin and half Rose's Lime Juice and nothing else."

Stir with ice 2 oz. gin and 1/2 oz. Rose's lime juice. Strain into sour glass.

gin. A distilled spirit made from grain and flavored with juniper and other aromatics. Gin was first made as a medicine in Holland by Franz de le Boë (1614–1672), also known as Doctor Sylvius, professor of medicine at the University of Leiden. Sylvius redistilled a pure alcohol with the oil of the juniper berry *(Juniperus communis),* the result of which he called *"Genièvre"* (French, from the Dutch, *jenever,* "juniper berries"). He believed the new spirit would have therapeutic effect, a claim that made its creator famous and created an immediate market for the then inexpensive spirit, which was sometimes called "Hollands" or "Schiedam" (after a gin-distillery center near Rotterdam).

The English imported gin, which they called "Dutch courage," but during Queen Anne's reign (1702–1714) the spirit was produced locally and became the favorite—and least expensive—alcoholic drink sold throughout England, especially after the monarch raised excise taxes on foreign spirits and lowered them on domestic. "London Dry Gin" used to mean a gin produced in or near that city, and such spirits differed in taste from the heavier Dutch gins. These lighter London-style gins became just as popular in the English colonies and have remained the preferred American variety ever since.

English gins run 80 to 97 proof, slightly lower than American gins, and their taste has a bit more character than ours. (The English also make a rarely seen sweetened gin called "Old Tom," which purists insist is the correct spirit for a Tom Collins cocktail.)

During Prohibition those who opposed enforced temperance would often make liquor illegally at home, and so-called bathtub gin,—that is, liquor mixed in one's bathtub—was the easiest spirit to produce. By obtaining a doctor's prescription for pure alcohol on some pretext of illness, one merely had to flavor the liquid with juniper berries, or their extract, and other botanicals such as coriander, lemon peel, or angelica. Glycerin was often added to soften the home brew's rawness.

Commercially produced gin in America may be either distilled or made by combining distilled spirits with botanical oils, a process called "compounding." By law all gins must have the flavor of juniper, though sloe gin, which is really a cordial and not a gin, is allowed to carry the name by tradition.

Gin is almost never aged, although there are some "golden gins" produced whose color comes from brief aging.

Gin is principally mixed with other spirits or citrus juices to make cocktails such as the dry MARTINI, the GIBSON, the GIMLET, the RAMOS GIN FIZZ, and others. The United States is the biggest producer of gin, and we import more British gin than any other country. About 10 percent of the liquor market in the United States is in gin, about 40 million gallons per year.

ginger *(Zingiber officinale)*. This native plant of tropical and subtropical regions of Asia, especially Indomalaysia, is no longer extant in its wild form, but its cultivated root is valued for its pungent, aromatic spiciness and is a seasoning used throughout the world in everything from curries to desserts.

The name derives from the Sanskrit *śṛṅgaveram* ("horn root"), Greek *ziggiberis,* Latin *zinziberi,* and on to Middle English *gingivere.* Ginger was well known to the ancient Romans, but it nearly disappeared in Europe after the fall of the Roman Empire. Marco Polo brought ginger back from the Orient, and afterwards the European appetite for spices made it once again a treasured and expensive condiment. Legend has it that Queen Elizabeth I of England invented the "gingerbread man," a cookie in the shape of a man, especially popular during Christmastime.

There was no ginger in the New World, but the English brought it to the American colonies early on, and ginger cookies were handed out to the Virginia voters to persuade them to elect certain candidates for the House of Burgesses. Ginger became a popular spice in Caribbean and Creole cookery, but in the rest of the country it was more often used in cakes, breads, and cookies. Virginian William Byrd in 1711 remarked that he "ate gingerbread all day long," and Amelia Simmons's *American Cookery* (1796) gives a recipe for molasses gingerbread. Eliza Leslie's 1828 volume, *Seventy Five Receipts,* listed both a common gingerbread and an enriched LAFAYETTE GINGER BREAD with lemon juice and brown sugar. Fannie Merritt Farmer, in her 1896 *Boston Cooking-School Cook Book,* speaks of three available grades of ginger—"Jamaica, best and strongest; Cochin [Indian], and African."

Today fresh ginger root is available in American markets, but Americans usually depend on dry, powdered ginger for use in cakes and cookies. Crystallized ginger is often found in specialty shops, and candied ginger was long served in the North as an after-dinner digestive. Ginger ice cream was a flavor popular in New England, though now rarely seen.

Booker T. Washington, founder of the Tuskegee Institute in Alabama, recalls the childhood he spent as a slave and how he envied the white people's enjoyment of ginger cakes: "I remember that at one time I saw two of my young mistresses and some lady visitors eating ginger-cakes, in the yard. At that time those cakes seemed to me to be absolutely the most tempting and desirable things that I had ever seen; and I then and there resolved that, if I ever got free, the height of my ambition would be reached if I could get to the point where I could secure and eat ginger-cakes in the way I saw those ladies doing" (*Up From Slavery* [1901]).

GINGERBREAD:
Sift together 1 tsp. powdered ginger and 1 cup flour. Cream 1/2 cup butter with 1/2 cup brown sugar. Add flour mixture and blend well. Beat in 1/2 cup molasses and 1 well-beaten egg. Dissolve 1 tsp. baking soda in 1/2 cup boiling water and add to batter. Mix well, then bake in well-greased shallow pan at 350° for about 20 min. or until inserted knife comes out clean.

ginger beer. A nonalcoholic beverage flavored with fermented ginger. Ginger beer was popular in England at the beginning of the nineteenth century and later in America as a substitute for real beer. A MOSCOW MULE is a cocktail made with ginger beer and vodka.

In a large earthenware vessel put 2 oz. pounded ginger root, 1/4 pt. lemon juice, 1 lb. sugar, and 1 gallon boiling water. Cool to 110°, then add 1 oz. yeast dissolved in a little water. Let ferment for 1 week. When fermentation ends, pour through strainer into bottles. Makes 1 gallon.

ginger champagne. A substitute cocktail without alcohol made with ginger flavoring. The drink has been known by this name since at least 1842.

gingersnap. A cookie made from ginger and molasses. *Snap* probably derives from an informal meaning for something easy, from German, or Middle Dutch, *snappen,* "to seize quickly." The word was first printed in 1805.

Gingerbread men may be made in the same way as gingersnaps, except that they are cut into human shapes either with a knife or a cookie cutter for that purpose. They are often decorated with icing for eyes, mouth, and buttons.

Boil a cup of molasses and blend in 4 tbs. butter, a pinch of salt, 2/3 tsp. baking soda, and 1 tsp. powdered ginger. Cool, then add enough flour to make a dough that can be rolled very thin. Cut out into 2-in. cookie shapes and bake in a 400° oven for about 15–20 min. The cookie should be very crisp when cooled. (*The Buckeye Cookbook* [1883] warns that "Snaps will not be crisp if made on a rainy day.")

glycerin. Also, "glycerol." An additive, derived from fat and oil molecules, for retaining the moisture of foods to which it is added, such as marshmallow, candy, and baked goods.

golden Cadillac. A cocktail made from Galliano, white crème de cacao, and heavy cream. The name derives from the golden color of the drink and its richness, both characteristics associated with the American luxury car, the Cadillac. In 1956 Columbia Pictures produced a motion picture entitled *The Solid Gold Cadillac,* and the cocktail may date from that period.

In an electric blender mix with crushed ice 1 oz. Galliano, 2 oz. crème de cacao, and 2 oz. heavy cream. Pour into cocktail glass.

goose. Any of a variety of wild or domesticated large birds of the family Anatidae, especially of the genera *Anser* and *Branta*. The word is from Old English, *gōs*.

Geese were plentiful in the New World, but they have never been successfully mass-marketed and must be raised on small farms or taken in the wild, where the following species are found: Canada goose *(Branta canadensis);* brant *(B. bernicla),* a western subspecies of which is the black brant; emperor goose *(Philacte canagica);* white-fronted goose *(Anser albifrons);* snow goose *(Chen caerulescens);* and Ross's goose *(Chen rossii).*

Geese are almost always roasted, but because of their fattiness have never achieved much popularity with Americans.

gordos. A trapper's term for wheat pancakes. But Blanche and Edna V. McNeil in *First Foods of America* (c. 1936) indicate that gordos were made from chili, meat, frijoles, avocados, and masa, while "gorditas" ("little fat ones" in Spanish) were masa cakes made with cheese, chili, and avocados.

gorp. A mixture of dried fruit, seeds, and nuts. The origin of the name is unknown but was first printed in 1968.

goulash. A Hungarian-American stew of meat and vegetables seasoned with paprika. The Hungarian word is *gulyás,* which originally meant "shepherd," then was synonymous with the kind of stew he ate. Its first printed reference in English was in 1866. In America the dish is often called "Hungarian goulash." It may be made with beef, veal, lamb, or chicken. The F.D.A. requires canned or packaged goulash to contain at least 25 percent meat.

> Brown 2 lb. beef in 1/4 cup butter or lard. Add 2 chopped onions and sauté until golden. Add 1 cup beef stock, 1 tsp. salt, 1 tsp. paprika, and, if desired, 1 chopped green pepper. Cover and cook for about 1 hr., then add 6 small peeled potatoes. Continue cooking till meat and potatoes are tender. Serve with buttered egg noodles.

graham flour. An unsifted, whole wheat flour containing the bran of the wheat kernel. It is named after Reverend Sylvester Graham (1794–1851), a tenacious advocate of temperance, healthy nutrition, and the virtues of home baking with this kind of flour. So influential was Graham's theory that he and his followers' appearance in Boston drew a protesting group of local bakers who were routed only after Graham's people had pelted the demonstrators with lime.

Graham set up "Graham hotels" serving strictly controlled meals quite in line with the belief of the temperance movement that food should not contain any stimulants or seasonings that might enflame the blood. Graham began his crusade in 1830, and within four years people were talking of "Graham bread." By 1882 a flat, slightly sweet cookie called a "Graham cracker" was well known, and the cookbooks of the nineteenth century always included recipes for such foods made with graham flour.

Graham's legacy survives today mostly in the form of the cookies named after him and graham cracker crust, a pastry crust that is used often in lemon meringue pies, Key lime pies, cheesecakes, and other confections. Graham crackers made by Nabisco Brands, Inc., of East Hanover, New Jersey, have long been one of America's most popular cookies.

GRAHAM CRACKER CRUST:
Combine 1 1/2 cups graham crackers with 1/4 cup sugar and 1/3 cup melted butter and blend until the texture of coarse meal. Press into pie tin and bake for 8 min. at 375°. Cool.

grape. Any of a large number of species of fruit berries from vines in the genus *Vitis,* 90 percent of which are Vinifera grapes, a variety encompassing at least five thousand varieties. The word is from the Germanic.

The earliest colonists found America abundant with wild grapes. In fact, it has been estimated that North America has 50 percent of the world's wild grape species, including *V. labrusca,* with its characteristic "foxy" taste and aroma, and *V. rotundifolia,* the MUSCADINE grape.

The settlers on the eastern coast immediately set to make wine from the native grapes, but found that their own European Vinifera vines fared poorly. On the western coast, however, the Spanish missionaries successfully introduced Vinifera varieties and made a great deal of wine from the 1780s onward. In the nineteenth century many new varieties were imported to California, and these thrived until the blight of *Phylloxera vastatrix* hit in the 1870s and devastated many vineyards, as it had in Europe before the vines were grafted onto resistant American roots. The story of American wine making is told in fuller detail under the main entry, WINE.

In those same years a grape industry had been building in New York and the West, providing table grapes, jellies, jams, preserves, juices, and raisins. The most popular table grape varieties include Almeria, Calmeria, Cardinal, Emperor, Italia, Muscat of Alexandria, Ribier, Thompson Seedless, and Tokay. Most grape juice, jelly, jams, and preserves are made with Concord grapes, a Labrusca hybrid. Most raisins are made from either Thompson Seedless or Muscat of Alexandria.

Garden-variety grapes include: the mustang or winter grape *(V. candicans),* the post-oak or turkey grape *(V. lincecumi),* the little mountain *(V. berlandieri),* the sweet mountain *(V. monticola),* the frost or sour grape *(V. cordifolia),* the sweet winter or ashy grape *(V. cinerea),* the adobeland or dog ridge grape *(V. champini),* the Texas Panhandle large grape *(V. doaniana),* the solonis, bush, or gulch grape *(V. longii),* the sand bush, sugar, or rock grape *(V. rupestris),* and the riverside or riverbank grape *(V. riparia).*

grapefruit *(Citrus paradisi).* Also called "pomelo." A tropical tree bearing a yellow, globular fruit that grows in grapelike clusters that give it its name, first mentioned in print in 1814 in *Hortus Jamaicensis* by John Lunan, who also noted that the fruit had the flavor of a grape. The fruit was originally confused with the true pomelo (or pummelo), known taxonomically as *C. grandis,* which was also called the "shaddock" after an English Captain named Shaddock brought seeds from Indonesia to Barbados in 1696. But the grapefruit that Lunan described was not the pomelo, although it may have been a mutant of it.

The grapefruit was introduced to Tampa, Florida, in 1823 by a French count named Odette Philippe, but it achieved no gastronomic notice until well into the nineteenth century, when the first shipments of the fruit were made to northern markets. The first commercial plantings in Florida were in 1885, and by 1900 the grapefruit had taken on some interest as an alternative to oranges, and, with the introduction of the Marsh seedless variety, it became all the more attractive as a breakfast fruit. In 1924 the pink-fleshed Thompson seedless was marketed, followed five years later by a red variety named "Red Blush."

Today the United States produces between 75 percent and 90 percent of the world's crop, mostly in Florida. More than half of the crop is canned or made into fruit juice or frozen concentrate. Grapefruit are eaten fresh and, occasionally, broiled with sugar.

grape pie. A pie made from eastern grapes of the Labrusca variety and its hybrids. This pie in some form was originally made by the Indians living along the vine-rich regions of Canandaigua Lake in New York, and it is rarely made anywhere else in the United States.

grasser. A head of grass-fed cattle.

grasshopper pie. A dessert pie made with green crème de menthe cordial, gelatin, and whipped cream. It derives its name from the green color of the cordial. The pie is popular in the South, where it is customarily served with a cookie crust, and probably dates from the 1950s.

The recipe below is from Nika Hazelton's *American Home Cooking* (1980):

> Crumble 1 1/2 cups chocolate cookies very fine, combine with 1/4 cup melted butter, and 1/8 tsp. cinnamon. Press into buttered pie pan to create a thin crust. Sprinkle 1 1/2 tsp. unflavored gelatin over 1/3 cup milk and mix. Stand bowl in double boiler and dissolve gelatin. Beat 4 egg yolks till thickened, beat in 1/4 cup sugar, 1/4 cup green crème de menthe, 1/4 cup crème de cacao, and blend completely. Stir in gelatin, chill mixture till quite thick, fold in 1 cup whipped cream, pour into pie crust, and chill overnight. Serve with a sprinkling of chocolate curls.

gravy. A sauce, usually flour-based, served with meat, poultry, and other foods. The word is from Middle English, *gravey,* from Old French, *grave,* which, according to the *American Heritage Dictionary of the English Language,* is a misreading of *grane,* perhaps "(dish) seasoned with grains," from *grain,* "spice." In America *gravy* is a more common term than *sauce* or *sop* and has been since the middle of the nineteenth century. By 1900 the word had metaphoric connotations of money obtained with little or no effort, so that to be on the "gravy train" was to acquire money gratuitously, often through political graft.

The F.D.A. requires processed gravy to contain at least 25 percent meat stock or broth or at least 6 percent meat.

grayling *(Thymallus arcticus).* Also, "Arctic grayling." A cold-water fish found throughout the Arctic and northern United States, where it has been widely introduced. The name of the fish, first used in the fifteenth century, comes from its color. Although graylings are no longer marketed commercially, they were from 1860 to 1880 a mainstay of the diet of the lumberjacks in Michigan, when, according to A. J. McLane in *The Encyclopedia of Fish Cookery* (1977), "enterprising merchants hauled them away by the wagonload to feed lumbercamps, or down the Au Sable and Lake Huron in the live wells of houseboats to supply restaurants of Detroit and Chicago." Ecological and climatic changes have decreased the fish's population considerably, so that today the grayling is mainly a sport fish.

Green Goddess. A salad or salad dressing made from anchovies, mayonnaise, tarragon vinegar, and other seasonings. The salad was created at San Francisco's Palace Hotel (now the Sheraton-Palace) in the mid-1920s at the request of actor George Arliss (1868–1946), who was appearing in town in William Archer's play, *The Green Goddess* (which had opened in New York in 1921 and was twice made into a motion picture [1923 and 1930] starring Arliss).

This recipe is from the Sheraton-Palace:

Mince 8–10 anchovy fillets with 1 green onion. Add 1/4 cup minced parsley, 2 tbs. minced tarragon, 3 cups mayonnaise, 1/4 cup tarragon vinegar, and 1/2 cup cut chives. Chop romaine, escarole, and chicory and mix together dressing and greens in a bowl that has been rubbed with garlic. The salad may be topped with chicken, crab, or shrimp.

green lamb. Rancher's term for a newborn lamb.

greenling. A southern name for a tart green apple.

greenling (Family Hexagrammidae). Also, "sea trout." A fish of the Pacific that ranges from Baja, California, to the Aleutians, the two dominant species being the kelp greenling *(Hexagrammos decagrammus)* and the painted greenling *(Oxylebius pictus).* Greenlings are often made into steaks and broiled or grilled.

green meat. Rancher's term for meat that has not been aged.

grenadine. A sweet syrup with a deep red color and the flavor of pomegranates, from which it takes its name (French, *grenadier*). Grenadine may be bought with a small amount of alcohol (about 5 proof) or with no alcohol, and it is used both as a sweetener and coloring for cocktails. The first printed English reference was in 1852.

grillade. A dish of veal or beef round braised with seasonings and served with grits. It is, in fact, usually referred to in Louisiana as "grillades and grits" and is a specialty of that region. *Grillade* is a French term meaning "broiled meat," usually ham, but veal or beef are more usual in America.

> Pound 2 lb. veal or beef that has been cut into pieces about 2–3 sq. in. and brown in 2 tbs. oil, then remove. Brown 1 1/3 tbs. flour in the same amount of hot oil to make a roux, add 1 tbs. oil, brown 1 chopped onion, 1/2 chopped green pepper, 1 chopped celery stalk, 2 cloves minced garlic, a pinch of thyme, 2 tsp. chopped parsley, and 1/8 tsp. cayenne pepper. Add 1 coarsely chopped tomato that has been peeled and seeded, stir in 1 1/2 cups water, salt, and pepper, bring to a boil, then simmer for about 10 min. Add meat, cover, and simmer until meat is cooked through and tender. Serve with grits.

grits. Finely ground dried, hulled corn kernels that are prepared in a variety of ways as a side dish, pudding, soufflé, and breakfast food. Grits are a form of HOMINY and are often called "hominy grits." The word is from Old English, *grytt,* for "bran," but the Old English word *greot* also meant something ground. Americans have used the word *grits* at least since the end of the eighteenth century.

Grits have been called an "institution" in the South, but they are rarely encountered in the North. Satisfying and filling, grits are a traditional southern breakfast food, but they are just as often served as a side dish. Grillades and grits is a Louisiana specialty of braised meat and buttered grits.

> BOILED GRITS:
> Soak 1/2 cup grits in 1 cup cold water overnight. Add 1/2 tsp. salt, 1/2 cup cold water, heat and stir till boiling, then lower heat to simmer and stir. Cover and let thicken, adding some more hot water to keep consistency from getting too thick. Serve with butter.
>
> GRITS SOUFFLÉ:
> Heat 1 1/2 cups water with 1 cup milk, add 1/2 cup grits, and 4 beaten egg yolks, and stir until thickened. Cool, then add 1/4 cup Parmesan cheese, Tabasco sauce, and salt and pepper to taste. Fold in 4 stiffly beaten egg whites, pour into buttered soufflé dish, and bake at 425° for about 30 min.

grog. A mixture of hot water and rum, often with the addition of spices and citrus fruit. The name supposedly derives from a British Admiral named Edward Vernon (1684–1757), whose nickname was "Old Grog" and who tried to prevent scurvy among his crew by giving them a rum-and-water mixture, a concoction that did nothing for scurvy but warmed the seamen's souls and gave the world "Old Grog's drink."

The United States Navy, following the British Navy's lead, included in the sailors' rations "one half pint of distilled spirits per day," and this was usually served from a "grog tub," kept locked away until seven bells, when the master's mate pumped the spirits and water into it. As described by the chaplain on the U.S.S. *Constitution* ("Old Ironsides") in the early nineteenth century:

> Shortly after eight bells, as the drum rolls, all move aft, towards the grog tub. Around this point of time concentrate half the meditations of the day. I often place myself at the tub, to watch the rolling eyes, and the look of supreme gratification with which they swallow their half pint. . . . A rope is drawn athwartships, near the tub; each as his name is called, and crossed, takes his allowance which must be drunk on the spot. From this, they pass to dinner. The whole operation is superintended by the officer of the deck.

On land grog became a very popular stimulant among workers in the iron mills of the Northeast and was an ordinary drink for others. Americans usually sweetened the grog with molasses, which gave it the name "blackstripe," a variation on "blackstrap," which was a cold mixture of molasses and rum in New England.

In a heated mug combine 1 oz. rum, 1 tsp. molasses, and top with boiling water.

grouper (Family Serranidae). A common name for a carnivorous member of the sea BASS family having over four hundred species. Only two genera of true groupers, *Epinephelus* and *Mycteroperca*, including about one hundred species, are of culinary interest. The name is from the Portuguese, *garoupa*, its first printed mention in English being in 1671. In California the rockfish *(Sebastichthys)* is also called a grouper.

The groupers of culinary importance in North America include the black grouper *(Mycteroperca bonaci)*; JEWFISH *(Epinephelus itajara)*; Nassau grouper *(E. striatus)*; red grouper *(E. morio)*; spotted cabrilla *(E. analogus)*; and yellowmouth grouper *(M. interstitialis)*, the most common market species of the South and especially popular in the Carolinas and Florida.

growler. A bucket or pitcher used to carry beer from a tavern to one's home. The term appeared in the last quarter of the nineteenth century. The vessels, suggests Flexner in *I Hear America Talking* (1976), were so called "perhaps because they made a growling, grating sound when they slid across the bar."

grub. A colloquial expression for any kind of food, often heard in the West among cowboys, ranchers, miners, and loggers.

The term is quite old, however, deriving from Middle and Old English words meaning "to dig" and suggesting a person who had to dig for roots to eat. To *grub* in this sense goes back at least to the fourteenth century, and the *Oxford English Dictionary* shows *grub* as a slang term for food as far back as 1725.

Grubstake refers to the practice of a benefactor who gambled on (staked) a prospector's chances for finding precious metals by providing money with which to buy food and provisions for the search. The term dates back at least to 1863.

grunt. A very old colonial dessert made with berries and a dough steamed in a kettle.

> Cook 1 cup blackberries or blueberries in 1 cup water and 1/2 cup sugar for about 5 min. till soft, then place in a buttered mold. Sift 3 tbs. baking powder with 1 1/2 cups flour and 1/4 tsp. salt. Cut in 1 tbs. butter to make a coarse meal, then stir in 1/2 cup milk to form a dough. Place dough over berries, cover, and set in a kettle of boiling water to steam for about 1 hr. Serve with a hard or foamy sauce. Serves 6.

A grunt is also an American fish of the family Pomadasyidae, genus *Haemulon* and allied species, deriving its name from the grunting sound it makes. (It is not the same fish as the Dutch *grunt* [*Cyprinus gobio*].) The pigfish *(Orthopristis chrysopterus)* is a species of eastern American grunt, so called because of its piglike mouth. So, too, is the sargo *(Anisotremus davidsonii),* abundant in Pacific waters, a species of grunt. The first mention of the grunt was in 1713 as the "Gray Grunt" in *Synopsis Piscium.*

Grunt is also a slang expression from the Old West meaning pork or ham, sometimes bacon. "Cluck and grunt" would be eggs and bacon, imitating the sounds made by the animals who provide them. Finally, *grunt* is a slang term from the late-1940s meaning a check or bill for a restaurant meal.

guacamole. A dip made from avocados and chili pepper. Guacamole is a staple of Tex-Mex and Mexican-American menus (the word is from Mexican Spanish via Nahuatl, *ahuacamolli,* "avocado sauce") and became especially popular in the 1960s and 1970s as an appetizer at parties and buffets. The first printed reference to the word in English was in 1920.

> Remove the pits from 2 avocados and mash the flesh with 2 tsp. lime juice, 1/2 tsp. salt, 2 chopped scallions, 1/2 chopped and seeded tomato, 1 minced garlic clove, a minced green chili or pickled jalapeño, and 1/2 tsp. coriander (cilantro). Serve with corn chips or over lettuce leaves as a salad.

gum. A variety of thickening agents and stabilizers, such as guar, locust bean, arabic, ghatti, karaya, tragacanth, and others, used in ice cream, beverages, puddings, salad dressings, candy, and other foods.

gumbo. A Louisiana soup or stew usually containing okra and any of a variety of meats, seafood, and vegetables. The dish reflects the influence of an amalgam of cultures, including those of the Indians of the region, the French and Spanish settlers, and the African slaves who gave it its name (from the Bantu, *gombo,* akin to Umbundu, *ochinggombo,* "okra"). The word *gumbo* first appears in American print in 1805, and throughout the nineteenth century the dish is mentioned with affection and relish. By 1823 people also spoke of "gumbo filé" (or "filé gumbo"), which was a gumbo thickened with filé powder (ground sassafras leaves) as used by the Choctaw Indians.

There are several forms of gumbo, incorporating meats and vegetables, vegetables alone, shrimp and crawfish, and, usually, okra pods. There is no such thing as an "authentic" gumbo, except that the tastes of such dishes seem to share a common heritage of heartiness. Even gumbo z'herbes (a corruption of the French, *aux herbes,* "with herbs"), traditionally served on the meatless Maunday Thursday, is usually described as containing only vegetables, but the "Gombo aux Herbes" recipe given in the esteemed volume, *The Picayune's Creole Cook Book* (1901), contains veal brisket and ham. Gumbo z'herbes also traditionally contains seven greens for good luck.

SEAFOOD GUMBO:
(From the Gumbo Shop restaurant in New Orleans) Peel and devein 3 lb. shrimp and chill. Boil shrimp shells and 1 ham bone in 2 qt. water to make a stock. In a skillet sauté 1 qt. okra cut into small pieces in 1 tbs. oil for about 30 min. In a large kettle make a roux with 2/3 cup oil and 1/2 cup flour, add 2 chopped onions, 1 chopped bell pepper, 2 chopped celery stalks, 2 chopped garlic cloves, and 1/4 cup chopped parlsey, and sauté until tender. Add 1 16-oz. can stewed tomatoes, cook 15 min., then add sautéed okra, the ham-and-shrimp stock, 2 small boiled crabs broken in quarters, salt and pepper, 2 bay leaves, 2 tbs. Worcestershire sauce, and 1/2 tsp. cayenne pepper. Bring to a boil, then simmer for 2 hr., stirring occasionally. Add shrimp and continue cooking till done. Serve over steamed rice.

TURKEY FILÉ GUMBO:
Brown 1 lb. smoked sausage in 2 tbs. oil. Remove from skillet and put in kettle with about 1 qt. or more turkey broth, from which turkey meat has been removed. Brown 1 lb. diced ham in 4 tbs. fat from sausage, then add ham to broth. Sauté 1 large chopped onion in skillet oil, then add 2 minced cloves garlic. Sprinkle in 4 tbs. flour and stir to blend, then add 1 16-oz. can stewed tomatoes. Add this all to broth and cook for 30 min. Add several shucked oysters if desired, simmer 15 min., put in turkey meat, and add 1 tbs. filé powder dissolved in 1/4 cup cold water. Thicken sauce.

GUMBO Z'HERBES:
In enough water to cover (about 1 gallon), boil cleaned, trimmed bunches of spinach, mustard greens, watercress, parsley, carrot tops, chicory, scallions, cabbage, and beet tops (or any variation totalling seven greens) for 2 hr. Strain greens, reserve water, chop greens finely. In a kettle make a dark roux from 4 tbs. flour and 4 tbs. oil or lard. Add 1 lb. boiled ham and 1 diced onion, and cook for 5 min. Add greens, simmer 15 min., add cooking water, 2 bay leaves, 2 minced cloves garlic, 1 tsp. thyme, salt and pepper, and 1 tsp. cayenne pepper, and simmer for another hour. Add 1 pt. oysters, if desired, during the last 15 min. of cooking. Serves 6.

gun-wadding bread. A light bread eaten by cowboys.

gut-eaters. Cowboy slang for Indians because of some tribes' taste for the entrails of animals.

hake (Genus *Urophycis*). With more than a dozen species, the hake is a member of the cod family and is found in both eastern and western waters. The two main species in the Atlantic are the white hake *(Urophycis tenuis)* and the red hake *(U. chuss),* which when washed ashore in winter are picked up by people who live along the shore, who call them "frostfish." The Pacific hake *(Merluccius productus)* is abundant on the coast from Alaska to Baja, California. The name is from Middle English.

halvah. Also, "halavah." A confection of mashed sesame seeds and honey. Halvah is of Turkish origin and was first sold in America at the turn of the century by Turkish, Syrian, and Armenian street vendors. (The word is from the Turkish, *helve.*) The candy soon became a favorite of the Jewish immigrants in New York, and today halvah is still associated with Jewish DELI-CATESSANS, even though one of the most popular commercial brands still depicts a turbaned Turk on its wrapper. The word was first printed in 1846.

Halvah is often sold in oblong bars from which slabs may be sliced according to one's request or in cellophane-wrapped smaller bars.

ham. The smoked or cured dried thigh of the hind leg of the hog. The word is from Old English.

Hams in America are cured in a variety of ways. Dry curing involves salting the meat heavily and allowing it to absorb the salt over a period of time. Sweet-pickle curing involves immersing the meat in a sweet brine. Injection curing, which is today the most common practice, involves a sweet-pickle cure coupled with injections of brine into the meat's interior in order to speed the process. After curing the hams are then smoked (though not all hams are so treated), the degree of smoking differing from region to region and ranging from a few hours to many weeks. The woods used for smoking are usually hickory or maple, though some large companies use sawdust or liquid smoke-flavorings. Most hams are then cooked, either partially or fully, and carry labels such as "fully cooked," "heat-and-serve," and "ready-to-eat," meaning they require no further cooking and may be eaten straight from the can or wrapper. *Sugar-cured ham* is a term that entered the language in the 1830s.

Most hams are prepared "urban style"—that is, made on a large scale—resulting in meat that is less expensive, because the processing is shorter and less complicated, and, usually, blander in taste. "Country-style" hams or "country-cured" hams (first recorded in 1944) go through more complex curings and smokings in rural sections of Virginia, Georgia, Tennessee, Kentucky, Vermont, and other states. The famous Smithfield ham is coated with salt, sodium nitrate, and sugar, refrigerated for five days, salted again, refrigerated again for one day per pound of meat, washed, refrigerated for another two weeks, smoked for ten days, and then aged six to twelve months. In order to carry a Smithfield label, a ham must be prepared in this manner in the town of Smithfield, Virginia, though the hogs may come from the surrounding area. This ham is sometimes called the "Virginia ham," but that name is more generally applied to a specific method of roasting a smoked ham, as given below. Kentucky country ham is called "old ham."

In the South ham steaks or ham slices are often served with REDEYE GRAVY made from the drippings.

BAKED VIRGINIA HAM:
In the outer surface of a ready-to-eat ham cut a grid pattern of gashes. Sprinkle with brown sugar, stud with whole cloves, top with pineapple slices, and bake, basting occasionally, for 1 hour. at 350°.

hamburger. Also, "burger." A grilled, fried, or broiled patty of ground beef, usually served on a "hamburger bun" and topped with ketchup, onions, or other condiments. Hamburgers, along with HOT DOGS, are considered the most identifiably American of food items, despite its German-sounding name. Certainly ground meat, served either raw or cooked, is not indigenous to America or Germany, but the name obviously derives from the German city of Hamburg, where some sort of pounded beefsteak was popular by the middle of the nineteenth century. *The Dictionary of American English* traces *Hamburg steak* to 1884 in an article in the Boston *Journal,* but chef Louis Szathmáry in his book *American Gastronomy* (1974) contends that he has seen an 1836 menu from Delmonico's restaurant in New York with just such an item on it. By the 1890s *Hamburg* (or *Hamburgh*) *steak* specifically referred not to a ground-meat patty but to a piece of beef that had been pounded so as to tenderize the meat by breaking up the fibers. Both Oscar Tschirky in *The Cook Book by "Oscar of the Waldorf"* (1896) and D. A. Mary Johnson (Bailey) Lincoln in her *Boston Cook Book* (1896) refer to such a treatment, with fried onions enfolded by the edges of the meat, which was then broiled.

In one of the most widely used cookbooks of the day, *Mrs. [Sarah Tyson] Rorer's New Cook Book* (1902), however, Hamburg steak is described as beef put twice through a meat grinder and mixed with onion and pepper. This is closest to the present concept of what a hamburger should be.

The first appearance in print of *hamburg* was in 1903, and, according to

James Villas in *American Taste* (1982), a "hamburger steak" was featured at the 1904 Louisiana Purchase Exposition in St. Louis, Missouri. By 1912 ground-meat patties we now call "hamburgers" were being served in a soft yeast bun having the approximate shape of the patty itself, and soon the suffix *-burger* was attached to all sorts of other foods, such as lamb, chicken, clam, and, the most famous and colloquially successful, cheese (known since at least 1938), which is a hamburger topped with a slice of American cheese that is melted in the cooking process. *The Dictionary of American Slang* notes that the suffix came to mean "any hot sandwich served on a bun, often toasted, with many condiments. . . . Occasionally a 'burger' is associated with a famous person, event, or historic spot [such as the] Ike-burger[,] somewhat pop[ular] during [the] first presidential campaign of Dwight D. Eisenhower [1952]."

Still, the word *steak* was used with *hamburger* well into the 1920s. In his novel *A Farewell to Arms* (1929), Ernest Hemingway makes such a reference to World War I versions of the dish.

"Hamburger stands" came along with the opening of a chain of roadside restaurants called White Castles (the first in Witchita, Kansas, in 1921) and the popularity of the hamburger grew rapidly with the increase in the number of Americans traveling the roads in automobiles. The dish—now loaded down with "the works," that is, onion, pickles, ketchup, and other condiments—was a standard item in inexpensive restaurants, and without its roll took on haughty pretensions at high-class restaurants, where it was called "chopped steak."

By the 1930s Americans were calling hamburgers "Wimpy burgers"—inspired by an insatiable hamburger addict named J. Wellington Wimpy from the Popeye comic strip drawn by Elzie Segar since 1919 and featured in movie cartoons after 1929. Even today *Wimpie* is a synonym for a hamburger in England, and there is a chain of Wimpy restaurants in the United States.

By the 1940s the hamburger was firmly entrenched as a quintessential American dish—beefy (though sometimes made with filler and usually with fat or gristle), easy to eat while on the move, and found almost everywhere in the country. In his annotations to H. L. Mencken's *The American Language* (1974), Raven I. McDavid, Jr., notes that "the ultimate horror, *Trumanburger* [after President Harry Truman (1945–53)], coined during the dying days of the meat rationing in 1946, consisted of mashed baked beans."

A fresh leap of popularity came in the 1950s with the opening of the McDonald's chain of hamburger stands in Des Plaines, Illinois. Modern, spanking clean, with an assembly-line efficiency and youthful atmosphere, these restaurants, immediately identifiable by their golden arches set outside the front-door parking lot, ushered in a new era of drive-in eating, featuring prepackaged hamburgers with the condiments already added. (The original McDonald's, opened in 1955, was closed in 1983; the year before, the parent chain took in $7 billion in revenue.) McDonald's spawned competitors like Burger King and Wendy's throughout the United States, and although such places sold other items, a "burger and fries" (french-fried potatoes) is still the most common order.

Today hamburgers are just as likely to be made at home from beef patties or ground meat purchased at a market and broiled, fried, or barbecued and served year-round.

Hangtown Fry. A dish of oysters, eggs, and bacon supposedly concocted during the California Gold Rush of 1849 when a recently lucky miner brought a sack of gold to the Cary House restaurant in Hangtown and ordered the most expensive meal in the place. When the chef suggested oysters and eggs—which were very high priced items at the time—the miner asked that bacon be added for good measure, and the dish gained local celebrity as the Hangtown Fry. (Hangtown, now called Placerville, got its name from the notoriety of several public hangings held during the Gold Rush days.)

> Dredge a dozen oysters in seasoned flour, then in a beaten egg, then in bread crumbs. Fry in butter, then add 8 beaten eggs and cook till firm. Season with salt and pepper. Turn and cook on the other side. Serve with bacon. Serves 4.

happy hour. The period of one or two hours before dinner when people enjoy a cocktail or other beverage. The term, which has been used by bars and taverns over the last twenty years, refers to a 1920s connotation of the word *happy* with being slightly intoxicated.

hard sauce. A dessert topping, dating in print to 1899.

> Cream 1/4 lb. butter with 1 lb. confectioners' sugar. Blend in 2 beaten eggs, then add 1 tsp. vanilla, and, if desired, rum or brandy to taste. To make a "foamy sauce," cream the butter with 1/2 lb. confectioners' sugar and slowly add 1 beaten egg and 1/4 cup hot water. Flavor with vanilla and, if desired, rum or brandy, and heat over hot water till thickened. Serve warm.

hardtack. Also, "sea biscuit," "sea bread," "ship biscuit," and "pilot bread." A hard biscuit made with flour and water but no shortening or yeast. The word is a combination of *hard,* for the firm consistency of the biscuit, and *tack,* an English word meaning "food." The first mention of hardtack in print was in 1836, but in 1833 there was mention of "soft tack," referring to loaves of bread.

Hardtack was long part of the staple diet of English and American sailors, because of its ability to keep for lengthy periods of time at sea.

Other more recent slang terms for hardtack include *hard Tommy, artillery, dog biscuits, jawbreakers,* and *pantile,* the last being the name of a roofing tile. Hardtack and molasses is called "dandy funk."

hartshorn. A source of ammonia used in baking cookies or, as "salt of harts-horn," as smelling salts. Once the word meant literally the ground horn of a hart's (male deer's) antler, but ammonium carbonate was later used as a substitute, which also went by the name of "salt of hartshorn." This is still available in American pharmacies and used occasionally in making cookies.

"Hartshorn jelly" is a nutritive jelly once made from hartshorn and later from calves' bones.

A recipe given for hartshorn jelly in Susannah Carter's *The Frugal House-wife* (1796), an English cookbook well known in America, is as follows:

"Take a large gallipot with hart's horn, then fill it full with spring water, tie double paper over the gallipot, and set in a baker's oven with household bread. In the morning take it out, run it through a jelly bag. Season with juice of lemons, double refined sugar, and the whites of eight eggs well-beaten. Let it have a boil and run it through the jelly bag again into jelly glasses, putting a bit of lemon peel into the bag."

Harvard beets. A dish of beets cooked in vinegar, sugar, and cornstarch. The name probably comes from the deep crimson color of the cooked beets, similar to the color of the Harvard football team's jerseys. The dish is more than fifty years old, but its origins are still unknown. A letter to the *New York Times* on the subject, printed on January 13, 1982, insisted that the dish was conceived at a seventeenth-century English tavern called Harwood's, whose customers included a Russian emigré who, in 1846, opened up a restaurant in Boston under the same name. But the emigré kept pronouncing his establishment's name more like "Harvard" than "Harwood," so the dish he brought from England became known as "Harvard beets." There is no evidence to support this story, however.

Gently wash a dozen beets and simmer till tender, about 40 min. Drain and chop up or dice. Mix together 1/2 cup sugar, 2 tsp. cornstarch, and 1/2 cup vinegar, and bring to a boil, then simmer for 5 min. Pour over the beets and reheat, then toss with 2 tbs. butter.

Yale beets, of even more obscure origins, are boiled beets prepared exactly as above except for the substitution of 1/2 cup orange juice and 1 tbs. lemon juice for the vinegar.

Harvard cocktail. A drink whose name derived from Harvard University in Boston, Massachusetts, probably in the 1930s after Prohibition ended.

Shake together with ice 3/4 oz. brandy, 3/4 oz. sweet vermouth, a dash sugar syrup, and 2 dashes orange bitters. Strain into chilled cocktail glass.

Harvey Restaurants. Originally, eating houses opened at the Santa Fe Railroad stations throughout the Southwest by Englishman Fred Harvey, who came to the United States at the age of fourteen to work on the railroads. Appalled at the conditions under which the workers and travellers had to eat, he opened a clean dining room with good food above the Topeka, Kansas, station in 1876. By 1912 Harvey had opened a dozen hotels, sixty-five railroad restaurants, and sixty dining cars. The waitresses at such establishments were called "Harvey girls" (in 1946 Metro-Goldwyn-Mayer made a motion picture by this title), and by 1928 there were Harvey diners and, by 1941, Harvey House restaurants.

Harvey Wallbanger. A cocktail that supposedly originated at Pancho's Bar in Manhattan Beach, California, and was named after a late-1960s surfboard enthusiast named Harvey, who consoled himself after the loss of a tournament with several of these cocktails, which thereupon caused him to bang into the wall on his exit.

The name and drink are now a trademark of "21" Brands, Inc., which is the importer of Galliano liqueur.

> Shake together with ice 2 oz. vodka, 1/2 tbs. Galliano, 4 oz. orange juice, and 1/2 tsp. sugar, pouring the mixture over ice cubes in a glass, and floating some Galliano on top. Some prefer to omit the sugar.

hash. A dish of chopped pork or beef combined with various chopped-up vegetables and seasonings. Hash is generally considered an odds-and-ends kind of dish and was thought of as such when the word first came into English in the mid-seventeenth century, from the Old French word *hacher,* "to chop," after which it was soon found in America as a form of shepherd's pie or other melange of meat and vegetables.

By the middle of the nineteenth century hash became associated with cheap restaurants called "hash houses" or "hasheries" (an 1850 menu from the Eldorado Hotel in Hangtown, California, lists "Low Grade Hash" for seventy-five cents and "18 Carets Hash" for a dollar) and the workers in such places were called "hash slingers." By the turn of the century "corned beef hash" was being ordered, sometimes called "cornbeef Willie." By the 1930s the curious jargon of lunch counters and diners was referred to as "hashhouse Greek," owing to the large numbers of Greeks who owned such establishments.

Hawaii. The food of Hawaii is a diverse blend of all the island and mainland cuisines, especially those of Polynesia, Japan, China, and Korea, wed to Portuguese and American tastes. Hawaii was settled by Polynesians who themselves derived from the Indomalayan region. Except for the bat *('ope'ape'a),* which was inedible, Hawaii had no indigenous animals, and all present animals on the islands were at one time or another brought to Hawaii. These included the DOG *('ilio),* which was bred for food, the pig *(pua'a),* domesticated fowl *(moa),* and other animals.

Fish, which is a mainstay of the Hawaiian diet, was plentiful in the island waters, and every species was eaten, for no poisonous fish existed in the region. Turtle *(honu),* porpoise *(nai'a, nu'ao, pahu),* sperm whale *(palaoa),* octopus *(he'e),* squid *(muhe'e),* crayfish *(ula),* crabs *(papa'i),* and shrimp *('opae)* were relished by the natives.

Wild plant foods were numerous and included the tree fern *(hapu'u),* the wild raspberry *('akala),* lambs'-quarters *('aweoweo),* and seaweed *(limu),* while other plants were introduced into the region, such as coconut *(niu)*, breadfruit *('ulu)*, banana *(mai'a)*, taro *(kalo)*, sweet potato *('uala, uwala)*, yam *(uhi)*, Polynesian arrowroot *(pia)*, and sugar cane *(ko)*.

Taro was easily the most important staple of the Hawaiian natives, and today it is still pounded into a thick, fermented paste called POI.

Hawaiian agriculture has made fruit and nuts one of the state's most important industries, with pineapple, papayas, and macadamia nuts the major exports.

The luau is a Hawaiian feast of some dimensions, and the featured dishes are often *poi, lomi-lomi* salmon, and *kahlua* pig, which is cooked in a covered, smokey pit.

Hawaiian snacks are varied among CRACKSEEDS of dried fruit, MALASADOS (a Portuguese-inspired doughnut), and MANAPUA (a stuffed yeast-dough bun). A traditional dessert of the state is *haupia,* a kind of gelatinous square pudding made from fresh coconut milk and cornstarch.

Hawaiians drink the same beverages as do the mainlanders, with the addition of indigenous beverages that include an abundance of fruit juices, drinks made with coconut milk, and Kona coffee, made from plantation beans on the island of Hawaii. There is some wine produced in Hawaii, both from grapes and from pineapple.

hazelnut. The nut of any of a variety of shrubs or trees of the genus *Corylus,* especially the American hazelnut *(C. americana),* the beaked hazelnut *(C. cornuta),* and the California hazelnut *(C. californica).* The name is from the Old English, *hæsel.*

The hazelnut is sometimes called the "filbert," because it supposedly ripens on St. Philbert's day, August 22.

Up until about 1940 most hazelnuts were imported to the United States from Sicily and Naples, but a native industry has since developed in Oregon and Washington. The nuts are often ground or roasted to be used in pastries and desserts.

headcheese. A sausage made from a calf's or pig's head and molded in its own jelly and seasoned. Headcheese is usually served as an appetizer or, according to C. Major's *Dictionary of Afro-American Slang* (1971), as a lunch meat in black communities.

In England headcheese is called "brawn," from a Germanic word referring to flesh or muscle. In French, however, the item goes by the name *fromage de tête de porc,* "cheese of the pig's head." Both the French and American usages refer to the crumbly, cheeselike texture of the meat, and its first appearance in American print was in 1841.

health food. A vague term first used in 1882 describing food that is supposedly healthier than most of the processed, packaged, or prepared food sold in the market. Sometimes *health food* is a synonym for "organic" or "natural foods," equally vague terms that suggest foods grown or raised without any ADDITIVES, pesticides, or special treatment whatsoever, but the term covers a wide range of food items, from fresh vegetables and fruits to herb teas and vitamin supplements. In fact, the average "health food store," a trend of the 1960s, 1970s, and 1980s, holds shelves full of vitamin and mineral supplements, literature on various diets, and expensive grain cereals.

The Federal Trade Commission has taken no position on the term *health food* but has proposed that such a phrase be prohibited in advertising food products, a claim that may cost the consumer more than twice what a food item without the "health food" label would.

"Organic foods" were popularized after 1948 by J. I. Rodale, publisher of *Organic Gardening and Farming* magazine.

heavenly hash. A dessert made of vanilla wafers and whipped cream popular in the Midwest.

> Beat 2 eggs with 1 cup confectioners' sugar and 1/2 cup butter, and mix with 1/2 pt. whipped cream and 3/4 cup walnuts. Place a layer of vanilla wafer cookies in a pan, add the whipped cream mixture, then another layer of wafers. Chill till firm and serve with more whipped cream.

Herman. A Midwest colloquialism for a bread starter, often kept over decades.

hero. Also, "hero boy" and "Italian hero sandwich," but see below for other variations. A loaf of Italian or French bread sliced lengthwise and filled with a variety of meats and cheeses, spices, lettuce, peppers, and other items. A meatball hero would contain meatballs and tomato sauce; a veal parmesan hero would contain a breaded, fried veal cutlet, mozzarella cheese, and tomato sauce.

In the 1930s Clementine Paddleford noted that the name derived from the hyperbole that one must be a hero to eat such a sandwich. In other parts of the country, however, the same item is known by other names. A "grinder" (first printed appearance in 1954), a "submarine," and a "wedge" are common, as is a "hoagie" (most often associated with Philadelphia, and first mentioned in print in 1955). In the South one hears it called a "po' boy" or "poor boy," since it is a relatively inexpensive item for a great deal of food. In New Orleans poor boys are made with thin slices of well-cooked meat such as shoulder roast in a rich gravy placed on a small, sliced French loaf with mayonnaise, tomatoes, and shredded lettuce. The most famous in that city is called the "peacemaker" or "la mediatrice" ("the mediatrix"), because in the nineteenth century husbands coming home late from the saloons would bring their wives a sandwich made with fried oysters and seasonings such as tartar sauce or cayenne. A "Cuban sandwich" is a Miami, Florida, version made with pork, pickles, and other condiments, while a *medianoche* ("midnight") is served on an egg roll there.

Still another New Orleans version is the "muffuletta," supposedly created at the Central Grocery. It is made on a round loaf of bread specially baked in the local bakeries, and contains salami, provolone cheese, ham, minced garlic, and a mixture called "olive salad," made from chopped green olives, pimientos, chopped Greek olives, oregano, and parsley.

herring. Any of various fishes of the Clupeidae family, but especially the *Clupea harengus.* The name *herring* is from the West German, *hēringaz,* and an Old English form has been known at least since the eighth century.

The herring is an important figure in European history; wars have been fought for control of its grounds, and there was even a Battle of the Herrings in 1429 at Rouvray, France between the British and the French. The Hanseatic League dwindled in power with the decline of the herring in the Baltic, and by 1665 the Dutch raided St. John's, Newfoundland, to halt the English herring industry that had developed there. In America fishermen sought the fish both in the Atlantic and Pacific, and in 1877 United States fleets paid England $5.5 million for the rights to fish the waters of the Gulf of St. Lawrence and Newfoundland. The agreement was not supported by Newfoundland sailors, who proceeded to cut the herring nets of the Americans, which precipitated the Fortune Bay Riot.

Herrings come in all sizes, but the two main species for American consumption are the Atlantic herring *(Clupea harengus),* also called "sea herring," and Pacific herring *(C. pallasii),* both ocean fish. The alewife or spring herring *(Alosa pseudoharengus)* of the Atlantic coast spawns in freshwater streams and is of some commercial interest when smoked or pickled.

The following terminology for herring preparations are used in the United States:

Bismarck herring. Cured with its skin on in strong vinegar, this herring made from schmaltz (see below) fishes derives its name from a German process of the nineteenth century.

bloater. A golden, hot-smoked, dry-salted herring whose name derives from its swollen, at appearance.

hard-salted or hard-cured herring. A lean herring cured in salt alone.

kipper. A brined, air-dried, cold-smoked fat herring; the name probably comes from its copperlike color, which in Old English is *coper.*

pickled herring. In the United States this term refers to a herring in VINEGAR and spices, but elsewhere it refers to a dry-salted herring cured in brine or blood pickle.

rollmops. See main entry.

schmaltz herring. A herring containing at least 18 percent fat, but usually more, and filleted and traditionally served with sliced onions, boiled potatoes, and black bread. The word is from the German for "melted fat."

hibachi. A Japanese brazier using charcoal as its burning medium whose name is Japanese for "fire bowl." The hibachi became a faddish implement for cooking meats and fish in America in the 1960s. Ingredients are marinated in soy sauce and other seasonings and grilled over the open fire.

hickory. Any of a variety of trees of the genus *Carya,* with seventeen species, thirteen of them native to North America. Of culinary importance is the native PECAN *(C. illinoiensis),* but the word *hickory* derives from a Virginia Indian name for a food made from crushed hickory nuts, *pawcohiccora.*

highball. A cocktail served in a tall glass, usually containing a carbonated beverage. The term's origin is obscure, though some have suggested it derives from the railroad semaphore signal having a large ball on top that means "Go ahead," which dates back at least to 1897. By 1932 Americans were familiar with "highball glasses," and the *Sears, Roebuck & Co. Catalog* of 1944 sold them by that name.

hip flask. A slender container, usually made of metal, for holding liquor. Its shape made it easy to insert in one's hip pocket and keep out of sight during the days of Prohibition. The term first appeared in print in 1923.

historical flask. A molded glass flask, used to hold liquor, decorated with American emblems, symbols, and nationally known figures, such as presidents of the United States. Historical flasks first appeared in the early nineteenth century and came in the colors light green, aquamarine, amber, and, occasionally, olive amber.

hoarhound candy. Also, "horehound." A candy, shaped as balls, drops, or squares made from hoarhound, an aromatic plant *(Marrubium vulgare),* and often used as a lozenge for sore throats.

> To 3 cups hot water add 3 oz. hoarhound and simmer for 20 min. Strain, then add 3 1/2 lb. brown sugar and cook till the syrup reaches the hard-ball stage (265° on a candy thermometer). Pour into a buttered pan and cool, then cut into small balls or squares. Makes about 5 doz.

Hoboken special. Pineapple soda with a scoop of chocolate ice cream. The term refers to Hoboken, New Jersey, presumably for no other reason than that this 1920s drink was popular in that section of the country.

hogfish *(Lachnolaimus maximus).* Also, "hog snapper." A fish of the wrasse family with a hoglike snout, found from Brazil to North Carolina and particularly popular in Florida. North Carolinians also refer to the "pigfish" *(Orthopristis chrysopterus),* so called because of its grunting sound, as "hogfish."

hominy. Dried, hulled corn kernels cooked in a variety of ways in breads, puddings, and other preparations. It was one of the first foods European settlers readily accepted from the Indians, and the word, from one or another Algonquian words, such as *rockahominie* ("parched corn") or *tackhummin* ("hulled corn"), was used as early as 1629. Different terms describe hominy that has been treated or ground in different ways. Great hominy, also called "whole hominy," "pearl hominy" (from its pearly appearance), and "samp" (from the Narraganset, *nasàump*, for "corn mush"), is coarsely ground and prepared by scalding shelled corn in water and wood ash to separate the hulls, called the "eyes." The corn is dried and then boiled till soft and porridgelike. Sometimes lye is used instead of wood ash, and this is often called "lye hominy." If the corn is ground more finely, or ground twice, the result is called "hominy grits" or, as is usual in the South, just GRITS. Further grinding results in cornmeal. (Since grits are a major food item in the South, they are treated in more detail under the main entry.)

Hogs and hominy is an old southern dish of hominy and fried pork.

BAKED HOMINY:
Sauté 1 minced small onion in 1 tbs. butter till limp. Beat 2 eggs with 1 cup cream, salt, and pepper, stir in onion and 28 oz. drained hominy. Bake 30 min. at 350°. Let stand 5 min. Serves 6.

honey. A sweet liquid produced by bees from flower nectar. Honey, whose name comes from Old English, *hunig*, was the first and most widespread sweetener used by man.

Although America has always had many species of bees, including some that were honey producers, Waverly Root in *Food* (1980) notes that the Spaniards found the Aztecs and Mayas consuming honey made by the species *Melipona beecheii*. But it was not until the 1630s that honey was available to New England settlers, who gathered honey from the introduced *Apis mellifica*, possibly Italian or Dutch varieties, which the Indians called "English" or "white man's flies." In *Food and Drink in America* (1981), Richard J. Hooker cites a chronicler's description of New York in 1670: "you shall scarce see a house, but the South side is begirt with Hives and Bees." By 1812 the honey bees had moved as far as Texas, where in 1821 Stephen F. Austin found a bee tree that provided his party with a gallon and a half of honey. By the middle of the nineteenth century L. L. Langstroth had invented the movable frame hive, which made the collection of honey far easier than it had been, and an industry flourished soon afterwards.

Today there are several hundred kinds of honey sold in the United States in three basic forms: comb, which comes straight from the hives; chunk, which is bottled with bits of the honeycomb; and extracted, which is usually pasteurized to prevent crystallization. Honey's flavor comes from the type of nectar used, and these may include, as James Trager lists in *The Enriched, Fortified, Concentrated, Country-Fresh, Lip-Smacking, Finger-Licking, International, Unexpurgated Foodbook* (1970), "orange-blossom honey from Florida, raspberry honey and strong buckwheat honey from New Jersey, chewy dandelion honey from Colorado, tupelo honey from the swamps of Florida and Georgia, firewood honey (pale-gold and molasses-thick) from Oregon and Washington, river-willow honey from the banks of the Mississippi, . . . manzanita honey from California, sage-blossom honey from Arizona, gallberry honey from Georgia, heartsease honey from Illinois, tulip-tree honey from Maryland, linden honey from New York, anise-hyssop honey from Iowa, spearmint honey from Indiana, milky-white guajillo honey from Texas, and alergoba honey from Hawaii."

honeydew. A variety of muskmelon, *Cucumis melo,* having a pale, yellowish skin and light green flesh. Its name comes from the fragrant, sticky sweetness of its flesh. The honeydew is a winter melon, first brought to America about 1900 and originally called the "French White Antibes."

hooch. Also, "hootch." A cheap whiskey. The term, which became widespread during Prohibition, has been cited back to 1897. It was derived from the name of a Chinook Indian tribe, the Hoochinoo, that made a form of distilled spirits bought by United States soldiers who had recently occupied the new Alaskan territory and who had been forbidden liquor by their government. By 1877 the soldiers were using the term *hoochinoo,* which, in the Gold Rush era after 1896, was shortened to *hooch.*

hopping john. Also, "hoppin' John." A southern dish made of COWPEAS and rice, served traditionally on New Year's Day to ensure good luck for the year. The origin of the name is obscure, but several stories abide. One ascribes the name to the custom of inviting guests to eat with the request to, "Hop in, John." Another suggests it derives from an old ritual on New Year's Day in which the children in the house hopped once around the table before eating the dish. The first mention of the dish by name was in 1838.

In his booklet *Rice & Beans: The Itinerary of a Recipe* (1981), John Thorne suggests that the name is a corruption of *pois à pigeon,* a French term for "pigeon peas," which flourished in the Caribbean but not in the American South, resulting in an etymological dissolve into "hopping john."

Whatever the origins of the name, the dish quite definitely was a staple of the African slaves who populated southern plantations, especially those of the Gulla country of South Carolina, and one will find similar dishes throughout the Caribbean. In Puerto Rico, for instance, such dishes are called *gandules,* and RED BEANS AND RICE is a staple of Louisiana cookery, just as black beans and rice (called *moros y christianos,* "Moors and Christians") is a famous Cuban dish. See also LIMPIN' SUZAN.

> Rinse 1 cup dry cowpeas in 8 cups water and boil for 2 min. Remove from heat and let stand for 1 hr., then drain, reserving 6 cups of the cooking water. In a skillet sauté 6 pieces of bacon, 1 chopped onion, and 1 chopped clove of garlic, then stir in cowpea mixture. Season with salt and pepper and add cooking water. Stir in 1 cup rice, bring to a boil, then simmer for 1 hurt., stirring occasionally. Serves 8.

horse *(Equus).* A hoofed mammal up to five-and-one-half feet at the shoulder and weighing up to eleven hundred pounds. Horses were brought to America by the Spanish, and wild horses, called "mustangs" in the West, are all descendants of these domesticated herds. Because of the horse's utility for both the white and the red man from the beginning of American history, it was never used for food, except in times of starvation, and Americans continue to respect the horse for its beauty, strength, and herding abilities.

Horse meat, then, is a rarity in the United States, though common in Europe and the Middle East, where American slaughterhouses send most of their available horsemeat. In fact, most of the sixteen American firms that sell horse meat are owned by Europeans. Until recently it was illegal in many states to sell horse meat. In 1981 about 280,000 horses were killed for meat, compared with 35 million cattle and 88 million hogs.

horse's neck. A strip of lemon or orange peel cut from the fruit in a continuous spiral and usually served as a garnish in a cocktail. The term is also a euphemism for "horse's ass," but it has not been established when a drink by the name "horse's neck" first appeared. A nonalcoholic variety was made with just ginger ale and the lemon peel, but there are recipes that add bourbon, blended whiskey, or gin.

hot bricks. A drink of WHISKEY, boiling water, and a ball of butter. Also called "stirrups," it was a drink of Louisville, Kentucky, now obsolete. *Hot bricks* was also a nineteenth-century term for something very dangerous.

hot brown. A sandwich of chicken, bacon, or ham with a cheese sauce, created at Louisville's Brown Hotel.

hot dog. Also, "frankfurter," "frank," "weenie," "wienie," "wiener," "dog," "red hot." A pork or beef sausage, sometimes skinless, served on a soft yeast roll. The hot dog is, with the hamburger, considered one of the quintessential American food items—inexpensive, easy and fast to cook, readily purchased all over the country, and ideal for eating while standing up. Most Americans eat hot dogs with combinations of mustard, pickle relish, and sauerkraut. Sometimes the hot dog is eaten without the roll but with beans, a dish called "franks and beans." Small frankfurters wrapped in puff pastry are called "pigs-in-a-blanket" and are served at cocktail parties or catered parties.

The hot dog is either boiled, grilled, or fried, and in Baltimore some make split, deep-fried versions called "frizzled hot dogs."

A great deal of etymological research has gone into the term *hot dog*, but there is still no certainty as to just who first used the words to describe the sausage, which in various forms had been a favorite of German-Americans since the middle of the nineteenth century, when it was known as "Wienerwurst" from the German for "Vienna sausage." By 1904 hot dogs were also called "wieners," and by the 1920s people were attending "wienie roasts," parties at which the attendees roasted their own sausages over an open fire.

Frankfurter (from the German city of Frankfurt) is reputed to have been introduced in St. Louis in the 1880s by a German immigrant named Antoine Feuchtwanger, who popularized the sausage in a roll in this country.

A crucial moment in the promotion of the item came at the turn of the century at New York City's Polo Grounds, where director of catering Harry Magely Stevens is reputed to have heated the roll, added the condiments, and exhorted his vendors to cry out, "Red hots! Get your red hots!" (Credit for the introduction of the heated roll has also gone to Charles Feltman's Coney Island stand in Brooklyn, New York.) Stevens himself said the term *hot dog* was coined by Hearst sports cartoonist T. A. ("Tad") Dorgan, who often caricatured German figures as dachshund dogs and who, by 1906, was drawing talking sausages in his newspaper's pages, playing off the suggestion that the cheap sausages sold at Coney Island and elsewhere contained dog meat. So accepted was this myth of the sausages' contents that the Coney Island Chamber of Commerce in 1913 banned the use of the term *hot dog* from all signs there. If Dorgan was the originator or instigator of the term, it would have had to have been well in advance of the *Oxford English Dictionary*'s earliest citation of the term in print: 1900.

The greatest promotion of the item was at Nathan Handwerker's frankfurter stand at Coney Island called Nathan's Famous (today a franchise operation with many branches in the Northeast). The sausage became so associated with his concession that people began calling the item a "Coney Island" (a term reserved thirty years before for fried clams). By the 1920s "hot dog stands" were well known throughout the United States, and it had become one of Americans' favorite foods, particularly at sporting events, county fairs, and carnivals. July has been National Hot Dog Month since 1957.

Today frankfurters are almost never made at home, though they are eaten in 95 percent of American homes, usually sold ready to eat but generally heated through by boiling or grilling in butter. Grilling hot dogs outside on a BARBECUE is a very popular method of cooking them, and American children enjoy inserting a stick through them and cooking them over an open fire. "Corn dogs" are fried with a cornmeal batter. A "Kansas dog" is served with mustard and melted cheese, while a "Chicago-style dog" comes in a poppy seed bun with several relishes. "Tube steak" is a serviceman's term for hot dog.

hot fudge. A thick topping for ice cream sundaes containing chocolate, butter, and sugar kept hot so as to have a slight melting effect on the ice cream. John Schumacher, current owner of an ice cream parlor in Los Angeles called C. C. Brown's, contends that hot fudge was invented by the original proprietor soon after opening the place in 1906. In the East credit for one of that region's first hot fudge recipes has been claimed for Sarah Dow, who bought Bailey's ice cream parlor in Boston in 1900 and started making the confection soon afterwards.

In a double boiler heat 1/2 cup milk, 1/4 cup butter, and a dash of salt. Add 2 cups bittersweet chocolate and stir till smooth. Remove from heat, add 1 tsp. vanilla extract, and stir. Keep warm for serving.

hot rock. Cowboy term for a biscuit.

hot sauce. Any of a number of commercially bottled seasoning sauces (usually from Louisiana) made with chili peppers, salt, and perhaps vinegar. One of the first was named after Maunsel White, a planter who brought slave-made hot sauce with him to the Gem Restaurant in New Orleans before the Civil War.

hot scotch. An alcoholic drink made with a little Scotch whisky and hot water, so called at least since 1882.

house pie. A pie of cooked crushed apples, including the peel and core. It dates back to the mid-eighteenth century.

Hubbard squash (*Cucurbita maximus ohioensis*). Also, "Ohio squash." A winter SQUASH with a very thick, bumpy, green-to-orange skin and yellow-orange flesh, it was supposedly brought to America from the West Indies. The origin of the name was explained by James J. H. Gregory in a letter published in the December 1857 issue of the *Magazine of Horticulture:*

> Upwards of twenty years ago, a single specimen was brought into [Marblehead, Massachusetts], the seed from which was planted in the garden of a lady, now deceased; a specimen from this yield was given to Captain Knott Martin, of this town, who raised it for family use for a few years, when it was brought to our notice in the year 1842 or '43. We were first informed of its good qualities by Mrs. Elizabeth Hubbard, a very worthy lady, through whom we obtained seed from Captain Martin. As the squash up to this time had no specific name to designate it from other varieties, my father termed it the "Hubbard Squash."

huckleberry. Any of a variety of deep-blue native American berries of a tree in the genus *Gaylussacia,* often confused with the blueberry. The name may be a variation of *whortleberry.*

Henry David Thoreau praised the huckleberry among the finest fruits of the wild and cautioned interested eaters:

> If you would know the flavor of huckleberries, ask the cow-boy or the partridge. It is a vulgar error to suppose that you have tasted huckleberries who have never plucked them. A huckleberry never reaches Boston; they have not been known there since they grew on her three hills. The ambrosial and essential part of the fruit is lost with the bloom which is rubbed off in the market cart, and they become mere provender.

Those unfamiliar with the huckleberry and blueberry may have difficulty telling them apart, the latter having a softer texture and many tiny seeds. On the West Coast what is referred to as the "mountain huckleberry" is actually the evergreen blueberry *(Vaccinium ovatum).* The common huckleberry *(G. resinosa)* is itself called the "black huckleberry," while the bush huckleberry *(G. dumosa)* is also called the "gopherberry."

Like the blueberry, the huckleberry is most often eaten raw, in muffins, in breads, or in pies, this last called in slang "fly pie."

One cannot mention the word *huckleberry* without its immediate association to one of America's favorite novel characters, the hero of Mark Twain's *The Adventures of Huckleberry Finn* (1884).

huevos rancheros. A Mexican dish of fried eggs set on tortillas and covered with a tomato-and-chili pepper sauce. The dish has become a staple of Mexican-American menus, especially as a brunch or luncheon item. The name is from the Spanish for "ranch eggs."

> Briefly sauté 2 tortillas on both sides, drain and keep warm. Fry two eggs, place on the tortillas, and cover with a sauce of 1 tomato, 1 chopped clove of garlic, 1 chopped red or green chili pepper, 1 chopped onion, salt, and pepper blended together and cooked with 1 tbs. oil for about 5 min. Often shredded Monterey Jack or Cheddar cheese is sprinkled on top.

humble pie. A pie made from the innards of deer. There is a double pun in the name, for *umble* is a very old English word for the heart, liver, and gizzard of a deer, the kind of food eaten by servants and hunters while the lord of the house ate venison. And since certain British dialects delete the *h* in the word *humble* when speaking, "humble pie" would be pronounced " 'umble pie," or a dish for those of few pretensions.

The English brought the dish to America, and in Susannah Carter's *The Frugal Housewife,* published in Boston in the eighteenth century from an English cookbook, a recipe for humble pie includes the entrails of the deer together with beef suet, apples, 1/2 lb. sugar, salt, mace, cloves, nutmeg, and more than a pound of currants.

It is no longer a dish to be found in America, except as a curiosity or as a version of the English steak and kidney pie.

Humboldt dressing. A dressing of crab butter, mayonnaise, and seasonings to be mixed with a dish of crabs. Supposedly created in the 1940s by a Eureka, California, woman named Humboldt who sold crabs from a stand, although it might also have originated in the town of Humboldt, California.

> Mash crab butter from 2 crabs, stir in 1/2 cup mayonnaise, 1 tsp. Worcestershire sauce, 4 dashes hot pepper sauce, 1 cup diced celery, 1/2 cup chopped parsley, and 2 tbs. chopped scallion. Cover and chill for 30 min.

hurricane. A cocktail made with passion fruit flavoring, dark rum, and citrus juices. The drink was created as a promotional cocktail that was featured at

Pat O'Brien's French Quarter Bar in New Orleans, Louisiana. There is even a hurricane glass in which the cocktail is served.

Fill a hurricane glass with crushed ice, add 2 oz. Jero's Red Passion Fruit cocktail mix, 2 oz. lemon juice, 4 oz. dark rum, 1 orange slice, and a maraschino cherry.

O'Brien's has since given birth to other cocktails, with names like the "cyclone," the "squall," and the "breeze."

hush puppy. A dumpling of cornmeal that is deep-fried, especially popular in the South. Although it is not confirmed, the general assumption regarding the origin of the term is that it dates from the period of scarcity following the Civil War, when cooks would toss scraps of corn batter to hungry dogs with the words, "Hush, puppies!"

The *Morris Dictionary of Word and Phrase Origins* gives another account, based on a southern reader's letter to the effect that in the South the aquatic reptile called the salamander was often known as a "water dog" or "water puppy" (also "dwarf waterdog" [*Necturus punctatus*] and "mudpuppy" [*N. maculosus*]), because of their squat, stout legs. These were deep-fried with cornmeal dough and formed into sticks, and, so the account goes, they were called "hush puppies" because eating such lowly food was not something a southern wife would want known to her neighbors. The term is apparently not that old, however, appearing in print for the first time only in 1918, according to the *Dictionary of Americanisms*.

Cornmeal hush puppies, however, are traditionally served with fried catfish and are considered one of the true delicacies of southern down-home cookery.

Sift together 1 1/2 cups cornmeal with 1/2 cup flour, 2 tsp. baking powder, and 1/2 tsp. salt. Beat 1 egg in 3/4 cup milk, and add 1 grated onion. Mix with cornmeal and flour till well blended, then drop from a tablespoon into hot fat. Fry till golden brown, drain, and serve hot.

hydrolyzed vegetable protein (HVP). A flavor enhancer used in processed foods like soup, frankfurters, and stews. It is vegetable protein (such as from the soybean) that has been chemically broken down to the amino acids.

ice. Water that has been frozen solid. Ice has been long used as a preservative, as a substance with which to cool food and drinks, and as a solidifier for ice cream and sherbets.

Since the nineteenth century Americans have always enjoyed abundant, available ice in various forms, first used in ice houses or ice cellars, where food was kept right through spring and summer through storage in structures filled with ice blocks cut in winter and well insulated with straw and sawdust.

From 1806 till the 1850s the ice-cutting industry was dominated by the "Ice King," Frederic Tudor of Boston, who eventually shipped ice as far away as China. Tudor's business was increased considerably when Nathaniel Wyeth invented an ice cutter with parallel saw-tooth runners, dragged through frozen ponds and lakes by horses. He also made iceboxes for the home as of the 1830s, and these insulated chests, supplied by "ice men," who brought hundred-pound blocks of ice on horse-drawn "ice wagons," became common household fixtures. The delivery of ice was part of a standard of life enjoyed by most Americans well into the twentieth century, when electric refrigerators with freezers became affordable to everyone.

Artificial ice was made by refrigeration in ice plants, the first of which was built in 1865 in New Orleans, and by 1875 restaurants had their own ice-making machines. Much later, about 1925, dry ice (carbon dioxide) became available for purchase in bulk, though it is almost never used at home.

Ice takes various forms in the preparation of food and drink. Shaved ice or chipped ice was once standard in bars and restaurants, where a bartender might actually chip his own from a large block. Ice crushers are mechanical or hand-cranked tools for making crushed ice, often used for blending or shaking cocktails. After the Second World War ice cubes predominated in bars as they have in home ice boxes.

"Aged ice" is commercially made ice that has been frozen very hard in order to retain the coldness. This form of ice is available in groceries or vending machines.

Many Europeans consider Americans' passion for ice a national characteristic. It is true that Americans drink few beverages aside from coffee and tea
that are not served ice-cold, whereas in Europe room-temperature drinks are
more usual.

The ice bucket, known since before 1919, is a bucket of ice in which one
places wine bottles to chill.

icebox pie. A crusted, creamy pie that is frozen or chilled firm. It became a
popular item by the 1920s, when Americans began buying refrigerators that
made such confections easy to make.

> Scald 2 cups milk with 1 1/2 squares baking chocolate. Mix in 2/3 cups sugar, 3 tbs.
> cornstarch, 1/2 tsp. salt, and then stir in milk and cook in double boiler for 10 min.
> till thickened. Stir a small amount of the liquid into 3 beaten egg yolks, being careful
> not to curdle them, then add the rest of the liquid. Stir and cook for 2 min. Add
> 2 tbs. butter and 1 tsp. vanilla, then cool. Beat well and pour into pastry shell, top
> with whipped cream and chill till quite firm.

ice cream. A dish made from cream, sugar, and flavorings chilled to a
semisolid consistency and consumed as a dessert or snack food. The specific
phrase *ice cream* dates in print to 1744, in a description by a Virginian who
sampled some "with the Strawberries and Milk" at Governor Thomas
Bladen's mansion in Annapolis, Maryland. Ice cream, in various forms, is
much older and goes back to the ancient Greeks and Romans, who cooled their
wine with mountain snow and ice. Marco Polo brought back from the Orient
a recipe for a frozen dessert based on milk, and there is evidence that some
form of ice cream was brought by Catherine de Médicis from Italy to France.
About 1700 a pamphlet of ice cream and sherbet recipes was published entitled
L'Art de Faire des Glaces, and by then the major capitals of Europe were well
familiar with the dish. By the 1770s confectioners were selling ice cream in the
American colonies, and George Washington owned something called a
"Cream Machine for Making Ice" at Mount Vernon. Washington's fancy for
ice cream is evident in the record that he spent at least two hundred dollars
on the confection during the summer of 1790.

Thomas Jefferson has often been credited with bringing "French-style" ice
cream, made with egg yolks, to America, and he certainly had an ice-cream-
making machine he called a *"sorbetière"* at Monticello, where he followed a
recipe that called for a stick of vanilla (which Jefferson also brought back from
Europe), two bottles of cream, and an egg custard mixture, boiled, stirred,
reheated, strained, and put in an "ice pail."

President James Madison's wife, Dolley (1768–1849), is said to have popularized ice cream by making it a frequent dessert at the White House between 1809
and 1817 (although she had also helped the bachelor Jefferson with his White
House parties after 1801). But the dish had been making considerable headway
on its own, both in recipe books of the eighteenth century and in confectioners'
shops, very often run by Italians. Consequently, ice creams were often called

"Italian ice creams" or "Neapolitan ice creams" throughout the nineteenth century, and the purveying of such confections became associated with Italian immigrants.

Philadelphia became renowned for its ice cream, and the phrase *Philadelphia ice cream,* used since the early nineteenth century, came to mean a specifically American style of rich ice cream. One proud Philadelphia confectioner of the nineteenth century, James W. Parkinson, who also opened the grand Parkinson's Broadway Saloon selling ice cream in New York City, wrote of the prejudicial distinctions made between American and French frozen desserts (as well as other foods): "The admission is well nigh universal that the French 'Made Us,' and that we are 'The Sheep' of French 'pastures.' . . . So deeply rooted is this sentiment in the public mind, . . . that when an American confectioner or caterer makes any invention in his craft, he feels that to secure its sales, and to establish its popularity, he must give it a French name." Parkinson had little reason to fear French competition, for he was enormously successful and claimed proudly to have created the first pistachio ice cream. He nevertheless played it safe occasionally by listing *biscuit glacé* among his confections.

The availability of ice in America made ice creams and sherbets equally available to everyone, whereas they had continued to be expensive items in Europe. By 1808 ice cream was available every day in New Orleans, where it was first sold at the Exchange Coffee-House. In 1835 English traveler Harriet Martineau reported "towers of ice cream" available daily in Kentucky. Two years later Englishman Frederick Marryat marveled at seeing "common laborers" lapping up ice cream on their midday break.

A breakthrough in ice cream production came in 1846 when a small, compact ice cream freezer was invented by an obscure woman named Nancy Johnson. The freezer was cranked by hand and made ice cream making a pastime (though still a chore) of American homelife. For some reason Johnson did not patent her invention, but in 1848 William G. Young did, calling it the "Johnson Patent Ice-Cream Freezer" (later known as the "Johnson-Young" ice cream maker).

By midcentury ice cream had become relatively cheap to buy at the market, thanks to the efforts of Baltimore ice cream manufacturer Jacob Fussell, who began by using an oversupply of cream to make the confection and to undercut the confectioners' prices by more than half in 1851. He opened ice cream plants in several eastern cities, while his associate Perry Brazelton moved the industry into the Midwest. By the end of the century Americans were eating five million gallons of ice cream a year, prompted by technological improvements in mechanical ice cream makers.

By the 1870s Americans were going to ice cream parlors and stopping at ice cream stands. In 1874 the ice cream soda, made with milk, a flavored syrup, and a scoop of ice cream, was first featured by Robert M. Green at the Franklin Institute in Philadelphia. Americans also loved "milk sherbets" (from the Turkish, *sherbet,* and Arabic, *sharbah,* "drink"), which if made without milk were called "ices" or "Italian ices" (these last were scooped into pleated paper cups and licked).

MILK SHAKES, malteds, and frappés came along towards the end of the nineteenth century too, as did the sundae and the ice cream cone. The origins of both items have been argued over the years. Paul Dickson, in his *Great American Ice Cream Book* (1972), cites two main contenders for the honor of creating the sundae, although he refers to several others with less credibility. The first claim concerns the Evanston, Illinois, civic moralists of the 1890s who inveighed against drinking soda water on the Sabbath, prompting confectioners to create a dish that would not corrupt public morals—scoops of ice cream with flavored syrups or toppings—called "Sundays." The other claim dates to the same period, when a man named George Hallauer of Two Rivers, Wisconsin, ordered such a dish at Ed Berner's soda fountain. The ice-cream-and-syrup confection became so popular that other parlor owners had to serve it, and George Giffy, a fountain owner in Manitowoc, Wisconsin, began serving it only on Sundays as a loss leader.

Although the original name was spelled with a *y* (the dish early on was called the "Soda-less Soda"), the *-ae* ending, contends Dickson, "came about when those who orated from the pulpit on the sinful soda went to work on the sacrilegious use of the name of the Sabbath for its stand-in." In any case, by 1900 soda fountain suppliers were selling tulip-shaped sundae dishes.

The ice cream cone is equally as confusing as to its origins. It seems clear that the cone (a wafer rolled to hold a scoop of ice cream) became popular at the 1904 St. Louis World's Fair, but there are several claims as to just who started hawking it there. Some authorities credit a Syrian immigrant named Ernest A. Hamwi with the invention, which was actually a Persian pastry, *zalabia,* that Hamwi rolled to hold ice cream when another concessionaire ran out of ice cream dishes. Another claim was made by David Avayou, a Turkish ice cream parlor owner from New Jersey, who got the idea from seeing ice cream eaten in paper cones in France and who then purveyed the wafer cones at the St. Louis Fair. Still another contender at that same exposition, Abe Doumar, claimed to have created the cone from waffles at a stand in the "Old City of Jerusalem" section of the fair; he called them "Cornucopias."

There are other stories too, but Dickson believes the most creditable claim is that of Italo Marchiony, an Italian immigrant who once offered documentary evidence that he took a patent on an ice cream cone as of December 13, 1904, but had made them since 1896. It would appear, writes Dickson, "that the Marchiony patent wins for him the credit as American inventor of the ice cream cone, but since he never achieved any success or popularity with his invention the distinction of introducing it to a waiting America goes to a group of men—which one is not sure—at the St. Louis Fair of 1904," where there were at least fifty ice cream booths selling five thousand gallons a day.

Today cones are made in a variety of shapes. The sugar cone has a cookie-like texture, while the waffle cone is lighter and more airy. Sometimes the latter is colored with food dyes.

A good deal of American ice cream was sold by street vendors in large cities. The slang term for their product as of the 1880s was *hokey-pokey*, which may derive from the Italian, *"O che poco!,"* "Oh, how little!" because the "hokey-pokey man" who sold this cheap ice cream was often of Italian descent (although the term may have something to do with the connotation of cheating, as in *hocus-pocus*).

By 1919 Americans were eating 150 million gallons of ice cream, and it became known as an "American typical food," like hamburgers and hot dogs. In those years there also appeared a new kind of ice cream with a very soft consistency, at first called "frozen fluff," then "frozen custard," and, by the 1960s and 1970s, "soft ice cream," dispensed like a paste from a machine and swirled into cups and cones.

People would go to a soda fountain and order "hand-packed" ice cream (ice cream that was scooped from large containers behind the counter and packed in a cardboard container). Otherwise the ice cream was packed at a factory and shipped, often with a considerable lag of time between its manufacture and its sale. Ice cream cakes were layer cakes filled with ice cream rather than icing, custard, or cream, and banana splits (which came in about 1920) were dishes of sliced bananas topped with scoops of ice cream, different syrups, ground nuts, and MARASCHINO cherries in profusion.

The first chocolate-covered ice cream bar was invented by Christian Nelson in Onawa, Iowa, in 1919. Nelson, a Danish immigrant who became a schoolteacher and part-time candy store owner, dubbed his confection the "I-Scream Bar" ("I scream, ice cream!" was recorded as a street cry of New York children as long ago as 1828), and in 1921 became partners with an Omaha ice cream company superintendent named Russell Stover, who changed the item's name to "Eskimo Pie," in a reference to the Alaskan Eskimos' frigid climate. By 1922 the company was selling a million ice cream bars a day. After a period of trouble defending their patent from imitators, Nelson and Stover's company became a subsidiary of U.S. Foil, which wrapped the confection in bright, shiny aluminum foil.

In the 1920s there also appeared ice cream sandwiches, slabs of ice cream wedged between a cakelike chocolate cookie, and in San Francisco the IT'S IT ice cream bar, a similar item made with oatmeal cookie layers. (In the 1980s a huge success was made by an ice cream sandwich using chocolate chip cookies called the "Chipwich.")

Credit for the first person to put ice cream on a stick goes to a Youngstown, Ohio, parlor owner named Harry Burt, who called his creation—a chocolate-covered ice cream bar set on a wooden stick—the "Good Humor Ice Cream Sucker," which was sold by vendors driving clean white trucks. After Burt's death in 1926, several Cleveland businessmen bought the company and began selling national franchises, which proliferated and made the "Good Humor man" a summertime fixture in American communities.

About the same time Frank Epperson, an Oakland, California, lemonade-powder maker, accidentally left some of his juice on a windowsill while visiting friends in New Jersey. This frozen juice bar was to become the Popsicle (at first called by its inventor the "Epsicle"), a patent later sold to the Joe Lowe Corporation. (Frozen juice bars had been known in the nineteenth century, including one called the "Hokey Pokey," but none was marketed well until the Popsicle in 1923.)

Ice cream sales suffered during the Depression of the 1930s, but the small-town soda fountain survived even as many of the large and opulent pharmacy fountains lost ground. Promoted as healthful and wholesome by the industry, ice cream took on a positively sanitary image in the 1940s, and Hollywood movies pictured ice cream soda fountains as oases of innocent Americana. In World War II newspapers printed photos and stories of GI's and sailors who missed nothing back home so much as ice cream. By 1946 Americans annually were consuming more than twenty quarts of ice cream per capita.

In the 1950s Americans began buying more ice cream in groceries and in the new supermarkets than in soda fountains and drugstores, and the flavor and texture of American ice creams began to change as large companies cut costs by adding stabilizers, more air, and artificial ingredients. Supermarkets and large food corporations marketed their own brands nationally, at the same time that a number of smaller companies began in the 1960s to sell "premium ice creams"—many resembling the kinds made before the 1950s—with rich flavors of chocolate, vanilla, and other old favorites. Companies like Howard Johnson's, a restaurant chain, advertised "28 Flavors," and Baskin-Robbins thirty-one. These premium, and very high priced, ice creams and sherbets begat a new generation of small shops selling "homemade ice creams" that purported to be more "natural" and certainly more delicious than the supermarket varieties. In 1973 Steve Herrell, owner of Steve's ice cream parlor in Somerville, Massachusetts, began blending his customers' choice of cookie and/or candy morsels into his ice cream and called the item a "Mix-in," a copyrighted trademark he sold with the store in 1977. This idea, under other names (including "Smoosh-in," the new term used at Herrell's next shop, in Northampton, Massachusetts), became very popular in the 1980s in the new ice cream shops opening in towns and suburban shopping malls.

Each year Americans consume about 14.5 gallons of ice cream per capita, having hit a peak in 1975 and declined somewhat since then.

VANILLA ICE CREAM:
In a double boiler combine 1 qt. light cream, 3 cups sugar, and 3 tsp. vanilla extract. Heat until cream is scalded, remove from heat, and add 2 qt. light cream. Cool, then chill or put through ice cream freezer.

FRENCH VANILLA ICE CREAM:
Beat 6 egg yolks till light and thickened, add 1 cup sugar till dissolved. Beat 6 egg whites till stiff, stir in egg mixture, add 8 cups light cream, 1 cup sugar, and cook in double boiler for about 15 min. Add a dash of salt, 4 tsp. vanilla extract, and cool. Put through ice cream freezer.

LEMON MILK SHERBET:
In 8 tbs. lemon juice dissolve 1 1/3 cups sugar. Blend in 3 1/2 cups milk and put through ice cream freezer.

icing. A term often interchangeable with *frosting* and preferred in America to describe the sugar-and-water mixture used to decorate and cover cakes. Icing may also contain other ingredients and flavorings such as marshmallow, chocolate, nuts, and fruit.

The word is akin to *ice,* for the icing becomes firm or glazed after being applied. *Frosting* actually precedes *icing* in print, the former appearing in 1756, the latter in 1769, and icing was long considered a somewhat lighter, decorative glaze than frosting. But in America it became normal to use *icing* (and the verb *to ice*) to describe either form of the confection.

WHITE ICING:
Dissolve 2 cups sugar in 1 cup water, cook, covered, in a saucepan for about 3 min., uncover and cook to 238° on a candy thermometer.

FLUFFY ICING:
Combine 2 unbeaten egg whites, 1 cup sugar, 1/3 cup water, and 1/4 tsp. cream of tartar in double boiler. Cook while beating till soft peaks are formed. Add 1 tsp. vanilla.

CHOCOLATE ICING:
Combine 1 cup confectioners' sugar with 2 tbs. butter. Stir in 1/4 cup milk, 1 beaten egg, 1 tsp. vanilla, and 2 1/2 squares chocolate that have been melted and cooled. Set in bowl of ice water and beat for about 3 min.

imitation. Under F.D.A. regulations, the word *imitation* must be used on the labels of all products that are not as nutritious as the product which it resembles and for which it is a substitute.

immigrant butter. A cowboy's term for grease, flour, and water.

Indian bread. As described by Adams in *Western Words,* "A tasty strip of fatty matter extending from the shoulder blade backward along the backbone of a buffalo. When seared in hot grease and then smoked, it became a tidbit the buffalo hunter used for bread. When eaten with lean or dried meat, it made an excellent sandwich." The term also referred to cornmeal bread.

Indian pudding. A cornmeal pudding dessert made with milk and molasses. The name comes from the fact that corn was called "Indian corn" by the early English settlers, and anything containing corn or cornmeal might have the adjective *Indian* so applied. This dish was called *"sagamite"* by the Indians, and, in the late seventeenth century, "hasty pudding" by the colonists. *Indian pudding* was first printed in 1722.

Scald 4 cups milk in a double boiler, stir in 1/3 cup cornmeal and cook, stirring, over boiling water for 15 min. Stir in 1/4 cup dark molasses, cook for 5 min., and remove from heat. Stir in 1/4 cup butter, 3/4 tsp. salt, a pinch of ginger or cinnamon, if desired, and 1 beaten egg. Pour into buttered baking dish and bake at 350° for about 2 hr. till set. Serve with whipped cream or vanilla ice cream.

Indian whisky. A very low grade alcoholic spirit that white men sold to the Indians during the days of the Missouri River trade of the nineteenth century. One recipe (from E. C. Abbott and Helena Huntington Smith's *We Pointed North* [1939]) suggests the horrifying nature of this brew:

> Take one barrel of Missouri River water, and two gallons of alcohol. Then you add two ounces of strychnine to make them crazy—because strychnine is the greatest stimulant in the world—three bars of tobacco to make them sick—because an Indian wouldn't figure it was whisky unless it made him sick—five bars of soap to give it a head, and half-pound of red pepper, and then you put some sage brush and boil it until it's brown. Strain this into a barrel and you've got your Indian whisky.

ingredients statement. A listing on a food product's label, mandated by the Federal Trade Commission, that must include the ingredients in order of predominance, that is, the most abundant ingredient must be listed first.

Ingwer kuche. A Pennsylvania Dutch ginger cake.

> Mix together 1 cup sugar, 1 cup molasses, 1 beaten egg, 2 tbs. butter, 1 cup cream, and 4 cups flour. Add ground ginger according to taste. Add 1 tsp. baking soda. Bake in an iron pan.

in the weeds. Restaurant waiter's lingo for having too much work to do that night.

invert sugar. A sweetening additive blended from dextrose and fructose and used in candy, soft drinks, and other foods.

Irish coffee. A blend of hot coffee, Irish whiskey, and whipped cream. According to a plaque outside the Buena Vista bar in San Francisco, "America's first Irish coffee was made here in 1952. It was inspirationally invented at Shannon Airport [Ireland] by Joe Sheridan. It was fortuitously introduced by [newspaper writer] Stan Delaplane. It was nurtured to a national institution by [the bar's owner] Jack Koeppler." It was first mentioned by this name in English print in 1950.

> Rinse out an 8-oz. goblet with hot water, place 2 tsp. sugar in goblet, and pour in 1 1/2 oz. Irish whiskey and 5 oz. strong hot coffee. Stir, then top with whipped cream.

isinglass. A transparent gelatin made from the air bladder of fishes, such as the STURGEON. Isinglass was used until the present century to make jellies and clarify liquors. The name is from the obsolete Dutch, *huizenblas,* and ultimately from German, *hūsōn,* "sturgeon," plus *blase,* "bladder." Its first mention in English was in 1545.

isleta bread. A Pueblo Indian bread shaped like a bear's claw, hence the alternate names "bear claw" or "paw bread."

Italian beef stand. An inexpensive restaurant or streetside stand selling sliced beef in a spicy gravy. Italian beef is a speciality of the Midwest, especially Chicago. The name merely refers to some vague idea of how Italians would serve their beef—highly seasoned—but there is no such dish in Italy.

It's It. An ice cream sandwich made from vanilla ice cream between two oatmeal cookies, covered with chocolate and frozen hard. This confection originated in 1928 at the Playland-at-the-Beach amusement park in San Francisco, and credit for its creation is given to park owner George Whitney. San Franciscans still remember a "trip to the It stand," and today the confection is available in food stores and supermarkets under its original name, made by the It's-It Ice Cream Company in that city.

izer cookie. A cookie baked on a long wafer iron that is impressed with figures of designs that then appear on the cookie. The term derives from the Dutch word *izer* (or *yser*), meaning "iron," and the cookies were made by the Dutch of New York and others of Dutch ancestry in America.

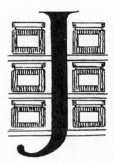

jack (Genus *Caranx*). Any of a variety of ocean fish that includes the POM- PANO, most of which are not significant food fishes in the United States. The origin of the name is obscure, the first mention being in 1587. The principal eating fishes of this type include the amberjack *(Seriola dumerili);* the bar jack *(Caranx ruber);* the blue runner *(C. crysos);* the crevelle *(C. hippos),* also called "jack crevelle" or "crevelle jack"; the jack mackerel *(Trachurus symmetricus),* also called the "horse mackerel," though it is not a true mackerel; the rainbow runner *(Elagatis bipinnulatus);* the yellow jack *(C. bartholomaei);* and the yellowtail *(S. dorsalis).*

jake. An alcoholic beverage made from Jamaican ginger during the Prohibi- tion era. The name comes from its allusion to Jamaica.

jambalaya. A main dish of rice, pork, ham, sausage, shrimp, crayfish, and seasonings—or any combination of the above. Jambalaya is one of the most famous Cajun-Creole creations, with as many versions and incorporating as wide a variety of ingredients as any dish in American gastronomy. Most linguists believe the name came from the Spanish word for ham, *jamon,* a prime ingredient in the first jambalayas of the eighteenth century, but others prefer the beloved story of a gentleman who stopped by a New Orleans inn late one night to find nothing left for him to dine upon. The owner thereupon told the cook, whose name was Jean, to "mix some things together"— *"balayez,"* in the dialect of Louisiana—so the grateful guest pronounced the dish of odds-and-ends wonderful and named it "Jean Balayez."

The word itself first appeared in print only in 1872, and *The Picayune's Creole Cook Book* (1901) calls it a "Spanish-Creole dish." Missouri Creoles call it "jambolail." But today it is a great favorite and synonymous with Louisiana cuisine.

Jambalaya may be made with beef, pork, chicken, shrimp, oysters, crayfish, or any number of other ingredients, and none is more authentic than the next. Most will use the local sausage called "chaurice" (or CHORIZO), and green pepper and chili or cayenne pepper are fairly standard. Louisianans are passionate about jambalaya and even hold an annual jamabalaya cook-off in the old Cajun town of Gonzales, the self-proclaimed Jambalaya Capital of the World.

The following recipe, from The Gumbo Shop in New Orleans, is a good amalgam of several styles of jambalaya:

> Sauté 1/2 lb. sliced smoked sausage and 1/2 lb. cubed ham in 1/4 cup hot oil till browned. Remove from saucepan and then sauté 1 cup chopped onions, 1 cup chopped bell pepper, 1 cup chopped celery, 1 cup chopped scallion, and 2 cloves minced garlic in meat drippings till soft. Add one 16-oz. can drained tomatoes, 1 tsp. thyme, 1 tsp. black pepper, 1/4 tsp. cayenne, 1 tsp. salt, and cook for 5 min. Stir in 1 cup converted rice. Mix together liquid from tomatoes, 1 1/2 cups chicken stock or water, and 1 1/2 tbs. Worcestershire sauce to equal 2 1/2 cups. Bring to boil, reduce to simmer, add 2 lb. raw, peeled shrimp, ham, and sausage, and cook uncovered for about 30 min.

Jeff Davis. A northerner's slur first used during the Civil War for the kinds of inferior and substitute foods southerners were forced to consume because of the deprivations caused by the conflict. The name derives from the name of American statesman Jefferson Davis (1808–1889), who, as president of the Confederacy during the war, was an object of northern scorn. Thus, "Jeff Davis coffee" was a substitute made from wheat grain rather than coffee beans, and to call someone a "Jeff Davis" was to label him a southern ignoramus. The term is not found in southern cookbooks of the nineteenth century, but "Jeff Davis pie" and "Jeff Davis pudding" have since lost all those unfortunate connotations, and one will easily find recipes for such dishes today.

The following recipe, from a Washington, D.C., woman named Florence Berryman, printed in the *D.A.R. Cookbook* (1949), is said to have gone back "three generations" in her family, suggesting that Jeff Davis pie was well known during Davis's own lifetime. A similar pie or tart in the South, based on English recipes known also in New England, was called "chess pie."

> Cream 1 cup butter with 2 cups sugar. Mix 3 beaten egg yolks with 1/2 cup milk, 2 tbs. flour, and the juice of 1 lemon. Add to creamed butter. Pour into pie plate with bottom crust and bake at 300° till set. Make a meringue and cover the pie, then brown in oven.

Other recipies call for more spices and raisins and nuts to be added to the batter.

Jell-O. A trademark of General Foods Corporation of White Plains, New York, for a gelatin dessert made from sugar, gelatin, adipic acid, disodium phosphate, fumaric acid, artificial color, natural flavor with BHA, and artificial flavor.

A patent for a "gelatin dessert" was taken out in 1845 by Peter Cooper, but such packaged desserts did not become popular until Orator Woodward of

LeRoy, New York, brought out Jell-O in 1902. The rights for the product were purchased in 1925 by the Postum Cereal Company (now General Foods).

Some slang terms for gelatin desserts of this type include *shivering Liz, shimmy,* and *nervous pudding.*

jelly. A sweet, semisolid translucent condiment made by boiling fruit juice and sugar with pectin or gelatin. Jelly is used as a spread on toast or as a dessert filling. Sometimes it is added to sauces or gravies, and mint jelly is customarily served with roast lamb or lamb chops.

The word *jelly* derives from Middle English, *geli* or *gely,* and ultimately from the Latin, *gelare,* "to freeze."

F.D.A. standards require that commercial jelly must contain not less than forty-five parts by weight fruit ingredients to fifty-five parts sweetening.

Jam differs from jelly in that the former is made with fresh or dried fruit rather than juice and has a thicker texture. The word may derive from the verb *jam,* in the sense of forcing something to congeal together.

Preserves differ from jams and jellies by containing pieces of the fruit, although jams and preserves are treated under the same heading in the F.D.A.'s *Code of Federal Regulations,* Title 21 (revised April 1, 1982).

Commercial jellies, jams, and preserves are usually made by adding pectins rather than relying on the natural pectins of the fruit. Grape jelly, made with Concord grapes, is the most popular of commercial jellies.

GRAPE JELLY:
Wash 4 cups underripe Concord grapes and remove stems. Place in a kettle with 1/2 cup water. Boil until soft, about 5 min., and strain through a jelly bag. Add 3/4 cup sugar and dissolve. Cook at a simmer till liquid begins to gel, 10–30 min. depending on desired texture. Boil jelly jars, pour in jelly to 1/4 in. from top, cover with paraffin, and close.

jelly bean. An egg-shaped candy with a chewy texture made by boiling sugar with a flavoring like fruit juice and setting it with gelatin or pectin. Jelly beans were first advertised in the July 5, 1905, edition of the *Chicago Daily News* at nine cents a pound.

jelly roll. A dessert of sponge cake rolled around a jelly filling, with currant or raspberry traditionally used in the preparation. Jelly cakes were known at least since the 1860s, but jelly rolls were not cited in print until 1895.

Combine 3/4 cup flour, 1 tsp. baking powder, and 1/2 tsp. salt. In another bowl beat 4 egg whites with 1/3 cup sugar till stiff. Beat 4 egg yolks till light with 1/2 cup sugar. Add 1/2 tsp. vanilla. Fold egg whites into flour, then this mixture into egg yolks till well blended. Spread over buttered pan lined with waxed paper, bake 15 min. at 375° till springy. Invert cake on clean cloth sprinkled with confectioners' sugar, carefully roll cake, then cool on rack. Unroll cake, spread with jelly, roll again, and sprinkle with more confectioners' sugar. Serves 8–10.

jerky. Beef that has been cut thin and dried in the sun. The word comes from the Spanish *charqui,* which itself came from a Peruvian word, *quichua.* It first appears in English in 1707 as a verb, then as a noun in the nineteenth century.

Jerky was a staple food among the Indians on the plains. It is very rich in protein and may be cooked in a soup or smoked.

Jerusalem artichoke *(Helianthus tuberosus).* A tuber with lumpy branches, reddish brown skin, and a slightly sweetish flavor. The tuber is not a true ARTICHOKE and has nothing to do with Jerusalem, for it is a native American sunflower, which in Italian is *girasole,* the name given the plant when it was introduced to the garden of Cardinal Farnese in Rome about 1617. In 1620 the Italian word had been transformed into the English "Artichocks of Jerusalem," and, thereafter, "Jerusalem artichokes."

The plant had been noted by Samuel de Champlain in 1605 as a garden vegetable of the Indians on Cape Cod, but the settlers who came after him developed little interest in the tuber. Very few Americans are familiar with the food at all, though some commercial growers have tried to market it under the less foreign-sounding name of "sunchokes."

Jerusalem artichokes are chopped up raw and used in salads, or they may be boiled or steamed and served with butter.

jewfish *(Epinephelus itajara).* Also, "giant sea BASS." A large, greyish brown GROUPER that may weigh up to seven hundred pounds, found near Florida and in the Gulf of Mexico. The first mention of the name in print was in 1697, when William Dampier, in his *Voyages and Descriptions, A Voyage to New Holland,* wrote, "The Jew-Fish is a very good Fish, and I judge so called by the English, because it hath Scales and Fins, therefore a clean Fish, according to the Levitical Law." (See main entry, KOSHER, for Jewish dietary rules.)

Jim Hill mustard. A northwestern term for a wild mustard discovered in the 1890s, when James Jerome Hill (1838–1916) built the Great Northern Railroad to Seattle, Washington.

Johannisberg Riesling. A white Vinifera grape, properly called the "White Riesling," that goes into some of Germany's finest white wines. It has been increasingly planted as a wine grape in the United States, especially in California where it is vinified either as a dry, spicy wine or as a LATE HARVEST sweet dessert wine with a high alcohol content.

Johnny Marzetti. A baked dish of ground meat, tomato, and macaroni. It was created at the Marzetti Restaurant in Columbus, Ohio, in the 1920s, and named after the owner's brother, Johnny.

> Brown 1 1/2 lb. ground beef with 1 chopped onion, add 1 can tomatoes, 1 can
> mushrooms, 1 can tomato paste, and 1/4 lb. Cheddar or mozzarella cheese. Cook

till tender and well blended, place on top of 8 oz. boiled noodles, sprinkle with cheese and bread crumbs and bake at 300° for about 40 min. Serves 8.

John Chinaman. A cowboy term for boiled rice, so called because the Chinese in nineteenth-century America subsisted on the grain. It has been a slang term for Chinese immigrants since the 1820s.

jolly boy. A nineteenth-century New England fried cake. Jolly boys were sometimes split in half, buttered, and served with maple syrup.

Stir 1/2 tsp. baking soda into 1 cup sour milk, then add 1 beaten egg and 1/2 cup molasses. Mix in 2 1/2 cups cornmeal or rye meal to form a biscuit dough. Drop balls of dough into hot oil and fry until golden brown. Makes about 25.

jook. A rice gruel sold in inexpensive Chinese-American "jook house" restaurants in San Francisco's Chinatown. Such places became popular just after World War II. See also JUKE.

jujube (*Ziziphus jujuba*). Also, "Chinese date." The fruit of an Old World tree having dark red skin and yellowish flowers. The term, which comes from the Middle English, *iuiube,* and, ultimately, from the Greek, *zizuphon,* also applies to several varieties of candies that are fruit-flavored and chewy, though not necessarily similar in taste to the jujube fruit.

A commercially produced candy called "Jujubes" (which probably took its name from the ju-ju gum that gave the tiny morsels their chewy texture) came on the American market sometime before 1920 and was followed by "Jujyfruits," which were shaped like candy berries, in 1920. Both candies are produced by the Heide company of New Jersey.

juke. Also, "jook" or "juke house." A roadside saloon, usually of a very low grade and long associated with Florida, where most jukes were operated. The word, which found its way into print only in 1935, derives from the African Wolof, *dzug,* "to lead a disorderly life," and many of the jukes were frequented by blacks.

By the 1940s *to juke* meant to go around to various bars and taverns, often in search of prostitutes. The word survives today in *juke box,* an automatic record player operated by dropping a coin in a slot and pushing buttons that indicate a listed song.

The food in such places usually included barbecue ribs and sandwiches, aside from liquor and beer, and jukes became known for their bold and intimidating signs, such as the one printed outside a Florida juke—"You can drink in here, but you go outside to get drunk"—or this one printed on the ceiling of an Alabama juke—"What the hell are you looking up here for?"

jumble. Also, "jumbal." A cookie with nuts "jumbled" up in the dough. Jumbles, among the first American cookies, came in various shapes, sometimes dropped on a baking sheet, sometimes cut with a cookie cutter. The first printed recipe appeared in 1892.

Blend 1/4 cup butter with 2 cups flour. Blend in 2 beaten eggs, 1/2 cup grated coconut, 1/2 tsp. rose water, and 3/4 cup walnuts. Make a stiff dough. Drop by teaspoon onto a buttered baking sheet and bake for 10 min. at 450°.

kaiser roll. Also called "Vienna roll." A crisp, puffy, light roll used to make sandwiches in delicatessans or eaten as a breakfast roll. The name is from the German, *kaiser,* "emperor," and refers to the crownlike appearance of the roll.

The kaiser roll originated in Vienna (some say it was named after Franz Josef [1830–1916], Emperor of Austria from 1848 to 1916) and was brought to America by German and Jewish immigrants. Today the confection is usually called simply a "hard roll" and is often topped with poppy seeds. The roll is not often seen outside the Northeast.

kamikaze. A cocktail made with citrus juices, Cointreau, and vodka. The name derives from the Japanese term, meaning "divine wind," for the Japanese pilots of the last years of World War II who would commit suicide by crashing their planes into American ships; metaphorically, drinking such a cocktail would be a suicidal act.

The drink may have once had less dramatic associations. According to bartender Tony Lauriano, he created the drink at Les Pyrénées restaurant in New York City in 1972 to honor the Broadway show *Jesus Christ Superstar,* after which the cocktail was named. Later the same ingredients came to be mixed into what was called the "kamikaze," but the person who coined that name is unknown.

> Shake with ice the juice of 1 lemon and 1 lime, 1 1/2 oz. Cointreau, and 1 1/2 oz. vodka. Garnish with sprig of mint.

Kansas City fish. Cowboy term for fried salt pork.

kedgeree. An East Indian dish brought to America by seamen that was originally composed of rice, lentils, eggs, and spices. New Englanders had added cod or other fish by the eighteenth century. The word comes from the Hindi, *khichrī,* from the Sanskrit, *khiccā.*

In a double boiler combine 2 cups cooked rice, 2 cups cooked cod, 4 chopped hard-boiled eggs, 2 tbs. minced parsley, 1/2 cup heavy cream, 1 tsp. salt, and 1/8 tsp. pepper. Heat thoroughly. Serves 6.

Kentucky breakfast. A colloquial slur defined as "three cocktails and a chaw of terbacker."

ketchup. Also, "catsup" and "catchup." A variety of condiments, the most common of which contains pickle and tomato. The word derives from Chinese, *ket-tsiap,* "pickled fish sauce," which was picked up by English sailors in the seventeenth century and first mentioned in print in 1711. Since in America most ketchups were made with tomato (bottled tomato ketchups were sold as of 1876 by the F. & J. Heinz Company of Pennsylvania), *tomato ketchup* as a description was little used after the end of the nineteenth century. Few Americans make their own ketchup any longer, though the bottled variety has come to be thought of as a necessary condiment with hamburgers, and much facile criticism of American food is aimed at the frequency with which Americans pour ketchup on their food, even though it is a traditional item both here and in England. "Tomato soy" is a nineteenth-century form of ketchup.

The following recipe is from Jacqueline Harrison Smith's *Famous Old Receipts* (1908):

Peel 4 qt. tomatoes and place in a kettle with 2 qt. vinegar, 6 chopped red peppers, 4 tbs. salt, black pepper, 2 tbs. dry mustard, and 3 tbs. allspice. Boil for 4 hr. till thickened. Bottle, seal, and serve as a condiment for meat and fish.

kidney bean *(Phaseolus vulgaris).* A species of kidney-shaped bean, the most familiar being reddish brown in color. The word was first printed in 1548.

kielbasa. Also, "kolbasy" and other spellings, or "Polish sausage." A pork sausage (sometimes containing beef or veal) seasoned with garlic. Kielbasa is sold in long links and is usually smoked and precooked, then eaten in smaller chunks. The word is from the Polish for the same sausage. *Kolbasa* is a Russian alternative. The term was first printed in the 1920s.

The word was also mentioned in American print in Saul Bellows's 1953 novel, *The Adventures of Augie March:* " 'Just catch the picture of this lousy classroom, and all these poor punks full of sauerkraut and bread with pig's-feet, with immigrant blood and washday smells and kielbasa and home-brew beer.' "

kishka. A Jewish-American baked sausage made with meat, flour, and spices. The word, from the Russian for "intestines," was first printed circa 1936.

knish. A Jewish-American pastry stuffed with mashed potato, cheese, buckwheat groats, or chopped liver. *Knish* is a Yiddish word that comes from the Russian, *knyš,* or Polish, *knyz.* The ubiquity of the knish in New York's Jewish community led to the lower section of Second Avenue being nicknamed "knish alley." A. Gross's *Kibitzer's Dictionary* (1930) humorously defines *knishes* as "dyspepsia." The word was first printed in 1916.

> Mix 1 cup mashed potatoes with 1 beaten egg, 1 tbs. chicken fat, 1/2 tsp. salt, a pinch of pepper, 1 tbs. minced onion, and enough flour to make a dough that is stiff enough to be shaped into oval patties about 4 1/2-in. long. Make a depression in the center of each patty, fill with cooked chopped chicken liver, mashed potato, cheese, or buckwheat groats, and enclose filling with folds of dough. Brush the dough with egg yolk, bake on a greased sheet at 350° for about 20 min. Makes about 6.

knockwurst. The usual American spelling for the German word for smoked beef and/or pork sausage *knackwurst*, whose name refers to the crackling sound the skin of the sausage makes when bitten into. The sausage also goes by the name *Regensburger* in Germany. Knockwurst may be boiled, grilled, or steamed and is often eaten with sauerkraut. *Knockwurst* first appears in English in 1929.

Know Your Cans. A cowboy game in which players had to recite from memory the exact ingredients listed on the labels of canned foodstuffs, with every punctuation mark in the right place.

kosher. A Yiddish term for food prepared according to strict Jewish dietary laws. The word is from the Hebrew *kāshēr*, meaning "proper," and has taken on colloquial meanings in America to mean "correct" or "honest" or "acceptable."

According to kosher laws, meat and milk may not be eaten together, a prohibition that even necessitates separate cooking utensils and dishes both in the home and at food-processing plants. There are also "clean" and "unclean" animals that are listed in Leviticus and Deuteronomy, kosher animals being those that have a cloven hoof and chew their cud. A nonkosher *(trayf)* animal chews its cud but is not cloven-hoofed. Fish with scales and fins are kosher, birds of prey are not.

Slaughter of animals must be done according to a ritual, the *schochet*, by the slashing of the throat, and the meat must then be stamped by a supervisor, the *mashgiach*.

These laws are biblical in origin, and, as Leo Rosten notes in *The Joys of Yiddish* (1968):

> Eating and drinking, to the ancient Jews, involved grave religious obligations, and strongly reinforced the idea of the Jews as a people "set apart," chosen by the Lord as "Mine . . ." "holy unto Me" (Leviticus). The strict observance of dietary rules was believed to strengthen the dedication of a Jew to his role as one of God's instruments for the redemption of mankind.

Kossuth cake. A sponge cake filled with whipped cream or ice cream, covered with icing, and set in individual paper cups. According to tradition, the cake was created in 1851 by an East Baltimore confectioner to honor the arrival in that city of Louis Kossuth (1802–1894), a Hungarian revolutionary leader who sought funds from the Marylanders. (Legend has it that he collected only twenty-five dollars.)

K ration. A packaged food item of World War II containing, according to its creator, physiologist Ancel Keys, all the necessary nutrition for a serviceman in the field. The term was first printed in 1940.

kreplach. A dumpling containing chopped meat or cheese, often served in soup. The word derives from the German, *kreppel.* Kreplachs are by tradition served on Purim, Rosh Hashanah, and the day before Yom Kippur. In its use as a Jewish dish, the word was first mentioned in 1892.

> Mix together 1 beaten egg, 1 cup flour, and 1/4 tsp. salt, and knead into an elastic dough. Roll out very thin and cut into 3-in. squares. Mix together 1 cup chopped cooked beef, 2 tbs. minced onion, 2 tbs. chicken fat, and 1/2 tsp. salt, place some in each half of the squares, then fold them to form triangles. Secure edges with a fork and boil in salted water for 20 min. Serve in soup or fry in hot fat. Makes 24.

kugel. A noodle or potato pudding served on the Jewish Sabbath. The word is from the German. If made with noodles, the more frequently prepared of the two varieties, the dish is called "lukshen kugel." Raisins are sometimes added to sweeten the dish. *Kugel* first appears in English print in 1846.

> Cook 1/2 lb. noodles in boiling water and drain. Beat 3 egg yolks with 2 tbs. chicken fat, 2 tbs. sugar, and 1/2 tsp. salt, then fold into noodles. Beat 3 egg whites till stiff, fold into noodle mixture. Pour into greased pan, bake in 350° oven for about 30 min., then brown under flame. Serves 6.

kumiss. Also, "koumyss," "koumiss," and other variants. A beverage of fermented milk, possibly originating with the Mongols, having an acrid flavor and a small bit of alcohol present. Kumiss was thought to have some digestive benefits. The word comes from the Russian, and was first printed in English around 1600. "Laban" is a similar item.

> Dissolve 4 oz. sugar in 1 gallon skimmed milk, pour into 1-qt. bottles, add 2 oz. dry yeast to each bottle, and seal tightly. Set bottles in warm place to ferment, then in cool cellar, set on their sides. Fermentation takes about 3 days.

lactic acid. A spoilage inhibitor, added to cheese, desserts, carbonated drinks, and Spanish olives, that imparts a tart flavor to foods.

la cuite. Cooked sugar syrup in the last stage before it blackens and becomes bitter. The term is used among Louisiana Cajun cooks and derives from the French word for "cooking."

Lady Baltimore cake. A white cake filled with nuts and raisins and covered with a vanilla-and-egg-white frosting.

There are several stories of how the cake was named, but the most accepted version concerns a cake by this name baked by a Charleston, South Carolina, belle named Alicia Rhett Mayberry for novelist Owen Wister, who not only described the confection in his next book but named the novel itself *Lady Baltimore* (1906). In *American Food* (1974) Evan Jones notes that "it may also be true that the 'original' recipe became the property of the Misses Florence and Nina Ottolengui, who managed Charleston's Lady Baltimore Tea Room for a quarter of a century and annually baked and shipped to Owen Wister one of the very American cakes his novel had helped to make famous." Alicia Rhett Mayberry, in *200 Years of Charleston Cooking* (ed. Lettie Gay, 1930) says the recipe came from the Woman's Exchange when Wister wrote his novel.

> Cream 1/2 cup butter and 1 1/2 cups sugar, adding 1 cup water gradually, then 3 cups flour and 2 tsp. baking powder. Fold in 4 stiffly beaten egg whites and 1 tsp. vanilla. Bake in 3 buttered cake pans in a 375° oven.
>
> Boil 1 1/2 cups sugar and 1/2 cup water in a double boiler till syrup forms a thread. Beat well and pour slowly over 2 stiffly beaten egg whites. Beat until mixture may be spread on the cakes. Sprinkle on 1/2 cup raisins, 5 diced figs, 1/2 cup chopped pecans, and 1/3 cup candied cherries.
>
> Boil 2 cups sugar with 1/2 cup water in double boiler. Boil till syrup forms a thread, and beat well. Slowly pour over 2 stiffly beaten egg whites and 1 tsp. vanilla. Spread completely over layered cake.

ladyfinger. A light sponge-cake biscuit. The name comes from the usual shape of the confection, which is long and narrow, light and delicate. (Okra is sometimes called "ladies fingers" too.) The word often appears in the possessive, *Lady's finger,* and the plural, *ladies' fingers,* and was first mentioned by John Keats in his poem, *The Cap and Bells* (1820). Ladyfingers have long been a popular confection in America, where some recipes call for the pastry to be pushed through a pastry tube.

> Beat 1 egg white with a pinch of salt till foamy, add 1 1/2 tbs. sugar and beat till stiff. Beat 1 egg yolk with 1/2 tsp. vanilla and 1 1/2 tbs. sugar till light. Fold in whites and yolks together, then fold in 1/4 cup flour. Spoon long "fingers" onto ungreased paper set on a cookie sheet and bake about 10 min. at 350°. Cool, dust with confectioners' sugar. Makes 12.

Lafayette ginger bread. Also called "Mary Ball Washington's ginger bread." A cakelike ginger-and-spice bread made by George Washington's mother when General Lafayette paid her a visit at her Fredericksburg, Virginia, home in 1784.

> Cream 1/2 cup butter, 1 cup brown sugar, and 1 cup molasses with 1/2 cup warm milk, 2 tbs. powdered ginger, 1 1/2 tsp. cinnamon, 1 1/2 tsp. mace, 1 1/2 tsp. ground nutmeg, and 1/4 cup brandy. Sift 3 cups flour with 1 tsp. cream of tartar and 3 beaten eggs, and add to butter mixture. Add the juice of 1 orange and its grated rind, 1 tsp. baking soda in 2 tbs. water, and 1 cup raisins. Blend thoroughly. Bake in a buttered 12-by-9-in. pan at 350° for about 45 min. Serves 15.

lagniappe. A Creole term for a small extra gift or bonus, such as a free roll given when one buys a dozen. It has been used in Louisiana at least since 1849 and is taken from the Spanish *la ñapa,* "the gift," by way of the Peruvian Quechuan word *yápa,* "addition." In *Life on the Mississippi* (1883), Mark Twain wrote:

> We picked up one excellent word—a word worth traveling to New Orleans to get; a nice, limber, expressive, handy word—"Lagniappe." They pronounce it lanny-*yap.* It is Spanish—so they said. We discovered it at the head of a column of odds and ends in the *Picayune* the first day; heard twenty people use it the second; inquired what it meant the third; adopted it and got facility in swinging it the fourth. It has a restricted meaning, but I think the people spread it out a little when they choose. It is the equivalent of the thirteenth roll in a "baker's dozen." It is something thrown in, gratis, for good measure. The custom originated in the Spanish quarter of the city. When a child or a servant buys something in a shop—or even the mayor or the governor, for aught I know—he finishes the operation by saying:
> "Give me something for lagniappe."
> The shopman always responds; gives the child a bit of licorice-root, gives the servant a cheap cigar or a spool of thread, gives the governor—I don't know what he gives the governor; support, likely.
> When you are invited to drink—and this does occur now and then in New Orleans—and you say, "What, again?—no I've had enough," the other party says, "But just this one more time—this is for lagniappe." . . . If the waiter in the

restaurant stumbles and spills a gill of coffee down the back of your neck, he says, "F'r lagniappe, sah," and gets you another cup without extra charge.

Lalla Rookh. A nineteenth-century dessert made with eggs, spirits, and whipped cream, although there are many variations. A 1910 cookbook by San Francisco chef Victor Hitzler of the Hotel St. Francis listed Lalla Rookh as nothing more than a crème de menthe cordial poured over ice in a sherbet glass to be served as a digestive between courses.

The name comes from a long poem about a beautiful princess of India, *Lalla Rookh* (1817), by Thomas Moore. The poem, praised for its "barbaric splendors" and exotic details, was a great success in both England and America, and this rich dessert was named after the poem's heroine.

In a saucepan heat 5 egg yolks with 1 cup sugar, stirring until thickened. Cool, then add 3/4 cup brandy and 1/4 cup rum. Fold in 1 qt. whipped cream and 5 stiffly beaten egg whites. Mix in a pinch of nutmeg, pack in ice and salt, and freeze.

lamb. A sheep *(Ovis aries)* less than a year old, usually slaughtered between four and twelve months for its meat. The word is from the Germanic, *lambiz-*.

The meat of the lamb is considered one of the most desirable foods by many people, but it has never achieved much acceptance in America, where beef, pork, and veal are preferred. Americans have also tended to slaughter their lambs somewhat later than Europeans and Asians, so that the taste is not as delicate as it is in other countries. Also, the social divisiveness and bloodshed caused by the introduction of sheep herds into the steer country of the western territories in the nineteenth century gave lamb a bad reputation for most of the last century. In fact, Americans in 1981 ate only 1.4 pounds of lamb per person as compared to 77.2 pounds of beef and 65 pounds of pork. When lamb is eaten, it is usually in the form of a roast or in lamb chops, much of it shipped in frozen from New Zealand.

There are three categories of lamb recognized in the United States: baby or hothouse lamb, which is milk-fed and usually slaughtered under six weeks of age; spring lamb, milk-fed and slaughtered at under four months; and lamb, weaned on grass and slaughtered under one year; after one year the animal's meat is termed "mutton," which is not very popular in America. Most United States lamb is sold as spring lamb, which federal regulations require be slaughtered between the beginning of March and the close of the week containing the first Monday in October. A very small amount of baby lamb comes from Pennsylvania and New Jersey.

Lamb is customarily served with mint jelly in the United States, and its greatest popularity is as the Easter meal.

lambs'-quarters *(Chenopodium album)*. Also, "lamb's quarters," and as a single word. A species of a wild plant, called "pigweed," "goosefoot," and "wild spinach," that originated in Europe and spread throughout the American West. The Hopi Indians packed the leaves around foods to be baked in order to keep in moisture, but others used them in stews or in salads. They may also be cooked like spinach, and the black seeds of the plant were used for breads. In the Southwest the plant is sometimes called by its Spanish-Mexican name, *quelites*. The word was first printed in 1773.

Lane cake. A layer cake with a fluffy frosting and containing coconut, chopped fruits, and nuts in the filling. The cake was named after Emma Rylander Lane of Clayton, Alabama, who published the original recipe under the name "Prize Cake" in her cookbook *Some Good Things to Eat* (1898). But, according to Cecily Brownstone, author of the *Associated Press Cookbook* (1972) and friend of Mrs. Lane's granddaughter, the original recipe is very imprecise. In various forms it has become popular throughout the South.

According to Mrs. Lane, the cake "is much better . . . made a day or two before using."

Beat 2 cups sugar, 1 3/4 cups butter, and 2 tsp. vanilla till light. Combine 3 1/2 cups flour, 4 1/2 tsp. baking powder, and 1 1/2 tsp. salt and add to butter mixture, alternating with 1 1/2 cups milk till smooth. Fold in 8 stiffly beaten egg whites. Divide batter and pour into 3 buttered and floured cake pans. Bake for 20 min. at 375°, then cool. Melt 1/2 cup butter with 1 cup sugar, 1/3 cup bourbon, and 1/3 cup water, bring to boil, dissolve ingredients together, and stir half the mixture into 9 lightly beaten egg yolks. Return to saucepan and cook till thickened. Remove from heat, then stir in 1 cup chopped raisins, 3/4 cup chopped pecans, 1/2 cup chopped maraschino cherries, 1/2 cup flaked coconut, and 3/4 tsp. vanilla. Cool to room temperature, then spread over cake layers and on top. Combine 1 cup sugar, 1/3 cup water, 1/4 tsp. cream of tartar, and a dash of salt in a saucepan and bring to boil, stirring till sugar is dissolved. Add 1 tsp. vanilla, then pour mixture very slowly into 2 beaten egg whites. Frost the cake with this icing.

larrup. Cowboy term for MOLASSES, which was also called "long sweetenin'." The origin of the name is unknown, though the same word in dialectical English means a "beating."

Late Harvest. A term used by American winemakers to indicate a wine made from grapes picked late in the fall, after the grape has been attacked by the mold *botrytis cinerea*. The mold allows moisture to escape and concentrates the sugars in the grapes, resulting in a very sweet, almost syrupy wine having high alcohol content. In California, Late Harvest wines are often made from the JOHANNISBERG RIESLING grape.

latke. A Jewish pancake, usually made from potatoes, traditionally served at Chanukah. The dish commemorates the biblical story of the Jewish Macca-bees' defeat of the Syrians in 165 B.C. They found in the Temple of Jerusalem only enough oil to burn for one night, but the oil miraculously burned for eight nights. The oil used for frying the latkes symbolizes this miracle.

This tradition developed among the Ashkenazi Jews of northern and east-ern Europe, many of whom came to America in the late nineteenth century and who carried the tradition with them. The potato latke has been made for over two hundred years, after the potato, brought from America in the sixteenth century, was accepted by Europeans as an edible food.

> Wash 6 potatoes and dice. Dry them, then grate, retaining some of the juice. Grate 1 small onion, add 1/2 tsp. salt and 1 egg. Blend well. Mix in 3 tbs. matzo meal with 1/2 tsp. baking powder, and blend into potatoes. Drop spoonfuls of the mixture into hot fat and cook till browned on all sides. Drain. Serve with applesauce or sour cream. Serves 4.

leather. An early American confection made from dried-fruit "butters" or purées baked slowly and cut in long strips resembling strips of leather.

> Cook 1 lb. of fruit, such as peach or apricot, in simmering water till tender. Rub through a sieve or food mill, add 1 part brown sugar or honey to 4 parts fruit purée, then simmer for 5 min. Spread in thin sheets over a buttered baking pan and let dry out thoroughly in a slow, 250° oven for 2 hr. Cool, sprinkle with confectioners' sugar and, if desired, roll up. Serves 4.

Lebkuchen. A Pennsylvania Dutch spiced drop cake made especially at Christmastime.

> Boil 1 qt. honey in a pan, then mix 3/4 lb. sugar with 1/4 lb. citron, 1/2 lb. ground almonds, 1/4 lb. orange peel, 1 oz. cinnamon, 1 pkg. yeast, 3 tbs. cherry brandy, some nutmeg, and 2 1/4 lb. flour. Knead for 15 min. Let stand overnight. Roll out and cut into 2-in. squares. Bake in a tin dish.

lecithin. An emulsifier and antioxidant found in animal and plant tissues and used in baked goods, chocolate, ice cream, and other foods. Lecithin also keeps oil and water from separating.

Lee cake. A white cake flavored with citrus rind and juice, supposedly based on recipes of cooks for General Robert E. Lee (1807–1870), commander of the Confederate Army in the Civil War.

> Beat 10 eggs till light in color and add 1 lb. sugar and 1 lb. flour, alternating the two ingredients. Grate in the rind of 1 lemon and add its juice, mix well, pour batter into cake pans, and bake at 350° till inserted knife comes out clean. Make icing of 1 lb. powdered sugar, 2 beaten egg whites, and the juice and rind of 1 orange. Coat layers of cake, sides, and top.

leek *(Allium porrum).* An onionlike plant of the lily family having green leaves and a white bulbous stalk. It is eaten as a vegetable, usually boiled, but has had little popularity in the United States until recently. Wild leek *(A. tricoccum)* is found in eastern North America. The word in Old English is *lēac.*

lemon *(Citrus limon).* A yellow-skinned, tangy citrus fruit native to Asia. Its juice, pulp, and rind are used in a wide variety of dishes, desserts, drinks, and COCKTAILS. The word is from the Persian, *līmūn,* and first appears in print about 1400. Lemonade is sweetened juice and water.

Lemons have been cultivated around the eastern Mediterranean for at least twenty-five hundred years, and after the Crusades they became a desirable fruit in Europe, where they began to be grown in Sicily, Spain, and other Mediterranean countries. Legend has it that Columbus brought lemon seeds to Florida, and Spanish friars grew the fruit in California, where it flourished in the middle of the nineteenth century—especially the Eureka (possibly first cultivated in California or brought from Sicily) and the Lisbon (brought from Australia). In 1874 James W. Parkinson, writing of American dishes at the Philadelphia Centennial, noted that citron (*C. medica*), a lemonlike fruit, had "lately been transplanted in California, and promise[s] in the near future to equal the best."

Today California produces about 80 percent of the American lemon crop, with Florida and Texas also contributing. The common or acid lemon is the variety most used in the food industry and at home.

LEMON MERINGUE PIE:
(A nineteenth-century dessert that has become one of the standards of the American kitchen) Combine 1/3 cup cornstarch, 1/8 tsp. salt, and 2/3 cup sugar, stir in 1 1/2 cups water, and cook over medium heat until mixture thickens and comes to a boil for 1 min. Remove from heat. Beat 4 egg yolks, stir in 2 tbs. of cornstarch mixture, then stir eggs into the rest of the cornstarch, being careful to stir out lumps. Add juice of 2 lemons and grated rind of 1 lemon. Cook in saucepan till thickened, but do not boil. Pour into pie crust and cool 10 min. Beat 1/2 cup sugar into 4 egg whites until stiff, mold on top of pie, bake in 400° oven till top is lightly browned. Cool.

SHAKER LEMON PIE:
(From the American Harvest restaurant in New York City) Slice 2 lemons paper thin, with rind. Remove seeds, place slices in bowl with 1 1/2 cups sugar, let stand overnight. Beat 4 eggs, fold into lemon mixture, pour into pastry crust, cover with top crust, slit vents, and brush with light cream. Bake for 15 min. at 450°, reduce heat to 350° and bake for 30 min. Cool.

LEMON ICE:
(Particularly popular in Italian-American neighborhoods where it is customarily sold at pastry shops in summer) Combine 3 cups water with 1 1/3 cups sugar, boil for 5 min., then cool. Add 1/2 cup lemon juice. Freeze in ice cream freezer, stirring occasionally to prevent cream from solidifying completely.

lettuce. Any of a variety of plants in the genus *Lactuca,* especially *L. sativa,* cultivated for its leaves, which are used in salads. The word is from the Latin, *lactuca,* which in Middle English became *letus.*

England had cultivated lettuce as of the fifteenth century, but Christopher Columbus may have been the first to bring it to America. Lettuce was grown only in home gardens until the twentieth century, when Americans' new appetite for salad made commercial production profitable. In 1982 Americans ate 23.8 pounds per person. Today lettuce is raised in twenty of the states, cultivated in four main botanical varieties:

head or cabbage lettuce *(L. s. capitata).* This variety includes the butterhead, of which the Bibb (named after amateur breeder John B. Bibb of

Frankfort, Kentucky) and the Boston are the principal horticultural varieties; and the crisp head, which includes the Imperial and iceberg varieties.

leaf lettuce *(L. s. crispa).* This variety includes the oak leaf and salad bowl lettuces.

Romaine or Cos lettuce *(L. s. longifolia). Romaine* derives from Old French for the city of Rome, whereas *Cos* refers to the Greek island of Cos, or Kos, from which it may have originated.

celtuce or asparagus lettuce *(L. s. asparagina).* Rarely seen in America.

liberty-cabbage. A colloquialism created during World War I as a patriotic substitute for the German *sauerkraut.* The term was, as Mencken notes, "a complete failure."

Liederkranz. A strong-smelling cow's-milk cheese of distinctly American origins. The word means "wreath of song" in German and derives from the name of a New York singing society that received some of the first samples made in 1892 by Emil Frey, a Swiss-born dairyman from Monroe, New York. He sent the cheese to his boss, delicatessen owner Adolph Tode (Todi?), who supplied the members of the Liederkranz club with packages of the new item. Liederkranz was an instant success, and its popularity caused production to flourish where there was more milk available, in Van Wert, Ohio.

light foods. Also, "Lite" foods. A vague term describing food items having a fewer number of calories than representative items that have not been processed in the same way. For instance, light beer (which makes up 18 percent of the domestic market) may contain only one-third the calories of regular beer; light canned fruits may have fifty calories per half-cup, rather than regular canned fruits' eighty-five; light ketchup may have half the calories of regular ketchup.

lima bean *(Phaseolus limensis).* A green, flat bean, called the "butter bean" in the South, which takes its name from the city of Lima, Peru, where it was cultivated very early. The bean was introduced to North America, where it was enjoyed by the Indians long before the arrival of the European settlers; it is the principal ingredient of SUCCOTASH. It is first mentioned in print in 1756 and in William Cobbett's *American Gardener* (1819).

Lima beans are eaten fresh but are more often boiled and buttered. California produces most of the United States lima bean crop.

lime *(Citrus aurantifolia).* A tangy green citrus fruit similar to the lemon. Its name derives from the Arabic, *līmah,* and was first mentioned in English in 1638. Indigenous to Southeast Asia, the lime was introduced to Europe through Italy. In *Fading Feast* (1981), Raymond Sokolov writes, "Whether Columbus brought seeds of *C. aurantifolia* with him to Haiti in 1493 is a matter of conjecture, but it seems probable, since limes were flourishing on that island in 1520. Limes then spread gradually across the West Indies, westward to Mexico and northward to the Florida Keys, where trees were well established by 1839."

These "Key limes" became a major commercial crop after 1906, but a hurricane in 1926 destroyed many of the groves. The groves were replanted with a more practical crossbreed called the "Tahiti" (or "Persian" or "Bearss") lime, which had been grown in California since the 1850s and in Florida since 1883.

Today almost all limes grown in America are of the Tahiti variety, while true Key limes are a rarity grown only on private, noncommercial plots in the Florida Keys.

Americans use limes as a flavoring for desserts and cocktails and to enhance the flavor of fish and salads. The most famous confection made with limes is Key lime pie, a tangy pie made with condensed milk and piled high with meringue or whipped cream. Because of the unavailability of true Key limes, except in the Florida Keys, Key lime pies are almost never made with anything but Tahiti limes.

Key lime pies were first made in the Keys in the 1850s. Jeanne A. Voltz, author of *The Flavor of the South* (1977), explains that the recipe developed with the advent of sweetened condensed milk in 1856. Since there were few cows on the Keys, the new canned milk was welcomed by the residents and introduced into a pie made with lime juice.

The original pies were made with a pastry crust, but a crust made from graham crackers later became popular and today is a matter of preference, as is the choice between whipped cream and meringue toppings. There are three recipes for Key lime pie in the Key West Women's Club collection, *The Key West Cook Book* (1949), only one of which refers to a graham cracker crust, and two of which do not require the pie to be baked. One has no topping, one whipped cream, and one meringue. The following recipe is from the Pier House restaurant in Key West:

KEY LIME PIE:
In a bowl combine 1 1/4 cups graham cracker crumbs, 1/3 cup sifted confectioners' sugar, and 6 tbs. unsalted butter, melted and cooled. Press the mixture into a pie plate to form a crust, bake in 350° oven for 10 min. till lightly browned, then cool on rack. Beat 4 egg yolks till light in color, stir in one 14-oz. can sweetened condensed milk, 1/4 cup lime juice, 1/2 tsp. cream of tartar, then another 1/4 cup lime juice. Spoon into shell and bake at 325° till it sets, about 10–15 min. Freeze for at least 3 hr. Beat 4 egg whites with 1/4 cup sugar till stiff, spread over pie, and bake in hot oven (450°) until meringue is golden.

limpin' Suzan. A southern dish of red beans and rice, a corollary to the more familiar HOPPING JOHN. The recipe given below is from Bob Jeffries's *Soul Food Cookbook* (1969):

Cover 1 lb. red beans with water and let soak for several hours. Drain, add 1 chopped onion, 1/4 lb. salt pork, and water to cover. Cook till tender, remove 1/2 cup of the beans and 2 tbs. of the liquid and mash into a purée. Add pepper and salt and 3–4 cups cooked rice. Cook through till heated, and top with the rest of the beans. Serves 6–8.

linguine. Also, "linguini." A flat pasta about one-eighth of an inch wide. Linguine, a staple of Italian-American restaurants, is usually served with a red or white clam sauce. The word was first printed in English in 1948.

liquor. A distilled spirit. The word, originally from the Latin, derives from Middle English *lic(o)ur*. Liquor is a general term for spirits that includes WHISKEY, BRANDY, RUM, VODKA, GIN, and CORDIALS. Malt liquor is brewed like BEER from malt, but has a higher alcohol content than beer, though it is usually nowhere close to the proof of most liquors.

American slang for liquor constitutes a freewheeling, sometimes hilarious compendium of imaginative speech, with entries running into the hundreds for general terms and into the thousands for specific cocktails (most of which have not worn well nor become part of the bartender's repertoire). For specific cocktail names, look under main entries, for example, MARTINI, MANHATTAN, PIÑA COLADA, and others. The following list includes general terms for spirits, followed by dates indicating when they came into use or were first recorded in print: *Jersey lightning* (1780), *anti-fogmatic* (1789), *phlegm cutter* (1806), *firewater* (1817), *rotgut* (1819), *red eye* (1819), *coffin varnish* (1845), *tanglefoot* (1859), *tarantula juice* (1861), *sheep dip* (1865), *pick me up* (1867), *shot* (1906), *belt* (1921), and *panther sweat* (1929).

Little Joe's. A dish made of ground meat and spinach, with various seasonings according to taste. It would seem to be a variation on the kind of thrown-together dish elsewhere called SLOPPY JOE or JOE MAZZETTI, but John Thorne in his *Simple Cooking* newsletter (1982) states, "Little Joe's is a popular San Francisco dish, named after the restaurant where, as legend has it, the meal was tossed together from leftovers in the kitchen late one night for a hungry customer."

> In 2 tbs. oil sauté 1 chopped onion till soft. Add 1 lb. ground beef and break up, cooking till gray. Add 1 cup cooked spinach, salt, and pepper, and cook till spinach is wilted. Beat 2 eggs with a dash of Tabasco sauce, add to beef and cook till eggs have set. Sprinkle with Parmesan cheese if desired, then spoon onto crisp rolls. Serves 4.

liverwurst. A sausage made with chopped liver that has a very smooth texture and is usually sliced in slabs. The word is derived from the German, *Leberwurst*, "liver sausage," and was first printed in American English in 1869. Originally it was called "Braunschweiger," because it came from Germany's Brunswick Province (Braunschweig); it has long been associated with German immigrants.

Liverwurst is seasoned with onions, pistachios, and other spices, smoked, and packaged, usually to be spread on a sandwich or served as a canapé or cold cut. Occasionally it is sold fresh.

lobscouse. A beef-and-potato stew described by Marjorie Mosser in her *Foods of Old New England* (1957) as "one of the most frequently used dishes in the galleys of New England sailing ships."

> Cut up 2 lb. bottom-round beef, 1 qt. potatoes, 1/2 lb. salt pork, 4 onions, cover with water and boil for 1 hr. Add 4 cups chopped corned beef, cook an additional 1/2 hr. Serves 6.

lobster. Any of a variety of crustaceans of the genus *Homarus* having five pairs of legs, including two large front claws. The name comes from the Old English, *loppestre,* and Latin, *locusta.*

The American lobster *(Homarus americanus)* is today one of the most expensive food items in the market, owing to the difficulty of obtaining sufficient quantities to meet the demand. But when the first Europeans came to America the lobster was one of the most commonly found crustaceans. They sometimes washed up on the beaches of Plymouth, Massachusetts, in piles two feet high. These settlers approached the creatures with less than gustatory enthusiasm, but the lobsters' abundance made them fit for the tables of the poor. (One observer remarked that "the very multitude of them cloys us.") In 1622 Governor William Bradford of the Plymouth Plantation apologized to a new arrival of settlers that the only dish he "could presente their friends with was a lobster . . . without bread or anything els but a cupp of fair water."

Lobsters in those days grew to tremendous size, sometimes forty or more pounds. (A record-holding forty-two-pounder was taken in Virginia in 1935 and is now hung in Boston's Museum of Science.) New Englanders might easily pick them off the beach for their tables, and ships carried them to other ports. When ships in New York harbor were bombarded during the Revolution the lobsters went to other waters, only to return at the cessation of hostilities.

The taste for lobster developed rapidly in the nineteenth century, and commercial fisheries specializing in the crustacean were begun in Maine in the 1840s, thereby giving rise to the fame of the "Maine lobster," which was being shipped around the world a decade later. In 1842 the first lobster shipments reached Chicago, and Americans enjoyed them both at home and in the cities' new "lobster palaces," the first of which was built in New York by the Stanley brothers. Here men made the consumption of several lobsters at one sitting a mark of one's affluence and joy in the good things of life. Diamond Jim Brady thought nothing of downing a half-dozen, in addition to several other full courses. (The March 1982 issue of *Yankee* magazine listed a professional wrestler named "Andre the Giant" as the all-time lobster-eating champion after he put away forty of the crustaceans at Custy's Restaurant in North Kingstown, Rhode Island. The news elicited a response from Tom Shovan of Woodlands, California, who claimed he had at the same restaurant once eaten sixty-one lobsters at a sitting. Shovan demanded from the magazine a "correction to this gross misstatement that would lead the naive to believe that a mere 40 lobsters are enough to satisfy a truly voracious appetite!")

By 1885 the American lobster industry was providing 130 million pounds of lobster per year. Soon afterwards the population of the lobster beds decreased rapidly, and by 1918 only 33 million pounds were taken. Today, thanks to conservation efforts, the production is again above 70 million pounds, while millions of pounds of other lobsters come from South Africa, South America, Mexico, Australia, and elsewhere, usually in the form of "spiny lobsters," sometimes called "crawfish" but distinct from our native freshwater CRAY-FISH. The so-called Maine lobster does not come only from Maine anymore either, but from beds in Canada as well.

The average American lobster weighs between one and two pounds, although many eastern steak and lobster houses carry them at five or more pounds. Frozen lobster tails, usually broiled and served with clarified butter, are brought in in great quantities from South Africa. Other preparations of lobster range from simple boiling or steaming to elaborate dishes, like lobster Newburg, that require the removal of the meat from the tail and claws (Americans usually do not eat the meat and innards of the body) and combining it with cream, seasonings, sherry, and other ingredients.

Besides the American lobster, the following also figure in culinary preparations in the United States, when available:

lobsterette (Family Nephropidae). Lobsterettes are smaller members of the lobster family, ten species of which are found in the Atlantic and Caribbean, including the Caribbean lobsterette *(Metanephrops binghami)*, the Florida lobsterette *(Nephrops aculeata)*, and the red lobsterette *(Metanephrops rubellus)*. In Europe these are called the *"langoustine," "scampo,"* "Dublin Bay prawn," and other names.

Spanish lobster *(Scyllarides aequinoctialis)*. Also, "shovel-nosed lobster," "sand lobster," "slipper lobster," "buccaneer crab," "gollipop," and other names. Rare in the United States, this lobster is brought in frozen from Southeast Asian waters.

spiny lobster *(Panulirus argus)*. A favorite Floridian species, the spiny lobster ranges from the Carolinas to the Caribbean and is related to a Californian species, *P. interruptus*. At market spiny lobsters are often called "rock lobsters."

lobster à l'américaine. A dish of lobster prepared with a sauce of tomatoes, brandy, white wine, cayenne pepper, and seasonings. It is certainly of French, not American, origins, and in France is called *"homard à l'américaine."* Some gastronomes insist that it is actually a dish of Breton, or Armorican, origins, and that *à l'américaine* is an incorrect transcription of *à l'armoricaine*. Robert Courtine, however, in his book, *The Hundred Glories of French Cooking* (1973), shows that the error was probably the other way around, pointing out that "no menu from any important restaurant, either in Paris or elsewhere, has ever been found with *armoricaine* antedating *américaine*. No, the latter has always preceded the former."

Courtine goes on to repeat the story told by the "Prince of Gastronomes," Maurice-Edmond Sailland (called "Curnonsky"), of how the dish was in fact created. Chef Pierre Fraisse had begun his cooking career in the United States, where he often prepared lobsters. Fraisse, known by the more American name "Peters," opened his own restaurant in Paris around 1860. One evening a group of Americans came in late and Fraisse, having little left to work with, prepared a dish with lobsters that he called, in deference to his guests, *"homard à l'américaine."*

Sauce à l'américaine is often used with other fish dishes.

Cut the claws off a lobster and cut the tail into even rings. In 4 tbs. oil sauté the meat with salt and pepper till the shell has turned red. Remove from pan. To pan with oil add 1 finely chopped onion, 2 chopped shallots, and 1/4 clove crushed garlic, and sauté till limp. Pour off the oil, add 1/2 cup white wine, 1/2 cup water, and 2 tbs. brandy, and burn off the alcohol. Add 2 peeled, seeded tomatoes, 3 sprigs of tarragon, and 1/8 tsp. cayenne. Place the lobster pieces on top, cover, and cook for 20 min. Remove lobster and place on serving platter. Remove tarragon. Over high heat reduce sauce in pan by half. Mash the lobster roe (called "coral") and green tomalley with 2 tbs. butter, a pinch of chervil, and a pinch of tarragon. Add to sauce in pan and stir to bind. Bring to boil, add 2 tbs. butter and 2 tbs. brandy, and pour over lobster. Garnish with chopped parsley and serve with rice.

lobster Newburg. A rich dish of lobster meat, sherry, egg yolks, cream, and cayenne pepper. The dish was made famous at Delmonico's restaurant in New York in 1876 when the recipe was brought to chef Charles Ranhofer by a West Indies sea captain named Ben Wenberg. It was an immediate hit, especially for after-theater suppers, and owner Charles Delmonico honored the captain by naming the dish "lobster à la Wenberg." But later Wenberg and Delmonico had a falling out, and the restaurateur took the dish off the menu, restoring it only by popular demand but renaming it "lobster à la Newberg," reversing the first three letters of the captain's name. Chef Ranhofer also called it "lobster à la Delmonico," but the appellation "Newberg" (later "Newburg") stuck, and the dish became a standard in hotel dining rooms in the United States. It is still quite popular and is found in French cookbooks, where it is sometimes referred to as *"Homard sauté à la crème."* The sauce itself is used with other shellfish and such a preparation retains the name à la Newburg." In some recipes the lobster is not sautéed in butter, but only boiled. The first printed recipe appeared in 1895.

Cook 2 lobsters in salted water till tender. Cool, then cut up meat into slices and sauté with 6 tbs. butter. Salt to taste and add a dash of Tabasco or 1/4 tsp. cayenne pepper. Pour in 1 cup heavy cream and 2 tbs. sherry and boil, reducing to half. Remove from heat and add 3 beaten egg yolks to thicken the sauce. Reheat, finishing it with a little more butter.

lollipop. A hard clear candy attached to a stick usually made of rolled paper. It is a favorite children's snack and has been so since it was introduced in England in the 1780s. The name comes from an English dialect word, *lolly,* for the tongue, and the *pop* is probably associated with the sound made when the candy is withdrawn from the mouth.

The Tootsie Roll Pop, a lollipop with a soft chocolate candy center, is a trademark of Tootsie Roll Industries, Inc., in Chicago, Illinois.

lomi-lomi salmon. A salted salmon dish of Hawaii often served at large feasts called "luaus." Lomi lomi means "massaged."

> Soak 1 lb. salted salmon in water and refrigerate overnight. Remove the skin, drain the fish, and cut up into small pieces. Add 5 large chopped, peeled, seeded tomatoes, 1 finely chopped Maui onion, and 2 finely chopped scallions. Squeeze all these ingredients through fingers until well blended. Serve ice cold. Serves 6.

London broil. Flank steak that is broiled and cut into slices, though the term may also refer to a cut of beef appropriate for cooking in this manner. The name obviously derives from the English city of London but first saw print in America in 1946, and seems specifically American in origin.

longhorn. Also "Longhorn" or "Texas Long Horn." This breed of cattle, itself a symbol of the state of Texas and the nickname given people from that state, was so called by 1834 for the wide stretch between the horns of the steers. Longhorns were the first domesticated cattle in the United States, having been brought via the Caribbean and Mexico from Spain in the early 1500s. The wild cattle roamed as far north as the Red River, and by 1830 there were about eighty thousand of them in Texas. Twelve years later a herd of longhorn was driven to New Orleans, and in 1867 the steers began the great cattle drives from Lockhart, Texas, to Abilene, Kansas, that in their prime resulted in ten million of the breed being raised throughout the Midwest.

But the longhorn's history was short-lived. The breed was overshadowed by the imported English breeds, the Angus and the Hereford, which were easier to ship and had a richer taste to the beef. By the 1920s the longhorn was pretty much forgotten as a meat-producing steer. The breed has been kept alive by federal wildlife preserves and members of the Texas Longhorn Breeders Association of America, which lists sixteen hundred members. Currently there are close to fifty thousand longhorns in the United States. See also BEEF.

Long Island Iced Tea. A cocktail of various clear spirits like vodka, gin, and tequila with Coca-Cola and lemon. Its origins (1970?) are unknown.

long neck. A beer bottle with a long neck, long known in the Southwest and particularly popular in Texas. Beer drinkers carry the bottle around by the neck with considerable swagger and do not drink from a glass.

love and tangle. Deep-fried doughnut that has been twisted and entwined.

love apples. A romantic term for tomatoes, so called because of a mistranslation of the Italian *pomo dei Moro* ("apple of the Moors," because tomatoes came to Italy from Morocco) into the French *pomme d'amour,* meaning "love apple." Certain aphrodisiacal attributes thereby have accrued to tomatoes with no justification. The word was first printed in 1578.

low mull. A meat-and-vegetable stew whose ingredients vary according to the person preparing it. The origin of the word may derive from a colloquial verb, *to mull,* "to make a muddle or mess" of something, used at least since 1821. Or the name may be a shortened form of *mulligan stew.* A recipe, reproduced below, from Marjorie Mosser's *Foods of Old New England* (1957) notes that, despite its lengthy cooking time, "the time is thought by New England huntsmen to be well spent."

> Cut beef or pork into cubes. Fill a pot halfway with water and bring to a boil. Add raw onions, celery, and sliced bacon. Fry more bacon and add to pot. Sauté onions in bacon fat and add to pot. Add 1 can tomatoes, 1 can condensed tomato soup, the juice of 1 lemon, garlic, allspice, cloves, paprika, salt, pepper, pickled red pepper, Tabasco sauce, Worcestershire sauce, ketchup, potatoes, and then the cubes of meat. Add butter, olive oil, sherry, and raw onions. Cook for 3 or 4 hr. and serve on a bed of rice.

lox. A Jewish-American version of smoked SALMON. The word is from the Yiddish, *laks,* from Middle High German, *lahs.* According to Leo Rosten in *The Joys of Yiddish* (1968), "the luxurious practice of eating *lox,* thought to be so typical of East European Jews, actually began for them in New York. *Lox* was entirely unknown among European Jews and is rare to this day there —and in Israel." The word first appeared in English in 1941.

Lox is sliced very thin and usually served on a bagel with butter and cream cheese. The preferred variety is the Pacific salmon cured in saturated salt brine.

lumberjack pie. A pie made with various vegetables and deer meat. The term is used by New England loggers.

lunch. The midday meal. The word originally referred to a chunk or lump of something, including perhaps a slice of food, and in its first appearance in print (1591) it was related to the Spanish, *lonja,* for "slice." By the seventeenth century it was often used to designate a piece of food or a light meal, but when the word *lunch* first appeared in print as an abbreviation of *luncheon* (1812), it was considered something of a fashionable colloquialism. Americans picked up the word quickly, however, and used it as a synonym for the midday meal taken quickly, as a worker might on the job. Before the 1820s the midday meal was called DINNER and the evening meal *supper.*

The midday meal at home was generally the heaviest meal of the day, but workers found neither the time nor the stomach for lengthy dinners while on the job, and so the custom of eating a sandwich or going to a lunch room or CAFETERIA became common, although more affluent business people of the nineteenth century would indulge in lavish midday dinners at city restaurants where six or more courses were not unusual.

For most Americans today lunch is a fairly light meal, with the largest meal of the day saved for the evening. The tax-deductible "business lunch" has become an American institution, and opponents of lengthy, lavish restaurant lunches at taxpayers' expense have called such exemptions unfair to the average wage earner who may not deduct the cost of his lunch. Such business lunches have been characterized as "three-martini lunches" since the 1960s, sarcastically referring to the number of cocktails imbibed. The administrations of both Presidents Jimmy Carter and Ronald Reagan tried unsuccessfully to limit the business lunch as a tax deduction, but the business and restaurant communities argued successfully that lunch in a restaurant was most conducive to doing business, and, they insisted, the days of the three-martini lunch had been replaced by meals accompanied by white wine or bottled water.

lunch counter. An inexpensive, casual restaurant serving simple food at a counter, although most lunch counters also have tables or booths. The term, first recorded in 1869, has many synonyms—*lunch stand, hash house, short-order restaurant, snack bar, lunchroom,* and *lunch,* superseded in the 1930s by *luncheonette.* The term may also be used to refer to a "diner," which is a lunch counter set up in an old railroad dining car.

Lunch counters have provided etymologists and linguists with one of the richest stores of American slang, cant, and jargon, usually based on a form of verbal shorthand bandied back and forth between waiters and cooks. Some terms have entered the familiar language of most Americans—*BLT* (a bacon, lettuce, and tomato sandwich), *stack* (an order of pancakes), *mayo* (mayonnaise), and others—but most remain part of a bewildering and colorful language specific to the workers in such establishments. The following list is culled from various sources, including Supplement Two of *The American Language* (1948), by H. L. Mencken, who wrote, "The queer lingo used in transmitting orders from table to kitchen was noted by a writer in the *Detroit Free Press* so long ago as Jan. 7, 1852, *e.g., fried bedpost, mashed tambourine* and *roasted stirrups.* In 1876 J. G. Holland, then editor of *Scribner's,* discussed it in his Everyday Topics, p. 386. It was richly developed by the colored waiters who flourished in the 1870s and 80s, but is now pretty well confined to the waitresses and countermen who glorify third-rate eating-houses."

Many of these terms are shared by workers in soda fountains or ice cream stores.

AC. A sandwich made with American cheese.
Adam and Eve on a raft. Two poached eggs on toast.
Adam's ale. Plain water.
alive. Raw (said of oysters).

all the way. A sandwich made with lettuce, mayonnaise, onion, and butter; also, a chocolate cake with chocolate ice cream.

Angel food cake and wine. Also, "Lord's Supper." Bread and water.

A-pie. Apple pie.

Arizona. Buttermilk (so called, according to Robert Shafer in "The Language of West Coast Culinary Workers," *American Speech* [April 1946], because "a waitress thinks any man drinking buttermilk ought to be in Arizona for his health").

axle grease. Also, "skid grease." Butter.

baby. Also, "moo juice," "Sweet Alice," and "cow juice." Milk.

belch water. Seltzer or soda water.

bird-seed. Cereal.

black stick. A chocolate ice cream cone.

blonde. Coffee with cream.

blue-bottle. Bromo Seltzer, a trademark for a digestive aid of bicarbonated soda that comes in a blue bottle.

blue plate special. A dish of meat, potato, and vegetable served on a plate (usually blue) sectioned in three parts.

Bossy in a bowl. Beef stew, so called because "Bossy" was a common name for a cow.

bottom. Ice cream added to a drink.

bowl of red. A bowl of chili con carne, so called for its deep-red color.

bow wow. A hot dog.

break it and shake it. Also, "make it cackle." Put a raw egg in a drink, especially a milkshake.

breath. An onion.

bridge. Also, "bridge party." Four of anything, so called from the card-game hand of bridge.

bucket of hail. A small glass of ice.

bullets. Also called "whistleberries" or "Saturday nights." Baked beans, so called because of the supposed flatulence they cause.

bun pup. A hot dog.

burn it and let it swim. A float, made with chocolate syrup and ice cream floated on top.

burn one. Put a hamburger on the grill or add chocolate.

burn one all the way. A chocolate milk shake with chocolate ice cream.

burn the British. A toasted English muffin.

Canary Island special. Vanilla soda with chocolate ice cream.

carfare. Also, "subway." A worker's tip or percentage of the check as a gratuity. The meaning referred to the money to provide transportation home.

cat's eyes. TAPIOCA.

CB. A cheeseburger.

China. Rice pudding.

chopper. A table knife.

city juice. Water.

CJ. A cream cheese and jelly sandwich.

clean up the kitchen. Hash or hamburger.

c.o. highball. Castor oil. See HIGHBALL.

coke pie. Coconut pie.

cold spot. A glass of iced tea.

Coney Island chicken. Also, "Coney Island." A hot dog, so called because hot dogs were popularly associated with the Coney Island stands at which they were sold.

cowboy. A western omelette or sandwich.

cow feed. A salad.

creep. Draft beer.

crowd. Three of anything (possibly from the old saying, "Two's company, three's a crowd").

deadeye. Poached egg.

dog and maggot. Cracker and cheese.

dog biscuit. Cracker.

dog's body. A pudding of pea soup and flour or hardtack.

dough well done with cow to cover. Buttered toast.

draw one. Coffee.

easy over. Eggs turned over and cooked briefly.

echo. Repeat the order.

eighty-one. A glass of water.

eighty-six. "Do not sell to that cusomer" or "The kitchen is out of the item ordered." Perhaps from the practice at Chumley's Restaurant in New York City of throwing rowdy customers out the back door, which is No. 86 Bedford Street. The term predates its first appearance in print circa 1967.

Eve with a lid on. Apple pie, referring to the biblical Eve's tempting apple and to the crust that covers it.

fifty-five. A glass of root beer.

fifty-one. Hot chocolate.

filet. Served with ice cream.

first lady. Spare ribs, a pun on Eve's being made from Adam's spare rib.

five. A large glass of milk.

fly cake. Also "roach cake." A raisin cake or huckleberry pie.

forty-one. Lemonade.

Frenchman's delight. Pea soup.

gentleman will take a chance. Hash.

GAC. Grilled American cheese sandwich. This was also called "jack" (from the pronunciation of GAC); a "Jack Benny" (after a radio comedian) was cheese with bacon.

George Eddy. A customer who leaves no tip.

go for a walk. An order to be packed and taken out.

gravel train. Sugar bowl.

graveyard stew. Milk-toast.

groundhog. Hot dog.

hamlette. An omelette made with ham.

Harlem. Also, "Harlem soda." A soda made with chocolate, named after the section of New York City known for its predominantly black population. A "Harlem midget" was a small chocolate soda.

hemorrhage. Ketchup.

high and dry. A plain sandwich without butter, mayonnaise, or lettuce.

high, yellow black and white. A chocolate soda with vanilla ice cream.

hold the hail. No ice.

hops. Malted milk powder.

hot cha. Hot chocolate.

hot spot. Tea.

houseboat. A banana split, made with ice cream and sliced bananas.

ice the rice. Add ice cream to rice pudding.

in the alley. Serve as a side dish.

in the hay. A strawberry milkshake, punning on hay as straw.

Irish turkey. Corned beef and cabbage.

java. Coffee.

jerk. An ice cream soda, referring to the jerking motion of a seltzer spigot.

joe. Coffee.

L.A. Serve an item with ice cream.

looseners. Prunes, so called because of their supposed laxative effect.

lumber. A toothpick.

maiden's delight. Cherries, so called because *cherry* is an old slang term for the maidenhead.

make it virtue. Add cherry syrup to a cola soda.

mama. Marmalade.

M.D. Dr. Pepper, a commercially produced soda.

Mike and Ike. Also, "the twins." Salt and pepper shakers.

Mud. Also, "murk." Black coffee or chocolate ice cream.

Murphy. Potatoes, so called because of their association with the Irish diet of potatoes, Murphy being a common Irish name.

natural. A commercially produced soda called "7-Up," from the combination of 5 and 2, called a "natural" in the dice game craps.

Noah's boy. A slice of ham, because Ham was Noah's second son.

no cow. Without milk.

O.J. Also, "Oh gee." Orange juice.

on the hoof. Meat done rare.

on wheels. An order to be packed and taken out.

pair of drawers. Two cups of coffee.

Pittsburgh. Toast or something burning, so called because of the smokestacks evident in Pittsburgh, a coal-producing and steel-mill city.

PT. A pot of tea.

put out the lights and cry. Liver and onions. Also, "nigger and halitosis," a racial slur of the era.

radio. A tuna fish salad sandwich on toast, punning on "tuna down," which sounds like "turn it down," as one would the radio knob.

sand. Sugar.

seaboard. Item wrapped for take-out, referring to "cardboard."

sea dust. Salt.

shoot it yellow. Add lemon syrup or slice of lemon to a cola soda.

shoot one from the south. Make an especially strong cola soda.

sinkers and suds. Doughnuts and coffee.

squeeze one. Orange juice.

stretch one. A cola soda.

through Georgia. Add chocolate syrup; because of Georgia's large black population.

to the left. Lemon syrup, customarily set to the left of the cola-syrup pump.

to the right. Cherry syrup, customarily set to the right of the cola-syrup pump.

twenty-one. Limeade.

Vermont. Maple syrup, because maple syrup comes primarily from Vermont.

warts. Olives.

wreath. Cabbage.

yum-yum. Sugar.

zeppelins in a fog. Sausages in mashed potatoes.

macadamia nut. Also, "Queensland nut." The seed of a tropical tree, *Macadamia ternifolia,* originally native to Australia but now forming the third largest crop of Hawaii. The tree is named after chemist John MacAdam (1827–1865), who promoted the plant's cultivation in Australia. The alternate name, "Queensland nut," derives from Australia's second-largest state.

According to S. A. Clark in *All the Best in Hawaii* (1949), the nut was brought to Honolulu, Hawaii, from Tasmania about 1890 by E. W. Jordan. The name *macadamia* was first used in print in 1904.

Originally the tree was used merely as an ornamental shrub, but researchers at the Hawaiian Agricultural College forty years later discovered the nuts' culinary value, leading to widespread planting for commercial harvesting.

Today macadamia nuts are usually roasted and salted, eaten as snacks, or used in salads and fish and meat preparations.

macaroni. A form of dried pasta that is usually tubular or shaped in some way, in contrast to the long, thin shape of spaghetti. The word is of Italian origins (from *maccherone,* which means "mixture of elements" but serves as a name for the pasta too) and has been known in English at least since the sixteenth century. (The reference to macaroni in the famous eighteenth-century American song, "Yankee Doodle Dandy,"—"stuck a feather in his hat and called it macaroni"—refers not to the pasta but to a slang term of the period for a fop or dandy, after the London Macaroni Club.) Thomas Jefferson sent his emissary, William Short, to Naples for a macaroni machine (though Short returned with a spaghetti machine instead).

Macaroni is eaten in America in the traditional Italian manner—that is, with various sauces (most often tomato)—but a specifically American dish is macaroni and cheese, which is made by placing a layer of boiled macaroni in a buttered baking dish and grating over it American, Cheddar, or Swiss cheese, then baking it until the cheese has melted. This dish was first made in the nineteenth century and continues to be very popular.

Macaroni salad is a dish of cold macaroni to which is added mayonnaise and various vegetables and seasonings, like celery, onions, peppers, tomatoes, chives, and pimiento.

McGinty. A pie made in Oregon from dried apples. The recipe below is from Mrs. John James Burton and dates back to the 1870s. The name probably derives from a common name for loggers and miners in the Northwest territory of those days.

> Wash, core, and skin 1 lb. dried apples, then soak overnight. Stew in water to cover, purée or push through a sieve, then add enough brown sugar to make a rich, thickened purée. Cool, add 1 1/2 tbs. cinnamon. Line a pie pan with a pastry crust, place fruit mixture in crust, cover with top crust, make gashes in top crust, and press edges together. Cook in hot oven for 15 min., then reduce heat. Serve hot with cream.

mackerel. Any of a wide variety of fishes in the family Scombridae. As a food fish the Atlantic mackerel *(Scomber scombrus)* is the most important mackerel in the United States. It travels in large schools, ranging from Labrador to Cape Hatteras, and is known for its swiftness. The name *mackerel* derives from Old French, *maquerel,* and has been found in print in English since the beginning of the fourteenth century.

Most American mackerel used to be salted, much of which was done in Boston; hence, salted mackerel was called "Boston mackerel." It was not until ships stocked ice in their holds that the mackerel was sold fresh. In 1885 a fishery at Eastport, Maine, brought in a hundred million pounds. As with other fish of this era, overworking the sea resulted in a decline in population, with the result that the mackerel has gone through cycles of scarcity and proliferation. The most important species for the table include the cero *(Scomberomorus regalis),* also called "painted mackerel"; chub mackerel *(Scomber japonicus),* also called "hardhead"; king mackerel *(Scomberomorus cavalla),* also called "kingfish" and "cero"; Spanish mackerel *(S. maculatus);* and "wahoo" *(Acanthocybium solandri),* whose etymological roots are unknown and which in Hawaii is known as *ono* ("sweet").

maggot. Cowboy term for sheep. The derogatory nature of the name was due to the cattle-raising cowboy's intense hatred for the sheep ranchers whose herds took up much of the valuable grazing land of the Great Plains.

maid of honor. A custard tart made with damson plums or other fruits. This popular early-American dish came from England, where the tarts were named after the maids of honor at the court of Elizabeth I (queen 1558–1603) and are associated with the palace at Richmond, Surrey.

> Roll out pastry for a 2-crust pie and line 10 tart shells about 3 1/2-in. in diameter. Beat 2 eggs with 1/2 cup sugar. Soften 1/2 cup almond paste with 2 tbs. dry sherry, 2 tbs. butter, and 1 tbs. lemon juice and add to egg batter. Mix in 2 tbs. flour. Drop a tsp. of fruit jam or preserves into each shell, pour batter over each, and bake for 45 min. at 350°.

mai tai. A cocktail made from lime, curaçao, and rum, created in 1944 by Victor "Trader Vic" Bergeron, then owner of an Oakland, California, restaurant called Hinky Dinks and later owner of Trader Vic's. In his book, *Trader Vic's Bartender's Guide* (revised, 1972), Bergeron tells how the drink came about:

> I was at the service bar in my Oakland restaurant. I took down a bottle of seventeen-year-old rum. It was J. Wray Nephew from Jamaica—surprisingly golden in color, medium bodied, but with the rich pungent flavor particular to the Jamaican blends. The flavor of this great rum wasn't meant to be overpowered with heavy additions of fruit juices and flavorings. I took a fresh lime, added some orange curacao from Holland, a dash of rock candy syrup, and a dollop of French orgeat for its subtle almond flavor. I added a generous amount of shaved ice and shook it vigorously by hand to produce the marriage I was after. Half the lime shell went into each drink for color; and I stuck in a branch of fresh mint. I gave the first two of them to Ham and Carrie Guild, friends from Tahiti, who were there that night.
>
> Carrie took one sip and said, "Mai Tai—Roa Aé." In Tahitian this means "Out of this world—the best." Well, that was that. I named the drink "Mai Tai." . . .
>
> Anybody who says I didn't create this drink is a dirty stinker.
>
> Squeeze juice of 1 lime into an old-fashioned glass, add 1/2 oz. orange curaçao, 1/4 oz. rock candy syrup, 1/4 oz. orgeat syrup, 1 oz. dark Jamaican rum, and 1 oz. Martinique rum. Shake with shaved ice. Decorate with lime shell, fresh mint, and fruit stick.

maître d'. A shortened form of *maître d'hôtel,* a head waiter who usually takes reservations at a restaurant and decides who sits where. The term is from the French, meaning "master of the hotel," first printed in English in 1950.

Maître d'hôtel butter. A classic preparation of butter mixed with pepper, salt, lemon juice, chopped parsley, and occasionally with chives. It is used as a garnish for grilled meats and fish.

malasado. A puffy pastry made from an egg batter that is deep-fried and rolled in sugar. It is based on similar pastries brought by the Portuguese immigrants, and each year the Portuguese Society of Hawaii holds a contest to make the best version. The term is from two Portuguese words, *mal,* "bad," and *assado,* "baked," and may have originated when scraps of Portuguese sweet bread dough were hastily thrown into hot fat, thereby making a "badly baked" bread.

manapua. A dough bun, filled with pork, bean paste, and other stuffings, that is steamed and usually sold from roadside stands in Hawaii.

Man at the pot! A cowboy expression directed at a colleague who went to refill his cup with coffee. On hearing this call he was duty bound to fill his companions' cups too.

Manhattan. Also, "Manhattan cocktail" or "manhattan." An alcoholic drink of bourbon or blended whiskey with sweet vermouth and bitters.

The *Oxford English Dictionary* traces the drink back to 1890, but a writer in the *New Yorker* in 1948 referred to seeing a Supreme Court justice drinking such a cocktail in a Washington bar back in 1886, and the drink is certainly older than that. Spirits authority Emanuel Greenberg traces the origin of the drink to a banquet given by Winston Churchill's American mother, Jennie, at New York's Manhattan Club: "It was a bash celebrating Samuel Tilden's election as governor of the state [in 1874], and the bartender whomped up a new drink for the occasion, thoughtfully naming it for his place of employment."

In the nineteenth century the drink had more vermouth in it than its drier modern version, of which there are several variations. The basic Manhattan recipe is as follows:

Stir 2 oz. bourbon or blended whiskey, 1/2 oz. sweet vermouth, and a dash or two of bitters with cracked ice. Strain and pour into chilled cocktail glass. Garnish with maraschino cherry.

A Perfect Manhattan used 1/4 oz. sweet vermouth and 1/4 oz. dry vermouth with the whiskey, while a Dry Manhattan substitutes dry French vermouth entirely for the sweet vermouth. A Sweet Manhattan is synonymous with a regular Manhattan, except, perhaps, for the amount of sweet vermouth added. A "Scotch Manhattan," more often called a ROB ROY, is made with Scotch instead of bourbon or blended whiskey.

mannitol. A sweetener used in chewing gum and on low-calorie foods.

maple. A sweet syrup or sugar made from the sugar maple tree *(Acer saccharum)*, also called the "hard maple" or "rock maple." The word is from Old English, *mapel (treow)*. Although Europeans were familiar with various species of maple tree in their own countries, they were unaware of the American sugar maple's virtues as an agent for such a delicious sweetener as the Northeastern Indians obtained merely by slashing the bark and letting the sap drip out. This technique was learned by the early colonists, who found maple syrup and sugar a fine substitute for the expensive sugar imported from the West Indies. By the 1720s there was a good deal of "sugaring" of maple trees going on among settlers, who waited for the sudden thaw of the late New England winter when the sap would begin flowing through the trees. The colonists would gash the tree trunks, guide the sap into troughs, and boil it over fires.

Maple sweeteners became even more popular after the passage of the 1764 Sugar Act, which imposed high duties on imported sugar. After the Revolution, New England maple production boomed, providing products like maple candy, beer, wine, and molasses. Abolitionists urged their fellow citizens to eat more maple sugar than West Indian sugar in order to "reduce by that much the lashings the Negroes have to endure to grow cane sugar to satisfy our gluttony."

Maple products remained principal forms of sweetening well into the nine-teenth century, especially after tin cans became available in which to pack the syrup. Before then, most maple was turned into sugar loaves. Today most of the maple sugar and syrup produced comes from Vermont, though a good deal of the syrup used on American foods like PANCAKES is no longer maple syrup at all. In 1887 P. J. Towle of St. Paul, Minnesota, produced a blend of maple and sugar cane syrup that was less expensive than pure maple syrup. He packed it in a tin can, shaped like a log cabin of the kind his childhood hero, Abraham Lincoln, grew up in, and called it "Log Cabin Syrup." Since then many syrups have been produced from other sweeteners, and these must be labelled "pancake syrups."

The sugaring of maple trees has long been a New England social ritual. Both professional and amateur sugarers will head for a grove of maple trees, called a "sugar bush," to collect the sap, return to a "sugar house" to boil it down, and hope for a "sugar snow," that is, a late snowfall that prolongs the running of the sap in the trees. It takes about thirty-five gallons of boiling sap to produce one gallon of syrup. Often a late-season "sugar in the snow" party is held, during which maple syrup is poured on fresh snow and eaten like an ice.

Maple syrup is graded Fancy (the finest), Grade A, Grade B, and Unclas-sified, a dark syrup used in commercially produced maple and blended syrups.

Maple sweeteners are used on breakfast dishes like pancakes, WAFFLES, BACON, and sausage and in candies, cakes, ice cream, and many other confec-tions. Vermont and New York produce more than two-thirds of the country's maple syrup. In 1981 New York made 331,000 gallons and Vermont 545,000 gallons.

MAPLE SUGAR:
Boil 1 pt. maple syrup, then reduce heat to a simmer and stir for about 10 min., until candy thermometer registers 240°. Cool by stirring over a pot of cold water until it thickens to light taffy stage. Return to medium heat to liquefy again, pour into candy or other molds, cool for 15 min., and turn out.

maraschino. A cordial made from the fermented juice of the Dalmatian marasca cherry or a maraschino-flavored preserved cherry. The cordial runs 60 to 78 proof. The cherry is used as a garnish in cocktails like the old-fashioned and the Manhattan, as well as a flavoring for some cakes and cookies.

The word comes from the Italian, *marasca,* referring to the cherry tree from which the drink is made, and first saw English print in 1791.

margarine. Also, and correctly, "oleomargarine." A blend of animal and vegetable oils and fats mixed with milk and salt to form a semisolid often used as a substitute for BUTTER. Americans use far more margarine than butter.

The word comes from the French *margarique,* referring to margaric acid, a fatty substance, and its pearly color (from Greek, *margaron* pearl). *Oleo* too derives from the French, *oléo,* for "oil." Originally the product was called in French *oléomargarine,* first made by French chemist Hippolyte Mège-Mouries in the 1860s for a contest sponsored by Napoleon III to find a substitute for butter. By 1867 a French patent had been filed, by 1869 a British one, and by 1873 an American one. Dairymen in the United States fought the use of margarine as a substitute, but it was widely manufactured by the end of the century. American margarine is usually made from corn, cottonseed, or soybean oil that is refined, deodorized, hydrogenated, homogenized, chilled, and reworked with salt, then often enriched with vitamins A and D. Although regular margarine is of about the same caloric count as butter, diet margarines are sold. In the 1960s a low-cholesterol margarine made from polyunsaturated fats was developed, and the current popularity of margarine is largely due to this innovation.

Margarita. A cocktail made from tequila, Triple Sec or Cointreau, and lime juice. According to *The Tequila Book* (1976), by Marion Gorman and Felipe de Alba, there are several claims as to the creation of the drink. One story traces the Margarita to the bar at the Caliente Race Trace in Tijuana, Mexico, about 1930. Another credits *Doña* Bertha, owner of Bertita's bar in Tasca, Mexico, as having made the drink about 1930. Former Los Angeles bartender Daniel Negrete claims to have originated the cocktail at the Garci Crespo Hotel in Puebla, Mexico, in 1936 and named it after a girlfriend named Margarita. Still another story gives the credit to a San Antonio, Texas, woman, Margarita Sames, who used to order such a drink at the Flamingo hotel bar in Acapulco, Mexico, where she and her husband had a house throughout the 1950s. Yet another claim pinpoints the drink's birthplace as The Tale of the Cock restaurant in Los Angeles in the early 1950s. Whatever its origins, the Margarita was the cocktail that increased American interest in tequila in the 1960s, particularly among college students in the West. *Webster's Ninth* gives the first appearance of the word as 1963. The recipe below is from *The Tequila Book:*

> Chill a stemmed cocktail glass and dip the rim in salt. In a metal shaker put a scoop of chopped ice, 1 1/2 oz. tequila, 1/2 oz. Triple Sec or Cointreau, and 1 oz. lime juice (preferably from a Key lime). Shake gently a few times, strain into glass, and garnish with lime peel, if desired.

marinara. A spicy, quickly cooked pasta sauce of Italian origins but far more popular in American restaurants featuring southern Italian cuisines than in most of Italy. The first printed American reference was in 1948.

The name means "mariner's style" and is perhaps associated with the custom of plopping the fresh catch of the day into steaming cauldrons of tomato, onion, and spices for the evening meal.

> In a large skillet heat 1/2 cup olive oil. Add and brown 4 mashed cloves of garlic. Put through a sieve 3 1/2 cups Italian canned tomatoes and add to skillet. Add

1 1/4 tsp. salt, 1 tsp. oregano, 1/4 tsp. chopped parsley, and 1/8 tsp. pepper. Cook uncovered on medium heat for about 15–20 min., till tomatoes have broken down and thickened.

Marlborough pie. An apple-and-cream pie, sometimes called "Marlborough pudding" or "Marlborough tart" since there is no top crust. The pie is a Massachusetts specialty, often served at Thanksgiving dinners, although the origin of the name is obscure. There is a town of Marlborough in Connecticut, while Massachusetts, New Jersey, New Hampshire, and New York all have towns called "Marlboro."

Combine 1 cup applesauce with 3 tbs. lemon juice, 1 cup sugar, 4 beaten eggs, 2 tbs. butter, 1/2 tsp. nutmeg, 1 cup cream, and 1/4 cup sweet sherry. Pour into a 9-in. pie crust and bake at 400° for about 10 min., then at 325° for about 45 min. more. Cool till the filling gels.

marmalade. A form of thick jam that contains pieces of the fruit used. The name comes from the Portuguese *marmelada,* meaning "quince jam," ultimately from the Greek, *melimēlon,* "honey-apple," and first appears in English print in 1524.

Early marmalades were in fact made with quince, but Seville orange had become the preferred flavor by the eighteenth century and remains so today.

ORANGE MARMALADE:
Wash and scrub the skin of 1 lb. Seville oranges, scald in boiling water for 2–3 min., remove peels, and cut into shreds. Remove pith, divide fruit into segments, then place pits and pith in a cheesecloth bag. Mash fruit, then simmer pulp, peel, juice, and cheesecloth contents in 2 pt. water for about 2 hr. Warm 1 lb. sugar in a low oven. Reduce orange mixture by about one-third, remove from heat, squeeze bag, and remove from mixture. Add sugar, bring to a boil, add brandy or whiskey if desired, and cook rapidly for 10 min. Test a small bit by pushing with finger to see if it wrinkles. If it does not, cook for a few more minutes. Remove scum. Let mixture stand for 15 min. to form skin on top of marmalade. Stir, then pour into hot, sterilized jars to brim. Seal tightly or with paraffin.

marshmallow. A pasty, sweet confection made from corn syrup, gelatin, and sugar. It was once made from the root of the marshmallow plant (*Althaea officinalis*), from which the word derives its name via Old English, *merscmealwe,* "marsh" and "mallow." As a confection *marshmallow* dates back at least to the 1880s. In America it is used as a topping and filling for cakes, candies, and desserts and as marshmallow morsels packaged in various sizes to be used in salads, desserts, and hot chocolate or cocoa. Marshmallows are also regarded as a child's sweet treat when inserted on a stick and roasted over an open fire till crispy on the outside and melting within.

Soak 1 envelope gelatin in 1/2 cup cold water for 5 min. Bring 3/4 cup water and 2 cups sugar to a boil till liquid forms a thread when dropped from spoon. Add gelatin and let stand away from heat till cooled. Add a dash of salt and 1 tsp. vanilla extract. Beat till white and thickened, pour into pans dusted with powdered sugar to a depth of about 1 in. Let cool, then turn onto greased marble, cut in cubes, and roll in powdered sugar.

martini. A cocktail made from gin and dry vermouth and served with a twist of lemon peel. It is not known when the drink was invented, but the first claim for something called the "Martinez" was made in *The Bon-Vivant's Companion, or How to Mix Drinks* (1862), by "Professor" Jerry Thomas, a bartender at San Francisco's Occidental Hotel. Thomas's recipe called for shaking together 1 dash bitters, 2 dashes maraschino liqueur, 1 oz. Old Tom gin, 1 wineglass vermouth, and 2 small lumps of ice, all garnished with a slice of lemon. For those who prefer it sweeter, he advised, add 2 dashes gum syrup.

Others say that the drink was named after a bone-chilled traveler on his way to Martinez, California. Little credence is given to the association of the name with a Swiss breechblock single-shot rifle, used by the British Army as of 1871, named after its inventor Friedrich Von Martini (the drink was said to have the "kick of a Martini"). The *Oxford English Dictionary* lists the name *Martini* as first appearing in 1894.

Most probably the name is somehow connected to the Martini vermouth company (later Martini & Rossi), which had been making vermouth since 1829.

The early forms of the drink were composed of one part gin and one part vermouth, either sweet or dry, but as the years went on the martini became drier and drier. A pre-Prohibition recipe calls for two parts gin, one part dry vermouth, and a dash of orange bitters, and before World War II the gin had reached four parts to each part vermouth. After World War II the bitters vanished in the cocktail, and the vermouth was reduced to a literal shadow of its former self, with gin-to-vermouth ratios of five-, six-, or seven-to-one becoming standard. There is one drink, called the "Montgomery," that has a ratio of fifteen-to-one, which is so called after England's World War II Field Marshall Bernard Law Montgomery's preference for having fifteen troops for every German troop in battle. Another, called the "naked martini," is no more than gin on the rocks with a lemon twist. This mania for dryness has led to joke recipes that direct the bartender to pour in some vermouth, swirl it around, toss it out, and pour in the gin, or the command for the bartender merely to look at the bottle of vermouth.

Martini fans will argue over the merits of their drink having a lemon twist or an olive as the perfect garnish, but there is general agreement that the addition of a white sour cocktail onion makes the drink a GIBSON. The "martini sandwich," devised by John Kepke, of Brooklyn, consists of a martini between two glasses of draft beer.

The vodka Martini has become very popular in the decades since 1960, made more so by the fictional British spy James "007" Bond (created by Ian Fleming), who preferred vodka to gin in his martini.

Maryland stuffed ham. A dish of boiled ham with slits in the meat, into which is stuffed cabbage, onions, mustard, hot pepper, and other seasonings. It is available only in southern Maryland, and, more specifically, will be found in St. Mary's County. Traditionally served at Easter, the dish may date from the time of Maryland's founder, George Calvert, Lord Baltimore (1580?–1632), who reportedly enjoyed stuffed ham as a boy in Yorkshire, England. In an article on the subject published in the *New York Times* (December 5, 1982), Mary Z. Gray notes that "Stuffed Chine," calling for a ham cut to the bone to be slit and stuffed with herbs before being boiled, was a familiar recipe in Elizabethan England. She also records a story that Maryland stuffed ham may have originated in the early eighteenth century, "when a slave at St. Inigoe's Manor House dished it up as a special Easter treat for the Jesuit Fathers emerging from their Lenten fast."

Preparation of the dish is time-consuming, requiring that a whole corned ham be cut with ten or so deep slits into which a mixture of cabbage, kale, onions, mustard seed, celery seed, crushed hot pepper, and various other seasonings is stuffed by hand. More of the mixture is packed around the ham, which is then placed in a cloth bag, covered with water, and simmered for several hours. After cooling, the bag is cut away and the ham is refrigerated overnight, then served, usually cold, the next day.

masa. A finely ground, parched corn that has been treated with lime. Masa is a staple flour among Hispanic-Americans and is traditionally used in the making of southwestern breads, tortillas and tamales. The word comes from the Spanish for "dough." The flour can easily be found in Hispanic markets, where it is sold dry, and occasionally one might find the traditional blue cornmeal masa, which has a nuttier, richer flavor than the white.

matzo. Also, "matzah" and other spellings. Unleavened bread made in thin sheets perforated for easy breaking apart. Matzo is the traditional bread of the Jewish Passover, a holiday commemorating the flight from Egypt of the Israelites, who had no time to wait for their bread to rise. The tradition has been passed on, as commanded in Exod. 12:15, "For seven days you shall eat unleavened bread." The word is from the Hebrew, first appearing in English print in 1846.

Today matzo is enjoyed year-round by Jews and non-Jews as a snack or cracker.

mayonnaise. A mixture of egg yolks, oil, lemon juice or vinegar, and other seasonings. Mayonnaise is used as a salad dressing, in sandwiches, on canapés, in dips, and in some sauces and desserts. The name is French, but its origins are obscure. Antonin Careme in his *Le Cuisinier parisien* (1833–1834) insisted the name should really be called *magnonaise,* from the word *manier,* "to stir." *Larousse Gastronomique,* however, believes the word is a popular corruption of *moyeunaise,* itself derived from an old French word, *moyeu,* which means "egg yolk." The *Oxford English Dictionary* lists the origins as "uncertain," while the *American Heritage Dictionary of the English Language* mentions that the dressing is "possibly named in commemoration of the capture in 1756 of the city of Mahon, capital of Minorca, by the Duke of Richelieu." The first appearance of the word in English print was in 1841.

In France there are several classic mayonnaise dressings, but in the United States most people think of bottled mayonnaise, the first important examples of which were made by Richard Hellmann in 1912 at his New York delicatessen and by The Best Foods, Inc., in California. The two merged under the Best Foods name (now owned by CPC International) and now produce a "real mayonnaise" that is sold east of the Rocky Mountains as "Hellmann's" and west of the Rockies as "Best Foods." The two brands account for about 43 percent of all the bottled mayonnaise sold in the United States.

The F.D.A. Standards of Identity require that mayonnaise have not less than 65 percent vegetable oil, whereas mayonnaise-type salad dressings (sometimes called "spoonable salad dressings") must contain not less than 30 percent vegetable oil.

Beat 3 egg yolks until thickened and light yellow. Add 1 1/2 tsp. dry mustard, a dash of cayenne, and 3/4 tsp. salt. Beat in 1/4 cup vinegar or lemon juice, then gradually add 1 1/2 cups olive oil mixed with 1 1/2 cups salad oil. Beat in another 1/4 cup vinegar.

Maytag Blue. A blue-veined, tangy, smooth-textured cheese from Iowa made from the milk of holstein-friesian cows. The cheese was first made in 1941 by Robert and Frederick Maytag in cooperation with Iowa State University.

meat. According to the United States Department of Agriculture, "meat comes from the muscles of cattle, sheep, swine, and goats." Skeletal meat refers to the muscular cuts of tissue that had been attached to the animal's bone structure. A "meat food product" or "meat product" is "any food suitable for human consumption made from cattle, sheep, swine, or goats containing more than 3% meat." Meatloaf is a baked loaf of chopped meat and bread, first in print in 1899.

meat by-product. Also known as "variety meat." The edible and wholesome parts of cattle, swine, sheep, and goats, other than skeletal meat. The United States Department of Agriculture requires that meat by-products be listed on labels.

melba toast. Also, "Melba toast." A very thin, crisp, dry toast first made in 1897 by chef Georges Auguste Escoffier of London's Savoy Hotel for Australian opera singer Nellie Melba (1859–1931), after whom Madame M. L. Ritz, wife of the hotel's owner, César Ritz, named the dish.

The toast became a standard item served with salads or on a restaurant's bread dish, and in the United States it is now packaged in cellophane and sold at groceries.

Curiously, Nellie Melba does not mention the famous toast in her autobiography, *Melodies and Memories* (1925), nor does Escoffier in his recipe book, *Le Guide Culinaire* (1921).

Slice stale bread very thin, dry in a warming oven, then toast in a slow oven or under a grill.

mess. Although a *mess of food* may connote a sloppily presented meal of indiscriminate quality, the term *mess* actually goes back to the Latin *missus*, a portion or course of food. Later, in England, *mess* referred to a group of people eating together, and in America a "mess hall" or "mess tent" is a servicemen's dining room, for which a "mess sergeant" and "mess crew" prepared the food.

metate. A stone used by Indians, Mexicans, and frontiersmen to grind cornmeal. The word is from the Mexican, first printed in English in 1834.

Mexican breakfast. Southern term, intending a regional slur, for a cigarette and a glass of water, usually prescribed for hangover victims.

Mexican strawberries. Cowboy term for dried beans, which were often red.

Miami grill. A dish of veal chops, orange slices, bananas, and tomatoes, all grilled or broiled together. It is associated with Miami, Florida, and probably dates from the 1930s.

On a greased rack place 4 veal chops, 4 lamb chops, 4 salted tomatoes, and 4 peeled and buttered bananas. Broil for 10–12 min., turning once.

mickey. A potato roasted over an open fire. Mickeys were sold by street vendors during the first half of this century, and the name derives from the potato's association with the Irish immigrants, who collectively had been referred to as "micks" since the nineteenth century. The word's usage in print, in reference to the potato, dates back only to the 1940s but is probably much older.

Mickey Finn. Also, "Mickey." A bartender's term for a secretly concocted beverage designed to induce diarrhea in an unwanted customer. It is also a term for "knock-out drops," a drink that will induce unconsciousness in someone.

The origins of the drink are usually associated with San Francisco's Barbary Coast in the 1870s, when, according to Herb Caen in *Don't Call It Frisco* (1953), a discredited Scottish chemist-turned-bartender named Michael Finn helped shanghai sailors by serving them such potions. Sometimes these drinks contained Glauber's Salts, a horse laxative, or potassium tartrate, an emetic. There was even an infamous "Mickey Finn Case" involving the poisoning of an orchestra playing at a club on Fisherman's Wharf in San Francisco.

By the 1920s in some quarters *Mickey Finn* referred to a "double," or two servings of liquor at once.

mile-high cake. Generally, a tall cake of several layers, or cakes designed from recipes for baking at high altitudes. Mile High Ice Cream Pie was created at New Orleans's Ponchartrain Hotel.

milk. The white liquid produced by the mammary glands of cows, goats, sheep, and other animals, although in the United States almost all milk comes from cows. The word is from Old English, *milc.*

Although milk has been drunk by most of the world's people, especially infants and children, it was not known to pre-Columbian Indians for the simple reason that they had no milk animals, which were brought to the New World by the Spaniards and English. At first the Europeans drank mostly goat's milk, but, notes Richard J. Hooker in *Food and Drink in America* (1981), "by 1634 all the 'better' plantations of Virginia were said to have plenty of milk, butter, and cheese, and throughout New England milk was drunk, made into cheese, or eaten with samp, suppawn, fruits, and baked pumpkins."

Until the nineteenth century, however, milk was still treated with caution, especially in the South, where the heat quickly spoiled fresh milk. Plantation slaves drank skim milk, while their masters drank the first milk of the morning. In the North, where it was cooler, Dutch and German settlers enjoyed their milk, especially when made into cheese. Still, milk was frequently contaminated, especially in the cities, where dairies were often run by breweries that fed the cows on fermented mash and adulterated the milk with water, chalk, and other ingredients, leading to *Leslie's Illustrated Newspaper*'s pronouncement in 1858 that such actions constituted "milk murder." Indeed, even in the country people risked illness, even death, from a disease called "the milksick," "the milk evil," "milk poison," "the slows," and "the trembles" (from which Abraham Lincoln's mother died). Nevertheless, nutritionists and temperance leaders promoted the virtues of sanitary milk for their followers, and "milk men" delivered their product from "milk ranches" (later "dairy farms") by "milk wagon," pouring it into customers' "milk cans."

A safer form of milk was developed by Gail Borden (1801–1874), who had experimented with attar of meat and other concentrated foods but who made his fortune by creating condensed milk in 1856 after witnessing the deprivations of immigrant babies on a transatlantic crossing because the cows onboard had milksickness. Condensed milk was flavored with sugar and cooked under vacuum to remove 60 percent of the water, and it became standard issue among Civil War troops.

It was also during this period that French chemist Louis Pasteur (1822–1895) developed a process of killing off harmful microbes in milk. This became known as "pasteurization" and was widely adopted in the United States by the 1890s, so that European visitors marvelled at the amount of milk consumed here. State laws were soon instituted to regulate sanitary conditions in dairies—for example, inspections were mandatory in Newark, New Jersey, as of 1882. By 1908 25 percent of New York's milk and 33 percent of Boston's was being pasteurized. The milk bottle, patented in 1894 by Harvey Thatcher, was part of every American home, as was the store-bought milk carton by the 1930s. Milk was wholesome, nutritious, and available to everyone; it was sold fresh or canned, condensed or, as of the 1920s, "evaporated," which was not sweetened like condensed milk. Before long the United States became the world's leading producer of milk and milk products, with Wisconsin and California leading the way. By 1950 Americans were drinking six hundred glasses of milk per person per year, but in the years that followed consumption decreased, owing to concerns over too much fat and cholesterol in the American diet. When low-fat milk containing between 0.5 percent and 2 percent milkfat (whole milk contains about 3.8 percent) came on the market in the 1960s, milk consumption rose again. Skim milk (or "skimmed milk") has nearly all the fat removed.

About 45 percent of American milk is sold as fresh milk or cream, while about 20 percent goes to make cheese, 17 percent goes into butter, and 10 percent is used for frozen desserts. Slightly more than 2 percent is used for condensed or evaporated milk, and the rest for other uses.

Most American milk is homogenized, and some is treated with a relatively new process called "ultrapasteurization," by which the milk is heated for two seconds at 280°, which has the effect of killing some organisms but not affecting the taste. This process produces "long-life milk," able to be kept on a market shelf without souring for up to six months. Dried milk, powdered milk, or dehydrated milk is made from either whole or skim milk.

Buttermilk is made from the sour liquid containing some butterfat left after the making of butter. Markets also sell a cultured buttermilk made with a lactic-acid bacteria added to skim or partially skimmed milk. Acidophilus milk (or "LBA culture") is cultured with acidophilus bacteria and fortified with vitamins A and D. It is more easily digested by those people who cannot tolerate whole milk.

See also CREAM.

milk punch. Any low-proof drink made of liquor, sugar, and milk, usually served for brunches. Of rather recent origins, milk punches are an American streamlined version of EGG NOG and includes drinks with names like the "Milky Way" (1/2 oz. brandy, 1/2 oz. rum, 1/2 oz. bourbon, 6 oz. milk, and a dash of vanilla shaken with ice).

milk shake. A drink made with milk, a flavored syrup, and ice cream blended to a thick consistency. It is a favorite soda fountain item, only occasionally made at home.

When the term first appeared in print in 1889, milk shakes may have contained whiskey of some kind, but by the turn of the century they were considered wholesome drinks made with chocolate, strawberry, or vanilla syrups. In different parts of the country the item went by different names. One might order a "frappé" (from the French, past participle of *frapper,* to "strike" or "chill"), which in the nineteenth century, and to some extent today, refers to a frozen sherbetlike mixture of fruit juice and ice. *Frappé* is today synonymous with *milk shake* and often pronounced "frapp." One may also hear "frosted," "thick shake," and, in Rhode Island, CABINET. A "malted" is made with malted-milk powder—invented in 1887 by William Horlick of Racine, Wisconsin, and made from dried milk, malted barley, and wheat flour—and was promoted at first as a drink for invalids and children. By the 1930s a "malt shop" was a soda fountain not attached to a pharmacy. Date shakes are popular in southern California.

CHOCOLATE MILK SHAKE:
In an electric blender mix until smooth and thick 1 cup milk, 1/2 oz. chocolate syrup, and 2 scoops chocolate ice cream. To make a malted, add 1 tsp. malted milk powder.

mincemeat. Also, "mince." A mixture of chopped fruits, spices, suet, and, sometimes, meat that is usually baked in a pie crust. The word comes from *mince,* "to chop finely," whose own origins are in the Latin, *minuere,* "to diminish," and once *mincedmeat* referred specifically to meat that had been minced up, a meaning it has had since the sixteenth century. By the nineteenth century, however, the word referred to a pie of fruit, spices, and suet, only occasionally containing any meat at all. In colonial America these pies were made in the fall and sometimes frozen throughout the winter.

MINCEMEAT PIE:
In a saucepan combine 1 lb. peeled, cored, and chopped apples, 1/2 lb. raisins, 1/2 lb. suet, 1/2 lb. chopped walnuts, 1/4 lb. citron, 1/2 lb. currants, and 1 cup apple cider. Cook over low heat for 1 1/2 hr., stir in 1/4 tsp. each of cinnamon, ground cloves, nutmeg, and mace, and 1/2 cup brandy or rum. Let cool, then place in pie crust. Cover with top crust in lattice-work strips, bake for 45 min. at 350°, then cool on rack. Serves 8.

Minnehaha. A term for a variety of cakes, breads, or puddings that share little in common except the simplicity of ingredients and preparation. The name commemorates the Indian heroine of Henry Wadsworth Longfellow's epic poem, *Hiawatha,* published in 1855, after which the Minnehaha foods appeared in recipe books. There is scant mention of Minnehaha's culinary talents in the poem, only a reference to the "Yellow cakes of the Mondamin" served at the wedding feast of Hiawatha and Minnehaha. Perhaps the simplicity of the dishes connoted some idea of the kind of food Indians might have made in those days.

MINNEHAHA CAKE:
Cream 1 1/2 cups sugar with 1/2 cup butter, add 3 beaten eggs, 2 tsp. cream of tartar, 2 cups flour, and 1 tsp. baking soda dissolved in 1/2 cup milk. Pour batter into two

9-in. cake pans that have been buttered, lined with waxed paper, and rebuttered. Bake for 30 min. at 350°.

mint. Any of a variety of plants in the genus *Mentha* that bear aromatic leaves used for flavoring desserts, candy, gum, and other food. The name is from the Greek, *minthē*.

The two most popular varieties of mint, peppermint *(M. piperita)* and spearmint *(M. spicata),* are not native to America but were brought over early by the European colonists, and the species proliferated without much need of cultivation.

Mint jelly is a customary accompaniment to lamb dishes in America, and peppermint sticks are a favorite hard candy, often crushed to make peppermint stick ice cream, served with hot fudge sauce.

mint julep. A COCKTAIL made from bourbon, sugar, and mint. It is a classic drink of Kentucky and is traditionally served at the running of the Kentucky Derby on the first Saturday of May. The word was first printed in 1809.

The origin of the word *julep* is the Persian *gulāb,* "rose water," which is not an ingredient in the Kentucky cocktail but indicates a very sweet concoction known since the fifteenth century. Mint juleps were known in the United States by the end of the eighteenth century, long before bourbon became the ingredient most associated with the drink, and one will find mint juleps made with whiskeys other than bourbon, though this would be heresy in the state of Kentucky, where there is also great debate as to whether the mint leaves should be crushed in the traditional silver mug. Francis Parkinson Keyes once observed that, "like a woman's heart, mint gives its sweetest aroma when bruised. I have heard it said that the last instructions which a Virginia gentleman murmurs on his deathbed are, 'Never insult a decent woman, never bring a horse in the house, and never crush the mint in a julep.' " Recipes for both are given below:

Chill a silver mug (made in the South especially for juleps). Dissolve 1 1/2 tsp. confectioners' sugar in 1 tbs. water. Fill mug with crushed ice, pour in enough bourbon to cover, then stir in the sugar syrup. Garnish with sprigs of mint.

Crush together in a silver mug 6 mint leaves and 1 1/2 tsp. confectioners' sugar. Pack in crushed ice to the mug's brim, then pour in bourbon to top. Stir together, then chill mug in refrigerator for 1 hr. Garnish with mint leaf.

miracle. A nineteenth-century New England fried cookie.

Beat 3 eggs with 3 tbs. melted butter, 2 cups flour, a dash of salt. Roll dough very thin, sprinkle with sugar, and cut into even, large squares. Fold in two, cut into long strips about 1-in. wide, and twist together to form a link. Fry in hot oil till golden-brown.

Mission bell. A stevedore's term for a drinker of cheap wine, so called because of the widespread use of Mission grapes in such wines, especially in California.

mock turtle soup. A soup made from calves' brains to resemble true turtle soup. It is of English origins, made famous by the character of the mock turtle (with the shell of a turtle and the head of a calf) in Lewis Carroll's *Alice's Adventures in Wonderland* (1865). The recipe below is from Mrs. James T. Halsey of Philadelphia, as published in *Famous Old Receipts* (1908):

> Boil the brains of a calf in 3 gal. water and reduce to 3 qt. Add a bunch of parsley, thyme, onions, 1 tsp. allspice, 1 tsp. cloves, 1 tsp. mace, 1 tsp. nutmeg, black and red peppers, and 1 tsp. salt. Cook for about 40 min. at a simmer. Remove meat, cool, then mince the meat. Return to pot with 1/2 pt. sherry, 1/2 cup walnuts, and 1/2 cup tomato ketchup. Make a roux of flour, 1 tbs. butter, and 1 tbs. vinegar and add to pot. Reheat, serve garnished with brain fritters, 6 hard-boiled eggs, parsley, and pepper.

molasses. A sweetener made from refined sugar, including cane sugar, sugar beets, and even sweet potatoes. In the production of molasses, the sugar cane is crushed and the juice concentrated by boiling; after crystallization the residue that remains is molasses, the residue of the first boiling being the best grade for table use.

The word is from the Portuguese, *melaço,* as derived from the Latin, *mel,* for "honey." The first use of the word was in Nicholas Lichefield's 1582 translation of *Lopez de Castanheda's First booke of the historie of the discoverie and conquest of the East Indias,* which described "Melasus" as "a certeine kinde of Sugar made of Palmes or Date trees."

Molasses became the most common American sweetener in the eighteenth century because it was much cheaper than sugar and was part of the triangular trade route that brought molasses to New England to be made into rum, which was then shipped to West Africa to be traded for slaves, who were in turn traded for molasses in the West Indies. When France forbade their West Indies colonies to export molasses to the mother country (where they feared it would ruin the French brandy industry), the colonists began shipping molasses to America, and before long it was the principal sweetener of the British colonies. The Molasses Act of 1733 placed high duties on the substance, but widespread evasion of the tariff resulted in lowering tariffs in 1764. Nevertheless, John Adams said molasses was "an essential ingredient in American independence," because of England's attempts to tax the colonists in this manner.

Molasses remained Americans' most popular sweetener in the next century; it was used in drinks and confections and with meats, especially with pork, causing English traveler Frederick Marryat to write in his *Diary of America* (1839) that although the English "laugh at the notion of pork and molasses, . . . it eats uncommonly well. . . . After all, why should we eat currant jelly with venison and not allow the Americans the humble imitation of pork and molasses?" A sweetener like molasses was especially needed with salt pork in order to temper the strong taste of the meat.

By the 1830s new brides measured their popularity by the number of layers of molasses cake or stack cake the guests brought, and molasses cookies and candy were very popular.

By the end of the century molasses vied with MAPLE syrup and sugar as the sweetener of choice, but, when sugar prices dropped after World War I, both molasses and maple fell in popularity, so that today both are used as sweeteners in confections only when their specific taste is desirable, as in BOSTON BAKED BEANS.

Molasses used to be called "long sweetening," while a darker, less-refined variety was called "short sweetening." The darkest and least refined is called BLACKSTRAP or "mother liquor."

MOLASSES COOKIES:
Cream 8 tbs. butter with 1/2 cup sugar, then blend in 1 cup molasses. Sift together 4 cups flour, 1 tsp. salt, 1 tsp. baking soda, 1 tsp. cinnamon, 1 tsp. ginger, and 1/4 tsp. ground cloves. Roll out to 1/4-in. thickness, cut with cookie cutter, and bake on greased pan for 10 min. at 375°.

monkey bread. A sweet yeast bread, sometimes mixed with currants, formed from balls of dough, laid next to one another, which combine during baking. The origin of the name is unknown, though it has been suggested that the bread resembles the monkey puzzle tree *(Araucaria araucana),* whose prickly branches make it difficult to climb. There is also a fruit called "monkey bread" from the baobab tree *(Adansonia digitata)* of Africa, but there is no evidence of any connection between it and the baked bread. It is probable that the name comes from the appearance of the baked bread itself, which resembles a pack of monkeys jumbled together.

Nancy Reagan, First Lady of President Ronald Reagan, made monkey bread a traditional dish of the White House Christmas celebration; she claims that the bread is so called "because when you make it, you have to monkey around with it." The following recipe is from the First Lady:

Dissolve 1 pkg. dry yeast in 1/4 cup milk. Add 2 eggs, beat, then mix in 3 tbs. sugar, 1 tbs. salt, 3 1/2 cups flour, and 1 cup milk, and blend thoroughly. Cut in 6 oz. butter, knead well, and let rise to double. Knead again, let rise again for 40 min. Roll dough onto floured board, shape into a log, and cut into 28 pieces. Shape each piece of dough into ball and roll in 1/2 lb. melted butter. Butter and flour two 9-in. ring molds, place 7 balls of dough in each mold, place remaining balls of dough on top, and let rise again. Brush tops with 1 beaten egg, bake for 15 min. at 375°.

monkey gland. A cocktail made with orange juice, grenadine, gin, and an anise cordial. It became popular in the 1920s, when Dr. Serge Voronoff (1866–1951), a Russian emigré to Paris and director of experimental surgery at the Laboratory of Physiology of the Collège de France, was promoting the benefits of transplanting the sex glands of monkeys into human beings in order to restore vitality and prolong life. His book, *Life,* appeared in 1920, but by the mid-1920s his theories had been generally discredited.

The cocktail, which facetiously promised similar restorative powers, may have been invented at Harry's New York Bar in Paris by owner Harry MacElhone.

> Shake together with ice a dash of anise cordial, 2 dashes grenadine, and equal parts gin and orange juice. Strain into cocktail glass.

monkey rum. A spirit distilled from the syrup of sorghum. The first mention of this drink, which is produced in North Carolina, was in 1941.

monoglycerides. An emulsifier that prevents spoilage in bread and baked goods and prevents the separation of oil in peanut butter.

monosodium glutamate (MSG). An amino-acid flavor enhancer used in seafood, cheese, sauces, and other foods both at home and in processing. Monosodium glutamate is often found in Chinese food, giving rise to the "Chinese restaurant syndrome," meaning the sensations of dizziness, tightness of the chest, and burning some people feel when they eat food with MSG in it.

moonshine. Illegally distilled WHISKEY, especially that made with corn. The term—which refers to the time of day when the cover of darkness hid the activities of the "moonshiners," those engaged in such illicit whiskey making —dates back at least to 1860 and was later sometimes shortened to *shine* or *moon*. The number of moonshiners naturally increased during the Prohibition era. Moonshine is very potent, very raw, and often composed of dangerous elements, including battery acid, oil, and other ingredients used to speed up fermentation, thereby reducing the risk of being discovered. This unhealthy brew was called "scared wiskey." Federal revenue agents were called "revenooers" by the hill people of Appalachia and the Ozarks, where most moonshine was produced, and a great deal of folklore grew up around the people and object of this cat-and-mouse game, depicted in comic strips like Al Capp's "Lil Abner" and William de Beck's "Barney Google."

The melancholy romance of the moonshiner is evoked in this folk ballad called "Kentucky Moonshiner":

> I've been a moonshiner for seventeen long years.
> I've spent all my money on whiskey and beer.
> I'll go to some holler, I'll put up my still,
> I'll make you one gallon for a two-dollar bill.
>
> I'll go to some grocery and drink with my friends,
> Where the women can't foller to see what I spends.
> God bless those pretty women, I wish they were mine.
> Their breath smells as sweet as the dew on the vine.

moonshine. A dessert of egg whites and fruit preserves—a New England dish of the nineteenth century that has nothing to do with the illicit whiskey distilled in the South. It may be named after the silvery white flower called "everlasting" *(Anaphalis margaritacea),* which in the mid-nineteenth century was called "moonshine."

> Beat 6 egg whites, add 6 tbs. confectioners' sugar, then fold in 1 cup peaches or 1 cup jelly or preserves. In a saucer pour cream flavored with vanilla and sugar and place egg white mixture on top. Serves 6.

moose *(Alces alces* or *Alces americana).* A large, hairy, antlered, deerlike animal, standing up to seven-and-a-half-feet high at the shoulder and up to ten feet in length, that ranges from the coastal tundra of Alaska down to northwestern Colorado. Its name, according to the *American Heritage Dictionary of the English Language,* is from Natick Indian, *moos,* from Proto-Algonquian, *mooswa* (unattested), while Flexner in *I Hear America Talking* cites Passamaquoddy *moosu,* "he trims smoothly," referring to the manner in which the animal strips bark from trees. In 1603 the first printed reference to the animal was made; by 1637, it was called "Mose," and by 1672 "Moose Deer."

Although the Indians hunted moose for their meat, early white settlers showed little interest in the animal as food. Even so the moose's numbers dwindled in subsequent centuries, and the government finally had to step in to stave off extermination of the herds.

Today moose is rarely eaten, except as an exotic specialty in game restaurants. The meat is usually marinated and prepared as one would venison, or dredged in flour and pan-fried.

Moravian Christmas cookies. A traditional Moravian spice cookie served at Christmastime.

> Sift 2 1/2 cups flour, 1/4 tsp. ground cloves, 1/2 tsp. cinnamon, 1/4 tsp. nutmeg, and 1/4 tsp. salt. Cream 1 cup butter and add 1 1/2 cups sugar. Beat well, then add 2 beaten eggs and 1 tbs. brandy. Beat in the flour and chill for several hours. Roll out very thin and cut with cookie cutter. Place on buttered baking sheets and bake at 375° for about 8 min.

Mormon dip. Cowboy term for gravy made from milk. The name refers to the Mormons, members of the Church of Jesus Christ of Latter-Day Saints, who founded Salt Lake City, Utah, in 1841.

Moscow mule. A cocktail made from vodka and ginger beer. Its name refers to vodka's Russian heritage and ginger beer's zest, which combine to give the drink the kick of a mule.

The drink was created in 1947 by Jack Morgan, owner of a restaurant in West Hollywood, California, called the Cock 'n Bull, together with Jack Martin and Rudy Kunett of Heublein, a spirits distributor then trying to promote Smirnoff vodka. The drink helped spur the popularity of vodka drinks in the United States soon afterwards.

In a copper mug with ice cubes stir 3 oz. vodka, the juice of 1/2 lemon, a twist of lime peel, and a twist of cucumber peel. Fill with ginger beer. (Sometimes ginger ale is substituted.)

mountain dew. Illicit liquor, especially from the mountains of Kentucky and Tennessee, though the term originated in the whiskey-producing Highlands of Scotland. In America there is also a commercial soft drink, which is slightly lemony and carbonated, called "Mountain Dew."

The first American printed reference to the word was in 1878.

mountain oyster. The testicles of the bull, pig, or lamb. Sometimes called "Rocky Mountain oysters," they are usually breaded and fried in the West. The name derives from the general appearance of the final product and not a little euphemism. It is a term used both by cowboys and meat-packinghouse workers. See also CALF FRY.

Moxie. Trademark for a fairly tart or bitter soft drink concocted by Dr. Augustus Thompson in Union, Maine, in 1884 as a "nerve medicine." The word itself came to have the additional meaning of courage, nerve, or shrewdness by 1930, when Damon Runyon wrote in *Collier's* magazine, "Personally, I always figure Louie a petty-larceny kind of guy, with no more moxie than a canary bird."

muckamuck. An Alaskan Chinook Indian word for food. (When coupled to their word *hiu,* meaning "plenty," it means "plenty to eat." By extension, in American slang, a "high muckamuck" was not only someone who ate well, but also, at least since 1856, a very powerful politician. Today it also means any powerful person.)

muddler. A stick with a nubby end used to mash sugar or other ingredients at the bottom of a glass in making a cocktail or other drink. The word is from *muddle,* "to mix something up."

muffin. A small yeast cake usually sweetened with a bit of sugar. In England muffins were once called "tea-cakes," while in America muffins are served primarily for breakfast or as an accompaniment to dinner. Americans make plain muffins from flour, yeast, and sugar, but often add nuts and berries. Cornmeal muffins, blueberry muffins, and ENGLISH MUFFINS are particularly popular. Muffins are usually buttered.

The origins of the word are obscure, but possibly it is from Low German, *muffe,* "cake." The term was first printed in English in 1703, and Hannah Glasse in her 1747 cookbook gives a recipe for making muffins.

Combine 1 beaten egg, 1 cup milk, and 1/4 cup cooled, melted butter. In another bowl mix together 2 cups flour, 2 tbs. sugar, 1 pkg. yeast, and a pinch of salt. Add milk mixture and stir lightly. Add berries or nuts if desired. Bake for 25 min. at 400° till lightly browned. Makes 1 doz.

mulacolong. A stewed chicken dish of obscure Southern origins. In *200 Years of Charleston Cooking,* edited by Lettie Gay (1930), this dish is described thus: "The marching rhythm of this name is entrancing. Its origin is as mysterious as the flavor of the dish itself.

"A bird which has reached the age politely spoken of as 'uncertain' may serve as the *pièce de résistance* of any dinner and reflect glory on the hostess if it is prepared in this manner." The following recipe is from Gay's book.

Cut 1 fowl in pieces and fry until it is well browned. Then add 1 large chopped onion to the fat and allow this to brown also. Add 3 pints veal stock, which should be very strong, and 1 tsp. turmeric mixed with 1 tbs. lemon juice. Season with salt and pepper and cook until the chicken is tender. The stock should cook down so that it forms a rich gravy which should be served over the chicken.

mulberry. Any of a variety of trees in the genus *Morus,* especially the American red mulberry *(M. rubra),* which bears sweet berries used in making jellies, cordials, and pastries. The word is from Old English, *mōrberie,* via the Latin, *mōrum.*

Other varieties include the Mexican or Texas mulberry *(M. microphylla)* and the black mulberry *(M. nigra).*

mullet. Any of a variety of fish in the family Mugilidae, having more than a hundred species worldwide. The name is from Latin, *mullus,* for the "red mullet" or "goatfish" *(Mullus surmuletus* and *M. barbatus),* known in Hawaii as *kumu.* In the United States two species are important: the striped mullet *(Mugil cephalus),* also called "black mullet" in Florida and "gray mullet" in other parts of the world; and the white mullet *(M. curema).* Both are usually pan-fried or baked and in the South are often served as a breakfast fish.

mulligan. Hobo slang for a stew made from any food he can find, but usually containing meat, potatoes, and vegetables. The term has been in use at least since 1904 and may be commemorative of some real or fictional cook of the hobo camps. It has been suggested, too, that it comes from *mulligatawny* (from the Indian Tamil word *milagutannir,* "pepper water"), an Indian curry soup still widely enjoyed. But the association with a typical Irish name like Mulligan seems true to an earlier meat-and-potatoes concoction of the nineteenth century called "Irish stew."

A "mulligan-mixer" is a cook in a hobo camp (or jungle). *Mulligan* was also a word for a bottle of hot pepper seeds and water once used in saloons to intensify the flavor of beer—a use of the term that may well refer back to the Indian Tamil word noted above.

mulligan car. Logger's term for a railroad car set in the woods from which the workers would take their lunch.

munchies. A colloquial term for a craving for something to eat, especially snack foods like potato chips, pretzels, and popcorn. It may also refer to the snack food itself. *To get the munchies* was a phrase that was first heard in the 1960s, largely among marijuana smokers, whose appetites supposedly increased under the influence of the drug, a meaning first noted in print in 1971, although the word itself has been around since at least 1917.

Muscadine *(Vitis rotundifolia).* A native American grape vine that proliferates in the Southeast. There are several species, including the SCUPPERNONG, sometimes called the "bullace grape." The word is a variant of *muscatel,* or *muscat grape,* from Latin, *muscus,* "musk."

Muscadine grapes were the first to be vinified in America, and as early as the 1560s the French Huguenots who settled in Florida were making wine from them. The grapes grow in bunches and are usually not picked but knocked to the ground with sticks.

Although Muscadine grapes and wines have always been made in the South and elsewhere, their greatest propagation in the nineteenth century was in North Carolina, where Colonel Paul Garrett built a very successful wine business selling Virginia Dare Scuppernong wine. During Prohibition the propagation of Muscadine fell, and only after 1965, with the help of the North Carolina state legislature and State University at Raleigh, has the grape again been grown significantly. Many new varieties have been developed, including the Mish, the Hunt, the Creek, the Higgins, the Tarheel, and others, most now marketed as wine under the general name of "Scuppernong."

mushroom. Any of a large variety of fungi of the class Basidiomycetes. The word is from the Gallo-Roman, *mussiro,* which became *musseroun* in Middle English.

When the first European settlers arrived in America, they found the woods filled with wild mushrooms of thousands of varieties, but the fear of eating poisonous mushrooms has prevented Americans ever since from developing any interest in them whatsoever, relying only on the cultivated white or brown *Agaricus bisporus* for almost the entire crop offered at market. This variety was first cultivated in France at the beginning of the eighteenth century, probably by Louis XIV's agronomist, Olivier de Serres, near Paris. For this reason the mushroom was called *"champignon de Paris,"* or, outside France, the "Parisian mushroom." The English got hold of this fungus by the end of the nineteenth century and exported it to the United States, where in 1926 Lewis Downing of Downington, Pennsylvania, discovered pure white spores growing among his mushrooms. He propagated these new types and spawned an industry that has made Pennsylvania the leading producer of mushrooms in the country, especially in Butler and Armstrong counties.

These were the only cultivated mushrooms in the United States until very recently, when some success has been achieved in the growing of shiitake (sometimes called "Black Forest mushrooms"), enoke, and oyster varieties.

There has even been some reported success with experiments in growing truffles in Texas and Oregon, though American wild truffles do exist. Also found wild in the United States are morels, cepes (sometimes called "King Boletus," "red caps," and other names), chanterelles, gyromitra (or "false morels"), honey mushrooms, chicken mushrooms (or "hens of the woods"), western puffballs, and Chinese wood mushrooms. While cultivated mushrooms represent far less than 5 percent of the approximately 470 million pounds of mushrooms produced in this country, there is now an enormous amount of wild mushrooms being exported by the United States to Europe.

Americans eat mushrooms in salads, in sauces, and stuffed with a forcemeat of various ingredients and seasonings.

mussel. Any of a variety of both salt- and freshwater bivalve mollusks having a blue-black shell. The name derives from the Latin, *mūsculus*, meaning "little mouse," and in Middle English the spelling is *muscle*.

Mussels have not been a major American food item except in communities with Mediterranean heritages. The most common mussel used in cooking is the blue or edible mussel *(Mytilus edulis)*, which ranges from the Arctic Ocean to South Carolina and has been successfully introduced on the Pacific coast, where it joined the indigenous California mussel *(M. californianus)*.

Mussels are usually eaten steamed or cooked in a stew. They are the main ingredient of the soup BILLI-BI.

mustard. A condiment in either paste or powdered form made from the seeds of any of a variety of plants in the genus *Brassica*, especially the black mustard *(B. Nigra)*, the white mustard *(Sinapis alba)*, and brown mustard *(B. juncea)*, also called "Indian mustard."

The word in Middle English was *mustarde*, derived from the Latin, *must*, meaning the "must" of new wine, which was usually blended with early forms of mustard paste.

English mustards have long been popular in America, the first of note having been blended with various spices by a Mrs. Clements of Durham, England, in 1729, and another prepared in the nineteenth century by Jeremiah Colman of Norwich, England. American mustards have generally been milder than European mustards and fall into two categories: a brown paste having some pungency and a yellow paste flavored with sugar, vinegar, turmeric, and white wine.

Mustard greens are the leaves of the mustard plants, and in America the brown mustard plant, sometimes called "leaf mustard," is used in cooking by southerners and in SOUL FOOD.

mystery meat. A schoolchild's term for cafeteria food that is unidentifiable because of poor preparation or ingredients.

nacho. A small TORTILLA chip topped with cheese and chili peppers or chili pepper sauce. The word may be from the Spanish for "flat-nosed," and was first seen in American print in 1969.

Naples biscuit. A light dessert or tea biscuit similar to a LADYFINGER. Its name comes from the Italian city of Naples, suggesting this was the sort of biscuit found there. Naples biscuits have been known in England since the seventeenth century and soon thereafter in America.

> Sift 1/2 cup flour and 1/2 cup confectioners' sugar. Add gradually 2 beaten eggs. Bake in biscuit tins or lady-finger pans at 375° for 15 min. Cool and cut into a dozen cakes.

natural food. A term, which first appeared circa 1917, that purports to describe unadulterated or unprocessed foods or foods that have been grown without the aid of pesticides or added enrichments. There is, however, no consensus as to just what a "natural food" is. The Federal Trade Commission, after several attempts, has not come up with an acceptable definition, although a survey by the agency showed that people were willing to spend, on the average, 10 percent more money on foods they considered "natural." An unofficial definition by the commission suggests that such foods are free of artificial or synthetic ingredients and "minimally processed," meaning that only the form of the food has been altered—for instance, changing the texture by grinding, drying, or pulping.

Because of the vagueness of the term, many manufacturers decide for themselves what they may or may not add. As a result many "natural" foods may contain sugar, guar and carob gum, carrageenan, vitamin C, monosodium glutamate, artificial colors, and a long list of other substances.

To some people the term is synonymous with *health food*.

navy bean. Also called "pea bean" or "beautiful bean." The navy bean is one of several varieties of KIDNEY BEAN *(Phaseolus vulgaris)*. The name comes from the fact that it has been a standard food of the United States Navy since at least 1856. An old popular song claims that "the Army gets the gravy, but the Navy gets the beans, beans, beans, beans."

ned. A nineteenth-century slang term (now obsolete) for pork. An 1833 account says the term was thus used in Tennessee for bacon, and by the 1840s, when the United States cavalry entered the western Indian territories, soldiers were called "Neddies," because of the preponderance of pork in their diet.

negus. A sweet alcoholic beverage made from port and citrus flavors. It is said to have been named after Colonel Francis Negus (died 1732), and was so called in print by 1743. Legend has it that Negus averted a political free-for-all by diluting a dwindling bottle of wine that, in the words of the *Dictionary of National Biography,* was "passing rather more rapidly than good fellowship seemed to warrant over a political discussion" between Whigs and Tories.

> Heat 1 qt. port and pour into warmed pitcher. Add 1 sliced lemon, 1 1/2 oz. brandy, 1 tbs. sugar, a pinch of nutmeg, and 1 qt. boiling water.

nene *(Branta [Nesochen] sandvicensis).* A large Hawaiian goose eaten by the natives there in precolonial times.

New American cuisine. A phrase that developed in the early 1980s to describe foods made by American cooks with American ingredients but according to the principles of preparation, cooking, and presentation promulgated by the practitioners of France's *la nouvelle cuisine,* a trend of the late 1960s and 1970s by which lightness, expensive ingredients, untraditional marriages of foods, and less cooking time apparently transformed classical French technique. In America many *la nouvelle cuisine* chefs opened establishments featuring similar methods in the 1970s and 1980s, while hard on their heels came young American cooks who adapted such techniques and philosophies to the American larder. Because California chefs have been the leaders of the movement, "California cuisine" has become synonymous with New American cuisine.

New Bedford pudding. A pudding made from cornmeal, flour, eggs, and molasses. The name commemorates the town of New Bedford, Massachusetts. The recipe below is from Elizabeth H. Putnam's *Mrs. Putnam's Receipt Book and Young Housekeeper's Assistant* (1850), published in Boston.

> Combine 4 tbs. flour, 4 tbs. cornmeal, 4 beaten eggs, 1 qt. boiling water, a pinch of salt, and 1 cup molasses. Bake for 3 hr. at a low temperature, about 300°.

New England boiled dinner. A very hearty dish of various meats and vegetables that was originally made with salt beef but that may also contain poultry. It was traditionally served at noontime, but begun early in the morning when the meat would be boiled with cabbage in a kettle over an open fire. Later the other vegetables would go in, and, notes Evan Jones in *American Food* (1974), "Some Yankees call for a sprinkling of cider vinegar, but the most common accents are homemade horseradish sauce or strong mustard."

The first printed mention of the term was in the 1936 edition of Fannie Merritt Farmer's *Boston Cooking-School Cook Book.*

> In a large kettle place a 4–5 lb. corned beef, 2 cloves garlic, 1/2 tsp. black peppercorns, and enough water to cover. Bring to boil, reduce to a simmer, and cook about 3 hr. Taste for desired degree of saltiness; if too strong, remove some of the simmering liquid and add fresh water. Add 1 chopped rutabaga, 10 red potatoes, 5 chopped carrots, and 1 chopped head of cabbage. Cook till vegetables are tender. Serves 8–10.

New York System. A term used in Rhode Island to describe an establishment that sells hot dogs or wienies. According to Elaine Chaika of the University of Rhode Island:

> The wienies look as if they have been cut from a longer sausage at both ends. They are about four inches long, and are covered with a meat sauce. . . . At true New York systems the man at the grill—and it's always a man—wearing a white dirty apron, takes the order, then puts the required number of hot dog rolls (not "buns" here) on his arm, puts the wienies in the roll and then ladles on the sauce. . . . Those places that sell these things always have "New York System" in their names, such as "Olneyville New York System," "Mary's New York System," "Joe's New York System." So far as I can see, the only requirement for using that name is that one must sell sawed-off wienies with meat sauce, and have counters but no tables, a somewhat greasy griddle, and be open late at night.

nigger baby. A late-nineteenth-century candy made of hard black licorice molded into the shape of a baby. Later these candies were also made in chocolate, but the racial colloquialism was dropped in favor of "chocolate baby" only later in the twentieth century.

niggers-in-a-blanket. A cowboy dessert whose name derived from the dark raisins in the dough. A similar pastry made with blackberries goes by the same derogatory name in Louisiana.

nioi. A Hawaiian "chili water," made with chili peppers, water, and salt, that serves as a seasoning for various dishes.

noodle. Any of a variety of thin strips of paste made from flour, water, and sometimes egg. The word is from the German, *Nudel,* and was first recorded in English in 1779. The word may refer to German or Pennsylvania Dutch egg noodles or to Italian pasta as well as to Chinese and Japanese examples. *Spaghetti* ("little string") did not enter the English language until the nineteenth century.

EGG NOODLES:
Combine 1 beaten egg, 2 tbs. milk, and 1/2 tsp. salt. Pour into a bowl of 1 cup flour in which a well has been made, mix to make a firm dough, and roll out very thin on floured board. Let rest for 30 min., then cut into strips about 1/4-in. wide.

nosh. A Yiddish-American word meaning to munch on one's food. Used as a noun, the word refers to a snack of some kind. A "nosher" is a habitual snacker. The word is from the German, *naschen,* "to nibble," and first appeared as a verb in English in 1956. A British reference to a "Nosh restaurant" appeared in 1917.

nougat. A confection made from sugar or honey with ground almonds (sometimes walnuts or pistachios). Nougat takes either of two forms: the first is white nougat, prepared from boiled sugar, egg whites, nuts, and sometimes dried cherries; the other is a caramel-based almond nougat molded into shapes. Either may be used in making candies.

The name originates in the Latin, *nux,* for "nut." There is no truth to the old tale that a woman of the French town of Montélimar (known for its white nougat) created the confection in the eighteenth century to the approval of her friends, who complimented her with the words, *"Tu nous gâtes"* ("You spoil us"). The confection probably goes back to the Middle Ages, when it may have been introduced to Europe by the Arabs via Spain. The word does not appear in print in English until 1827, in a recipe book on Italian cookery.

In the United States nougat is principally used as a filling for commercially produced candies.

WHITE NOUGAT:
Heat 1/2 lb. honey with 1/2 lb. sugar to 260° on a candy thermometer. Add 1 tbs. orange water and 1 stiffly beaten egg white, and melt together to 240°. Add 1 lb. blanched, finely chopped almonds that have been slightly roasted. Place mixture in tin lined with greased waxed paper and cover with another sheet of waxed paper, then place a weight on top. Cool and cut into shapes.

nun's toast. A dish of hard-boiled eggs with a milk-and-flour gravy served over toast. It is sometimes synonymous with FRENCH TOAST, and both terms date from the nineteenth century.

Cut 4 hard-boiled eggs into slices. Sauté in butter 1 chopped onion and 1 tsp. flour, then add 1 cup milk till thickened. Add eggs, season with salt and pepper, and pour over toast.

nutrition labeling. A voluntary listing of substances in a food product that is printed on the label. (Such a list is mandatory by Federal Trade Commission rules only on products for which specific nutritional claims are made, such as said to be low in calories.)

The listing must include: serving size and servings per can; the amount of calories, protein, carbohydrates, and fat per serving; and the percentage per serving of the Recommended Daily Allowances (RDAs) for protein, vitamins A and C, thiamine, riboflavin, niacin, and the minerals calcium and iron; although other nutrients may be listed too, along with the cholesterol level per serving.

oat. Usually used in the plural. Any of a variety of grasses in the genus *Avena,* especially the common cultivated variety, *A. sativa,* developed from the common wild oat, *A. fatua.* The word is from Old English, *àte.*

In the United States 93 percent of the oat crop is used to feed animals, with about 42 million bushels going to make breakfast cereals, especially the porridge called "oatmeal," which is made from rolled oats—that is, oats with the husks ground off—after which the oats are steamed and rolled flat, which maintains their freshness longer.

The United States is the world's leading producer of oats, grown primarily in Iowa, Minnesota, Illinois, Wisconsin, and South Dakota.

octopus. Any of a variety of marine mollusks of the genus *Octopus,* having a saclike head and eight tentacles with rows of suckers. The name is from the Greek, *oktōpous,* meaning "eight legs."

Except in Hawaii, where they are called *"puloa"* and *"he'e,"* octopuses are not consumed by Americans to any great extent, although Italian and Portuguese immigrants enjoy them, usually in a stew or salad. The Atlantic octopus *(Octopus vulgaris)* and the common Pacific octopus *(O. dolfleini)* are the two North American species. They are sometimes called "devilfish" because of their strange appearance.

OCTOPUS SALAD:
(From Mario's restaurant, Bronx, New York) Have fish dealer prepare 4 baby octupuses for cooking. Add the octopuses, one at a time, to boiling water and remove when water returns to the boil. Cool briefly, return to boiling water, let water return to boil, remove, and cool briefly. Repeat one more time. In another pot of salted boiling water place all octopuses and simmer for 30 min. or until tender. Drain and run under cold water. Remove any nonfleshy parts and beak if found. Cut into bite-size pieces, add 5 cloves garlic, 2 cups chopped celery, 15 pitted California black olives, 1/2 cup olive oil, 10 tbs. lemon juice, salt, pepper, 1 tsp. red pepper flakes, 1/3 cup chopped parsley, and 1 tbs. chopped basil leaves. Toss and let stand about 1 hr. Serves 12.

O.D. gravy. A rural slang term of the South and Midwest that refers to brown gravy as "ox dung gravy" or "olive drab" gravy.

Ohio pudding. A pudding of sweet potatoes, carrots, and brown sugar, popular in Ohio.

> Combine 4 eggs with 1/4 cup brown sugar, 1/2 cup cooked mashed sweet potatoes, 1/2 cup carrots, and 1/2 cup squash, 1 tsp. salt, 1/4 tsp. pepper, 1 cup bread crumbs, 1 qt. light cream, and 1 tsp. vanilla extract. Pour into buttered pan and bake 1 1/4 hr. at 350°. Serve with a sauce made from 1/4 lb. butter beaten with 1 1/2 cups confectioners' sugar, 1/2 cup heavy cream, and 1 tbs. lemon juice. Serves 6.

okolehao. Also, "oke." An 80-proof Hawaiian cordial made from cooked *ti* roots *(Cordyline australis)*. Originally the liqueur was made by an Australian, William Stevenson, about 1790, but today it is produced commercially in column stills. Okolehao is not aged. It may be drunk straight, on the rocks, or in various Hawaiian-inspired cocktails.

okra *(Hibiscus esculentus)*. A tropical or semitropical tree bearing finger-shaped green pods. The word, derived from a West African native name, *nkruma,* was in use in America by the 1780s. Okra was brought to America by black slaves, who used it in stews or soups and cut it up as a vegetable. The most famous use for okra is in Louisiana GUMBO, whose name derives from either of two African words for the vegetable, the Bantu *gombo* or the Umbundu, *ochinggombo.* In this dish okra is often used as a thickener. Okra is particularly popular among American blacks in SOUL FOOD.

old-fashioned cocktail. A COCKTAIL made with WHISKEY, sugar, and BITTERS. According to an unsigned article in the *International Review of Food & Wine* (November 1978), the birthdate of the old-fashioned cocktail

> could be no earlier than 1881, the year in which Louisville's aristocratic Pendennis Club first opened its doors to its members, one of whom was the then-reigning patriarch of fine Kentucky Bourbon, Colonel James E. Pepper. The Colonel's grandfather, Elijah, had claimed twin birthdays for his distillery and the nation, and for generations his "Old 1776" brand of Bourbon would continue to be flogged [*sic*] under the proud slogan, 'Born with the Republic.' One might therefore surmise that the Old-Fashioned, created at the bar of the Pendennis and introduced in the East at the original Waldorf bar to honor Colonel Pepper some time in the 1890s, got its inspiration in part from Elijah's label.

Most aficionados of the old-fashioned insist a sugar cube be placed at the bottom of the glass (which is squat and holds about six ounces), but others prefer to use sugar syrup. The term was first printed in 1901.

> In an old-fashioned glass place 1 sugar cube in 2 tbs. water, add a dash of bitters, and 1 1/2 oz. of whiskey (usually bourbon or rye). Add ice cubes and a slice of orange. Many prefer the drink topped off with club soda and a maraschino cherry, although some like the addition of a small amount of an orange cordial.

olive *(Olea europaea).* An Old World evergreen tree bearing a small fruit that is eaten on its own or pressed to make OLIVE OIL. The word is from the Latin, *olīva,* and the Greek, *elaia,* first appearing in English about 1200. (The American olive or devil wood [*Olea americana*] and the Californian olive [*Oreodaphne californica*] are of no real culinary interest.)

The olive has long been cultivated throughout the Mediterranean, where it is a major food of the people's diet. It was first mentioned in records of seventeenth century B.C. Egypt. The Spaniards introduced olives to America, bringing them to California by the middle of the eighteenth century after having planted three saplings in Lima, Peru, as of 1560 that were the ancestors of all that followed.

Thomas Jefferson planted olives in 1774 at Monticello, calling the vine "the worthiest plant to be introduced to America," but these efforts and his subsequent plantings in South Carolina in 1791 came to naught, for the plants all died.

Nevertheless, the olive trees flourished in California, where technology has bred a tree that matures in fifteen to twenty years rather than the usual thirty required in the Old World. Although Italy and Spain are the largest producers of olives in the world, California does produce a substantial crop, mainly in the San Fernando and San Joaquin valleys. There, in contrast to European methods of leaving green olives to ripen to black on the vine, olives are picked in the fall at varying shades of green, given a lye cure, and, if marketed black, are oxidized in a ferrous gluconate solution. California green olives thus treated with lye are called "Spanish-style olives." The predominant olives used in California are the large Sevillano, the Manzanilla, the Mission (used mostly for olive oil), the Barondis, and the Ascolanos. Olives are often sold stuffed with pimiento slices or already pitted.

olive oil. An oil that is pressed from olives. It is a ubiquitous cooking ingredient around the Mediterranean, and much of it is imported to the United States from Italy and Spain. Olive oil is mono-unsaturated and has a distinctive taste of the olive. In Europe the grades of quality range from Extra virgin (the finest, having only 1 percent acid) to Fine (1.5 percent), plus others that have more than 3.3 percent acid. Pure olive oil is extracted by solvent and refined, while blended oils may contain only 10 percent olive oil. None of this nomenclature is retained in F.D.A. Standards of Identity. Very little olive oil is produced in the United States; most of what is produced here comes from California.

onion. Any of a variety of pungent vegetables in the genus *Allium,* having a white, yellow, or red bulbous head, that is grown and eaten around the world in a wide variety of ways and as a basic seasoning ingredient to thousands of dishes. The word is from dialectial Latin, *uniō,* which in Middle English became *unyon.*

Under the term *onion* fall GARLIC, LEEK, SCALLION, and SHALLOT. There are about seventy species of onion native to North America, and Hernando

Cortés found onions in Mexico in the sixteenth century. Father Jacques Marquette, who explored the southern shore of Lake Michigan in 1624, survived for a time by eating a wild onion the Indians called *"chicago,"* better known as the "tree onion" or "Egyptian onion" *(A. canadense)*. Although the Indians and the pioneers certainly savored a wide variety of native onions, commercial production in the United States has largely been limited to one variety, the common or seed onion *(A. cepa)*, brought from Europe in colonial times and now principally grown in California, Texas, and Oregon. Some of the other onion varieties in the American market include the pearl or button onion, the Red Italian onion, the Prizetaker onion, the Spanish onion, and the Bermuda onion, though these last two names are often applied to a number of varieties.

Americans chop up onions for soups, stews, and sauces, boil them, roast them, sauté them, and use them in salads and as condiments. French-fried onion rings are very popular with meat dishes.

FRENCH-FRIED ONION RINGS:
Slice 1 large onion into rings, soak in a mixture of 1 beaten egg and 1/2 cup milk. Dip into flour mixed with cornmeal, then into bread crumbs. Fry in hot oil till golden brown.

on the rocks. A term to describe a beverage being served with ice cubes. The phrase has become common usage in this century.

open dating. A system of dating products that outlines the various dates at which an item was packaged and should be discarded and past which it is no longer fit for consumption. The "pack date" tells when the food item was packaged; the "pull" or "sell date" indicates the last date on which the product should be sold, although some storage time in the home refrigerator is allowed for; the "expiration date" indicates the last date on which the food should be eaten or used; the "freshness date" is similar to the expiration date, but may allow for home storage. The "shelf life" of a product is the manufacturer's or grocer's indication of how long a product will last.

opossum. Also, " 'possum." A nocturnal marsupial of the family Didelphidiae that is fifteen to twenty inches long, weighs six to eight pounds, has gray fur, and inhabits the woodlands of much of the United States. The only species in North America is the Virginia opossum *(Didelphus virginiana)*, found mostly in the Southeast, California, the Northwest, and west of the Cascade-Sierra Mountains (where it was introduced in the 1920s). Its name is from the Algonquian for "white animal" and was used as early as 1610 by settlers. The opossum is no longer widely used as a food animal, though it is still occasionally eaten in the South either stewed or roasted and is a nostalgic dish for many American blacks.

Rub opossum with salt and pepper. Brown 1 chopped onion in 1 tbs. butter or lard. Add the chopped opossum liver and sauté until tender. Add 1 cup bread crumbs, 1/4 tsp. Worcestershire sauce, 1 hard-boiled egg, and 1 tsp. salted water and mix.

Stuff the opossum with this mixture, place bacon strips on the back, place in a roasting pan with 1 qt. of water and cook uncovered for 2 1/2 hr. at 350°.

orange. Any of a variety of trees in the genus *Citrus* bearing round, yellow-red fruit that is eaten fresh, made into juice, and used as a flavoring. The name is from the Sanskrit, *nāranga,* which became "orange" in Middle English.

The orange is one of the most important fruits of the world and one of the oldest cultivated. Originating in the Orient, the fruit was cultivated in China as early as 2400 B.C. These were bitter oranges *(C. aurantium),* later brought to Spain, where they became known as the "Seville orange." The sweet orange *(C. sinensis)* also originated in China and was also brought to Spain, possibly by the Moors in the eighth century.

Christopher Columbus brought Canary Islands orange seeds to Hispaniola in 1493, and plantings by the Spanish and Portuguese soon followed throughout the Caribbean, Mexico, and South America. Some believe that Ponce de León brought orange seeds to Florida, but the first recorded evidence of the fruit on North American soil credits Hernando de Soto with bringing the orange in 1539 to St. Augustine, Florida, where the trees flourished until Sir Francis Drake sacked the city in 1586 and destroyed them. These grew back quickly, but commercial plantings were of only minor importance for more than two centuries. In the West, meanwhile, Spanish missionaries brought oranges from Mexico into California and Arizona, but there, too, they were not developed into a commercial crop.

In Florida only one significant orange grower was to be found in the eighteenth century. His name was Jesse Fish, who in 1776 shipped sixty-five thousand oranges and two casks or orange juice to England.

It was not until the United States acquired Florida in 1821 that orange growing became a profitable business for Americans. Before long the territory around St. Augustine and Jacksonville's Saint Johns River supported a thriving crop of orange trees, and by 1830 the major eastern cities enjoyed relatively dependable shipments of the fruit, although much of the supply came from the Caribbean, especially from Cuba, until the 1880s. It became the custom in the period before the Civil War to give children a fresh orange in their Christmas stockings, and it remains a tradition to this day in some regions of the South.

The Florida groves increased in size until 1835, when a February freeze struck the orchards, wiping out all but one hardy variety—the Indian River —raised by Douglas Dummett, from whose orchard the entire Florida stock was begun again (and still again, in the winter of 1894–1895, when the Dummet grove was the sole survivor of another frost). The Parson Brown orange, developed by Reverend Nathan L. Brown of Webster, Florida, became extremely popular as an early-season variety.

By the 1880s orange production was growing rapidly, owing to the development of refrigerated ships that could carry the fruit from California and to the building of railroads into the heart of Florida. Also, a new orange, the navel (so called because of the bump on the skin of fruit, which prompted people to call it the "belly-button orange") entered California in 1873 from Bahia, Brazil, by way of Washington, D.C. (and is in fact called the "Washington Navel"). By the 1890s, the navel orange had become commercially important to the developing California orange industry—at a time when Florida was already shipping more than a billion oranges per year. By the 1920s nutritionists were promoting the benefits of orange juice, a fruit especially high in vitamin C, and the drink became as ubiquitous as coffee on American breakfast tables to such an extent that the industry's motto—"A day without orange juice is like a day without sunshine"—carried both figurative and literal truth. Indeed, after World War II orange juice became so popular that the sale of fresh oranges dropped 75 percent. Today most oranges grown are processed into juice, which more often than not reaches the consumer as a frozen concentrate that is sometimes reconstituted and sold in bottles or cartons.

Today the United States produces about 34 percent of the world's orange crop, with Florida contributing 73 percent of that figure, California 23 percent, and Arizona, Texas, and other states the rest. Ninety-three percent of the Florida crop goes into orange juice concentrate. Before 1950 California produced most of the juice orange crop, and Florida most of the eating oranges, but this has now been reversed. Of all the oranges produced, the sweet orange is by far the most important; the bitter variety is used primarily in marmalade. The most common sweet oranges grown include the Hamlin, the Pineapple, the Valencia, and the navel, but hybrids such as the King, Temple, Orlando, Mineola, Robinson, Osceoloa, Lee, Nova, and Page are also well established.

The mandarin orange (C. reticulata), with its principal United States varieties such as the Dancy, the Clementine, the Murcott, and the Ponkan, is also called the "tangerine" (because it was first imported to Europe from Tangier, the earliest recorded shipment being in 1841). The tangelo (also called the "red tangelo" or "honeybell")—developed by the Department of Agriculture in Minneola, Florida, in 1931—is a cross between a Dancy tangerine, a Bowen grapefruit, and an Orchid Island grapefruit.

The United States Department of Agriculture grades oranges U.S. Fancy and U.S. No. 1, though these are not mandatory gradings and do not appear on most oranges.

The most popular culinary uses for oranges in the United States are in fruit salads, sherbets and ices, soda, and as a flavoring for many desserts, cakes, cookies, and candies. There are also several orange-flavored substitutes for the real thing, some in powdered form.

orange blossom. A drink made with orange juice and gin. The orange blossom was created during the Prohibition era to cut the taste of the gin and was sometimes called the "Adirondack Special" or "Florida," the first probably because illicit spirits could be had in the Adirondack Mountains and the latter because of Florida's great orange crop.

Combine 8 oz. gin, 4 oz. orange juice, and 1/2 oz. sugar syrup over ice.

oregano *(Origanum vulgare).* Also, "pot marjoram" and "wild marjoram." A strongly flavored herb common in Europe and North America that is used in Italy and the United States as a seasoning in tomato sauces, stews, and other preparations. It is similar to sweet marjoram *(Majorana hortensis),* which is milder and sometimes used as a substitute.

The word *oregano* is from the Italian, *origano,* and Spanish, *orégano,* ultimately from Greek, *origanon.* As a seasoning it was not popular in the United States until after World War II, when returning soldiers brought back a taste for the spicy food of southern Italy requiring oregano for reproduction.

Oregon tea. A brew made from boiling water and the shrub yerba buena.

Oreo. A trademark name of the Nabisco Biscuit Company for a cookie composed of two thin chocolate cookies enclosing a white cream filling. The word was apparently made up by the company. Oreos were first sold on April 12, 1912, and have sold 100 billion since.

orgeat. An orange-and-almond flavoring used in cocktails and food. The word is from the French, originally from Latin, *hordeum.* In the eighteenth century, when it became known in England, the syrup was made with barley, but later it was sweetened and used as a PUNCH. Orgeat may be bought commercially.

> Crush together 1 stick cinnamon with 1/4 lb. almonds. Add 3 cups milk, 1 cup cream, and 1 tbs. rose water. Sweeten to taste, bring to a boil, strain, and serve in punch cups.

OTW. An abbreviation for "on the way," used by restaurant maîtres d'hôtel to note that a party is late but has indicated it is in transit to the restaurant.

Oxford John. A simmered mutton dish named after Englishman John Farley, who compiled the *London Art of Cookery* in the eighteenth century. It became a very popular dish in Virginia during those years.

> Cut a 6-lb. leg of mutton into very thin slices. Season with salt, pepper, and a sprinkling of mace. In a saucepan sauté 2 tbs. butter with 1/4 cup chopped parsley and 4 chopped scallions (green onions) till soft, then add meat to sear it. Add 1 cup beef consommé, the juice of 1 lemon, and 1 tbs. flour dissolved in 1/4 cup water. Simmer and add 1 tbs. butter. Cook until tender. Serves 8.

oyster (Genus *Ostrea*). Any of several edible mollusks found in brackish waters, marshes, inland waters, even on the roots of submerged trees and coral reefs. The name derives from the Greek, *ostreon.*

Oysters have long been considered a delicacy and have been cultivated for at least two thousand years. The American Indians of the coastal regions enjoyed them as a staple part of their diet, and the earliest European explorers marveled at oysters that were up to a foot in length. Cultivation began soon afterwards, and Virginia and Maryland have waged "oyster wars" over off-shore beds since 1632. Although the oyster may have been an expensive delicacy in Europe, it was a common item on everyone's table in America. By the eighteenth century the urban poor were sustained by little more than bread and oysters. Colonial citizens dined regularly on chicken and oysters, and the mollusk was an economical ingredient for stuffing fowl and other meats. By the middle of the next century English traveler Charles Mackay could write in his book *Life and Liberty in America* (1859) that "the rich consume oysters and Champagne; the poorer classes consume oysters and *lager bier,* and that is one of the principal social differences between the two sections of the community."

Americans were oyster mad in the nineteenth century, and as people moved and settled westward, the demand for the bivalves in the interior regions grew accordingly. This demand was met by shipping oysters by stagecoach on the "Oyster Line" from Baltimore to Ohio, followed after the opening of the Erie Canal in 1825 by canal boats laden with oysters. Canned or pickled varieties were available as far west as St. Louis, Missouri, by 1856.

An American who sat down to a dish of oysters was not satisfied by a mere half-dozen. A man who could not put away a dozen or more was not considered much of an eater, and soup recipes of the nineteenth century call for quarts of oysters. Eliza Leslie's *Directions for Cookery* (1837) required two hundred of the mollusks for a stew, and there are records of prodigious feats of oyster consumption—not the least of which was the capacity of James "Diamond Jim" Brady (1856–1917), a wealthy financier who thought nothing of downing three or four dozen a day, in addition to soup, fowl, game, vegetables, desserts, chocolates, and gallons of his favorite drink, orange juice. (Lest anyone think the days of the great oyster trenchermen are over, consider that in 1972 Bobby Melancon ate 188 oysters in one hour at the Louisiana State Oyster Festival in Galliano, Louisiana.)

Every coastal city had its oyster vendors on the streets, and "oyster saloons" or "cellars" were part of urban life. In New York City, where $6 million worth of oysters were sold in 1850, one looked for red-and-white-striped muslin balloons lighted by candles and set above basement restaurants where oysters were shucked day and night in quarters that might be remarkably ornate or rather sleazy. The city's "Canal Street Plan," named after a street in lower Manhattan, was an invitation to consume all the oysters a customer desired for the fixed price of six cents.

Such places were frequented not only by men on the town but also by families, who ate to the rear, away from the bar. A few more refined spots, like Downing's on Broad Street, catered to a high-class clientele with dishes like oyster pie, scalloped oysters, and poached turkey with oysters.

On the West Coast oysters, including the indigenous Olympia variety, were just as popular. The dish called the HANGTOWN FRY was created at the Cary House in 1849 from what were then the two most expensive items of those Gold Rush days—eggs and oysters. A San Francisco miner accidentally created the "oyster cocktail" about 1860 (and by extension the "shrimp cocktail") by dipping the bivalve in ketchup.

Most oysters in those days were simply roasted, grilled, made into a stew, or eaten raw, with side dishes of lemon juice, mustard, and other condiments. The oyster cracker did not come along until about 1873.

Throughout the middle of the century oysters remained plentiful. Even when other foodstuffs were scarce in the Civil War, Union soldiers in Savannah sated their hunger with buckets full of oysters brought to them by the Negroes they had liberated. In 1869 more than eighteen thousand pounds of oysters were sold during the racing season by one Saratoga, New York, hotel.

Nowhere was the oyster more appreciated than in New Orleans, where several classic oyster recipes, like OYSTERS BIENVILLE and OYSTERS ROCKE-FELLER, were created. *The Picayune's Creole Cook Book* (1901) lists nearly forty recipes for the mollusk, including the famous city specialty, oyster loaf, or La Médiatrice ("peacemaker"), so called because a husband who had stayed out too late would bring one home to his patient wife as an offering of peace.

The demand for oysters was so high that by the 1880s the eastern beds began to be depleted. Chesapeake Bay then produced 15 billion bushels of oysters a year, but by the end of the century many cultivators had gone out of business for lack of product and new sources in the South were tapped to placate the American appetite. Also, the increase in water pollution in cities became so bad as to cause real concern that typhus might be spread by shellfish that had been soaked in local water after delivery and before serving. "The great century of the oyster was over," wrote Richard J. Hooker in *Food and Drink in America* (1981). "The joyous and uninhibited eating of oysters by rich and poor, Easterner and Westerner, Northerner and Southerner, had ended."

While many species of oyster are now brought in to the American market, only four species are of widespread gastronomic interest. The Virginia oyster *(Crassostrea virginica)*—also known as "blue point," "Cape Cod," "Chincoteague," "Apalachicola," "Kent Island," "Lynnhaven" and many others—ranges from the Gulf of St. Lawrence to the West Indies, is two- to six-inches long, has a gray, coarse shell, and is widely cultivated. The coon oyster *(Lopha frons)* ranges from Florida to Brazil, has an oval, ridged shell, and attaches itself to coral in shallow waters and also to trees—a phenomenon Sir Walter Raleigh described to Queen Elizabeth's court to their disbelief. (The name comes from their main predator, the raccoon.) The California oyster *(Ostrea lurida)*, native to the West Coast, is purplish black or brown in color, has various shapes, and ranges from Alaska to Baja California. This species is more commonly called the "Olympia oyster" (from the Olympia Peninsula in the state of Washington) and is greatly valued for its flavor. The Japanese oyster *(Crassostrea gigas)*, also known as the "Pacific oyster," larger than the California variety, is long in the shell and gray with purplish streaks. It ranges from British Columbia to Morro Bay, California, and was introduced from Japan in 1902. Americans harvest 25 million pounds of oysters annually.

In restaurants specializing in oysters one will find many more varieties brought in. In *The Grand Central Oyster Bar & Restaurant Seafood Cookbook* (1977), the oyster offerings of this cavernous establishment underneath New York City's Grand Central Terminal include Cotuits, from Cotuit Harbor on the Nantucket Sound, Wellfleets, from Wellfleet Harbor in Cape Cod; Chincoteagues, Kent Islands, New Orleans, and Apalachicolas from the South; Olympias from Puget Sound; bluepoints and box oysters from Long Island; Malpecques from Prince Edward Island in Canada; and belons, a French oyster cultivated in Blue Hill, Maine.

OYSTER FRITTERS:
Mix together 1/4 cup flour, 2 beaten egg yolks, 2 tbs. cooled melted butter, salt, pepper, and 3/4 cup of the strained liquid from 3 doz. oysters. Let stand for 2 hr. Fold in 4 stiffly beaten egg whites, dip shucked oysters into batter, fry in hot fat, drain, sprinkle with parsley, and serve with lemon wedges.

OYSTER PIE:
Shuck 2 pt. oysters, strain liquid, and add sufficient water to make 3 cups of liquid. In a double boiler melt 6 tbs. butter, add 6 tbs. flour, salt, pepper, and a dash of celery salt. Cook till thickened, add oysters. Pour into buttered casserole, cover with pie crust, make slits in top, and bake about 20 min. at 450°.

OYSTER STEW:
(Recipe from Lila Gault's *Northwest Cookbook* [1978]) Shuck 1 pt. oysters, retaining liquid. In large kettle simmer oysters in liquid for 3 min. Add 1 cup heavy cream and 3 cups milk. Heat till bubbles form at edge, add 1 tsp. salt, 1 tbs. Worcestershire sauce, and cayenne pepper to taste. Remove from heat, add 2 tbs. butter, and garnish with chopped parsley. Serves 4.

oysters Bienville. A New Orleans dish of oysters with a béchamel sauce of green pepper, onion, cheese, and bread crumbs. Named after the founder of the city, Jean Baptiste Le Moyné, Sieur de Bienville (1680–1767), the dish was created in the 1930s or early 1940s by Roy Alciatore, owner of Antoine's restaurant there, and chef Pete Michel. The following recipe, taken from Roy F. Guste, Jr.'s *Antoine's Restaurant Since 1840 Cookbook* (1979), differs considerably from other New Orleans versions that contain cayenne pepper, bacon, shrimp, and other ingredients.

Melt 4 tbs. butter in a skillet. Sauté 1 1/2 cups minced bell pepper, 1 cup minced scallions, and 2 cloves minced garlic till limp. Add 1/2 cup dry white wine and bring to boil. Then add 1/2 cup chopped pimiento, 2 cups béchamel sauce, 2/3 cup ground American cheese, 1/2 cup bread crumbs, and salt and pepper to taste. Simmer for about 20 min. till very thick. Place 6 raw oysters on the half shell on each of six pie pans filled with rock salt. Cover oysters with sauce, bake in 400° oven for 10 min., till they begin to brown on top. Serve as an appetizer.

oysters Kirkpatrick. A dish of baked oysters, green pepper, and bacon. The creation of this dish is credited to chef Ernest Arbogast of the Palm Court (later the Garden Court) of San Francisco's Palace Hotel (now the Sheraton-

Palace Hotel), which was opened in 1875, burned down in the fire of 1906, and reopened in 1909. Named after Colonel John C. Kirkpatrick, who managed the hotel from 1894 to 1914, the dish was already well known by the end of his tenure, when Clarence E. Edwards wrote in *Bohemian San Francisco* (1914) that the dish was merely a variation on the "oyster salt roast" served at Mannings' restaurant on the corner of Pine and Webb Streets.

The following recipe from the Sheraton Palace is supposedly the original:

> Combine 1 cup ketchup, 1 cup chili sauce, 1 tsp. Worcestershire sauce, 1/2 tsp. A.1 sauce, 1 tsp. chopped parsley, and half a small chopped green pepper. Cut bacon slices into thirds, and cook halfway. Shuck oysters, dip them into sauce, and replace them in shells. Place oysters on a bed of rock salt, cover with bacon, and sprinkle on Parmesan cheese. Bake at 400° until bacon is crisp.

oysters Rockefeller. A dish of oysters cooked with watercress, scallions, celery, anise, and other seasonings. It is a specialty, created by Jules Alciatore in 1899, of Antoine's restaurant in New Orleans. Roy F. Guste, Jr., great-grandson of Alciatore, writes in *Antoine's Restaurant Since 1840 Cookbook* (1979):

> [In 1899] there was a shortage of snails coming in from Europe to the United States and Jules was looking for a replacement [he wanted] to be local in order to avoid any difficulty in procuring the product. He chose oysters. Jules was a pioneer in the art of cooked oysters, as they were rarely cooked before this time. He created a sauce with available green vegetable products, producing such a richness that he named it after one of the wealthiest men in the United States, John D. Rockefeller.

Rockefeller (1839–1937) was indeed one of the country's richest men, having built a fortune in the oil, steel, railroad, and banking industries.

The original recipe for oysters Rockefeller has never been revealed, but although many renditions include chopped SPINACH in the dish, Guste insists that spinach was not an ingredient of the original recipe. There does appear a recipe, however, in a 1941 compilation by Ford Naylor called the *World Famous Chefs' Cook Book,* in which the author contends, "Every recipe in this book, with few exceptions, is a secret recipe which has been jealously guarded. In many cases, its ingredients, proportions and blending have been concealed from the world for generations. Now, with as little change as possible in the directions of the chefs who produced them, these cherished recipes have been adapted for the use of the modern homemaker." The recipe for "Oysters à la Rockefeller" is given above the name "Antoine's Restaurant, New Orleans," and, allowing Naylor room for hyperbole and ambiguity of detail, it is possible that the following is quite close to the original recipe:

> "Select Louisiana oysters, open them and leave them on the half shell. Place the shells containing the oysters on a bed of rock salt in a pie pan. . . . Use the tail end tips of special onions [scallions], some celery, chervil, tarragon leaves, crumbs of stale bread, tabasco sauce and the best butter obtainable. Pound all these into a

mixture in a mortar, so that all of the fragrant flavorings are blended. Add a few drops of absinthe [substitute an anise cordial] and a little white wine. Then force the mixture through a sieve. Place one spoonful on each oyster as it rests on its own shell, and in its own juice on the crushed rock salt, the purpose of which is to keep the oyster piping hot. Then place the oysters in an oven with overhead heat and cook until brown. Serve immediately."

pack. A liquor made from molasses. It is most familiar in the region around New Orleans, though rarely seen now. The name comes from English Major General Sir Edward Michael Pakenham (1778–1815), who was killed at the Battle of New Orleans in January, 1815, during the War of 1812.

package goods store. Also, "package store." A store selling liquor in packages, as opposed to a bar dispensing liquor by the glass. The term came into use after the repeal of Prohibition in 1933, at a time when words like *saloon* and *barroom* still made some state legislators skittish. In many states such stores may also carry groceries and other items.

pail-fed. Cowboy term describing a calf fed on skimmed milk.

pair of overalls. Cowboy term for an order of two drinks served at once.

Palace Court salad. A salad of lettuce, tomato, and artichoke with a dressing of mayonnaise and crabmeat. The salad was created at the Palace Hotel (now the Sheraton-Palace) in San Francisco, though just when it first appeared on the menu is unclear. It may have been after 1909, when the restaurant there was named the Palm Court, or after 1942, when the name was changed to the Garden Court. The recipe below is used at the hotel.

> Prepare a bed of shredded lettuce a half-inch deep. On the center place a thick slice of tomato and a marinated artichoke bottom. Mix 1 oz. chopped celery with 5 oz. crabmeat, and fold in just enough mayonnaise to hold the mixture together. Season with salt, pepper, and lemon juice. Form the salad into a tower-shaped mound and place an artichoke bottom on top. Garnish with a crab claw or pimiento strip. Border the lettuce with chopped egg and garnish the plate with an asparagus spear, black olive, and lemon wedge.

palm heart. Also called "swamp cabbage." The edible shoot of the cabbage palm *(Sabal palmetto),* sometimes called the "palmetto," which flourishes in swampy land in Brazil and Florida. According to Howard Hillman in *The Cook's Book* (1981), "Palm hearts are quite bland, but extravagant; they are sometimes made into 'millionaire's salad,' so called not only because of the price but also because the fledgling tree has to be chopped down to get at its heart." The palm heart is usually boiled and eaten as a vegetable or mixed in a salad.

pancake. A flat cake cooked on a greased griddle and browned on both sides. Pancakes have long been a staple of the American breakfast table, and their history is as old as that of the Indians, who shaped a soft batter in their hands and called it, in the Narraganset, *nokehick* ("it is soft"), transmuted by early white settlers into *no cake*. Cornmeal pancakes were called "Indian cakes" as early as 1607. The Dutch in America made similar cakes from buckwheat, *pannekoeken,* which by 1740 were called "buckwheat cakes." English settlers brought with them the feast of Pancake Tuesday, an old name for Shrove Tuesday, the day before the Lenten fast begins. (In New Orleans this holiday was Mardi Gras.) Eating such rich, buttered cakes on this day was the last gasp of gourmandism before forty days of self-denial.

By 1745 Americans were also referring to "hoe cakes," perhaps because they were cooked on a flat hoe blade, and there were "rice cakes," "batter cakes," and "slapjacks" by the end of the eighteenth century. One of the most hotly debated versions of this simple cake is the "johnnycake," specifically associated with Rhode Island but well known throughout New England. The origins of the name have never been satisfactorily settled upon.

Johnnycake, known at least as early as 1739, may derive from an Indian word for flat cornmeal cakes, *joniken.* Other authorities vouch for the name being a derivative of *Shawnee cake,* after the Indian tribe of the Tennessee Valley. Still others say the word is from *journey cake,* because it might be carried on a long trip, but what we know as johnnycakes are hardly substantial or durable enough to pack in saddlebags for a long trek through the New England wilderness. It is also possible that *johnnycake* is a form of the Dutch *pannekoeken,* for a *j* could be easily interchanged for the *p,* and the word is often seen spelled "jonnycake," without the *h.*

Whatever the derivation, johnnycakes are made with cornmeal, and this brings up another point of debate with Rhode Islanders, members of whose legislature a century ago almost came to blows over the correct method of making the item. In Newport County, Rhode Island, johnnycakes are made with cornmeal, salt, and cold milk (see recipe below); in South County they are made with cornmeal, salt, and boiling water, resulting in smaller, thicker johnnycakes than those in the north. There is even a Society for the Propagation of the Jonnycake Tradition in the state that demands a true johnnycake be made with an obsolete strain of Indian corn called "whitecap flint corn," which is cultivated in very small quantities because of its low yield (twelve tons to an acre, as opposed to twenty tons for dent corn). In the 1940s the Rhode Island legislature again considered the johnnycake question by deciding that only those made with flint corn could be labelled "Rhode Island johnnycakes." (Johnnycake mixes are sold in packages.) As might be expected, Rhode Island holds a Johnnycake Festival each year in the last week of October.

Meanwhile the rest of the country has gone on naming and renaming flat, griddle-fried cakes in all manner of ways. Thomas Jefferson served them at Monticello, and Benjamin Franklin called the Rhode Island variety "better than a Yorkshire muffin." By the nineteenth century northerners were referring to "flapjacks" and "griddle cakes," which by the 1830s and 1840s were being made with white flour rather than cornmeal. American versions of French *crêpes* sought refinement through names like "Quire-of-Paper Pancakes," a thin Virginia variety made with a little white wine. Another Virginia example, made with the coloring of beet juices and slathered with fruit preserves, was called "Pink-Colored Pancakes." The word *pancake* itself was not in general usage till the 1870s, but afterwards became the predominant American term for these traditional favorites. In mining camps and logging camps, they were called either "flannel cakes" (perhaps because they had the texture of the flannel shirts the workers wore), "a string of flats," or "flatcars" (after the flat, open cars used by the railroads to ship lumber). Still another name used by lumberjacks was "sweatpads," possibly after the round, perspiration-absorbant pads women wore under their dresses. Southerners called cornmeal cakes "Crispus Attucks," after the black patriot killed in the Boston Massacre in 1770.

Whatever they were called, pancakes became an American passion, and, as one English traveler wrote, "It is hard for an American to rise from his winter breakfast without his *buckwheat cakes.*" American novelist James Fenimore Cooper made buckwheat cakes for Parisians in the 1820s.

So popular are they that nationwide chains of restaurants have opened up that specialize in pancakes in any number of forms, including "Silver Dollar" pancakes (small enough to be served in portions of six to a dozen), pancakes mixed with fruit, especially blueberries, or nuts, and pancakes topped with preserves, whipped cream, and often eggs.

The classic accompaniment to a stack of three pancakes is either crisply fried bacon or link sausage. MAPLE syrup is poured over the top, and one is also likely to find hash brown potatoes nearby, and, in the South, a side order of GRITS. Sometimes a garnish of orange slice is set on the plate.

PANCAKES:
Sift together 1 1/2 cups flour, 1/2 tsp. salt, and 2 1/2 tsp. baking powder. In another bowl mix 1 well-beaten egg with 1 cup milk and 3 tbs. butter, then pour into flour mixture, and stir just to moisten. Batter will be lumpy. Spoon out batter onto a hot buttered griddle in 4-in. rounds. When bubbles begin to show through top, flip over and cook until both sides are golden. Serve with butter and syrup.

BLUEBERRY PANCAKES:
Before baking press into the batter 1/2 to 3/4 cup fresh blueberries that have been slightly dusted with flour.

CORN PANCAKES:
Mix 1 cup yellow cornmeal in 1 cup boiling water. Add 2 tbs. bacon fat, 1 tbs. sugar, 3/4 cup flour, 1 tsp. salt, 1 tsp. baking powder, and, gradually, 1 cup milk. Add 1 beaten egg. Spoon batter onto buttered griddle as above. Serve with syrup or honey.

JOHNNYCAKES, NEWPORT COUNTY STYLE:
Mix 1 cup stone-ground white cornmeal, 1/2 tsp. salt, 1 1/2 cups cold milk, and 2 tbs. melted butter. Mixture will be thin. Spoon onto buttered griddle in 5-in. rounds and fry till golden.

JOHNNYCAKES, SOUTH COUNTY STYLE:
Mix 1 cup stone-ground white cornmeal with 1/2 tsp. salt, then slowly pour 1 cup boiling water over cornmeal and break up lumps with a fork. Add 1 tsp. sugar or molasses. Stir, then spoon onto buttered griddle, flip over, and fry till both sides are golden.

FLANNEL CAKES:
Cream 1/2 cup sugar with 1 tb. butter, add 2 cups milk with 1/2 cake of yeast dissolved into it. Add 1 beaten egg and enough flour (about 1 1/2 cups) to make a stiff, pancakelike batter. Let stand overnight. Batter will thicken still more. Stir and cook on buttered griddle, or, preferably, bake in muffin tins at 400° till brown.

pan drippings. The browned bits of fat and meat left in a pan after roasting or frying. Pan drippings are usually mixed with flour or cornstarch, water, and seasonings to make a GRAVY.

papaya (*Carica papaya*). A tropical American tree bearing a yellow fruit. The word, which is from the Spanish, was first recorded in English circa 1598.

The papaya was first noted by Christopher Columbus as a staple fruit of the West Indian diet, and other travelers soon brought its seeds to the Far East, including the Philippines and Nepal. In the United States it has only been grown successfully in Florida, Texas, and Hawaii. Usually eaten fresh as a fruit, papaya may also be boiled and served as a form of vegetable. Papaya's enzyme, papain, is widely used in granular form as a tenderizer for meats.

The papaya is sometimes called "pawpaw," but it is not the true PAWPAW (*Asimina triloba*).

paper bread. A Pueblo Indian bread having as one ingredient wood-ash lye.

parfait. A frozen dessert made from cream, eggs, sugar, and flavorings, or, as is more usual today, an ice cream sundae of several different ice creams garnished with various syrups or crushed fruits. The word comes from the French, meaning "perfect," and first saw print in 1894.

COFFEE PARFAIT:
Combine 2/3 cup sugar, 2 tbs. cornstarch, and a pinch of salt with 2 tbs. milk and 2 beaten egg yolks. Add 1 cup strong, cooled coffee, and cook in a double boiler till thickened. Chill, then blend in 1 1/2 cups whipped cream. Place in freezer till firm, and serve in tall glasses with whipped cream.

Parker House roll. A puffy yeast roll with a creased center, created at the Parker House hotel in Boston soon after its opening in 1855 by the kitchen's German baker, whose name was Ward. One story holds that Ward, in a fit of pique over a guest's belligerence, merely threw some unfinished rolls into the oven and came up with the little bun that made his employer, Harvey Parker, famous. Such light, puffy rolls, sometimes called "pocketbook rolls" because of their purselike appearance, were a novelty in their day and became a standard item in American dining rooms and tables. The following recipe is from the Parker House kitchen and makes four dozen rolls.

Mix 2 1/4 lb. flour with 1/4 lb. shortening, 2 1/2 oz. milk powder, 1/4 lb. sugar, and 1/2 oz. salt. Melt 1/2 oz. dry yeast in 3/4 qt. warm water, then add slowly to flour mixture. Beat till smooth. Let the dough rest for 1 1/2 hr., then knead it. Cut dough into 1-sq.-in. pieces, stretch each piece, and fold over. Arrange on a greased baking pan, let rise for 45 min., then bake in a 400° oven for 10 min. till golden brown. Brush with melted butter and serve.

parsley *(Petroselinum crispum).* A green herb with a grassy taste. It is usually sprinkled on dishes as a garnish, though its flavor enhances stocks and sauces. The word is from the Greek, *petroselinon,* "rock parsley," which in Middle English became *persely.*

Waverly Root in *Food* (1980) notes that Giovanni da Verrazano reported seeing parsley when he landed in what is now Massachusetts in 1524, adding, "vigilant writers since have insisted that this could not have been true, since parsley is an Old World plant. The rectifiers were perhaps wrong. There were Norsemen not far from Massachusetts, if not actually there, five hundred years before Verrazano, to say nothing of the Basque fishermen who came from parsley country to the Grand Banks off Newfoundland before Columbus ... where perhaps they let drop a seed or two [that] could easily have migrated from Newfoundland to Massachusetts in a couple of centuries." Root goes on to say, however, that no written record of parsley's presence in America occurs before 1806. Today two main varieties, the Italian *(P. c. neapolitanum)* and Hamburg or turnip-rooted parsley *(P. c. tuberoseum),* are grown in the United States. The latter is the most readily available nationwide; the former, grown in southern Louisiana, is essential to Creole and Cajun cookery.

parsnip *(Pastinaca sativa).* A plant having a white root that is boiled and eaten as a vegetable. The word is from the Latin, *pastināca,* which became in Middle English *pasnepe.*

The origins of the parsnip probably lie in northeastern Europe, though there is a wild parsnip found in the American West. Europeans brought parsnips to North America in the seventeenth century, first to Virginia in 1608, where the Indians soon learned to enjoy them.

The vegetable has never been particularly popular with Americans, but a particularly hardy and early-maturing variety developed here is called the "All-American." Parnsips are usually boiled and buttered.

partridge. America has no true partridge (any of a variety of Old World game birds in the genera *Perdix* and *Alectoris*), but many birds are called by this name in America. The terminology is further confused by the use of other names, such as "quail" or "pheasant," for the same birds. The bobwhite (*Colinus virginianus*), a name first recorded in 1837, was erroneously called a "partridge" in print as of 1587. The ruffed grouse (*Bonasa umbellus*), so called as of 1752, was also termed a "partridge" in print as of 1630. (The ruffed grouse has also been called on occasion a PHEASANT or "mountain pheasant.") The gray partridge (*Perdix perdix*), which *is* a true partridge, was introduced from Eurasia into the northern United States, but, as noted in *Harper & Row's Complete Field Guide to North American Wildlife* (Eastern edition), assembled by Henry Hill Collins, Jr. (1981), has "generally [been] unsuccessful in becoming established."

pasta primavera. A dish of noodles, macaroni or spaghetti, made with a sauce of quickly cooked vegetables. *Primavera* in Italian means "springtime," but there is no traditional or specific dish in Italian cuisine by this name. Pasta with vegetables in Italy would be referred to as *pasta al verdure,* or, as is more usual, according to the specific vegetables used—for example, *fettuccine con funghi e piselli* (fettuccine with mushrooms and peas). Pasta primavera became a very popular dish in America in the 1970s and 1980s, and, although there are other claimants for the invention of the dish, the version that gave it its name and spurred its popularity was created by Sirio Maccioni, owner of Le Cirque restaurant in New York City, who while on a visit to Canada on October 2, 1975, made the dish from several vegetables he tossed together. Maccioni was encouraged by food writers to add it to his menu in New York, and the newly christened dish became an immediate favorite and had its instant imitators.

> Steam 1 cup sliced zucchini, 1 cup sliced broccoli, 1 1/2 cups snow peas, 1 cup baby peas, 6 sliced asparagus stalks, and 10 sliced mushrooms. Rinse under cold water. Sauté in 1 tbs. olive oil 2 coarsely chopped tomatoes, 1/4 cup parsley, salt, and pepper for a few min. In another pan sauté 1/3 cup pine nuts and 2 tsp. minced garlic. Add to pan with garlic all vegetables except tomatoes. Simmer, add 1 lb. cooked spaghetti, 1/2 cup Parmesan cheese, 1/3 cup butter, 1 cup heavy cream, and 1/3 cup fresh basil. Toss, then pour tomatoes on top. Serves 6.

pastrami. CORNED BEEF that has been dried, rubbed with a mixture of coarse pepper and other spices, smoked over hardwood sawdust for two to twelve hours, then cooked by steaming. The word was first printed in 1936.

Pastrami, often served on sandwiches, is a Jewish-American delicatessan item. Its name is derived from the Rumanian word *păstra,* "to preserve."

pasty. A Cornish turnover that may contain a variety of meats and fillings. The dish has been known in England since the Middle Ages and is mentioned in Shakespeare's *Merry Wives of Windsor* (1598–1600?). It has its variants in Scandinavian and Russian cookery.

Pasties became a staple midday meal for the Cornish miners who settled in Michigan's upper peninsula in the middle of the nineteenth century, and there have been attempts to have the pasty declared the state's official food. May twenty-fourth has been declared Michigan Pasty Day, and people of the region will argue over every item that must go into a perfect pasty.

The Cornish miners would wrap the hot pasty (pronounced "pass-tee," not "pay-stee") in a napkin, then in newspaper, and place it in their metal lunch pails so that by midday the pasty would still be warm. There is some argument as to whether the pastry itself should be made with lard or suet, but most versions will contain a mixture of the following ingredients.

> Blend 3 cups flour with 1 cup suet and 1/4 cup lard. Add 1 tsp. salt and about 7 tbs. cold water to make a dough. Divide in four pieces and roll into 9-in. circles. Stir together 3/4 lb. coarsely ground beef chuck, 1/2 lb. coarsely chopped pork, 1 lb. diced peeled potatoes, 2 diced turnips, 1 chopped onion, 2 diced carrots, salt, pepper, and 2 tsp. butter. Spread on circles and fold the pastry together, crimping the top ridge. Bake at 350° on ungreased sheet for about 45–50 min., till browned.

pawpaw *(Asimina triloba)*. Also called "papaw." A tree native to northern Central America bearing a fleshy fruit. The name, which is probably derived from the Spanish, *papaya,* is often mistaken for the true PAPAYA *(Carica papaya),* and the first recordings in English of the fruit are variations of papaya. The word first appeared in print in 1624.

Pawpaws, with a taste that has been described as a cross between bananas and pears, grow on stream banks from temperate regions of New York down to Florida and into the Midwest, where it is sometimes called the "Michigan banana" or "custard apple."

pea *(Pisum sativum)*. A climbing plant having edible seeds enclosed in long pods. The word is from the Greek, *pison,* which in Middle English became *pese* in the plural.

The pea is one of the oldest cultivated plants in the world. Peas were supposedly brought to the West Indies by Christopher Columbus in 1493 and planted on Isabella Island, part of the Galápagos. By 1614 they were being cultivated at Jamestown, Virginia, and New England's first peas were planted by Captain Bartholomew Gosnold on the island of Cuttyhunk in 1602.

The most popular variety is called the "garden pea," the most popular forms being Layton's Progress, the Dwarf Telephone, Gradus, and Mammoth Melting Sugar, with the Great Lakes, Washington, and Oregon the highest producers. The sugar pea has been popular only among the Pennsylvania Dutch, while the COWPEA, sweet pea, and CHICK PEA are not peas, but plants in other genera.

Split peas are peas that have been dried so that the seeds split in two. They are customarily used to make split pea soup. Whole peas, fresh or frozen or canned, are boiled or heated and served with butter, onion, or other seasonings.

SPLIT PEA SOUP:

Wash 1 cup split peas, cover with water, and soak for 8 hr. Pour off water, retaining 4 cups with peas, and add 2 oz. salt pork, 1 sliced onion, 1 stalk chopped celery, 1 bay leaf, salt, and pepper. Bring to a boil, then simmer for 2 hr. Drain, reserve liquid, purée vegetables and combine again with liquid and 1 tbs. butter.

peach *(Prunus persica)*. A tree native to China that bears a sweet fruit with yellow flesh and a yellow-red, slightly fuzzy skin. The word is from the Latin plural of *persicum (persica) mālum,* "Persian apple," which in Middle English became *peche.*

The Romans imported the peach from the Persians, who got it from China and India. It was a popular, though rare, fruit in France and England through the seventeenth century. After the Spanish brought it to the New World in the sixteenth century, the peach thrived among the southern Indian tribes (the Natchez even named one of the months of the year after the fruit) and became just as popular with the northern tribes when they began planting it. In 1661 Philadelphia's William Penn told a friend that peaches proliferated in Pennsylvania—"not an Indian plantation without them"—and Thomas Jefferson planted French varieties at Monticello in 1802.

Commercial plantings began in Virginia in the nineteenth century, led first by Maryland and Delaware, then by Georgia. Peach brandy was a specialty of the Ohio Valley. Today peaches, second only to the apple as an American crop, are produced in California, New Jersey, Pennsylvania, Virginia, North and South Carolina, Georgia, Alabama, Michigan, Arkansas, and Colorado.

Most peaches are eaten fresh or canned, often in a sweet syrup, and peach bread and peach pie are both long-standing southern specialties. The two main varieties of peaches are the clingstone (so called because the fruit's firm flesh clings to the pit) and the freestone (which has a softer flesh). The most popular yellow varieties include Muir, Lovell, Rochester, Blake, Late Crawford, Crosby, and the largest variety, the Elberta. The most popular white peaches include the Mountain Rose, Alexander, Champion, Heath Cling, Cling, Oldmixon, Summer Snow, Iron Mountain, and Belle of Georgia. The most successful crossbreeds include the Golden Jubilee, Halehaven, Redhaven, Dixieland, Dixigem, Southland, and Goldeneats.

Nectarines, mostly raised in California and Oregon, are a variety of peach having a firmer flesh.

peach melba. A dessert of peaches poached in vanilla syrup and served with vanilla ice cream and raspberry sauce. The dish was created by chef Georges Auguste Escoffier (1846–1935) and named after Australian opera singer Nellie Melba (born Helen Mitchell; 1859–1931), but it is not clear exactly when or where. Many stories printed during the principals' lifetimes only served to obscure the truth. André L. Simon and Robin Howe, in *A Dictionary of Gastronomy* (1978), state unequivocably that Escoffier served poached peaches with vanilla ice cream at a party given at the London Savoy Hotel to honor Melba on her Covent Garden opening in *Lohengrin*. The authors add that Escoffier later "improved [the dish] by adding a purée of fresh raspberries and a sprinkling of shredded green almonds," which appeared "on a menu of the Carlton Hotel on its first opening in London on July 15, 1899." In *Melba* (1909), the singer's biographer, A. G. Murphy, spoke of Melba's 1898–1899 tour and noted that "by this time innumerable soaps and sauces, ribbons and ruffles, had been named after her." But Escoffier himself contended the dish was not created for Melba's *Lohengrin* debut, but instead that he put it on the menu merely because she so often demanded peaches and ice cream for dessert. Escoffier says the dish was created at the Ritz-Carlton Hotel in London and that the peaches were from the Montreal suburb of Paris, while the raspberry purée was merely a rendition of *sauce cardinal* with Kirsch added. To make matters more confusing, Melba herself treats the subject of the dessert in her autobiography, *Melodies and Memories* (1925), in a chapter devoted to her activities during the years 1904–1905, insisting that Escoffier made the dish for her at the Savoy Hotel, which Escoffier had left in 1898.

By 1905, however, the dessert must already have been fairly well known, for American author Edith Wharton mentioned the dish in her novel of that year, *The House of Mirth*. By 1906 the dish, called in French *"pêches Melba,"* was on Escoffier's menus and given as a recipe, which appears below, a year later in his book, *A Guide to Modern Cooking*. (The version mentioned by Simon and Howe as the one appearing on the menu in 1899 is listed in Escoffier's book as *"pêches cardinal."*) The dish became a favorite in American hotel dining rooms, and an already mixed "melba sauce" was being bottled by 1951.

"Poach the skinned peaches in vanilla-flavored syrup. When very cold, arrange them in a timbale on a bed of vanilla ice-cream and coat with raspberry sauce."

peachy. A CIDER made from peaches. It is quite possibly an American creation, since its first appearance in print was in S. Peters's *History of Connecticut* in 1781.

peanut. An edible, nutlike seed of the vine *Arachis hypogaea,* native to South America. Peanuts are widely enjoyed as a snack, as a sandwich spread called "peanut butter," and as an ingredient in candy. Peanut oil is often used in frying.

In his discussion of the peanut in his book, *Food* (1980), Waverly Root points out that the seeds were found in Peruvian mummy tombs and pictured on Chimu pottery, but other authorities believe that the seeds came originally from Brazil. The Incas may have been the first to cultivate the plant. The Spaniard Hernando Cortés saw peanuts in Mexico; Columbus found them in Haiti. The Spanish and Portuguese took the peanut to other parts of the world, including the Malay Peninsula, China, and Africa. In West Africa the Portuguese propagated the plant to feed the slaves bound for the New World, and the American colloquialisms *goober* and *pinder* (or *pindal*) are derived from African words, brought by the slaves, either for the peanut itself or for an African underground species, *Voandgeia subterranea,* and other plants. These words soon appeared in print in America, the former in 1833, the latter first in Jamaica in 1707 and in South Carolina in 1848. Other names for the peanut include "monkey-nut," found in England and, to a certain extent, in America; "ground-nut," first recorded in 1602, and "ground-pea," in 1769; and others. Root says that Thomas Jefferson was propagating peanuts in the 1790s, while the *Dictionary of American English* traces the first appearance of the word *peanut* in print to 1807.

Before the arrival of Europeans there were no peanuts on the North American continent, and it was not a staple crop until George Washington Carver (1864?–1943), founder of the Tuskegee Institute in Alabama, promoted it as a replacement for the cotton crop destroyed by the boll weevil in the 1890s. Carver discovered hundreds of uses for the peanut and demonstrated its high nutritive value in dozens of recipes for appetizers, main dishes, soups, and desserts. His list of the most popular peanut varieties includes the Spanish, Georgia, and Tennessee Red and the Virginia Running peanuts, this last referred to as the typical "American peanut."

By the end of the century peanut butter had been invented by a St. Louis doctor, and it was promoted as a health food at the 1904 St. Louis World's Fair. It soon became a favorite sandwich spread, usually layered with grape jelly, among American schoolchildren, and today more than half the American peanut crop goes into the making of peanut butter.

In the South peanut soup is very common, as is peanut cream gravy. Peanuts are boiled or they are eaten roasted out of their shells, salted or unsalted. They are mixed into stuffings, salads, cakes, cookies, puddings, pies, and candies and are a versatile ingredient in many of the most popular commercial candy bars. Peanut brittle came along at the turn of the last century; peanut stands were known as early as the 1860s, and vendors selling peanuts in paper bags have been a fixture in sporting arenas and circus tents in America for decades.

PEANUT BUTTER:

Commercial peanut butter contains a stabilizer that keeps the oil from separating, but homemade peanut butter may be made by grinding 1 cup dry-roasted peanuts in a blender with 1/4 cup vegetable oil or peanut oil. Add 1 tbs. sugar and a dash of salt.

PEANUT BRITTLE:

In a large pot bring to a boil 3 cups sugar, 1 1/4 cups white corn syrup, and 1 cup water (140–145° on a candy thermometer). Add 3 1/2 cups unroasted shelled peanuts and heat to 300°. Make a mixture of 1/2 tsp. salt, 1 tsp. baking soda, and 1 tsp. vanilla; when the temperature of the peanut mixture reaches 315°, add the salt mixture quickly. Then pour onto a marble slab or cookie sheet. Smoothe out, and, with hands in oiled gloves, begin to turn over and stretch the candy till it is very thin and smooth. Let stand until hard.

PEANUT PIE:
Beat 3 eggs with 1/2 cup sugar. Add 1 cup white corn syrup, 1 tsp. vanilla, 1 tsp. butter, a pinch of salt, 2 tbs. peanut butter, and mix for 5 min. Pour into a 9-in. pie shell, sprinkle top with 3/4 cup toasted peanuts, and bake for 45 min. at 300°.

PEANUT SOUP:
(Also known as Tuskegee soup, for its creator, George Washington Carver) Chop 5 scallions and sauté in 3 tbs. butter. Make a roux by blending in 3 tbs. flour, then add 1/2 cup peanut butter and 2 cups chicken stock, and stir till smooth. Add 1/2 cup cream and the juice from 1 qt. oysters. Add salt, cayenne pepper, and savory to taste, then finish with a dash of sherry, parsley, and shucked oysters.

PEANUT BUTTER COOKIES:
(These became known by the 1940s.) Mix 1 1/4 cups flour, 3/4 tsp. baking soda, 1/2 tsp. baking powder, 1/4 tsp. salt, 1/2 cup butter, 1/2 cup peanut butter, 1/2 cup sugar, 1/2 cup brown sugar, and 1 egg. Roll dough into small balls and drop on greased cookie sheet. Bake for 10 min. in 350° oven.

pear *(Pyrus communis).* A tree bearing a fruit with a spherical bottom and tapered top. The word is from the Latin, *pirum,* and, ultimately, from the Greek, *apios.* In Middle English it appeared as *pere.*

The pear originated in Asia, possibly China, and has been cultivated at least since 2000 B.C., with more than fifteen thousand species having since been developed from either the Chinese pear *(P. sinensis)* or the European pear *(P. communis).* Most American varieties have been developed from the latter, which was brought to the colonies in the seventeenth century by Jesuit missionaries, English settlers in Massachusetts, and the Dutch in New Amsterdam. In the West the pear was introduced by Spanish missionaries.

By far the most widely cultivated variety in the United States is the Bartlett, first mentioned in print in 1831. In Europe the Bartlett was called the "Williams' Bon Chrétien," because the fruit was supposedly brought to France in the fifteenth century by St. Francis of Paola (*bon chrétien* in French means "good Christian") and was perhaps propagated in England and on the continent by a horticulturist named Williams. Neither of these stories has been proven, but the pear acquired its American name thanks to Enoch Bartlett of Dorchester, Massachusetts, who promoted the variety in the United States. The Bartlett now accounts for three-quarters of United States pear production.

Other important varieties include the Seckel, the Comice, the Bosc, the Anjou, and the Kieffer. Americans eat pears fresh or canned in syrup, with ice cream, and cooked in cream and sugar. The largest producers of pears are California, Washington, Oregon, New York, Michigan, Illinois, Pennsylvania, and New Jersey.

pecan *(Carya illinoensis).* The nut of the tall hickory tree native to America, ranging from Illinois down to Mexico. After the peanut, the pecan is the most popular nut grown in this country and is used in pies, PRALINES, candies, and ice cream. The name comes from various Indian words (Algonquian, *paccan,*

Cree, *pakan,* and others) and was first mentioned in print in 1773. Thomas Jefferson introduced the tree to the eastern shores of Virginia, and he gave some to George Washington for planting at Mount Vernon. Pecan Pie is sometimes called Karo pie after the brand name Karo syrup so often used in its preparation.

PECAN PIE:
Beat 3 eggs till light in color with 1 cup sugar. Add 1 cup corn syrup, 1/2 cup melted butter, 1 cup pecans, 1/4 tsp. salt, and 1 tsp. vanilla extract. Pour into pie crust. Bake for 10 min. at 400°, lower heat to 350° and bake until set.

pemmican. An Indian food made from buffalo meat or venison dried and compressed into small cakes also containing some form of melted fat, berries, and sometimes bone marrow. This highly nutritious food that kept well on long journeys was introduced to the early pioneers, though they did not take to it with any particular relish. The pioneers' version often did not contain the meat.

The word comes from Cree Indian, *pemikân,* from *pimiy,* "grease," and was first used in print in 1791. A struggle between the hunters and fur traders of the Northwest Fur Company and the Hudson Bay Company, which lasted from 1812 to 1821, was referred to as the "Pemmican War," because it took place in the Indian country of the outer territories.

pepita. A word for a pumpkin seed, borrowed from the Spanish. Pepitas are usually toasted and eaten as a snack in the Southwest and are added to sauces for texture and flavor.

pepper. Primarily this word refers to the peppercorn of the vine of the family Piperaceae, first domesticated in India and now used around the world as a seasoning, especially the peppercorn of the *Piper nigrum,* from which both black and white pepper are made. The distribution of pepper throughout the world was once fought over by several European countries that tried to monopolize the trade. For a while in the early nineteenth century, Salem, Massachusetts, was a dominant pepper-trading port of the Western Hemisphere, to which peppercorns from Sumatra were brought in the fast clipper ships developed in New England.

The term *pepper* is also, erroneously, applied to a wide range of fruits of the Capiscum plants, including the chili, cayenne, paprika, pimientos, and sweet red and green peppers. These last two, *C. frutescens, grossum,* are far milder than the rest and are often eaten as a vegetable because they have a sweet, rather than a hot, flavor. In fact, the first mention of the green pepper in American print was as the "sweet pepper plant" in 1834. Bell peppers, so called because of their bell-like shape, grow well in the southeastern United States, and in the Midwest are called mangoes.

The word *pepper* is from the Greek, *peperi,* ultimately from the Sanskrit, *pippali,* "berry."

perch. Any of a variety of fish in the family Percidae. Perch are freshwater inhabitants, although their name is also applied offhandedly to some marine fish of the families Percichthyidae and Scorpaenidae. The name goes back to the Greek, *perkē.* The main varieties of culinary interest in the United States are yellow perch *(Perca flavescens);* white perch *(Morone americana),* which is a temperate bass; and ocean perch *(Sebastes marinus).*

perry. A pear CIDER made both still and sparkling. It is an ancient beverage in England and was very popular throughout the thirteen colonies in America.

persimmon *(Diospyros virginiana* and *D. kaki).* Also called "date plum." A tree chiefly of the tropics bearing a late-ripening orange-red fruit. The word is from the Algonquian, akin to the Cree word for dried fruit, *pasiminan,* first appearing in print as *putchamin* in 1612, then in its present form in 1709.

The earliest explorers and colonists of the New World were fascinated by the persimmon. Hernando de Soto, in about 1540, compared it with the Spanish red plum and preferred the persimmon. John Smith in Virginia at the beginning of the seventeenth century called it "one of the most palatable fruits of this land," something like an apricot. Not every settler agreed, for before the fruit is wholly ripe it is acidic and astringent to the taste; it achieves its succulent ripeness only late in the fall. The Indians made it into beer, which the colonists soon adapted, and bread, which the Indians of Missouri called *"stanica."* In the November 1981 issue of *Cuisine* magazine, Meryle Evans wrote: "In 1863 Logan Martin, an enterprising young southern Indiana farmer, took a gallon bucket of native persimmons to market in nearby Louisville, Kentucky, where they sold so quickly that he decided on the spot to raise the fruit commercially. Every autumn, for over forty years, 'Persimmon' Martin (as he came to be known) harvested and packed up over 2,000 gallons for shipment by railroad from his hometown of Borden to city markets as far away as New York." Today, near Martin's hometown, the people of Indiana hold an annual persimmon festival the last week of September.

The native American persimmon was eventually pushed aside as a commercial crop in favor of the Japanese persimmon *(D. kaki),* which may have been introduced to the United States in 1855 by Commodore Matthew C. Perry.

In the South persimmon seeds are ground to be used as a coffee substitute, and throughout the Southeast and Midwest persimmon pudding is a Thanksgiving tradition.

PERSIMMON PUDDING:
Wash and dry 2 persimmons, peel off skin, and force flesh through a colander. Combine pulp with 2 cups sugar, 1 1/2 cups sugar, and 2 beaten eggs. Combine 1 1/2 cups sifted flour, 1 tsp. baking powder, 1/8 tsp. salt, and 1 tsp. cinnamon. Combine 1 1/2 cups buttermilk with 1 tsp. baking soda. Combine 1/4 cup cream with 1 tbs. honey. Add buttermilk mixture to dry ingredients and add persimmon pulp, then stir in cream mixture. Add 4 tbs. melted butter, pour into buttered pudding pan, bake 1 hr. at 350°. Serve warm with whipped cream.

Petite Sirah. Also, "Petite Syrah." A red Vinifera grape planted in California. The true identity of this grape has not yet been discovered, though some believe it derives from the Duriff variety of the Rhone Valley in southern France. Used both in blending wines and as a varietal, the Petite Sirah has an intense, spicy aroma and a range of colors from light to deep red.

petticoat tails. A shortbread cookie of Louisiana brought to America by Scottish immigrants. The term dates from the French-influenced court of Mary Stuart (1542–1587), where the cookies were known as *petits gâtels* or *gâstels,* which later became *petits gâteaux,* "little cakes." The Scottish dialect transformed that sound into "petticoat tails," and the cookie is now made with scalloped edges that seem to resemble petticoat edges.

pheasant. Any of a variety of game birds in the family Phasianidae with characteristic long tails and colored plumage. Pheasants are native to the Old World, and there is some confusion in American terminology for the birds. The common term, *pheasant,* is from the Greek, *phasianos,* referring to the bird of the Phasis River in the Caucasus. In America, however, *pheasant* was applied by the early colonists to the ruffed grouse *(Bonasa umbellus),* which did not take this latter name until the middle of the eighteenth century. The Old World pheasant, specifically the ring-necked pheasant *(Phasianus colchicus),* was introduced from Europe and Asia, perhaps in the eighteenth century, but definitely by the nineteenth. L. Patrick Coyle, Jr., in *The World Encyclopedia of Food* (1982), writes that "George Washington imported pheasants from Europe in 1789 to stock his Mt. Vernon estate . . . [and] by the 1830s it was common enough to figure in cookbooks of the period." Waverly Root, in *Food* (1980), notes that Thomas Jefferson once proposed to raise French pheasants in Virginia, but it is not known if he succeeded. The usual date given for the introduction of the pheasant to America is 1881, when an American consul brought Shanghai pheasants home to his Oregon farm. Whenever the pheasant arrived in the United States, it proliferated so successfully that now it is found in more than thirty states.

The bird is usually roasted, and it can be bought frozen.

Philadelphia cheese-steak. A sandwich made with thin slices of beef topped with cheese and other condiments and served on a crisp Italian-style roll. It is a specialty of Philadelphia. Its origins have never been satisfactorily explained, although Pat and Henry Olivieri of Pat's restaurant claim to have created the item in 1930. An order for "cheese with" means the dish should be made with sautéed onions. The cheese is usually, though not always, American, sometimes squirted from a plastic cannister.

> Slice several pieces of rare beef very thin and sauté quickly on a griddle. Place thin slices of cheese on top of meat to melt, place on Italian-style roll, and add ketchup, if desired.

Philadelphia eggs. A dish described by Oscar Tschirky in *The Cook Book by "Oscar of the Waldorf"* (1896) as two split muffins topped with cooked white chicken meat, poached eggs, and hollandaise sauce.

Philadelphia pepper pot. A dish of tripe, pepper, and seasonings supposedly created during the severe winter deprivations of George Washington's ragged army in 1777–1778, when all the cook had to work with was tripe and pepper. The dish was named after the cook's hometown and was so well received by the starving troops that the dish became legendary and was later sold in the streets of Philadelphia by black women crying, "Peppery Pot! Nice and Hot! Makes backs strong, makes lives long!"

> Wash 3 lb. tripe thoroughly and bring to a boil in 4 qt. water. Cook on low heat for 6 hr., until tripe is soft, then allow to cool. Cut into small pieces. In another kettle place 1 1/2 lb. veal knuckle, 3 sliced carrots, 1/2 cup chopped celery, 2 tbs. chopped parsley, 1 chopped onion, 1 tsp. each marjoram, bay leaf, summer savory, and basil, 1/2 tsp. thyme, 3/4 tsp. whole black peppercorns, and 3 cloves. Cover with water and simmer for about 2 hr., till very tender. Strain, discard vegetables, cool, and skim fat from broth. Add tripe and 2 chopped potatoes. Simmer till potatoes are tender. Serves 6.

Philadelphia sticky bun. A nineteenth-century Philadelphia yeast bun flavored with cinnamon and brown sugar. In Philadelphia these sweet rolls are called "cinnamon buns."

> Dissolve 1 pkg. yeast in 1/4 cup lukewarm water. Scald 1 cup milk, then cool till lukewarm and add yeast and 1 1/2 cups flour. Mix, cover, and let rise for 1 hr. Add 4 tbs. cooled melted butter, 2 beaten egg yolks, 4 tbs. sugar, 1 tsp. salt, the grated rind of 1 lemon, and 3 cups flour. Knead, then cover and let rise till doubled. Roll dough to 1-in.-thick long rectangle, brush with a mixture of melted butter, 2 tbs. brown sugar, 1 tsp. cinnamon, and 3 tbs. red currants (if desired). Roll and cut into 1-in. slices. Crumble 3/4 cup brown sugar with 4 tbs. melted butter and spread in skillet. Place dough slices in skillet, let rise for another 60 min., or till doubled, then bake at 350° for 30 min. Turn out onto cooling rack. Makes 12 buns.

philpy. A South Carolina rice bread. The name is of obscure origins.

> To 1/2 cup flour add 1/2 cup milk and 1/2 tsp. salt. Mash 3/4 cup cooked rice and add to flour mixture with 2 tsp. melted butter and 1 beaten egg. Pour into buttered 8-in. layer pan and bake 45 min. at 450°. Cut into 6 wedges.

phosphoric acid. An acidifier and flavor enhancer used in soft drinks.

picadillo. A mincemeat stew of the Southwest whose name is taken from the Spanish word for hash.

> Cook 1/2 lb. ground beef and 1/2 lb. ground pork, 1 minced onion, 1 cup canned tomatoes, 2 minced cloves of garlic, 1 tbs. vinegar, salt, pepper, 1 tsp. ground cinnamon cloves, 1/4 tsp. ground cumin, 1 bay leaf, 1/2 cup seedless raisins, and 1/2 cup almonds. Add water if necessary to give a stewlike texture.

pickle. A food that has been preserved in a brine solution that has been flavored with herbs and seasonings. Although in America the word most often refers specifically to a cucumber preserved in this way, pickling may be done with fish and many other foods. Vinegar is most often the ingredient that defines the flavor of such items.

The word may derive from a Dutch fisherman named William Beukelz (died 1437), who is credited with inventing the pickling process. It was used in England as early as 1440 (*pekille,* in Middle English) and by the eighteenth century any preserved food item could be called a "pickle." In America pickled food became the product most associated with Henry J. Heinz, who put up fifty-seven varieties for sale to groceries around Sharpsburg, Pennsylvania, beginning in 1869. Fried dill pickles are a Mississippi specialty.

There are numerous varieties of cucumber pickles, including these main varieties in the United States: dill pickles, flavored with dill leaves and seed heads; sour pickles, fermented in a sour brine; sweet pickles, sugared as well as soaked in brine; kosher pickles, flavored with garlic; and gherkins, miniature pickles used mainly as a garnish.

MUSTARD PICKLES:
Cut into wedges 2 lb. green tomatoes, 20 small white onions, 2 red peppers, 1 lb. green beans, 1 1/2 cups cauliflower, and 3 carrots in julienne strips. Place in enough water to cover and add 1/2 cup salt. Let stand for several hours. Boil for 10 min., then strain. Make a paste of 4 cups cider vinegar, 4 tbs. dry mustard, 1/2 cup flour, 3 cups sugar, 1 tbs. turmeric, and 1 oz. pickling spices, add a little water, then pour over drained vegetables. Mix well and put in jars.

PICCALILLI:
Chop 4 qt. green tomatoes, add salt to cover, and drain. Chop 1/4 head of cabbage, 3 medium onions, and 3 green peppers and blend. Add 1 tsp. turmeric, 1 oz. mustard seed, 5 stalks celery, 1 cup brown sugar, and 1/2 oz. allspice. Cover with cider vinegar and cook for about 30 min. Put up in jars and seal.

PICKLED ONIONS:
Pour boiling water over 4 qt. small white onions to cover. Let stand a few minutes, drain, cover with cold water, and peel. Cover with 1 cup salt, let stand overnight, then cover again with cold water and drain again. Boil with 1/4 cup pickling spices, 2 cups sugar, and 2 qt. vinegar. Remove pickling spices, boil, then pour into jars and seal.

PEPPER HASH:
Chop 1 doz. green peppers, 1 doz. red peppers, and 1 doz. onions. Salt to cover and let stand overnight. Into 1/2 gal. vinegar put 1 cup sugar, 2 tbs. white mustard seed, 2 tsp. black pepper, and 2 tbs. horseradish and bring to a boil. Pour over the vegetables, mix, put up in jars, and seal.

pickled pork. Also, "sweet pickled pork." A Louisiana seasoning made from pork shoulder marinated in brine. It used to be made at home by a lengthy, arduous process extending over two weeks, but today it is prepackaged and sold in markets. It is considered an important ingredient in making red beans and rice. The following recipe is from John Thorne's booklet, *Rice & Beans: The Itinerary of a Recipe* (1981).

> Combine 1/2 cup mustard seeds, 1 tbs. celery, 1 dried hot pepper (or 2 tbs. Caribe chili powder or 2 tbs. Tabasco sauce), 1 qt. distilled white vinegar, 1 bay leaf, 1 tbs. kosher salt, 12 peppercorns, and 6 cloves garlic that have been peeled and flattened but left whole. Boil for 3 min. Let cool. Place 1/2 lb. boneless pork butt cut into 2-in. cubes (or 2 1/2–3 lb. country-style spare ribs individually cut) into pickling solution, stirring to remove all air bubbles. Completely submerge meat and refrigerate for 3 days, stirring occasionally.

picnic. A meal taken out of doors and away from home, often without benefit of tables, chairs, or other amenities. The word is borrowed from the French, *piquenique,* meaning much the same thing, and entered the English language about 1748.

In America picnickers usually pack a basket or hamper of cold foods, SANDWICHES, and cans or thermos bottles of beverages. Some people go to picnic areas specifically set up with outdoor tables in rural settings.

picnic ham. Also called "California ham." A shoulder cut of HAM so called since about 1910. The meat is sometimes also referred to as CALAS.

pie card. A union card used since the turn of this century by loggers to obtain lodging or a meal.

pie-washer. Baker's term for the worker who paints the top crust of pastry with a wash of water, milk, or egg to give the finished baked item a glossy look.

pigeon. Any of a wide variety of birds in the family Columbidae. There are at least three hundred species, a half dozen of which are found in North American skies, including the mourning dove *(Zenaida macroura),* also called the "turtledove," and the common ground dove *(Columbina passerina),* but none is of much culinary interest to most Americans, who regard pigeons as anything from a pet to an urban nuisance. At one time, however, the native passenger pigeon *(Ectopistes migratorius)* was highly esteemed as a game bird, and it may have been the most numerous bird on earth, with an estimated population of nine billion at its height. Almost immediately upon their arrival in the New World, European colonists hunted the passenger pigeon enthusiastically, and wholesale slaughter of the flocks continued unabated until well into the nineteenth century, when a shotgun could bring down a hundred of the birds in one burst. By 1900, however, only one wild bird was found, and the last passenger pigeon died in a Cincinnati zoo in 1914.

Today only young pigeons less than four weeks old, called "squabs," are of much culinary interest. They are raised on farms mostly for consumption in restaurants.

pigs' ears. Although this term may refer to a dish of pigs' ears, rarely served in the United States, it is more often used to describe a fried pastry popular in Louisiana, called by the French name *"les oreilles de cochons,"* especially by Cajun cooks.

> Combine 2 cups flour, 1 tsp. baking powder, and 1/2 tsp. salt. Beat 1/2 cup melted cooled butter into 2 beaten eggs, stir into flour mixture, divide into 2 doz. balls, and roll out to 6-in. diameter. Deep-fry in hot oil. When the pastry rises to the surface of the oil, pierce center with a fork and turn pastry. Fry till golden brown, drain. Cook 1 1/2 cups cane syrup to 230° on a candy thermometer, drizzle over pastries, and sprinkle with chopped pecans. Makes 24.

pig's vest with buttons. Cowboy term for salt pork or sow belly.

pike. Any of a variety of freshwater fish in the family Esox, five species of which are found in North America. The name is from Middle English, possibly referring to the spiked appearance of the fish. The pike has never been a popular eating fish in America, although it is highly praised by gastronomes as a fine food fish and is traditionally made into *quenelles* in French kitchens.

The main species in America include the northern pike *(Esox lucius),* and the muskellunge *(E. masquinongy),* whose name derives from the Algonquian, *maskinonge,* "big pike," and is often called "muskie" for short.

pilau. Also, "plaw," "pilaw," "pilaf," and "pilaff." Any of a variety of steamed rice dishes made of meat, chicken, fish, or vegetables in a broth.

The word comes from the Turkish, *pilāw,* from the Persian, *pilāw,* and from the Osmanli *pilav,* "rice porridge." The dish is known in numerous versions throughout the Middle East: the Greeks make *pilafi* with tomatoes, the Iraqis make a lentil version called *"mejedrah"* and the Iranians an apricot version called *"geisi pelo,"* the Poles cook *pilaw turecki,* and the dish found its way to France under the name *pilaff de crevettes,* made with shrimp.

The dish was spoken of by English writers in the seventeenth century, and by the eighteenth century it seemed to have taken hold in Britain, especially after the empire spread through the Middle East and into India. In America the dish became popular in the South because of the influence of the spice trade and the rice crop, and in Louisiana the French culinary influence was felt so strongly as to make *pilou français* or *pilaff de volaille* local delectables. Greek-Americans adapted their native dish to *pilafi tou fournou,* baked in an oven. Most pilaus use a touch of curry powder, though the Louisiana versions more often do not. Marjorie Kinnan Rawlings, in *Cross Creek Cookery* (1942), called pilau, which she pronounced "purr-loo," "almost a sacred Florida dish. . . . A Florida church supper is unheard of without it."

> In a Dutch oven cover 2 1/2 lb. chicken with water, add salt and pepper, bring to a boil and simmer, covered, for 1/2 hr. Remove, cool, and cut chicken meat into strips about 3-in. long. To 3 cups of the cooking liquid add 1 tsp. curry powder, 1/2

tsp. parsley, 2 tbs. butter, and 1 cup raw rice. Bring to a boil, lower heat, cook 10 min., add chicken, and cook 10 min. more.

piloncillo. A cowboy term, from the Spanish *pilón,* for a small loaf of unrefined sugar, in use at least since 1844.

piña colada. A cocktail made from light rum, coconut cream, and pineapple juice. It is especially popular during warm weather with boating enthusiasts and at southern resort areas. The term was first printed in 1923.

The piña colada (which in Spanish means "strained pineapple") originated at the Caribe Hilton Hotel in San Juan, Puerto Rico. Back in 1952 bartender Ramon Marrero was introduced to a new product called Coco López cream of coconut (containing coconut, sugar, water, polysorbate 60, sorbitan monostearate, salt, propylene glycol alginate, mono- and diglycerides, citric acid, guar gum, and locust-bean gum). After trying out various liquors with the product, he mixed pineapple juice and light rum with it, blended the mixture with crushed ice, and came up with a sweet, creamy drink that did not really catch on until 1954, when it was served to a group of government officials at a convention there.

Another Puerto Rican claimed to have invented the piña colada in 1963 at the bar called La Barrachina in San Juan's Old City, where there still hangs a plaque that announces "The House Where in 1963 THE PIÑA COLADA Was Created by Don Ramon Portas Mingot." But Mr. Marrero's 1952 claim seems clearly more authoritative, and, therefore, here is his original recipe.

> Pour 2 oz. light Bacardi's rum, 1 oz. coconut cream, 1 oz. heavy cream, and 6 oz. unsweetened pineapple juice into a blender with a cup of crushed ice. Blend for about 15 sec. and serve in a large glass with a garnish of pineapple stick and maraschino cherry. (An almost identical drink, the Bahia, invented at Trader Vic's restaurant in San Francisco, substitutes 1 oz. white Jamaican rum and 1 oz. light Puerto Rican rum for the Bacardi rum in this recipe.)

pineapple *(Ananas comosus).* A tropical plant bearing a large ovular fruit with spiny skin and swordlike leaves. The word derives from its appearance, which resembles a pinecone, and its first appearance in print, in 1398, actually referred to a real pinecone. Not until 1664 did the fruit known by this name enter the printed language.

The pineapple is native to America and was first discovered by Christopher Columbus on the island of Guadeloupe in 1493, and called by him *"piña de Indes,"* "pine of the Indians." Indians of Paraguay and Brazil, especially the Guaraní tribe, had domesticated the plant and called it *"naná,"* ("excellent fruit") from which the Latin term for the pineapple derived.

In 1519 Ferdinand Magellan found the pineapple in Brazil, and by 1555 the fruit was being exported from that country to England. It was also widely dispersed throughout Asia's tropics, growing in abundance in India by 1583, and it proliferated in the West Indies, where, in Barbados in 1751, George Washington tasted and preferred it to any other tropical fruit.

The pineapple was introduced to Hawaii by Captain James Cook in 1790, but it was not commercially cultivated there because of the difficulty of shipping between the islands and the United States. Throughout the nineteenth century the fruit was a rarity for most Americans, even though it was grown in Florida. In the 1880s, however, widespread cultivation was encouraged in Hawaii with the onset of the steamship trade in the Pacific, and it became the largest crop of those islands, especially after the establishment in 1921 of the Hawaiian Pineapple Company by James D. Dole, cousin of the islands' president from 1894 to 1898, Sanford B. Dole.

Pineapple became more readily available in the American market when it was introduced in cans as of 1910. Today pineapple is Hawaii's largest crop, 75 percent of which is canned. The most popular variety there is the Smooth Cayenne, followed by the Red Spanish.

Americans eat pineapple fresh, as part of a salad or fruit cocktail, in sherbets, ice cream, and ices, in gelatin, in cocktails, and as a flavoring, including in cordials. Canned varieties include sliced rings, chunks, and crushed pieces. Pineapple juice is extremely popular and often used in mixed drinks like the MAI TAI and PIÑA COLADA.

pink lady. A cocktail, probably dating from the Prohibition era, made by mixing 1 part grenadine, 2 parts lemon or lime juice, 2 parts apple brandy, 6 parts gin, and 1 egg white.

pink sauce. A pink-colored sauce served with shrimp and dating probably from the 1950s.

> Blend 3/4 cup mayonnaise, 1 cup ketchup, 1 tsp. horseradish, 1/4 tsp. salt, 1 chopped onion, 1/4 tsp. garlic, 1/4 tsp. confectioners' sugar, 1/2 tsp. Worcestershire sauce, 1/4 tsp. Tabasco, 1/2 tsp. paprika, and pepper to taste.

pinole. Dried, ground, spiced and sweetened corn used in the Southwest, sometimes pronounced "panola." The term is Spanish-American, from Nahuatl, *pinolli,* and has been used north of Mexico at least since the 1840s.

It is also a term for a drink of the Southwest, described in Blanche and Edna V. McNeil's *First Foods of America* (c. 1936) with the following recipe:

> Mix 1/2 cup masa with a small amount of water to make a paste. Add 1/4 tsp. salt and sugar and chocolate to taste. Add water, boil for 10 min., then thin with milk. It is often served with buñuelos.

Pinot Noir. A red Vinifera grape that makes an intense, rich, tannic wine and that is also used to make champagne. It is the principal grape used in France's Burgundy and in recent years has become an important grape in premium wines of California and the Northwest (although American Pinot Noirs have thus far lacked the finesse and complexity of the French examples).

pipikaula. A Hawaiian dish made of beef jerky and soy sauce.

pistachio *(Pistacia vera).* A tree, native to Asia Minor, that bears green nuts within a pod that is often dyed a bright, pinkish red for commercial purposes. Pistachios are grown in the southwestern United States and California and are eaten as a snack or, very often, as a flavoring for ice cream, the first example of which was created by confectioner James W. Parkinson of Philadelphia, Pennsylvania, about 1840.

English use of the word dates back to the early sixteenth century.

pita. A round, flat bread easily slit open to form a pocket that may hold everything from chicken salad to chili con carne to bean sprouts to cheese. Its origins are in the Middle East, and it was first served in America in Greek, Turkish, Armenian and other small restaurants. Pita became popular in the 1960s and 1970s as an "ethnic" bread, whereas today it is easily found in groceries throughout the country.

> Dissolve 1 tbs. dry yeast in 1/2 cup warm water. When the yeast is proofed, add 1 cup more warm water, 2 tsp. salt, and 1 tbs. olive oil and mix well. Blend in 1 cup whole wheat or white flour and knead to an elastic dough. Place in an oiled bowl and let rise for about 1 1/2 hr., till doubled. Roll out the dough into a long cylinder, cut into a dozen sections and roll each into a ball. Roll each ball into a disc about 6 in. in diameter and let rest for about 15 min. Place on baking bricks in a 500° oven and cook about 3 min., till puffy. They will deflate somewhat on removal from the oven.

pizza. A flat pie made from a yeast dough topped with various cheeses, vegetables, meats, seasonings, and other ingredients. It is one of the most popular of all American meals and snacks, and it is made in restaurants called "pizzerias," sold frozen in groceries, or, occasionally, made at home.

Contrary to some assertions, the pizza is not an American creation, but its acceptance in this country has made it a far more widespread food item here than in its country of origin, Italy. The American promotion of pizza has resulted in its becoming an international favorite, from Tuscaloosa to Tokyo.

The term *pizza* is clouded in some ambiguity, but etymologists believe it derives from an Old Italian word meaning "a point," which in turn led to the Italian word *pizzicare,* meaning "to pinch" or "to pluck." The word shows up for the first time in a Neapolitan dialect, referring perhaps to the manner in which the hot pie is plucked from the oven.

Pizza has obvious analogues in Middle Eastern pita breads, and flat, seasoned yeast breads are known in many parts of the world (for example, Indian *naan,* Moroccan *Khboz Bishemar,* and Armenian *Lahma bi ajeen*), but it is useless to argue direct linkage to any such breads, because pizza is merely an elaboration of all these variants. The fact is that the pizza as we know it today could not have existed before the sixteenth century, when the tomato was brought to Italy from South America. Although the tomato was held in low esteem by most Europeans, the poor people of Naples, subsisting quite literally on their daily bread, added the new ingredient to their yeast dough and created the first simple pizza, which by the seventeenth century had achieved a local notoriety among visitors who would go to the poor section to taste this peasant dish made by men called "*pizzaioli.*" By the next century pizza was known outside Naples only as a curiosity, and it was not until the nineteenth century that mozzarella cheese (usually made from buffalo milk) became a standard ingredient. Legend has it that Neapolitan *pizzaiolo* Raffaele Esposito of the Pizzeria di Pietro was the first to make a mozzarella pizza to honor the visit of Queen Margherita, consort of King Umberto I, to Naples in 1889. This thereafter was called *pizza Margherita* and became very popular in that city.

But the pizza remained a local delicacy until the concept crossed the Atlantic in the memories of immigrants from Naples who settled in the cities along the eastern seaboard, especially in New York City. The ingredients these immigrants found in their new country differed from those in the old: in New York there was no buffalo-milk mozzarella, so cow's-milk mozzarella was used; *origano,* a staple southern Italian herb, was replaced in America by sweet marjoram; and American tomatoes, flour, even water were different. Here the pizza evolved into a large, wheellike pie, perhaps eighteen inches or more in diameter, reflecting the abundance of the new country.

These first American pizzas may have been made at home, but the baker's brick oven, preferably fueled with wood or coal, was (and still is) essential to making a true pizza, with its crispy crust, soft, breadlike middle, quickly seared topping, and bubbling cheese. Some weight should be given to the opinion that the first pizzeria in New York was Gennaro Lombardi's, opened in 1905 on Spring Street, but others quickly followed in the Italian communities around the city. Still, pizza and pizzerias and, later, "pizza parlors" were little known outside the large cities of the East until after World War II, when returning American G.I.'s brought back a taste for the pizzas they had had in Naples along with the assumption that pizza, like spaghetti and meatballs, was a typical Italian dish, instead of a regional one.

Pizza became very popular after World War II, especially as the fast-food business grew. Along with hamburger and hot dog stands, the pizzeria became a fixture in many American cities and, later, part of commercial chains that expanded throughout the country in the 1960s and 1970s.

Cookbooks of the early twentieth century that give recipes for Italian dishes do not list pizza, but by the 1950s they could be found in American collections as popular as *Ford's Treasury of Favorite Recipes from Famous Eating Places* (1954).

Chicago-style pizza, created in 1947 by Ike Sewall and Ric Riccardo at the Pizzeria Uno in that city, is cooked in a heavy skillet. Sicilian-style pizza is usually cut into rectangles and has a thicker crust than standard pizza, which is often called "Neapolitan-style." This standard pizza, cut into six or eight wedges, is usually made for more than one person and may be topped with ingredients as various as cheese and herbs (often called a "plain pie"), anchovies, onions, mushrooms, sausage, pepperoni, small meatballs, mussels, and many others, in any combination. Often pizza is ordered by the slice, which may be folded in half and held in the hand or cut up with a knife and fork on a plate. (In Italy pizza is usually served on a plate as an individual portion to be eaten with knife and fork.)

Although it is impossible to achieve the same effect at home as one would with a professional pizza oven, the following standard recipe works well in the home kitchen.

Dissolve 1 pkg. yeast in 1/3 cup lukewarm water and let stand for 10 min. In a bowl mix 3 cups flour with 1 tsp. salt. Add the yeast mixture, blend, then add 2/3 cup lukewarm water to make a pliable, elastic dough. Form into a ball, cover with a clean cloth, and let rise till doubled in a warm place.

Meanwhile fry 2 cloves of garlic in 3 tbs. olive oil, add 1 1/2 cans of Italian tomatoes, 1 tsp. salt, 1/4 tsp. pepper, and 1/4 tsp. oregano. Cook for about 20 min., till tomatoes have broken down and thickened.

Roll out the dough onto a flat pan, spread tomato sauce over the top, then add 1 lb. chopped mozzarella cheese. Bake at 450° for about 20 min., until crust is crisp and cheese is melted. To brown cheese, quickly place pizza under broiler flame.

ENGLISH MUFFIN PIZZA:
On a toasted English muffin spoon some tomato sauce (see recipe above) and sprinkle grated mozzarella cheese on top. Grill in broiler till cheese is melted.

CHICAGO (OR "CHICAGO-STYLE") PIZZA:
Brush a 2-in.-deep pizza pan with oil, sprinkle with cornmeal, press basic pizza dough onto bottom and sides. Cover and let rise 30 min. Spread tomato sauce over dough, top with 4 oz. sliced pepperoni, sprinkle with shredded Kasseri or provolone cheese, 1/2 cup chopped, pitted Greek olives, 1/2 cup chopped Italian peppers, 1 chopped green pepper, and 2 cups shredded mozzarella. Bake for 45–60 min. at 450°, till crust is browned and topping is bubbly. Cut into wedges. Serves 8–10.

pizza strip. A strip of thick dough topped with tomato sauce and Parmesan cheese. Pizza strips are usually bought in Italian bakeries in New England, especially Rhode Island, and are eaten hot or cold.

plum. Any of a variety of shrubs or trees in the genus *Prunus* bearing a smooth-skinned, red, yellow, or purple fruit with a soft, pulpy flesh. The word is from Old English, *plūme*, ultimately from Latin, *prūnum*. The word in Latin once probably referred specifically to the fruit, but later many varieties in the genus were differentiated by various names, of which "plum" was one. There are hundreds of varieties of plum today, but those of culinary interest in the United States include the European plum *(P. domestica)*, brought to America in colonial times; the native American plum *(P. americana)*; the damson *(P. damascena)*, originally imported by the Romans from Damascus about the first century A.D.; and the Japanese *(P. salicina* or *triflora)*, brought to the United States in 1870. Other varieties introduced from other countries include the sloe or blackthorn *(P. spinosa)*, the bullace *(P. instituta)*, the gage *(P. italica)*, and the cherry *(P. cerasifera)*.

Other main species native to North America include the Canada *(P. nigra)*, the Chickasaw *(P. angustifolia),* the Alleghany or American sloe *(P. alleghani-ensis),* and the beach plum *(P. maritima),* this last plum found in New England.

Principal hybrids include the Italian Prune, the Stanley, the Burbank, the Underwood, the Monitor, and many others.

Plums are usually eaten fresh. The traditional Anglo-American plum pudding (for recipe, see PUDDING) contains no plums (the word *plum* once meant a fruit of any kind).

A prune is a plum that has been dried either in the sun or by artificial heat. The word prune comes from the Greek, *proumnon,* which became in Middle English *prouynen.*

pocket soup. Also, "cake soup." A soup that was boiled down into a jellylike mass that could be put in a pouch and later reconstituted with hot water. A recipe in the *Lady's Companion* of 1753 calls for boiling a leg of veal until the liquid in the pot thickens to a jellied stage when cooled. This is strained and poured into cups, which are then placed in a pan of boiling water till jellied. The gel is then cooled and turned onto a piece of "new flannel," in order to absorb the moisture. The result was a very concentrated, strong jelly that was turned back into soup by the addition of hot water and salt.

poi. A pasty preparation of taro, breadfruit, sweet potato, or banana. This staple of the Hawaiian diet, often referred to as the "staff of life" there, serves as the first solid food for infants and is recommended for everything from longevity to bee bites.

Today most poi is made with taro root, commercially produced and packaged in cellophane bags. In Hawaii's early days taro was washed and cooked (cooked taro was called *"aipa'a"*), then peeled, scraped, and pounded laboriously into a paste by the men of the tribe, who sat with taro on one side and water on the other, mashing the root into a firm mass called *"pa'i-'ai."* Poi was made by adding water to this mass and by kneading, usually followed by a period of a few days' fermentation, which imparted a sour taste to the paste.

Before World War II Hawaiians could purchase poi in white cotton bags, which had to be strained free of its fiber in a "poi strainer" hung on a clothesline. Today packaged poi has a more pliable texture, and it is scraped in a bowl with some water to achieve a consistency referred to as a thin "one-finger poi," a thicker "two-finger poi," or a still thicker "three-finger poi." As one can tell by these names, poi is eaten by dipping one's fingers into the paste and is served as a condiment with main dishes of meat or fish or as a breakfast food or dip for CANAPÉS. The longer the fermentation of the poi —"one-day," "two-day," and "three-day" poi—the more sour it becomes.

Breadfruit poi is called *"poi 'ulu";* sweet potato poi, *"poi 'uala";* and banana poi, *"poi mai'a."*

poke. A Hawaiian dish of diced fish marinated in various sauces. Hawaiian-style poke comes with chopped seaweed, "Korean-style" with chili, and "onion-style" with Maui onions. Also, short for the salad herb pokeweed *(Phytolacca Americana)* from the Algonquian, *puccoon*.

Polish sandwich. A sandwich of Polish-style sausage (such as KIELBASA) in a soft roll. It is particularly popular in and around Baltimore, Maryland.

pollock *(Pollachius virens).* Also, "Boston bluefish." Ranges the North Atlantic south to Chesapeake Bay. The name is from the Scottish, *podlok*.
    Walleye pollock *(Theragra chalcogramma).* Also, "Alaska pollock." Ranges from Japan to central California. This variety is usually sold salted rather than fresh. *Walleye* refers to its whitish gray eyes.

polysorbate 60. An emulsifier used in baked goods and other processed desserts to prevent spoilage. It also prevents oil and water from separating.

pomegranate *(Punica granatum).* A tree native to Asia bearing a red, tough-skinned fruit containing many seeds and a pulpy, sour-sweet flesh. The name derives from the Old French, *pome* ("apple") plus *grenate* ("many-seeded").
    The fruit has been highly esteemed ever since biblical times, when its many seeds symbolized fertility to the Jews. The pomegranate was brought to America by the Spanish and was quickly dispersed into the wild. It was found growing in Frederica, Georgia, in 1773 and earlier in California. Although efforts were made in the 1860s to propagate an Afghan variety in Washington, the pomegranate thrives only in the American South, where it is a crop of minor commercial importance.

pommes de terre soufflées. Also, "pommes soufflées" or "puffed potatoes." Potatoes that are sliced thin and deep-fried twice so as to give them a puffy, crisp texture. The term is French, meaning "puffed potatoes," and there are two stories as to the dish's origins.
    Larousse Gastronomique attributes the dish to an unnamed chef at a restaurant in Saint-Germain-en-Laye near-Paris, where in 1837 a new railway was being inaugurated. While waiting for the train to arrive for the meal ordered by the railway company, the chef prepared some fried potatoes, only to remove them from the hot oil on the news that the train was having difficulty getting up the hill. When the party finally arrived, the chef put the now cold potatoes back into the hot oil and to his delight watched them puff up. "The famous analytical chemist Chevreul," *Larousse* explains, "who was informed of this phenomenon, studied it experimentally and established the conditions under which it occurred and could be reproduced at will."
    But the man who brought these potatoes to America, Antoine Alciatore, owner of Antoine's restaurant in New Orleans, told of how he came by the

recipe from the man who created it, Chef Collinet, under whom Alciatore apprenticed at the Hôtel de Noailles in Marseilles. Collinet had waited for the train at Saint-Germain-en-Laye and for the arrival of King Louis Philippe (1773–1850). Having cooked Louis's favorite potatoes, Collinet discovered that the king had been taken off the train as a precautionary measure and put on a carriage that would arrive late. When the king finally did arrive, the chef fried the cold potatoes again and produced the puffy crisps that became instantly popular.

> Wash and peel 2 lb. potatoes, cut lengthwise into 1 1/4-in. slices about 1/8-in. thick. Soak in cold water, drain, and dry. Place a layer of potatoes in oil heated to 275°, moving the slices around until they begin to puff up. Remove potatoes, drain, and let cool for a few minutes. Replace the potatoes in 400° oil till puffed up and crispy. Remove, drain, salt and serve.

pompano *(Trachinotus carolinus* and *Alectis crinitus).* A saltwater fish of the jack family (Carangidae). The pompano is esteemed as one of the favorite catches of the Gulf Coast and Florida, although it may be found as far north as Massachusetts. Most are taken at about four to five pounds.

The African pompano *(Alectis)* is also called the "threadfin" or "threadfish," but the Florida pompano, sometimes called the "Irish pompano," is the more easily found at market. A similar fish, the "permit" *(Trachinotus falcatus),* which may run up to fifty pounds, is not a pompano and is rarely treated with the same kind of culinary respect. The poppy fish *(Palometa simillima)* is sometimes called the "California pompano."

The name *pompano,* from the Spanish, *pámpano,* has been used at least since 1778. Mark Twain called the fish "delicious as the less criminal forms of sin." In New Orleans the fish is sometimes called "sole."

The most notable way to prepare the fish is as pompano en papillote, created by Jules Alciatore, owner of Antoine's restaurant in New Orleans, to honor Brazilian balloonist Alberto Santos-Dumont (1873–1932). According to Deirdre Stanforth in *The New Orleans Restaurant Cookbook* (1967), the dish was a version of one Alciatore's father, Antoine, had made in honor of the inventors of the balloon, Joseph Michel (1740–1810) and Jacques Étienne Montgolfier (1745–1810), two brothers who inflated a linen bag with hot air in 1783. This dish was called "Pompano Montgolfier." The later dish became a specialty of Antoine's and, soon afterwards, of other restaurants in New Orleans and America. Movie director Cecil B. De Mille enjoyed the dish so much while filming *The Pirate's Lady* in New Orleans in 1937 that he had it written into the script, even though the story took place long before Antoine's opened in 1840.

POMPANO EN PAPILLOTE:

In 3 tbs. butter sauté 1 cup scallions till wilted, add 1 cup raw, peeled shrimp, and 1 cup white wine and bring to boil. Mix in 1 cup crabmeat and 2 cups fish velouté sauce, salt and pepper, and a dash of cayenne. Simmer for 10 in. and allow to cool. Poach 6 pompano fillets with water to cover, 1 sliced onion, 2 tsp. salt, 5 whole peppercorns, 1/2 cup wine, 2 bay leaves, and the juice of 1 lemon. Cut 6 heart-shaped pieces of white parchment paper about 10-in. high and 14-in. wide. Spoon some of sauce into center of one half of a paper heart, top with a fillet, fold over the other half of the paper, and seal edges. Place on greased baking pan, bake for 15 min. at 400°, till paper begins to brown. Before serving cut open top of paper. Serves 6.

Pompey's head. A roll of ground meat with a sauce of tomatoes and green pepper. In *The White House Cookbook* (1964) the dish is described as having been "popular before automatic ovens were invented because it could cook unattended for hours." The name apparently refers to the broad head of Roman statesman and general Gnaeus Pompeius Magnus, called "Pompey the Great" (106–48 B.C.).

Mix 1 lb. sausage meat with 1 lb. ground beef, season with salt and pepper, and form into a roll. Dust with flour and brown in a 450° oven. Add 2 cups chopped tomatoes, 1 cup chopped celery, 1 tbs. chopped onion, 1/2 green pepper to pan, and bake, covered, for 1 1/2 hr. at 350°, basting occasionally. Serve with vegetables poured over it.

pony. A short bar glass shaped like a small sherry or brandy glass that is often used for cordials or for measuring one ounce of liquid. The term may also refer simply to a small drink of straight liquor, a meaning that dates back at least to 1849.

pooch. A cowboy dish made from tomatoes, sugar, and bread.

poor doe. Tough venison, in cowboy slang.

poor-man dishes. A very vague term for a wide variety of stews, pies, soups, desserts, and other foods, possibly because they are made with simple, inexpensive ingredients.

popcorn. Also, "popped corn." Corn kernels heated in oil until they burst open into white, fluffy-textured balls.

Popcorn was brought to the first Thanksgiving in 1621 by Chief Massasoit's brother, Quadequina. At first called by the early colonists "popped corn," "parching corn," or "rice corn," it became commonly known after 1820 as "popcorn," and was a popular treat for Americans, who not only ate it as a snack but strung it on Christmas trees. By the 1870s people were adding molasses to make crunchy popcorn balls, and in 1896 the firm of F. W. Rueckheim and Brother of Chicago came up with a combination of popcorn, molasses, and peanuts that they called "Cracker Jack" (the confection had been sold without that name at Chicago's 1893 Columbian Exposition), which came from a contemporary slang term for anything considered excellent. Before long Cracker Jack was a staple food item at baseball games throughout America, and the cry, "Getcha' peanuts, popcorn, and Cracker Jack!" is still heard at every circus, sporting event, and carnival in the land.

Popcorn machines were soon fixtures on street corners and, particularly, in movie theaters, where popcorn became an absolute requisite for an enjoyable evening. By 1918 the Butter-Kist popcorn machine, which coated the popcorn with melted butter, was also common. Today popcorn is often made at home with nothing more than corn kernels and a pot, though electric popcorn poppers and cellophane packages of popcorn are sold too. Americans ate forty-two quarts per person in 1982.

pope's nose. Also, "parson's nose." The rump of a cooked fowl. The phrase is a demeaning term for both parts of the anatomy, for it was originally meant as a slur against Catholics during the reign of James II of England, although *parson's nose* seems to predate it. In America "parson's nose" (called by New England poet Henry Wadsworth Longfellow an "epicurean morsel") was the more common slang term.

pop-out. A prepackaged, frozen meal sold to many commercial airlines for use on their flights. The food pops out of the package and is then arranged on a tray to be heated aboard the aircraft.

popover. A light, hollow muffin made from an egg batter similar to that used in making YORKSHIRE PUDDING. The name comes from the fact that the batter rises and swells over the muffin tin while baking. The first appearance of the word in print was in 1886.

In *American Food* (1974), Evan Jones writes: "Settlers from Maine who founded Portland, Oregon, americanized the pudding from Yorkshire by cooking the batter in custard cups lubricated with drippings from the roasting beef (or sometimes pork); another modification was the use of garlic, and, frequently, herbs. The result is called Portland popover pudding, individual balloons of crusty meat-flavored pastry."

Most popovers, however, are not flavored but merely set in buttered muffin tins. They are served at breakfast or with meats at lunch and dinner.

> Combine 1 cup sifted flour and 1/4 tsp. salt. Beat until very smooth 2 eggs and 1 cup milk, then blend well with flour. Pour into buttered muffin tins and bake in 450° oven for about 20 min. Reduce heat to 350°, bake 10–15 min. till puffy and brown.

pop wine. A term of recent years used to describe a sweet, fruit-flavored wine that is usually quite inexpensive.

porgy. Any of a variety of marine fishes of the family Sparidae. Porgies are small-mouthed, have strong teeth, and inhabit sandy bottoms both inshore and offshore. The name, according to the *American Heritage Dictionary,* derives from the Spanish, *pargo,* which goes back to the Greek *phagros,* "sea bream," by which the porgy is known outside the United States. A. J. McLane, however, in his *Encyclopedia of Fish Cookery* (1977), asserts that the name is "strictly American, derived from the Narraganset Indian word *mishcuppauog.*

Pauog meant fertilizer, for which the fish was widely used." But the first instances of the word in English print were in 1671 and in Sir Hans Sloane's 1725 book, *A voyage to the islands Madera, Barbados, Nieves, S. Christophers, and Jamaica, with the natural history . . . of the last.* Since the Narraganset Indians were a tribe of North America, and specifically of what is now Rhode Island, the appearance of the word in a text on the Caribbean throws McLane's contention into doubt.

The fish has always been enjoyed in the South, with more than 20 million pounds marketed annually along the Atlantic coast, and in the nineteenth century they were hawked on the streets of southern cities like Charleston, South Carolina, the setting for the American opera *Porgy and Bess* (1935), about a crippled black man named Porgy.

The main species of culinary interest in the United States include the scup *(Stenotomus chrysops),* whose name derives from the Narraganset word *mish-cùp;* jolthead porgy *(Calamus bajonado);* Pacific porgy *(C. brachysomus);* and sheepshead *(Archosargus probatocephalus).*

pork. The edible flesh of a pig or hog. The word derives from the Latin, *porcus.*

Pork is the most widely eaten meat in the world, and from the time the first settlers came to the New World it was the predominant meat in the American diet. Pigs have been domesticated since the Stone Age, and wild pigs, called "peccaries" or "javelinas" *(Tayassu tajacu* or *T. peccari),* may have crossed the Bering Strait from Russia to disperse throughout North and South America.

Hernando Cortés (1485–1547) found pigs in Mexico, but the first domesticated pigs were a herd of thirteen brought from Spain to Tampa, Florida, in 1539 by Hernando de Soto (c. 1500–1542), and from these all North American domesticated pigs are descended. Some of these Spanish pigs escaped into the forests and turned wild. They are called RAZORBACKS and are not related to the peccaries.

English, French, and all other colonists found pigs easy to raise, for they foraged on their own and lived off scraps. By 1640 Massachusetts had already built a small salt pork trade. Salting and smoking was the standard method of treating a butchered hog, and salt pork became the dominant meat in the colonial diet; it was used for its oil and its meat as bacon, in stews, as flavoring, in pies, roasted, boiled, barbecued, and in all manner of preparations. The HAMS of Virginia became famous for their succulent flavor, especially those of Smithfield, where the pigs forage in the peanut fields.

Southerners ate every part of the hog, saving every piece for some special dish like RED BEANS AND RICE, a Louisiana delicacy traditionally made on Monday with the hambone left over from Sunday's dinner. Families had pork barrels in their cellars, and the term *pork barrel legislation* came to mean laws passed by a region's congressman designed specifically to help his local constituency. To be living "high on the hog" meant that one was eating the best meat on the pig, while others had to subsist on belly BACON meat.

Thomas Jefferson, with his usual curiosity, experimented with new breeds by crossing Virginia hogs with Calcutta varieties, soon cornering the local market and overcharging his neighbors, who began calling him the "hog governor" and in defiance hung his Monticello fence with pig entrails.

By the 1830s the streets of major cities were crisscrossed with hog tracks, for they were allowed to feed on the garbage, and English traveler Francis Marryat noted of a Fourth of July in New York that the three-mile-long stretch of Broadway was lined on both sides of the street with booths selling roast pig. During the same era Cincinnati became the major pork-packing center, earning its nickname "Porkopolis." Pork itself was sometimes called in slang "Cincinnati olive."

The demand for pork increased during the Civil War, when hog production doubled to provide meat for the Union troops while soldiers of the Confederacy starved for lack of it. After the war a new industry arose in meat-packing, led by Gustavus Franklin Swift and Philip Danforth Armour, who independently set up companies in Chicago in 1875. Chicago soon became the center of the industry for the entire United States, which was served with pork in abundance thanks to the newly developed refrigerated railroad cars. (Long into the present century *Chicago* was a slang term for pork.) Still, those pioneers who set out for California after the Civil War always packed a full load of salt pork, which they usually cursed for its monotonous appearance in their diet as they crossed the Great Plains.

With the increase in available beef during the same period, however, pork began to recede in popularity, tied as it was to a coarse and boring diet of the poor. By the twentieth century beef began to compete favorably in price and was preferred at the table, so that Americans ate less and less pork as the decades wore on. Today, though pork consumption is again on the rise, 40 percent of Americans eat little or no pork at all, but Americans consume about sixty-five pounds per person per year, compared with seventy-seven pounds of beef.

Today pork is served in a wide variety of ways, as roast pork or ham, as spareribs, chopped up in a southern-style BARBECUE, in sausages, in stews, as chops, and in a wide range of ethnic foods. The innards, especially the intestines, called CHITTERLINGS, are an important part of SOUL FOOD. The Department of Agriculture grades pork No. 1, No. 2, and No. 3. The various cuts of pork are listed below:

primal loin. This cut runs along the pig's back and is the preferred meat. It includes the sections from which come Canadian bacon and the best spareribs, as well as the tenderloin, sirloin, center loin, blade (or rib) loin, and the finest chops. The chops from this section are often called "country style."

primal leg. From this section is cut the meat to make fresh ham—that is, pork roasted as is—and the ham that is to be cured and smoked, which is cut into the butt end and shank end.

primal Boston (or shoulder) butt. This section comprises the Boston butt and the picnic ham.

primal picnic shoulder. A cut from the foreleg that is usually sold cured and smoked, though some of the meat is sold as an arm roast.

primal side pork. Also called "pork belly." This section provides bacon.

primal spareribs. These lie under the primal side pork. A slab of between two and five pounds is cut into spareribs.

For information on HAM, see main entry.

port. A fortified wine usually made in America with ZINFANDEL and other grape varieties. The name comes from the city of Oporto, Portugal, where the original port was made. In the United States Portuguese ports are labelled "Porto" to distinguish them from American bottlings. Port wines began to be fortified with brandy in the eighteenth century, after which their distribution became dominated by the British shipping trade.

American ports generally contain between 18 and 20 percent alcohol and 5 to 10 percent residual sugar. Most are produced in California, and some, since the 1970s, are marketed as vintage ports.

Port is traditionally served with the cheese course or after dinner, although some light ports are enjoyed as aperitifs.

porterhouse. Also, "porterhouse steak." A beefsteak cut from the thick end of the short loin, containing a T-bone and part of the tenderloin. The name derives from the taverns or alehouses of the eighteenth century that were called "porterhouses" (because porters in London's Covent Garden market drank ale in such places). The steak itself was popularized around 1814 by a New York City porterhouse keeper named Martin Morrison. It soon became the most popular form and cut of steak in America.

Portuguese sweet bread. A white loaf of bread sweetened with sugar and sometimes baked with slices of sausage. The Portuguese, who call it *"pao doce,"* brought it to American communities on the East Coast as well as to the Hawaiian Islands in the nineteenth century.

> Combine 1/3 cup sugar, 1 tsp. salt, 2 pkgs. yeast, and 1 cup flour. In saucepan over very low heat combine 1/4 cup butter in 2/3 cup milk until warm, then gradually beat into flour mixture, increasing speed of mixer. Beat in 6 eggs and 1 1/2 cups more flour to make a thick batter, then stir in about 2 1/2 cups more flour to make a soft dough. Turn onto floured surface and knead till elastic, about 10 min., using more flour as necessary. Shape into ball, turn into greased bowl, cover, and let double. Punch down dough, cut in half, shape into 2 loaves, and place on buttered cookie sheet. Let double again, brush tops with milk, and bake 35 min. at 350°. Cool.

Porty Reek long-lick. A New England sailor's slang term for molasses. *Porty Reek* refers to Puerto Rico, where sugar was produced. *Long-lick* probably referred to its dense, viscous texture and was also used by westerners. *Long-tailed sugar* was a variant of the phrase.

posset. A drink of sweetened hot milk, wine, or ale. The word is from Middle English, *poshet* or *possot.* It was a popular drink in the fifteenth century and continued to be well into the nineteenth, though it is rarely seen today. Sometimes posset contains egg, in which case it is called an "egg posset."

WINE POSSET:
Boil 1 qt. milk with 1/2 pt. dry white wine until milk curdles. Strain off whey, dissolve 1 tbs. sugar in it, and press curdled milk through a sieve. Sprinkle with nutmeg and ground cloves and beat in sweetened whey. Serve hot.

potato *(Solanum tuberosum).* A native South American plant having a rough-skinned, starchy tuber that is widely propagated and eaten in a great variety of ways as a vegetable. The word comes from the Spanish, *patata,* which derives from the Taino word *batata,* but this is only the beginning of the many confusions surrounding the potato and its history. When Christopher Columbus explored the West Indies he found a tuber, which is now called the SWEET POTATO *(Ipomoea batatas),* called in the Taino language *"batata."* This tuber was immediately transported back to Spain and propagated there. The confusion arose when John Gerard's *Herball* in 1597 listed the white potato as a North American plant, and for a good while afterwards it was assumed that there were white potatoes in North America. This, however, was not the case. The white potato is native to South America and was cultivated perhaps five thousand years ago in Peru. It was this plant that the Spanish found cultivated by the Incas, who called it *"papa,"* and which the conquistadores believed were a form of truffle. These tubers were soon sent back to Spain from Ecuador, may have reached France about 1540, and were mentioned in print in 1553 by Pedro de Cieza León in his *Crónica del Perú.*

Legend has it that Sir Walter Raleigh's men brought the white potato back from Virginia in 1586, but there is no evidence of the white potato's existence in North America at that time. Waverly Root in *Food* (1980) suggests a plausible explanation of the legend by noting that Sir Francis Drake picked up Raleigh's disgruntled colonists in 1586 on his way back from Cartagena, Colombia, from where he had taken some white potatoes. These were of considerable interest to Thomas Hariot, one of Raleigh's men, and it was Hariot who gave the tubers to John Gerard, who thereupon planted them in his own garden and ten years later reported that this white potato had come from Virginia.

Whatever happened in Virginia and England, Raleigh has been credited with planting the first white potatoes in Ireland soon afterwards, where they were grown to prevent famine, as they were in Germany and elsewhere. Those who had no fear of starving would not eat the potato, fearing it was at worst poisonous and at best unappetizing.

The white potato finally entered North America by way of Irish Presbyterians, who brought it to Boston in 1719 and then began propagating it in Londonderry, New Hampshire. By 1762 it was a field crop in Salem, Massachusetts, and by 1770 it was grown for commercial sale back in England. It was not even eaten in Spain until the middle of the eighteenth century. By then Americans had learned to distinguish the white potato from the orange tuber that originally took its name. The latter variety was by the 1740s called the "sweet potato."

Still, the white potato had few admirers well into the nineteenth century. It was considered fit only for the poor and largely associated with the Irish, who in their own country had staved off starvation with the potato in 1740 and continued to live on it almost to the exclusion of every other food. In fact, the potato was so closely associated with the Irish that the slang term for the tuber became the same as the slur word for an Irishman—*mickey.*

When the Irish Potato Famine hit in 1845, owing to a failure of the crop, the only solution for the poor was to emigrate to America, which they did by the millions for decades following.

By the mid nineteenth century the potato was no longer feared for its poisonous properties, and cookbooks began carrying a few recipes for potatoes as vegetables. Even fried potatoes were called by Sarah J. Hale, in the 1857 *Mrs. Hale's New Cook Book,* "an admirable way of dressing potatoes," and potato chips, called SARATOGA CHIPS, had become popular in that same decade. FRENCH-FRIED POTATOES came along near the end of the century, by which time Americans consumed great quantities of the tuber—two hundred pounds per person per year by 1900. Cookbooks listed scores of ways to prepare them—boiled, mashed, baked in their skins, cooked in the fat of a roast beef, and sliced up to be baked in cream, called "scalloped potatoes." In large eastern cities street vendors would roast them over coals and children would cook them on a stick over an open fire. They were boiled and made part of hot or cold German potato salad, and the idea of Swiss *roesti* became American hash (or hashed) browns—potatoes that are shredded or chopped and cooked with butter and bacon and onion in a skillet.

During World War II dehydrated potatoes became a staple part of the serviceman's diet. Later these were a commercial success in the grocery. After the war frozen french-fried potatoes supplanted freshly made french fries in most homes and restaurants, especially at FAST-FOOD stands, where thinly cut shoestring potatoes are generally sold. Today Americans eat about 120 pounds of potatoes per year, 75 pounds of that amount fresh.

The three main varieties produced are the Russet Burbank, the Variety Katahdin (used mostly for boiling and canning), and the Kennebec (usually used for potato chips or for baking and boiling). The Idaho potato is considered the finest in the world by many connoisseurs. Other important potato-producing states include Washington, Maine, California, North Dakota, Oregon, Minnesota, Wisconsin, and New York.

Popular homegrown varieties include the Red Pontiac, the Norgold Russet, and the White Cobbler.

MASHED POTATOES:
Boil 4 washed, peeled potatoes cut into chunks, drain, and mash coarsely. Add 1/3 cup cream or milk, 3–4 tbs. butter, salt, and pepper, and mash to a smooth consistency.

HASH-BROWN POTATOES:
Boil 4 washed, peeled potatoes and shred or cut into coarse chunks. In a skillet cook 4 strips of bacon till crisp, then remove and drain. Pour off all but 3 tbs. bacon fat, sauté 2 shredded onions till limp, remove from pan, and add to potatoes. Crumble bacon and add to potato. Add salt and pepper to taste. Melt 1/4 lb. butter in skillet till foamy, pour in potato mixture and pat down tightly. Turn up flame to high and cook until bottom side of potatoes is browned and crisp. Invert potatoes on a warmed plate.

potato salad. A cold or hot side dish made with potatoes, mayonnaise, and seasonings. It became very popular in the second half of the nineteenth century and is a staple of both home and food-store kitchens. Hot potato salad was associated with German immigrants and was often called "German potato salad."

COLD POTATO SALAD:
In a bowl stir together 1/2 cup mayonnaise, 2 tbs. milk, 1/2 tsp. salt, 1/4 tsp. pepper, 2 1/2 cups cooked cubed potatoes, and 1/2 cup chopped celery and mix thoroughly. Chill for 2 hr. Makes 3 cups.

HOT POTATO SALAD:
Cook 6 potatoes in salted boiling water, peel, and slice. In a large skillet sauté 4 strips bacon, 1/4 cup chopped celery, and 1/3 cup chopped onion till browned. In a saucepan heat to boiling 1/4 cup chicken stock, 1/2 cup vinegar, 1/3 tsp. sugar, salt and pepper, and 1/8 tsp. sweet paprika. Pour into skillet, add potatoes, and stir thoroughly. Cook till well blended and slightly thickened. Serve with chopped parsley. Serves 6.

potato snow. Described by Eliza Leslie in *Directions for Cookery* (1837) as potatoes that have been boiled, thoroughly dried, then pushed through a sieve but afterwards not mixed in any way.

potlikker. Southerners, particularly blacks, call the liquid left over from a meal of greens, field pea, pork, or other items "potlikker." Often served on its own as a vitamin-rich broth, potlikker was a staple among the field hands of the South and is now an essential ingredient of modern SOUL FOOD.

A passion for potlikker (first cited in 1744) is a requisite for political office in the South, for, as Marjorie Kinnan Rawlings observed, "a man addicted to the combination [of potlikker and cornbread could] claim himself a man of the people." Governor Huey Long of Louisiana, in an all-night filibuster on the subject of authentically made potlikker, once claimed that fried corn pone must be dunked into the broth for the best results, although opponents countered that the corn pone should be crumbled into the potlikker. Franklin D.

Roosevelt jokingly suggested that the issue be referred to the platform commit-
tee at the 1932 Democratic National Convention.

As for the spelling of the word, Lieutenant Governor Zell Miller of Georgia
corrected a 1982 article in the *New York Times* with the following blast:

> I always thought The New York Times knew everything, but obviously your editor
> knows as little about spelling as he or she does about Appalachian cooking and soul
> food. Only a culinarily-illiterate damnyankee (one word) who can't tell the differ-
> ence between beans and greens would call the liquid left in the pot after cooking
> greens "pot liquor" (two words) instead of "potlikker" (one word) as yours did. And
> don't cite Webster as a defense because he didn't know any better either.

pot luck. A meal composed of whatever is available. In the West it meant food
brought by a cowboy guest.

potpie. Also, "pot pie." A crusted pie made with poultry or meat and, usually,
chopped vegetables. The term, which first appeared in American print in 1792,
probably refers to the deep pie pans or pots used to bake the pies in, and it
has remained primarily an Americanism. The most popular pot pies have been
chicken, beef, and pork. The first frozen pot pie was made with chicken in 1951
by the C. A. Swanson company.

CHICKEN POT PIE:
In a kettle cook 1 quartered chicken in 2 cups chicken broth for 30 in. Cool, reserve
broth. In another pot cook 1 doz. small onions in 1 cup chicken broth for 10 min.,
add 4 chopped carrots, 1 cup peas, and 1/2 cup chopped celery. Cook 20 min., then
remove from heat. In a saucepan make a roux of 6 tbs. butter with 6 tbs. flour,
stirring about 1 min. Stir in reserved chicken broth, season with salt and pepper,
cook about 7–10 min., till thickened, and remove from heat. Remove chicken meat
from bones, place in vegetable mixture, and blend in roux. Pour into pastry-lined
deep-dish pan, cover with top crust, slit air vents for steam to escape, and bake 10
in. at 450°, then lower heat to 350° and cook another 20 min., until crust is golden
brown.

pot roast. A meat that is browned and cooked with vegetables and gravy in
a deep pot or saucepan, usually covered. Pot roast was once an appetizing way
to cook beef from beasts that had been work animals rather than food animals
or other inferior cuts of meat. Today, the availability of good beef makes pot
roast a delicious, hearty dish, though lesser cuts of meat are still used for the
cooking. Beef brisket, bottom and top round, and chuck are the usual choices.

Brown a 4- to 5-lb. chuck roast in 1/4 cup fat. Add 2 sliced onions, salt, pepper,
1 tsp. minced garlic, 2 bay leaves, and 3 cups beef bouillon. Cover, bring to a boil,
reduce to simmer and cook 2 hr. Add 1 lb. chopped carrots and 1 lb. small white
onions, and cook for 30 min. more. Remove meat and vegetables. To pot add 2 tbs.
cornstarch in 1/4 cup water, and stir thoroughly. Bring to a boil, cook for 1 min.
or till thickened. Serve gravy with sliced meat and vegetables. Serves 6 to 8.

poultry. Defined by the United States Department of Agriculture as "all domesticated birds (chickens, turkeys, ducks, geese, guineas)."

poultry byproduct. Any edible part of a domesticated other than the sex glands and POULTRY MEAT.

poultry food product. Also called "poultry product." Any food suitable for human consumption made from any domesticated bird and containing more than 2 percent poultry meat.

poultry meat. The white and dark meat portions of deboned poultry, excluding fat, skin, and other edible poultry parts.

pound cake. A plain white-cake loaf whose name derives from the traditional weight of the ingredients—one pound of flour, one pound of butter, one pound of sugar, and one pound of eggs—although these measurements are generally not followed in most modern recipes. Its first printed mention was in 1747 according to *Webster's Ninth,* and it has remained a popular and simple cake to make to this day.

> Cream 1/2 cup butter with 1 cup sugar till light and fluffy. Add 1 3/4 cups flour, 3 egg yolks, a pinch of salt, and 1 tsp. vanilla extract. Pour into loaf pan and bake at 350° for about 45 min.

pousse-café. A drink made by pouring successive layers of cordials on top of one another, creating a rainbow effect of color. The term is French, meaning "push down the coffee," and in France a *pousse-café* is merely a cordial, brandy, or other digestive alcohol. In America, however, it is a bibulous tour de force, its success depending upon the specific densities of the cordials, with the heaviest going on the bottom and graduating with the lighter ones towards the top. A tall, slender cordial glass (or special pousse-café glass) is needed, and care must be taken in pouring each cordial so as not to disturb the one under it. A typical pousse-café might be layered in the following order: Kirsch, grenadine, orange curaçao, green *crème de menthe,* purple *crème de cassis,* and yellow *crème de bananes.* The word was first printed in 1880.

prairie beeves. Cowboy term for a buffalo.

prairie bitters. A popular Old West beverage, also considered medicinal, made by cowboys from the gall of the buffalo and water.

prairie chicken. The greater prairie chicken *(Tympanuchus cupido)* and the lesser prairie chicken *(Tympanuchus pallidicinctus)* are grouse of the open plains of the West. The bird was named as early as 1691, and the Lewis and Clark expedition of 1804 referred to it as the "prairie hen" or "prairie fowl." Later they were also called "prairie grouse."

prairie dog (Genus *Cynomys*). A rodent of the short-grass prairies found throughout the West and Southwest. Prairie dogs were as much a nuisance to the people of the range as they were a source of endless fascination. Although not usually eaten, they sometimes found their way onto a cowboy's barbecue spit or in a stew. The name was first printed in 1774.

prairie oyster. A cocktail made by dropping 1 unbroken egg yolk into a tumbler, adding 2 tsp. Worcestershire sauce, 2 dashes Tabasco sauce, a pinch of salt and pepper, and 1 tsp. malt vinegar. It is considered by bartenders to be a good cure for the hiccups. The term (also, sometimes, *prairie cocktail*) has been part of western lingo since the late nineteenth century.

praline. A confection made from almonds or pecans and caramel. It is a great favorite in the South, especially in New Orleans, and derives from the French preparation of *pralin,* caramelized almonds and sugar pounded into a fine, crumblike texture. Both terms come from the name of French diplomat César du Plessis-Praslin, later Duc de Choiseul (1598–1675), whose cook suggested that almonds and sugar aided digestion. The American Creoles substituted pecans for the almonds.

The confection is first mentioned in print in 1727, though the term had various meanings by 1809, when one chronicler told of pralines made from corn and sugar.

Combine 3 cups light brown sugar with 1/4 cup water and 1 tbs. butter. Heat to a temperature of 238° on a candy thermometer, add 1 cup pecan meats, remove from heat, and stir till mixture loses glossiness. Drop in spoonfuls on waxed paper.

prawn (*Macrobrachium acanthurus*). A crustacean similar to a SHRIMP but with a more slender body and longer legs. The name is from Middle English, *prayne.* At market the term *prawn* is often used to describe a wide variety of shrimp that are not prawns at all. The only native American species is found in the South, ranging from North Carolina to Texas. Prawns are cultivated in Hawaii.

pretzel. A crisp, salted biscuit usually twisted into a loose knot, though often made in sticks. The word is from the German, and some believe it refers to the Latin word *pretium,* "reward," as in a little gift to a child. Others trace the roots to the Latin, *bracchium,* "arm."

Pretzels can be traced back to Roman times, and they have long been traditional in Alsace and Germany. Legend has it that a monk of France or northern Italy first twisted the pretzel into its unusual shape about 610 A.D. in order to imitate the folded arms of someone praying. The Dutch probably brought the pretzel to America, and there is a story that in 1652 a settler named Jochem Wessel was arrested for using good flour to make pretzels to sell to the Indians at a time when his white neighbors were eating bran flour. The first mention of the word *pretzel* in American print was about 1824, and the first commercial pretzel bakery in the United States was set up in 1861 by Julius Sturgis and Ambrose Rauch in Lititz, Pennsylvania. Most pretzels are twisted by machine, introduced in 1933.

Today pretzels come in a variety of shapes and sizes, from sticks, called "thins," to rings and saltless, hard, thick teething pretzels, or "baldys." Especially popular in New York and the eastern cities are puffy yeast pretzels sold by street vendors and at candy stores. In Philadelphia these same pretzels are usually eaten with a squirt of yellow mustard.

prickly pear. Also called "prickly cactus." Any of a variety of cacti in the genus *Opuntia* bearing an ovular fruit with a spiny skin—hence its name, first recorded in print in 1612. It is a native to the New World tropics and is grown in the southeastern United States, where it is eaten in salads or made into jams, jellies, and pickles.

progressive dinner. A meal in which each different course is eaten at a different neighbor's house. The practice became popular in the 1950s with the expansion of suburban housing developments.

Prohibition. An era lasting from 1920 to 1933 during which the United States government forbade the manufacture, sale, or transportation of intoxicating liquors. Prohibition began with passage of the Eighteenth Amendment to the federal Constitution on January 16, 1919, which went into effect one year later, and was repealed by the Twenty-First Amendment on December 5, 1933.

The Prohibition era (called by President Herbert Hoover [1874–1964; in office 1929–1933] the "Noble Experiment") was the result of intense pressure by temperance groups across the country, especially the Women's Christian Temperance Union, founded in 1874 in Cleveland, Ohio, and a Washington, D.C., lobbying organization called the Anti-Saloon League, founded in 1893. There had also been a minor but insistent political challenge mounted by the Prohibition Party, founded in 1869, which ran candidates in several presidential elections but failed ever to receive a large percentage of the popular vote.

The temperance advocates, whose main argument was against the deleterious effects of alcohol on the drinker and, by extension, on the family, the society, and the nation itself, sought to turn America "dry." Maine had become a model for other states when it forbade the sale of liquor in 1841. Most of the South followed after the Civil War, and, by the First World War, most of the Midwest, arguing that precious grain be reserved for the war effort rather than for distilleries. There was also a deliberate anti-German sentiment against the beer brewery owners, most of whom had German backgrounds. Finally, bowing to temperance pressures or drawing support from temperance funds, the House of Representatives and the Senate passed a joint resolution on December 5, 1917, to propose the ratification by at least thirty-six states of the Eighteenth Amendment. By January 16, 1919, the amendment was ratified and was put into effect one year later (after Congress had overridden President

Woodrow Wilson's veto), with additional legislation under the Volstead Act (named after its sponsor, Minnesota Representative Andrew J. Volstead [1860–1947]) to enforce it.

The law was stringent: an intoxicating liquor was defined as "any beverage containing 1/2 of 1% alcohol," which effectively put an end to the legal manufacture and sale of beer and wine as well as hard liquor. This aspect of the law crippled the hopes of building a great wine industry in America just when it seemed possible to do so. California and New York grape growers shifted to selling their fruit to home winemakers (allowed under the law originally to placate Virginia apple farmers who sold their fruit to make cider), leading to an enormous two-thirds increase in wine consumption. Beer consumption, however, declined drastically to three-tenths of what it had been before Prohibition.

Alcohol could still be sold for medicinal purposes, and many people found sympathetic pharmacists who were willing to sell alcohol or alcohol-based tonics to those who sought to drink them for more convivial purposes. Sacramental wine was also allowed to be used in Catholic and Jewish services, and a good deal of New York State's wine production shifted to reaching this market.

The sale of illegal spirits soared, and the sale of bad spirits kept pace, causing 11,700 deaths in 1927 alone. The bootlegger, a smuggler of whiskey, became a kind of folk hero to those who found evasion of an unpopular law to be in the tradition of American individuality and resourcefulness. The most fashionable spots in the major cities were SPEAKEASIES selling illicit liquor, often to prominent people in society and politics who publicly denounced the abuses of alcohol. In New York alone there were 32,000 speakeasies, many of them horrid places, others clubbish and genteel, where "Café Society" congregated. It has been estimated that Americans drank $32 billion of illicit liquor during the Prohibition era.

The same law that kept such speakeasies thriving throughout the 1920s drove many legitimate restaurants out of business, including some of the famous opulent dining establishments of the pre-Prohibition era, such as Delmonico's, and the development of fine cuisine suffered accordingly because of the lack of fine wines to accompany it.

Prohibition led immediately to opposition, mostly in the form of gangsters who controlled the importation of illegal spirits and the manufacture of the same. By also controlling distribution and many of the establishments that sold these spirits, the criminal underworld was able to coerce public officials, police, and the common people into maintaining a vicious circle of lawlessness, bloodshed, and corruption at every level of society.

Clearly the Noble Experiment was a failure, and small concessions, such as allowing in 1932 the public to buy beer and wine containing 3.2 percent alcohol (called "McAdoo wine" after the bill's sponsor, Senator William Gibbs McAdoo of California), did nothing to modify the wrongs that Prohibition had unwittingly wrought. Finally, on December 5, 1933, the Twenty-First Amendment repealed the Eighteenth and the Volstead Act, although it was not until 1966 that all statewide prohibition laws were finally repealed. Today there are still many counties, particularly in the South and Midwest, that are dry.

proof. A term that describes the alcoholic strength of a spirit. The word originates in its meaning "to pass a test," as described in *Grossman's Guide to Wines, Beers, & Spirits,* by Harold J. Grossman, revised by Harriet Lembeck (1977):

> Before making distilled spirits became a science, the primitive distillers had a very simple method for determining the potable strength of the distillate. Equal quantities of spirit and gunpowder were mixed and a flame applied. If the gunpowder failed to burn, the spirit was too weak; if it burned too brightly, it was too strong. But if the mixture burned evenly, with a blue flame, it was said to have been proved.

In America approximately one-half the proof listed on the label of a spirit indicates its alcoholic content at a temperature of 60 degrees Fahrenheit. One proof gallon equals one measured wine gallon at 100 proof. Since each degree of proof equals 1/2 percent alcohol, an 80-proof spirit would contain 40 percent alcohol.

propyl gallate. An antioxidant used in vegetable oils, meat products, chewing gum, and other foods.

prosciutto. An air-cured or dry-cured ham that originated in Parma, Italy. Prosciutto is sliced paper-thin and eaten raw, usually with ripe melon. Since an embargo prohibits the importation of Italian raw ham, American companies have manufactured a similar product they call "prosciutto," which is made according to the same method. The word appeared in the 1920s.

protose steak. A steak substitute made from vegetable protein. It was eaten by Jewish-Americans who were prohibited by kosher dietary laws from eating meat at certain times.

ptarmigan. A bird of the genus *Lagopus* that inhabits the arctic and subarctic regions. The name is originally from the Scottish Gaelic, *tarmachan,* which was transformed into a specious Greek form derived from *pteron,* "wing." The bird is hunted and roasted by the Alaskans.

pudding. A term describing several different desserts, usually cooked, including cakelike confections such as plum pudding; or a dish of suet crust containing fruits and sugar; or a spongy steamed dish; or a pastry crust filled with chopped meats, like kidney; or YORKSHIRE PUDDING, a crisp breadlike side dish made from a flour-and-egg batter cooked in pan drippings; or, as is most usual in contemporary usage, milk-based dessert made with flavorings like chocolate or vanilla cooked with a starch until thickened and then cooled until well set.

Eighteenth- and nineteenth-century cookbooks refer to any and all of these as puddings. The word seems to derive from the Old French, *boudin,* "sausage," and, ultimately, from the Latin, *botelīnus,* for many puddings were a form of encased meat or innards. The earliest examples of the word in English refer to such dishes. Dr. Johnson's *Dictionary* (1755) defines the word as "a kind of food very variously compounded, but generally made of meal, milk, and eggs." One of the earliest American desserts was a quickly thrown together mixture of cornmeal, milk, and molasses called "cornmeal mush" or "hasty pudding," known at least since 1691. (Harvard's literary society has been called the Hasty Pudding Club since 1795.) "Plum pudding" did not contain plums (*plum* in the seventeenth century referred to raisins or other fruits).

In the present century a pudding almost always means a soft-textured, milk-based dessert, the most popular being those packaged commercially and a large number of which, called "instant puddings," require no cooking at all. "Tapioca pudding" (or "tapioca," from the Tupi word, *tipioca,* "residue") is made with a starch from the cassava root. A Hawaiian pudding called *haupia* is made with coconut milk. "Indian pudding" is an old colonial dessert based on cornmeal, which used to be called "Indian meal." "Noodle pudding" is particularly savored by Jewish-Americans, and "sweet potato pudding" is beloved in the South.

CHOCOLATE PUDDING:
Combine 3 tbs. cocoa, 4 tbs. cornstarch, 1/3 cup sugar, and a pinch of salt in a saucepan. Add 1/2 cup light cream and blend well. Scald 1 1/2 cups milk and stir into cocoa mixture till thickened, then add 1 tsp. vanilla extract. Pour into dishes and chill. Serves 4.

BREAD PUDDING:
Combine 4 eggs, 2 cups sugar, and 3/4 cup vanilla extract till light in color. Melt 3/4 lb. butter in 1 1/2 qt. milk, beat in with egg mixture, and pour over 4 cups cubed stale bread. Add 3/4 cup raisins and let soak for 1/2 hr. Pour into buttered dish, place in hot water bath, and bake for 1 hr. at 350°. Serve with custard sauce or whipped cream.

INDIAN PUDDING:
Scald 5 cups milk and pour slowly over 1/3 cup cornmeal. Cook in double boiler till slightly thickened, then add 1 tsp. salt, 1/2 cup molasses, and a pinch of grated nutmeg. Pour into buttered dish and bake at 300° for about 2 hr. or until set. Serve with whipped cream or ice cream.

SUET PUDDING:
Mix 1 tsp. baking soda with 1/2 cup buttermilk, then blend in 1 cup chopped suet, 1 cup molasses, 1 1/2 cups flour, 1 cup bread crumbs, 1 tsp. salt, 1 cup preserved fruit, and a dash of cinnamon. Pour into buttered pudding mold, cover tightly, place in kettle of boiling water and cover. Steam for 3 hr.

PLUM PUDDING:
Combine 1 cup sifted flour, 3/4 lb. raisins, 1/3 cup candied fruits, 1/2 cup chopped almonds, 1/2 cup sugar, 1 tsp. baking powder, 1/2 tsp. each of allspice, cinnamon,

ground cloves, and nutmeg, and 1 tsp. salt. Blend well, then add 1 cup molasses, 3 beaten eggs, 1 cup chopped suet, and 1 cup brandy or rum. Pour into buttered pudding mold, cover, place in kettle of boiling water, cover, and cook slowly for 6 hr. or until set. Serve with hard sauce. This pudding is often doused with warmed brandy or rum and ignited at the table.

TAPIOCA:
Combine in a double boiler 1/2 cup quick tapioca and 1 pt. milk and stir over heat till tapioca is clear. Beat in 1 egg yolk, 1/8 tsp. salt, 1 tsp. vanilla extract, and 1/3 cup sugar. Stir until thickened, remove from heat, fold in 1 stiffly beaten egg white, and chill. Brown the top under a broiler just before serving.

pueblo bread. A white flour bread made by Indians of the Southwest, specifically the Pueblo Indians of New Mexico. The dough, made with flour, salt, yeast, and water (and sometimes eggs), is allowed to rise overnight in a metal washtub or large basin. The loaves are shaped by the women of the tribe into various forms of animals or sunbursts. The hot embers from the fire of pine branches are cleared out of the adobe oven so the bread may be put in to bake for about an hour.

pumpernickel. A dark bread made from rye flour. Pumpernickel was originally made in Westphalia, Germany, and in that country is called *Schwarzbrot,* "black bread." It is firm, slightly acidic in flavor, and of varying densities and textures. The word was first printed in 1839.

The term is of somewhat obscure etymology. The *American Heritage Dictionary* cites "German *Pumpernickel:* early New High German *Pumpern,* a fart (imitative) + *Nickel,* 'devil,' general pejorative; so named from being hard to digest." The *Morris Dictionary of Word and Phrase Origins* states the word was a combination of *Pumper,* the sound "made by a person falling," and *Nickel,* a "dwarf" or "goblin." A "pumpernickel," therefore, was a dolt or fool. Theodora FitzGibbon, in her *Food of the Western World,* cites a story that the word is a corruption of the phrase *"pain pour Nicole"* ("bread for Nicole"), after Napoleon's horse Nicole's fondness for black bread.

Pumpernickel was brought by German immigrants to America and is now found in most supermarkets, though the best is usually found in German or Jewish neighborhood bakeries.

pumpkin *(Cucurbita pepo).* A trailing vine and its fruit, having a yellow-orange rind and flesh. The name is from the Greek, *pepōn,* for a large melon. An English word for the pumpkin, *pompion* or *pumpion,* had been in use at least since 1545, whereas in America *pumpkin* did not make an appearance in print until 1647.

Pumpkins were among many squashes eaten by the Indians and introduced early on to the European settlers. In fact, pumpkin pie, still one of the country's favorite desserts, was served at the Pilgrims' second Thanksgiving in 1623 and has become a traditional Thanksgiving food. The colonists made pumpkin beer, and pumpkin soup was also popular. Pumpkin seeds are roasted and eaten as a snack.

Pumpkins may be cooked like other squashes, roasted with butter and brown sugar, or boiled as a side dish. Most Americans today use canned pumpkin filling for their pies.

The sugar pumpkin is also used as a Halloween jack-o'-lantern.

PUMPKIN PIE:
Combine 2 cups cooked pumpkin with 2/3 cup sugar, 1 1/2 tsp. cinnamon, 1/2 tsp. nutmeg, 1/4 tsp. ground cloves, and 1/2 tsp. salt. Blend 3 eggs with 1/2 cup heavy cream and 1/2 cup milk, then mix in pumpkin. Pour into pastry crust and bake for about 45 min. at 400° till inserted knife comes out clean. Serve with whipped cream.

punch. An alcoholic beverage mixture of various ingredients. Today the term usually refers to a bowl of a citrus- or fruit-based party drink containing any number of liquors, sparkling wine, or champagne.

The word originally came from the Hindi, *panch,* meaning "five," in reference to the five original ingredients used—lime, sugar, spices, water, and a fermented sap called "arrack." British sailors had picked up the drink and spoken of punch as of the early seventeenth century. It soon became a popular beverage in the West Indies and North American colonies, where it might be mixed with wine, milk, hot water, and, most often, rum. At the large Caribbean plantations enormous bowls of punch—described by one onlooker as big enough "for a goose to swim in"—were served at lavish social gatherings, and people of the day already were arguing as to what made a perfect punch. An advertisement in the *Salem Gazette* for 1741 by a West Indies trader proclaimed that his orange juice was preferred by many punch enthusiasts to lemon. Few would agree on the exact proportions of "planter's punch," which supposedly originated among Jamaican planters. Planter's punch is a mix of "sour-sweet-strong-and-weak," in a ratio that is the subject of debate among aficionados of the beverage.

Fish House punch, created at The State in Schuylkill, founded in 1732, is another punch hotly debated as to its original ingredients. Many other punches became associated with specific regiments, navy crews, and Ivy League universities. "Sangaree" (from the French, *sang,* "blood"), also spelled "San garee," was a colonial punch made with red wine and fruits (sometimes ale), an early version of Spanish SANGRÍA, which became popular in the 1960s as a party punch.

Nonalcoholic punches, usually made with club soda or ginger ale and various fruits, are still popular at children's parties in America.

SANGAREE:
To 1 bottle of dry red wine in a bowl add 1 cup crushed strawberries or peaches, the juice of 1 lemon, 1/3 cup sugar, a pinch of cinnamon, and ground cloves. Chill for one hour. Strain and fill glass, then top off with club soda and stir.

PLANTER'S PUNCH:
Stir over ice 1 part lime juice, 2 parts grenadine, 3 parts dark rum, and 4 parts orange juice.

NAVY PUNCH:
Mix 6 oz. lime juice, 2 pt. liquid sugar, and 3 pt. dark rum and blend over an ice chunk. Garnish with fruit and a sprinkle of nutmeg.

MILK PUNCH:
Mix together 3 oz. liquor of one's choice, 1 cup milk, and 1–3 tsp. sugar. Shake with ice, strain into cup, and sprinkle with nutmeg. If a hot punch is desired, the ingredients may be heated or boiling milk may be poured into the other ingredients.

pupu. Also, "pu pu." A Hawaiian term for various appetizers, such as macadamia nuts, barbecued meats, coconut chips, and won ton. In Chinese-American or Polynesian-American restaurants a "pu pu platter" is usually a plate of appetizers spread around a lighted burner, into which one sticks the morsels for heating.

quail. Any of a variety of New World game birds—none of which are related to the Old World quail, such as *Coturnix coturnix,* though all are in the order Galliformes and family Phasianidae. The common name *quail* derives from the Gallo-Roman *coacula,* probably from the sound made by the bird. In Middle English the word was written as *quaille.*

There is some confusion in American terminology for quail, especially since the most familiar variety, the bobwhite *(Colinus virginianus),* is called "quail" in the North and "partridge" in the South. (For further information, see PARTRIDGE.) *Quail* was first applied to this fowl in print in 1625; *bobwhite* is first recorded in 1837 and *bobwhite quail* in 1920. The term *bobwhite* derives from the sound the bird makes, as Americans perceive it. This same bird has also been called the "blue quail" in the Southwest.

Other American quails include the mountain quail *(Oreortyx pictus),* Montezuma quail *(Cyrtonyx montezumae),* gambel's quail *(Lophortyx gambelii),* also called "redhead," California quail *(L. californicus),* and scaled quail *(Callipepla squamata).*

Other varieties of quail are raised on farms in the United States, primarily the Pharoah, Egyptian, or Japanese quail, most of which are grown now for food rather than as game birds. Quails are usually roasted or grilled and are often served with wild rice.

quaking custard. A cream custard of New England around which are garnished egg whites. The name refers to the quivering texture of the dish.

quiche. A pie or tart having an egg filling and a variety of other ingredients. The word is French, probably from a German dialect word, *Küche,* "cake." Quiche is certainly a dish of French origins, especially of Lorraine. In fact, the first quiche recipes to become popular in America were those for the egg-onion-and-bacon tart called "quiche lorraine," which was extremely fashionable in the 1970s as a luncheon, brunch, or appetizer dish in the United States. Since then quiches have been adapted to contain all manner of ingredients, from peppers and cheese to vegetables, sausage, and other meats. There are even retail stores specializing in a variety of quiches, which may be cooked as a large tart or as individual tarts.

Combine 4 beaten eggs, 2 cups cream, 6 strips of cooked bacon cut into small pieces, salt, and pepper. Pour into unsweetened pastry crust, dot with butter, and bake at 375° for about 30 min. till set and slightly browned on top.

quick bread. A bread, biscuit, muffin, or other baked good without yeast or too much sweetness. The term was first printed in 1918.

rabbit. A herbivorous, long-eared mammal of the Leporidae family that is found both wild and domesticated in America. Wild rabbits are up to sixteen-inches long and weigh two to three pounds. The New World genus *Sylvilagus* includes the cottontail, the marsh, and the swamp rabbit. The Idaho pygmy rabbit *(S. idahoensis)* is found in the Great Basin of the United States. The jackrabbit and snowshoe rabbit are actually hares, though of the same family. The word in Middle English was *rabet.*

The rabbit was in America long before Europeans arrived, and the Aztecs worshipped a rabbit god; the North American Indians certainly ate them. Although Americans have always eaten rabbits, their association in the present century with pets and the image of the anthropomorphic Easter Bunny have made many people squeamish about cooking such beloved animals. Nevertheless, they are still hunted and valued for their meat, which should be taken young. The best domesticated rabbits for eating are about two months old and can be roasted whole, sautéed, fried, or broiled. Mature rabbits should be stewed and are best marinated before cooking. Americans consume about 50 million pounds of rabbit meat each year.

RABBIT STEW:
Disjoint a young rabbit and season inside and outside with salt and pepper. Melt 1 tbs. butter in pan and brown rabbit meat. Add 1 tbs. flour and simmer for 2 min. Add 1/2 cup red wine and 1/2 qt. chicken stock to cover the rabbit. Boil, then add 2 cloves of garlic, 2 cloves, 1 bay leaf, and a pinch of thyme. Cover and bake at 350° for 45 min. Add white onions and 1/2 cup mushrooms and return to oven for 15 min. Serves 4.

raccoon *(Procyon lotor).* Also, "coon" or "'coon," or "racoon." A grayish brown furred mammal with black, masklike markings found throughout North America. The name comes from the Virginian Algonquian Indian, *aroughcoune, arathkone,* and is first noted in English as early as 1608.

Raccoon was once enjoyed by the early colonial settlers of the East and South as a matter of course and continued to be enjoyed regularly by westerners. Today it is something of a delicacy among hunters and is almost never found commercially. Louisiana blacks used to call a dish of raccoon sprinkled with gin and served with mashed potatoes "drunk coon."

Remove the fat and scent glands from a dressed raccoon. Place in a large kettle with enough water to cover. Salt water well and let stand for 24 hr. Drain, cover with fresh, unsalted water, and boil for 1 hr. Drain, place in roasting pan, and season with salt and pepper. Stuff with bread crumbs mixed with thyme, rosemary, and sage. Lay strips of salt pork on the back and bake uncovered for 2 hr. at 375°.

radish. Any of a variety of plants in the genus *Raphanus,* especially *R. sativus,* bearing pungent roots usually eaten raw in salads. The word is from the Latin, *radix,* "root."

The wild radish *(R. raphanistrum)* is common in both Europe and North America, but the origins of the cultivated species, *R. sativus,* is unknown. An Oriental radish, the *daikon,* is sometimes seen at market in the United States and is grown privately by Asian immigrants.

railroad cookie. A cookie swirled on the inside with cinnamon and brown sugar. The origin of the name may derive from the dark tracks of filling that look like railroad tracks. The cookies were mentioned in a Missouri recipe book as early as 1875.

Cream 1 cup butter with 2 cups brown sugar. Beat in 2 eggs, 1 tsp. baking soda, 1/4 tsp. salt, 1 tsp. cinnamon, and 2 cups flour. Add 2 more cups flour (dough will be stiff), divide dough, roll out to 1/8-in. thickness, spread with date filling, roll up, and slice to 1/4-in. thickness. Bake 15 min. at 350°.

raisin. A sweet, dried grape. Raisins are eaten plain, mixed with nuts, cooked in cakes, pastries, breads, and puddings, and mixed with cereals, especially bran flakes, as a breakfast dish.

The word comes from the Latin, *racēmus,* which became *raisin* in Middle English.

California produces the most raisins of any region in the world, mostly from THOMPSON SEEDLESS and Muscat of Alexandria grapes. Raisins are sun-dried in the vineyards, then graded, cleaned, and packed, sometimes lightened in color with sulfur dioxide.

Ramos gin fizz. A cocktail made from cream, gin, lemon juice, orange flower water, and egg whites. It was first made by Henry C. Ramos, a New Orleans bar owner who had purchased the Imperial Cabinet (or Cabaret?) soon after he had arrived in the city in 1888. The drink became famous for its preparation at the hands of the Imperial's squad of bartenders, who during Mardi Gras of 1915 numbered thirty-five. (Rima and Richard Collin in *The New Orleans Cookbook* [1975] cite Meyer's Restaurant as the place where Ramos concocted the drink, although since 1935 the Roosevelt Hotel, now the Fairmont Hotel, has held the trademark on the name "Ramos Gin Fizz.")

Most authorities on the cocktail recommend a long shaking time for the ingredients to achieve the proper texture.

> Shake with crushed ice 1 tbs. confectioners' sugar, the juice of half a lemon, the juice of half a lime, 1 egg white, 1/2 oz. heavy cream, 1 1/2 oz. gin, a dash vanilla extract, a dash seltzer, and 3 drops orange flower water. Continue shaking till foamy and of a consistent texture—about 5 min. Pour into a highball glass. (The ingredients may be mixed in an electric blender for 1 1/2 min.)

ramp *(Allium tricoccum).* A wild onion native to North America with a long green leaf and slender white bulbs resembling the scallion. The word is an Elizabethan dialect rendering of the wild garlic, *rams* or *ramson,* and is first mentioned in English print in 1826, though it was used earlier by the English immigrants of America's southern Appalachia Mountains.

Ramps grow from South Carolina to Canada. "To many West Virginians," according to E. Kemp Miles in an article in *Gourmet* magazine (April 1983), "ramps are the harbingers of spring. The first appearance of the flat green leaves of this wild leek jutting through the snow signals the beginning of feasts and festivals where bushels of the pungent stalks are consumed, both raw and cooked, along with quantities of ham, eggs, and potatoes."

Ramps are somewhat stronger than scallions, but are eaten raw, as well as in preparations where onions, scallions, or shallots would be called for.

rankins. A nineteenth-century cheese pudding.

> Combine 1 cup buttermilk, 6 tbs. grated cheese, 3 tbs. bread crumbs, 3 tbs. butter, 1/3 tsp. salt, 1/3 tsp. dry mustard, a pinch of cayenne pepper, and a pinch of ground pepper. Bring to a boil, cool, then add 2 beaten egg yolks and fold in two stiffly beaten egg whites. Bake 15 min. in a 375° oven.

raspberry. Any of a variety of plants in the genus *Rubus* bearing fleshy, dark-purple or red berries. The name derives from an earlier word, *raspis,* and was first recorded as *raspberry* in the early seventeenth century.

America offered a wide variety of wild raspberries to the early colonists, who nevertheless imported their European variety, *R. idaeus,* for cultivation. The American red raspberry *(R. i. strigosus)* was known in Massachusetts and first listed as of 1621 among the region's wild fruits. The black raspberries *(R. occidentalis* of the East and *R. leucodermis* of the West) are the other major varieties grown in the United States, chiefly in Michigan, Oregon, New York, and Washington.

Americans eat raspberries fresh or frozen, in pies, ice cream, sherbets, and ices, and make them into sweet dessert sauces, such as melba sauce (see PEACH MELBA).

ratafia. A sweet cordial made from the infusion of fruit kernels in alcohol. The word is from the French, via West Indian Creole, and in France *ratafia* more specifically refers to sweetened aperitifs made from wines such as Burgundy and champagne. It first appeared in print in English in 1699 to describe a cherry brandy made with peach and apricot pits. (By 1845 there was also a "ratafia biscuit" to be eaten with the cordial.) "It is claimed," *Alexis Lichine's New Encyclopedia of Wines & Spirits* (1981) notes, "that the name was applied to any liqueur at the ratification of a treaty or agreement," but this seems highly unlikely.

Ratafia was a popular nineteenth-century homemade cordial, but it is now rarely seen. There have been some efforts in California wineries to produce a French-style ratafia aperitif.

rattlesnake. (Genera *Sistrurus* and *Crotalus*). Any of a number of venomous snakes, found in North America, whose tails have interlocking links that make a rattling sound when shaken by disturbed vipers. Rattlesnakes are found throughout the country and include such species as the massasauga, timber, pygmy, Eastern and Western diamondback, red diamond, sidewinder, rock, speckled, black-tailed, twin-spotted, tiger, Mojave, and western rattlesnakes.

Although they have never been particularly relished as food by most Americans, rattlesnakes have held a certain gastronomic interest among hunters, woodsmen, trappers, and cowboys, who usually put them in a stewpot or grill them.

The recipes are from the Horse & Hound Inn in South Salem, New York.

RAGOUT OF RATTLESNAKE:
Remove head and skin snake, cut into 1-in. pieces, sprinkle with flour and sauté till lightly browned. Add 1 diced tomato, 1 stalk chopped celery, 1 chopped onion, salt, and pepper. Season with 1/2 tsp. thyme, 1/2 tsp. chili powder, and 2 cloves chopped garlic. Add equal amounts of dry red wine and beef broth to cover stew. Bring to boil, then simmer for about 2 1/2 hr.

BARBECUED RATTLESNAKE:
Remove head and skin snake, cut into 2-in. pieces, and parboil for 1/2 hr. in a broth seasoned with salt, pepper, and herbs. Combine juice of 1 lemon, 1/2 cup honey, 2 tbs. Worcestershire sauce, 2 tbs. red wine vinegar, 1 chopped chili pepper, 1 clove chopped garlic, salt, and pepper. Baste snake with mixture and cook on grill.

raw bar. A stand or bar serving uncooked shellfish.

razorback. A wild hog of the southeastern United States that is descended from domesticated hogs brought over by the Spanish in 1539. The razorback was again domesticated by the American pioneers, who made bacon from its meat. It is not the same animal as the American wild pig—the peccary or javelina. *Razorback* was first printed in 1849.

red beans and rice. A Louisiana dish of kidney beans and rice flavored with a ham bone and traditionally served on Monday after a Sunday dinner of ham. The dish originated with Louisiana's Negro cooks, who call it "red and white," but it has also become associated with the Creoles and can be found in numerous New Orleans restaurants on Mondays. As John Thorne notes in his booklet *Rice & Beans: The Itinerary of a Recipe* (1981), "Although red kidney beans are often used in making red beans and rice, strict purists aver that they have too strong a flavor for the dish, and that the small South Louisiana red bean is preferred." Similarly, purists insist on using Louisiana PICKLED PORK (or sweet pickled pork), a packaged seasoning made from pork shoulder marinated in brine. There is also considerable debate as to whether the beans and rice should be cooked together or separately. *The Picayune's Creole Cook Book* (1901), from which the following recipe is taken, prefers the latter method.

> Wash 1 qt. dried red beans and soak overnight in cold water. Drain off water, place beans in a pot and cover with at least 2 qt. fresh water, and heat slowly. Add 1 lb. ham or salt pork, 1 chopped carrot, 1 minced onion, 1 bay leaf, salt, and pepper, and boil for at least 2 hr. When tender mash beans, place meat and vegetables on top, and serve on a bed of white boiled rice. May be served as an entrée or side dish.

redeye gravy. Also, "red-eye gravy" and "red ham gravy." A gravy made from ham drippings, often flavored with coffee. It is a traditional southern gravy served with ham, biscuits, and grits and takes its name from the appearance of a "red eye" in the middle of the reduced gravy. It has been popular at least since the 1930s, and the term was in print by 1947.

> Remove ham steak from skillet in which it has fried and add 1/2 cup water (some insist on ice water) or 1/2 cup strong black coffee. Scrape up ham drippings and cook about 3 min., stirring constantly. Pour over ham, biscuits, or grits.

redhorse (Genus *Moxostoma*). Any of a variety of reddish brown fishes of which eighteen species inhabit the eastern rivers, including the river redhorse *(M. carinatum),* silver redhorse *(M. anisurum),* shorthead redhorse *(M. macrolepidotum),* torrent sucker *(M. rhothoecum),* rustyside sucker *(M. hamiltoni),* golden redhorse *(M. erythrurum),* and black redhorse *(M. duquesnei).* It is a popular food fish, and South Carolinians make a "redhorse bread" with cornmeal and redhorse.

red sauce. This term may refer either to an Italian-style tomato sauce or to a tomato-flavored clam sauce, also a standard item in Italian-American cookery. Both terms have become well known since the end of World War II. See also WHITE SAUCE.

> TOMATO SAUCE:
> In 2 tbs. olive oil sauté 2 minced cloves garlic for 1 min. Remove garlic and then sauté 1 finely chopped onion till limp. Return garlic to pan, add 3 1/2 cups canned seeded tomatoes, 1 1/4 tsp. salt, 1/2 tsp. pepper, 1 tsp. oregano, 1/4 tsp. chopped parsley, and 1 bay leaf. Bring to a boil, lower to simmer and cook for at least 30 min., adding a small amount of water if necessary for texture.

RED CLAM SAUCE:
In 1/4 cup olive oil sauté 1 chopped clove garlic for 1 min., stir in 3 1/2 cups canned seeded tomatoes, and add 1/2 tsp. salt, 1 tsp. chopped parsley, 1/4 tsp. oregano, salt, and pepper. Simmer for 10 min., then add 1 cup chopped clams with clam broth. Simmer till clams are tender and tomatoes well broken down.

red snapper Vera Cruz. Red snapper cooked with chili peppers, tomatoes, and other seasonings. In Mexico this dish is called *"huachinango a la vera-cruzana,"* but it has also become a popular item in Mexican-American restaurants across the country.

Salt and pepper 4 red snapper fillets and sauté in 3 tbs. olive oil. Remove from pan and keep warm. Add 1 tbs. olive oil to pan and sauté 1 chopped onion, 2 chopped garlic cloves, 4 peeled, seeded, and chopped tomatoes, the juice of 1 lime, a pinch of oregano, and 2 red or green chili peppers that have been seeded. Cook for 10 min., return fish to pan and simmer, covered, for 10 min. Serve with rice. Serves 4.

refried beans. A Mexican-American dish of mashed, cooked pinto beans, usually served as a side dish or as a filling for various tortilla preparations. The term *refried* is actually a mistranslation from the Mexican *frijoles refritos,* which means "well-fried beans." The term was first printed in 1957.

Cook 4 cups pinto beans in water to cover till tender, and place in a skillet with 4 tbs. lard or bacon fat. Mash down the beans, adding a little of the bean liquid. Add 2 minced garlic cloves, salt, and pepper. Cook over medium heat for about 30 min., till edges are crispy. Turn out onto a warm plate. Serves 6.

relish. Any of a variety of spicy, often PICKLE-based condiments served as a side dish or spread on a food item. The word, which first appears in English in 1798, is from the Middle English for a "taste" and is derived from Old French, *reles,* "something remaining," ultimately from the Latin, *relaxāre,* "to relax" or "loosen." As Theodora FitzGibbon notes in her encyclopedia, *The Food of the Western World* (1976), "In Britain [*relish*] usually means a thin pickle or sauce with a vinegar base. In the United States the term also embraces finely chopped fruits or vegetables with a dressing of sugar, salt, and vinegar; this is not only served as an adjunct to a main course, but may also constitute the first course of a meal, as apple relish, garden relish, and salad relish."

American relishes would include CHOW-CHOW, picalilli, KETCHUP, watermelon rind, chutneys, and the many pickle-based bottled varieties that are customarily spread on hot dogs and hamburgers.

rémoulade. Also, "remolade." A mayonnaise dressing or sauce of French origin flavored with mustard and other seasonings. The word is a variant of the Picard dialect, *ramolas,* "horseradish." In New Orleans cookery the sauce is made spicier than the French version and often contains hard-boiled eggs. If chopped parsley is added it may be called a "green remoulade" or *"rémoulade verte."* Different versions will include different ingredients.

Mix 2 cups mayonnaise with 1/4 cup hot mustard, 1/4 cup horseradish, 1/2 tsp. cayenne, 2 chopped shallots, and 2 tbs. Worcestershire sauce. Chill and serve over fish, meat, or shrimp.

restaurant. A dining room or other eatery where one pays for a meal. The concept of a public place selling full meals is of rather recent origins, for although inns and taverns of one form or another have long histories, the main business of such places was either as a dispenser of spirits or as a traveler's waystop that sold food only incidentally. The word *restaurant* is French, from the verb *restaurer,* "to restore," and was only used to describe a full-fledged public dining room in Paris as of 1763. The first appearance of the word in American print—a reference in *The Prairie* (1827), by James Fenimore Cooper, to "the most renowned of Parisian restaurants"—predates the first English appearance by several years.

The taverns and inns of England had since the sixteenth century served food, usually one set meal each day called the "ordinary," which also came to mean the establishment themselves. These were common in colonial America too, as were the coffeehouses and men's clubs first set up in London in the seventeenth and eighteenth centuries. The White Horse Tavern in Newport, Rhode Island, established in 1673, claims to be the oldest continuously operating tavern in America. It was at New York City's Fraunces Tavern, run as a tavern by Samuel Fraunces since 1763, that George Washington bade farewell to his troops on December 4, 1783.

After the Revolution in France, many chefs once attached to the homes of the aristocrats opened public restaurants. The concept caught on in France's ally, the United States, where in 1794 French chef Jean "Julien" Baptiste Gilbert Payplat, once cook for the archbishop of Bordeaux, opened a French-style restaurant in Boston. The distinction of such an establishment was that a Bostonian might choose to dine there on any evening, not merely because he was traveling through town and had nowhere else to eat before his next stop, as one did at a hotel (a word first applied in America to Corre's Hotel in New York City, opened in 1794), where dining rooms began to improve rapidly as of the turn of the century. The Tremont House in Boston in 1829 was heralded at its opening for its two-hundred-seat dining room.

The idea of a public restaurant not attached to a hotel was given its true impetus by John and Peter Delmonico, two Swiss brothers, the first an ex–sea captain, the second a pastry shop manager, who emigrated to the United States in 1825 and in 1827 opened up a small, six-table coffee-and-pastry shop called Del's on Williams Street in New York City. Slowly the brothers built a discerning clientele who enjoyed the European confections, and the wines and spirits served along with them, and in 1831 the brothers opened a full-fledged restaurant with a French chef and a number of then exotic dishes that included salad and green vegetables served in the French manner. Delmonico, or, as it was better known, Delmonico's, became the beacon of good taste and lavish meals, and the brothers' success begat ten more restaurants under their family name, each one more grandiose than the last, usually run by a relative imported for the purpose of maintaining tradition.

Everyone of importance went to Delmonico's, where the finest wines and the greatest array of game were offered on a daily basis. The menu (a term first recorded in America in 1830) went on for several pages, with nearly thirty poultry dishes, eleven beef dishes, and sixteen pastries listed. The influence of French cooking on the Delmonico's menus set a mold for American deluxe dining rooms that has been maintained ever since. Delmonico's lent its name to many dishes, like DELMONICO POTATOES, Delmonico bombe, and Delmonico steak.

After English novelist William Makepeace Thackeray dined at Delmonico's, he called it "a sin to spend so much money on your belly." The restaurant even impressed the difficult-to-please Charles Dickens, who, until his visit to Delmonico's in 1868, had done little but complain about the barbarities of American dining rooms. One wonders what Dickens might have thought of a breakfast given by importer Edward Luckmeyer five years later, at which swans swam in a lake constructed in the middle of an eighteen-foot-wide table, complete with a gold birdcage made by Tiffany. It was at Delmonico's in 1866 that Samuel F. B. Morse sent the first transatlantic telegraph cable.

Delmonico's had its imitators in New York, like Rector's and Louis Sherry, and other cities followed suit, especially New Orleans, whose own French heritage enabled Antoine Alciatore to succeed immediately when he opened Antoine's in that city in 1840. Elsewhere the best restaurants were those opened in hotels, like Boston's Parker House, Niagara's International Hotel (where waiters served to the sound of a full band), Denver's Brown Palace, and many others around the country. In such establishments the food was served course by course, and with military efficiency.

In lesser public dining rooms meals were served at a furious pace and with all courses set on the table at once. English traveler Basil Hall noted that at one New York City lunchroom in 1827 two complete dinners were served to two sets of customers within twenty minutes. Crucial to the development of American hotel dining room service was the idea of the "American Plan," initiated around 1830, by which guests at hotels had to pay for their meals whether they ate them in the hotel or not. Guests on such a plan enjoyed four large meals a day at set hours, served by waiters tottering under huge platters of food and served in cavernous dining halls that were often segregated by sex. Little of the food was prepared with much sophistication, and it was consumed by the hundreds of guests present with amazing speed.

Eating out in America was an exercise of one's capacity to consume enormous amounts of food, whether it was at a restaurant like Delmonico's (where twelve-course meals were rather ordinary affairs) or at "lobster palaces" and "beer halls" of the post–Civil War era, where customers ate and drank their fill very cheaply. Dickens once commented on the American passion for shellfish, saying he saw "at every supper at least two mighty bowls of hot stewed oysters, in any one of which a half-grown Duke of Clarence might be smothered easily." Game was equally relished by the gastronomes of the day, and a typically lavish meal, like the one served to President Ulysses S. Grant at Chicago's Parker House, might include young bear, Maryland coon, leg of elk, and loin of buffalo.

Women were not admitted to all dining rooms, and until the 1870s separate rooms were provided for them to take their meals at eastern hotels. All-male establishments like saloons and barrooms often gave away a FREE LUNCH in order to attract customers, and the fare might have included anything from crackers and cheese to caviar (then a very inexpensive item).

Coffee shops were prevalent as early as the 1830s, and lunchrooms as of the 1820s. Snack bars came in about 1895, while CAFETERIAS began in the Midwest about the same time. The first AUTOMAT was opened in Philadelphia in 1902.

Americans have always prided themselves on their mobile eateries, from the chuck wagons used on the range to the urban lunch wagon and food-purveying street vendors of the post–Civil War period. The first dining cars on American trains were known as of 1838, but the truly lavish and impeccably appointed dining car (later called the "club car") was the creation, in 1868, of George Pullman, who named his first mobile restaurant after Delmonico's. Many of these railroad dining cars were sold after 1900 to be made into diners, which were set on a stationary foundation, and these became representative symbols of American roadside hospitality after the automobile became part of most people's lives and traveling the highways part of the national destiny. Diners were at first modest transformations of dining cars, but later examples, from the streamlined trains of the 1920s and 1930s, were wonderful examples of Art Deco adaptive architecture. In the East diners were often bought and run by Greek immigrants who had previously run inexpensive hash houses or coffee-shops, and some of the LUNCH COUNTER slang and jargon was once referred to as "hash-house Greek."

The cheap, fast restaurant in America might well be understood by the straightforward emblem (often in neon lights) reading EATS, which was set on many such establishments. This might apply to chili or taco stands, night-owl restaurants (places open late at night), or burger joints. The idea of serving customers in their cars (called "curb hopping") was probably begun in Miami, Florida, in the 1920s, but it was widespread throughout the United States by the 1930s, when one would go to a drive-in for hamburgers, hot dogs, milk shakes, and other quickly prepared dishes, called "fast food" in the 1960s. The hamburger stand itself took on a new allure when franchised chains like White Castle (begun in the 1920s) began selling a standardized product. Another concept for rushed customers was the one-arm lunch room (started about 1912), at which the eater sat at a chair with armrests on which the food was placed.

Prohibition effectively put a brake on the evolution of fine dining at restaurants in America, and many of the old-fashioned establishments of the Gilded Age were forced to close, including Delmonico's itself, which went out of business in 1923. Speakeasies took up the slack, ranging from terrible "dives" to society saloons like New York City's "21" Club, which after Prohibition went on to become a serious restaurant.

In the 1930s restaurants again started to acquire an affluent clientele, although the tastes of such people were either basic or informed only by the amount of money something on a menu cost. At the other end of the scale were the cheap immigrant restaurants that catered to Americans' idea of what Italian, Greek, Chinese, German, and other cuisines were, resulting in standard dishes, like chow mein, spaghetti and meatballs, and goulash, that had little to do with the traditions of the cooking of the countries from which these dishes were supposedly "imported."

New York still dominated the rest of the country for the sheer number and variety of restaurants, although New Orleans had developed its own Creole-Cajun-French cuisine and restaurants that resembled few that could be found elsewhere. San Francisco, which had enjoyed something of a gastronomic reputation before the 1906 earthquake, slowly built up its renown for good American food after that disaster. It was not until the 1970s that Los Angeles began to diverge from its self-perpetuated image as the capital of FAST FOOD.

The 1930 World's Fair in New York City had an effect on American restaurants, for it brought in excellent chefs from all over the world who served imaginative cuisine to a public generally ignorant of authentic European dishes. The manager of the French Pavilion restaurant, Henri Soulé, opened his own restaurant in New York called Le Pavillon, which became the bellwether of French classic dining rooms for the entire country, although the restaurant's influence was not significant outside New York until the 1960s.

In that same decade a new gimmick became popular—"theme restaurants," in which the style, design, decor, and food itself was all made to coalesce around a central idea, such as the "Wild West," a Roman garden, or a pirate's cove. A company called Restaurant Associates, begun in the 1950s, opened sleek, well-thought-out dining rooms with names like the Forum of the Twelve Caesars, the Trattoria, and the Four Seasons, all wed to motifs that were carried through from menu items to ashtrays. Such restaurants were widely imitated around the country, often by franchise chains.

In the 1960s a renewed interest in foreign cuisines gave Americans "ethnic restaurants"—Indian, Thai, Korean, Mexican, and a variety of Chinese restaurants featuring regional cuisines—as well as "health food restaurants" specializing in salads, vegetables, and, often, amateur cooks. The traditional European restaurateurs refined their cooking so that, for example, Italian restaurants began specializing in "northern Italian cuisine," as opposed to the southern Neapolitan and Sicilian cookery that had previously dominated. The 1970s brought in a spate of French restaurants practicing the tenets of *la nouvelle cuisine,* which was a deliberate reaction against the staid clichés of the classic menu as interpreted by kitchens in French and American hotel dining rooms for decades. This, in turn, led to a so-called NEW AMERICAN CUISINE, promoted by young American chefs and glossy magazines as using

American ingredients in new, often startling combinations and with French techniques. California chefs led this movement in the late 1970s.

Today there are more than fifteen thousand restaurants in New York City alone, and other major cities have made the installation of new deluxe restaurants a mark of their sophistication, while to a certain extent traditional American cookery has been neglected.

In 1981, the average American ate out 3.5 times per week, and spent 33 percent of his food budget eating outside the home.

rhubarb. Any of a variety of plants with long stalks in the genus *Rheum*, although the leaf stem of *Rheum rhaponticum* is the species of culinary interest. The etymology of the word goes back to the Greek, *rha*, which probably derived from the former name for the Volga River, Rha, where rhubarb was grown. In Middle English *rha* became *rubarbe*, possibly through an alteration of the Latin term *rha barbarum*, meaning "barbarian rhubarb."

Rhubarb is of Asian origins, and, although it had been cultivated at monasteries for its medicinal values, Europeans showed little culinary interest in the plant. It was not until the nineteenth century that the plant began showing up in London markets. At that time in the United States its pouch of unopened flowers, which the Alaskan Eskimos customarily ate raw, was of some gastronomic interest. Rhubarb pie, first mentioned in print in 1855, was to become one of the two most popular preparations of the food; the other was stewed, sweetened rhubarb served as a dessert. So popular was rhubarb pie that the plant is often called the "pie plant." It has been particularly relished by the Pennsylvania Dutch.

In the United States rhubarb is grown either as a hothouse or field variety, the latter more flavorful and more deeply pink in color. A pie made with rhubarb and strawberries or angelica is a traditional American dish.

RHUBARB PIE:
Combine 4 cups chopped rhubarb, 1 1/3 cups honey, 7 tbs. flour, 4 tbs. angelica, and 1/2 tsp. salt. Pour into pastry crust, dot with butter, cover with another crust, bake at 450° for 10 min. Reduce to 350° and cook another 50 min.

rice *(Oryza sativa)*. A cultivated cereal grass that is one of the most important foods of the world, especially in Asia, where it forms a large part of the diet. The word is from the Greek, *oruzon*, via the Sanskrit, *vrīhi;* in Middle English it appears as *rys*.

Although rice was a popular food in Italy, Spain, and France by the Renaissance, it did not make much of a stir in England, which nevertheless encouraged experiments to grow the crop in its American colonies, the first in 1622. In 1647 William Berkeley sowed half a bushel of rice in Virginia and reaped thirty times that amount in his first harvest. But the crop eventually failed. South Carolina is generally credited as the birthplace of the rice industry in America, based on a legend concerning the arrival in 1685 at Charleston of a Captain John Thurber, who had been blown off course. Thurber gave some

Madagascar rice to one of the city's foremost citizens, Henry Woodward, who planted it in his garden. Some stories tell of the rice dying, others of it flourishing. Another tale credits a Dutch captain with bringing the grain to Charleston in 1694, while still another gives the honor to a man named Ashby, who planted one hundred pounds of seed in South Carolina and sent back sixty tons to England in 1698.

However rice got to South Carolina, the state remained the leading rice-producing region for two hundred years. During the American Revolution the British captured Charleston and shipped the entire rice crop home, leaving no seed behind. Thomas Jefferson smuggled some Italian rice seed out of Europe in 1787 and brought it back to the Carolinas. The industry eventually revived and a favorable trade was established with England in the early nineteenth century, during which time every southern state east of the Mississippi began growing rice, the exception being Louisiana, which did not produce a rice crop till 1889, although it had been introduced there as early as 1718. California also produced rice as early as 1760, but the territory between the Pacific and the Mississippi took on the crop slowly: Texas was not cultivating the grain until 1850 and ten years later referred to the crop as "providence rice," because low-lying regions depended wholly on collected rainwater for irrigation.

By 1905 Arkansas was growing rice, and the industry took off quickly in the Sacramento Valley in California as of 1912. Missouri followed in 1920 and Mississippi in 1949. Today very little rice is grown in the original delta lands of the southern Atlantic states, with Arkansas, Louisiana, Texas, and California the major producing states. South Carolina, ironically, is no longer a major producer. Today the United States rice growers' total crop is about 10 billion pounds and the United States is the world's leading exporter of rice, even though America produces less than 2 percent of the world's crop.

WILD RICE (*Zizania aquatica*) is discussed under its main entry.

Americans of the South and Southwest eat the most rice in the United States, for it is a staple food of Hispanic-American, Creole, and Delta cookeries. In Charleston, South Carolina, rice is part of a long tradition. Samuel Gaillard Stoney, in *Charleston: Azaleas and Old Bricks* (1937), records that "on every proper Charleston dinner table [there is] a spoon that is peculiar to the town. Of massive silver, about fifteen inches long and broad in proportions, it is laid on the cloth with something of the reverential distinction that surrounds the mace in the House of Commons at Westminster. . . . If you take away the rice-spoon from the Charleston dinner table, the meal that follows is not really a meal."

Rice is combined into seafood and meat preparations, in pancakes called "rice cakes," in breads, puddings, and dumplings, or served simply boiled and buttered. It is the basis of many American dishes, like DIRTY RICE, PILAUS, JAMBALAYA, and REDS BEANS AND RICE.

Carolina rice is a long-grain variety. Brown rice is the unpolished grain of rice containing the wheat germ and outer layer of bran, which gives the seed a brownish coloring.

RICE PUDDING:
Combine 2 tbs. cooked rice with 1 tbs. raisins, and place in buttered pudding pan. Beat 2 egg yolks, add 1/2 cup sugar, 2 cups milk, and 1 tsp. vanilla. Pour over rice and bake for 40 min. at 325°. When done sprinkle with cinnamon.

rickey. A drink whose basic ingredients are lime juice and soda water. In its nonalcoholic form, a sweet syrup is usually added. In its alcoholic form, sugar is traditionally forbidden and a spirit is added, usually gin, though bourbon, blended whiskey, or applejack are sometimes used. Adding sugar would make the drink a TOM COLLINS.

The *Dictionary of Americanisms* dates the first appearance of the word in print at 1895. In his abridged edition of Mencken's *American Language* (1974), Raven I. McDavid, Jr. notes that "authorities agree that the drink was named after a distinguished Washington guzzler of the period, but his identity is disputed, as is the original form of the *rickey.*" One attribution is to a "Colonel" Rickey from Kentucky, with no further information on the subject; another names him "Joe Rickey."

In an old-fashioned glass mix with 1 ice cube 2 oz. gin, 1 oz. fresh lime juice, club soda, and a twist of lime.

CHERRY LIME RICKEY:
Place 3 tbs. cherry syrup in a tall glass, add 1 1/2 tbs. lime juice, 1 tbs. bar sugar, and ice cubes. Fill with club soda or seltzer and garnish with a slice of lime.

rivel. A Pennsylvania Dutch soup made by adding to 6 cups chicken or beef broth a combination of 2 cups sifted flour, 1/2 tsp. salt, and 1 beaten egg. Cook together for about 10 min. Serves 6.

Rob Roy. A cocktail made with Scotch, sweet vermouth, and bitters. The cocktail, sometimes called a "Scotch manhattan," is named after the legendary Robert Macgregor (1671–1734), hero of a Sir Walter Scott novel (1817) named after him and known as "Rob Roy" for his red hair. The drink's name was first printed in 1919.

Shake 3/4 oz. Scotch whiskey, 3/4 oz. sweet vermouth, and 2 dashes bitters with cracked ice. Strain and pour into chilled glass. In a dry Rob Roy dry vermouth is substituted for sweet.

rock and rye. A liqueur with a blended whiskey base, to which is added rock candy syrup and sometimes fruits, and having a proof of 60 to 70. It was used in the nineteenth century as a digestive aid.

Combine 1 pt. whiskey, 1/2 pt. glycerine, and 1/2 lb. powdered rock candy. Bottle and seal.

rock candy. A hard candy made by cooling a concentrated sugar syrup. It is often sold crystallized around a piece of string or a stick. It is sometimes used to make rock and rye, the liqueur.

Dryden & Palmer of Norwalk, Connecticut, has manufactured rock candy since 1880 and claims to be the only company still doing so.

rocky road. A confection of milk or dark chocolate mixed with marshmallows and nuts. Its name derives from the texture of the finished product. It is also the familiar name of a similarly flavored ice cream produced by the Baskin-Robbins Company.

> In a saucepan mix 2 cups milk chocolate or dark chocolate morsels, one 14-oz. can sweetened condensed milk, and 2 tbs. butter. Heat till chocolate is melted. Remove from heat. Combine 5 1/2 cups small marshmallows with 1 1/2 cups unsalted roasted peanuts or chopped almonds, then fold into chocolate mixture. Spread into a pan lined with waxed paper and chill for about 2 hr., till firm. Remove from pan, peel off waxed paper, and cut into squares. Makes 8 doz.

Roffignac. A cocktail made with whiskey, grenadine or raspberry syrup, and soda water. It is a New Orleans beverage named after an early mayor of that city, Louis Philippe Joseph de Roffignac.

An oyster dish made with mushrooms, red wine, shrimp, and scallions also goes by this same name.

rollmops. A marinated herring fillet that is stuffed and rolled and served as an hors d'oeuvre. The name comes from Germany, a combination of *rollen,* "to roll," and *mops,* "pug dog"—perhaps so called because of its stubby appearance.

> Spread individual herring fillets with mustard, then place chopped onion, a slice of pickle, and some capers on top. Roll into snug packages and tie with a string or secure with a toothpick. Marinate the rollmops in a boiled solution of 1 cup vinegar, 1 cup water, 1 tsp. sugar, 2 bay leaves, and 1 tbs. pickling spices.

Romano. A cow's-milk cheese that originated in Italy but is made in several American dairy states. The name derives from the city of Rome, and there are several varieties, including Pecorino Romano (which is quite sharp and salty) and a Wisconsin-made flattened ball of cheese called Piccolo Romano ("Little Roman"). Romano is fairly firm and is usually used as a grating cheese for pasta, salads, and other dishes.

rooster spur pepper *(Capiscum frutescens fasciculatum).* A hot red pepper, cometimes called the "bird pepper," whose name derives from its resemblance to the spur of a rooster's claw. These peppers are not commercially grown but raised in home gardens in the South.

The rooster spur pepper took on some political clout in 1978, when Attorney General Griffin Bell snuck some sausages seasoned with the pepper past Secret Service officers and into the White House, to the delight of President Jimmy Carter, (1924– ; held office 1977–1981), who asked Bell for more. As a result the Justice Department was deluged with requests for the recipe, which came from a farmer named H. S. Williams in Haralson, Georgia.

Sending rooster spur pepper condiments to politicians has been something of a small tradition in the South, maintained in Mississippi for half a century by J. C. Luter, Sr. of Walthall County, whose pepper sauce was famous as of the 1920s.

ROOSTER SPUR PEPPER SAUCE:
Clip several rooster spur peppers from a bush, leaving short stems. Wash, drain, and pack tightly in bottles. Pour boiling water over the peppers and into the bottles and let stand till scalded. Drain water, add a pinch of sugar and salt, then pour hot vinegar over peppers to fill the bottles. Seal tightly.

Roquefort dressing. A salad dressing made with Roquefort or blue cheese.

Combine 1 lb. Roquefort, 2 tbs. lemon juice, 1/2 cup heavy cream or sour cream, 1 tbs. chopped chives, Worcestershire sauce and Tabasco sauce to taste, and a dash of garlic salt.

roux. A mixture of a starch (flour, cornstarch, or arrowroot) and a fat that is browned in a saucepan until thickened and that serves as the base of a sauce or gravy. The word is French, from Latin, *russus,* "red." Roux has a particular fascination for Louisiana cooks, who contend it is the ingredient that distinguishes their finest preparations. These Creole roux are cooked far longer than most French *roux* and achieve a deep honey color (although there is also a white roux, which is pale in color because it is cooked quickly and not allowed to brown).

Combine 4 tbs. butter or lard with 4 tbs. flour in a skillet and cook, stirring constantly, over a very low flame until it is a rich brown color throughout. This may take 20–45 min.

Ruby Cabernet. A red Vinifera grape used to make a medium-bodied red wine. It was developed in 1946 by Harold Paul Olmo at the University of California at Davis from crossing CABERNET SAUVIGNON and Carignane. Most Ruby Cabernet wine is produced in California's Central Valley.

rugola. Also, "arugola," "arugala," and others. An herb, *Eruca sativa,* known in England as "rockets." The name is derived from the Italian regional words for the herb, *rucola* or *ruccetta.* The word first appeared in English print as of 1973. The herb is native to Eurasia but was brought to America by the Italian immigrants of the late nineteenth century, and it is still very much localized in this country within cities with large Italian populations. It is eaten with salad dressing and often with tomatoes. It should not be confused with "rocket salad," an American winter cress.

rum. A spirit distilled from fermented sugar cane, principally molasses. There are several types of rum, ranging from light to full-bodied, most produced in the islands of the Caribbean but also on Java in Indonesia (called "Batavia Arak") and in Guyana along the Demerara River. Although some heavy rums may be distilled at 190 proof, federal regulations require a minimum of 80 proof.

Rum was first made in the Caribbean, possibly in Barbados, around 1600, after Christopher Columbus brought sugar cane to the West Indies from the Azores. These first rums were made by the Spanish, but the rum trade was quickly picked up by various Europeans. By 1639 the spirit was called "kill-devil." The word *rum* is of somewhat obscure origins: some believe it may derive from the Latin, *saccharum,* for "sugar." The *Oxford English Dictionary* suggests *rumbustion* and *rumbullion* are earlier forms. The first use of the word was in 1654, long before the date of another story sometimes cited to explain the origin of the name, the legend that in 1745 British Admiral Edward Vernon (also credited with providing the word GROG) tried to cure his crew's scurvy by switching their beer ration to the molasses-based spirit. The grateful seamen nicknamed their captain "Old Rummy," for *rum* was then a slang term for "the best."

The rum trade was exceptionally important in the colonial era, and by 1657 rum was even being produced in New England. The spirit was shipped to Europe and sold or traded in Africa for slaves to work the American plantations, which produced the molasses to make more rum.

Until gin replaced it as a cheap drink in the eighteenth century, rum was the predominant alcohol of the poor and a subject of frequent jeremiads from the pulpit. It was often drunk at breakfast or mixed with other ingredients to make early forms of cocktails, such as shrub, flip, punch, and grog. "Bombo" (possibly named after British Admiral John Benbow [1653–1702]), made from rum, hot water, and molasses, was popular in North Carolina, while "black-strap," a mixture of rum and molasses, was favored in New England, where pungent rums were called "stink-a-bus." "Samson," referring to the most powerful of Biblical heroes, was rum mixed with cider.

Rum was given out at political rallies; in fact, George Washington gave out seventy-five gallons of rum to voters during his successful campaign in 1758 for representative in the Virginia House of Burgesses. By 1775 Americans were drinking four gallons of rum per person per year, but this was soon to change. The British had passed in 1733 the Molasses Act, which imposed high duties on the colonists; this was followed by the Sugar Act in 1764, which cut the duties on molasses, but made the importation of sugar, wine, and coffee very expensive. Both acts were strictly enforced against smugglers. These laws had a crippling effect on the New England distilleries and further hastened the general dissent that led to revolution in the next decade. One story has it that Paul Revere fortified himself with two drafts of Medford rum at Isaac Hall's distillery before beginning his famous ride to warn the colonists of a British invasion on the night of April 18, 1775.

After the war America's favorable trade relations with the British West Indies was disrupted and the price of rum rose. Also, a strong temperance movement was building in the new country that effectively prevented the recovery of the New England distilleries. Domestic production was further impaired by war between France and England and America's own War of 1812 with England. The abolition of the slave trade in 1808 destroyed any possibility for economic viability in United States rum production, although a low-grade drink made from molasses, called "tafia," was produced in New Orleans during the nineteenth century.

Rum continued to be very popular, however, and, after the reestablishment of the United States Navy in 1794, an act of Congress decreed that every sailor's ration should include "one half pint of distilled spirits per day, or in lieu thereof, one quart of beer per day." Rum was preferred, usually drunk in the form of grog and mixed with water. The Navy Department tried to substitute whiskey for rum as an economic measure, but it was years before the latter spirit was accepted by most sailors. The grog ration was reduced throughout the nineteenth century, after a panel of surgeons in 1829 had found it inexpedient and demoralizing. Finally, after urging from Assistant Secretary of the Navy Gustavus V. Fox, Congress resolved on July 14, 1862, that the "spirit ration shall forever cease and thereafter no distilled spiritous liquor shall be admitted onboard vessels of war, except as medicine." The grog ration ended when President Abraham Lincoln signed the resolution on September 1, 1862, though the confederate navy kept up the ration throughout the Civil War. (The British Admiralty did not abolish the ration until August 1, 1970.)

Today Americans obtain most of their rum from the Virgin Islands, where rum has been made since the repeal of Prohibition in 1933. Seventy percent of the rum comes, however, from Puerto Rico, which makes light White or Silver rums and more flavorful Amber or Gold rums, all hovering around 80 proof, and "liqueur rums," which are dry and robust. There is still some rum made in Massachusetts (about two hundred thousand gallons), but the Bureau of Alcohol, Tobacco, and Firearms of the United States Treasury dropped the appellation "New England rum" from the United States Standards of Identity list in 1968. Nevertheless, New Englanders continue to consume more rum than any other Americans. Currently Americans drink about 30 million gallons of rum, mostly light. The spirit constitutes about 7 percent of the liquor market.

Today rum is usually mixed with other ingredients to make cocktails like the DAIQUIRI, the PIÑA COLADA, EL PRESIDENTE, and the CUBA LIBRE. Rum and Coke (rum mixed with Coca-Cola) is particularly popular among young Americans, and hot buttered rum is consumed in winter. Listed below are some of the more popular rum drinks.

beachcomber. A drink dating possibly from the 1930s. Shake with ice 1 oz. maraschino, 2 oz. lemon juice, and 8 oz. rum.

between the sheets. The name probably refers to the cocktail's supposed ability to force one to bed, but see THREE SHEETS IN THE WIND for another alternative. Shake with crushed ice 1 part Triple Sec, 2 parts lime juice, 3 parts brandy, and 3 parts Gold rum. Serve with lemon twist.

hot buttered rum. In Kenneth Roberts's novel, *Northwest Passage* (1937), a character says of this old New England favorite,

And it ain't a temporary drink. . . . No matter how much you drink of anything else, it'll wear off in a day or so; but you take enough hot buttered rum and it'll last you pretty near as long as a coonskin cap. . . . After a man's had two-three drinks of hot buttered rum, he don't shoot a catamount; all he's got to do is walk up to him, kiss him just once; then put him in his bag, all limp.

Roberts's recipe is as follows: Heat a tumbler, add 1/2 inch hot water, and dissolve 1 tsp. sugar in it. Add a jigger of New England rum, 1/2 tsp. cinnamon, a pat of butter, and more hot water.

rumrousal. A New England milk punch made by combining 1 qt. Jamaican rum, 3 qt. milk, 1 1/2 cups honey, and 1/2 pt. bourbon. The origin of the name is unknown.

rum tum tiddy. A New England blend of tomato soup and Cheddar cheese served as a main course.

To 2 cups of tomato soup add 1/2 lb. sharp Cheddar cheese and cook in a double boiler till cheese is melted. Add 1/4 tsp. dry mustard and 1 beaten egg. Stir briefly, then serve on buttered toast.

Russian dressing. A salad dressing made from mayonnaise, pimiento, chili sauce, green pepper, and chives. It is so called possibly because the mixture was thought to resemble those found in Russian salads, but it is American in origin, first found in print in 1922.

Combine 1/2 cup mayonnaise with 1/4 cup chili sauce, 1 tbs. chopped pimiento, 1 tbs. chopped green pepper, and 1 tsp. chopped chives.

rye 'n' Injun bread. Also, "Rhineinjun bread." A New York Dutch bread made from 1 qt. unbolted Rhode Island rye meal and 2 qt. Narraganset cornmeal. According to Alice Morse Earle's *Colonial Recipes in Old New York* (1926), the bread was cooked in a fireplace and covered with hot ashes. Its first mention in print was in 1805.

rye whiskey. One of the first whiskeys made in America, rye must be made from at least 51 percent rye grain, which can be mixed with corn and barley, and must be aged in barrels for at least a year. The word *rye* is often casually used for blended whiskeys that do not have the legal 51 percent rye grain, but to print such an appellation on the label would be forbidden by law.

The first distilleries to make rye whiskey were set up in the eighteenth century by Scots and Irish settlers in western Pennsylvania. The first appearance of the term in print was in 1785.

saccharin. An artificial sweetener that is 350 times sweeter than sugar. Saccharin is used in processed foods and as a substitute for sugar. Created at the turn of the century, it is now manufactured by the Sherwin-Williams Companies and currently accounts for about 70 percent of the artificial-sweetener market in America. The chemical makeup of saccharin is $C_7H_5NO_3S$, and the name derives from Latin, Greek, Pali, and Sanskrit root words meaning "sugar."

sago. A starch from the sago palm *(Metroxylon, Arenga,* and *Caryota)* used as a thickener for puddings and other desserts. The word is from the Malay, *sagu,* and first appears in English print in 1580.

salad. A dish of leafy vegetables dressed with various seasonings, sauces, and other vegetables or fruits. The word is from the Latin, *sāl,* for "salt," because the first salads of Rome were dressed with little more than simple salt. In Middle English the word became *salade,* and throughout the nineteenth century *salat* is often used in American cookbooks. In England a salad composed of lettuce or other leafy vegetable only is called a "green salad" and is served as an accompaniment to cooked meats or poultry, whereas a "green salad" in America has, at least since 1891, meant a separate salad course, usually served before the main course, with a simple dressing of oil and vinegar. In France and elsewhere in Europe salads are customarily served after the main course and before the cheese.

Americans had very little interest in salad for most of their history, and more often than not after the Civil War a salad was largely composed of poultry or seafood and vegetables surrounded by only a few lettuce leaves. The wealthy, however, began enjoying European-style salads in the new restaurants opening in the large cities, especially in New York, where Delmonico's restaurant specialized in novel salad dressings and the WALDORF SALAD of the Waldorf-Astoria hotel was an instant sensation.

"Moulded" or "congealed" salads, made with gelatin or aspic and sugar or sweet fruits, were common in the late nineteenth century. The Shakers had long made "fruit salads," which might not have had any greens at all, and these became a popular luncheon dish in place of a first course. The Germans brought POTATO SALADS, and the Italians made tomatoes the most popular ingredient of all in twentieth-century salads, especially with the availability of excellent fruit and vegetables from California then entering the market. California was also the inspiration for a great number of famous salads, such as the GREEN GODDESS, PALACE COURT, and (via Tijuana, Mexico) CAESAR SALAD. So pervasive was the California influence that a salad has become a common main course item in itself, called "chef's salad" and including ham and hard-boiled eggs, on many menus as well as at many hosts' tables. Restaurants in the 1970s developed the idea of the "salad bar," a long counter of greens, seasonings, vegetables, and condiments at which the customer arranges his own salad on whim. Some sandwich fillings made with mayonnaise are also called salads, as, for example, tuna salad, chicken salad, or egg salad. In the 1970s and 1980s cold pasta salads, particularly those made with tortellini, mayonnaise, and dill, became fashionable.

Dressings have ranged from the very simple oil and vinegar, called FRENCH DRESSING since 1900, to elaborate sauces that might contain orange slices and marshmallows. Only in the recent past have endive, escarole, rugola, and other European greens become popular.

For individual salads or dressings see main entries.

salami. A well-seasoned, often smoked sausage of various kinds most often used as a cold cut or sandwich meat. The name is from the Italian, *salame,* "salted pork," and Vulgar Latin, *salāre,* dating in English print at least to 1852. Since foreign sausages are not allowed to be brought into the United States for health reasons, many varieties of Italian salami have been reproduced here, although usually somewhat less spicy. Most are made from a combination of pork and beef, the best known being Genoa salami, which derives its name from the kind of sausage made in Genoa, Italy. Mortadella is a bologna-style sausage that is larded with pork fat. The name is from the Latin, *murtātum,* a sausage made with myrtle and berries, first appearing in English in 1613.

saleratus. An early-nineteenth-century form of BAKING POWDER. Used as a leavening agent, it was an improvement over pearlash (used in the eighteenth century) and predated baking soda, which came along in the 1870s. Saleratus (which in Latin means "aerated salt") was first made from potassium bicarbonate, then sodium bicarbonate, and it imparted an undesirable bitterness. One may still hear of old-fashioned saleratus bread and biscuits, although one will no longer find saleratus in a grocery store.

Salisbury steak. A patty made of ground beef and seasonings that is usually broiled. The dish was named after Dr. J. H. Salisbury, who at the end of the nineteenth century advocated eating beef three times a day for health benefits.

The Salisbury steak is often cited as an early example of what was soon to become the HAMBURGER.

Combine 1 lb. chopped beef with 1 minced onion, 1 tbs. chopped parsley, salt, and pepper. Shape into ovals about 1 1/4-in. thick and broil on one side. Press in fried bacon bits on the other, and then broil that side till bacon is crisp and the inside is cooked as desired. May be served with a pan gravy. Serves 2.

Sally Lunn. Also, "Sally Lunn bread." A bread, made from flour, yeast, eggs, and sugar, of English origins and usually associated with the city of Bath, where a woman named Sally Lunn is supposed to have sold these tea cakes in the eighteenth century. Others suggest the name derives from French, *soleil* and *lune*, "sun and moon," or *soleil* and *une*, "sun-one," because of their golden bright, puffy appearance. The first appearance of the name in English print was in 1780. In 1827, William Hone's *Everyday Book* remarked that Sally Lunn was a Bath woman who sold the bread "about thirty years ago" on the streets and whose business was bought by a local banker and musician who made up a song about her.

Sally Lunn bread recipes are found throughout American cookbooks of the nineteenth century.

Scald 1 cup milk, cool till warm, dissolve 1 pkg. yeast in the milk, and set aside. Cream 1/2 cup butter with 1/3 cup sugar till light. Beat 3 eggs into butter and add 4 cups sifted flour and 1 tsp. salt, alternating with the milk mixture. Cover and let rise to double. Beat again and pour into a 10-in. tube pan. Let rise to double again, then bake at 350° for 45 min.

salmagundi. Also, "salmagundy." A dish of chopped meat, eggs, anchovies, onions, and vinegar served on lettuce. The word is from the French, *salmigondis,* for a "hodgepodge," and first appears in English print in 1674. Salmagundi was a popular English and American colonial dish.

In boiling water cook 12 white onions till tender. Drain and cool. Mix together 3 cups cooked chicken cut into strips, 4 chopped hard-boiled eggs, 8 anchovies, 1 tbs. chopped parsley, 1/2 cup salad oil, 1/4 cup white wine vinegar, salt, and pepper. Add white onions and mix together well, then pour over lettuce leaves. Serves 6.

salmon. Any of a variety of fish of the genera *Salmo* and *Oncorhynchus* having eight species in United States waters. The name is from Latin, *salmō,* which became the Middle English *samoun.* As with many of America's fishes, the salmon was noted for its size and abundance by the first white settlers, only to be fished out or driven out by pollution. Today this once ubiquitous fish is an expensive delicacy.

The salmon was extremely important to the Indian diet, and as Waverly Root points out in *Food* (1980), "in several of the Indian languages the word for 'salmon' was also the word for 'fish.'" The great majority of the fish consumed by the Northwest Indians was salmon, cooked in scores of ways, including planking the fish on driftwood or alderwood and allowing the embers of a fire to cook the flesh. Salmon was also dried and smoked, then stored in seal bladders, a preparation white settlers called "Siwash cheese."

The superstitions about salmon that abounded among the Chinook Indians were based on the fear that if the salmon disappeared, the tribes would starve to death. They removed the heart and burned it, lest it be eaten by dogs, who would defile the fish's spirit; menstruating women or girls could not eat salmon. In *American Cooking: The Northwest* (1970), Dale Brown wrote that "the Chinook Indians believed . . . that anyone involved in preparing a corpse for burial could drive the fish away, and to avert this danger went so far as to bury the infirm alive."

Viking seafarer Eric the Red was amazed at the size of the Atlantic salmon he found when he sailed American waters in the tenth century, and early European settlers bemoaned the constant diet of salmon they endured, even to the point of having a clause written into indentured servants' contracts that forbade the serving of salmon more than once a week.

The waters of the East and West swarmed with salmon. When Lewis and Clark made their way through the Columbia River in the Northwest territory they found their boats blocked by thousands of enormous salmon that had died spawning. In New England it was not considered a true celebration of the Fourth of July if steamed salmon was not part of the feast. In Hawaii, LOMI-LOMI salmon is equally beloved. By 1840 salmon was being canned in New England and shipped across the country, and then the Californians reversed the transport about 1864. By the end of the nineteenth century salting plants had proliferated on the Columbia River.

By 1889 the Maine coast salmon catch totalled 150,000 pounds, but by the First World War overfishing and pollution had reduced the Northeast's salmon fisheries so severely that in New York one might find only cod and trout sold fresh at market. The salmon became fewer in number in the East and began to dwindle in the West too, so that by 1950 only about a thousand pounds—about eighty-two fish—were taken in Maine. In 1964 fishermen discovered a large salmon feeding ground off Greenland. This revived hopes of a resurgence, but domestic fisheries do not produce nearly enough salmon for the market, with only about 17 million pounds landed in the Columbia River in recent years. Today all Atlantic salmon come from Canada or Europe.

The main species of salmon in American waters include the Atlantic salmon *(Salmo salar);* the Chinook salmon *(Oncorhynchus tshawytscha),* also called "spring," "king salmon," and "quinnat salmon"; the pink salmon *(O. gorbuscha);* the chum salmon *(O. keta),* the word *chum* (origins unknown) referring to bait, which is also called "dog salmon" because the Athabascan Indians of the Yukon fed it to their dogs; the coho *(O. kisutch),* also called "silver salmon" (the origins of the word *coho* are unknown); and the sockeye salmon *(O. nerka),* also called "blueback" or "red salmon" (the word *sockeye* is from dialectical Salish, *suk-kegh*).

Domestic smoked salmon comes from the Pacific and is often labelled "Nova," "Novy" or "Novie" in imitation of true Nova Scotia salmon, which is rarely seen in United States markets. The Pacific fish is wet-cured, that is, it is placed in a salt brine, while the Atlantic, which is almost never encountered at market anymore (except if the salmon is from Canadian or European waters), is dry-cured with salt and sugar. Indian cure or Indian hard cure is a process of brining and cold-smoking Pacific salmon once used by the Northwest Indians. Kippered salmon is mildly brined and hot-smoked. *Squaw candy* is a colloquial term for strips of Pacific salmon salt-brined and hot-smoked. Kennebec salmon (the name derives from the Kennebec River in Maine) merely refers to a preparation of poached salmon steaks.

See also LOX.

saloon. A place where alcoholic drinks are sold by the glass and drunk either at a bar or a table. The term comes from the French, *salon,* "room," and in England for a long while it meant just that, especially a large, public room. But in America the term had come to mean a bar or tavern by the 1840s, and *saloon keeper* was an acceptable term by 1860. By the time of Prohibition the word had taken on a particularly unsavory connotation, so that after the repeal of Prohibition in 1933 Americans continued to use other terms, like *bar, tavern, lounge,* and others. By the 1960s *saloon* had a distinctly antique ring to it and establishments that used the word in their names often were trying to convey a certain "turn-of-the-century" connotation about the barroom.

salsa. A general term for seasoned sauces, usually made with chili pepper, in Mexican-American and Tex-Mex cookery. Salsa is used for dipping or as a condiment to main courses. The word is Spanish.

> Chop up 1 tomato with 1 onion, 4 green or red chilies, and 2 cloves garlic. Add salt to taste and let marinate for 1/2 hr.

salsify *(Tragopogon porrifolius).* Also called "vegetable oyster" or "oyster plant." A native European plant with an edible taproot. The name is derived from the French, *salsifis,* and Italian, *salsifica.* Some believe the root has a faint oysterlike flavor (nineteenth-century cookbook author Mrs. Sarah Tyson Rorer wrote that vegetarians would make a mock oyster soup from it), and it was once very popular as a vegetable. Recently there has been a resurgence of interest in the plant.

> Wash and scrape salsify roots and plunge into 4 cups salted cold water with 1 tbs. vinegar. Boil 15 min., let stand, then cut into thin slices lengthwise. Dot with butter, salt, and pepper, cover with cream sauce and bread crumbs, and bake in 350° oven for 20 min. Salsify slices may also be placed in batter and fried, in which form they resemble oysters.

salt. Sodium chloride, widely used as a seasoning, a curing medium for meat and fish, and the basis for pickling brine. Salt appears in a wide range of foods, from cheese to applesauce, and in many foods where one would not expect to find it, such as in sweet desserts. The food-processing industry in America adds salt indiscriminately to food items that home cooks would rarely salt. As a result, one-fourth to one-half of Americans' salt intake comes from processed food; only one-third is added directly at home in cooking or serving. The rest is ingested through some foods and some drinking water in which salt is naturally found. Americans consume an average of about two teaspoons per day, or eight-and-a-half pounds per year, an amount that has raised some concern among health officials and led in recent years to a reduction by some food processors of the salt added to their products.

Salt (Old English, *sealt;* Latin, *sal*) is an ancient seasoning and a valued one, having at certain times in history been used as money and barter. It is obtained from the evaporation of seawater (called "sea salt") and is also dug out of the earth in crystalline form (called "rock salt").

The early settlers in America brought salt with them, as well as salted meat and pork called "salt horse." Importing salt from England, France, Spain, the Canary Islands, and the West Indies was preferred to early attempts at domestic salt making. "Bay salt," from seawater evaporation, was preferred for curing meat and fish, while the salt used for seasoning at home was generally referred to as "table salt." Later, salt was obtained from the Great Salt Lake in Utah, but during the Civil War the seizure by Northern troops of the saltworks in the Great Kanawha and Holston valleys cut off the South's supply, causing widespread spoilage of meats and other foods for the Confederacy and forcing some Southerners to scrape the floors of smokehouses for the residue dripped from ham and bacon cured with the substance.

A "salt cellar" was not only a treasured repository at an American dinner table of the eighteenth and nineteenth centuries, but also functioned as a centerpiece and social "borderline," with honored guests sitting above it with the host and lesser guests positioned below it.

A "salt lick" is a natural deposit of salt licked by animals in the wild, also called, depending on the territory, a "deer lick" or "buffalo lick." A "salt marsh" is a low-lying coastal grassland subject to tidal flooding.

"Salt rising bread" is a bread of the 1830s and 1840s made from flour, water or milk, and salt, which had a leavening effect.

Salt is packaged and sold in a variety of ways. Seasoned salts are those flavored by onion, garlic, celery, pepper, monosodium glutamate, and other substances. Kosher salt is a large-grained, coarsely crushed salt used by Orthodox Jews according to kosher food laws. Iodized salt contains cuprous iodide or potassium iodide, added as a public health measure to prevent goiter due to insufficient iodine in the American diet.

salteur liquor. Diluted spirits given to the Indians by early fur traders.

salt hoss. Cowboy's term for corned beef.

salt potato. A small new potato that has been soaked or boiled in a brine solution. It is a specialty of Syracuse, New York, once a great salt-producing center. Originally the potatoes were soaked in the residue of the brine used in the production of sodium carbonate (washing soda) by the Solvay process. Today the potatoes may be boiled in heavily salted water at home or purchased already packaged at a grocery.

sand dab *(Citharichthys sordidus).* Also, "Pacific sand dab." A flounderlike flat fish found from the Bering Sea to Cape San Lucas, Baja California. It is a delicacy of the Pacific, usually dredged in flour, salt, and pepper, sautéed in butter, and served with a dip of vinegar, parsley, and garlic or merely sprinkled with lemon. The first mention of the fish by this name in print was in 1891.

sandwich. A dish of sliced bread and any variety of meats, cheese, relishes, jellies, vegetables, lettuce, and condiments. It is primarily a LUNCH item for most Americans and is far more popular here than in its country of origin, England, where it was named after a notorious gambler in the court of George III named John Montagu ("Jemmy Twitcher"), Fourth Earl of Sandwich (1718–1792), who during twenty-four-hour betting marathons would order bread-and-meat dishes that he could eat while continuing to gamble. The combination came to be named after him about 1762, but it was not known in America till some time later. Eliza Leslie's *Directions for Cookery* (1837) listed ham sandwiches as a supper dish, but it was not until much later in the century, when soft, white bread loaves became a staple of the American diet, that the sandwich became extremely popular and serviceable. By the 1920s white loaf bread was referred to as "sandwich bread" or "sandwich loaf."

Most American sandwiches are made with this type of presliced bread, sometimes toasted, sometimes trimmed of its crusts to make "tea sandwiches" for afternoon teas. There are also toasted sandwiches, often made with melted cheese, and "open-faced" sandwiches, usually made with one slice of toast, slices of meat or poultry, and a gravy. These are also called "hot sandwiches." Sandwiches are usually made on buttered bread.

Some of the most popular and obvious sandwich makings would include: peanut butter and jelly; corned beef or pastrami, usually on rye bread with mustard; turkey with mayonnaise and lettuce; American or Swiss cheese; tongue, usually with mustard; bologna, usually with mustard; liverwurst on pumpernickel or rye; ham and cheese with mustard; bacon, lettuce, and tomato, called a "BLT," usually with mayonnaise; tuna fish, always made with canned white tuna and sometimes mixed with mayonnaise; and cream cheese and jelly. See also CANAPÉ and CLUB SANDWICH.

CHICKEN SALAD SANDWICH:
Combine 1 cup cooked, chopped white chicken meat with 2 tbs. chopped celery, a few capers, 2 tbs. chopped green pepper, and enough mayonnaise to bind the mixture. Add salt and pepper to taste. Spread on white sandwich bread that has been lightly toasted.

HOT ROAST BEEF SANDWICH:
On buttered toast place several thin slices of rare roast beef. Salt and pepper to taste, then cover with a ladle of brown gravy made from the pan juices of the beef. Often served with mashed potatoes.

GRILLED CHEESE SANDWICH:
Butter two slices of sandwich bread and place between them one or two slices of American or Swiss cheese. (Some like to add crisp bacon and tomato.) In a skillet melt 2 tbs. butter till foamy, place the sandwich in the skillet and place a light weight on top to press down the sandwich and melt the cheese. When browned, turn over, place weight on top, and cook until other side is also browned and the cheese melted. (Instead of using a weight, a small cover over the sandwich may also be used.)

REUBEN:
(Named after Reuben's delicatessen in New York City.) Place slices of corned beef and Swiss cheese on rye bread, add sauerkraut, cover with rye bread, and cook as grilled cheese sandwich.

EGG SALAD SANDWICH:
Combine 1 chopped hard-boiled egg with 1 tsp. chopped green pepper, 1 tsp. pimiento, 1 tsp. chopped celery, and mayonnaise to bind. Spread on buttered toast.

sangría. A drink made from red wine, fruits, and, sometimes, brandy. The word is Spanish for "bleeding" and refers to the drink's blood-red color. Sangría originated in Spain, where it is made in batches and often served in a pitcher, a practice that has become just as popular in the United States.

The drink took on a certain faddishness after being introduced by Alberto Heras, supervisor of the Spanish Pavillion at the 1964 New York World's Fair (his recipe is given below). It was a very popular party drink throughout the 1960s and 1970s, including a commercially bottled sangría called "Yago."

Empty bottle of red Spanish wine into a pitcher, add 2 tsp. sugar, and mix till dissolved. Add 1 lemon cut in slices, 1/2 orange cut in slices, 1 1/2 oz. Cointreau, 1 1/2 oz. Spanish brandy, ice, and one 12-oz. bottle of club soda. Stir, then let chill for 15 min. Pour sangría into wine glasses without the fruit.

sapsis. A porridge flavored with beans. It was made by Indians on the eastern coast of North America and may still be found in New England states.

Saratoga potatoes. Also, "Saratoga chips." Thinly sliced, deep-fried potatoes. "Potato chips" have been known since the 1840s, but they were sliced fairly thick in those days. According to most authorities the thin potato chip was created in 1853 at the Moon's Lake Lodge in Saratoga, New York (another story places it at the Montgomery Hall hotel in the same town), when chef George Crum supposedly sliced his potatoes as thin as possible to placate the request of a particularly stubborn customer for thinner potatoes. The next day the chips were given out free in paper cones to customers, and a sign was put on the bar reading, "Help Yourself." They became very popular across the country, and after a while the term *potato* *chip* meant a very thin, fried potato, usually served cold as a snack and most often purchased at a food store. They are now a staple of informal parties, served with beer, soft drinks, and aperitifs. Except at restaurants, they are rarely prepared fresh and hot.

> Slice peeled potatoes as thin as possible, place in ice water, and let stand for several hours. Fry in hot oil till crisp and golden. Drain on paper, sprinkle with salt, and serve hot or cold.

sardine. Any of a variety of small species of fish in the HERRING family. The name derives from the Greek, *sardinos,* which became the Middle English *sardeyn.*

Canning of the fish began on the island of Sardinia. Today sardines are air-dried and coated with oil, then canned, occasionally with other seasonings such as mustard or chili.

Most American sardines now come from Maine, after a long period during which the industry was dominated by Pacific companies. The Pacific sardine *(Sardinops sagax)* population has declined significantly since the 1930s, however.

sarsaparilla. Also, "sassparilla." A carbonated beverage, which first appeared in the 1840s, made from the smilax plant or ginger flavors. The name comes from the Spanish words for a bramble *(zarza)* and a small vine *(parrilla).* The soft drink is still found today, though it is not as popular as it once was.

sashimi. A Japanese dish of carefully sliced raw fish. It became known in America in the era of jet travel during the 1960s. Today most Japanese restaurants in major American cities have a sushi bar serving sashimi.

sassafras *(Sassafras albidum).* An aromatic tree of the laurel family, native to North America. The bark of the root is dried and used as a flavoring for root beer and as a brew called "sass tea." The leaves were pounded by the Choctaw Indians to make filé powder, an essential ingredient in the Creole stew called "filé gumbo."

The tree was given the name *sasafrás* by the Spaniards, who may have taken it from an Indian word or confused it with the *Saxifrage* genus of plant. By 1602 it had taken on its English spelling, though it had been mentioned in print as of 1577.

The Food and Drug Administration banned the sale of sassafras tea when it was found to have carcinogenic properties, and the leaves may no longer be used as a flavoring for root beer or other beverages, although extracts of the plant are considered safe.

sauce piquante. A spicy Louisiana tomato-based sauce customarily cooked with shellfish, turtle, or frogs' legs. The term is from the French, *piquante,* "sharp" or "tart."

In 2 tbs. oil sauté 2 chopped onions, 2 chopped cloves garlic, and 1 chopped bell pepper. Then add 1 stalk chopped celery, 1 can tomato paste, 2 chopped scallions, salt and pepper, and 1/4 cup vinegar. Bring to a boil, then lower to a simmer. Add meat from shellfish, turtle, or frogs' legs and enough water to cover meat. Cook until meat is tender and sauce is reduced. Serve over rice.

sauerkraut. Also, "sourcrout." A chopped cabbage that is salted and then fermented in its own juice. The word, which in German means "sour cabbage," is first mentioned in American English in 1776, and the dish was long associated with German communities in the United States. It is still widely enjoyed, especially with pork dishes and as a condiment on hot dogs. It is usually bought in groceries rather than made at home.

Sauvignon blanc. Also, "Fumé blanc." A white Vinifera grape that makes a fruity, spicy wine. It is used extensively in the white wines of Graves in Bordeaux and in the Loire Valley. In California it has achieved great success in the last ten years, especially after the Robert Mondavi Winery of the Napa Valley substituted the name "Fumé blanc" in the late 1960s to make it sound more attractive to American ears.

saxifrage. Any of a variety of plants in the genus *Saxifraga* bearing a leafy, lettucelike green. The word is from the Latin, *saxifragus*, "rock-breaking," because the plant grows in the crevices of rocks. The main North American variety is the mountain lettuce *(S. micranthidifolia)*, also called "branch lettuce" and "deer-tongue." Two other varieties, *S. virginiensis* and *S. pennsylvanica*, proliferate along the eastern coast.

Saxifrage is cooked as a vegetable and added to soups. In the South it is often fried with bacon and onions.

Sazerac. A cocktail made with whiskey, sugar, bitters, and an anise-flavored cordial. It is a famous drink of New Orleans and took its name from a French brandy of the firm Sazerac-du-Forge that was imported to the city by John Schiller, who opened his Sazerac Coffee House in 1850 at No. 13 Exchange Alley in the French Quarter. In 1870 Schiller's bookkeeper, Thomas Handy, bought the establishment and changed the name to the Sazerac House. About the same time Handy changed the original recipe for the cocktail to include a slight taste of ABSINTHE, a dash of red Peychaud BITTERS (introduced to New Orleans by pharmacist A. A. Peychaud in the 1790s), and, ironically, replaced the Sazerac brandy with American blended whiskey. (Leon Lamothe, another importer, has been mentioned as the man who added the absinthe back in 1857, but this seems rather early.)

By the 1880s the drink had caught on and had achieved so much notoriety beyond New Orleans that a newspaper of the day printed this piece of advice:

"When you get to New Orleans, my son, drink a Sazerac cocktail for me and one for yourself."

"And a third one?"

"For the devil, my son, for no living mortal can accomplish that."

The recipe was further changed when absinthe was banned from sale in the United States in 1912 because of its harmful effects on the body and anise-flavored liqueurs like Spanish Ojen or Louisiana Herbsaint were substituted. Some bartenders made the drink with bourbon instead of blended whiskey, and it is rarely made with brandy anymore.

The name *Sazerac* became a trademark of the Sazerac Company, Inc., and the "original" recipe is still served at the Sazerac Bar in the Fairmont Hotel (formerly the Roosevelt). The real Sazerac cocktail is sold by the Sazerac Company, using a proprietary recipe. Following is a substitute recipe:

> Combine 1 1/2 oz. rye or bourbon, 4 tsp. bar sugar, 1/2 tsp. Peychaud bitters, and ice cubes. Pour 3 dashes of Herbsaint into a chilled old-fashioned glass, coat the sides, then pour out. Pour the mixed ingredients into the glass and garnish with a lemon twist.

scallion. A general term for any of a variety of onions, including the shallot, the leek, and the white onion. The name comes from the Latin, *Ascalōnia,* referring to Ascalon, where a certain onion was grown. The word shows up in English in the fourteenth century.

In the United States the word *scallion* usually refers to *Allium fistolosum,* a bulbless onion also called the "spring onion" or "green onion." In Creole and Cajun cookery, however, the word is used to describe a young shallot, as explained in the recipe book of *American Cooking: Creole and Acadian* (1971):

> In Louisiana, which produces about 90 percent of the shallots grown in the United States, the shallot crop is sold and used in its green form. For this reason, perhaps, a special problem of terminology has developed there. Since the green shallot is the most readily available form of scallion in Louisiana, the term scallion is usually restricted to that vegetable in Creole and Acadian cooking. Elsewhere in the United States, the term scallion usually refers to a green or bunching onion, while a shallot is the mature vegetable, usually reddish brown, clove-shaped and dried.

scallop. Any of a variety of marine mollusks of the family Pectinidae. Scallops are usually sold in American markets dead and without their coral.

The name derives from Old French, *escalope,* "shell," which refers to the shell in which the mollusk lives.

In the eastern United States there are four species: the deep sea scallop *(Placopecten magellanicus);* the lion's paw *(Nodipecten nodosus);* the calico scallop *(Argopecten gibbus);* and the bay scallop *(A. irradians).* The first and last in this group are the most often encountered at market in the East, with the latter generally preferred for its delicacy of taste.

In the western United States one finds the pink scallop *(Chlamys herica);* the hinds' scallop *(C. rubida);* the Iceland scallop *(C. islandica);* the speckled scallop *(A. circularis aequisulcatus);* the kelp-weed scallop *(Leptopecten latiauratus);* and the giant rock scallop *(Hinnites giganteus),* which may measure up to six inches.

In American kitchens scallops are either breaded and deep-fried or cooked according to French recipes such as *coquilles Saint-Jacques,* with cream and seasonings.

scampi. A Venetian term that in America refers to shrimp cooked in garlic, butter, and white wine, which may be listed on a menu as "shrimp scampi." The true *scampo (scampi* is the plural) of Italy is a small lobster or prawn, of the family Nephropidae, which in America is called a "lobsterette." These shellfish are available in United States waters, first introduced in 1962 by deepwater shrimp fishermen of Florida, but are not generally found in markets. The term *scampi,* then, has come to mean any shrimp—usually of medium size —cooked in butter, to which is added finely chopped garlic and a dash of dry white wine. It is a staple feature of Italian-American restaurants.

Schichtkuche. A Pennsylvania Dutch "layer cake," typical examples of which are the King's cake and the Queen's cake.

KING'S CAKE:
Add 16 egg yolks and 1 lb. sugar to 1 lb. whipped cream. Stir for 1 hr., then add 1 lb. fine flour and stir for 1/2 hr. Add 1 lb. Sultana raisins, 1 lb. dried currants, and 3 oz. finely cut citron shell. Add 9 stiffly beaten egg whites. Bake 1 hr.

QUEEN'S CAKE:
Mix together 1 lb. sugar, 1 lb. flour, 1 lb. butter, and 8 eggs that have been separated and beaten separately, the whites until they are of a thick consistency that holds to the whisk. Add 1/2 lb. currants, 1 ground nutmeg, and an equal amount cinnamon and bake.

schmaltz. A Yiddish-American term for melted fat, most often chicken fat, first printed in 1935. The word is of German origin.

schmear. A Yiddish term for a daub or smear of a condiment, like cream cheese spread on a bagel or sandwich, used at least since the 1960s.

school breakfast program. A federally sponsored program to provide income assistance to impoverished families, whereby children are fed breakfast at school at no or little charge.

school lunch program. A federally sponsored program providing 23 million schoolchildren with subsidized lunches.

schooner. A drinking glass popular in the last half of the nineteenth century. It held a pint or more of beer. The word probably derives from the large size of a type of ship of the same name.

scoff-law cocktail. A drink made of Canadian whiskey, dry vermouth, and grenadine. According to the *Chicago Tribune* for January 27, 1924, "Hardly has Boston added to the gaiety of nations by adding to Webster's Dictionary the opprobious term of 'scoff-law,' when Jock, the genial manager of Harry's Bar in Paris, yesterday invented the Scoff-Law Cocktail, and it has already become exceedingly popular among American prohibition dodgers."

> Shake together with ice 1 dash orange bitters to a mixture made up of 1/3 Canadian whiskey, 1/3 dry vermouth, 1/6 lemon juice, and 1/6 grenadine. Strain and pour into cocktail glass.

scrapple. Also, "Philadelphia scrapple." A porridge-and-pork breakfast or brunch dish that is chilled and served in slices. It is an old Pennsylvania Dutch dish often served with apple slices and brown sugar, the name being a diminutive of "scrap." The Pennsylvania Dutch also called it "pawnhaus" (finely chopped food) and, later, "poor-do," since it was made often from leftovers. It was introduced at least as early as 1817 to the city of Philadelphia, where it became an immediate favorite, especially among the upper-class gentry.

> Cover 1 1/2 lb. boneless pork with water, bring to boil, and simmer for 2 hr. Remove and slice and then mince meat. To 3 cups of the cooking liquid add 1/2 tsp. pepper, 1 tsp. sage, and 1/2 tsp. salt. Return meat to broth. Mix 1 1/2 cups cornmeal with 1 cup water, stir into meat mixture, and cook on low heat till thickened, then 10 min. more. Rinse a 9-by-5-in. loaf pan with cold water, put in meat mixture, and chill. Unmold and slice. Brown in bacon fat. Serves 6–8.

screwdriver. A drink made with vodka and orange juice. It has been popular since the 1950s, but its origins are obscure. According to one story the name came about when an orange-juice salesman in Bakersfield, California, asked a bartender to mix orange juice with vodka and to serve the drink to six customers, five of whom liked the concoction, but one of whom tasted it and said, "I'd just as soon swallow a screwdriver."

A more frequently cited story—though with no more evidence to back it up—contends the drink was created by American oil-rig workers in the Middle East who mixed vodka with orange juice packed in cans that they opened with screwdrivers, which were also used to stir the drink's ingredients.

> In a glass with ice cubes pour 1/2 oz. vodka and 3 oz. orange juice. Stir.

scripture cake. A cake made with ingredients as listed in certain verses of the Bible. Though known throughout the American colonies, it was a traditional confection among the Baptists. The recipe below is from a Pennsylvania woman, as published in *Famous Old Receipts* (1908):

> Combine 1 cup butter (Judg. 5:25), 3 1/2 cups flour (1 Kings 4:22), 3 cups sugar (Jer. 6:20), 2 cups raisins (1 Sam. 30:12), 2 cups figs (1 Sam. 30:12), 1 cup water (Gen. 24:17), 1 cup almonds (Gen. 43:11), 6 eggs (Isa. 10:14), 1 tbs. honey (Gen. 43:11), a pinch of

salt (Lev. 16:13), spices to taste (1 Kings 10:10), and 2 tbs. baking powder (1 Cor. 5:6). [It is interesting to note that, since baking powder was only invented in the 1850s, the biblical reference uses the verse, "Your boasting is unseemly. Do you not know that a little leaven ferments the whole lump?"] Follow Prov. 23:14, Solomon's advice for making good boys: "Thou shalt beat him with a rod."

scrod. Also, "scrode." A young COD or a young haddock, specifically one that has been split and prepared for cooking. The word may derive from obsolete Dutch, *schrood,* "slice" or "shred," but the sometimes encountered variant *escrod* is more obscure. The Parker House hotel in Boston, famous for its simple preparation of the dish (see recipe below), calls it "schrod."

Although cod was a staple fish of old New England, this term for a young example seems to be of rather recent origins, appearing in print, according to the *Dictionary of Americanisms,* for the first time in 1841. Today it is still a specialty of New England.

Marinate a 12-oz. fillet of cod (or haddock) in 1/2 pt. milk, 1 tsp. lemon, 1/2 tsp. Worcestershire sauce, salt, and pepper for about 1 hr. Mix 3 tbs. vegetable oil with 1/2 tsp. paprika, dip the fish into this mixture and then in 1/2 cup bread crumbs. Place in a baking dish with a little white wine and 2 tbs. butter. Bake for about 12 min.

Scuppernong. A species of Muscadine grape used to make wines and jellies, or the wine made from such a grape. The Scuppernong is grown throughout the South, particularly in North Carolina, where the name covers almost all wines made from various Muscadine grapes.

The origins of the word *Scuppernong* are given in Leon D. Adams's *Wines of America* (2nd edition, revised, 1978):

Scuppernong was named for a town, which was named for a river, which was named for a tree. "Ascopo" was the Algonquian Indian name for the sweet bay tree. "Ascuponung," meaning place of the Ascopo, appeared on old maps of North Carolina as the name of the river in Washington County, near Albemarle Sound. Later maps spelled it Cuscopung, then Cusponung, next Scuponing and Scupuning, until by 1800 the spelling of the river had become Scuppernong. The grape, however, was merely called the White Grape until James Blount of the town of Scuppernong took the census of Washington County in 1810 and reported 1,368 gallons of wine made there in "this small but very interesting branch of our infant manufactures." An article in the Raleigh (North Carolina) *Star* for January 11, 1811, commenting on Blount's report, was the first to call it "The Scuppernong Grape."

Wine has been made from the Scuppernong since the 1560s, when the French Huguenots who settled in Florida fermented the grapes, which were exceptionally abundant and needed only to be knocked to the ground from the high, prolific vines. Sir Walter Raleigh's men discovered the vine growing in Virginia's Roanoke Island in 1584 and introduced it elsewhere. (Supposedly the original vine Raleigh's men propagated still exists on Roanoke and is called the "Mother" or "Raleigh vine.")

The fame of the Scuppernong wines was fostered by a North Carolinian named Captain Paul Garrett (1863–1940), who, after working as a salesman for his uncle Charles Garrett's winery, established his own winery called Garrett & Company in 1900. By 1903 he had four more and was becoming rich selling Scuppernong, which he first called "Escapernog," then "Minnehaha" and "Pocahantas," and, finally, "Virginia Dare," after the first child born of English parents in America. (Dare, born in 1587 of Ananias and Elenor Dare, vanished with the rest of Raleigh's settlers on Roanoke after four years of deprivation.) Garrett's wines became the most popular in the country until certain states and then the country went dry with Prohibition. Garrett had plantings of Scuppernong in other states, but after Prohibition the grapes were scarce in the East, and Virginia Dare no longer tasted the same. By 1966 propagation of the Scuppernong had fallen to a few hundred acres in North Carolina. Since then, with the help of the state legislature and State University in Raleigh, there has been renewed interest in the Scuppernong, in addition to several other Muscadine varieties that now go under the name Scuppernong.

The original Scuppernong is a greenish bronze grape grown in bunches that produces a distinctive, amber-colored wine that is most often sweetened. If blended with other Labrusca grapes, it tends to mute the foxy taste of the finished wine.

sea lion. Cowboy term for wild longhorn cattle that crossed from Mexico into Texas. The name refers to their ability to swim in the Gulf of Mexico.

sea pie. A stew of pork, veal, or fowl mixed with sweet dried apples, molasses, and dumplings. The dish is served in New England and so called, according to Josephine H. Pierce in *Coast to Coast Cookery* (1951), "because a sea captain told how to make it." A recipe may be found in Mary Randolph's *Virginia Housewife, or Methodical Cook* (1836).

sea plum. Cowboy term for an oyster.

sea urchin. Any of a variety of marine echinoderms of the class Echinoidea having a soft flesh encased in a spiny shell. The names derives from its resemblance to a hedgehog, which in Middle English was *(h)irchon,* and Latin, *(h)ēricius.*

Sea urchins are unappreciated by most Americans, but Mediterranean immigrants buy most of the catch at market. This includes the following species: purple sea urchin *(Arbacia punctulata),* keyhole urchin *(Mellita quinquiesperforata),* green sea urchin *(Strongylocentrotus droebachiensis),* giant red urchin *(S. franciscanus),* purple sea urchin *(S. purpuratus,* a Pacific species different from the eastern variety above), white sea urchin *(Lytechinus variegatus),* and heart urchin *(Moira atropos).*

seed cake. A nineteenth-century cake made from caraways. The following recipe dates from *Mrs. Winslow's Domestic Receipt Book for 1865:*

> Combine 4 cups flour, 1 1/2 cups cream, 1/2 cup butter, 3 eggs, 1/2 cup caraway seeds, 1 tsp. baking soda, and 1 tsp. rose water and make a dough. Cut with biscuit cutter and bake at 350° for about 20 min.

seltzer. A plain, naturally or man-made carbonated water with no taste of its own, drunk plain or as a mixer in everything from soda fountain confections to alcoholic drinks. The word was first printed in 1741.

Carbonated waters have been known for hundreds of years. The word *seltzer* comes from a bottled mineral water called *"Selterser Wasser,"* made from the waters of the Prussian town, Nieder Selters.

Man-made carbonated water was created by Joseph Priestley in 1767, and Swedish chemist Torbern Bergman produced commercial quantities of carbonic gas in 1770. By 1807 such man-made sodas were sold around New York by Yale University's Professor Benjamin Silliman, and in 1832 an English immigrant to New York named John Matthews crafted a practical, small machine to carbonate water for use in pharmacies. It was called a "soda fountain," and its use in drugstores was evidence of the era's belief in seltzer's medicinal and curative value.

Flavors were soon added to seltzers, and such mixtures were called "soda pop" by the 1840s, but the word *seltzer* has continued to mean an unflavored carbonated water to this day. Seltzer was served both at fountains and in siphon bottles that became standard items at the home bar, a practice that has all but disappeared. Today seltzer is distinguished from club soda by having less or no salt added. The term *club soda,* and also *sparkling water,* came into use after the repeal of Prohibition in 1933, when the association with elegant supper or private clubs deliberately removed the drink's medicinal connotations.

In New York seltzer was sometimes called "Jewish champagne" because of its popularity among Jews, who called it *grepsvasser,* "belch water," and who drank it to help the digestion of their fatty diet and to adhere to kosher rules against mixing meats with milk. In the early part of this century in New York one would go to a candy store and ask for a "two-cents-plain," a glass of seltzer for two pennies.

semmel. A Pennsylvania Dutch yeast roll, whose name is borrowed from the German for "roll."

> Mix 1/2 pkg. yeast in 1/4 cup warm water. Add to 1/2 cup cooled, cooked mashed potatoes and stir in 1/2 cup sugar. Let stand 4 hr. Add 1/2 cup butter to 2 cups scalded milk. Cool, add 2 beaten eggs, 1/2 cup sugar, and 1/2 tsp. salt. Beat into yeast mixture, add 6 cups flour, cover, and let rise 8 hr. Roll dough into a square 1/4-in. thick. Brush with melted butter and cut into 2-in. squares, then turn up corners. Place on buttered baking sheet and let rise to double. Bake at 450° for 20 min. Brush with butter and sprinkle with confectioners' sugar and cinnamon. Makes about 30.

Senate bean soup. A white bean soup served for half a century in the United States Senate restaurant, which is operated for the senators and their guests.

Credit for its creation has gone to Senator Fred T. Dubois of Idaho in the 1890s and to Senator Knute Nelson of Minnesota, who served from 1895 to 1923.

> Soak 2 cups dried pea beans overnight, drain, cover with boiling water, and cook till tender. Drain, return to pot with hambone and 3 qt. water. Bring to boil, simmer for 2 hr., then add 3 cooked mashed potatoes, 3 chopped onions, 2 chopped garlic cloves, and 3 chopped stalks of celery. Cover, simmer for 1 hr., remove hambone, and scrape off meat into soup. Stir in 1/4 cup parsley. Serves 12.

sesame (*Sesamum indicum*). A tropical Asian plant whose small, flat seeds are used to make oil and cookies and as a garnish for some breads and rolls. The name is from the Greek. In the South the seeds are called "benne," from an African word, and are much used in SOUL FOOD. Benne cookies or cakes are sometimes called "good luck cookies" in South Carolina.

> BENNE COOKIES:
> Combine 2 cups flour, 1 1/2 tsp. baking powder, 1/4 tsp. salt, and 1/4 tsp. nutmeg. Cream 1/2 cup butter with 1/4 cup sugar till light, then add the grated rind of 1 orange or lemon. Beat 1 egg with 1/3 cup milk and blend into butter and flour mixtures. Place by tablespoons on a greased cookie sheet and bake for 10 min. at 350°. Combine in a saucepan 1/2 cup honey, 1 tbs. butter, and 2 tbs. sesame seeds, and cook until the mixture reaches 290° on a candy thermometer. Dip cookies in glaze or brush glaze over tops of cookies. Makes about 3 doz.

seven sweets and seven sours. Side dishes of sweet, spiced fruits and sour pickles served as accompaniments to main dishes in Pennsylvania Dutch meals. They do not strictly have to be seven in number; more is better, and less is quite all right, as long as there are several from which to pick and choose, such as spiced apples, cantaloupe, CHOW-CHOW, peppers, and COLE SLAW.

Seyval Blanc. A white French hybrid grape officially named "Seyve-Villard 5–276" after its creator Bertrand Seyve (1895–1959), whose father owned a nursery with Victor Villard, whose daughter married the younger Seyve. It has become a notable wine grape in New York's Hudson Valley and elsewhere.

shad. Any of a variety of fishes of the herring family in the genus *Alosa*. The name is from the Old English, *sceadd*. The American shad (*Alosa sapidissima*) is the most important shad from a culinary standpoint, although early in this country's history the common availability of the fish was such that settlers considered it a fish of last resort, and it has been suggested that the Indians used the fish for fertilizer, a technique they recommended to the Pilgrims. But by the time of the American Revolution shad was much appreciated, and Washington's troops had the fish as part of their rations in 1776.

Parties were held by the Indians to celebrate shadtime, which occurred in spring. The Indians dried the shad and may have "planked" it on wood to cook it slowly. But specific credit for this method of cooking has been given to the

State in Schuykill, a fishing and cooking society formed in 1732. The fish fillets are seasoned and wrapped with bacon, then nailed to greased hardwood planks set at an angle near a hot ash fire made from charcoals. Shad roe, traditionally served with lemon, sorrel, and boiled potatoes, is particularly appreciated by gourmets, who cook it in a variety of ways.

By the nineteenth century shad was a popular fish, and, after several attempts, the American shad was introduced in 1871 to western waters, where it thrived in the Sacramento and Columbia rivers. By 1889 4.5 million pounds of shad were taken, although some, like Henry David Thoreau, noticed a decline in the quality of the fish in certain waters. The pollution caused by industries on the rivers drove out or killed the large fish, but, as Thoreau wrote, "Perchance, after a few thousands of years, if the fishes will be patient and pass their summers elsewhere meanwhile, Nature will have leveled the Billerica dam and the Lowell factories, and the Grassground River run clear again, to be explored by new migratory shoals."

The shad have rebounded since their nadir in the years that followed the end of the nineteenth century and are now found in eastern markets, though often they are imported from western fisheries.

shallot *(Allium ascalonicum).* An onionlike plant of the lily family used to flavor a wide variety of dishes and having a more delicate flavor than onion. The word is from the Latin, *Ascalōnia,* referring to a kind of onion grown in Ascalon. The herb was first mentioned in English print in 1664, then also called "Spanish garlick."

The shallot is a native of Central Asia, possibly introduced to England in the thirteenth century, though long known to the Romans. It is now widely planted in the United States and is an essential part of most European immigrant cookeries.

In Creole and Cajun cookery, however, the term SCALLION is often applied to the green shallot, that is, the shoots of the shallot before it matures.

Most of the mature shallots found in the American market are grown in New Jersey and New York, with others imported from Mexico and France.

shark. Any of a variety of voracious marine fishes under the order Squaliformes or Selachii. The origin of the name is obscure. Feared for their legendary attacks on man (which in truth are exceptionally rare), the shark has not garnered much attention as a food fish in America, although the United States government in 1916 tried to promote the dogfish shark species *(Squalus acanthias* and *Somniosus microcephalus)* as a nourishing fish having large amounts of protein. After World War I this momentary infatuation with the shark died out, although another peak of favor was reached just before World War II, when the liver of the shark was especially sought for its nutrients. In 1982 about 24.5 million pounds of shark were caught commercially. Some fishermen have tried to pass off meat from the mako *(Isurus oxyrhynchus)* and blue shark *(Prionace glauca)* as SWORDFISH steaks, and soupfin shark *(Galeor-*

hinus zyopterus) is often used to make the Chinese dish shark's fin soup. Many other sharks are poor eating and may in fact cause sickness.

she-crab soup. A soup made from blue crabs, crab roe, sherry, and vegetables. It is a specialty of Charleston, South Carolina, and Savannah, Georgia, both of which claim credit for the dish's creation, probably at the beginning of the nineteenth century. The female crab's roe gives the soup a slightly sour, tangy flavor that marks it as distinct from other crab soups. State law, however, forbids taking she-crabs with mature eggs, so cooks often use male crabs and immature females and then add eggs from unfertilized females (which are allowed to be caught). Crumbled egg yolk is sometimes used to give the traditional orange color of the roe to the soup.

> In a saucepan cook 1 grated onion, 1/2 tsp. mace, 2 grated celery stalks, salt, and pepper in 2 tbs. butter. Add 1 cup crabmeat and heat through thoroughly. Heat 2 cups milk and add to crab mixture. Stir and add 1/2 cup cream, 2 tbs. Worcestershire sauce, and 2 tbs. flour dissolved in water. Add 3 tbs. sherry and cook for 30 min. Serves 4.

sheeny destroyer. Slang for pork, derived from the derogatory word for Jews, *sheeny* or *sheenie,* probably from the German *schin,* "a cheat" or "miser." Since Jews are not allowed under religious law to eat pork, serving them such a dish would "destroy" them. The term probably dates from the period 1910 to 1930. In a similar vein, an order of two pork chops was sometimes called "a couple of Hebrew enemies."

sherry. A fortified wine originally made in Spain and now produced in the United States most often by a process of "baking" that gives the drink its characteristic burnt flavor.

Sherry was first made in and around the town of Jerez in Spain's Andalusia, and the word *sherry* is an Anglicized rendition of the town's name, for the British were major shippers of Spanish wines. By the sixteenth century the wine was called "sherris-sack," the word *sack* perhaps having been derived from Old French, *sec,* "dry." H. Warner Allen in *A History of Wine* (1961), however, suggests that it comes from the Spanish, *sacar,* meaning "to take out" or "export," an opinion shared by Pauline and Sheldon Wasserman in their *Guide to Fortified Wines* (1982). Sack was the wine beloved by Shakespeare's Falstaff, who attributed his own "excellent wit" to the wine's powers. But by the beginning of the seventeenth century *sherry* was fast replacing *sack* (which is today a registered trademark of sherry shippers William & Humbert).

Americans of the colonial era much preferred Madeira and port to sherry, and the sherries that later became favored were the sweeter Spanish varieties like *olorosos* and "creams," whose high alcohol content also coincided with Americans' tastes after the end of Prohibition in 1933. American sherries are made by three basic methods. The most frequently used is the baker's method, by which dry or sweet white wine is fortified with brandy and then heated to between 120° and 140° for between 45 and 120 days. (A variation on this method, called "weathering," exposes the wine and brandy to outdoor weather conditions.) The second process is the traditional Spanish *solera* system, by which the wines are constantly blended with other, older wines in a complex tier system involving stacked barrels, with the newest and freshest wines on top. The third method is the "submerged *flor*" process, by which new wine is continuously pumped over the yeast (*flor,* in Spanish) that develops on the top of the wine, thereby giving the sherry a yeasty, tangy flavor without the benefits of aging.

American sherries are made from a variety of grapes, including Mission, Malaga, Palomino, Concord, and others, while traditional Spanish sherries are made with Palomino Blanco and Pedro Ximénez varieties, with some producers using Mantuo Castellano and others to a lesser degree.

Americans usually drink sweet sherries, either as an aperitif, on the rocks, or after dinner as a cordial.

Shirley Temple. A nonalcoholic beverage usually made for children who enjoy the idea of drinking an "adult" cocktail before dinner. It is named after child actor Shirley Temple (1928–), who began making movies in 1932 and three years later had attained the position of the "Number One" box-office star in the United States. Her curly-haired image was world famous and hundreds of products, from dolls to clothes, appeared with her name or face on them. She was held up to children as a model of good behavior, and, thus, a cocktail called a "Shirley Temple" would be considered the very essence of innocence. The drink probably took this name in the 1930s or, possibly, in the 1940s, by which time Shirley Temple had grown into parts that called for her to portray winsome, good-natured teenage girls.

Occasionally one will hear such nonalcoholic cocktails referred to as "pussyfoots." A term of some derision in its meaning of an indecisive or weak person, this word may have been coined by President Theodore Roosevelt (1858–1919). It appeared in print for the first time in 1893 as a verb, later, in 1934, as a noun. One of the greatest enforcers of temperance laws in the 1890s, William Eugene Smith, was called "Pussyfoot" for his zeal in sending offenders to jail, especially in Oklahoma.

> In a cocktail or champagne glass pour 1/2 oz. grenadine syrup, fill with ginger ale, and garnish with a maraschino cherry.

shit on a shingle. A G.I. term for creamed CHIPPED BEEF. Civilians often refer specifically to SALISBURY STEAK by this term.

shoofly pie. A pie made of molasses and brown sugar, so called supposedly because one had to "shoo away the flies" from this sweet dessert. It is probably of Pennsylvania Dutch origins, but was not mentioned in American print till 1926.

Line a pie plate with a pastry crust. Combine 1 1/2 cups sifted flour, 1 cup brown sugar, 1/8 tsp. salt, and 1/4 cup cold butter to make a crumbly blend. Dissolve 1/2 tsp. baking soda in 1/2 cup molasses, then add 3/4 of the crumb mixture. Pour into pie pan, top with the rest of the crumbs, and bake in a 350° oven for about 30 min., till firm.

shortnin' bread. A southern quick bread made with a shortening like butter or lard.

Mix 2 cups flour with 1/2 cup brown sugar and blend till crumbly. Work in 1/4 lb. butter till dough is smooth. Divide, pat into a circle 1/2-in. thick, prick the top, and cook in ungreased pan at 350° for about 30 min.

shrimp. Any of a wide variety of ten-legged crustaceans of the suborder Natantia. It is the most popular shellfish in the United States, which harvests about 370 million pounds annually, more than any other country; in addition, the United States imports another 200 million pounds.

The word *shrimp* derives from Middle English, *shrimpe,* meaning "pygmy" or the crustacean itself.

Americans have always eaten shrimp, but its tendency to spoil quickly had for most of our history confined its availability to regions having access to the sea or rivers. Fresh shrimp are available in the South, but almost all the shrimp Americans buy at market or in restaurants is in fact frozen. Only in the twentieth century, with advances in refrigeration onboard trawlers (which began plying the waters for lengthy voyages only in 1917), did shrimp become readily available in American markets, with New York City consuming the lion's share of the catch—about a million and a half pounds a week.

Most shrimp comes from Atlantic waters, though there is some from Alaska and from the rivers of the South. The main species for culinary use include seven species in the Atlantic—the edible shrimp *(Penaeus aztecus, setiferus,* and *duorarum),* also called, respectively, "brown," "pink," and "white" shrimp; the Caribbean shrimp *(P. schmitti);* the sea bob *(Xiphopeneus kroyeri);* the royal red shrimp *(Hymenopenaeus robustus);* and the rock shrimp *(Sicyonia brevirostris)*—and in the Pacific the side-stripe shrimp *(Pandalopsus dispar);* the pink shrimp *(P. borealis* and *P. jordoni);* the coon-stripe shrimp *(P. danae);* and the spot shrimp *(P. platyceros).*

Americans eat shrimp boiled and served plain or with a ketchup sauce seasoned with chili pepper and horseradish (called a "shrimp cocktail"), deep-fried, grilled, baked in various sauces, and in many other forms. In New Orleans shrimp RÉMOULADE is a traditional dish and "shrimp boils" popular social affairs. Many preparations originally made with lobsters are adapted for shrimp. Shrimp SCAMPI, rarely made with true scampi, is a dish of shrimp sautéed in garlic and oil or butter.

shrimper's sauce. A tomato sauce made by the shrimp fishermen of the South. The following recipe is given in the Federal Writers Project American Guides volume on the *Mississippi Gulf Coast* (1939).

Fry 1 cup chopped salt pork in 1/2 cup oil, add 3 French onions, 1 can tomato sauce, 3 cups boiling water, 1 tsp. chili powder, 2 cloves minced garlic, 1 sprig of thyme, 1 tsp. celery salt, salt, and pepper, and cook about 30 min.

shrimps de Jonghe. A seasoned shrimp dish that originated at Jacques', a Chicago restaurant run by two Belgians named de Jonghe.

Cream 3/4 cup butter with 1 tsp. salt, 1 mashed clove of garlic, 1 cup bread crumbs, 1/4 cup parsley, 1/2 cup sherry, and a dash of cayenne and paprika. Shell and devein 3 lb. shrimp, then boil till half-cooked. In 8 small cooking tins place some of the bread crumb mixture, top with the shrimp, layer on more of the bread crumbs, and bake at 375° for 20–25 min.

shrimp wiggle. A dish of creamed shrimp popular in New England. *Wiggle,* slang for something done in a hurry, refers to the dish's ease and quickness of preparation. In *American Cookery* (1972), James Beard comments, "For many years this was in the repertoire of every coed with a chafing dish and every girl who had a beau to cook for."

Combine 1 tbs. butter, 1 tbs. chopped onion, 1 cup boiled rice, and 1/2 can tomato soup in a double boiler. Add a dash of red pepper, salt and pepper to taste, 1 cup cream, 2 cups shelled, deveined shrimp, and 2 cups peas. Heat through and serve on crackers, toast or in pastry shells.

Siberia. A section of a restaurant dining room that is considered either socially inferior or merely poor seating. While not all American restaurants have such undesirable sections or tables, much fuss is made over those that do, and some people would rather not sit down at all than to be escorted to Siberia.

The term is said to have originated in the 1930s, when a society woman named Peggy Hopkins Joyce entered the class-conscious El Morocco nightclub in New York and found herself being led to a less than desirable table. "Where are you taking me," she asked the maître d'hôtel, "Siberia?"

In most society restaurants the most treasured tables are usually situated along the banquettes that line the room as one enters, though in other restaurants a good table, called an "A" table, may be a corner table or one that is regularly occupied by a person of some celebrity.

sidecar. A cocktail made from brandy, orange-flavored liqueur, and lemon juice. The drink seems to have originated at Harry's New York Bar in Paris, but the date and inspiration of the invention are uncertain. The bar's owner, Harry MacElhone, claimed the drink was concocted in 1931 for a customer who always arrived in a motorcycle sidecar. But David A. Embury, in *The Fine Art of Mixing Drinks* (third American edition, 1958), says it was invented by a friend of his during World War I and was "named after the motorcycle sidecar in which the good captain customarily was driven to and from the little bistro where the drink was born and christened."

Embury recommends a blend of one part Cointreau or Triple Sec, two parts lemon juice, and eight parts cognac or Armagnac. But the more usual mix is as follows:

> Shake together with ice 1 part Triple Sec, 1 part cognac, and 1 part lemon juice. Strain and serve in cocktail glass.

Singapore sling. A cocktail of gin, cherry brandy, Cointreau, Benedictine, and citrus juices. It was supposedly created by bartender Ngiam Tong Boon of the Long Bar in Singapore's Raffles Hotel in 1915 and is sometimes called the "Singapore Raffles gin sling" or the "Raffles bar gin sling." There are many variants; one admirer of the drink has said the original was topped off with club soda, but the official Raffles version given below is without any such additive.

> Into a shaker with 4 ice cubes put 1 oz. gin, 3/4 oz. cherry brandy, a "few drops" Cointreau, the juice of 1/2 a medium-size lemon, 2 oz. fresh pineapple juice, 1 or 2 drops bitters, and 1 dash grenadine. Cover and shake for 10 sec., pour into a 10-oz. glass with 2 ice cubes. Garnish with a wedge of pineapple and maraschino cherry.

singles bar. A bar or lounge dispensing alcoholic beverages and frequented by single—that is, unmarried—people who go to such places specifically to meet other single people of the opposite sex. Although bars have long been social centers, it was not until the 1960s that working women in large cities began to visit such establishments without worrying about public opinion. By the 1970s, however, the term *singles bar* had taken on a pejorative connotation.

sirloin. A cut of beef from the upper part of the loin between the rump and the porterhouse. Between six and eight one-inch-thick sirloins may be taken from the hip, though many Americans prefer a two-inch steak. If aged correctly, sirloin is one of the best steak cuts for tenderness and flavor.

Depending on the way a butcher cuts the meat, different kinds of sirloin may be produced. When cut across the grain, the steaks will be called "pin-bone," "flat bone," "round bone," and "wedge bone," from the shape of the hip bone they contain. By cutting with the grain the butcher produces boneless roasts called "tenderloin," "top sirloin," and "bottom sirloin." A whole, uncut sirloin is called a "king-sized roast," weighing between twelve and twenty pounds.

Sirloins are usually broiled or grilled, though they can be pan-fried.

The origin of the word is from Old French, *surlonge* (*sur,* "above," and *longe,* "loin"). A cherished but wholly inaccurate legend attached to the name has to do with an English king who knighted a piece of beef "Sir Loin." Thomas Fuller's *Church History* (1655) maintained that the monarch in question was Henry VIII, but Jonathan Swift vouched for James I. Neither is correct. There are references to the word as far back as 1554. In France this cut is referred to as the *"contre-filet"* or *"faux-filet."* In many parts of the United States a sirloin is called a "New York cut."

skully-jo. A dish made by the Portuguese settlers in Provincetown, Massachusetts, from dried cod or haddock cured in the sun till, in the opinion of one observer, "it's hard enough to bend lead pipe around." The children of the region would chew it instead of candy. It is rarely made anymore.

skunk egg. Cowboy term for an onion.

sloppy Joe. A dish of ground beef, onions, green peppers, and ketchup made in a skillet and often served on a hamburger roll. It is sometimes called a "skilletburger."

The origins of this dish are unknown (circa 1960s?), and there probably is no Joe after whom it is named—but its rather messy appearance and tendency to drip off plate or roll makes "sloppy" an adequate description, and *Joe* is an American name of proletarian character and unassailable genuineness.

> Cook 1 lb. ground beef in a skillet with 2 tbs. butter. Mix in 1/4 cup flour, 1 tbs. chopped onion, 1/4 cup chopped green pepper, 1 cup chopped celery, 1/4 cup ketchup (or canned tomato soup), 2 tsp. salt, 1/2 tsp. pepper, and 3 cups water. Boil together till tender and well blended.

slow elk. Cowboy's term for beef butchered without the owner's knowledge.

slumgullion. Also, "slum." A term from the California Gold Rush days used by miners for any disgusting or makeshift food or drink. It first appears in print in 1850 (and as *slum* in 1874), and in *Roughing It* (1872) Mark Twain wrote of being offered a drink of slumgullion by a station keeper in Nebraska who said it was like tea. But, Twain remarked, "there was too much dish rag, and sand, and old bacon-rind in it to deceive the intelligent traveller." Nevertheless, Twain admired whoever it was who named it.

slump. A dish of cooked fruit and raised dough, known since the middle of the eighteenth century and probably so called because it is a somewhat misshapen dish that "slumps" on the plate. Louisa May Alcott, author of *Little Women,* named her Concord, Massachusetts, home "Apple Slump" and recorded this recipe:

> Pare, core, and slice 6 apples and combine with 1 cup sugar, 1 tsp. cinnamon, and 1/2 cup water in a saucepan. Cover and heat to boiling point. Meanwhile sift together 1 1/2 cups flour, 1/4 tsp. salt, and 1 1/2 tsp. baking powder and add 1/2 cup milk to make a soft dough. Drop pieces of the dough from a tablespoon onto apple mixture, cover, and cook over low heat for 30 min. Serve with cream.

small beer. A beer of low alcoholic content. The term is more widely used in England, where it first saw print in 1568, than in the United States.

smelt (Family Osmeridae). A silvery, small, slender fish found in North American oceans, rivers, and lakes. The name is from the Anglo-Saxon, *smoelt,* meaning "smooth" or "shining." Smelts are a very perishable fish and are often sold frozen. They are best coated with seasoned flour and beaten egg and pan-fried in butter or oil. It requires about a dozen to make a pound. The main North American species are:

rainbow smelt *(Osmerus mordax).* Also, "ice fish." A smelt found along the Atlantic coast, measuring about seven to eight inches long and having a silver band. It was introduced to the Great Lakes drainage in 1912, where it has proliferated.

eulachon *(Thaleichthys pacificus).* Also, "candlefish" (because its oiliness made it a good candle when dried by Indians, who inserted a bark wick through the fish). Found from the Bering Sea to central California at lengths up to twelve inches, the eulachon is often marketed as "Columbia River smelt" in the Northwest. The name *eulachon* is from a Chinook Indian dialect word, *vlâkân,* for the fish, and one encounters renderings such as *ulchen* and the colloquial American *hooligan* (which itself is a word for a ruffian). Because of their fattiness, eulachon are sometimes dried out in a warm oven after being fried.

surf smelt *(Hypomesus pretiosus).* Also, "silver smelt." Found from Alaska to Southern California, the surf smelt grows to about ten inches and is netted on sandy beaches of the outer coast.

Other, less well known smelts include: night smelt *(Sprinchus starski),* found from Alaska to central California; delta smelt *(Hypomesus transpacificus),* in the San Joaquin and Sacramento river systems; longfin smelt *(Sprinchus thaleichthys),* similar to the night smelt; Pacific smoothtongue *(Leuroglossus stilbius),* a Pacific species; whitebait smelt *(Allosmerus elongatus);* and pond smelt *(Hypomesus olidus),* found in Alaska and Canada. The top smelt and the jack smelt are Pacific silversides of the family Atherinidae, of a different order from other smelts, and deep-sea smelts are of the family Bathylagidae, but closely related to true smelts.

smorgasbord. A buffet meal of Swedish origins that has become in this century a very popular party spread. The word comes from the Swedish, *smörgåsbord,* a "bread and butter table," and first appeared in American print in 1919. The idea soon caught on, so that by 1941 the West Hartford Ladies Aid Society's *Swedish American Cook Book* listed several suggestions for a smorgasbord, including the following items: butter balls, Swedish rye bread, pumpernickel, hardtack, pickled herring, baked ham, smoked tongue, lingonberries, radish roses, omelettes, *Rulle Pulse* (rolled pressed lamb), liver *pastej* (liver pâté), jellied veal, head cheese, hot Swedish meatballs, Swedish pork sausage, brown beans, Swedish fish pudding, smoked salmon, stuffed eggs, potato salad, *sill* salad (herring salad), meat and potato sausage, fruit salad, Swedish apple cake, and coffee with cream.

Today smorgasbords may still contain many of these same items, as well as dishes from other countries.

smothered. A word used to describe any of a variety of dishes in which the meat, poultry, or fish is "smothered" with a gravy and/or vegetables while baked, braised, or cooked in a covered skillet. One authority, Craig Claiborne, believes the term may derive from the use of a weighted-down plate to cover the dish as it cooks.

SMOTHERED CHICKEN:
Cut a 3-lb. chicken into pieces and dredge in a mixture of 3/4 cup flour, 1 1/2 tsp. salt, and 1/4 tsp. pepper. Brown chicken in 4 tbs. butter, add 1/2 cup water, cover, and simmer for about 1 hr. till very tender. During the last 20 min. of cooking, add 1 cup green peas, 2 tbs. pimiento strips, and 1/2 cup onions. Reduce sauce and spoon over chicken. Serves 4.

snack. A meal or food item eaten hurriedly or casually, which might include anything from a candy bar to a hamburger. The word, also used as a verb, *to snack,* derives from the Dutch, *snacken,* "to bite," and in English first meant a small portion of liquor. By the eighteenth century it had acquired its present meaning. Snack bars, where one bought a snack, were known as of 1895, though this term was more popular in England than in America until well into the twentieth century.

snake-head whiskey. A cheap whiskey known among cowboys. The name came from the assumption that the drink's potency was due to the addition of snake heads in the distilling barrel.

snapper. A bony fish of the Lutjanidae family. There are 250 species in the world, of which fifteen are found in United States waters from North Carolina to the Gulf of Mexico. Snappers are usually pan-fried. The most popular American species for eating are:

gray snapper *(Lutjanus griseus).* Also called "mangrove snapper." Found in southern United States waters, the gray snapper may weigh from under a pound up to ten pounds.

mutton snapper *(Lutjanus analis).* Also, "muttonfish." The mutton snapper, found from south Florida to the tropical Atlantic, is olive-green and has range-red sides and brick-red fins. Though it is rarely seen in American markets, it is good baked.

yellowtail snapper *(Ocyurus chrysurus).* This yellow-striped, shallow-water snapper is usually about one-and-a-half pounds in size and rarely weighs over five pounds. Its main popularity has traditionally been around Key West, where it was long considered a breakfast fish because it was sold early in the morning after the catch. It is excellent pan-fried with a squeeze of Key lime over it. The yellowtail snapper is not to be confused with a form of TILEFISH, found in American waters further north, that goes by the name "yellow snapper."

red snapper *(Lutjanus campechanus).* By far the most popular of the species in America, the red snapper is found from North Carolina down through the Gulf of Mexico, and although it can grow to thirty-five pounds, the typical specimens found in markets weigh between four and six pounds. This beautiful red-pink fish takes well to most forms of cooking. It is quite similar to the silk snapper (*L. vivanus*), which is often called "red snapper" at market. The Creole *rouget* is red snapper, not kin to the French *rouget* (red mullet).

A red snapper recipe popular in Florida calls for the fillets to be marinated in a baking dish with 1/2 cup chopped onions, 1/4 cup fresh orange juice, 2 tsp. grated orange peel, and 1 tsp. salt for about 30 min. Sprinkle a pinch of nutmeg and black pepper on the fish, then bake for about 10 min. in a 400° oven.

snickerdoodle. A New England cookie made with flour, nuts, and dried fruits. The name is simply a nineteenth-century nonsense word for a quickly made confection.

Sift 3 1/2 cups flour with 1/2 tsp. salt, 1 tsp. baking soda, 1 tsp. cinnamon, and 1/8 tsp. nutmeg. Cream 1 cup butter, add 1 1/4 cups sugar slowly, beat in 3 beaten eggs, stir in flour, then add 1 cup chopped nuts, 1/2 cup currants, and 1/2 cup raisins. Drop in spoonfuls onto buttered cookie sheet, and bake at 350° for 12–15 min. Makes about 10 doz.

snow ball. Also, "sno' ball." A scoop of vanilla or other flavor of ice cream rolled in shredded, sweetened coconut that is chilled and served with a topping of chocolate syrup, or a ball of shaved ice with fruit syrup.

snow cone. A confection of crushed ice or freshly fallen snow drizzled with a fruit syrup and usually served in a paper cone. It is a traditional treat of summer, especially among Hispanic Americans.

snow cream. A southern confection especially popular with blacks, snow cream is nothing more than freshly fallen snow that is scooped up and mixed with a variety of flavorings like vanilla, sugar, and cinnamon. Some devotees claim that only the first snow of the season should be used, though some claim that it is the third snow of the season that is the purest.

In New England children pour cooked maple syrup over snow and let it harden. This is called "sugar-in-snow."

sober side of the bar. The bartender's side.

soda. Also, "soda pop" and "soft drink." Carbonated water, usually flavored and colored. The first carbonated waters were from natural sources and sold at the end of the eighteenth century as "soda water" at "soda fountains." By 1809 the drink was being sweetened and flavored to make items like "ginger pop," also called "ginger beer" (which once had a slight alcoholic content), and, later, "ginger champagne" or "ginger ale" (which does not). In 1812

English author Robert Southey commented on the new word *pop* as deriving its meaning from the sound made when the cork is drawn from the bottle.

By 1819 a patent was issued for "carbonated mead," and in 1824 one for SARSAPARILLA. In the 1830s the first man-made carbonated waters became available, and lemon, strawberry, vanilla, and other flavors were popular. Birch beer came along in the 1880s to compete with Charles E. Hires's Herb Tea, later changed to Root Beer (a previously common term for a soda flavored with various roots and herbs) and advertised as "The National Temperance Drink." Temperance advocates succeeded in prohibiting alcoholic beverages from the 1876 Centennial Exposition in Philadelphia, thereby boosting the sales of sodas, which came in a wide range of flavors. By 1854 cream soda was vanilla flavored. In 1889 a cream soda was cited as ice cream in soda water—"a favorite drink of American women."

In 1881 there appeared Imperial Inca Coca, made from extracts of the cola, or kola nut, and the leaf of the coca plant. Five years later an Atlanta, Georgia, a pharmacist named Dr. John Smyth Pemberton began making a beverage from the same ingredients, which his bookkeeper, Frank M. Robinson, named Coca-Cola, registered as a trademark in 1893. Another pharmacist, Asa G. Candler, bought the rights to the soda syrup and immediately began promoting the drink as a refreshment, whereas it had previously been sold as a medicinal aid to cure hangovers and headaches. A myth has persisted that Coca-Cola (since 1909 called "Coke" for short) once contained small amounts of cocaine, but although trace elements of cocaine may have found their way into pre-1900 batches of the drink, cocaine has never been part of the formula and improved purification methods after 1900 removed any possibility of such elements entering the product.

Another pharmacist, Caleb Bradham of New Bern, North Carolina, came up with a similar concoction in 1898, which he sold as "Brad's drink" to his local customers. He changed the name in 1903 to Pepsi-Cola and began manufacturing and bottling the beverage in 1904; three years later the Pepsi-Cola Company had forty franchises, and the drink, usually sold by horse-drawn cart, began to be purveyed by motor vehicles, and auto racer Barney Oldfield was enlisted as a spokesman for the drink.

Coca-Cola and Pepsi-Cola went on to become great American success stories after World War I, thanks to a developing taste for such drinks and a drop in the price of SUGAR (although Pepsi-Cola had several difficult years because Bradham had overbought sugar when it was at its most expensive). Both companies also used advertising and marketing with amazing results. Pepsi-Cola was the first company to broadcast a jingle on radio, and every American was soon able to sing along with the words,

> Pepsi-Cola hits the spot.
> Twelve full ounces,
> That's a lot.
> Twice as much for a nickel, too,
> Pepsi-Cola is the drink for you.

(The lyrics indicated that "Pepsi," as it was called for short, sold twelve ounces for the same price Coca-Cola charged for six ounces, then the standard of the industry.)

Both products became among the best-known American food items in the world, and one or the other, or both, can be found around the globe, including, in Pepsi-Cola's case, as a franchise in the Soviet Union. The formulas for these drinks are considered to be among the world's best-kept industrial secrets, with only a handful of people knowing different parts of the formulas. Coca-Cola sells about 265 million eight-ounce servings of their product per day. Pepsi-Cola sold 1.1 billion cases in 1981.

Other significant soda drinks in the American market would include: 7-Up, a lemon-lime-flavored drink originally marketed in St. Louis, Missouri, by C. L. Grigg in 1929 under the name Bib-Label Lithiated Lemon-Lime Soda (the reason for 7-Up's name has never been divulged by Grigg, though Stuart Berg Flexner in *I Hear America Talking* [1976] notes that a card game by that name was known since the 1820s); Canada Dry Ginger Ale (introduced in 1904); Royal Crown Cola; Dr Pepper; and, in New York, a coffee-flavored soda called Passaro's Famous Manhattan Special.

Diet sodas have become very popular in the last twenty years with trademark names like Tab, Pepsi Light, Diet 7-Up, Fresca, and others, which represent about 13 percent of the $25 billion soda industry business.

soda beer. A nineteenth-century substitute for real beer.

> For 5 min. boil together 2 oz. cream of tartar, 2 lb. sugar, the juice of 1/2 lemon, and 3 pt. water. Cool and add 3 stiffly beaten egg whites and 1/2 cup flour, 1/2 oz. wintergreen essence, and 1/2 oz. lemon essence. Stir to blend and bottle. Use 1 tbs. of soda beer for each glass of water or soda.

soda jerk. Also, "soda jerker." A person who prepares sodas and other confections behind the counter at a soda fountain. The word dates back at least to 1916 and comes from the jerking motion the hand had to make on the soda spigots then in use in order to fill glasses.

sodium nitrite ($NaNO_2$). A preservative used in bacon and other cured meats. It is made by the transformation of sodium nitrate ($NaNO_3$) by sodium carbonate.

sole. Any of a variety of flatfish of the family Soleidae. Some confusion has been created by the use of the name "sole" for other species, and restaurant terminology does not always adhere strictly to the rigors of taxonomic nomenclature. The word comes from Old French, *sole,* referring to the shape of the foot, which the fish's flat form resembles.

The true soles of American waters—four species—are rarely sold as food fish, while American flounders of various species are often called "sole." These include butter sole *(Isopsetta isolepsis);* English sole *(Parophrys vetulus);* petrale sole *(Eopsetta jordani);* rex sole *(Glyptocephalus zachirus);* sand sole *(Psettichthys melanostictus);* and the best known, Dover sole *(Microstomus pacificus),* which is a common name for the major fish of the sole market, but it is not the true Dover sole *(Solea vulgaris)* of Europe.

Americans enjoy sole sautéed or grilled with BUTTER, sometimes breaded, and very often prepared according to classic French recipes, such as SOLE MARGUERY, *sole meunière* (with butter and *fines herbes*), and sole *amandine* (with slivers of blanched almonds).

sole Marguery. Or, *"filets de sole Marguery."* Fillets of sole served in a sauce made with egg yolks, butter, and white wine and cooked with mussels and shrimp.

Although it is decidedly a French creation—by chef M. Mangin of the Café de Marguery in Paris—and is listed in Escoffier's *Le Guide Culinaire* and in *Larousse Gastronomique,* sole Marguery is far more popular in the United States than in France, and much of its celebrity derives from the story of how it came to these shores.

Diamond Jim Brady, one of the most flamboyant American gourmands at the turn of the century, returned from Paris to his favorite New York restaurant, Rector's, with the news that he had enjoyed a remarkable dish called *"filets de sole Marguery."* George Rector thereupon withdrew his son from Cornell Law School and sent him off to Paris to get the recipe by working in the kitchens of the Café de Marguery, where he labored for more than a year before he was able to "get the hang of the famous sauce." The young Rector worked fifteen hours a day until he produced a version of the dish that seven master chefs pronounced perfect. He immediately quit his Parisian post, sailed for America, and was greeted in New York harbor by Rector's Russian Orchestra, his father, and Brady, whose first words were, "Have you got the sauce?" Rector made the sauce that night at a fabulous banquet, and Brady pronounced the dish "so good I could eat it on a Turkish towel," and proceeded to down nine portions.

The dish immediately became a sensation and a standard item on American deluxe restaurants' menus.

Ironically, the recipe given by the originator, M. Mangin, to *Larousse Gastronomique,* differs from that published by George Rector, Jr. in his book, *The Girl from Rector's* (1927). Here is the recipe from Mangin:

> Fillet two fines soles. Use the bones and trimmings to make a white wine *fumet,* flavored with a little chopped onion, a sprig of thyme, quarter of a bay leaf and a little parsley. Season with salt and pepper. Simmer for 15 minutes. Add to this *fumet,* which should be strained and concentrated, the strained cooking liquor of a quart of mussels cooked in the usual way (using white wine).
>
> Place the fillets of sole, seasoned and lightly flattened, on a buttered baking dish. Sprinkle over a few tablespoons of the aforesaid *fumet.* Cover with buttered greaseproof paper and poach gently.

Drain the fillets well. Set them in an oval dish and surround with a double row of shelled mussels and shrimps. Keep hot, covered, while the sauce is prepared.

The sauce. Strain the *fumet* to which will have been added the cooking juices of the soles. Boil down by two-thirds. Remove from heat, allow the sauce to cool a little, then add 6 egg yolks. Whisk the sauce over a gentle heat, like a hollandaise, incorporating about 3/4 pound of the finest butter, slightly melted. Season the sauce and strain. Coat with it the fillets and garnish. Glaze in a hot oven.

Here is Rector's recipe:

Cut the fillet with a very sharp knife. There are four fillets to a fish. Take the rest of the fish and put them into a big boiler with plenty of leeks, onions, carrots, turnips, lettuce, romaine, parsley, and similar vegetables. The whole mass is reduced by boiling from eight to twelve hours. This leaves a very small quantity of a jellylike substance, which is the essence of the fish. If properly prepared, only a handful of jelly will be obtained from two hundred fish.

In another pan we place the yolks of four dozen eggs. Work a gallon of melted butter into this, stopping every ten minutes to pour in a pint of dry white wine of good Bordeaux quality. Add from time to time a spoonful of the essence of fish. This is stirred in and cooked in a double boiler in the same way as you would make a hollandaise sauce.

Strain the sauce through a very fine sieve. Season with a dash of cayenne salt. At no time in the preparation of the sauce should it be allowed to come to a boil.

Now we take the fillets, which should be kept on ice to retain their freshness until the sauce is ready. Place them in a pan with just sufficient water to float them a little. About half an inch of water should be sufficient to cover them. After they simmer for ten minutes or less remove and place on a silver platter. Garnish the dish on one end with small shrimp and on the other with imported mussels from northern France.

Pour a liberal amount of the sauce over the whole platter. Sprinkle with chopped parsley and place under the grill for the purpose of allowing it to glaze to a golden brown. Then serve.

son-of-a-bitch stew. Also, "son-of-a-gun stew." A slang term among cowboys, loggers, miners, and other westerners for a stew made pretty much from whatever was available at the moment or from kitchen scraps.

sop. Gravy. A colloquialism of the West, *sop* may also refer to a habitual drunkard.

sopaipilla. A deep-fried fritter usually served with honey. Sopaipillas, whose name is from the Spanish, are a staple of Mexican-American menus. Yet in *Jane Butel's Tex-Mex Cookbook* (1980), the author notes that "history reveals they originated in Old Town, Albuquerque, [New Mexico,] about 300 years ago." Diana Kennedy, in her *Recipes from the Regional Cooks of Mexico* (1978), writes, "For years I have been denying to aficionados of the *sopaipillas* of New Mexico that they have a Mexican counterpart. I have now discovered that they *can* be found, though rarely, in the state of Chihuahua. . . . I have yet to see them on any restaurant menus in the north." A good sopaipilla is supposed to resemble a puffed-up pillow; if cut into a round shape, it is called a "buñuelo." *Sopaipilla* was first found in American print circa 1940.

> Mix 2 cups flour, 1 tbs. baking powder, and 1/2 tsp. salt. Cut in 1 tbs. lard till of a crumbly texture, then gradually add 2/3 cup lukewarm water. Knead into smooth ball and let rest for 10 min. Divide in two, then roll into thin sheets. Cut into 2 1/2-in. squares and fry in hot oil till golden brown. Drain and serve with honey, cinnamon, or powdered sugar. Makes about 3 doz.

sorbic acid. A preservative that prevents the growth of mold. Taken from the berries of the mountain ash tree, sorbic acid is used often in cheese, syrup, wine, and dried fruits.

sorbitan monostearate. An emulsifier that prevents water and oil from separating and prevents discoloration in heated chocolate. It is found in many dessert products.

sorbitol. A sweetener and thickener added to diet drinks, candy, chewing gum, and other foods.

sorghum. Any of a variety of Old World grasses in the genus *Sorghum* that is grown both for animal forage and for a sweet syrup. The word is from Vulgar Latin, *syricum (grānum),* "Syrian grain," although the grain may have originated in Africa. It is first mentioned in English print in 1597.

Sorghum may have been brought to the United States from Africa, probably around 1700, but it was not an important crop until settlers moved west of the Mississippi, where forage for cattle and sheep was needed in the Great Plains. Sweet sorghum *(S. vulgare saccharatum),* also called "sorgos," was made into sorghum molasses, first recorded in print as of 1860. This was an important sweetener throughout the nineteenth century, but it decreased in popularity as refined cane sugar became cheaper and more available after World War I. The grain is still grown in the southeastern United States to some degree.

sorrel. Any of a variety of plants in the genus *Rumex,* especially the French sorrel *(R. scutatus),* whose leaves are used in salads and as a seasoning for soups, sauces, and other preparations.

The word is from Old French, *surele,* from *sur,* "sour," because of its tangy taste, and in Middle English appeared as *sorel.*

Wild sorrel in the United States is rare, but the plant is widely cultivated in many states, often as a pasture fodder.

soul food. Although this term applies to traditional foods eaten by American blacks, especially in the South, it is of rather recent vintage, circa the mid-1960s, when it became associated with the growth of ethnic pride in black culture, of which food was a significant part. The term comes from the fraternal spirit among blacks that their culture, heritage, and cooking gives them an essential "soulfulness" that helps define the black experience in America.

Soul food dishes include CHITTERLINGS, black-eyed peas, collard greens, HOMINY, GRITS, ham hocks, and more. As Bob Jeffries, in his *Soul Food Cookbook* (1969), notes, "While all soul food is southern food, not all southern food is soul."

soup-en-famille. A vegetable-and-beef-brisket soup served in Louisiana. The term is from the French for "family soup."

soup kitchen. Originally an army term for a MESS kitchen, used since 1851; during the Great Depression it was used to describe a charitable organization's kitchen, where free soup and bread were served to the poor and unemployed. Today they are officially called "emergency food programs."

sour. A drink made with liquor, sugar, and citrus juice and usually shaken with cracked ice. Sours first became popular in the middle of the nineteenth century, at first made with brandy and by the end of the century with whiskey. The bar at the "21" Club in New York began mixing sours with bourbon and honey in the 1950s, in homage to society woman Princess "Honey Child" Wilder. A sour glass is a squat bar glass that holds six ounces.

> WHISKEY SOUR:
> Over cracked ice, shake together 3/4 oz. lemon or lime juice, 1 tsp. powdered sugar, and 1 1/2 oz. bourbon or blended whiskey. Strain into sour glass, add cocktail cherry and slice of orange. Scotch, gin, brandy, rum, vodka or other spirits may be used instead of bourbon or blended whiskey.

sourdough. A white bread made with a sour starter made from flour, water, and sugar. The use of a sour starter is a method of bread baking that goes back at least six thousand years, for yeast had to be sustained from bread batch to bread batch. Legend has it that Columbus brought a starter with him to America, and the technique was certainly a standard method of baking in the early days of this country. With the advent of commercially available yeast and baking powder in the nineteenth century, the use of such starters was confined to those pioneers who moved farther and farther from settlements. These included the prospectors of the Yukon during the Alaskan Gold Rush of the 1890s, and it was then that the term *sourdough* became associated not only with the bread such pioneers made but also with the prospectors themselves, and, later, by extension, all Alaskans.

Because many of these prospectors set out by boat from San Francisco, sourdough bread is often associated with that city to this day, and it is still a San Francisco specialty.

Although sourdough starter can be purchased, it can be made by mixing together one cup flour, one cup water (Alaskans often use potato water), and one tablespoon sugar and letting it stand in a warm place for two or three days. It will begin to ferment and have a sour smell. This starter can be continued and preserved by each week adding a bit more flour and water to the mixture and storing it in the refrigerator.

Sourdough starter may also be made by combining a package of dry yeast with one cup lukewarm water. Stir to dissolve completely, then blend in one cup flour and one tablespoon sugar. Cover and let stand for two to three days in a warm place.

In the West some starters are said to have been handed down from one generation to another.

SOURDOUGH BREAD:
Mix 1 1/2 cups starter with 1 cup warm milk, 1 1/2 tbs. sugar, 2 tsp. salt, and 3 tbs. butter or shortening. Knead well with 4 1/2 cups flour. Place in greased bowl and let rise in a warm place till doubled in bulk. Punch down and let rise again for 45 min. more. Shape into two loaves and bake on greased pan at 375° for about 45 min.

sourdough bullet. Cowboy's disparaging term for a poorly made biscuit.

Southern Comfort. A trademark for a cordial made from freshly pitted peeled peaches and bourbon, which is bottled at 100 proof. It was supposedly made and named by Louis Herron, a bartender in St. Louis, Missouri, about 1875, when it was originally called "Cuff and Buttons," then a phrase that meant the equivalent of "white tie and tails," or formal dress.

southern fried chicken. Chicken parts that are floured or battered and then fried in hot fat. This description does little justice to what is perhaps the best-known and best-loved southern dish of all. There are hundreds of recipes for southern fried chicken that may deviate on any or every variable, from the seasoning to the skillet to the fat to the cooking time, and significant debates may be heard in the South over the best accompaniment for this simple but delectable dish. Some will use Tabasco or lemon or garlic in the seasonings; some swear by lard, others by shortening; some insist gravy should never be served with the chicken, while others wouldn't serve the dish without it; some will swear it is best eaten hot from the skillet, while others prefer it cold the next day; some will argue that the best fried chicken is not fried at all, but battered or bread-crumbed and then baked in an oven. In the summer 1982 number of *Gastronome* magazine seven "experts"—including North Carolina-born James Villas and Mississippi-born Craig Claiborne—considered the various ways to make southern fried chicken, with advice on everything from how to keep the skin crisp to how to dredge in a brown paper bag.

Southerners were not the first people in the world to fry chickens, of course. Almost every country has its own version, from Vietnam's *Gà Xaò* to Italy's *pollo fritto* or Austria's *Wiener Backhendl,* and numerous fricasees fill the cookbooks of Europe. And fried chicken did not become particularly popular in the northern United States until well into the nineteenth century: Miss

Leslie did not mention it in her 1837 Philadelphia cookbook, and Fannie Merritt Farmer's 1896 cookbook refers only to "Fried Chicken" as a fricassee served with "Brown Sauce" or as oven-baked "Maryland Chicken." But by the first quarter of this century southern fried chicken was well known and appreciated throughout the country, as Lettie Gay, editor of *200 Years of Charleston Cooking* (1930), bears witness: "If you say the words 'south' and 'chicken' to most northerners they think of fried chicken. But in Charleston chicken is cooked in many ways."

The Scottish, who enjoyed frying their chickens rather than boiling or baking them as the English did, may have brought the method with them when they settled in the South. The efficient and simple cooking process was very well adapted to the plantation life of the southern black slaves, who were often allowed to raise their own chickens. Louisiana blacks called a breakfast of fried chicken and grits a "Sunday breakdown."

The idea of making a sauce to go with fried chicken must have occurred early on, at least in Maryland, where such a match came to be known as "Maryland fried chicken." By 1878 a dish by this name was listed on the menu of the Grand Union Hotel in Saratoga, New York, and, Richard J. Hooker notes, "In B. C. Howard, *Fifty Years in a Maryland Kitchen* (Baltimore, 1873), p. 52, the only fried chicken recipe calls for a sauce made of butter, cream, parsley, salt and pepper." Except for the sauce, Marylanders make their fried chicken in as many different ways as do the rest of the cooks in the South— dusted with flour, rolled in cornmeal, patted with bread crumbs, or even dipped in an egg batter. This last method was harshly criticized by novelist and Virginian William Styron, who wrote, "There is a school, developed mainly in the State of Maryland, which holds that, before cooking, the chicken parts should be immersed in some sort of 'batter.' This is absolute rubbish. Southern fried chicken should have after cooking a firm, well-developed crust—this is one of its glories—but the 'batter' principle simply won't hold up after pragmatic examination."

The cooking oil itself is of significance in such debates, with most authorities supporting the idea that a certain amount of BACON fat is advisable to give the chicken full flavor. Some, like Styron, demand undiluted bacon fat, while others, like James Villas, suggest a few tablespoons mixed in with some Crisco shortening. Peanut or other vegetable oils are also popular.

Most southerners would argue that southern fried chicken is never "deep-fried," but, rather, fried in just enough oil to reach halfway up the sides of the chicken parts. Some suggest frequent turning, while others advise one side be completely cooked at a time. Some prefer to cover the skillet in order to keep in the moistness, while others believe this will make the chicken steamy. Almost everyone agrees the frying pan itself should be a black, well-seasoned skillet.

However southern fried chicken is cooked, it is always eaten with the fingers —a habit that is obviously practical but that probably kept the dish out of the more delicate ladies' cookbooks of the nineteenth century. It is to southern fried chicken that the colloquial phrase *finger lickin' good* (adopted by one commercial fried-chicken company as their slogan) is most often applied.

Once a recipe has been decided upon, next comes the matter of what southern fried chicken demands as an accompaniment. Cole slaw is often cited, as is corn on the cob in season. There is one sect that likes it with rice, but most southerners would feel more comfortable with mashed potatoes and gravy made from the giblets and pan drippings of the chicken.

Southern fried chicken has been known to get dipped into honey as well, and biscuits are often found within reach.

After all this debate one would think it is a difficult dish to prepare well, and many Americans have avoided the problem (and the mess of frying) by buying their fried chicken in groceries, where it is most often found frozen, or at restaurant chains that specialize in cooking the dish.

Here are several southern fried chicken recipes requiring varying methods and ingredients.

BASIC SOUTHERN FRIED CHICKEN:
In a paper bag put 1 cup flour, grind a generous amount of black pepper, and add 2 tsp. salt. Cut a tender chicken into pieces and soak in cold milk for 1/2 hr. Place the chicken pieces in the paper bag and shake till they are all coated. In a skillet of hot oil, fry the chicken pieces on one side till golden brown. Turn and brown the other side. Drain on paper bags and serve hot.

CHICKEN IN BATTER:
In a bowl place 1 1/3 cups flour, 1 tsp. salt, some freshly ground black pepper, 1 tbs. melted butter, and 2 beaten egg yolks. Add 1/2 cup flat beer. Refrigerate for several hours. Thin batter with a little milk or beer if too thick. Dip chicken pieces into batter and let rest on a rack for about 20 min. Fry in hot oil first on one side, then the other, till golden brown.

OVEN-FRIED CHICKEN:
Soak chicken pieces in milk for a few hours, then dredge the pieces in a mixture of 1 cup flour and 1 cup bread crumbs or cornmeal. Sauté the chicken lightly in 4 tbs. butter, then transfer to a baking pan and baste with the pan juices. Bake in a 350° oven for 30 min. or until tender, turning pieces occasionally.

GIBLET GRAVY:
Chop up the giblets of the chicken. Pour off all but about 2 tbs. of the oil in which the chicken pieces have been fried, retaining the browned bits in the pan. Stir in 1 1/2 tbs. flour, blend, and cook till brown. Add the giblets and sauté briefly. Add 1 cup milk gradually, scraping free the brown bits and giblets in the pan and thickening the sauce. Salt and pepper to taste. This gravy should be served on the mashed potatoes, or, if making Maryland fried chicken, on the chicken itself.

southern style. A colloquial expression used in reference to chicken cut in uniform pieces for eating with the fingers.

Southside. A cocktail made by shaking over crushed ice the juice of 1 lemon, 2 tsp. sugar syrup, and 2 oz. Jamaican rum. A Northside substitutes orange juice for the lemon juice. The drink may have originated in Chicago, possibly in the 1950s.

soy protein. A substance made from soybeans that is often used as a binder or extender in meat and poultry products like sausages, luncheon meats, soups, sauces, and gravies. According to the United States Department of Agriculture, "Soybeans are processed into three basic soy protein products: soy flour, soy protein concentrate, and isolated soy protein, each of which may be converted to textured vegetable protein. Whenever soy protein is added to a meat or poultry product, its presence is noted in the ingredients statement on the label."

speakeasy. A term popular during PROHIBITION to describe an establishment selling illegal alcoholic beverages. In order to gain entrance you had to speak in a low voice through a small opening in the back door and tell the attendant inside who it was who sent you to the place.

The term itself may derive from the English *speak-softly-shop,* an underworld term for a smuggler's house where one might get liquor cheaply, its usage in this sense having been traced back to 1823. But with the onset of Prohibition in America, speakeasies sprang up overnight, sometimes in shabby sections of town, but often in the best neighborhoods, and many of these establishments were actually fine restaurants in their own right. New York's "21" Club was a speakeasy during this period and had two bars, a dance floor, an orchestra, and dining rooms on two floors. The term *Café Society* was coined in February 1919 by gossip columnist Maury Paul ("Cholly Knickerbocker") right after Prohibition's onset to describe a new, chic crowd in New York that, in the words of Lucius Beebe, "found itself living frankly, unabashedly, and almost entirely in saloons."

Not all speakeasies enjoyed such favorable notoriety.

French diplomat Paul Morande, visiting New York for the first time in 1925, reported his experience at a speakeasy:

> There is a truly New York atmosphere of humbug in the whole thing. The interior is that of a criminal house; shutters are closed in full daylight, and one is caught in the smell of a cremation furnace. Italians with a too familiar manner, or plump, blue jowled pseudo-bullfighters, carrying bunches of monastic keys, guide you through the deserted rooms of the abandoned house. Facetious inscriptions grimace from the walls. There are a few very flushed diners. At one table some habitués are asleep, their heads sunk on their arms; behind a screen somebody is trying to restore a young woman who has had an attack of hysteria. . . . The food is almost always poor, the service deplorable.

Designed to shut down all saloons, the Volstead Act instead spurred more illicit ones to open, so that, thanks to a thoroughly entrenched system of graft and police corruption, New York had more than thirty-two thousand speakeasies within its boroughs—twice the number of saloons closed.

spiedie. A sandwich of French bread enclosing grilled, skewered cubes of marinated beef or lamb, it is a specialty of Binghamton, New York. The name probably derives from the Italian word *spiedo,* "kitchen spit."

spinach *(Spinacia oleracea).* A dark green plant with rippling leaves eaten raw in a salad or boiled as a vegetable. The plant is native to Asia, and the name derives from the Arabic, *isfānākh,* appearing in English print about 1530.

Of the two main groups of spinach, the prickly-seeded and the smooth-seeded, the former is the most widely cultivated in the United States, with about half the production coming from California. The Spanish brought spinach to the New World.

New Zealand spinach *(Tetragonia implexicoma)* is not a true spinach and is grown only to a small extent on the West Coast.

The bitter taste of spinach has made the plant a particular anathema to American children, who have long been coaxed into eating it as a vegetable by reminding them that the cartoon character Popeye, created by Elzie Crisler Segar in 1919, derived his extraordinary strength from spinach.

spoon bread. Also, "spoonbread" or "spoon cornbread." A soft, custardlike dish usually made with cornmeal. The term may come from an Indian word for porridge, *suppawn,* or from the fact that the dish is usually eaten with a spoon. Its first mention in print was in 1906.

> Sift together 1 cup cornmeal, 1/2 cup flour, 2 tbs. sugar, 1 1/2 tsp. salt, and 2 tsp. baking powder, then mix in 2 beaten eggs and 2 cups milk. Blend well. In a baking pan melt 4 tbs. butter and pour in the cornmeal batter. Pour 1 cup milk over top, then bake for 45 min. at 375°.

spot *(Leiostomus xanthurus).* Also, "spot fish," "red drum," "Lafayette," and "Cape May goody." An eastern freshwater fish that ranges from Maine to Texas. Its black spot behind the gill cover gives it its name, which has been in use at least since 1875. Spot is a favorite fish in Virginia and the South.

spotted pup. Cowboy dish made from cooked rice and raisins.

spotted sea trout *(Cynoscion nebulosus).* A variety of WEAKFISH found in southern waters. It is not a true TROUT but its black spots give it a similar appearance, and it is sometimes marketed as "gray trout."

spring house. A house built over a cold spring to keep dairy foods cool, the term dating back at least to 1755.

spring roll. A Chinese-American appetizer made of crisp dough wrapped around a filling of various ingredients such as vegetables, meat, shrimp, and seasonings. Sometimes synonymous with the "egg roll," it is considered somewhat more "authentic" than the latter.

The name comes from the Chinese tradition of serving them on the first day of the Chinese New Year, which is also the first day of the lunar year's spring.

spritzer. Originally a drink made with Rhine wine and club soda or seltzer, but today a spritzer may be made with almost any dry white wine. The name comes from the German, *spritzer,* a "squirt." The drink became very popular in America in the 1960s, at a time when many people were just being introduced to wine. Often it is ordered as a "white wine spritzer."

spud. A colloquial name for a potato. The word comes from a Middle English word for a short knife, and, later, a spade with which to dig up a tuber such as the potato. The term as used in England in the nineteenth century was a slur against Irishmen, as it was later in America, because of Ireland's dependence on the potato for food. Americans also called a person who picked potatoes a "spud-glommer," especially in Idaho, one of the biggest potato-producing states.

There is no truth to the story that the term comes from a nineteenth-century organization formed to discourage the growing and eating of potatoes—the Society for the Prevention of Unwholesome Diet, whose initials were S.P.U.D.

spud with the bark on. Logger's term for an unpeeled potato.

squash. Any of a variety of plants and their fruits of the genus *Cucurbita.* This term includes the native American summer and winter squashes as well as pumpkins, gourds, and zucchini. The name is from the Narraganset, *asquatas-quash,* meaning "eaten raw, green," and refers specifically to the summer varieties *(C. pepo).* The word *squash* first appeared in print in 1634.

The European settlers were introduced to squashes by the Indians, and John Smith, who traveled through Virginia in 1607, commented that the fruits, called by the Indians there *"macocks,"* were similar to English muskmelons.

Squashes were a staple of the Indian diet throughout the continent. The oldest evidence of their being used as food, dating back to between 7,000 and 5,500 B.C., was found at the Ocampo Caves in Mexico, whence they were carried to North America, where evidence of squash has been found in the burial mounds of Indians of Ohio, Kentucky, and Virginia from two thousand years ago.

Early botanists disagreed on or confused the terminology of squashes, so that one may find some varieties described with various overlapping Latin names for three basic species: *C. pepo, C. maxima,* and *C. moschata.* The English, meanwhile, call them "vegetable marrow." In America squashes are generally separated at market into winter and summer varieties, as noted below.

Summer squashes include the yellow or orange crookneck, the turban squash, the zucchini, the spaghetti squash (so called because its fibers look like strands of spaghetti), and the pattypan (also called cymling and scalloped squash). The winter squashes include the HUBBARD SQUASH, the winter crook-neck, the butternut, the acorn squash, and the sugar pumpkin.

BAKED SQUASH:
Cut a squash in half and scoop out seeds and fibers. Sprinkle squash with brown sugar and 1 tbs. butter and a pinch of salt. Bake at 350° for 1 hr. till tender.

squid. Any of a variety of marine cephalopod mollusks of the genera *Loligo, Rossia,* and others, which is similar to the OCTOPUS but has instead ten legs. The origin of the word is unknown. In Hawaiian the squid is called *"muhe'e."*

In the United States squid consumption is largely confined to ethnic restaurants and Mediterranean immigrants' homes. The most important species for food is the common Pacific squid *(Loligo opalescens)* found in California waters. Most Americans know squid better by its Italian name, *calamari,* which in restaurants usually indicates squid served in a zesty tomato sauce or chopped up with other seafood as a cold salad dish.

squirt. A drink of liquor or wine, fresh fruit or fruit syrup, and seltzer or club soda, made deliberately sweet.

WHISKEY SQUIRT:
Crush half a peach with 1 tbs. sugar syrup, 1 tsp. curaçao, and 1 1/2 oz. bourbon or blended whiskey. Shake with crushed ice and fill glass with seltzer or club soda.

starch. A thickening agent, often made from corn, but also from potato, flour, arrowroot, and other substances. Starch is used in soups and stews, in making a roux, and in other dishes. Modified starch, created in the laboratory, will dissolve in cold water, which regular starch will not do.

state doin's. Trapper's term for food.

States' eggs. In the early days of the western frontier eggs had to be shipped from eastern states to those cow-country territories not then part of the Union.

steam beer. A beverage produced on the West Coast in the mid-nineteenth century by a process that circumvented the shortage of ice needed to make lagers. In *The Great American Beer Book* (1978), James D. Robertson describes the process:

Fermentation proceeds at a relatively high temperature (60°–68° F.) and barley malt is used exclusively. Within twelve to eighteen hours after the yeast has been added to the wort in the fermenting tubs, the beer comes into "krausening," where it is kept from six to eight hours. It is then run into the clarifier for two to three days . . . for completion of fermentation. If fermentation has been proper, at the end of this stage the beer shall have undergone a reduction of fifty to sixty percent and be quite clear in appearance. From the clarifier, the beer is racked directly into barrels, where it receives an addition of about twenty percent of krausen, together with some fining. In four to six days the beer has raised a sufficient amount of "steam" in the barrels (some fifty pounds per square inch), and some bleeding of pressure must be done. In olden days these barrels were shipped to saloons, rested a few days, and then tapped for the trade. Steam beer is made today by only one West Coast firm [The Anchor Brewing Company of San Francisco, begun in 1896] and the product is bottled. . . . Steam beer has a golden brown color, sharp hoppy taste, full body, and a lingering malt finish.

steer. A young ox castrated before maturity, or, as one cowboy put it, "a male cow who had been operated on so he could never be a family man."

sticky. A sweet pastry popular in South Carolina.

Make pastry dough for 2 pies, roll out thin, cut into 12 squares about 3 1/2 in. in size. Divide 1/2 lb. butter into 12 pieces, place on squares, and pour 1 cup sugar on pastry. Fold corners into center, close edges, place closely together on a greased pan, and bake at 350° till browned.

stifle. Also, "stiffle." A New England stew made with salt pork and vegetables or seafood. The word probably suggests the "stifling"—that is, smothering of the ingredients—in the cooking process. "Eel stiffle" is described by Josephine H. Pierce in *Coast to Coast Cookery* (1951) as "a scalloped dish made with eels, onions, potatoes and salt pork. A favorite on Martha's Vineyard [in Massachusetts]." Pierce also notes that a similar stew without the eel is known on Cape Cod as "Halleluia," the biblical exclamation for good news, though this may be a bit of hyperbole or sarcasm.

stirabout. A form of porridge whose name is formed from the two words *stir* and *about*. The Pennsylvania Dutch of the nineteenth century made this dish with vegetables, saffron, and chicken broth, but in the mining towns of the Northwest it was a simpler affair, no more than a breakfast of oatmeal mush thinned with milk and salt. In the Federal Writers Project volume entitled *Copper Camp: Stories of the Greatest Mining Town, Butte, Montana* (1943), the authors report that stirabout was brought to that locale by Irish miners and dished out at the Clarence Hotel and Florence Hotel, where servings were "computed in tons" and every boarder ate two to three bowls each morning and carried more to the mines for lunch.

To a kettle of 6 cups boiling chicken broth add 4 cups sliced peeled potatoes, 2 tbs. chopped parsley, 1 cup chopped celery, salt, pepper, and 1/8 tsp. saffron. Reduce heat, and then simmer for 20 min. Beat 2 eggs with 1/2 cup flour, drop into simmering broth by teaspoonfuls, then cover and boil another 7 min. Serves 6.

stone boiling. A Pueblo Indian method of cooking by placing hot stones into a basket with food.

stone crab (*Menippe mercenaria,* although *Lithodes maja* is also called by this name). Also, "Moro crab." A crab with very hard claws filled with sweet, white meat. The stone crab is one of the delicacies of the southern United

States and particularly of Florida. Since only the claws are eaten, fishermen twist them off and throw back the crab, which grows new claws within eighteen months. Usually the claws are then boiled and either put on ice or frozen, because cooks have found that freezing removes the unpleasant taste of iodine frequently noticed in the meat. The claws are usually served cold.

Damon Runyon said of the crustacean, "The stone crab is much larger than the northern crab and has a shell harder than a landlord's heart." It has become especially associated with a restaurant in Miami Beach that popularized the dish in the 1920s—Joe's Stone Crab Restaurant, opened in 1913 by Joe Weiss and designated a historical landmark in 1975. Here hundreds of people sit in a cavernous room and wait for a platter of crab claws served with cole slaw, mustard-mayonnaise, and hash-brown potatoes. The claws' knuckles are broken with a mallet in the kitchen and then served cold with a dipping sauce of melted butter and lemon or a mustard sauce. Before 1920 the crab was eaten only by Miamians and others in the Florida and Gulf Coast communities. *Stone crab* first appeared in print in 1709.

stone fence. Also, "stonewall." An alcoholic drink made from apple cider or applejack and a whiskey such as rum. The *Dictionary of Americanisms* traces *stone fence* to 1843, but Washington Irving mentions the drink in his *Knickerbocker's History of New York* (1809). According to the *Better Homes and Gardens Heritage Cook Book* (1975), "stonewall was the favorite drink of Ethan Allen and his Green Mountain Boys."

> Combine 1 1/2 oz. applejack with 1/2 oz. dark rum. It may be poured over crushed ice.

straight. An alcoholic spirit of any kind drunk with no other ingredients, except, in some cases, ice. Americans have used this word at least since the middle of the nineteenth century. In England a drinker would say "neat" instead.

strawberry. Any of a variety of plants in the genus *Fragaria* bearing a red berry with a soft, pulpy flesh. The word is from Old English, *strēawberige,* possibly because the low-lying plant's runners resemble straw.

Strawberries have been eaten by man for thousands of years, but little trouble was taken to cultivate them before the Renaissance in Europe. In the New World strawberries were abundant, and the Indians made them into bread and held feasts at the harvest of the fruit. Jacques Cartier mentioned seeing wild strawberries along the banks of the St. Lawrence River in Canada in 1534, and a white strawberry was noted in 1536 to be growing in Massachusetts and New York.

The native American strawberry, called the "Virginia strawberry," "meadow strawberry," or "scarlet strawberry" (*F. virginiana*) by the white settlers and "*wuttahimneash*" by the tribes of the eastern coast of America, was admired by the first colonists and plants were soon sent back to Europe, perhaps as early as 1600. (France had samples as of 1624.) In 1607 Captain John Smith reported, "Captain Newport and my selfe with divers others, to the number of twenty-two persons, set forward to discover the [James] River, some fiftie or sixtie miles, finding it in some places broader, and in some narrower . . . the people in all places kindly treating us, daunsing and feasting us with strawberries, Mulberies, Bread, Fish, and other their Countrie provisions. . . ." Roger Williams of Rhode Island marveled at the great size of his region's strawberries—"four times bigger than ours in England," he wrote.

A second American berry was discovered by the Spanish explorers of Central and South America, where they found Indians cultivating a very large berry the conquistadores called *"frutilla."* This strawberry was of little interest until French navy engineer Amede Frézier rediscovered it while exploring Peru and Chile in 1712 and sent some back to the royal gardens in France and some to Brittany. This strawberry was widely proliferated throughout the Pacific coast, as far as Alaska, and also in Hawaii, and in English took the name "beach" or "Chilean strawberry" *(F. chiloensis).* Frézier's plants did not bear fruit in France because he had unknowingly brought only female examples of a species that needed a separate male in order to breed. Thirty years later an accidental crossing of these same berries with the already established Virginia strawberries in France resulted in an excellent hybrid that became known as the "pine" or "pineapple strawberry" *(F. ovalis),* now one of the major cultivated varieties.

In the United States few people bothered to cultivate berries because they were so plentiful in the wild. After Englishman William Cobbett visited the United States, he reported in *A Year's Residence in America* (1818) that "strawberries grow wild in abundance; but no one will take the trouble to get them." By one estimate there were only fourteen hundred acres of cultivated strawberries in America at the beginning of the nineteenth century, and the wild strawberry patch was a well-established fixture in rural areas and home gardens. Cultivation did begin, however, in the early years of the nineteenth century, and strawberries became something of a luxury, especially when served with cream. President Martin Van Buren (1782–1862; held office, 1837–1841), who was often accused of trying to turn the White House into a highfalutin palace, was criticized before his election for using public money to grow strawberries for his delectation.

New York became a strawberry market after the Erie Railroad brought in eighty thousand baskets in a single night in June of 1847, and widescale cultivation began in America four years later, with the development by Albany, New York, horticulturist James Wilson of the hardy Wilson variety. By the 1880s more than one hundred thousand acres were under cultivation for the fruit, and the refrigerated railroad cars perfected in that era meant that the perishable strawberry could be shipped to the Midwest. A strawberry industry began to grow in Arkansas, Louisiana, northern Florida, and Tennessee, and today strawberries are grown in all fifty states, with the majority coming from California.

The main species is the hybrid *F. ovalis,* the main varieties of which include the Aroma, the Beaver, the Blakemore, the Catskill, the Dorset, the Fairfax, the Howard 17, the Klondike, the Klonmore, the Lupton, the Marshall, the Massey, the Missionary, the Redheart, the Fairpeake, the Swanee, the Tennessee Beauty, the Florida Ninety, and the Tioga.

Americans eat strawberries fresh or frozen in syrups, particularly on strawberry sundaes (first recorded in 1904), and STRAWBERRY SHORTCAKE, as well as a flavoring for various desserts, especially ice cream. There are many strawberry festivals held throughout the United States each year, a tradition dating back to the 1850s.

strawberry shortcake. A dessert made with a biscuit pastry, strawberries, and whipped cream. The name derives from its being made "short," that is, crisp, by the use of lard or another fat, a meaning of the word that dates back to the fifteenth century. In England *shortcake,* mentioned in Shakespeare's *Merry Wives of Windsor* (1598), is usually synonymous with *shortbread,* which is crisp and a traditional specialty of Scotland. In America, however, *shortcake* meant a rich pastry enclosing fruits, to which Washington Irving in his story, "The Legend of Sleepy Hollow" (1821), may have referred when he wrote of a table laid with "sweet cakes and short cakes, ginger cakes and crumbling cruller, and the whole family of cakes." By the 1830s strawberry shortcake was known and soon became one of the best-loved American desserts.

The recipe below is adapted from Marjorie Kinnan Rawlings's *Cross Creek Cookery* (1942).

Sift twice 2 cups flour, 1/4 cup sugar, 4 tsp. baking powder, and 1/2 tsp. salt. (Add a few grains of ground nutmeg if desired.) Work mixture with 5 1/3 tbs. butter till coarse and crumbly. Add 1 well-beaten egg, then 1/3 cup milk, and blend to make a dough. Turn into buttered pan and pat into shape. Bake 15–20 min. at 400°. An hour before serving cut up 1 qt. fresh strawberries, saving about 1 doz. whole. Add 3/4 cup brown sugar. Let stand in a warm place for 1 hr. Split the shortcake hot from the oven into 2 layers, butter each side, lay on strawberries and juice, cover with other shortcake layer, and top with whole strawberries and whipped cream.

streak-of-lean. Also, "streak-o-lean." A southern Negro term for salt pork.

streusel. A crumb topping of flour, butter, and spices that is sprinkled and baked on breads, cakes, and muffins. The term is from the German, *Streusel,* "something strewn together," and these toppings are certainly of German origin, although they are sometimes referred to as "Danish" or "Swedish."

Blend together 3/4 cup brown or white sugar with 1/2 cup flour and 1/3 cup butter till mixture becomes like meal. Add pinches of nutmeg, cinnamon, powdered cloves, or other spices if desired. Sprinkle over sliced fruit, breads, cakes, muffins, and other baked goods, and brown in oven.

string bean. Also called "snap bean" or "green bean." A long, slender green bean *(Phaseolus vulgaris),* so called because of its stringy tendrils. The term is first recorded in 1759, and *snap bean* (because of its crisp sound when cracked) is first recorded in 1770. String beans are widely eaten in the United States, usually boiled and buttered.

The yellow variety of string bean was called the "wax bean" as of about 1900.

striped bass *(Morone saxatilis).* Also, "rockfish" and "striper." A North American fish whose name derives from the dark stripes along the length of its body. They are considered one of the principal game fish of the world. (For distinctions among BASS, see main entry.)

The striped bass was one of the many fish early European settlers marveled at for its size and abundance, and Captain John Smith, who sailed into Chesapeake Bay in 1607, wrote enthusiastically of striped bass "so large, the head of one will give a good eater a dinner, and for the daintinesse of diet they excell the Marybones of Beefe." The Pilgrims were nourished on striped bass heads and salted the bodies for winter, also using the fish for fertilizer to such an extent that the Massachusetts Bay Colony General Court put a stop to the practice in 1639, because the fishes were quickly dwindling in number. In those days the striped bass grew to an enormous size, sometimes six-feet long and well over a hundred pounds. By the nineteenth century the bass had become one of the sportsmen's favorite fishes, and waters of both coasts were full of this elusive challenger to the talents of the best fishermen. (The fish had been introduced to the Pacific in 1879.)

The striped bass is prepared in a variety of ways and takes especially well to poaching.

strudel. A rolled pastry filled with nuts, STREUSEL mixture, fruit, or cheese, brought to America by German immigrants. The name is from Middle High German, meaning a "whirlpool." Apple strudel is the most common form of the pastry. The word was first printed in English in 1927.

Combine 3 cups flour, 1/2 tsp. salt, and 1/2 cup butter to make a crumbly meal. Add 1 beaten egg mixed with 2/3 cup water, then knead for 5 min. Cut in half and let stand 1 hr. On floured cloth roll half the dough into a large square, brush with melted butter, let stand 5 min., then begin to work the edges out from the middle to make a very thin dough. Brush with butter. Mix 2/3 cup sugar, 2 tsp. cinnamon, and 1 cup ground almonds or walnuts. Peel and slice 6 cups apples, lay half of them along one edge of the dough, and sprinkle with half the sugar-cinnamon mixture and 1/4 cup dried currants. Fold a flap of dough over the apples, then lift cloth so that dough slowly rolls. Seal ends. Repeat with the rest of the dough and other ingredients. Brush tops with egg whites and bake at 350° for 45 min. Sprinkle with confectioners' sugar.

stuffing. A packed combination of meats, vegetables, grains, fats, or other ingredients inserted in the cavity of meat, poultry, or fish. The word comes from the verb *to stuff,* and first appears in English print in 1538, displacing the customary *forcemeat* (from the French, *farcir,* "to stuff") used in the English tradition. After the 1880s, however, Victorian propriety in America made the term *dressing* more acceptable; both *stuffing* and *dressing* are still used interchangeably today, with the former finding more adherents in the East and South.

Turkeys and most roast poultry and game are stuffed, usually with bread or cornmeal crumbs and various seasonings. Oysters were a very popular nineteenth-century stuffing, and pecan or rice stuffings were often used in the South. Italian-Americans may use a stuffing of sausage, onion, and mozzarella cheese, while dried fruit, potatoes, and apples are customary among German-Americans.

PECAN STUFFING:
Sauté in 4 tbs. butter 1/4 cup chopped onion, 1 1/2 cups cooked white rice, 1/2 cup pecan halves, 1/2 tsp. salt, and 1/4 tsp. pepper. Toss to moisten.

CHESTNUT STUFFING:
Remove 3 lb. roast chestnuts from shells, sauté in butter, and cover with boiling water to simmer for about 35 min. Drain, put half through a blender or ricer; chop other half in small pieces. Cover 1 cup raisins with boiling water and let stand 1 hr., then drain. Add 1 tbs. sugar and 1 grated lemon rind. Cook 3 tbs. finely chopped onions in butter till limp, add 6 cups bread crumbs, 1 tsp. salt, and all ingredients. Toss, adding hot water if necessary for texture.

BREAD STUFFING:
Sauté 1/2 cup chopped onions in 1/2 cup butter, season with salt and pepper, and remove from heat. Combine 6 cups bread crumbs, 1 tsp. salt, 1/2 tsp. pepper, 1 tsp. each of thyme, rosemary, summer savory, and bay leaf, 1/3 cup chopped parsley, and 1/2 cup chopped celery. Add onions and toss, adding hot water as necessary for texture.

OYSTER STUFFING:
Drain 1 pt. oysters and retain liquid. Cut oysters in half. Sauté in 8 tbs. butter 2 cups chopped onion, 1 1/2 cups chopped celery, 1 cup chopped green pepper, 1 tbs. minced garlic, 1/2 tsp. thyme, 1/2 tsp. rosemary, 1 crushed bay leaf, and 1 cup chopped parsley. Cook with onion for about 5 min. Add oyster liquid, cook for 5 sec., remove from heat, and add 5 cups bread crumbs, salt and pepper, and 2 beaten eggs. Blend well, adding water if necessary for texture.

sturgeon. Any of a variety of fishes in the family Acipenseridae. It is a very large fish particularly known for its roe, which is turned into CAVIAR. The name is from Germanic, *sturjōn,* and has been used in English at least since the thirteenth century.

The sturgeon in North American waters amazed the early European settlers, who found two-hundred-pound examples in the Hudson River, and Captain John Smith, who explored the Virginia coastline in 1607, wrote, "We had more Sturgeon, than could be devoured by Dog and Man." Sturgeon was an everyday food for southerners: "The supplies seemed limitless," wrote

Richard J. Hooker in *Food and Drink in America* (1981). "Stories were told of men becoming physically tired from pulling fish from the rivers, of catches with hooks of 600 sturgeon, and of immense takes on the rivers with seines, eelpots, weirs, and fish pots."

In the nineteenth century the sturgeon became the source of a booming American caviar business, but by 1900 supplies of both the Atlantic and Pacific sturgeons were almost totally depleted. So far the resurgence of the fish has been only modest, and it is still illegal in California to catch them for commercial purposes.

Today the sturgeon that does come to market is generally smoked, frozen, or packed in jars with pickling spices. Most come from the Northwest, though the Atlantic sturgeon *(Acipenser oxyrhynchus)* is taken in the waters of South Carolina and Georgia. The main species marketed for consumption are the white sturgeon *(A. transmontanus)*, the green sturgeon *(A. medirostris)*, and the lake sturgeon *(A. fulvescens)*.

succotash. A cooked dish of corn and lima beans. More popular in the South these days than elsewhere, it is still often found in cafeterias.

The term first made its appearance in print in 1751, an Americanism formed from the Narraganset Indian word *misickquatash* (and other Indian words, for example, *sukquttahash* and *msakwitash*) referring to various ingredients in a stew pot, and, more specifically in the Narraganset, to an ear of corn.

So American is the term that President Ronald Reagan once lumped "South Succotash" in with "Podunk" as epithets for an out-of-the-way, insignificant small town, which immediately got up the dander of the six hundred people who actually live in a place called Succotash Point, Rhode Island, on Narragansett Bay.

> Cook 1 cup fresh corn kernels till tender in boiling water. Do the same with 1 cup lima beans. Mix together with 1/2 tsp. salt, 1/8 tsp. pepper, 1 tbs. salt pork or butter, and 1/4 cup milk, and cook together till hot but not boiling. Serves 4.

A recipe for Delaware succotash, appearing in *The American Heritage Cookbook* (1980), contains tomato and nutmeg.

sucker. Any of a variety of fish in the family Catostomidae. These fishes derive their name from the sucking, protractile mouth that attaches itself to whales, sharks, other fish and boats. The freshwater varieties of sucker are so called because their method of eating is to suck up the algae and crustaceans of their diet. The first mention of such fish in print was in 1772, referring to species in the Hudson River.

The principal suckers of culinary interest include: blue sucker *(Cycleptus elongatus)*, ranging throughout the Midwest and South; the bigmouth buffalo *(Ictiobus cyprinellus)*, also called "redmouth" and "gourdhead buffalo"; black buffalo *(I. niger)*, also called "bugler," "prairie buffalo," and "rooter"; smallmouth buffalo *(I. bubalus)*, also called "highback", "channel buffalo," and "razorback"; black redhorse *(Moxostoma duquesnei)*; golden redhorse *(M. erythrurum)*, spotted sucker *(Minytrema melanops)*; and white sucker *(Catostomos commersoni)*.

Not related to these species is a marine fish of the family Echeneidae, the remora. The remora takes its name from the Latin words *re-*, "back," and *mora*, "delay," because they held back and delayed a ships' passage. Remoras are also called "suckerfish."

suffering bastard. A name used for two entirely different cocktails. An American drink of this name was created by a Los Angeles restaurateur of the 1930s named Don the Beachcomber (born Don Richard Beaumont Gantt), who specialized in creating rum drinks like the missionary's downfall, the vicious virgin, and the ZOMBIE. His suffering bastard was made with lime juice, 1/2 oz. curaçao, 1/4 oz. sugar syrup, 1/4 oz. orgeat syrup, 1 oz. light rum, and 1 oz. medium rum, all shaken with crushed ice and garnished with cucumber peel, fresh mint, lime shell, and a fruit stick.

The other suffering bastard is attributed to the bar at the Shepheard Hotel in Cairo, Egypt, where it was originally called the "suffering bar steward." The name changed when it became associated with the hard-pressed British and Australian defenders of Tobruk in North Africa during World War II. In this drink 2 oz. cognac or brandy, 2 oz. dry sherry, and ginger ale are poured over ice in a tall tumbler and decorated with fresh mint.

sugar. There are more than a hundred substances that may be described as "sugars"—including honey, dextrose, corn syrups, levulose, lactose, sorbitol, mannitol, maltitol, xylitol, total invert sugar, turbinado sugar, and scores of others—but common white sugar, called "sucrose," is the one most used in the American home. The word *sugar* (which derives ultimately from Sanskrit *sárkarā*) refers to sweet, water-soluble carbohydrates extracted from plants such as cane and sugar beets, maple sap, fruits, sorghum, and other sources.

Until the Middle Ages honey was the only sweetener known in Europe, but sugarcane products, including molasses, were used in Asia at least as early as 800 B.C. The Arabs brought sugarcane to the West, and the Crusaders may have brought some back too. By the fifteenth century Venice was importing it from Alexandria, and sugar became a sensation throughout Italy, where it was used to sweeten not only desserts but hors d'oeuvres, meats, and macaroni as well. In 1498 the Portuguese explorer Vasco da Gama brought back sugarcane from his voyage to India, heralding an expansion of sugarcane production into the Cape Verde and Canary islands and Madeira. But four years before that Christopher Columbus had planted pieces of cane in the New World that were to flourish and change the course of Caribbean history, for soon the Spanish introduced the plant to Hispaniola, Cuba, and other islands, the Portuguese to Brazil, the English to Barbados, and the French to Martinique, establishing both a profitable sugar trade and a slave trade to support it. As Reay Tannahill points out in *The Fine Art of Food* (1968), "Sugar became so important to trade that in the 1670s the Dutch yielded New York to England in exchange for the captured sugar lands of Surinam, and in 1763 France was prepared to leave England with the whole of Canada, provided she had Guadeloupe returned to her." By 1520 there were at least sixty sugar factories on the island of Saint Thomas alone. Whole native populations, such as the Caribs and Arawaks of the Greater Antilles, were forced into slavery on the sugar plantations, causing the virtual extermination of these tribes. The Europeans then turned to Africa for slave labor, bringing more than 10 million wretched souls to work the New World's plantations. Soon a reciprocal trade network was set up between the islands, the North American colonies, and Europe, with New England selling codfish (with which to feed the slaves) to the islands, the islands shipping sugar and molasses to New England and Europe, and New England sending cod and rum made from molasses to Africa in return for a fresh supply of slaves. "King Sugar" ruled an empire of human misery. Many abolitionists urged people to refrain from using sugar, and some sugar vendors advertised their product as "East India sugar not made by slaves."

France's loss of the Sugar Islands of the West Indies to England after 1761 severely crippled Louis XV's prosperity and was one of the significant reasons his successor entered America's War of Independence on the colonists' side. Despite the outcome of the war, however, France never did regain much of the Caribbean sugar trade.

Sugarcane never brought North American farmers much profit, though it was grown in the South in Louisiana, Alabama, Mississippi, Florida, and Georgia until competition from the Caribbean and the Far East after the Civil War pretty much wiped out the domestic industry. Today only Louisiana has a sugarcane industry, but it accounts for less than one-half of one percent of the world's output of sugar. Some cane is still grown in other southern states to make sugar syrup.

Although white sugar was always popular with Americans, it was often more expensive than alternatives like molasses, maple syrup in the Northeast, and "muscovado" (from Portuguese *mascavado,* unrefined sugar), an unrefined product derived from sugarcane juice that was considerably cheaper than white sugar. After the lifting of sugar tariffs in the 1880s sugar came down in price and afterwards became a cheap commodity all Americans could easily afford. Consumption doubled between 1880 and 1915. Today Americans ingest about ninety pounds of sugar per person per year, a drop from a decade ago. Americans get about 24 percent of their calories from sugars of various kinds, of which only 3 percent comes from fruits and vegetables and 3 percent from dairy products, causing many nutritionists to advise against too much consumption of what they call "empty calories." Sugar has also become the leading ingredient added to processed foods in the United States, and 65 percent of the refined sugar now produced is utilized by the food and beverage industries.

The following list includes the most common sugars and sweeteners:

sucrose. Obtained from cane or sugar beets, sucrose is a compound of glucose and fructose, is 99.9 percent pure, and is sold granulated or powdered.

raw sugar. A coarse, light brown granulated sugar evaporated from cane juice. Only purified raw sugar may be sold.

turbinado sugar. Produced by separating raw sugar crystals and washing them with steam, turbinado sugar must be refined to remove impurities.

brown sugar. Less refined than white sugar, brown sugar consists of sugar crystals contained in molasses syrup with natural color and flavor. It may also be made by adding syrup to white sugar and blending. It may be found in groceries in either a light or dark brown shade, the latter having a somewhat stronger taste.

total invert sugar. A mixture of glucose and fructose, made by a process called "inversion," by which acids or enzymes split sucrose. Total invert sugar is sweeter than sucrose and comes in liquid form; it helps to prolong the freshness of baked goods.

honey. An invert sugar formed by the action of bees' nectar enzymes and composed mainly of fructose, glucose, maltose, and sucrose.

corn syrup. Also, "corn sirop." Produced by the action of enzymes and/or acids on cornstarch, corn syrup is often used in baking and desserts.

levulose. Also, "fructose," which is called "fruit sugar." A commercial sugar sweeter than sucrose and used in cooking.

dextrose. Also, "glucose" or "corn sugar." A commercial sugar made from the action of heat and acids, or enzymes, on starch. Dextrose is often blended with regular sugar.

lactose. Also, "milk sugar." Made from skim and whey milk for commercial purposes, lactose is found in mammals' milk and is used mainly by the pharmaceutical industry.

sugar alcohol. Also, "polyol." Any of the natural fruit sugars like sorbitol, mannitol, maltitol, and xylitol that are commercially produced from sources like dextrose.

confectioners' sugar. A highly ground form of powdered sugar (which would be labelled "XXX") that is labelled "XXXX," ideal for making icings and other confections.

colored sugar. Also, "confetti sugar." Any sugar variously colored for cake and dessert decoration.

flavored sugar. Any sugar scented with aromatics such as lemon, vanilla, or cinnamon, often added to tea or coffee.

maple sugar. See MAPLE.

sukiyaki. A Japanese dish of meat and vegetables simmered together. Sukiyaki is a standard item in Japanese-American restaurants. The word translates as "broiled on the blade of a plow," from the practice of Japanese farmers who often cooked their meals in the fields on such a utensil. Today, however, the dish is not broiled but stir-fried and simmered.

Sear 2 1/2 lb. beef that has been cut in thin strips in a wok or skillet with 2 tbs. oil. Remove, then add to wok 1 can bamboo shoots, three chopped scallions, 4 sliced onions, 1 can Japanese noodles (or shirataki threads), 1 chopped tofu (bean curd) cake, 1 cup Japanese soy sauce, 2 cups water, 3 tbs. sugar, and 1/2 cup *saké*. Add beef. Simmer till tender.

sunfish. Any of a variety of North American freshwater fishes in the family Centrarchidae or marine fishes in the family Molidae. Their brightly colored bodies give these fishes their name, which was first mentioned in print in 1629 referring to the sea species, and in 1685 (by William Penn) referring to the North American freshwater variety. The most important sunfish for culinary reasons include: the bluegill *(Lepomis macrochirus);* the black crappie *(Pomoxis nigromaculatus)* and white crappie *(P. annularis),* also called "speckled perch," "calico bass," "strawberry bass," "bachelor perch," "paper-mouth," and, in Louisiana, "sac à lait" ("milk sack")—the word *crappie* is from a Canadian French name for the fish, *crapet*—the flier *(Centrarchus macropterus);* the green sunfish *(Lepomis cyanellus);* the longear sunfish *(L. megalotis);* the pumpkinseed *(L. gibbosus);* the redbreast sunfish *(L. auritus),* also called the "robin," "sun perch," and "yellow belly sunfish"; the redear sunfish *(L. microlophus),* also called the "shellcracker"; the rock bass *(Ambloplites rupestris),* also called the "redeye bass" or "goggle-eye"; and the warmouth *(L. gulosus),* also called the "stump knocker."

sunflower. Any of a variety of plants in the genus *Helianthus,* especially the common sunflower *(H. annuus),* native to the New World, bearing seeds that are dried or roasted to be eaten as a snack or pressed to make an oil. The word derives from its bright yellow flowers surrounding a dark center and was first recorded in English in 1597. Sunflower oil is first mentioned in print in 1819.

Sunflowers were cultivated by the American Indian long before the arrival of the Europeans, but Russia became the world's largest producer. Although it is the official state flower of Kansas, the states producing the largest sunflower crops are North Dakota, Minnesota, and California.

supermarket. A large self-service food market that also sells many nonfood items. The supermarket is the principal retail food store for Americans. The various items and brands are arranged on open shelves along long aisles, and customers line up at cash registers near the exit to unload their purchases from a rolling metal gridwork basket. The items are totalled up as they move along a conveyor belt and then placed in brown paper bags by a store attendant called a "packer." Often the bags will be placed on another conveyor belt that brings them outside to a spot where customers can easily stop their cars to pick up the bags.

The supermarket is a specifically American notion built on the ideas that efficiency is increased by self-service, that variety is a tempting and competitive manner of advertising on the spot, and that the mobile nature of the American consumer is conducive to shopping in large retail stores with easy access by automobiles. In the last fifteen years such stores have become popular in Europe too, often under the same term, *supermarket,* in various languages.

The first self-service market was opened in 1916 by Clarence Saunders on Jefferson Avenue in Memphis, Tennessee. Items were prepackaged, labelled, and priced and the store was kept impeccably clean, in contrast to the traditional rustic grocery store where many items were sold loose, priced according to how much one bought, and often delivered to one's home.

The self-service idea did not really catch on, however, till the 1930s, when supermarkets were sometimes referred to as "cafeteria-type" markets. In 1930 a grocery-chain manager in Herrin, Illinois, named Michael Cullen opened the King Kullen supermarket in an abandoned garage in Jamaica, New York, that was ten times the size of the average grocery. Cullen carried both fresh meat and groceries, promising to keep prices down through volume sales, and by 1932 King Kullen had seven more markets. By 1936 America had more than twelve hundred markets under different names in eighty-four cities.

The first mention of the word *supermarket* in American print occurred in 1937. The term became as firmly entrenched as the concept, so that by 1950 America had more than ten thousand supermarkets, their growth encouraged by the postwar "baby boom" and the movement of the middle class to the suburbs.

The average supermarket was by then more than thirty thousand square feet, with chains like A&P, Safeway, Grand Union, and others dominating the food-buying habits of the country. In significant ways these large chains influenced what Americans ate to the extent that pretty much the same offerings of those in the West were enjoyed by those in the East, North, and South. By the 1960s supermarkets were carrying everything from imported foods to lawn furniture, and many had sections selling delicatessan-style items, fresh bread, and cooked foods.

But by the 1970s competition and overexpansion caused the supermarkets to lose money, even though sales in 1981 totaled $150 billion. Profit margins, never very high, fell to half what they had been in the 1950s and 1960s, and some chains went bankrupt.

To some extent many Americans began to regard the supermarket as depersonalized and lacking in the nostalgic charm of the older neighborhood groceries, and in cities increasing numbers of "gourmet" or delicacy shops were opened, carrying better-quality (and higher-priced) merchandise. But the supermarket is still an essential part of Americans' gastronomic and social life.

suption. A southern Negro word for "flavor" in food, perhaps a variant of the word *sup,* "to eat."

surf-n'-turf. A dish of meat and seafood served on the same plate. The meat is usually beef, the seafood lobster. This combination has led to several colloquial variants, including "pier-n'-steer," "lob-steer," "beef-n'-reef," and others, used as menu listings or restaurant names. These began to appear in the 1960s and 1970s.

swamper. Cowboy's term for a cook's helper.

swamp seed. Cowboy's name for rice.

Swedish meatball. A meatball covered with a brown gravy. Swedish meatballs are usually served at buffets and SMORGASBORDS, a custom that reflects their Swedish origins. They have been served in American homes at least since the 1920s.

> Grind together 3/4 lb. beef, 1/4 lb. pork, and 1/4 lb. veal. Soak 1 1/2 cups soft bread cubes in 1 cup light cream for several min., then mash into meat with 1/2 cup chopped onion, 1 beaten egg, salt, pepper, 1/4 cup chopped parsley, and a dash of ginger and nutmeg. Form into meatballs about 1 in. in diameter. Sauté meatballs in 3 tbs. butter till browned, then remove. Melt 2 tbs. butter in same skillet, scrape meat drippings, stir in 2 tbs. flour, cook briefly, and add 1 1/3 cups beef bouillon. Cook till thickened, return meatballs to skillet and cook, basting often, for about 30 min.

sweet potato *(Ipomoea batatas)*. A vine native to the New World tropics, the yellow or orange tuber of which is eaten as a side dish in various forms. Sweet potatoes may be baked, boiled, candied, mixed in a pie or in biscuits, and topped with marshmallows. They are an important crop of the American South, though grown elsewhere in the United States too, with two types being dominant—the "pale" sweet potato and another, darker-fleshed type called, erroneously, "yam." (The true yam [*Dioscorea bulbifera*] is a different tropical vine whose tuber may grow to lengths over seven feet and which is generally sweeter than the sweet potato. It is rarely seen in the United States, except, perhaps, in Latin-American markets.) The confusion with the true yam came from the habit of slaves calling the American sweet potato by an African word (either Gullah, *njam,* Senegal, *nyami,* or Vai, *djambi*) meaning "to eat." The word was first recorded in America in 1676.

The earliest records of the cultivation of the sweet potato, dated to around 750 B.C., come from Peru, but it was grown throughout South and Central America by the time Christopher Columbus arrived in the New World. He found the tuber in Saint Thomas, where it was called *"aje"* or *"axi";* on Hispaniola *("ages");* in the Yucatan *("camote");* and in Arawak *("batatas").*

The Taino word *batata* was soon transformed into several European words, including the Spanish *patata,* French *patate,* and English *potato.* These words first meant specifically the sweet potato, not the white potato that was introduced much later to the North American colonies. John Gerard in his *Herball* (1597) called sweet potatoes "common Potatoes," and, according to the *Oxford English Dictionary,* he termed white potatoes "Virginia Potatoes," and, later, "Bastard Potatoes." But, as Waverly Root points out in *Food* (1980), Gerard could not have meant the white potato, for "not only did [it] not exist in Virginia, it did not exist anywhere in North America." (For further information on the white potato, see POTATO.)

The sweet potato, meanwhile, had already been shipped back to the Old World, perhaps as early as 1493 in Columbus's ship, and was cultivated in Spain by the middle of the sixteenth century. England got its first taste of the tuber in 1564, when Sir John Hawkins brought it back from "the Indies of Nova Hispania," although Henry VIII might have sampled some Spanish varieties earlier. By the end of the century Shakespeare wrote of them in *Merry Wives of Windsor,* and sweet potato pie was an English delicacy.

But the term *sweet potato* was not in use in America until the 1740s, by then distinguished from the white potato that had come to Boston about 1719 with Irish immigrants. Long before then the sweet potato was being shipped to ports in Massachusetts from as far away as Bermuda. Root says earliest evidence for the cultivation of the tuber in North America dates to 1648, and probably back to 1610. It was in cultivation in New England by 1764 and much earlier in Virginia.

In the nineteenth century George Washington Carver devised more than a hundred uses for the sweet potato, which he noted was also called the "Indian potato," the "Tuckahoc," and the "hog potato," and listed table varieties that included the "Dooley yam," "Triumph," "Pumpkin yam," "Porto Rico," and "Nancy Hall." By the 1880s Americans were enjoying candied sweet potatoes, along with less lavish preparations of boiled, roasted, or mashed tubers.

The sweet potato has long been associated with southern and soul cooking, and it is still traditional to serve it with the Thanksgiving meal.

In *Invisible Man* (1952) Ralph Ellison reminisced about the sweet potatoes of his childhood:

At home we'd bake them in the hot coals of the fireplace, had carried them cold to school for lunch; munched them secretly, squeezing the sweet pulp from the soft peel as we hid from the teacher behind the largest book, the *World's Geography.* Yes, and we'd loved them candied, or baked in a cobbler, deep-fat fried in a pocket of dough, or roasted with pork and glazed with the well-browned fat; had chewed them raw—yams and years ago. More yams than years ago, though the time seemed endlessly expanded, stretched thin as the spiraling smoke beyond all recall.

SWEET POTATO PIE:
Boil 1 lb. sweet potatoes, remove the skins, mash, and beat. Blend with 3/4 cup brown sugar, 1/4 tsp. salt, and 1 tsp. ground cinnamon. Beat in 3 eggs, 3/4 cup milk, 3/4 cup heavy cream, and 1 tbs. butter. Spoon into pie plate line with a pastry crust and bake at 400° for about 45 min.

CANDIED SWEET POTATOES:
Boil, peel, and cut up 6 sweet potatoes. Place in a buttered pan, sprinkle with 3/4 cup brown sugar, 1/2 tsp. grated lemon rind, and 1 1/2 tbs. lemon juice, and bake in 375° oven for about 20 min. Serves 4.

SWEET POTATO BISCUITS:
Boil, peel, and mash 1 cup sweet potatoes. Beat in 4 tbs. butter, 2/3 cup milk, 1 1/4 cup flour, 4 tsp. baking powder, 1 tbs. sugar, and 1/4 tsp. salt to make a dough. Cut with biscuit cutter and bake on buttered pan at 450° for 15 min.

sweetsop *(Annona squamosa)*. Also called "sugar apple." A tropical American tree bearing a yellow-green fruit with sweet yellow pulp, which is grown to some extent in Florida. The word first appears in print in 1696.

swellfish (Family Tetraodontidae). Any of a variety of fish that can inflate themselves with air or water, which gives them their name, as well as others, like "puffer," "blowfish," "globefish," and "sea squab." Swellfish are often poisonous to eat. The two main American species are the smooth puffer *(Lagocephalus laevigatus)* and the northern puffer *(Sphoeroides maculatus)*.

Swiss steak. Sliced BEEF rump or round baked with tomatoes, onions, peppers, and sometimes seasonings such as thyme, rosemary, basil, or chili. In England it would be called "smothered steak," but there is really no direct corollary for the dish in Switzerland, the closest being *carbonades*. The name may derive instead from an English term, *swissing,* which refers to a method of smoothing out cloth between a set of rollers, because Swiss steak is usually pounded and flattened before cooking. The term was first printed in 1924.

Rub 2 lb. sliced round steak with 1/2 tsp. sugar and 1/2 lemon. Mix 1/2 cup flour, salt, and pepper, and pound into the meat. Sear the slices, then place in casserole. Sauté 2 sliced onions, 1 chopped green pepper, and 3 chopped celery stalks in 3 tbs. oil till tender. Add a 1-lb. can of stewed tomatoes, 1/4 tsp. rosemary, and 1/4 tsp. basil. Cook till tomatoes break down. Spoon over the meat, cover, and cook at 300° for 1 1/2–2 hr. Serves 4.

switchel. A colonial drink made from molasses, rum, and water.

Combine 1 cup light brown sugar, 1 cup wine vinegar, 1/2 cup light molasses, 1 tbs. ground ginger, and 1 qt. cold water. Stir.

swizzle. A tall drink, usually made with rum. Its origins are unknown, but the term perhaps is onomatopoeia that refers to the sound of mixing the drink in a glass. *Swizzle* has been used to describe a drink since the early nineteenth century, and it also came to mean drunkenness. A "swizzle stick," first mentioned in 1879 in print, is a kind of small paddle used to stir a drink.

swordfish. Any of a variety of large marine fish in the family Xiphiidae. Swordfish is one of the great game fishes and is found throughout the world. The name refers to the fish's swordlike upper jaw and has been used in English at least since 1400. The fish usually referred to under this name is *Xiphias gladius,* which is found in the waters of both the Atlantic and Pacific coasts. Although expensive because of the difficulty in landing the large fish, the swordfish has always been enjoyed by Americans, even though in the 1960s the Food and Drug Administration announced that it found dangerously high levels of mercury in the majority of specimens it examined. This is no longer believed to be of major concern.

In New England swordfish steaks are traditionally broiled or grilled.

Sydney Smith's salad dressing. A salad dressing of potatoes, mustard, olive oil, egg yolks, onions, and anchovies. The recipe—which came from a doggerel poem by English clergyman and founder of the *Edinburgh Review,* Sydney Smith (1771–1845)—was quite popular among American cooks in the nineteenth century.

> Two boiled potatoes strained through a kitchen sieve,
> Softness and smoothness to the salad give;
> Of mordant mustard take a single spoon,
> Distrust the condiment that bites too soon!
> Yet deem it not, thou man of taste, a fault
> To add a double quantity of salt.
> Four times the spoon with oil of Lucca crown,*
> And twice with vinegar procured from town;
> True taste requires it and your poet begs
> The pounded yellow of two well-boiled eggs.
> Let onion's atoms lurk within the bowl
> And, scarce suspected, animate the whole,
> And lastly in the flavored compound toss
> A magic spoonful of anchovy sauce.
> Oh, great and glorious! Oh, herbaceous meat!
> 'Twould tempt the dying Anchorite** to eat,
> Back to the world he'd turn his weary soul
> And plunge his fingers in the salad bowl.

syllabub. An egg nog made with wine. It was once a popular drink at American Christmas parties, though it is rarely seen today. *The American Heritage Cookbook* (1980) contends the name "is derived from wine that came from Sillery in the Champagne region of France, and from 'bub,' an Elizabethan slang word for bubbling drink." The term first appears in print in 1537.

Combine 2 cups white wine, 5 tbs. grated lemon rind, 1 cup sugar, and 1/3 cup lemon juice. When sugar is dissolved, add to a blend of 3 cups milk and 2 cups light cream, then beat till frothy. Beat 4 egg whites with 1/2 cup sugar until stiff. Pour wine mixture into bowl and top with mounds of egg white. Sprinkle with nutmeg.

*Olive oil.
**Hermit.

Tabasco. A hot sauce made from chili peppers, salt, and vinegar. Tabasco is a trademark, "McIlhenny's Tabasco Sauce," established in 1868. *Tabasco* is a Mexican Indian word meaning "damp earth" and is the name of a Mexican state on the Gulf of Campeche.

The chili peppers used were originally imported from Mexico and now are grown on a hillock called Avery Island, owned by the Avery and McIlhenny families in Louisiana. The peppers are salted, mashed, fermented in barrels for three years, and then churned with vinegar and bottled. Tabasco is so thoroughly identified with the McIlhenny name that many recipes specifically refer to this brand.

taco. A crisp tortilla shaped into a U and filled with various stuffings. Tacos are often served as a snack but also as a main course when served with refried beans, rice, and chili sauce. The word is Mexican-Spanish, meaning a "wad" or "plug," but colloquially refers to a light meal or snack. Small Mexican-American restaurants, especially those found along the road, are often called "taco stands," and there is at least one major franchised chain of such establishments featuring the item.

Tacos are usually bought in packages at a grocery and are quite crisp, though in Mexico they are generally more pliable. The various fillings for a taco, usually doused with a hot chili sauce, include ground beef, chicken, pork, chorizo sausage, tomato, cheese, lettuce, guacamole, onion, and refried beans. The word was first printed in English in 1934.

Tailgate picnic. A meal served outdoors off the folded-down rear door, or tailgate, of a station wagon, an American car designed to carry several family members or a large load. The term dates in print to 1941.

The food is varied and of a kind found at any picnic—salads, sandwiches, fried chicken, beer, soft drinks, coffee, cakes, and anything else that strikes the fancy. With the demise of the large American station wagon, this social get-together may itself fade in the years to come.

taffy. A confection made from sugar, butter, and flavorings that has a chewy texture obtained by twisting and pulling the cooked ingredients into elasticity.

The British term for such candy is *toffee* or *toffy,* possibly from *tafia,* a cheap West Indian rum made from molasses and used originally to flavor candy. The *Oxford English Dictionary* notes that *taffy* (the preferred word in Scotland, Northern England, and America) seems to refer to an older form of the candy. By the 1870s "taffy bakes" and "taffy pulls," at which young people would gather to stretch the candy between them, had become social occasions.

English toffees are often harder than American taffies. Saltwater taffy, popularized at the Atlantic City boardwalk in New Jersey in the 1880s, had a small amount of saltwater added to the mixture.

Combine 3 cups sugar, 1 cup water, and 1 cup corn syrup in saucepan. Stir, add a dash of salt, and 4 tbs. butter. Bring to boil till candy thermometer reaches 264° (or less for a somewhat chewier texture). Turn onto marble slab, add 1 1/2 tsp. vanilla, and begin to turn the edges of the taffy towards the center, then, with greased fingers begin turning and twisting the taffy to incorporate air and firmness of texture. When the taffy can hold its shape on the slab, cut into pieces.

take-out. A term for food that is bought at a restaurant but taken elsewhere to be eaten. The term has been in use only since the 1940s and became widespread only since the 1960s. Synonyms would be *carry-out food* and *take-home food.*

tamale. A term describing a wide range of dishes based on a cornmeal flour dough that is placed inside corn husks and then steamed. Tamales are of Mexican origin and were enjoyed by the Aztecs (the word comes from the Nahuatl, *tamalli*) in several versions, from appetizer to sweet dessert. In Mexico they are traditionally served in restaurants on Sunday nights and as ceremonial food on All Saints' Day. As early as 1612 Englishman Captain John Smith mentioned a kind of tamale made by the Indians of Virginia, and by 1691 note was made by others of a bean-filled tamale of the Southwest. By 1854 the dish had been described in Bartlett's *Personal Narratives.*

Coarsely chop 2 lb. pork and cover with water, bring to boil, then simmer till tender. Drain, reserving 1 1/2 cups stock. Shred the pork and sauté in 4 tbs. oil till brown, then stir in 2 tbs. flour till brown. Stir in a sauce made from 1 chopped tomato, 1 chopped garlic clove, 1 chopped red or green chili pepper, 1 chopped onion, salt, and pepper puréed in a blender. Add 3 chopped green or red chili peppers, 1/4 tsp. oregano, salt, and pepper, and simmer for about 30 min. Make a dough of 1 1/2 cups lard creamed with 1 1/2 tsp. salt. Mix 4 1/2 cups masa with 2 1/2 cups warm water. Beat into lard. Place portions of the dough into a dozen corn husks, spread portions of meat mixture on dough, and fold opposite sides of husks toward center. Peel dough from husks and seal, then close husks around dough to seal into a packet. Steam for 1 1/2 hr. Serves 12.

tamale pie. A dish of cornmeal mush filled with chopped meat and a hot chili sauce. The term first appeared in 1911.

tansy. Also, "tansey." A pudding made from the juice of the tansy plant (of the genus *Tanacetum,* especially *T. vulgare*), or any such confection made with a tart fruit. The word is from Middle English, derived from Old French *tanesie,* and, ultimately Latin, *athanasia,* "elixir of life."

Tansy cake was known in England at least since the fifteenth century. As a pudding, tansy was first mentioned circa 1450, said to be eaten at Easter to commemorate the "bitter herbs" of the Passover.

In America the dish often lacked the ingredient that gave it its name, substituting instead a tart fruit such as the cherry. It was a popular dessert at George Washington's Mount Vernon home in Virginia.

> Drain 2 cups tart cherries. To the juice add 2 tsp. lemon juice, 1/8 tsp. nutmeg, 2 tsp. cornstarch, and 1/4 cup water. Cook till thickened, then add the cherries and mix. Place in greased 1-qt. pan. Beat 2 eggs with 1/3 cup sugar and 1/4 cup butter, then add 1/4 cup bread crumbs. Pour over cherries and bake for about 40 min. at 375°. Serves 6.

Taos lightnin'. Also, "Touse." A variety of distilled spirits originally made at San Fernández de Taos, now Taos, in New Mexico. The Spanish called it *aqua ardiente,* or "burning water," and it was enjoyed by the early trappers in that region.

taro (*Colocasia esculenta,* family Araceae). Also, "dasheen," "eddo," and many other regional names. A tropical plant with broad leaves and a starchy, edible root. The name comes from the Tahitian and Maori and was first mentioned by Captain James Cook in 1779 after finding the plant in the Sandwich Islands of the Pacific. The plant is cultivated in the southern United States, and there are at least one thousand varieties in the world.

Taro was a staple of the high islands of Polynesia and Hawaii, where it is called *"kalo,"* and treated with the respect that made it the islands' most important food. The corm of the plant was used for food, with some of the leaves and stalks occasionally cooked as greens. Taro's most important use in Hawaii to this day is in the preparation of POI, and it is also made into cakes and biscuits and fried in butter.

tarragon (*Artemisia dracunculus*). A Eurasian herb used as a seasoning in soups, sauces, salads, and other foods. The name is from the Greek, *drakontion,* "adderwort," which became in Middle English *tragonia* or *tarchon.*

Although tarragon is used as a seasoning in the United States, it is little grown here except in home gardens, where it was first reported in 1806. In many home gardens the variety grown may actually be the false or Russian tarragon (*A. dracunculoides*), which has a less pungent flavor.

tautog (*Tautoga onitis*). Also, "blackfish." A fish of the wrasse family (Labridae), found on the Atlantic coast. It is of little commercial value. The name comes from the Narraganset, *tautauog.*

tea. A beverage made by steeping the leaves of various shrubs or herbs, but specifically of the shrub *Thea sinensis* (or *Camellia sinensis*). The word derives from the Ancient Chinese *d'a,* as transmuted by the early Dutch traders in that region. The word first appears in English print in 1598.

Tea was extremely popular with the American colonists of the eighteenth century, so that the passage of the Townshend Acts in 1767 by the British, levying a three-pence-per-pound tax on tea imported to the colonies, followed in 1773 by the Tea Act that nearly gave the British East India Company a monopoly on the selling of tea, was cause for great dissent and opposition to British policies. Protests erupted in Boston on the night of December 16, 1773, when a group of colonists dressed in Indian outfits boarded three English ships and threw the tea shipments into the harbor. This became known as the Boston Tea Party by the 1830s. Patriots took to drinking "liberty tea," made from loosestrife leaves, or turned to COFFEE.

After the Revolutionary War United States shippers established a trade with China in 1784 and had shipped more than a billion pounds of tea three years later. The British still dominated the tea trade, however, until 1859, when Americans George Huntington Hartford and George Gilman eliminated the wholesaler and bought tea directly from ships and sold it directly to their customers for one-third the price charged by their competitors. They established the Great Atlantic and Pacific Tea Company, later to grow into a chain of supermarkets under the name "A&P."

By the 1860s Americans were enjoying iced tea, especially in the South, where even today hot tea is often prepared by heating up iced tea for those few who want a cup of the beverage.

The tea bag was first marketed in 1902 and quickly replaced loose tea in the decoction of the leaves. Although few Americans adopted the British custom of having "afternoon tea," first enjoyed in the 1840s, by 1915 young women attended "tea dances" during World War I and afterwards many women invited their friends for "tea parties," often as part of a fashion show at a club.

By the 1930s Americans could buy instant tea, made from processed granules (and often containing sugar) that needed only water from the tap to produce the beverage.

Tea leaves have never been successfully cultivated in the United States, the last significant attempt having been made by C. U. Shepard and the Department of Agriculture at Summerville, South Carolina, from 1890 to 1916.

Herb (or herbal) teas made from sassafras, ginger, and other herbs have long been a part of American history. They received a great boost in popularity during the "natural foods" movement of the 1960s when such decoctions were thought to be soothing and beneficial to one's health (for more information see HEALTH FOOD).

Teas are generally named after their type and size of leaf or their region of origin; most are blends of several varieties. Orange pekoe tea is the most readily found in the United States.

tenderizer. A substance used to make meat more tender, usually taken from an enzyme, papain, of the papaya plant. As a powder, this substance will partly digest up to 300 times its weight in lean meat with which it comes in contact, but it is deactivated when heated. Although it is considered no substitute for proper aging, a powdered tenderizer can improve inferior cuts of meat.

tenderloin. The most tender fillet of beef cut from the hindquarter in the primal short loin. Tenderloin is almost entirely free from fat, marbling, or bone, and sometimes is sold as part of the porterhouse steak. Butchers may also refer to this cut as "filet mignon," "chateaubriand," and "tournedos."

Colloquially, the term has long been associated with sections of cities where vice and graft run rampant, originally referring to an 1880s section of Manhattan from Madison Square (Twenty-third Street) to Longacre Square (Forty-second Street). The story goes that a police captain named Williams, on learning he was being transferred from Wall Street to this graft-ridden precinct, remarked, "I've had nothing but chuck for a long time but now I'm going to get some tenderloin."

Tennessee whiskey. A straight whiskey that must be made from at least 51 percent of a single grain, usually corn, and made by a sour-mash process similar to that used for bourbon. The term has been in use at least since the 1840s.

tepary *(Phaseolus acutifolius latifolius).* A New World vine bearing a bean that is particularly grown in the Southwest and Mexico. The origin of the word is obscure, mentioned in Spanish as of 1716. It has been suggested that the name is from a Papago word, *'stäte päve,* "wild pave."

tequila. A liquor distilled from the Central American *Agave tequilana* plant. The name comes from the Tequila district of Mexico, where the best tequila traditionally is made. The agave (in Spanish, *maguey*) plant contains a sweet sap at its heart called *"aguamiel"* ("honey water") that is fermented into *madre pulque* ("mother pulque"), which tastes something like sour milk, and drunk locally. It may also be made into a brandy called *"vino mezcal,"* which is tequila. The fermented and double-distilled spirit is drawn off at 104 to 106 proof and reduced to 80 to 86 proof when shipped to the United States, most of it unaged. The word was first printed in English in 1849.

According to Michael Jackson's *Pocket Bartender's Guide* (1979), tax records of the town of Tequila show that three barrels of "mezcal wine" were shipped across the border to Texas in 1873. American troops brought it back from their campaign against Pancho Villa in 1916. During a GIN shortage in 1944 in this country tequila enjoyed a brief popularity, but it was not until the 1960s, when it became a faddish drink among California university students, that the sales of the spirit really grew, especially as the basis for the MARGARITA cocktail. In 1970 only one million gallons of tequila were exported to this country, but by 1982 shipments had soared to 8 million gallons.

The "classic" way (sometimes called the "Mexican Itch") to drink straight tequila, which required the ingredient of dried crushed worms from the agave plant placed in a shaker of salt, was described by Green Peyton in his book *San Antonio: City in the Sun* (1946): "You gulp the Tequila, sprinkle the mummified condiment on the back of your hand, swallow it, suck on a small piece of lime, and then sit down for a while to recover your senses."

tequila sunrise. A cocktail made from tequila, orange juice, and grenadine. According to *The Tequila Book* (1976), by Marion Gorman and Felipe de Alba, the drink may have originated at the Agua Caliente racetrack bar in Mexico during the Prohibition era, when Californians would drive there to play the horses and have a few drinks. After a night of carousing the visitors would need a pick-me-up at sunrise, and the addition of one's morning orange juice to tequila seemed appropriate.

Another tequila drink, the tequila sunset, must have come some time afterwards.

TEQUILA SUNRISE:
In a shaker with crushed ice combine 1 1/2 oz. tequila, 1 oz. grenadine, and 3 oz. orange juice. Shake, strain into a wine glass that has been chilled, and garnish with lime slice.

TEQUILA SUNSET:
In a blender with crushed ice combine 1 1/2 oz. orange juice, 1 1/2 oz. pineapple juice, and 1 oz. tequila. Blend for about 30 sec. Pour, without straining, into a chilled wineglass whose rim has been sugared.

Tex-Mex. A combination of the words *Texan* and *Mexican,* first printed in 1949, that refers to an adaption of Mexican dishes by Texan cooks. It is difficult to be precise as to what distinguishes Tex-Mex from true Mexican food, except to say that the variety of the latter is wider and more regional, whereas Tex-Mex is a more standardized cookery popular throughout the state and, now, throughout the entire United States. The best-known Tex-Mex dishes might be found at a roadside taco stand or at a fine home, and they might include TACOS, TORTILLAS, CHALUPAS, BURRITOS, corn bread, TAMALES, TOSTADOS, NACHOS, ENCHILADAS, and various forms of chili, the most specific Tex-Mex version being CHILI CON CARNE, or, as Texans call it, "a bowl of red." Central to Tex-Mex cooking is the CHILI pepper, which may go into anything from bread to jelly.

Texans refer to this kind of food as "Meskin," really a local pronunciation of *Mexican,* and many of the same dishes may in other parts of the country be called "Mexican-American."

Thanksgiving. A national American holiday centered around a family feast commemorating the first harvest of the Plymouth Colony in 1621 after a winter of great suffering and near starvation. The colony had been established the year before, and, in thanks to God for their survival, Governor William Bradford

(1590–1657) declared a feast be held between the settlers and the Indians of the region, led by Chief Massasoit (c. 1580–1661) of the Wampanoag tribe, which had signed a treaty with the Pilgrims.

Massasoit arrived at the feast, which probably lasted several days, with ninety-nine braves, bringing many of the dishes, including popcorn. Governor Bradford sent out four men to catch game, but it is not known for sure whether the fowl consumed on the first Thanksgiving included turkey, which has since become the traditional main course of Thanksgiving celebrations. It is known that oysters, eel, corn bread, goose, venison, watercress, leeks, berries, and plums were eaten, all accompanied by sweet wine.

The next recorded Thanksgiving in the Plymouth Colony was on July 30, 1623, at which turkey was definitely served, along with cranberries and pumpkin pie.

Thanksgiving was not held as a regular feast, but it became traditional in New England to give thanks on a day set aside for that purpose; Connecticut had its first Thanksgiving in 1649, the Massachusetts Bay Colony in 1669, and by the 1780s the feast day was popular throughout the region. President George Washington proclaimed the first nationally observed Thanksgiving for November 26, 1789.

In 1827 Mrs. Sarah Joseph Hall, editor of Boston's *Ladies' Magazine* and later of *Godey's Lady's Book* of Philadelphia, campaigned to turn Thanksgiving into a national holiday. President Abraham Lincoln declared August 6 the appropriate day in 1863, but a few months later changed the date to the last Thursday of November. This tradition was maintained until 1939, when President Franklin Delano Roosevelt changed the date to the third Thursday in November in an effort to stimulate sales in retail stores by heralding the advent of Christmas a week earlier. In December 1941 Congress changed it back again to the last Thursday in November.

The traditional Thanksgiving meal for most Americans is eaten at home and includes many of the same dishes enjoyed at the first Thanksgiving— the turkey having been well established as the feast's main course by the 1820s.

Thompson Seedless. A white Vinifera grape used as a blending grape in sparkling wine and brandy, as well as a popular table grape. It was introduced in 1872 by farmer William Thompson of Yuba City, California, and it became the most widely planted variety of grape in the state.

Thousand Island dressing. A salad dressing based on RUSSIAN DRESSING with various additions of pickles, cream, green peppers, and other seasonings. Webster's first lists the name in 1924; it probably derived from the Thousand Islands in the St. Lawrence River that cuts between New York and Ontario, where the dressing may have first been concocted.

It has also been suggested that the bits and pieces of seasonings and ingredients resemble a multitude of islands in a sea of dressing.

Fold 1 qt. mayonnaise into 1 qt. chili sauce, add 1 chopped pimiento, 5 chopped hard-boiled eggs, 1 pt. chopped sweet pickles, and 2 chopped green peppers. Mix well.

three sheets in the wind. Also, "three sheets to the wind." An expression meaning "to be drunk." It derives from a sailor's tacking of the sails by means of a chain or rope called a "sheet" attached to the lower corner of the sail. If the sail fluttered freely, it was said to be "in the wind." If three sheets were thus free, the sail would not be under control, causing the ship to weave and sway in the wind.

thyme. Any of a variety of herbs grown in New England in the genus *Thymus*, of the mint family, especially the garden or black thyme *(T. vulgaris)*, the lemon thyme *(T. citriodorus)*, and the wild thyme *(T. serpyllum)*. The word is from the Greek, *thumon*.

Thyme is used as a seasoning in soups, sauces, salads, and other dishes. It is customarily added to chowder.

tilefish. Any of a variety of marine fish in the family Branchiostegidae, with four species in the United States. The name is actually short for a species known in taxonomic Latin as *Lopholatilus chamaeleonticeps*, although the tilelike spots on the fish probably also influenced the name, which appeared in print in 1881. This species is found from Chesapeake Bay to Maine and was first noted off the New England coast in May 1879. In 1882 the fish had totally disappeared, possibly as a result of a climatic change in the water temperature, but it came back in abundance five years later and is readily available at market today. The main species of culinary interest include the common tilefish named above, the blackline tilefish *(Caulolatilus cyanops)*, the sand tilefish *(Malacanthus plumieri)*, and the ocean whitefish *(C. princeps)*.

tipsy. Also, "tipsy parson" in the South. A sponge cake spread with almonds, soaked in sherry, and served with custard. It was a dish of the late nineteenth century. The name apparently refers to the alcohol content, which if taken in large doses would make the imbiber "tipsy" or slightly drunk.

tiswin. A fermented beverage made by the Apache Indians. The name is also spelled *"tiswino"* or *"tesquino"* by the New Mexican Indians. Tiswin is made by fermenting dried corn with water, PILONCILLO cones of brown sugar, and spices such as cinnamon and orange peel.

toasted ravioli. A St. Louis, Missouri, specialty of meat-filled pasta dough that is deep-fried golden brown.

toddy. Although there are many variations, a toddy is usually a heated mug of whiskey flavored with citrus fruits and spices. The word comes from the Hindi, *tāri,* for the fermented or fresh sap of a palm tree, and the English traders picked up the word in India. Originally the drink was made cold, but cold days at sea made the idea of a hot toddy more convivial onboard. Scottish poet Robert Burns was the first to note the drink in print, in 1786.

> Dissolve 1 lump of sugar in a glass half-filled with boiling water, add 1 1/2 oz. rum or whiskey, 2 cloves, a stick of cinnamon, and lemon rind.

to go. When an American orders food in a restaurant "to go," he means he wishes to have the food packaged so that he may take it elsewhere to eat. TAKE-OUT orders are a standard feature at drive-ins, fast-food restaurants, Chinese and Mexican restaurants, and pizzerias.

togue. A Maine term for a large lake trout, first noted in print in 1839.

togus. A New England dish of the nineteenth century made from milk, cornmeal, and molasses, whose name possibly derives from an Indian word. The *Pentucket Housewife* (1882) lists the ingredients as 3 cups milk, 1 cup sour milk, 3 cups cornmeal, 1 cup flour, 1/2 cup molasses, and 1 tsp. baking soda. The dish is steamed for 3 hours and eaten with butter and sugar.

Toll House cookie. A cookie made from flour, semisweet chocolate chips, brown sugar, and nuts. It is by far the most popular of all American cookies.

In 1930 Mrs. Ruth Wakefield and her husband purchased a 1709 tollhouse on the outskirts of Whitman, Massachusetts, a halfway point for travelers between Boston and New Bedford. Mrs. Wakefield turned the house into the Toll House Inn, and one day in her kitchen, while experimenting with an old American recipe for Butter Drop Do cookies, she happened to cut up a bar of Nestlé Semi-Sweet chocolate into small chips and added them to the batter. Instead of melting, the chocolate bits retained their texture in the baking and gave the cookie a flavor that soon was to make her famous. The Toll House cookie was born (Wakefield originally called it the "chocolate crunch cookie"), and people began writing to her for the recipe. With her permission the Nestlé Company began printing the recipe on their semisweet chocolate bar wrappers, and, in 1939, it began packaging bits of uniformly shaped chocolate chips. Today Nestlé produces 250 million morsels a day in three factories, and it has been estimated that half the cookies baked at home in America are chocolate chip, making them as famous as the proverbial apple pie. In fact, after Canadian diplomats had secretly helped six Americans to escape from Iran during the hostage crisis of 1980, the grateful people of America sent a large bag of chocolate chip cookies to the Canadian embassy in Washington.

The Toll House Inn is still in private hands; the recipe given below is still printed on the Nestlé semisweet morsel package.

> Combine in a bowl 2 1/4 cups unsifted flour, 1 tsp. baking soda, and 1 tsp. salt. In another bowl combine 1 cup butter, 3/4 cup sugar, 3/4 cup brown sugar, and 1 tsp. vanilla extract. Beat till creamy, then add 2 eggs. Gradually add the flour mixture and blend in well. Stir in 12 oz. Nestlé semisweet chocolate morsels (2 cups) and

1 cup chopped nuts. Drop by rounded teaspoons onto ungreased cookie sheet. Bake in 375° preheated oven for 8 to 10 min. Makes 100 2-in. cookies.

BLONDIES:
A variation in the shape of these cookies is achieved by spreading the dough into a greased 15-by-10-in. baking pan. Bake at 375° for 20 min., then cut into 35 2-in. squares.

Tom and Jerry. A beverage made from eggs, sugar, brandy or bourbon, and whiskey, topped with milk or boiling water. The name apparently comes for no particularly good reason from Pierce Egan's *Life in London, or the Days and Nights of Jerry Hawthorne and his Elegant Friend Corinthian Tom* (1821). Before the decade was out *Tom-and-Jerrying* connoted rowdy, drunken behavior, and a "Tom and Jerry shop" was a low beerhouse of the day. In 1862 American bartender Jerry Thomas, in his *How to Mix Drinks,* gave the first recipe for a Tom and Jerry, and Thomas has been credited by some for inventing the drink. It is no longer a popular drink.

"Tom and Jerry mugs" were ceramic cups with handles.

Separate 6 eggs. Beat 1/4 lb. sugar into yolks till the mixture is light yellow, then pour in 2 oz. whiskey. Beat egg whites till stiff and fold into mixture. Ladle into a cup, add 2 oz. brandy or bourbon to each mug, and fill with boiling milk or water. Stir and sprinkle on nutmeg and a dash of brandy, if desired.

tomatillo. A berry of the family Physalis that resembles a small, unripe tomato. It is known under various names in Mexico—*tomate verde, tomate de cáscara,* and *fresadilla*—and canned in the United States as *"tomatillo entero"* or *"tomatito verde"* and "peeled green tomato." (There is also a shrub in Chile [genus *Solanaceous*] called *"tomatillo."*) When ripe, tomatillos turn yellow, but the green fruit is preferred for coloring sauces.

tomato. The fleshy, juicy, usually bright red fruit of the plant *Lycopersicon esculentum.* Tomatoes are used in a wide variety of ways—including fresh, in salads, in sauces, as juice, and in other preparations. The word is from the Nahuatl, *tomatl,* and first appears in English print about 1604, though then the tomato was also referred to as a "love apple." (The Italian name for the fruit is still *pomodoro* or "golden apple," because the first examples to reach Europe were yellow varieties.)

The tomato is probably native to Peru and Ecuador, but it was widely established throughout Central America by the time the Spanish arrived in the early sixteenth century. Because the tomato is taxonomically a member of the deadly nightshade family, Solanaceae, Europeans approached the idea of eating the fruit with extreme caution. The Spaniards had brought the tomato back to their own country early in the century, and from there to Italy (though some authorities posit that the fruit may have gotten to Italy via Neapolitan sailors). By 1544 Pierandrea Mattioli had described the tomato as a kind of eggplant, but later changed his description to *mala insana,* "unhealthy apple." Indeed, most Europeans continued to believe the tomato was poisonous—or at the very least an exotic fruit or vegetable to be cooked cautiously and eaten sparingly.

Tomatoes were not cultivated in North America until the 1700s, and then only in home gardens. Thomas Jefferson was raising tomatoes by 1782 and noted that others in Virginia grew them for private consumption. Nevertheless most people of that century paid little heed to tomatoes, and only in the next century did they make their way into American cookbooks, always with instructions that they be cooked for at least three hours or else, as Eliza Leslie wrote in her *Directions for Cookery* (1848 edition), they "will not lose their raw taste." Nineteenth-century cooks used them in KETCHUPS or in sauces, but did not recommend eating them raw. Waverly Root, in *Food* (1980), notes that "the Thorbun seed catalog gave directions for growing tomatoes in 1817, but offered only one variety; by 1881 it would be selling thirty-one." By 1865 northern markets offered tomatoes year-round. In 1893 the Supreme Court decreed that, for trade purposes, the tomato could be classified as a vegetable, though it is in reality a fruit.

Tomato sauces became popular with the arrival of Italian immigrants in the late nineteenth and early twentieth centuries, and after 1900 the tomato itself finally gained credibility as a flavorful, healthy food, aided by southern farmers who began propagating the fruit on a widespread basis. By 1929 Americans were eating thirty-six pounds of tomatoes per capita per year. The tomato has become the most widely planted of all home-garden fruits or vegetables and is now grown in every state in the union.

Fresh tomatoes at market are most likely to come from Florida, New Jersey, Texas, California, or Alabama, with the principal varieties being Fireball, Big Boy, Manapal, Floradel, and Pinkshipper.

Tomatoes grown primarily for canning are raised in California and include the Bouncer, New Yorker, Red Top, Campbell 1327, and San Marzano. Home-grown varieties include the Red Cherry, Bonney Best, Marglobe, Jubilee, Rutgers, and Beefsteak.

Many Americans who have grown their own tomatoes or who remember the tomatoes of other decades believe that the various hybrids and commercially cultivated tomatoes marketed today have lost a great deal of their natural flavor in return for easy availability on a year-round basis and a high yield. As John L. and Karen Hess observe in *The Taste of America* (1977):

> More and more of the produce grown in those far-off factories of the soil is harvested by machine. It is bred for rough handling, which it gets. A chemical is sprayed on trees to force all the fruit to "ripen"—that is, change color—at once, in time for a monster harvester to strike the tree and catch the fruit in its canvas maw. Tomatoes are picked hard green and gassed with ethylene in trucks or in chambers at the market, whereupon they turn a sort of neon red. Of course, they taste like nothing at all, but the taste of real tomatoes has so far faded from memory that, even for local markets, farmers now pick tomatoes that are just turning pink. This avoids the spoilage that occurred when they used to pick tomatoes red-ripe.

Tom Collins. A cocktail made with gin, citrus juice, and soda water, customarily served in a tall glass called a "Tom Collins glass" or "Collins glass." The drink is supposedly named after the bartender who created it, though the moment of creation is highly speculative. The first American reference to the drink is in 1909, but H. L. Mencken, in *The American Language*, Supplement I (1945), can only guess that it came out of the post–Civil War era. The original Tom Collins was supposedly made with Old Tom gin, which was slightly sweet, but another drink, the John Collins, was customarily made with Holland gin, with its more pronounced, aromatic flavor. The problem is that the first printed reference to a John Collins is in 1865, and, suggests the *Oxford English Dictionary*, it may be of American origins. Mencken writes of the John Collins, "Who John Collins was I do not know. Sidney J. Baker, author of A Popular Dictionary of Australian Slang; Melbourne, n.d., tells me that the *John Collins* was known in Australia so long ago as 1865, but he does not list it in his dictionary." The "fizz" is a similar drink made with crushed ice in the blend and dates back at least to the 1860s.

Whichever cocktail came first, American bartenders at the beginning of the twentieth century mixed both, making a John Collins with dry London gin and a Tom Collins with Old Tom gin. This latter gin gradually disappeared from the American market, however, and the dry London gin replaced it. After a while both drinks went by the name "Tom Collins," and today the cocktail is made with dry gin.

Still later a carbonated citrus soda appeared called "Tom Collins mix," which most bartenders use instead of fresh citrus juice and sugar.

In a glass with ice cubes stir 1 tbs. sugar syrup, the juice of 1 lemon, and 3–4 oz. gin. Fill glass with soda water or seltzer.

Tom Fuller. A dish of cooked corn, peas, beans, and dried venison similar to succotash. It was originally an Indian dish of the Mississippi region called "sofkee." The reason for the name "Tom Fuller" is unknown, but it was popular in the beginning of the nineteenth century in the southern Appalachian Mountains.

tortilla. A flat, unleavened cake made of cornmeal or white flour cooked on a griddle and used in a variety of dishes of Mexican origin, including as a bread, in a casserole, or as a sandwichlike holder for other foods. Tortillas are a staple of Mexican-American and TEX MEX cookery. The word comes from the Spanish-American diminutive for the Spanish *torta*, "round cake." (In Spain, the *tortilla española* is more like an omelette.) The word was first printed in English in 1699.

In the United States tortillas are usually bought in groceries and are rarely made at home, except in the Southwest. In Arizona, where a great deal of wheat is grown, they are often made from white flour and are called *"tortillas de harina de trigo,"* as opposed to those made with cornmeal flour, *"tortillas de masa harina."* When a tortilla is filled with meat and sauce and rolled, it is called a TACO, which is sometimes fried in hot lard. An ENCHILADA is somewhat more elaborate, with CHILI peppers and cheese as well as other ingredients in the stuffing. A simple stuffed tortilla recipe follows:

> Brown 1 lb. ground round beef in 2 tbs. peanut oil. Add 2 lbs. canned tomatoes, 1 can tomato paste, 2 cloves chopped garlic, 2 tsp. oregano, 1 tsp. salt, 1/2 tsp. ground coriander (cilantro), 1 tsp. salt, 1/2 tsp. pepper, and 1/2 tsp. chili powder. Simmer for 1/2 hr. On each tortilla place a slice of Monterey Jack cheese, some of the meat filling, and bake 15–20 min. at 350°.

tortoni. An Italian-American ice cream with crushed almonds or macaroons sprinkled on top. The confection originated in the eighteenth century at the Café Napolitain in Paris, and was named after the owner, Tortoni. After the arrival of Italian immigrants in New York, the ice cream became featured in every Italian-American restaurant (and often called "biscuit tortoni"). The word was first printed in English in 1944.

Tortoni can be made simply by mixing finely chopped almonds into vanilla ice cream and topping the cup with more chopped almonds before freezing. Macaroons may be substituted for the almonds.

tostado. A deep-fried corn chip popular as a snack in Mexican-American and Tex-Mex cooking. The name is from the Spanish for "toasted."

> Cut corn tortillas into wedges, fry in hot oil, drain, and sprinkle with salt, and, if desired, minced garlic. Serve with guacamole and other appetizer dips or sauces.

trade whiskey. Whiskey traded to the Indians in the nineteenth century. The term later became associated with any cheap, inferior spirit.

trapper's butter. Trapper's term for bone marrow of a killed animal, which was often made into a thickened broth.

Treasure Cave. A blue-veined cheese, also called "Minnesota Blue," ripened in sandstone caves. It is produced by the Treasure Cave Blue Cheese Company in Fanibault, Minnesota.

Trenton cracker. A light, puffy, round cracker made from wheat flour, vegetable shortening, salt, and yeast. It is a traditional Eastern cracker used in oyster stews.

The Trenton cracker was first made in 1848 by Adam and John Exton, two English immigrants who created the item in their Trenton, New Jersey, bakery. They called it the "Exton Oyster and Butter Cracker and Wine Scroll Biscuit." Within a short time more than thirty competitors were making imitations, including Ezekiel Pullen, owner of the Pullen Cracker Company in Trenton. This company was later sold and in 1887 became The Original Trenton Cracker Company, which in 1962 bought exclusive rights to the Exton products. Today the crackers are stamped before baking with the company's initials, *O.T.C.,* which is now a trademark of the company, now located in Lambertville, New Jersey.

The crackers are still served in chowders and stews or eaten buttered with a small bit of horseradish. They are called "Trentons" for short.

triggerfish. Any of a variety of fishes of the family Balistidae that is found in Atlantic waters and is enjoyed in the South as fillets. Triggerfish have a second, "trigger," spine that releases the first spine—hence, the name, first listed in John Ogilvie's *Imperial Dictionary, English, technological, and scientific* (1882).

tripe. The stomach of a cow, sheep, or pig. Its name is from the Old French, *tripe,* and first appears in English in the fourteenth century.

Owing to its perishable nature and the difficulty of cleaning it, tripe has never been a popular meat with most Americans, although it has some ethnic interest among Mediterranean immigrants and Chinese in this country. The only American recipe of note, given below, was developed at Boston's Parker House hotel.

> Boil a piece of tripe (about 8 oz.) till tender, cool, then soak in milk for 2 hr. Sprinkle with 2 tbs. white wine, 1 tbs. oil, 1/2 cup bread crumbs, 1 tsp. vinegar, a dash of paprika, and salt, pepper, and thyme to taste. Broil till golden brown. Serve with a mustard sauce made by combining 1 cup demi-glaze, 2 tsp. Dijon mustard, 1 oz. white wine, 1/2 oz. white vinegar, I small shallot finely minced, peppercorns, and 2 tbs. heavy cream.

trout. Any of a variety of fishes of the genera *Salvelinus* and *Salmo* cultured throughout the world both for sport and for food. The name derives from the Latin, *tructa.*

As did sturgeon and salmon in the colonial era, trout became an everyday food for the first settlers, and there seemed little reason to imitate the efforts of the French, which culminated in 1852 with the construction of the first public-owned trout hatchery, to propagate fish commercially. American anglers merely had to dip their lines in the rivers and come up with large, beautiful fish perfect for pan-frying on the spot; America's first great fishing author, Frank Forester, complained in his *Fish and Fishing* (1849) that Americans did not take their fly-fishing with all due seriousness. A hatchery was set up in 1864 at Mumford, New York, by Seth Green, for the days when anglers filled their baskets with forty trout in an afternoon were almost over. When the end came—as a result of industrial pollution and invasion of the trout streams, as well as overfishing—it came quickly, and after the Civil War the trout population decreased at a depressing rate. It was the introduction of the German brown trout *(Salmo trutta)* to North America in 1883, and Seth Green's stocking of his own hatcheries with that fish in 1886, that caused a comeback of the trout in America, and before long the native rainbow trout

(Salmo gairdneri) was being introduced as far away as New Zealand and South Africa.

Protective measures also helped restore the trout populations, and, since American anglers had by then become serious about their sport, efforts were made to maintain the balance of nature in trout streams.

Some of the finest literature on trout has come from American authors, from specialists like George Michel Lucien La Branche, Charles Zebulon Southard, Arthur Flick, Sparse Grey Hackle, and Ernest Schwiebert, to out-doorsmen like Zane Grey (who wrote mostly fishing books in his later life), John Steinbeck, and Ernest Hemingway, whose "Big Two-Hearted River" is a classic short story for its description of the challenge and beauty of the sport.

The trout species of the most culinary interest include: the brook trout *(Salvelinus fontinalis)* and the brown trout, both found in nearly every state in the union; the cutthroat trout *(Salmo clarki),* so called because of slash marks on the throat; the DOLLY VARDEN *(Salvelinus malma);* the golden trout *(Salmo aguabonita);* the lake trout *(Salvelinus namaycush),* in Maine called the "togue" (from a Canadian French name probably derived from an Indian word) or the "mackinaw" (possibly from its coloring, which resembles a plaid mackinaw coat or cloth, which itself refers to an island in Michigan called Mackinac) or the "gray trout" (in Canada); and the rainbow trout.

Trout in America is prepared in a variety of ways, from simple pan-frying or grilling to French recipes such as *amandine* (with almonds) and *meunière* (with browned butter) to the Swiss *truite au bleu,* by which a freshly caught trout is cooked in a court bouillon that turns the skin blue.

truck farm. Also, "truck garden." A garden producing vegetables intended for sale in the market. Today there is a double meaning to the word. Originally the word *truck,* derived from an Old French word *troque,* for "barter," referred to the vegetables themselves. By the eighteenth century in America people referred to "market truck," meaning fresh produce brought to the market. Much later, motorized heavy vehicles designed for carrying loads were called "trucks" too, probably from the Latin word *trochus,* "wheel." When such vehicles began carrying fresh produce to city markets it was quite natural for the term *truck farm* to take on a double meaning, both for the vegetables themselves and for the means of conveyance.

tuna. Also, "tuna fish." Any of a variety of marine fishes of the genus *Thunnus,* although the name is also applied to some related species. The name is derived from the Latin, *thunnus,* and is a variation on the English name for the fish, "tunny." The *Oxford English Dictionary* says *tuna* is "Spanish American" and a "name in California for the tunny." *Webster's Ninth* cites circa 1884 as the earliest printed reference.

The tuna is a member of the mackerel family (Scombridae), with six species available at market in the United States, where most of the catch has been from

Pacific waters. Not until 1960 were significant commercial catches made in the Atlantic, and the industry continues to be centered in California.

The most important species for culinary interest include: the albacore *(Thunnus alalunga),* the most desirable tuna for the canning industry, which labels its product "white-meat" tuna; the bluefin tuna *(T. thynnus),* the largest tuna, weighing up to sixteen hundred pounds; the bonito (*Sarda sarda* in the Atlantic and *S. chiliensis* in the Pacific), which cannot legally be labelled "tuna" and must be put in brine before cooking (its name is from the Spanish for "beautiful"); the false albacore *(Euthynnus alletteratus),* also called the "little tunny" or "bonito"; the kawakawa *(E. yaito);* the skipjack tuna *(E. pelamis),* also called "oceanic bonito," "watermelon," "oceanic skipjack," "Arctic bonito," and, in Hawaii, *"aku";* and the yellowfin tuna *(Thunnus albacares),* which in Hawaii is called the *"ahi"* and which is the principal fish of the California tuna industry.

Canned tuna is designated as "solid" or "fancy" (with several large pieces), "chunk" (smaller pieces), and "flaked" or "grated."

The F.D.A. Standards of Identity require that "white tuna" must be limited to albacore; "light," any tuna not darker than the Munsell color value 5.3; "dark," all tuna darker than the value 5.3. "Blended" applies to a blend of tuna flakes.

Tuna may be canned in oil or water and may be seasoned.

Americans eat tuna fresh, but most often it is served from a can as a filling for a tuna fish sandwich or a tuna fish salad, in both cases mixed with mayonnaise.

turkey *(Meleagris gallopavo).* A large, native North American game bird widely domesticated here and abroad. With its brownish feathers and wattled head and neck, the turkey is certainly an unattractive fowl, but its associations with colonial American history and its indigenous character throughout the United States caused Benjamin Franklin to remark, "I wish the Bald Eagle had not been chosen as the representation of our country. . . . The turkey is . . . a much more respectable bird, and withal a true original native of America."

The turkey proliferated throughout Mexico, the Southwest, and the East. The Plains Indians and New England tribes caught the bird in the wild with little trouble, whereas the Aztecs and Indians of the Southwest had domesticated the birds very early so that by the time the Spaniards arrived in Mexico the turkey was a staple part of the Indian diet.

It is not known who first brought the turkey back to Europe (according to Waverly Root, there is a turkeylike bird woven into the Bayeux tapestries of 1087), but by the first quarter of the sixteenth century Spanish explorers had brought the bird home. One English chronicler of the seventeenth century noted that turkeys were brought to England about 1524, giving rise to the ditty, "Turkeys, Carps, Hoppes, Piccarell, and Beer, Came into England in one year." By 1570 Englishman Thomas Trusser could vouch that the domesticated turkey already formed part of the common farmer's "Christmas husbandlie fare," and across the channel the bird was highly esteemed.

It is not entirely clear how the bird got its name. The *American Heritage Cookbook* suggests *turkey* is a corruption of *furkee,* an Indian name for the bird. But most authorities believe the name was the result of the bird's being confused with the guinea fowl, which the Portuguese had brought to Europe from Guinea, through the dominion of Turkey, so that both birds were called "turkeys" in the sixteenth century. Even after the confusion was cleared up and the American fowl took the name "turkey," the Linnaean system devised in the eighteenth century christened it with the Latin word for the guinea fowl, *Meleagris.*

The turkey thrived in Europe under various names: the French called it *"d'inde"* (later *dinde*), "of India"; the Germans called it *"calecutische Hahn,"* "Calcutta hen"; the Indians themselves called it *"peru,"* with no reference to the country of that name.

Captain John Smith, who explored the Virginia territory during the first two decades of the seventeenth century, spoke of turkeys brought to feasts by the Indians, but at least one authority doubts that the Indians brought turkeys to the famous 1621 feast that initiated the tradition of THANKSGIVING in the Plymouth Colony. It is curious that the colony's governor, William Bradford, did not mention the bird in his transcript of the feast's menu (which probably extended over days), but another attendant, Governor Edward Winslow, described how the settlers brought in their harvest and sent out "foure men on fowling," who "killed as much fowle as, with a little helpe beside [possibly from the Indians], served the Company almost a weeke." It is a safe assumption that these fowl included wild turkeys. Turkey was certainly served at the Pilgrims' next Thanksgiving, on July 30, 1623. The term *Thanksgiving turkey* was in circulation by 1829, and Thanksgiving itself was referred to as "Turkey day" by 1916.

In the early days turkey was a frequently served dish, usually a wild bird, sometimes weighing up to forty pounds, and by 1820 turkeys were cheaper than chickens in Kentucky. In other parts of the colonies, however, the wild turkey was nearly wiped out by hunters, so that by the end of the eighteenth century the bird had virtually disappeared east of the Connecticut River.

Domesticated turkeys filled the void rapidly, and turkey was readily available to most people year-round. But the bird's association with Thanksgiving became so distinct after President Abraham Lincoln proclaimed the last Thursday in November as the official holiday that many Americans eat turkey only on that day, and, perhaps, on Christmas.

Today turkeys are raised on large farms and sold both fresh-killed or frozen, their average weight being between eight and sixteen pounds. Most of these are young hens of the White Holland breed, for mature "tom turkeys" are increasingly rare. Breast meat is the most valued part of the turkey by Americans, and one may buy such meat separately, sometimes smoked. Other turkey meat may be compressed into turkey roll, used for sandwiches.

There is even a "self-basting turkey," injected with oils beneath the skin. In some instances, the poultry producer also inserts a small, plastic thermometer in the bird's skin that pops out when the turkey is cooked to the right temperature. In 1982 Americans consumed about 190 million turkeys.

American recipe writers have over the years come up with all manner of methods of cooking a turkey, from covering it with foil to placing it on a rack, from turning the bird on its back to cooking it in a very slow oven. The simplest way to cook a turkey is to wash and clean the bird, stuff it, baste it with butter, place it in a large roasting pan, and set it in a 450° oven for fifteen minutes. Turn down the heat to 350° and continue cooking and basting until a fork inserted in the leg joints shows the juices running clear.

Any number of side dishes are traditionally served with turkey—cranberry sauce, sweet potatoes, turnips, and, of course, the stuffing.

TURKEY HASH:
Sauté 1 cup coarsely chopped onions in 2 tbs. butter till limp and translucent. Add 1 cup diced cooked potatoes and cook for 5 min. Add 1 cup coarsely chopped turkey meat, salt, pepper, and 1/4 cup chopped green pepper. Press down into skillet and pour in 1/3 cup heavy cream. Cook over medium heat till crusty on the bottom. Turn out onto a plate.

turnip *(Brassica rapa).* An Old World plant bearing a large yellow or white root that is usually boiled and served as a vegetable. The word comes from the Latin, *nāpus,* which in Middle English became *nepe,* and is first recorded as *turnip* in 1533.

The turnip, native to Asia Minor, was eaten in Europe in the Middle Ages and cultivated in England by the seventeenth century. The French and English brought the plant to America, though the root was of little culinary interest until the eighteenth century. The common turnip *(B. rapa),* also called the "white turnip" for its coloring, is the most available variety in United States markets, though in the South the rutabaga *(B. napus rutabaga),* also called the "big yellow" or "Canadian turnip," is particularly well liked, often mashed and served with butter. (The name *rutabaga* comes from dialectical Swedish, *rotabagge,* "baggy root.")

There are records of turnip cultivation in Canada as of 1540, and Virginia had them by 1609, but it took another century and more before they found their way into southern soil. They were very successful with the Indians, who preferred them to their native Indian turnip *(Arisaema dracontium,* also called "green dragon" or "dragonroot," and *A. triphyllum,* called "jack-in-the-pulpit," "starchwort," and "bog onion"). Today the turnip is widely planted throughout the United States.

Turnips greens are often cooked with bacon as a vegetable.

turnover. A pastry filled with fruit preserves, chopped meat, or cooked sauce.

Roll out pastry crust to a thickness of about 1/8 in. and cut into 4-in. circles. Place a fruit mixture like preserves or sauce on the side of each circle, moisten pastry edges, fold over, and seal. Prick top and bake for 15 min. at 450° till golden.

turtle (Order Testudinate). Any of a large number of fresh- or saltwater reptiles having a shell, a horny beak, and a wide array of colorings. There are about 225 species in the world, found at sea, in lakes, rivers, ponds, woodlands, fields, and pastures. The most treasured—and today one of the rarest—for the American connoisseur has always been the diamondback terrapin *(Malaclemys terrapin),* whose name comes from a Virginian Algonquian name, *toolepeiwa,* and its diamond-shaped polygonal scutes with concentric ridges on its back. The green turtle *(Chelonia mydas)* of the Caribbean is also eaten in the South with great favor, while other species—such as the southeastern alligator snapping turtle *(Macroclemys temminckii),* the common snapping turtle *(Chelydra serpentina),* and the loggerhead *(Caretta caretta)*—are also considered good food turtles. The eggs from various species, too, are of culinary interest.

The word *turtle* may derive from the French, *tortues,* from which we also get *tortoise.* Europeans have depended on the West Indies, South America, Africa, and Australia for these delicacies.

The earliest explorers of North America commented on the variety and numbers of turtles here, and Thomas Hariot, who wrote *A Briefe and True Report of the New Found Land of Virginia* (1588), spoke of turtles a yard in breadth and found the meat and eggs good eating. By the seventeenth century turtle meat was being exported back to England, where it became an expensive item of exotica. But in America turtle was cooked by most coastal settlers, who used the meat as steaks, in stews, or in soups. So popular was the turtle that Eliza Leslie, in her *Directions for Cookery,* published in Philadelphia in 1837, noted that turtle soup was a time-consuming, difficult process best left to a "first-rate cook" or ordered in a "turtle-soup house." This appetite for turtle led quickly to the near extinction of several species, including the diamondback terrapin, and before the middle of the nineteenth century the American rich had joined their European peers in the consumption of the few turtles that were caught. As a result, turtle dishes became the pride of the elite social clubs in cities like Baltimore and Philadelphia, whose wealthy citizens argued over the correct way to treat a tortoise. Marylanders insisted a turtle should be the base for a sherry-tinged clear consommé, while their northern neighbors preferred the turtle meat in a cream sauce. According to Evan Jones, members of Philadelphia's Rittenhouse Club and Baltimore's Maryland Club met with an impartial jury in 1893 to decide the matter of taste: the turtle consommé won.

By 1920 the prices for terrapin had grown so high that even the wealthy found them too much, and, fortunately, the species has since then been restored to a certain extent.

In other parts of the country other species have been consumed; in Florida the green sea turtle has been prized as steak meat or used for turtle soup. Today sea turtles are being commercially raised, especially in the Cayman Islands. Turtle eggs are also a Southern delicacy.

When available at all, turtle is today found frozen, canned, or in prepared soups.

TURTLE SOUP:
Brown 1 lb. chopped turtle meat in a kettle, add 1 cup water, bring to a boil, then simmer, covered, till tender. In a saucepan mix 2 stalks chopped celery, 2 chopped carrots, 1 chopped onion, 2 cups chopped cabbage, 8 peppercorns, 3 sprigs parsley, 2 bay leaves, 2 cloves garlic, 1 1/2 tsp. salt, and 5 cups water. Bring to boil, cover, simmer for 1 hr., then strain. Stir in turtle meat, add 1/2 cup dry sherry, heat, and serve. Serves 6.

CREAM OF TERRAPIN SOUP:
Melt 4 tbs. butter in saucepan with 1 tbs. flour, remove from heat and stir in 2 cups milk and salt and pepper to taste. Add 2 lb. chopped terrapin meat, simmer for about 5 min., stir in 1/2 cup heavy cream, cook till thickened, then add 1/4 cup dry sherry.

tutti frutti. A maceration of fruits and brandy especially popular in the South, where ladies would add one of each fruit of the season to one pint brandy along with an amount of sugar equal to a quart of fruit. The mixture would be stirred each morning and kept for the season.

Tutti frutti is also an ice cream flavored with various fruits. The term is from the Italian, meaning "all fruits," and in America dates from the 1870s. There was also a gumball candy called by this name in New York City in the 1880s.

TV dinner. A meal of meat, poultry, or fish, together with vegetables and dessert, all precooked and packed on an aluminum plate, frozen, and sold in groceries and supermarkets. The meal has simply to be heated in the oven, and its self-contained character makes it easy to eat it away from the dining-room table while watching television. The first TV dinners appeared in the early 1950s, the most notable brand produced by the C. A. Swanson Company, which marketed a turkey-and-mashed-potatoes meal under the trademark "TV Dinner" in 1953.

twin mountain muffins. A New England muffin, the recipe for which appeared in Fannie Merritt Farmer's *Boston Cooking-School Cook Book* (1896).

Cream 1/4 cup butter, add 1/4 cup sugar and 1 well-beaten egg. Sift 3 tsp. baking powder with 2 cups flour and add to first mixture, while gradually adding 3/4 cup milk. Pour into buttered pan and bake in 350° oven for about 30 min.

underwears. A cowboy's term for sheep.

Universal Product Code. A printed series of symbols on a prepackaged food item in a retail store that identifies the type of product, manufacturer or distributor, contents, and price. The symbols are printed in binary forms that are scanned by a low-powered laser beam near the cash register. The laser converts these symbols into an electronic code that is then imprinted and tallied on the cash register's tape. This allows for fewer mistakes for the customer, higher efficiency for the store, and an automatic record of sales and inventory. There is even one Universal Product Code (UPC) scanner, called "Positalker," that enunciates in a female voice the price of each item as it passes by the laser beam.

upside down cake. A cake that is baked with its filling or flavoring on the bottom and then inverted before serving. The first mention in print of such a cake was in 1930, and was so listed in the 1936 *Sears, Roebuck and Co. Catalog,* but the cake is somewhat older.

Sometimes, as in the recipe below, the cake is cooked in a skillet.

Melt 1/4 cup butter in a skillet and add 1 cup brown sugar to dissolve. Remove from heat and add 1 cup pecans or walnuts. Layer with sliced pineapple. Combine 1 cup cake flour and 1 tsp. baking powder. Beat 4 egg yolks, 1 tbs. melted cooled butter, and 1 tsp. vanilla. Beat 4 egg whites till stiff, fold in 1 cup sugar and egg yolk mixture, then add flour gradually. Pour onto pineapple slices in skillet, bake 30 min. at 325°, remove from oven and invert on cake plate. Serve with whipped cream.

u'u *(Myripristis murdjan).* A popular Hawaiian fish of the Pacific reefs.

valley tan. Trader's term for a whiskey made by the Mormons of Salt Lake Valley.

vanilla *(Vanilla planifolia).* Also called "vanilla bean." The seed pod of a tropical American orchid. It is a frequently used flavoring, especially in desserts.

The word is from the Spanish, *vainilla,* "little sheath." Vanilla was brought to Europe by the Spanish conquistadores returning from Mexico. The word is first mentioned in English in 1662 as a flavoring used by the Indians with their chocolate, but although it became a highly desirable substance in France and England, Americans were not much familiar with vanilla until ice cream became popular in the late eighteenth century. Thomas Jefferson discovered its virtues in France and on arriving back in the United States in 1789 sent for some pods from Paris, which must have come from Central America in the first place.

By the nineteenth century Americans developed a passion for vanilla, especially as an ICE CREAM flavoring, and today America uses more vanilla than any other country. The supply of vanilla beans, however, does not meet the demand, so substitutes, especially "vanilla extract," are commonly used. Vanilla extract (or "essence"), created by Joseph Burnett in 1847, is made by soaking vanilla beans in grain alcohol and water (requirements stipulate that bottled extract must contain at least 35 percent alcohol; "vanilla flavoring" may contain less than 35 percent alcohol). There is also a concentrated vanilla extract that may be used as a flavoring for regular vanilla extract.

Vanillin is a flavoring obtained either from vanilla itself or from various balsams and resins; it is chemically a crystalline compound, $C_8H_8O_3$.

veal. The meat of a slaughtered calf. The word is from the Latin, *vitellus,* which became in Middle English, *veel.*

Esteemed as a delicate meat since biblical times, veal achieved its greatest popularity in Italy. By the Renaissance it was valued in France, Germany,

Austria, Holland, and elsewhere in Europe, where the high price of the meat never dissuaded connoisseurs from enjoying it. In America, where beef cattle were not plentiful until the middle of the nineteenth century, veal was not much appreciated. Also, the abundance of grass and fodder in America's Midwest promoted the growing of cattle to their full size for beef, while in Europe the availability of pastureland was severely restricted, thereby making the slaughter of an unweaned calf more the norm.

Veal was eaten, especially in the South and Midwest, but it was often ill treated by overcooking. It was only with the arrival of Italian and German immigrants in the late nineteenth and early twentieth centuries that an appetite for veal developed in the eastern cities, with *schnitzels* and veal scallopine showing up on restaurant menus. Consumption of veal by Americans in the 1940s was nearly ten pounds per capita per year, but, largely owing to the high cost of the meat, consumption had fallen to 1.6 pounds by 1981. It is still mostly eaten in Italian and French restaurants, where adaptions of Old World recipes have resulted in dishes like VEAL PARMESAN and VEAL FRANCESE, whose names are unknown abroad.

The three basic categories of veal are "bob veal," usually the meat of a calf up to one month old; "veal," between one and three months; and "baby beef" or "calves' meat," between three and twelve months. These categories are not strict, however, and the terminology is inexact.

The best veal, called "milk-fed veal," is usually considered that from un-weaned calves. A feeding system called the "Dutch method" (because it was developed in Holland) raises the calves on a special formula of milk solids, water, and nutrients, producing an anemic animal.

The main cuts of veal include the primal leg (for veal scallops), the primal loin (for chops), the primal rib (for chops and roasts), the primal shoulder (for veal rolls or blade roasts), the primal shank (for braised dishes like the Italian menu item *osso buco*), the primal breast (for riblets and veal breast), and the primal flank (for stew meat).

veal francese. A dish of pounded veal scallops cooked in butter and white wine. The cutlets are often dipped in egg and flour before cooking.

The name is Italian, meaning "veal in the French style," which seems to indicate nothing more than the use of white wine in the recipe and a lighter treatment than in many Italian-American recipes for veal scallops, which are often covered with tomato sauce, cheese, and ham (see VEAL PARMESAN). There is not a specific or traditional dish in Italy by this name.

> Pound 4 veal scallops till thin and tender, sauté in 2 tbs. butter till browned, then remove from skillet. Add to skillet 1 tbs. butter and 1/2 cup dry white wine, scraping brown bits from skillet. Reduce, burn off alcohol, pour sauce over veal scallops, and serve with a slice of lemon and a bit of chopped parsley.

veal parmesan. Also, "veal parmigiana." A dish of pounded veal scallops that are breaded, sautéed, topped with mozzarella cheese and tomato sauce, and heated until the cheese is melted. Although it is a dish in the Italian style and a staple of Italian-American restaurants, there is no dish specifically by this name in Italy. The name probably derives from Parmesan cheese, a grating cheese originally made in Parma, Italy, and now made there and in the United States, though the dish does not necessarily contain Parmesan cheese.

> Dip veal scallops in an egg-and-milk mixture, then in a plate of bread crumbs. Sauté in butter or olive oil till browned. Top with a thin slice of mozzarella cheese and some tomato sauce, and either bake in a 400° oven or put under broiler till cheese is melted.

vegetable liver. A Jewish-American dish made of eggplant and seasonings as a substitute for chopped chicken liver, which is forbidden at certain times under KOSHER dietary laws.

vegetable oil. Any oil made from various vegetables and seeds, such as sesame, safflower, corn, peanut, soy, and olive, used both for cooking and for salad dressings. These oils are pressed in large cylinders that squeeze out 95 percent of the oil in the seed or are extracted through a method invented in Germany in 1870 by which the seed is treated with a bath of solvent such as hexane. The often seen term *cold-pressed* has no real authority, though it is often used by the food-processing industry to indicate a superior method of oil extraction. The fact is that all oils reach at least 130–150° F. during pressing.

The usual distinction between an "oil" and a "fat" is that the former is liquid and the latter solid. Saturated oils are those in which each of the molecule's carbon atoms is paired with two attached hydrogen atoms; if there are less than two hydrogens per carbon, the oil is unsaturated, in which case adjacent carbon atoms make a double bond. If there is one double bond in the oil molecule, the oil is monounsaturated; if there are two or more double bonds, it is polyunsaturated. These differences are mainly the concerns of nutritionists who fear that the more saturated the oil, the greater the likelihood that it will be turned into cholesterol by the body. Generally speaking, most vegetable oils are polyunsaturated. A hydrogenated oil is one in which the polyunsaturated oils are saturated with hydrogen in order to stabilize them.

"Crude" or "virgin" oils are not processed after pressing.

vegetable (plant) protein. According to the United States Department of Agriculture guidelines, "Vegetable protein products derived from soybeans may be used as binders or extenders in such meat and poultry products as sausages, luncheon meats, soups, sauces and gravies. Sometimes, they are the main ingredients in meat and poultry product substitutes."

veggies. A slang term for vegetables. It has been in use only in the last two decades and perhaps derives from the pseudomaternal admonishment to "eat your veggies."

venison. The flesh of the deer, which is usually marinated and cooked as a steak, a stew, or a barbecue. The word is from the Latin, *venatio,* "hunting," which in Middle English became *veneso(u)n.*

Venison was eaten by the Indians, who stored it for the winter, as Captain John Smith noted on his travels in Virginia in 1607. The woods were filled with deer and the early colonists followed the Indians' example of drying the meat by grilling it over fires. By the nineteenth century venison was a common meat in large cities' markets, but few could vouch for its freshness and so treated the meat with marinades and heavy, highly seasoned sauces that lessened its gaminess.

Today venison is readily available in restaurants during the season, but it is illegal to sell a deer freshly killed by a private hunter unless inspected by government inspectors.

ROAST VENISON:
Marinate a 3-lb. venison roast in a mixture of 2 1/2 cups beef bouillon, 1 1/2 cups red wine, 3 cloves chopped garlic, 1/2 tsp. basil, 1 bay leaf, and 10 peppercorns for 3 days, making sure the entire roast is covered with liquid. Remove from liquid, pat dry, then coat with a mixture of 1/2 cup flour, 2 tsp. salt, 1/4 tsp. pepper, 1/4 tsp. thyme, 1/2 tsp. paprika, and 1/4 tsp. marjoram. Brown meat in hot fat, then pour marinade over meat and bake at 350° for 3 hr.

vermouth. An aromatized wine flavored with various herbs and spices and made in either dry or sweet varieties. The word comes from the German, *Wermut,* "wormwood," which was once customarily used in the manufacture of vermouth, though it is now considered poisonous. Today's vermouths are made with herbs and spices like cinnamon, gentian, cloves, artemisia, quinine, orange peel, camomile, and angelica root.

France and Italy are generally conceded to make the best vermouths, but some are made in the United States, including some under license from European companies. The word was first printed in 1806.

veto. A beverage of the 1840s. It was mentioned in the *New Orleans Picayune* in 1841, though it is not known precisely what the ingredients were, nor the origin of the name.

vichyssoise. A potato-and-leek cream soup served cold. Vichyssoise was created by Chef Louis Diat at the Ritz-Carlton Hotel in New York City. In *American Food* (1975), Evan Jones says the soup was first served in 1910, while the *American Heritage Cookbook* (1980) adds, "[The soup] was served for the first time to Charles Schwab, the steel magnate" for the opening of the hotel's roof garden. But there are several things wrong with these assertions: Diat did come to work at the Ritz-Carlton sometime in 1910, but the restaurant did not open until December 14 of that year, and this was not the roof-garden restaurant in any case. Nor was Charles M. Schwab (1862–1939) present. Also, the menu for that opening night's meal was listed in the *New York Times* the next day; the soup served was a turtle soup, not leek and potato. The *Times* also noted that the meal was overseen not by Diat but by Auguste Escoffier, the renowned chef who had opened Ritz hotels in Paris and elsewhere. Lastly, Diat himself remarked, in his book *Louis Diat's Cookbook* (1946), that "One of my earliest food memories is of my mother's good Leek and Potato soup made with plump, tender leeks I pulled myself from the garden. . . . When I first came to this country I actually couldn't find any [leeks]. I finally persuaded one of my vegetable suppliers to find someone who would grow leeks for me." It is unlikely that Diat found someone to grow leeks quickly enough to have them in time for the opening in 1910.

Curiously enough, Diat does not mention his famous soup by name in his 1946 cookbook, published at a time when many French chefs in New York had tried to change the name to *crème gauloise* because of their hatred for the wartime government established at the city of Vichy, after which Diat had named the soup because he had grown up nearby. Nor did he give the date he created the soup in his earlier book, *Diat's Cooking à la Ritz* (1941). Elizabeth David, however, in her *French Provincial Cooking* (1960), gives, without comment, the date 1917 as the year of the soup's creation, and *Webster's* cites that year as the first printed reference.

The recipe below is from Diat's 1941 volume, in which the full, formal name of the soup is *crème vichyssoise glacée:*

> Finely slice the white parts of 4 leeks and 1 medium onion, brown very gently in 2 oz. sweet butter, then add 5 medium potatoes, also finely sliced. Add 1 qt. water or chicken broth and 1 tbs. salt. Boil for 35–40 min. Crush and rub through a fine strainer. Return to fire and add 2 cups milk and 2 cups medium cream. Season to taste and bring to a boil. Cool, then rub through a very fine strainer. When soup is cold, add 1 cup heavy cream. Chill before serving. Finely chopped chives may be added when serving. Serves 6.

victuals. Also, "vittles," so spelled because of the usual pronunciation of the word, meaning "food or provisions." It is from Latin, *victualia*.

vinegar. A pungent, sour, acidic solution of fermented wine, apple cider, or other substances. Vinegar is the result of a conversion by bacteria of alcoholic solutions into acetic acid. The word is from the Latin, *vīnum*, "wine," plus *acer*, "sharp," which in Middle English became *vinegre*.

Vinegar is used as a flavoring, especially in salad dressings, and as a pickling solution. It is made by any of three methods, called the "slow process," the "generator process," or the "submerged process" (this last developed since World War Two). Homemade vinegar must utilize a starter known as "mother of vinegar."

In Europe most vinegars are based on wine, and the United States produces this kind too, sometimes by winemakers who age the vinegar in oak casks. Distilled white vinegar (also called "white vinegar," "grain vinegar," or "spirit vinegar") is made from grain alcohol diluted with water to a strength of about 5 percent acidity. The H. J. Heinz Company, established in 1869, claims to have produced the first bottled distilled white vinegar, which is today the largest selling of its type in the United States. The most commonly produced vinegar in this country, however, is apple cider vinegar, diluted with water to a table strength of 5 percent acidity.

vinegar candy. A popular nineteenth-century confection made by combining 1 cup sugar, 1/2 cup water, 2 tbs. white vinegar, 1 tbs. molasses, 2 tbs. butter, and 1 tbs. chocolate. Boil for about 20 min. and turn out on buttered sheet. Cut up into small candy pieces.

vinegar pie. Mix 1 beaten egg, 1 tsp. flour, 1 tsp. sugar, 1 tbs. white vinegar, 1 cup cold water, and a pinch of ground nutmeg. Pour into a pie crust, top with another pie crust, brush with cold water, and bake at 375° until filling is set and the crust is browned.

vodka. A distilled spirit made from potatoes, corn, or other grains. It is usually neutral in flavor and, in America, bottled at proofs between 80 and 100.

The word *vodka* is from a Russian diminutive, *voda,* meaning "little water," and although some claim the spirit originated in Russia, other authorities believe its birthplace was Poland, at the end of the tenth century. *Zhizennia voda* ("water of life") is first mentioned in Russian records in the twelfth century, but the spirit was also being made in Finalnd, Czechoslovakia, and other regions of Eastern Europe. Its prominence in the czarist Russian courts was legendary, and in the sixteenth century Ivan the Terrible opened "taverns," where the general populace could enjoy vodka. Western Europeans became familiar with the spirit during the Crimean War (1853–1856), but vodka was still a rarity in the West until well into the twentieth century.

Vodka first came to America with Russian émigré Rudolph Kunnetchansky, son of a Ukranian plantation owner who supplied the P. A. Smirnoff Company (which supplied the Czar's vodka) with grain-neutral spirits. Kunnetchansky fled Russia during the Revolution of 1917 and settled in the United States, where he changed his name to Kunett and became a salesman for Standard Oil, then a manager for Helena Rubenstein Cosmetics. He also bought the rights from Vladimir Smirnoff, then in Paris, for $2,500 to produce and sell Smirnoff vodka in the United States and with Smirnoff's help set up the first American vodka distillery in Bethel, Connecticut, in 1934. In 1939, after years of low sales, the Smirnoff Company was sold to G. F. Heublein and Brothers for $14,000 plus royalties.

Still there was little interest in vodka among Americans, even though the BLOODY MARY cocktail had achieved some success after the end of Prohibition. It was not until well after the Second World War that interest in the spirit picked up, and cocktails like the MOSCOW MULE helped spur a taste for vodka. By the 1960s vodka sales soared, buoyed by a new generation of young Americans who found the lack of a distinct flavor in the spirit perfectly suited to their taste, mixing vodka with all sorts of fruit juices and tonic waters. Even the vodka martini became faddish, especially after the success of Ian Fleming's series of spy books in the 1960s about James "007" Bond, a suave British agent who preferred vodka to gin in his MARTINIS.

By 1975 vodka had become the best-selling spirit in the United States (a position it has held ever since), with about 32 million cases sold each year, less than 2 percent of it imported.

American vodkas are distilled to be odorless, colorless, and nearly tasteless, although a few flavored vodkas are made in small quantities. American vodkas are unaged, distilled from a fermented mash, and highly purified. If colored, that fact must be noted on the bottle's label. There are today more than three hundred brands of vodka, both foreign and domestic, available on the United States market.

Volstead cocktail. According to Harry MacElhone's *ABC of Mixing Drinks* (reprinted in various editions from 1919 to 1939), "This cocktail was invented at Harry's Bar, Paris, in honour of Mr. Andrew J. Volstead (who brought out the Dry Act in the U.S.A.) and was the reason for sending such a large number of Americans to Europe to quench their thirst." (See PROHIBITION.) The drink is made with "1/3 Rye Whiskey, 1/3 Swedish Punch, 1/6 Orange Juice, 1/6 Raspberry Syrup, 1 dash of Anisette."

waffle. A light batter cake cooked on a griddle with a special weblike pattern. Waffles are a popular breakfast dish served with butter and maple syrup. The word is from the Dutch, *wafel,* and first appeared in English print circa 1701. The item was known to the Pilgrims, who had spent time in Holland before sailing to America in 1620, and "waffle parties" became popular in the latter part of the eighteenth century. Thomas Jefferson returned from France with a waffle iron, a long-handled patterned griddle that encloses the batter and gives it its characteristic crispness and shape. A century later vendors on city streets sold waffles hot and slathered with molasses or maple syrup.

Waffles continued to be extremely popular breakfast items in the twentieth century, and electric waffle irons made the timing of the cooking easier. At the 1964 World's Fair "Belgian waffles," made with yeast and thicker than the usual waffle, were an immediate sensation and they are sold today at stands, county fairs, carnivals, and other fast-food outlets. In the South waffles are also made with rice or cornmeal (sometimes called "Virginia waffles"). Raised waffles are also made with yeast. In Baltimore, Maryland, kidney stew on waffles is a traditional Sunday specialty.

> Combine 1 cup flour, 1 1/2 tsp. baking powder, a pinch of salt, 1/2 cup milk, and 1 beaten egg yolk. Mix in 1 tbs. melted, cooled butter, then fold in 1 stiffly beaten egg white. Pour onto a well-buttered waffle iron and cook until golden brown. Serve with butter and maple syrup.

Waldorf salad. A salad with a mayonnaise dressing, apples, and celery, though walnuts are traditional too. The dish was supposedly created by maître d'hôtel Oscar Tschirky of the Waldorf-Astoria hotel in New York City, which opened in 1893. By 1896, when Tschirky compiled *The Cook Book by "Oscar of the Waldorf,"* the recipe—given without comment—called for only apples, celery, and mayonnaise, and the salad later became a staple item in most hotel dining rooms and other restaurants. At some point in the next two decades chopped walnuts were added, for they are listed by George Rector in the ingredients for the salad in *The Rector Cook Book,* which appeared in 1928, after which walnuts became standard in the recipe, including the one given in *The Waldorf-Astoria Cookbook* (1981), by Ted James and Rosalind Cole.

OSCAR'S ORIGINAL WALDORF SALAD RECIPE:
Peel 2 raw apples, cut into small pieces about 1/2-in. square, cut some celery the same way, and mix with the apple. Add "a good mayonnaise."

walleye *(Stizostedion vitreum).* A North American freshwater fish whose wide, bright eyes give it its name, from the Middle English, *wawil-eghed.* It is sometimes called "yellow pike," "dory," and "pike perch," although it is not a pike or a John Dory. According to A. J. McLane in *The Encyclopedia of Fish Cookery* (1977), the walleye was apparently introduced into the Chemung River, a tributary to the north branch of the Susquehanna at Elmira, New York, in 1812 by a Jesuit priest. "The reproduction of these walleyes," writes McLane, "was so successful that they literally swarmed in the pools and eddies of the entire river system, and 'Susquehanna salmon' were soon in greater favor than shad." For a long while afterwards the walleye was called a "salmon."

walnut. Any of a variety of trees in the genus *Juglans* bearing a nut that is eaten on its own, in pastries and desserts, in stuffings, and as a flavoring for ice cream, syrups, and other foods. Cordials and oils are also made from walnuts.

The word is from the Latin, *nux gallia,* "Gaulish nut" (referring to a nut from Gaul), which in Middle English became *walnot.*

The native American black walnut *(J. nigra)* was eaten by the Indians three thousand years ago, about the same time that the Persian walnut *(J. regia)* was being recorded in Babylon. Other native American varieties include the butternut or white walnut *(J. cinerea),* the little walnut *(J. microcarpa),* the Arizona walnut *(J. magor),* the California walnut *(J. californica),* and the Hinds *(J. hindsii)*—eleven other species are native to Central and South America. Nevertheless, nearly 100 percent of the walnuts produced in the United States come from California, but most of those are of the Persian variety, also called the "English walnut" because of its wide propagation by the English.

Walnuts are often combined with maple syrup or flavoring to make maple-walnut ice cream. Walnut fudge appeared just after World War I.

wanigan. The cook's boat that followed a river drive of logs. *Wanigan* was also used by sheepherders to mean the supply wagon. The word comes from the Ojibwa Indian *wannikan,* "man-made hole," because it originally referred to a large supply chest. The word was first printed in 1848.

Washington pie. Also, "Martha Washington pie," "Washington cake," and other variants. A cake of several layers spread with fruit jelly or marmalade. The name derives from Martha Washington (1731–1802), who in her day was a prominent hostess and fine cook, basing many of her preparations on two old recipe collections, *A Booke of Cookery* and *Booke of Sweetmeats,* given to her by her first husband, Daniel Custis, in 1749. These collections, passed on to her granddaughter, Nelly Custis, in 1799, have been reprinted by Karen Hess as *Martha Washington's Booke of Cookery* (1981) and contain several cake recipes, none of which much resembles the Washington cakes of the nineteenth century that supposedly were variants of a cake Martha Washington was said to have made for her granddaughter's wedding in 1799. The following recipe is adapted from one of these nineteenth-century preparations.

> Beat together 1/2 lb. butter with 3/4 lb. sugar until light. Add the rind of half a lemon, then beat in 6 eggs, one at a time. Mix 3 tsp. baking powder with 3/4 cup cream, stir into batter, then add 4 cups flour and blend well. Pour into 4 cake pans and bake at 350° until an inserted knife comes out clean, about 30 min. Cool, then spread layers with fruit jelly or marmalade.

Another kind of Washington pie was described by H. L. Mencken as being "about two inches thick and [sold] in blocks about two inches square. It was made of stale pies, gingercakes, etc., ground up and rebaked." The dish is mentioned in the Ladies of the First Baptist Church's *Pentucket Housewife* (1882).

wasp nest. Cowboy's term for a light bread.

watermelon *(Citrullus vulgaris)*. A vine native to Africa bearing a large, green-skinned fruit with bright pink flesh and black seeds. The name derives from the great amount of watery juice in the fruit and first appears in English in 1615.

Cultivated for thousands of years in the Middle East and Russia, the watermelon was brought to America by the African slaves. In fact, watermelons have long been associated with American blacks, not always in a complimentary way, for much of the graphic and cartoon art of the nineteenth century pictured blacks as docile people content to walk barefoot and eat watermelon. The word itself has sometimes been used as a slur word for blacks, and one slang term for the fruit is "nigger special." (Another, nonracial colloquial name for the fruit is "August ham," because of its size and time of appearance.)

The watermelon has been widely cultivated in California, Indiana, and Texas. It is usually eaten fresh in the summertime, although pickled watermelon rind is a traditional American relish.

WATERMELON RIND OR PICKLE:
Cut away 1 lb. of watermelon rind and cut into chunks. Cover with cold salted water and boil till softened. Drain, cover again with cold water, and cook until very tender. Dissolve 3/4 lb. sugar in 1 cup hot water, add rind and 1 sliced lemon, bring to a rapid boil, and cook till rind turns clear. Add 2 tbs. vinegar, 1/2 oz. whole cloves, and cook till clear. Chill.

weakfish *(Cynoscion regalis)*. Also, "sea trout" and "squeteague" (the latter from the Narraganset). A variety of marine fish found in the Atlantic. It seemed to have vanished from American waters after 1800 and did not reappear in force until 1870, with remarkable numbers swarming off New York City's Rockaway Beach in 1881. The fish again disappeared in the 1950s and came back in 1972. It has since made progress as a desirable food fish in eastern restaurants.

The name is from Obsolete Dutch, *weekvische,* probably referring to the soft mouth of the fish, although an English encyclopedia of the 1830s suggested that Americans called the fish by that name because it was "considered by some as a debilitating food."

western. A sandwich composed of an omelette with green pepper, chopped ham, and onions on white bread or toast. It is sometimes called a "western omelette" or, in Utah, a "Denver." The term for this sandwich was first printed in 1951.

wheat. One of the most important grains of man, with several varieties in the genus *Triticum.* The word is from Old English, *hwǣte.*

There is no evidence that wheat existed in the New World before Columbus brought it to Isabela, Puerto Rico, in 1493, and it was introduced to Mexico by Hernando Cortés as of 1519. The Spanish missionaries brought the grain to Arizona and California in the eighteenth century. In the East wheat was sown unsuccessfully by the Pilgrims, who made do with corn, and in Virginia tobacco was a more profitable crop, so wheat was relegated to a minor role in that colony. It was not until it was planted in the Mississippi valley in 1718 by the Company of the West that wheat became an important American crop, increasingly so during the Civil War, when the mechanized northern harvesters brought in far more wheat for their troops than the southerners could with manual labor. The North was even able to export wheat and flour to Europe during the hostilities.

Today the Soviet Union is the world's leading producer of wheat, followed by the United States, which in recent years has exported a great deal of wheat to the Soviet Union.

Wheat is turned into flour, cereals, pasta, and enough kinds of food to provide one-quarter of the total food requirements of man.

The principal varieties of United States wheat include:

hard red spring wheat. High in protein and gluten, this is excellent for making bread flour.

hard red winter wheat. A thinner kernel than hard red spring wheat, also good for bread flour.

soft red winter wheat. Starchier than hard wheat, this is good for pastry flour.

durum wheat. High in gluten, durum wheat is ground to make semolina for pasta.

Commercial forms of wheat include:

bran. The outer covering of the wheat kernel, used to make cereals.

bulgur. Also called "wheat pilaf," bulgur is the ground whole kernel, often used in Middle Eastern dishes.

cracked wheat. Another form of crushed whole wheat kernels.

wheat germ. The embryo of the wheat kernel, often used as a nutritional supplement for cereal and other foods.

whelk. Any of a variety of marine snails in the family Buccinidae having a thick turreted shell and a large foot that is used as food. The name is from Old English, *weoloc*. Whelk is not commonly eaten by Americans except at Italian restaurants, where it is listed on menus as *"scungilli."* The two species of culinary interest are the waved whelk *(Buccinum undatum)* and the channeled whelk *(Busycon canaliculatum)*.

Whelk is usually prepared with garlic and tomato sauce or served with lemon, oil, and vinegar as part of a cold salad.

whip. A dessert of whipped cream to which has been added sugar and lemon juice.

> Combine 1 cup sugar with the juice of 3 lemons. Add 1 pt. heavy cream and whip until stiff. Serve in glasses.

whiskey. An alcoholic distilled spirit from grains such as corn, barley, or rye. In the United States several grain spirits are produced, but the only true American whiskeys (that is, those that are produced only within the United States) are BOURBON, TENNESSEE WHISKEY, and BLENDED WHISKEY (often erroneously called RYE), each of which should be consulted under those names.

The word *whiskey* comes from the Gaelic, *uisgebeatha,* "water of life." When it specifically refers to Scotch (produced only in Scotland), the word is spelled without the *e,* although this spelling has been adopted as standard for all domestic whiskeys by the Bureau of Alcohol, Tobacco, and Firearms. Still, Americans continue to spell domestic and Irish grain spirits *whiskey.*

The earliest European settlers in America brought distilled spirits with them, and rum was commercially produced in New England very early. By 1640 there was a distillery on New York's Staten Island, but the industry grew rather slowly, with rye and barley the principal grains used. Many farmers used their excess grain to this end, and during the Revolutionary War whiskey was used as a medium of exchange.

In 1791 Alexander Hamilton passed a federal excise tax on whiskey that resulted, three years later, in an uprising of mostly Scottish-Irish farmers in western Pennsylvania who opposed this incursion into their livelihood. President George Washington was forced to call out the militia to quell the revolt, called the "Whiskey Rebellion," thereby demonstrating the federal government's resolve in enforcing the new laws of the land.

Today the best American whiskeys continue to come from those regions where the water passes through layers of limestone, as it does in the principal whiskey-producing states of Pennsylvania, Indiana, Tennessee, Maryland and Kentucky.

The principal types of American whiskey are defined as:

straight whiskey. Whiskey distilled at 160 PROOF or less, aged at least two years in new, white, charred oak barrels. The addition of water brings the alcohol down to no lower than 80 proof, with a minimum of 51 percent of the volume being the grain. A spirit that has reached a proof above 160 is called a "neutral spirit" and should not possess any discernible flavor, aroma, or body. About half the whiskey consumed in the United States is straight whiskey.

bottled-in-bond. Only straight whiskeys are "bottled-in-bond," a term that has nothing to do with guaranteeing quality but is instead a means of aging whiskey without having to pay tax on it until the spirit is ready for sale. The Bottled in Bond Act of 1894 required that the whiskey be aged at least four years (usually higher in practice), bottled at a minimum of 100 proof, and kept under the supervision of the Internal Revenue Service in a "bonded warehouse." When the distiller removes the whiskey from the warehouse, he then pays the tax.

light whiskey. Whiskey distilled at 161 to 189 proof, stored in used or uncharred new oak containers. This category was established in 1972. Most light whiskey is made from corn, and it may be called a "blended light whiskey" if mixed with less than 20 percent straight whiskey on a proof-gallon basis.

whiskey mill. A frontier saloon.

whistle berries. A cowboy's term for beans, perhaps because of the flatulence they often cause.

white bass (*Morone chrysops*). A freshwater fish similar to the STRIPED BASS. White bass are particularly popular in lakes and rivers of the Midwest, where pan-frying is the most usual preparation.

white chocolate mousse. A dessert made from white chocolate, cream, egg whites, and sugar. It was created by chef Michel Fitoussi in 1977 on the occasion of the second anniversary of the Palace restaurant in New York City and quickly became popular in other restaurants around the United States; it also began an interest in white chocolate (actually a form of flavored cocoa butter) as a confectionary ingredient.

Whip 1 qt. heavy cream till stiff. Chill in refrigerator. Cook 1 lb. sugar with 1 cup water to 250° on a candy thermometer. Beat 1 cup egg whites till almost stiff, pour in sugar syrup, and blend until almost cool. Cut 2 lb. white chocolate into small cubes, fold in egg whites and whipped cream. Purée 4 pt. strawberries with sugar to taste and a little Kirsch. Spoon sauce onto plate, spoon mousse onto sauce, and top with strawberry or raspberry. Serves 10.

whitefish. Any of a variety of freshwater fishes in the genus *Coregonus,* although other related species are usually called by this name. Whitefish are members of the salmon family, and the most important species gastronomically include the cisco, whose name derives from the Ojibwa, *pemitewiskawet,* "oily-skinned fish" and of which there are several species—the cisco *(Coregonus artedii),* also called "lake herring"; the deepwater cisco *(C. johannae);* the longjaw cisco *(C. alpenae);* the shortjaw cisco *(C. zenithicus);* the shortnose cisco *(C. reighardi);* and the blackfin cisco *(C. nigripinnis);* the lake whitefish *(C. clupeaformis);* the mountain whitefish *(Prosopium williamsoni),* also called the "Rocky Mountain whitefish"; and the round whitefish *(P. cylindraceum),* also called "Menominee whitefish" (after the Menominee River in Michigan).

white lady. A drink of equal parts lemon juice, white crème de menthe, and Cointreau, shaken over ice and strained into a cocktail glass. The original was created by bartender Harry MacElhone in 1919 at London's Ciro's Club, but he changed the formula in 1929 at Harry's New York Bar in Paris to substitute gin, which is more readily found today, for the white crème de menthe. Sometimes the drink is made with the addition of half an egg white.

white sauce. This term may refer to a sauce made from a roux of flour, butter, and milk or cream or to a light, clear sauce made with clams and clam broth that goes with spaghetti, usually LINGUINE. The former usage is far older than the latter, which has been heard in Italian-American restaurants only since World War II. See also RED SAUCE.

WHITE SAUCE:
In 2 tbs. butter blend 2 tbs. flour, over a low heat, till well incorporated, then stir slowly into the roux 1 cup milk or 1/2 cup milk and 1/2 cup cream. Season with salt and pepper, simmer till thickened.

WHITE CLAM SAUCE:
In 1/4 cup olive oil sauté 1 sliced clove garlic for 1 min. Add 1/4 cup water, stir in 1/2 tsp. chopped parsley, salt and pepper, 1/2 cup minced clams, and 1 cup clam broth. Simmer till tender.

wild boar *(Sus scrofa).* A Eurasian swine with a thick, short, powerful body and upcurved tusks. It was domesticated in Europe about 1500 B.C. and introduced in its wild state to the United States by sportsmen. Waverly Root and Richard de Rochemont note in *Eating in America* (1976) that Hernando de Soto "landed near what is now Tampa [Florida] in 1542 with thirteen porkers in his supply train, and although other explorers and settlers of the American South brought pigs which eventually ran wild, Louisianans like to think of their wild boar as having a true Creole ancestry, that is to say, in this case, Spanish, with no native intermixture." Yet de Soto's swine were obviously domesticated boars or, more probably, simple hogs.

Wild boars proliferated throughout New Hampshire, North Carolina, and the Southwest (where they are called "javelinas") and are still hunted and, when taken, cooked in a stew or as a roast. The following recipe is from the Horse & Hound Inn in South Salem, New York.

WILD BOAR ROAST:
In a marinade of dry red wine, diced scallions, carrots, celery, basil, juniper berries, and other seasonings, place a haunch of wild boar and let sit in the refrigerator for 12–48 hr. Remove boar, wipe dry, cover with lard, season with salt and pepper, and roast at 400° till browned. Reduce heat to 325° and cook for 25 min. per pound, basting often with marinade. Strain drippings from pan for use in a Cumberland or gooseberry sauce.

wild rice *(Zizania aquatica).* Also called "Indian rice," "Tuscarora rice," and "Canadian rice." Not a true rice, but the grain of a tall aquatic grass grown in the northern part of the United States. The Indians of that region called it *"manomin"* or *"Meneninee."* It was called "crazy oats" by the French and "wild rice" by Americans as of 1778. Later it was also referred to as "water oats" or "water rice."

Wild rice is now cultivated in rice paddies, mostly in Minnesota, where it is most often cooked by the following method:

Cover 1 cup wild rice with boiling water, cover the pot and let stand for 20 min. Drain, repeat process three more times. Add salt to taste, drain, then dry briefly over a low heat. It is usually served with butter, but sliced almonds, mushrooms, or onions may be added, also.

wine. Fermented grape juice, although wine may also be made from other fruits. The word is from the Latin, *vīnum.*

The story of wine in most wine-producing countries is the history of a culture, but in America the story of wine is a spotty narrative of fits and starts, blind alleys, and intermittent, slow progress. Viticulture in this country has been a series of vignettes rather than a saga. Only within the last ten years have Americans begun to appreciate wine as an ordinary beverage with some extraordinary characteristics.

The earliest settlers in this country set about making wine almost as soon as they arrived. These were wines made from wild American grapes, the MUSCADINE *(Vitis rotundifolia)* and Labrusca, strong-flavored wines that were unfamiliar to the Europeans' taste. But the French Huguenots made wine from these grapes in the 1560s near Jacksonville, Florida, and Captain John Hawkins noted in 1565 that the Spanish settlers in Florida had made their own wine there. By the early 1600s Captain John Smith of Virginia could report "a great abundance [of vines] in many parts, that climbe the toppes of highest trees in some places. . . . Of these hedge grapes we made neere twentie gallons of wine, which was like our British wine, but certainly they would prove good were they well manured." There was certainly wine at the first Thanksgiving feast in 1621. Lord Delaware brought French vines to Virginia in 1619, and the Virginia assembly required landowners to plant ten vines and offered prizes for the best wines.

In the seventeenth century there were several failed attempts throughout the eastern colonies to grow wine grapes—in Maryland, in Massachusetts, in Pennsylvania, in Rhode Island, in New York, and throughout the South. Thomas Jefferson's wine producing attempts at Monticello in 1773 were unsuccessful, too, largely because he, like the other farmers of the day, tried to plant European Vinifera grapes that were not resistant to American disease, pests, and cold winters.

Meanwhile, wines were being successfully introduced in the West, particularly in California. As early as 1518 the Spanish explorer Hernando Cortés ordered grapes to be grown for wine in Mexico, a program so swiftly successful that the Spanish wine producers feared the competition and decreed that New World wines would be considered contraband. Nevertheless, the wines prospered.

Legend has it that wine vines were introduced into California by a Franciscan priest named Junipero Serra in 1769, when he founded the Mission San Diego. Research now shows that this was probably too early. In an article in *New West* magazine (September 24, 1979), Roy Brady showed that Father Serra did not choose the San Diego site until July 16, 1769, too late in the year to plant vines for successful propagation, and by 1772 Serra lamented the lack of wine at the mission in his letters to his superior. By 1777 Serra was certain that wine could be made at the mission, and in a letter of March 15, 1779, Father Pablo de Mugártegui refers to "vine cuttings which at your request were sent to us from the lower country" having been planted. Brady surmises that the first vines actually arrived in 1778, brought aboard Don José Camacho's ship, the *San Antonio,* and were planted at San Juan Capistrano and that the first wines were ready for drinking in 1783, from a year-old vintage.

The grape the Spanish used in California was a species of Vinifera called "Mission" or "Criolla." Leon D. Adams notes in *The Wines of America* (1978) that "ampelographers say it probably grew from a seed brought from Spain via Mexico by the *conquistadores,*" since there is no precise counterpart for the grape in Europe.

Native American grapes were propagated back East, with the first plantings of an indigenous grape made by James Alexander of Pennsylvania, and named after him, in the 1730s. By 1793 the first commercial wine producing was being done northwest of Philadelphia along the Susquehanna River by the Pennsylvania Vine Company. Grape growing for wine expanded into the Midwest by 1804, when Jean Jacques Dufour planted Alexander grapes at Vevay, Indiana. By the 1820s there were vineyards in Ohio, the Hudson Valley of New York, Missouri, and North Carolina.

All these were wines made from varieties of Labrusca, which possess a very grapey flavor Americans called "foxy." This term, considered derogatory by growers of Labrusca, refers to the fox grape, *Vitis labrusca,* of the eastern United States. (Actually, all eastern wine grapes are by now crossbreeds, more properly called *Vitis labruscana.*) Purplish and large, the fox grape was first mentioned in 1657 and was described in 1682 by William Penn as "the great red grape (now ripe) called by ignorance, 'The fox-grape,' (because of the relish it hath with unskilful palates)." By 1864 Webster defined *foxy* as having the coarse flavor of the fox grape.

Vinifera grapes had failed consistently in the East, but in 1833 Jean Louis Vignes brought French vines to Los Angeles and grew them successfully, spurring more farmers to plant such varieties. After the Gold Rush of 1849, many failed miners stayed on in California to plant grapes, so that by 1863 there were more than 12 million vines in the state. There was even an industry bust in 1858 and 1859, and another in 1876, owing to an overproduction of wine. American wines by then were being shipped abroad in increasing numbers, and the French even feared United States competition in viticulture.

A great deal of credit for improving the California wine industry has been given to Hungarian-born Agoston Haraszthy, who came to America to run a successful vineyard in California's Sonoma County in 1857 and then returned to Europe, with the approval of the state legislature, to bring back one hundred thousand vine cuttings. It has often been charged that the legislature reneged on a promise to reimburse Haraszthy (who called himself "Count" with no documentation to back up the title) for his trip and cuttings, but Charles L. Sullivan showed in his article, "A Viticultural Mystery Solved; the Historical Origins of Zinfandel in California," printed in the summer 1978 number of *California History,* not only that Haraszthy did not bring back the Green Hungarian and ZINFANDEL grapes that would eventually become important varieties in California viticulture, but that he guaranteed the legislature his trip would not cost them a cent. Haraszthy's contributions to viticulture in the state were considerable in terms of technical methods and improved propagation, but there seems little reason now to christen him the "Father of California's Wine Industry," as some have in the past.

Sometime between 1858 and 1863 American vines were imported by Europeans for experimental purposes. These Labrusca vines carried with them a louse, the *Phylloxera vastatrix,* that attacked the susceptible European vines, almost completely destroying the vineyards over the next fifty years and eventually affecting the vines of Russia and Australia as well. Ironically, the vines of the eastern United States were resistant to the phylloxera, but those of California had never built up such a resistance, and in 1873 the lice attacked the vines in Sonoma and devastated many vineyards throughout northern California before it was checked at the turn of the century.

The phylloxera was stopped in Europe by grafting European vines onto resistant American roots, principally from the Midwest, so California vineyards began replantings with these same roots, halting the ravages of the lice.

In 1880 the California state legislature ordered the University of California to undertake a continuing program of intensive research in viticulture, a tradition that has made the school preeminent in the world today. California surpassed Ohio and Missouri as the largest wine-producing state in 1870, but wineries were thriving in the South, the Midwest, the Northwest, and even in Utah. After 1860 New York State's Finger Lakes became an important wine-producing region, and by 1876 American wines were winning medals in international expositions. American "champagne" was first made in Ohio in 1842 and a sparkling wine made from Catawba grapes by New York's Pleasant Valley Winery in 1865 won an honorable mention at the Paris Exposition two years later.

American wines had earned international respect, but Americans themselves drank very little wine and what was available was usually sold in bulk. Italian immigrants set up wineries in New York and California and made wine according to Old World methods, which sometimes included pressing the grapes with their feet, leading to appellations that were sometimes facetious, such as calling the harsh red wines of northern California "Chateau La Feet" (a pun on the prestigious French Bordeaux wine, Château Lafite) or, with a somewhat more belittling tone, "dago red" (from the ethnic slur "dago," which originally derived from the common Spanish name "Diego" but which by 1887 referred to an Italian). *Dago red* was used as a general term for red wines made from Zinfandel and other grapes and often marketed under the name "Chianti" (a red wine made in Italy's Tuscany region from Sangiovese and other grapes).

It was not the low reputation of more ordinary American wines that kept Americans from building a palate for table wine, but instead the growing temperance movement of the early twentieth century that first demonstrated its power in individual counties, then states, with Kansas having declared itself "dry" as early as 1880. By the First World War thirty-three of the forty-eight states forbade the sale of spirits and wine, and the passage of the Volstead Act in 1919 effectively crippled the rapidly developing wine industry, causing growers to switch to the production of "sacramental wine," used for religious rituals, or supplying home winemakers (as well as bootleggers) with grapes. One provision of the Volstead Act (Section 29), added at the behest of Virginia apple farmers, allowed private citizens to make up to two hundred gallons a year of homemade cider or nonintoxicating fruit juice, and the Department of Agriculture even amended its own crop reports to read "juice grapes" instead of "wine grapes." The popularity of homemade wine was so great that the California grape growers suddenly found what they thought was a disaster had turned into an astounding boom for their industry. By the end of PROHIBITION grape acreage in California was 35 percent greater than it had been when the Volstead Act was passed, and more than 90 million gallons of "nonintoxicating fruit juice" were being made at home each year, though the majority was made from inferior grapes the industry had been quick to provide.

Owing to an oversupply, there was a collapse of the California grape market in 1925, and many growers switched to other fruits like apricots. But most wineries went out of business during Prohibition, with only a hundred or so surviving the Great Experiment.

During this period wineries sold sacramental wine, wine bricks (compressed grapes), grape juice, and "Vine-Glow," a syrupy concentrate marketed in 1931 for the home winemaker (this last product was denounced in public forums and removed from the market soon afterwards). In 1932, on the verge of repeal, Senator William Gibbs McAdoo of California proposed to allow wine and beer to be sold at 3.2 percent alcohol, and the little wine that was made according to this formula was scornfully called "McAdoo wine."

Even after repeal, the wine industry took a long while to recover, largely because the growers had already switched to other crops or to inferior grapes. Sweet dessert wines gained in popularity, as did high-alcohol "fortified wines," with a 20 percent alcoholic content boosted by brandy. And, too, the legacy of Prohibition was still manifest in many states that chose to remain "dry" after repeal.

In 1935, however, Philip Wagner of Baltimore began bringing in hybrid grapes from France. A home winemaker himself, Wagner could not obtain his preferred Zinfandel and Carignane grapes from California after 1933 and he did not care for the Labrusca flavors of eastern grapes. He therefore imported the new French hybrids and began making wines that did indeed taste more like European wines. Wagner's first hybrids, created by Maurice Baco and Albert Seibel, became the basis for wide-ranging experimentation in New York during the 1960s, revitalizing the industry in that state, where sweet Labrusca wines had been made almost exclusively.

A small but ultimately significant boost was given American wines when New York City journalist Frank Musselman Schoonmaker began importing the best wines of California, Ohio, and New York and labelling them not with imitative and misleading names like "Burgundy," "Chianti," and "Sauterne" (American winemakers almost always spell the French wine "Sauternes" without the final *s*), but with varietal names based on the principal grape used— "Cabernet," "Catawba," "Riesling," "Grenache Rosé," and others, sold at premium prices to the best restaurants and wine stores.

In 1934 the California Wine Institute was formed to work towards national standards for winemaking in the United States. In 1938 the word *fortified* (which had a connotation of alcohol abuse) was banned from labels and advertising, and by 1954 the term was removed completely from federal regulations regarding wine. By the 1950s the prestige of the University of California's enology school at Davis was unparalleled in the world, and, thanks to their efforts, American wines improved year by year.

Still, Americans continued to drink more dessert wines than table wines, and by the mid-1950s per capita consumption was less than a gallon per year, much of that being softer versions of red wine called "vino" with an attempt to imbue such wines with an Italian cachet. Flavored wines with high alcohol and strange proprietary names like "Pagan Pink Ripple" and "Thunderbird" seemed ideal for the soda-pop palate of the postwar generation. Dozens of "pop wines" made from fruit juices and other flavorings became extremely popular in the 1960s.

It was during the same decade, however, that American wines took an astonishing leap in quality and reputation. In California established wine producing families and individuals like Sam Sebastiani, Robert Mondavi, André Tchelistcheff, Joe Heitz, and others pioneered the new technologies that utterly transformed the industry into a modern, efficient system capable of turning out varietal Vinifera wines of great character, long-livedness, and prices competitive with the best French wines.

This rise in quality coupled with a growing interest on the part of American consumers in their own wines, boosted the sales of table wines over dessert wines for the first time in 1968, and by 1972 per capita consumption had risen to a gallon-and-a-half per year. Land prices in the Napa and Sonoma valleys soared, investors bought up farms in an increasing number of wine regions in California, Washington, Idaho, and elsewhere, and there was increased activity in wine culture along the Hudson Valley in New York, as well as renewed efforts in Maryland, Virginia, Connecticut, Texas, and other states that had all but abandoned winemaking on a commercial scale. Even on the island of Maui in Hawaii a winery was opened by Emil Tedeschi, who used a hybrid called "Carnelian" made from Grenache, CABERNET SAUVIGNON, and Carignane grapes that flourished in the Pacific heat.

"Wine bars," where people could sample several different wines by the glass, opened in several major American cities, and in the 1970s there was a white-wine boom, in which Americans ordered white wine by the glass as a cocktail and bought drier and drier white wines by the bottle. White wines jumped from 17 percent of the American wine market in 1960 to 57 percent in 1981, with red wines dropping during the same period from 74 percent to 25 percent. (Rosé now accounts for about 18 percent of the market). California sells more than 69 percent of the wine drunk in America. Americans import about 23 percent of the wines they drink. The leading producer of American wines is the firm of Ernest and Julio Gallo of California, which in 1981 shipped 131.4 million gallons. Americans still drink fifteen times more soda than wine.

An increasing number of Americans are buying "light wines," which may have one-third less calories than regular wine, with sales in 1982 of about $20 million, or about 2 percent of all the California table wine sold in 1981. Light wines are produced in various ways, but most winemakers pick their grapes earlier, when the sugar level is lower than that at full ripening, thereby decreasing the alcohol content before fermentation. Other producers remove the alcohol after fermentation is completed. Light wines have been made commercially since December 1979, when California laws permitted a reduction of alcohol from a previous minimum of 10 percent down to as low as 7 percent, and in February 1981 vintners won the right in federal court to use the term *light* on their labels.

Varietal wines must contain, under federal regulations that went into effect on January 1, 1983, a minimum of 75 percent of the grape variety named on the label, although premium varietals have often been made using 100 percent of the grape named. Multivarietal labels listing two different grapes are also allowed, as long as the exact percentage appears on the label.

Estate bottled may be printed on wine labels when both the vineyard and the winery are in the same "recognized viticultural region," according to federal regulations; furthermore, the winery must own its own vineyard or have it under long-term lease, and all winemaking activities must occur on the premises. A specific geographical region—for instance, "Sonoma Valley"—may be listed on the label only if 85 percent of the grapes have been grown in that region. If a county is named—for instance, "Mendocino"—75 percent of the grapes must be grown in that county. The same percentage applies to state names appearing on labels (although California law mandates that 100 percent of the grapes come from the state for a California appellation).

"Chaptalization" (after a Napoleonic minister named Chaptal), a process of adding sugar to wine in order to increase its alcohol content through fermentation, has been forbidden in California since 1887 but is permitted in New York.

Home winemaking is allowed by the federal government if no more than one hundred gallons per year per adult, or two hundred gallons per household with two or more adults, are produced.

In 1981 Americans drank 2.2 gallons of wine per capita, which placed the United States thirtieth in the world in wine consumption.

The following is a list of the principal grape varieties grown in the United States for making wine. Those printed in small capital letters are major varieties having main entries elsewhere in this book. The names preceding numerals indicate the creator of the hybrid.

Aleatico (red Vinifera)
Alicante bouschet (red Vinifera)
Aligoté (white Vinifera)
Aurora (also, "Aurore"; white hybrid; Seibel 5279)
Baco noir (red hybrid; Baco No. 1)
Barbera (red Vinifera)
Cabernet Franc (red Vinifera)
CABERNET SAUVIGNON (red Vinifera)
Carignane (red Vinifera)
Cascade (red hybrid; Seibel 13053)
CATAWBA (native red Labrusca American hybrid)
Cayuga White (white hybrid)
Chancellor (also, "Chancellor Noir"; red hybrid; Seibel 7053)
Charbono (red hybrid)
CHARDONNAY (white Vinifera)
Chelois (red hybrid)

CHENIN BLANC (white Vinifera)
CONCORD (red Labrusca hybrid)
Cynthiana (also, "Norton" and "Virginia Seedling"; red hybrid)
De Chaunac (red hybrid; Seibel 9549)
DELAWARE (red Labrusca hybrid)
Diamond (white Labrusca hybrid)
Dutchess (white Labrusca hybrid)
Emerald Riesling (white Vinifera)
Flora (white Vinifera)
Foch (also, "Maréchal Foch"; red hybrid; Kuhlmann 188-2)
Folle Blanche (white Vinifera)
FRENCH COLOMBARD (also, "Colombard"; white Vinifera)
Gamay (also, "Napa Gamay"; red Vinifera)
Gamay Beaujolais (red Vinifera)
Gewürztraminer (white Vinifera)
Green Hungarian (white Vinifera)
Grenache (red Vinifera)
Grey Riesling (white Vinifera)
Grignolino (red Vinifera)
JOHANNISBERG RIESLING (also, "White Riesling"; white Vinifera)
Leon Millot (red hybrid; Kulhmann 192-2)
Malbec (red Vinifera)
Merlot (red Vinifera)
Mission (red Vinifera)
Moscato (white Vinifera)
Müller-Thurgau (white Vinifera)
MUSCADINE (gold or reddish black Labrusca)
Napa Gamay (red Vinifera)
Nebbiolo (red Vinifera)
Niagara (white hybrid)
Palomino (also, "Golden Chasselas"; white Vinifera)
PETITE SIRAH (also, "Petite Syrah"; red Vinifera)
Pinot blanc (white Vinifera)
Pinot gris (white Vinifera)
PINOT NOIR (red Vinifera)
RUBY CABERNET (red Vinifera)
SAUVIGNON BLANC (white Vinifera)
Sémillon (white Vinifera)
SEYVAL BLANC (also, "Seyval"; white hybrid; Seyve-Villard 5-276)
Sylvaner (also, "Sylvaner Riesling" or "Franken Riesling"; white Vinifera)
THOMPSON SEEDLESS (white Vinifera)
Tinta Madeira (red Vinifera)
Vidal blanc (white hybrid; Vidal 256)
Villard blanc (white hybrid; Seyve-Villard 12-375)
ZINFANDEL (red Vinifera)

wine brick. Dehydrated grapes pressed into a brick and later put in water for homemade wine, used during Prohibition.

witch. A nineteenth-century New England cookie described in *The Pentucket Housewife* (1882) as containing 2 eggs, 1 1/2 cups sugar, 1/2 cup butter, 1 tbs. milk, 1/2 tsp. baking soda, and 1 tsp. each of cinnamon, cloves, and allspice.

wohaw. Indian term for the cattle they first saw with the white men. The story goes that the Indians combined the trail calls "Whoa!" and "Haw!" into a general name for the beasts.

wolf fish. Also, "wolffish." Any of a variety of marine fishes in the genus *Anarhichas* having sharp teeth and an ugly appearance that has kept it from becoming a popular food fish. The name, derived from its appearance, is sometimes changed at the market to "ocean catfish." The first appearance in print of the *wolf fish* was in 1569.

In the United States the Atlantic wolffish *(Anarhichas lupus)* is found from Labrador to Nantucket.

woosher. Cowboy's term for a hog.

Wop salad. A salad of lettuce made with olives, oregano, capers, anchovies, garlic, and oil. It is a Louisiana specialty whose name derives from the ethnic slur term *wop,* from a Neapolitan word, *guappo,* "handsome man," used since the 1890s.

yakitori. A Japanese dish of skewered, broiled chicken pieces that have been dipped in a soy sauce marinade. Yakitori is a staple of Japanese-American restaurants. The word in Japanese means "grilled chicken."

Yale boat pie. A dish made with layers of meat, poultry, and shellfish set in a pastry crust. The name comes from Yale University in New Haven, Connecticut, and the recipe below is from *Jennie June's American Cookery Book* (1866) by J. C. Croly, who says, "This pie is excellent for a picnic or water excursion."

> Season with salt and pepper 3–4 lb. beef steak, then place in a large baking dish. Cut 2 chickens into pieces and place on top of steak, add 1 1/2 doz. oysters (without their liquid) and 6 sliced hard-boiled eggs. Dampen the bottom of the dish with ale, cover with mushrooms and 1/2 lb. meat glaze. Top with a pastry crust, bake at 400° till bubbling inside.

Yale cocktail. A drink made by mixing 3 dashes orange bitters, 1 dash Angostura bitters, and 2 oz. gin with ice and garnished with lemon peel. Named after Yale University in New Haven, Connecticut, though its origins are unknown; it probably dates from the post-Prohibition era of the 1930s.

yogurt. A creamy food made from MILK curdled with bacteria such as *Lactobacillus bulgaricus* and *Streptococcus thermophilus*. The word is Turkish, first mentioned in English in 1625.

Yogurt is a very old food, probably of Middle Eastern origins. Turkish immigrants are said to have brought yogurt to the United States in 1784, but its popularity dates only from the 1940s, when Daniel Carasso emigrated to the United States and took over a small yogurt factory in the Bronx, New York. He was soon joined by Juan Metzger, and the two sold their yogurt under the name Dannon (originally Danone, after Daniel Carasso, whose father was a Barcelona yogurt maker). In 1947 the company added strawberry fruit preserves to make the first "sundae-style yogurt." When nutrition promoter Benjamin Gayelord Hauser published an excerpt from his book, *Look Younger,*

Live Longer (1950), in the October 1950 issue of *Reader's Digest* magazine extolling the health virtues of yogurt, the product's sales soared. They leapt again in the 1960s, when so-called health foods were popularized by the "youth movement." Aside from the obvious nutritive values of the milk used, the health benefits of yogurt have not been conclusively proven, and in 1962 the F.D.A. forbade claims that yogurt had any therapeutic or weight-reducing value.

Today Americans eat about one billion cups of yogurt a year, often as a light lunch or dessert, and frozen yogurt is sold at special yogurt stores. Yogurt is also made at home, usually with a simple yogurt machine that uses already made commercial yogurt as a culture starter.

Swiss- or French-style yogurts usually have the fruit flavors already mixed in, rather than in a separate layer at the bottom of the cup. Strawberry yogurt is the most popular of all types.

Yorkshire pudding. A puffy, breadlike side dish made by cooking an egg-and-milk batter in the hot fat and pan drippings from a roast beef. It is a traditional English dish named after a northern county in England. The first recipe for Yorkshire pudding appears in Mrs. Hannah Glasse's *Art of Cookery,* printed in England in 1747 and widely circulated in America. The dish is now a traditional accompaniment to roast beef in this country as well.

> Combine 1 cup flour, 1/4 tsp. salt, and 1 cup milk. Add 2 beaten eggs, make a smooth batter, and let stand till roast beef is done. Pour off the hot fat, retaining about 1/2 in. in the pan. Pour in the batter evenly, bake at 450° until browned and puffy. Cut into wedges and serve with beef.

zephyrina. A North Carolina cookie baked by both the Indians and the early settlers of the territory. The name derives from Latin, *zephyrus,* for "wind," because of their light, airy quality.

> Combine 2 cups flour, 1 tbs. butter, salt, and enough water to make an elastic dough. Roll thin, cut into rounds, prick with fork, and bake till browned in a 375° oven.

Zinfandel. A red Vinifera grape that is usually made into a robust, fruity, tannic wine of unique flavor. It is the most widely propagated grape in California, growing in nearly every wine region in the state and one of American viticulture's finest wines. Zinfandel is also blended with other grapes to make a PORT or rosé, or, as "Blanc de Noir," made into a rosé itself. Occasionally one finds a "Late Harvest Zinfandel" that is a sweet dessert wine. Some light varieties are made in a fruitier style.

Until recently the origins of the Zinfandel grape were unknown. Although some thought it to be indigenous to the United States, others believed it of Hungarian origin. There is a record of William Robert Prince growing a grape by this name in New York as early as 1830; Prince said the grape was from Hungary.

Now, however, most evidence points to the Zinfandel having originated in Italy, and more specifically to the region of Puglia, where a grape called by the farmers there, *"Primitivo di Gioia"* (also called *"Zingarello"*), has been shown to be almost identical to the California variety. In his book, *Vino* (1980), Burton Anderson says that the *Primitivo* was "almost certainly of Greek origin," and that after the phylloxera plague wiped out the grape in the Salento peninsula, growers had to bring back the vine from Gioia. Today in Italy some winemakers produce a *Primitivo* they call by the American name of Zinfandel.

The best Zinfandels are from Northern California, which has medium to warm coastal climates. The wine, which was grown for decades in California by Italian immigrants, was sometimes characterized as undistinguished "dago red," but today Zinfandels are among the most sought-after and respected California bottlings.

zip code wine. A wine industry term to describe a French wine made from grapes not grown in a prestigious region like Burgundy but whose shipper's office *is* in such a region. Under French law only the regional zip code may be used on the label, not the region's name.

zombie. A drink made from various rums and citrus juices. It was created in the late 1930s by Don the Beachcomber (born Don Richard Beaumont-Gantt), whose restaurant in Los Angeles was known for its rum-based concoctions. The story goes that the zombie was created to cure a customer of his hangover. Several weeks later the customer showed up again, and, when asked how he'd enjoyed the drink, replied, "I felt like the living dead." The cocktail was thereafter called the zombie, after the legendary spirits that reanimate the bodies of dead people in voodoo mythology. The word is from Kongo, *zumbi*, "fetish."

> Shake together 3/4 oz. lime juice, 1 oz. pineapple juice, 1 tsp. sugar syrup, 1 oz. light rum, 2 oz. medium rum, 1 oz. Jamaican rum, 1/2 oz. 151-proof Demeraran rum, and 1/2 oz. apricot liqueur. Pour into a tall glass with shaved ice, garnish with a slice of orange and sprigs of mint. Serve with straw.

zoo. Hotel workers' slang word for the place where the help eats.

zorilla. An early longhorn breed of cattle, so called because its black coloring with white freckles on its sides and belly made it resemble the colorings of the polecat, which in Spanish is *zorrillas*.

zucchini. A summer SQUASH of the species *Cucurbita pepo,* which measures from four to six inches in length, has a smooth green skin, and grows from flowers that themselves are sometimes battered and fried. The word is derived from the Italian, *zucchino,* for a small squash. Zucchini only became known to Americans in the 1920s. By the 1950s it was a staple of Italian-American restaurant menus and served either stewed with tomatoes, battered and fried in olive oil, or cut into salads. Harrisville, New Hampshire, holds an annual "zucchini festival" at which the vegetable is carved into shapes and there is even a peeling contest.

zwieback. Dry toasted bread slices, long popular for their digestibility and often served to young children. The word is from the German for "twice baked" and first appears in English print in 1894. Zweiback is usually bought at the grocery.

> Cut small bread loaf into slices 1/2 in. thick. Place in pan and dry out in open oven at 200°. When dry, close oven door and increase heat slightly to brown slices.

A Bibliographic Guide

I might have ended this book with a complete list of every book, magazine, and newspaper I consulted in writing it, but that would be of interest only to the most indefatigable scholar, who has merely to leaf through the printed card catalogs of the New York Public Library and the Library of Congress to find the thousands of items under the category *American Cookery* I have *not* consulted. The catalog of the New York Public Library runs to well over a hundred pages, with a score of entries on each page. From these I chose to look at several hundred items I considered important, including cookbooks, histories, reminiscences, Army and Navy food-preparation manuals, commercial brochures, centennial exposition pamphlets, and articles on everything from Pennsylvania Dutch Christmas pastries to World War One ration regulations. In addition, I consulted works in every discipline from music and art to state histories and travel guides, as well as several biographies of famous people after whom a dish was apparently named. There were, of course, daily inspections of newspapers, magazines, government bulletins, and regional journals for serendipity's sake, while an idle glance at some cereal box might turn up a key piece of information I had sought for months.

Since any item of specific interest or particular scholarship is cited and credited in the text of this book, I believe it would be repetitious to list all references again in a bibliography. I have decided, then, to provide both the scholar and the general reader with a brief guide to the best and most important sources for my research, giving credit where it is heavily due while establishing a working bibliography for future scholarship in the field of American studies.

Unfortunately, I cannot include the names of the countless friends, acquaintances, restaurateurs, cooks, waiters, and waitresses who provided me with essential information. They are the living, walking repositories of American gastronomic traditions and manners. And that includes just about everyone.

ETYMOLOGY

For standard definitions and etymology, I relied first on *The American Heritage Dictionary of the English Language,* edited by William Morris, first published in 1969. (The college edition published in 1982 was consulted for new words, but the etymological information in it is not as thorough as that in the earlier edition.) Words were then checked for their first appearance in English in the *Oxford English Dictionary* and in *Webster's Ninth New Collegiate Dictionary* (1983), which added to and altered much of the material found in *A Dictionary of Americanisms,* edited by Mitford M. Mathews (1951). *The Dictionary of American English,* edited by Sir William Craigie, which appeared from 1936 to 1944, was used to a lesser degree in my research. Eric Partridge's *Dictionary of Slang and Unconventional English* (fourth edition, 1951) often contained words I could find nowhere else, while an even richer store of the national tongue was found in Harold Wentworth and Stuart Berg Flexner's *Dictionary of American Slang* (second supplemented edition, 1975). Also of interest was *The American Thesaurus of Slang,* edited by Lester V. Berrey and Melvin Van den Bark (second edition, 1953).

Every lover of words is equally a lover of H. L. Mencken's *The American Language,* first published in 1919, followed by a greatly expanded fourth edition in 1936 and two massive supplements in 1945 and 1948. All of this material was revised, brought up to date, and abridged by Raven I. McDavid, Jr., in a one-volume edition that appeared in 1963. Mencken's own original linguistic research was slight, dependent upon the standard texts and dictionaries available to him, and the significance of his work is indebted to hundreds of correspondents who added immeasurably to the corrections and revisions of the supplements. Mencken's real contribution was to pull all the strains of American English and linguistic scholarship together. As McDavid noted in his own revision of Mencken's work, "Much of [the development of linguistic science in North America] has been a response to the challenge which Mencken's work provided, through a realization among professional scholars that American English demanded serious and systematic investigation by the best minds, and that the fruits of this investigation might not only be interesting in themselves but have beneficent effects upon American letters and the American educational system."

Mencken made American linguistic studies exciting for the student and fascinating for the general reader, a tradition that has been maintained admirably by Stuart Berg Flexner, whose formal linguistic work on the *Dictionary of American Slang* and the *Oxford American Dictionary* (with Eugene Ehrlich, Gorton Carruth, and Joyce M. Hawkins; published in 1980) has been shaped into a more popular form in two remarkable works on Americana—*I Hear America Talking* (1976) and *Listening to America* (1982)—which in both narrative and illustration, with scrupulous attention to detail and a fine eye for anecdote, make the study of the American language as much a social history as an analysis of word origins.

The Morris Dictionary of Word and Phrase Origins, by William and Mary Morris (1977), has the same pleasure in it for the general reader, as does *The Merriam-Webster Book of Word Histories* (1976).

For the language of cowboys, miners, trappers, loggers, and other westerners I turned most often to Ramon F. Adams's *Western Words: A Dictionary of the American West* (1968), which was invaluable for its inclusiveness. For the language of black Americans I consulted Clarence Major's *Dictionary of Afro-American Slang* (1970). For Jewish-American words *The Joys of Yiddish,* by Leo Rosten (1968), wholly lives up to its title.

ENCYCLOPEDIAS, DICTIONARIES, ETC.

Two general encyclopedias were used extensively, the *Encyclopedia Britannica* (fifteenth edition, 1980) and the *Encyclopedia Americana* (1982). For information on animals, birds, and fish, I relied first on *Harper & Row's Complete Field Guide to North American Wildlife* (two volumes, 1981). *The Oxford Book of Food Plants,* by G. B. Masefield, M. Wallis, S. G. Harrison, and B. E. Nicholson, was consulted for fruits and vegetables, while A. J. McClane's *Encyclopedia of Fish Cookery* (1977) was an inexhaustible source of information on edible marine life.

I constantly turned to the following books for general information on cooking, ingredients, and origins of dishes: Theodora FitzGibbon's *Food of the Western World* (1976); Andre L. Simon's *Concise Encyclopedia of Gastronomy* (1952) and its revision by Robin Howe, *A Dictionary of Gastronomy* (1962); Prosper Montaigné's *Larousse Gastronomique* (1961); Patrick L. Coyle, Jr.'s *World Encyclopedia of Food* (1982); Tom Stopart's *Cook's Encyclopedia* (1980); and Howard Hillman's *Cook's Book* (1981). Special credit must be given to the late Waverly Root, who not only published excellent studies of the cuisines of France and Italy, but whose beautifully written and lavishly illustrated *Food* (1980) is an example to all food writers for style, wit, personality, and breathtaking scholarship. Sadly and ironically, Root's greatest work was cut by two-thirds for publication, and its glaring omissions make the reader wonder what fascinating information he is missing by having only such an abridgment of what is clearly Root's masterwork.

There is also much good information to be dug out of a quirky hodgepodge entitled *The Enriched, Fortified, Concentrated, Country-Fresh, Lip-Smacking, Finger-Licking, International, Unexpurgated Foodbook,* by James Trager (1970).

INDIVIDUAL TOPICS

For cheese history and description of types throughout the world, I consulted most often Evan Jones's *World of Cheese* (1979), and the same author's *Book of Bread,* written with his wife Judith Jones (1982) is just as good on the subject of baked goods. The subject of ice cream confections is lovingly covered in Paul

Dickson's *The Great American Ice Cream Book* (1972), while Ray Broekel's *Great American Candy Bar Book* (1982) is just as important and just as much fun on the subject of Milky Ways, Tootsie Rolls, and Hershey Bars.

My main sources of research on wines and spirits came from Harold J. Grossman's *Grossman's Guide to Wines, Beers, and Spirits* (sixth revised edition, 1977, by Harriet Lembeck); *Alexis Lichine's New Encyclopedia of Wines & Spirits* (1981); Leon D. Adams's *Wines of America* (second revised edition, 1978); *The Signet Book of American Wine* (1980), by "Peter Quimme" (John and Elin Walker); and *The Connoisseur's Handbook of California Wines* (1980), by Charles Olken, Earl Singer, and Norman Roby.

Although there is no completely authoritative book on cocktails and mixed drinks, I found the following extremely helpful for information and recipes: *The Fine Art of Mixing Drinks,* by David A. Embury (third American edition, 1958); *Trader Vic's Bartender Guide,* by Victor J. Bergeron (revised, 1972); *The Pocket Bartender's Guide,* by Michael Jackson (1979); *The Drink Directory,* by Lionel Braun and Marion Gorman (1982); and *Harry's ABC of Mixing Cocktails,* by Harry and Andy MacElhone (new edition, 1982).

HISTORIES, REMINISCENCES, AND ESSAYS

Little academic attention has been paid until recently to American gastronomy, and few history texts spend any time at all on the subject, the exception being Daniel J. Boorstein's *The Americans: The Colonial Experience* (1958), *The Americans: The National Experience* (1965), and *The Americans: The Democratic Experience* (1973). I consider it a serious omission that the *Harvard Encyclopedia of American Ethnic Groups,* edited by Stephan Thernstrom (1980), barely mentions the foods and culinary traditions of the immigrants to this country.

The full history of American gastronomy is told admirably in *Eating in America,* by Waverly Root and Richard de Rochemont (1976). Evan Jones's *American Food: The Gastronomic Story* (second edition, 1981) is eminently readable and full of fine recipes. Often overlooked but extremely valuable, despite its dry tone, is Richard J. Hooker's *Food and Drink in America: A History* (1981), and there is much useful information in *The American Heritage Cookbook* (1964), by Helen McCully and Helen Duprey Bullock, and in *The Better Homes and Gardens Heritage Cook Book* (1975), both of which are as important for their historical information as they are for their recipes.

The Time-Life series *American Cooking* (seven volumes, 1970–1973) was a landmark in American studies of our food and our culture.

Raymond Sokolov's *Fading Feast* (1981), originally commissioned as a series of articles for *Natural History* magazine, has much of the same flavor and treats many dishes and traditions that are indeed fast fading in this country for a variety of reasons. Jane and Michael Stern's *Goodfood* (1983) constitutes a rich store of Americana and anecdote along with its practical object of pointing the reader to the best American regional restaurants.

The Taste of America, by John L. and Karen Hess (1977), is an instructive and disturbing jeremiad aimed at those who would corrupt the traditions of American cookery, and it includes an excellent bibliography of eighteenth- and nineteenth-century works on cookery.

A book with a similar name but a more engaging author is *American Taste* (1982), by James Villas, one of a number of southern writers who have fondly kept alive the lore and traditions of southern cooking. This group would also include Craig Claiborne, whose *A Feast Made for Laughter* (1982) is an excellent memoir of a Mississippi childhood; Edna Lewis, who in *The Taste of Country Cooking* (1976) recalls Virginia; and Norma Jean and Carole Darden, who write of North Carolina in *Spoonbread and Strawberry Wine* (1978). James Beard's *Delights and Prejudices* (1964) does for Oregon what these southerners do for their states.

An excellent study of culinary and social history will be found in Michael and Ariane Batterberry's *On the Town in New York* (1973), and Jay Jacobs's *New York à la Carte* (1978) contains a very good short history of restaurants in that city.

For the best and most affectionate writing on American regional dishes, I turn to Calvin Trillin's *American Fried* (1974) and *Third Helpings* (1983).

COOKBOOKS AND RECIPE COLLECTIONS

The scholar may wish to consult Eleanor Lowenstein's *Bibliography of American Cookery Books,* 1742–1860 (1972) and Katherine Golden Bitting's *Gastronomic Bibliography* (1939) for long lists of American recipe books, but, as I have noted, the printed, bound catalogs of the Library of Congress and the New York Public Library are the most rewarding for their inclusiveness.

I shall list only some of the hundreds of cookbooks and recipe collections I have found most useful in my own research; this list is more for the general reader's interest than for the scholar's. I have not listed here very old or rare cookbooks. The majority of the books below are still in print or readily available at libraries.

Beard, James. *James Beard's American Cookery* (1972).
Brody, Jerome, intro. *The Grand Central Oyster Bar and Restaurant Cookbook* (1977).
Brown, Helen Evans. *The West Coast Cook Book* (1952).
Buckeye Publishing Company. *The Buckeye Cookbook* (1883; printed in facsimile, 1975).
Burton, Nathaniel, and Rudy Lombard. *Creole Feast* (1978).
Butel, Jane. *Tex-Mex Cookbook* (1980).
Claiborne, Craig. *The New York Times Cook Book* (1961).
Collin, Rima, and Richard Collin. *The New Orleans Cookbook* (1980).
Copping, Wilf, and Lois Copping. *The Country Innkeepers' Cookbook* (1978).
Early, Eleanor. *New England Cookbook* (1954).

Engle, Fannie, and Gertrude Blair. *The Jewish Festival Cookbook* (1954).

Exum, Helen. *Chattanooga Cookbook* (1970).

Farmer, Fannie Merritt. *The Boston Cooking-School Cook Book* (1896; facsimile edition, 1973).

Gault, Lila. *The Northwest Cookbook* (1978).

Gay, Lettie, ed. *200 Years of Charleston Cooking* (1930).

Hazelton, Nika. *American Home Cooking* (1980).

Hunter, Ethel Farmer. *Secrets of Southern Cooking* (1956).

Jeffries, Bob. *Soul Food Cookbook* (1969).

Kander, Mrs. Simon. *The Settlement Cookbook* (1936).

Kennedy, Diana. *The Cuisines of Mexico* (1972).

Key West Woman's Club. *The Key West Cook Book* (1949).

Lassiter, William Lawrence. *Shaker Recipes and Formulas for Cooks and Homemakers* (1959).

Lobel, Leon, and Stanley Lobel. *All About Meat* (1975).

McClane, A. J. *McClane's North American Fish Cookery* (1981).

Margittai, Tom, and Paul Kovi. *The Four Seasons* (1980).

Masterton, Elsie. *Blueberry Hill Menu Cookbook* (1964).

Muscatine, Doris. *A Cook's Tour of San Francisco* (1963).

Niethammer, Carolyn. *American Indian Food and Lore* (1974).

Parents' Club of Ursiline Academy. *Recipes and Reminiscences of New Orleans*. Vol. II (1981).

The Picayune's Creole Cook Book (1901; facsimile edition, 1971).

Puckett, Susan. *A Cook's Tour of Mississippi* (1980).

Sarvis, Shirley. *Crab and Abalone* (1968).

Taylor, Demetria. *Apple Kitchen Cook Book* (1979).

Voltz, Jeanne A. *The Flavor of the South* (1977).

Wolcott, Imogene. *The Yankee Cook Book* (1963).

Yardly, Maili. *Hawaii Cooks* (1970).

Index

black bottom sundae, 42
black brant, 178
black buffalo, 391
black cake, 43
black coffee, 119
black cow, 43
black crappie, 395
Black Diamond, 42
black drink, 43
black drum, 149
black duck, 150
Black Esopus Spitzenburg, 11
black-eyed pea, 131
blackfin cisco, 435
blackfish, 43, 403
Black Forest mushroom, 262
Black Gillflower, 11
black grouper, 183
blackhorn plum, 303
black huckleberry, 201
blackjack, 130–31
blackjack steer, 43
blackline tilefish, 408
black Mike, 43
black mullet, 261
black mustard, 263
black raspberry, 329
black redhorse, 331, 391
black-seed, 237
black stick, 237
blackstrap, 43, 183, 257, 342
blackstripe, 183
black-tailed rattlesnake, 330
black thyme, 408
black water, 131
blade cut, 32
blade roast, 110
Blakemore strawberry, 388
Blake peach, 288
Blanc de Noir, 447
blended light whiskey, 434
blended tuna, 416
blended whiskey, 44
Blenheim apricot, 17
blind, 150
blind pig, 44
blind tiger, 44
blintz, 44
bloater, 194
blonde, 237
blondies, 410
bloody Bronx, 58
Bloody Maria, 45
Bloody Mary, xxxiii, 44–45
Bloody Mary Quite Contrary, 45
Bloody Shame, 45
blowfish, 399
BLT, 236, 351
blueback, 348

blueback flounder, 163
blue-bottle, 237
blueberry, 45, 200
blueberry pancake, 283
blueberry pie, 45
blue blazer, 45–46
blue catfish, 80
blue cheese, 90
blue crab, 131
bluefin tuna, 416
bluefish, 46
bluegill, 395
blue lagoon, 46
blue meat, 46
blue mussel, 263
blue plate special, 237
blue point, 277, 278
blue quail, 325
blue runner, 212
blue shark, 362
blue sucker, 391
boardinghouse man, 46, 125
bob for apples, 11
bobotee, 46
bob veal, 423
bobwhite, 286, 325
bobwhite quail, 325
bock beer, 37
bog onion, 418
boiler, 46, 125
boilermaker, 46–47
boilermaker's delight, 47
boiling fowl, 96
bologna, baloney, boloney, 47
bolted meal, 47
bombed, 150
bombo, 47, 342
bonded warehouse, 434
bongo bongo soup, 47
bonito, 416
Bonney Best, 411
boova shenkel, 47
bop, 48
borracho, 48
borscht, 48
Borscht belt, 48
Bosc, 291
bosk, 48
Bossy, 237
Bossy in a bowl, 237
Boston baked beans, 48–49
Boston bluefish, 305
Boston brown bread, 49, 54
Boston butt, 49, 310
Boston coffee, 118
Boston cracker, 49
Boston cream pie, 49–50
Boston cut, 32
Boston lettuce, 228
Boston mackerel, 242

Boston shoulder, 49
Boston strawberry, 49
bottled beer, 35
bottled-in-bond, 434
bottled water, 50
bottle gourd, 69
bottom, 237
bottom fermented, 34
bottom round, 32
bottom sirloin, 367
boucherie, 68
boudin, 50
boula, 51
bounce, 51
bounce berry, 134
Bouncer tomato, 411
bourbon, 51–52
bourbon and branch water, 52
bourbon balls, 51–52
Bowen orange, 274
bowl of red, 101, 237
bow wow, 237
box oyster, 278
boysenberry, 42
Brabham pea, 131
bramble, 42
bramble jelly, 52
bran, 433
branch lettuce, 354
branch water, 52
Brandon puff, 53
brandy, 16, 53
brandy Alexander, 53
brandy smash, 53
brant, 178
brasserie, 53
Braunschweiger, 230
bread, 53–56
breadfruit poi, 304
bread line, 57
bread pudding, 321
breakfast, 56–57
breakfast cereal, 82
breakfast cream, 57
break it and shake it, 237
breath, 237
breeze, 202
brewery, 34
brick cheese, 57, 89, 90
bridge, 237
bridge party, 237
Brie, 90
broccoli, 57
broiler, 96
Bronx cocktail, 57–58
Bronx vanilla, 173
Brooklyn cake, 58
brook trout, 415
Brother Jonathan's hat, 58, 141
brown-and-serve, 55

brown bag, 58
brown bear, 30
brown coffee, 131
brownie, 58
brown mustard, 263
brown rice, 338
brown shrimp, 365
brown sugar, 394
brown trout, 415
Brown Turkey, 161
bruiss, 58
brunch, 58
Brunswick stew, 59
brush roast, 59
Brussels sprout, 59
brut, 84
bubble gum, 72, 95
bubble gum card, 95
bubbly, 86
buccaneer crab, 232
buck, 59
buck and breck, 59–60
Bucket of Blood, 44, 60
bucket of hail, 237
bucket of suds, 35
bucket shop, 60
buckwheat, 60
buckwheat cakes, 60, 282, 283
buffalo, xxix, 60–61
Buffalo chicken wings, 62
buffalo chip, 61
buffalo cider, 61
buffalo grass, 61
buffalo lick, 350
buffalo marrow, xix
buffalo pound, 61
bug juice, 62
bugler, 391
bulgur, 433
bulk process, 85
bullace grape, 262
bullace plum, 303
bull and bear, 62
bull cheese, 62
bulldog of the ocean, 46
bullets, 237
bullshot, 62
bun pup, 237
buñuelo, 63, 376
Burbank plum, 304
burbot, 63
burger, 187
burger and fries, 189
burgoo, 62–63
Burgundy, 440
burn it and let it swim, 237
burn one, 237
burn one all the way, 237
burn the British, 237
burrito, 64

busboy, 64
bush grape, 179
bush huckleberry, 201
business lunch, 236
buster, 131
butt end, 310
butter, 64–65
butter bean, 29, 228
butter cookie, 125
butterfish, 65
butterhead lettuce, 227
buttermilk, 65, 237
butternut, 384, 430
Butters' apple, 11
butterscotch, 65
butter sole, 373
button onion, 272

cabbage, 66
cabbage lettuce, 227
cabbage palm, 282
Cabernet, 440
Cabernet Franc, 442
Cabernet Sauvignon, 66–67, 442
cabinet, 67, 254
cackleberry, 67
cackler, 67
caesar salad, 67
café brûlot, 67–68
Café Society, 381
cafeteria, 68, 335
cafeteria-type market, 396
caffeine, 68
Cajun, 68–69
cake, 69
calabash, 69
calamari, 384
calas, 60–70
calcium propionate, 6, 70
calcium stearoyl lactylate, 70
cale-cannon, 70
calf fry, 70
calico bass, 395
calico scallop, 355
California bean clam, 113
California halibut, 163
California ham, 49, 69, 297
California hazelnut, 192
California mussel, 263
Californian chili, 101
California oyster, 277
California pompano, 306
California quail, 325
California-style cottage cheese, 130
California walnut, 430
Calimyrn fig, 161
Calmeria, 179
calves' meat, 423

cambric tea, 70
Camembert, 90
Campbell 1327, 411
Canada goose, 178
Canada plum, 303
Canadian bacon, 22, 310
Canadian coffee, 118
Canadian rice, 436
Canadian turnip, 418
canaigre, 70
Canal Street Plan, 276
canapé, 71
Canary Island special, 237
candlefish, 369
candy, 71–72
candy apple, candied apple, 73
candy bar, 72, 73–76
candy shop, 72
candy store, 73
canner, 31
canoe race, 76
cantaloupe, 76
cantina, 76
canvasback duck, 76–77, 150
Cape Cod oyster, 277
Cape Cod turkey, 77
Cape May goody, 382
caper, 77
capon, 96
cappuccino, 77
caramel, 71, 77–78
caramel sauce, 78
carbonated mead, 372
Cardinal, 179
carfare, 237
Caribbean lobsterette, 232
Caribbean shrimp, 365
caribou, cariboo, carraboo, 78
Carignane, 442
Carnelian, 441
Carolina rice, 338
Carolina tea, 43
carp, 78
carpetbag steak, 78–79
carrageenan, 6, 79
carrot, 79
carrot cake, 79
carrot tops, 79
carry-out food, 402
casaba, 79
Cascade, 442
casserole, 79
casserole cookery, 80
Catawba, 80, 440, 442
catfish, 80
Catskill strawberry, 388
catsup, catchup, 219
cat's eyes, 237
cattalo, 61
cauliflower, 80–81

Rocky Mountain whitefish, 435
rocky road, 340
roffignac, 340
rolled oats, 269
rollmops, 194, 340
romaine lettuce, 228
romano, 92, 340
Rome Beauty, 14
rooster spur pepper, 340–41
Root Beer, 372
rooter, 391
Roquefort dressing, 341
rosina, 171
Ross' goose, 178
rotgut, 230
rouget, 371
round bone, 367
round clam, 112
round whitefish, 435
roux, 341
Royal Ann, 94
Royal apricot, 17
royal red shrimp, 365
Ruby, 14
Ruby Cabernet, 341, 443
ruffed grouse, 286, 294
rugola, 341
rum, 341–44
rumrousal, 344
rum tum tiddy, 344
Russet Burbank, 313
Russian crab, 132
Russian dressing, 344
Russian tarragon, 403
rustyside sucker, 331
rutabaga, 418
Rutgers, 411
rye, 44
rye flour, 164
rye 'n' Injun bread, 54, 344
rye whiskey, 344

sac à lait, 395
saccharin, 5, 345
sacramental wine, 439
sagamite, 209
sage Cheddar, 87
sago, 345
salad, 345
salad bar, 346
salad bowl lettuce, 228
salami, 346
saleratus, 23, 346
Salisbury steak, 346–47, 364
Sallie, 125
Sally Lunn, 347
salmagundi, salmagundy, 347
salmon, 347–49
saloon, 26, 349, 281

salsa, 349
salsify, 349
salt, 5, 349–50
salt cellar, 350
salteur liquor, 350
salt horse, salt hoss, 350
Saltines, 133
salt lick, 350
saltmarsh, 350
salt of hartshorn, 189, 190
salt pork, 22
salt potato, 350–51
salt rising bread, 350
samp, 196
Samson, 342
sand, 240
sand bush grape, 179
sand dab, 163, 351
sand lobster, 232
sand sole, 374
sand tilefish, 408
sandwich, 351–52
sandwich bread, 351
sandwich loaf, 55, 351
sangaree, 323
sangría, 323, 352
Sanka, 119
San Pedro, 161
San Marzano, 411
Santa Gertrudis, 31
sapsis, 352
Saratoga potatoes, Saratoga chips, 313, 352–53
sardine, 353
sargo, 184
sarsaparilla, sassparilla, 353, 372
sashimi, 353
sassafras, 353
sass tea, 353
saturated oil, 424
Saturday nights, 237
sauce piquante, 353–54
saucer glass, 28
sauerkraut, sourcrout, 354
Sauterne, 440
Sauvignon Blanc, 354, 443
savor cabbage, 66
saxifrage, 354
Sazerac, xxix, 3, 354–55
scaled quail, 325
scallion, 355
scallop, 355–56
scalloped potatoes, 313
scalloped squash, 383
scampi, 356
scared whiskey, 258
scarlet strawberry, 386
Schichtkuche, 356
schmaltz, 356

schmear, 356
school breakfast program, 356
school lunch program, 356
schooner, 356
scoff-law cocktail, 357
scorcher, 125
Scotch Manhattan, 244
Scotch tender, 32
scoter, 150
scrambled egg, 154
scrapple, 357
screwdriver, 357
scripture cake, 357–58
scrod, scrode, schrod, 117, 358
scungilli, 433
scup, 309
Scuppernong, 262, 358–59
sea biscuit, 183
seaboard, 240
sea bread, 189
sea bob, 365
sea dust, 240
sea herring, 194
sea lion, 359
sea pie, 359
seasoned salt, 350
sea squab, 399
sea trout, 431
sea urchin, 359
sec, 85
Seckel, 291
seed cake, 359–60
seed onion, 272
self-rising flour, 23, 54
sell date, 272
seltzer, 360
Sémillon, 443
semisweet chocolate, 105
semmel, 360
semolina, 164
Senate bean soup, 360–61
serrano, 101
sesame, 361
seven sweets and seven sours, 361
7-Up, 373
Seville orange, 273
Seyval Blanc, 361, 443
shad, 361–62
shaddock, 180
Shaker lemon pie, 227
shallot, 362
shank end, 310
shark, 362–63
shaved ice, 203
Shawnee cake, 282
Shawn O'Farrell, Shawn O', 47
she-crab soup, 363
sheep dip, 230